# ORGANIZATIONAL BEHAVIOR AND CHANGE

## Managing Diversity, Cross-Cultural Dynamics, and Ethics

### Joseph W. Weiss
Bentley College

SOUTH-WESTERN
*
THOMSON LEARNING™

Australia · Cana~~~~~~~~~~~~~~~~~~~~~~~ingdom · United States

*Organizational Behavior and Change: Managing Diversity, Cross-Cultural Dynamics, and Ethics,* 2d ed., by Joseph W. Weiss

Vice President/Publisher: Jack W. Calhoun
Executive Editor: John Szilagyi
Developmental Editor: Ohlinger Publishing Services
Marketing Manager: Rob Bloom
Production Editor: Starratt Alexander
Manufacturing Coordinator: Sandee Milewski
Internal and Cover Design: Jennifer Lambert/Jen 2 Design
Cover Illustrator: © Christopher Baldwin/SIS
Production House: DPS Associates, Inc.
Printer: West Group Printing

Printed in the United States of America
2  3  4  5  03  02  01

For more information contact South-Western College Publishing, 5101 Madison Road, Cincinnati, Ohio, 45227 or find us on the Internet at http://www.swcollege.com

For permission to use material from this text or product, contact us by
• telephone:  1-800-730-2214
• fax:  1-800-730-2215
• web:  http://www.thomsonrights.com

Library of Congress Cataloging-in-Publication Data

Weiss, Joseph W.
   Organizational behavior and change : managing diversity, cross-cultural dynamics, and ethics / Joseph W. Weiss
       p. cm.
   Previously published: Minneapolis/St. Paul : West Pub. Co. c 1996.
   Includes bibliographical references.
   ISBN 0-324-02709-5 (alk. paper)
     1. Organizational behavior.  2. Organizational change—Management.  3. Diversity in the workplace.  4. Personnel management.  5. Business ethics. I. Title.

HD58.7 .W34 2000
658.4'06—dc21                                                                       00-038800

This book is printed on acid-free paper.

Dedicated to Hayat and Taya Weiss,
and to André Delbecq, friend and mentor

# PART 2    INDIVIDUAL PROCESSES  35

# PART 3 TEAM AND INTERPERSONAL PROCESS  133

A dominant theme affecting organizations is change. Change has become a constant. Effects of an emerging global economy, the Internet and different information technologies, increased industrial competitiveness, and new entrants of employees across national boundaries affect organizations significantly. The study of organizational behavior must, I believe, reflect and address these changes: thus, the title of this book, *Organizational Behavior and Change*.

The theme of planned change is integrated with classical organizational behavior topics throughout. A major premise of this book is that organizations and their individual participants must understand and use consultative perspectives on change in order to survive and succeed. Toward this end, Chapter 14 presents major change models that are integrated throughout the book.

Another innovation, which this book helped to pioneer, is the integration of the themes of international differences, ethical perspectives, and diversity, which are addressed in each chapter. These themes underlie organizational change. Also, part of the challenge for organizational members is to know how to relate, work, and produce effectively in continuously changing internal and external environments in socially responsible and ethical ways. Each chapter relates to these topics, and this edition enhances the coverage and practical integration of these three perspectives through new exercises and assessments with the aim of engaging, informing, and extending readers' knowledge and skills in OB areas.

## GOALS OF THE BOOK

The major goals of the book are straightforward:

- **To provide the reader with a contemporary, real-time, and conceptual approach to understanding organizational change by using OB theory and models.** This meant enlivening the text with the realization that information technology is part of almost all business and organizational changes. So, examples from current business presses and journals on this and other topics are included. Each classical topic has been updated to include current research and organizational experience that affects strategy, structure, teams, leadership, communication, and other dimensions of organizations and behavior that respond to changing environments.

- **To increase awareness and understanding of organizational change as it relates to the enterprise and to individuals and teams.** A challenge here was to present concept and practice in ways that linked the "big picture" of organizational change with individual and group behavioral dimensions. Since organizational transformation and change include the macro and micro levels of behavior, the approach in this book attempts to capture both dimensions.

- **To develop individual and team diagnostic and consultative skills.** In a sense, all members and participants in organizations are consultants. Consultative skills include both diagnostic and expert content areas. Each chapter introduces skill-based concepts and techniques that can be used to understand and change behavior when required.

- **To increase understanding and development of communication and problem-solving skills in diverse work groups.** National cultures interpret organizational reality and behavior in different ways. This book examines cross-cultural interpretations of communicating and working. Since effective communication in organizations is required to increase productivity, the text also presents methods for creating and enhancing synergy while recognizing cultural differences.

## FEATURES OF THE BOOK

Each of the 14 chapters begins with a set of **learning objectives** that previews content and guides the reader. Each chapter contains **stories and excerpts from contemporary business journals and presses** that discuss both present and potential issues that organizational members are likely to face in leading, communicating, organizing strategy and structure, motivating, and changing organizational behavior. Each chapter also presents sections that explore **international, diversity, and ethical perspectives** on behavior in organizations and provides **managerial checklists** and **diagnostic guides** for understanding different OB topics. In addition, action-oriented models and change models are presented in Chapter 14. The book integrates change models and perspectives in each section and summarizes several of these perspectives in Chapter 14. Finally, I have written and presented theory, concepts, and skills in a "**reader-friendly**," straightforward way. This is not always easy when presenting other people's ideas and works, although this text does, I believe, accomplish this goal.

## NEW TO THIS EDITION

The second edition of *Organizational Behavior and Change: Managing Diversity, Cross-Cultural Dynamics, and Ethics* has been updated and revised to reflect the most recent research, trends and examples in Organizational Behavior today. End of chapter summaries have been added. Scenarios, skill assessments, and topical insertions that engage students in individual and group exercises have been added to each chapter. In addition to these general revisions and updates, the following specific changes have been made.

## Organizational Changes

In order to enhance continuity and student apprehension of the material, the overall sequencing of the chapters has been changed and organized into four sections: PART 1 (Introduction and Overview) introduces the subject and text. PART 2 (Individual Processes) includes those chapters that relate directly to this subject. PART 3 (Team and Interpersonal Processes) deals with groups, teams, and behavior between individuals. PART 4 (Organizational Processes) includes topics that are more macro in nature. To facilitate the flow of the topics, the Communication chapter (Chapter 5 in the previous edition) has been moved to Chapter 6. In addition, Chapter 8 (Power and Politics) and Chapter 9 (Conflict and Negotiation) have been placed together in the text. Also, Chapter 8 (Power and Politics) has been moved to accompany the chapter on Leadership and Followership. Finally, Chapter 10 (Work, Jobs, and Job Design) has been moved to precede the chapters on Organizational Design and Organizational Culture and Careers and Socialization. Feedback from the first edition indicated that these chapter changes would more accurately reflect the order in which this course is being taught. Still, the chapters are self-contained units and the text remains flexible enough for professors to teach the material in the order they find most appropriate.

## New Additions and Revisions to Content

- Each chapter includes new research findings and new textual examples.

- Additional examples of diversity and diversity perspectives are included with practical exercises.

- Information technology trends and issues in the workforce are addressed in each chapter with examples as this topic relates to Organizational Behavior.

- Scenarios, "The Changing Workplace" exercises, and quick skill assessments are found throughout the text.

- Exercises and examples related to ethics have also been integrated in the chapters.

These comprehensive revisions are accompanied by several specific revisions in the following chapters:

- Chapter 1 has been significantly expanded to include material on e-commerce and information technology as it relates to Organizational Behavior. Recognizing the significant impact of information technology on business and OB is critical. Thus, the relationship between the two is clearly expressed in the introductory chapter of this text.

- Chapter 7 (Leadership and Followership) has been completely revised, eliminating a portion of the more academic discussion on classical leadership theories. We made these revisions so that this important chapter will fit more easily into a typical lecture period in a standard semester schedule, allowing both students and professors more time to focus on contemporary theories of leadership.

- Chapter 9 includes an expanded section on negotiating and negotiating skills.

- Chapter 14 has been streamlined to focus on change management techniques and exercises which students can use in their future careers.

## PEDAGOGY

The primary goal of any textbook is to enhance and engage students in their comprehension and understanding of organizational behavior as a dynamic subject. With this goal in mind several pedagogical features have been added to this edition:

- Boxed material, titled "The Changing Workplace," has been added to every chapter. Every chapter contains a minimum of three boxes, and some chapters feature as many as five. This material is designed to provide students the opportunity to apply the theories being presented in the chapter. This type of exercise reinforces material while allowing students to explore how OB Theory affects, or will affect, them in the workplace.

- Most chapters now contain an End of Chapter Scenario that presents a brief case and requires students to make decisions regarding how they would handle the situation and why. These scenarios were designed to improve critical thinking skills and develop problem-solving techniques by having students examine situations they will encounter in their careers.

- Extensive review questions have been added to the end of each chapter as well. These questions work in connection with the learning objectives to provide students with a comprehensive understanding of the chapter material.

## INSTRUCTOR SUPPORT MATERIALS

**Instructor's Manual.** This manual, prepared by Michael K. McCuddy of Valparaiso University, contains chapter outlines, learning objectives, lecture notes, lecture enhancements, explanations and possible answers to the text's boxed material, answers to the end of chapter review questions, additional suggested discussion questions, and suggested supplemental readings.

## ACKNOWLEDGMENTS

A number of people made this work possible. Three MBA graduate assistants helped engineer and deliver the first edition of the text. Brian Norris, whose influence is part of the fabric of the text, was instrumental in helping lay out the original plan and research of the book. Kathy Rusiniak helped with the second phase, that of researching, editing, and finalizing topics. Kathy's diligence proved vital. Finally, Pamela Costello helped transform research and drafts into a manuscript. Her professional managerial experience combined with research skills provided the needed launch energy. John Szilagyi, Executive Editor at South-Western College Publishing, helped guide and direct this second edition. The editorial efforts of Theresa and Kelly Curtis and their staff at Ohlinger Publishing Services gave impetus and closure to this second edition. In addition, I give special thanks to the following professors, whose reviews and critical suggestions helped clarify the text:

Nathan Bennett
Louisiana State University

Gay Blau
Temple University

Maureen Fleming
University of Montana

Virginia Geurin
University of North Carolina–Charlotte

Sandra Hartman
University of New Orleans

Mary Ann Hazen
University of Detroit Mercy

Avis Johnson
University of Akron

Linda Livingstone
Baylor University

Edward Marlow
Eastern Illinois University

Dean McFarlin
Marquette University

Fred Schuster
Florida Atlantic University

Richard Sebastian
St. Cloud State University

Gregory Stephens
Texas Christian University

Jacqueline N. Hood
University of New Mexico

Gregg Lattier
Lee College

Helen Juliette Muller
University of New Mexico

# Introduction and Overview

# 1

# Organizational Behavior in the 21st Century

---

## LEARNING OBJECTIVES

After studying this chapter, you should be able to:

**1** Describe four 21st century challenges to organizations.

**2** Define the field of organizational behavior.

**3** Explain advantages of studying OB.

**4** Show seven major management historical trends.

**5** Illustrate international perspectives on managing cultural synergy.

**6** Describe an organizational diversity change model.

**7** Describe five ethical perspectives in organizations.

**8** Describe three approaches for diagnosing organizations.

**9** Describe two change-management models.

**10** Understand the game plan of the book.

---

Organizational behavior (OB) is the study of how individuals, groups, and teams create, lead, and manage change effectively. A dominant theme of organizations in the 21st century is the *creation, integration,* and *management* of change. Information technology is a major force driving change. We are experiencing the rapid integration of information across all industries everywhere,[1] yet it is still people who invent, direct, guide, and manage change in their own careers and in the so-called boundaryless organization. This text relates organizational behavior topics to managing change in the contemporary business environment. Organizational behavior is a dynamic body of knowledge that can be used to understand and manage a wide range of concepts and behavioral interventions, including diversity, ethics, and technological change as a driver of performance and integration.

## TWENTY-FIRST CENTURY CHALLENGES

Corporations are changing more rapidly and radically now than at any time since the Industrial Revolution. Change is shaped by the interrelationships of (1) the forces of information technology and the Internet, (2) the emergence of a global economy,

(3) international competition, and (4) an increasingly diverse workforce. For industries and companies, these changes have created a competitive, survival environment that emphasizes increased product and service quality, decreased delivery time, and customer satisfaction. "Business @ the speed of thought"[2] is a major factor of competitive advantage. Another set of success factors that lead to competitive advantage are developing and sustaining world-class products and services with Internet speed and meeting and exceeding customer demand.

Organizations are adapting by reengineering,[3] reinventing, restructuring, and rethinking their strategies, structures, and expertise around Web-based, Internet-integrated business processes. Not all organizations are changing at the same pace or on the same scale. However, Internet-driven networks and software applications have produced a type of "digital Darwinism,"[4] (i.e., the competitive playing field is being leveled by information technologies; to play, companies must create new value-added applications and invent interactive services that transform transactions into unique and personalized experiences that competitors cannot replicate). Established companies are streamlining operations using the Internet to eliminate unnecessary processes, link communications to suppliers, and integrate communication within the firm by way of secured private on-line systems called *Intranets*. Peter Drucker describes the arrival of the new organization this way:

> The typical business 20 years hence will have fewer than half the levels of management of its counterpart today, and no more than a third of the managers. In its structure, and in its management problems and concerns, it will bear little resemblance to the typical manufacturing company, circa 1950, which our textbooks still consider the norm. Instead, it is far more likely to resemble organizations that neither the practicing manager nor the management scholar pays much attention to today: the hospital, the university, the symphony orchestra. For like them, the typical business will be knowledge-based, an organization composed largely of specialists who direct and discipline their own performance through organized feedback from colleagues, customers, and headquarters. For this reason, it will be what I call an information-based organization.[5]

The information-based organization has knowledge workers who are specialists and who resist command-and-control procedures based on the military model. Everyone takes responsibility in these workplaces. Structures become flatter. Clear, simple, common objectives that lead to action are required. Changing managerial roles include developing rewards, recognition, and career opportunities; creating a unified vision in the organization; devising a management structure for task forces; and ensuring the supply, preparation, and testing of top management people.[6]

The workforce also continues to rapidly change. "Workforce 2000" includes new and younger workers—many of whom are more technologically savvy than their predecessors. At the same time, there is an aging workforce (in the United States and in Japan, in particular). Half the workforce is composed of women, and an increasing number of minorities and immigrants are working. The accompanying job market will generate new jobs in information and service industries that require higher skills, and the new organization will recruit more disabled workers and will enable intermingling of diverse cultures in the workplace.[7] With the increasing diversity of workers, managers will need to create flexible organizational cultures, mentor employees, develop equal access and fast-track training programs, and implement sensitivity seminars. A knowledge of organizational behavior, tools, and techniques is central to these tasks.

Finally, because of the internationalization of business and continuous merger, acquisition, and divestiture activities, yet another aspect of managerial work is being revised. Rosabeth Moss Kanter calls the new managerial work and practices "post-entrepreneurial" because "they involve the application of entrepreneurial creativity and flexibility to established businesses."[8] Post-entrepreneurial practices include managers involving themselves in networks outside their hierarchy; adding value by deal making; brokering interfaces instead of building individual empires; and thinking cross-functionally and strategically to contribute to other facets of the business. Such managers serve as integrators and facilitators, not as watchdogs and interventionists; they sell their services and negotiate across boundaries with peers and partners and form alliances to build relationships involving joint planning and decision making. In their continual search for internal synergies, strategic alliances, and new ventures, these new-style leaders cultivate political skills that enable them to juggle a set of constituencies rather than control a set of subordinates.

The era of the **boundaryless** or seamless corporation has arrived. Emphasis is placed on developing cooperative relationships among internal, external, and virtual teams who are part of an expanding economic (or what may become a "Webonomic," i.e., Internet integrated) enterprise. High-performance teams are organized with empowered individuals who work creatively to add value to their company as well as to their units. A knowledge of organizational behavior and a repertoire of people skills are essential in building and sustaining face-to-face and virtual relationships.

## WHAT IS ORGANIZATIONAL BEHAVIOR?

The field of organizational behavior (referred to as OB) is the systematic study of attitudes, actions, and behaviors of individuals and groups in organizations. Systematic study means identifying the nonrandom patterns of individual and group behavior that contribute to, or detract from, work and organizational effectiveness. Effectiveness is defined as the extent to which individuals and groups, in performing their work, contribute to an organization's competitiveness, productivity, success, and social responsibility.

A major aim in attaining OB expertise is learning skills to diagnose, predict, and apply concepts and techniques for changing behaviors to increase organizational effectiveness. Ideally, OB knowledge and skills enable managers and employees working with customers, suppliers, vendors, and strategic alliance partners to create responsible win-win situations—that is, to create and sustain productivity, satisfaction, development, and success—for the organization and its stakeholders (those inside and external to the organization who have an interest, or stake, in its activities and outcomes).

The field of OB generally includes the following topics: leadership; team and group development; motivation; individual personality and learning behavior; interpersonal communication; conflict resolution; power and politics; job design and reward systems; and, more recently, diversity and ethics.

Organizational behavior is also concerned with the linkages and alignments among performance-related behaviors of an organization's individuals with groups and teams, the organization's leaders and constituencies, and external influencers (customers, suppliers, competitors, strategic partners). While OB remains focused on individual and group behavior (see Figure 1–1), the effects of change from other organizational dimensions (such as strategy and culture) and environments are also important influences on behavior.

As a field of study, OB is interdisciplinary. It draws on theory, research, and research methods from social psychology, sociology, anthropology, political science, engineering, and medicine. Because of this multidimensional background and the complexity of organizational problems, there is usually no one best way to predict or recommend solutions. A contingency approach is, therefore, generally preferred over absolute or single-dimensional answers. A contingency approach identifies possible cause(s) and multiple effect(s) of a problem and then defines situations under which a particular course of action can solve the problem. The idea is that, for any given problem, certain situations might require a more flexible, collegial style of

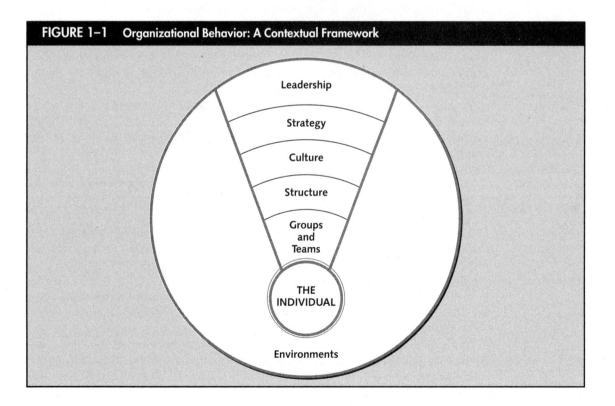

**FIGURE 1–1    Organizational Behavior: A Contextual Framework**

leadership while other situations might call for a supervisory, structured style of leadership.

Building on the contingency approach, the conceptual perspective of "reframing" organizations has more recently contributed to a broader understanding of organizational behavior.[9] In this perspective, the major schools of organizational thought are viewed from four "frames." These frames are

> *windows on the world and lenses that bring the world into focus. Frames filter out some things while allowing others to pass through easily. Frames help us to order experience and decide what action to take. Every manager, consultant, or policy maker uses a personal frame or image of organizations to gather information, make judgments, and determine how best to get things done. . . . Frames are also tools for action, and every tool has its strengths and limitations. . . . The truly effective manager and reader will need multiple tools, the skill to use each of them, and the wisdom to match frames to situations.[10]*

The four frames are used to make sense of an organization and to understand organizational behavior. They include (1) the structural frame (which emphasizes formal roles, relationships, and responsibilities and seeks to fit structure to situations); (2) the human resource frame (which examines individuals' needs, feelings, and prejudices and seeks to "find an organized form that enables people to get the job done while feeling good about what they are doing"); (3) the political frame (which studies the competition for power and resulting conflicts and seeks to develop solutions through bargaining, negotiation, and compromise); and (4) the symbolic frame (which studies organizations as tribes, theaters, or carnivals where "various actors play out the drama inside the organization" and which seeks "improvements in rebuilding the expressive or spiritual side of organizations . . . through the use of symbol, myth, and magic").[11]

The point and suggestion here are that your study of organizations and behavior and the factors and judgments that constitute "effectiveness" can and should include multiple perspectives, frames, and tools. Different frameworks will be emphasized throughout this text.

## WHY STUDY OB?

Peter Senge at MIT has had a significant impact on management thinking in his work on building "learning organizations."[12] Many of the skills that he maintains are required in a learning organization are central tenets of the field of OB. For example, his term "building shared vision" is the practice of unearthing shared pictures of the future that foster genuine commitment; "personal mastery" is the skill of continually clarifying and deepening our personal vision; developing "mental models" is the ability to unearth our internal pictures of the world, to scrutinize them, and to make them open to the influence of others; "team learning" is the capacity to "think together," which is gained by mastering the practice of dialogue and discussion; "systems thinking" is the discipline that integrates the others, fusing them into

## THE CHANGING WORKPLACE

### You're the Change Management Consultant

Use the organization where you work or one in which you have worked for this exercise.

Senior management from the company where you work or worked has contacted you and asked for help in *diagnosing* and drafting an initial *framework* for identifying bottlenecks and issues preventing your workgroup from pursuing aggressive goals and results.

Using any part(s) of Chapter 1, draft a memo to the responsible senior manager. In your memo, (1) identify the problem(s), issue(s) and/or opportunities you believe exist, and (2) show guidelines for uncovering obstacles and identifying opportunities. (Use specific work examples if possible. Share your memo with two members in your class. As you share your memos, ask these questions.

- How would your guidelines help diagnose the problem or plan the opportunities you outlined? Why?

- Would your guidelines be accepted by your present or previous organization? Why? or why not?

- What skills would be required to implement your framework?

- Do you currently have those skills? Would you use this framework if it were accepted? Explain.

a coherent body of theory and practice. These skills, which are used in learning organizations, are similar to many techniques in OB.

Concepts and skills learned in the study of OB will enable you to diagnose and implement actions for improving behaviors, activities, and human systems within your organization. Mastering OB gives you a common and analytic vocabulary for examining behavioral issues in organizations; a wide range of interdisciplinary theory, concepts, tools, techniques, and maps for discovering and diagnosing behavioral problems and issues; and ways of observing the interconnections between behavioral and other system components in organizations. How, for example, do strategy, structure, and rewards affect attitudes and actions? Or what specific methods, tactics, and people skills are needed for improving behavioral performance in different settings? Next, an overview of the evolution of OB within the context of management thought is presented.

## HISTORICAL OVERVIEW

How did the field of OB begin and evolve? What difference does it make? Understanding the historical context of OB and management helps to put theory and techniques in perspective. Some of the new trends may not be entirely new, and understanding how we got from "there to here" may help us better understand how to get from "here to there." Management, as well as OB theory and principles, changes with the environment and times. As we investigate the major schools of thought from the early 1900s into this millennium, we must also ask, What trends will the changing environment encourage in the twenty-first century?

The time line in Figure 1–2 illustrates the major schools and trends of management thought from the early 1900s to the present. You can see that OB originated in the 1920s (the human relations school of thought); it is indeed a product of the twentieth century.

A brief summary of these major influences follows, with each of them put in these contexts: (1) What were the dominant environmental conditions that gave rise to these trends? (2) What was the major focus of each trend? (3) To what extent and in what form does each trend survive?

### Scientific and Classical Management (1910-1920)

Turn-of-the-century America was witness to wrenching change in our national fabric. The agrarian society began to give way to an industrial one. Even so, the average level of education was 8.2 years.[13] Several major waves of immigration gave the melting pot characterization of our country renewed meaning. Social Darwinism, or survival of the fittest, was the prevailing ideology, as was individual worker productivity. Henry Ford's assembly line ushered in the age of mass production and, along with it, the beginnings of industrial engineering (1914). Employees were viewed as a function of the physical workplace and were studied in a systematic way.

Frederick W. Taylor's *The Principles of Scientific Management* (1911) and Henri Fayol's "Principles of Management"[14] were seminal works that spawned the scientific and classical management school of thought. The idea that each job could be made highly efficient was new, and the goal was to use rational and systematic methods of productivity to make this happen. Fayol's 14 principles of management became a cornerstone in the development of a new management science. The principles focused on (1) division of work (specialization); (2) authority (right to give orders, expect obedience); (3) discipline; (4) unity of command (subordinates receive orders from a superior); (5) unity of direction (one person in charge with one plan with same objective); (6) subordination of individual to organization's interests;

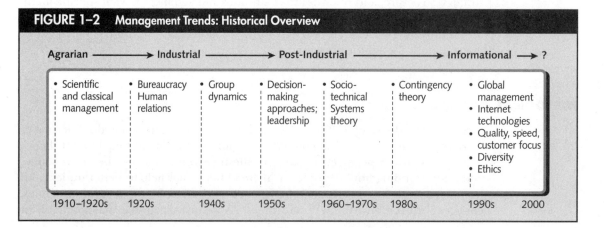

FIGURE 1–2    Management Trends: Historical Overview

Agrarian ⟶ Industrial ⟶ Post-Industrial ⟶ Informational ⟶ ?

| • Scientific and classical management | • Bureaucracy Human relations | • Group dynamics | • Decision-making approaches; leadership | • Socio-technical Systems theory | • Contingency theory | • Global management<br>• Internet technologies<br>• Quality, speed, customer focus<br>• Diversity<br>• Ethics |
|---|---|---|---|---|---|---|
| 1910–1920s | 1920s | 1940s | 1950s | 1960–1970s | 1980s | 1990s        2000 |

(7) remuneration (fair payment for work); (8) centralization (consolidation of managerial functions); (9) scalar chain (chain of command, authority); (10) order (personnel and materials located in designated places); (11) equity (equality of treatment); (12) stability of tenured personnel (limited turnover); (13) initiative (conceiving and ensuring the success of a plan); and (14) esprit de corps (harmonious relationships among personnel).

### Bureaucracy (1920-1940)

Max Weber is known as the father of the school of bureaucracy. Although his writings[15] were not translated into English until the 1940s, his principles of management were widely known and practiced in the United States in the 1920s. For Weber, bureaucracy was the blueprint of orderly systems for dividing responsibility, authority, and accountability. His idea was that with a unity of command, the application of consistent, thorough rules, and the expanded use of documentation and extensive worker training, work could be successfully accomplished as intended.

Today, bureaucracy has a negative reputation, more often indicative of bottlenecks, red tape, and inefficiency. In its mature phase, bureaucracy has led to bloated organizations and a redundant and excessive number of rules, all of which lead to a rigid organization type unable to meet the changing needs of the marketplace. Nevertheless, Weber's principles live on. Job descriptions, work manuals and procedures, organizational charts, and training programs are not dead. To Weber's credit, distinguishing the substance from the form of the job enables more effective human resource planning and activities.

### Human Relations and Group Dynamics (1940-1950)

By the end of the 1940s, two world wars had come and gone, and the Great Depression was over, leaving the United States with an enviable growth-oriented economy and a growing sense of prosperity. Although the authority of owners and managers was still unquestioned, unions were strong, and employees were no longer cogs in the industrial machine.

The Western Electric Company studies in 1924 presaged the dominance of the human relations school of thought and with it, the beginnings of OB, which really came into their own after World War II. But it was the famous "Hawthorne effect," identified by Roethlisberger[16] of Harvard in his 1927 study, that shifted the focus from studying only the productivity and efficiency of physical workplace characteristics to listening to employee groups and changing the quality of supervision.

Briefly, Roethlisberger's studies began (in the spirit of scientific management) by addressing the effects of lighting levels on worker productivity. Contrary to expectations, worker productivity remained the same or increased with decreased illumination. Interviews showed that employees' morale increased not from differing levels of illumination, but as a result of the presence of the researchers. The researchers also found that the presence of informal groups among workers sometimes had a positive effect on morale and performance. The close relationships between the quality of supervision, morale, and productivity led to new training programs.

Later in the 1940s, Kurt Lewin and his associates[17] expanded the use of employee interviews and group involvement in work method discussions to improve job roles and responsibilities. The role of work groups in studying and implementing organizational effectiveness programs became an important part of management and OB practices.

### Decision Making and Leadership (1950-1960)

The decade of the 1950s was conservative in the United States. Industries in the United States maintained their international sovereignty, and the economy was stable. The United States had evolved beyond an agrarian and industrializing society, and the post-World War II economy was one in which U.S. industries reigned supreme. The human relations school made progress in management thought, particularly in the areas of decision making and leadership. Organizational behavior continued as a focus of inquiry.

Herbert Simon and James March published studies in the late 1950s[18] that moved management thinking another step away from scientific and classical management thought and into the humanistic and subjective areas of decision making. Their concepts of bounded rationality and "satisficing" were widely accepted. Human rationality had limits and boundaries. Individuals, it was found, did not always seek optimal alternatives among the available choices or solutions. They instead sought good enough choices that satisfied their perceived need for solutions: Individuals "satisficed;" they did not optimize. The perfect world of rationality made way for imperfect individuals.

Leadership studies were another innovation of the 1950s. These studies reflected both an OB and a classical, scientific management orientation. For example, Douglas McGregor's now-classical theory X and theory Y[19] orientations to management argued that theory X was based on beliefs that people are lazy and naturally avoid work and responsibility. Thus, theory X leaders need to exert control and use punishment to obtain worker productivity. Theory Y held that employees are naturally responsible and self-directed. Theory Y leaders exert less control and facilitate employee involvement.

Bales' study[20] characterized leadership as a continuum with the task leader, who assists employees by clarifying and focusing on goals, on one end and the social leader, who emphasizes employee involvement and cohesion, on the other. These studies showed that leadership beliefs, assumptions, and behaviors affected both the way employees responded to direction and their productivity.

### Sociotechnical and Systems Theory (1960-1980)

The stable 1950s gave way to the politically turbulent 1960s as the Vietnam War rattled U.S. society and the economy. The 1970s experienced further shifts in the U.S. industrial landscape as global forces rudely awakened a lethargic continent: the oil embargo hit; "Japan, Inc." was born; and the average level of education of the U.S. workforce jumped to 12.6 years.

Systems theory was developed in the 1950s and 1960s.[21] A major premise behind this school of thought is that work systems are interdependent on the technology, organizational structure, and social and technical nature of jobs. E. K. Trist and K. W. Bamforth found that, although technology improvement and the accompanying job specialization in a British coal mine should have led to an increase in worker productivity, the opposite occurred. In fact, worker absenteeism increased when groups were organized more narrowly by specialization. Performance was found to be higher in close-knit control groups that continued to do a variety of tasks. Trist and Bamforth concluded that social and technical aspects of work systems could not be separated.

Another intriguing development was the work by D. Katz and R. L. Kahn,[22] who described organizations as open systems. In this view, the system is dynamic and open to its environment. The system is an interdependent set of individuals, groups, and teams working to transform new energy received as inputs from the environment into outputs. Information (feedback) regarding the outputs is used to return the organization (like an organism) to a balance or equilibrium. The business environment was finally recognized as an integral part of organizations, which were studied as sets of interdependent systems. However, little attention was paid in the 1960s and 1970s to international or global competition in the workplace, an oversight for which the United States paid dearly.

### Contingency Theory (1980-1990)

The 1980s were politically conservative but economically extravagant and reckless. Junk bonds financed mergers and acquisitions that were driven more by corporate raiders' greed than by corporate advantage. At the same time, many large U.S. corporations remained complacent toward Japanese competition in electronics, automobiles, and other critical industries. Nevertheless, management thought was awakening to the need for competitive change in this decade: Michael Porter's *Competitive Strategy* (1980) was a landmark work; Tom Peters and Bob Waterman's *In Search of Excellence* (1982) was another. The seeds for change were sowed.

Contingency Theory, developed in the 1960s, came into its own in the 1980s through the work of Henry Mintzberg and others.[23] The major premise underlying contingency theory is that it is the fit between an organization's structure and its environment that determines effectiveness. There is not necessarily one best approach, and a manager must be aware of shifting environmental threats and opportunities. Burns, Stalker, and Woodward (in the 1960s) originated contemporary contingency theory. Burns and Stalker distinguished between two management systems: organic (flexible, open, human) and mechanistic (machinelike).[24] Organic systems work best in dynamic, uncertain, and fluid environments, whereas mechanistic systems work in stable, unchanging environments with routine task requirements. Woodward[25] argued that organic structures respond best to craft or continuous process technologies (such as a gas refinery), while mechanistic organizations respond best to mass production technologies (such as heavy equipment). Mintzberg extended the fit between organization structure and technologies, goals, environments, age, workforce, and organizational size. In contingency theory, it is the manager who identifies and organizes the appropriate management system and resources to respond to environments, technologies, and tasks.

### Global Management, Customer Focus, Information Technology, Diversity, Business Ethics (1990-?)

From the early 1970s until the early 1990s, the United States struggled to recover from serious government overspending and underdevelopment of corporate competitiveness. The new realities of global competition shocked the traditional hierarchical systems of larger corporations such as IBM and General Motors. The Japanese, other Asians, and Europeans presented serious industrial competitive threats with new quality products and reduced cycle times (i.e., faster delivery time to market).

A U.S. turnaround occurred beginning in the 1990s. Downsizing, reengineering, paying attention to quality, and integrating information technologies—especially through the Internet online and software applications—turned productivity around. Entrepreneurial start-ups and consolidation of businesses and industries continue to blur traditional boundaries. Telecommunications, entertainment, television, computers, and smart devices running on the World Wide Web are creating virtual ways of doing business and competing on Internet time.

At the same time, workforce diversity remains a major integrating challenge as organizations strive to recruit needed brainpower and knowledge workers from any country. Also, the need to lead, manage, and work legally and ethically remains high on the agenda of major corporations.

Quality remains a key component of global competitive advantage. The Internet has shifted power from corporations to customers. As stated earlier, the Internet has personalized service while delivering quality products faster. Quality, consequently, has come to be defined as more than a characteristic of a product or service: It is a strategic and operational requirement for conducting business. Various definitions of quality reflect the pervasive influence of this concept: quality in value, conformance to specifications and requirements, fitness for use, loss avoidance, and meeting and/or exceeding customers' expectations.[26] In fact, total quality management (TQM) practices have caused a paradigm shift in the way people see, do, and evaluate their work. Core values of TQM center around customer-driven requirements, organizational leadership, continuous improvement of all services, employee participation and development, fast response, design quality, long-range outlook, partnership development, results orientation, and corporate responsibility and citizenship.[27]

Dr. W. Edwards Deming, the late quality management guru, instigated the movement toward quality—first in Japan, and then belatedly in the United States.[28] He formulated 14 guidelines that address the "seven deadly sins" of quality management: (1) lack of constancy of purpose; (2) emphasis on short-term profits and immediate dividends; (3) evaluation of performance, merit rating, or annual review; (4) mobility of top management; (5) running a company only on visible figures; (6) excessive medical costs; and (7) excessive costs of warranty.

Deming intended to make providing quality the central activity of an organization. These are his guidelines for doing so: (1) create constancy of purpose; (2) adopt a new philosophy; (3) end the practice of purchasing at lowest prices; (4) institute leadership; (5) eliminate empty slogans; (6) eliminate numerical quotas: (7) institute on-the-job training; (8) drive out fear; (9) break down barriers between departments; (10) take action to accomplish the transformation; (11) improve constantly and forever the process of production and service; (12) cease dependence on mass inspection; (13) remove barriers to pride of workmanship; and (14) retrain vigorously.

The point here is that discussions and research on organizational behavioral effectiveness must now pay attention to the question of quality requirements and follow-through in service and product delivery, and on thinking about and "doing business."

The fall of the Berlin Wall, the rise of regional trading blocs, the increased mobility of global workforces, and the integrating force of the Internet have stimulated the globalization, imagination, and change of management curricula. The field of OB, in particular, emphasizes cross-national dimensions in its topical areas (e.g., communication, negotiations, teamwork, organizational cultures). We must also address changing ways of communicating in virtual and geographically dispersed teams. We must ask how information technologies affect the way companies organize, do business, lead, and manage people.

Managing diversity in the workplace has also become an imperative because almost half of the workforce is composed of women. In the entire workforce, approximately 15 percent are nonwhite, 13 percent are older than 55, and the education gap among employees widens. Moreover, entrepreneurial and small organizations are increasing. In large organizations and with the increasing number of mergers and acquisitions, the diverse workforce must integrate. At the individual, group, and organizational levels, increased awareness and sensitivity training will enable managers and employees to create synergy and to enhance productivity by overcoming stereotypes, isolation, and discriminatory practices.

A resurgence in the importance of business ethics actually began in the late 1980s and continues today. Then new emphasis on the legal and moral rights and responsibilities of corporations and employees is, in part, a reaction and response to the effects of the perceived greed of 1980s business practices. Society in the United States, with the help of the media, has also become more informed and aware of illegal and unethical activities in businesses and government. Moreover, laws have evolved and are being enforced to protect employees against discrimination, sexual harassment, unsafe environments, and other wrongful activities. In the following sections, we discuss the international dimensions of OB, managing diversity, and ethics, and close by presenting a diagnostic approach with introductory models for managing change.

## MANAGING INTERNATIONAL DIMENSIONS OF OB

### Who Is "Us"?

In a global environment, professionals and managers who work in teams must learn to create synergy in cross-cultural working relationships (i.e., the whole equals more than the sum of the individual parts of a system). A synergistic workforce is not parochial (our way is the only way) or ethnocentric (our way is the best way) in its beliefs, attitudes, values, and behaviors. The workforce members will develop skills in recognizing, communicating, negotiating, and working effectively with members of different national cultures and traditions.

> *Workforce skills are critical. As every advanced economy becomes global, a nation's most important competitive asset becomes the skills and cumulative learning of its workforce. Consequently, the most important issue with regard to global corporations is whether and to what extent they provide Americans with the training and experience that enable them to add greater value to the world economy. Whether the company happens to be headquartered in the United States or the United Kingdom is fundamentally unimportant. The company is a good "American" corporation if it equips its American workforce to compete in the global economy. The world of commerce has changed: now, we are they and they are us.*[29]

Foreign-owned corporations employ more than 3 million Americans, and 10 percent of U.S. manufacturing workers. In 1989, foreign manufacturing affiliates created more jobs in the United States than U.S.-owned manufacturing companies.[30] Only 35 of the 100 largest public companies have their headquarters in the United States. Forty percent of IBM's employees are foreign. Whirlpool employs more than 43,000 (mostly non-American) people in 45 countries, and U.S. companies employ more than 11 percent of Northern Ireland's industrial workforce. More than 100,000 Singaporians are employed by 200 U.S. companies: General Electric is Singapore's largest private employer. Moreover, the United States' most profitable midsize firms increased overseas production investments 20 percent annually between 1981 and 1986. Eighty percent of U.S. industry now faces some form of international competition.[31]

### Toward Cultural Synergy

Synergy means that the whole is equal to more than the sum of its parts, 1 + 1 = 3. When multicultural teams can use their differences as a source of creativity to multiply productivity, synergy occurs. "Cultural synergy builds upon similarities and fuses differences resulting in more effective human activities and systems. The very diversity of people can be utilized to enhance problem solving by combined action. Those in international management have unique opportunities to foster synergy on a global basis."[32]

A first step toward thinking and acting in a culturally synergistic way is to understand and be aware of our own cultural assumptions, unspoken rules, attitudes, communication, and negotiation patterns. Table 1–1 lists the national persuasion styles of Arabs, North Americans, and Russians. The differences in persuasion styles among these three groups occur on eight dimensions: primary negotiating style, conflict, making concessions, response to opponents' concessions, relationships, authority, initial position, and deadlines. You can see how understanding your own communication and negotiation styles before you problem-solve with members from other cultures could be helpful. An American doing business with a Saudi Arabian, for example, may want to reconsider the meaning of relationship in the transactions.

| TABLE 1–1    National Styles of Persuasion | | | |
| --- | --- | --- | --- |
| | *North Americans* | *Arabs* | *Russians* |
| Primary Negotiating Style and Process | Factual: Appeals made to logic | Affective: Appeals made to emotions | Axiomatic: Appeals made to ideals |
| Conflict: Opponent's Arguments Countered with . . . | Objective facts | Subjective feelings | Asserted ideals |
| Making Concessions | Small concessions made early to establish a relationship | Concessions made throughout as a part of the bargaining process | Few, if any, small concessions made |
| Response to Opponent's Concessions | Usually reciprocate opponent's concessions | Almost always reciprocate opponent's concessions | Opponent's concessions viewed as weakness and almost never reciprocated |
| Relationship | Short term | Long term | No continuing relationship |
| Authority | Broad | Broad | Limited |
| Initial Position | Moderate | Extreme | Extreme |
| Deadline | Very important | Casual | Ignored |

**SOURCE:** Reprinted from *International Journal of Intercultural Relations*, Vol 1, E.S. Glenn, D. Wilmeyer, and K.A. Stevenson, "Cultural Styles of Persuasion,"1984 with permission of Elsevier Science.

Similarly, Table 1–2 compares the negotiation styles and underlying cultural differences of the Japanese, North Americans, and Latin Americans. In this table, 11 dimensions, which range from emotional sensitivity to how personal or impersonal decision making is considered, are identified. Again, you can see that the concept of teamwork to an American differs dramatically from that of a person from Latin America or Japan. Certainly, these characterizations do not necessarily apply to all Americans, Japanese, or Latin Americans, but, on average, these cultural traits are a valid starting point for understanding such differences.

With training in cross-cultural communication and negotiation differences, multinational work groups and teams can begin to use their differences as strengths instead of barriers in reaching decisions that benefit the organization.

**TABLE 1–2    Negotiation Styles from a Cross-Cultural Perspective**

| Dimension | Japanese | North American | Latin American |
|---|---|---|---|
| 1 | Emotional sensitivity highly valued<br>Hiding of emotions | Emotional sensitivity not highly valued<br>Straightforward or impersonal dealings | Emotional sensitivity valued<br>Emotionally passionate |
| 2 | Subtle power plays; conciliation | Litigation; not as much conciliation | Great power plays; use of weakness |
| 3 | Loyalty to employer; employer takes care of employees | Lack of commitment to employer; breaking of ties by either if necessary | Loyalty to employer (who is often family) |
| 4 | Group decision making by consensus | Teamwork provides input to a decision maker | Decisions come down from one individual |
| 5 | Face-saving crucial; decisions often made on basis of saving someone from embarrassment | Decisions made on a cost-benefit basis; face-saving does not always matter | Face-saving crucial in decision making to preserve honor, dignity |
| 6 | Decision makers openly influenced by special interests | Decision makers influenced by special interests but often not considered ethical | Execution of special interests of decision maker expected, condoned |
| 7 | Not argumentative; quiet when right | Argumentative when right or wrong, but impersonal | Argumentative when right or wrong; passionate |
| 8 | What is down in writing must be accurate, valid | Great importance given to documentation as evidentiary proof | Impatient with documentation, seen as obstacle to understand-general principles |
| 9 | Step-by-step approach to decision making | Methodically organized decision making | Impulsive, spontaneous decision making |
| 10 | Good of group is the ultimate aim | Profit motive or good of individual ultimate ultimate aim | What is good for group is good for the individual |
| 11 | Cultivate a good emotional social setting for decision making; get to know decision makers | Decision making impersonal; avoid involvements, conflict of interest | Personalism necessary for good decision making |

SOURCE: Reprinted from Casse, P. *Training for the Multicultural Manager: A Practical and Cross-Cultural Approach to Management of People* (Washington, D.C.: Copyright © 1982. Society for Intercultural Education, Training, and Research, SIETAR International). Used with permission.

### 3 Step Process: Cultural Synergy

A useful framework for understanding how to create cultural synergy is illustrated in Figure 1–3. This three-step framework can help managers and cross-national team members by explicitly (1) describing a situation or problem from two or more cultural perspectives (How do you see the situation?); (2) determining the cultural assumptions underlying each perspective (What are you assuming about the cause(s) of this situation? What are our perceptual similarities and differences?); (3) creating cultural synergy (What new or different alternatives and solutions can we create and implement to address the situation and solve the problem? Does the solution fit with your cultural assumptions?). The solution is then refined after obtaining feedback from the various cultural perspectives. Working toward synergy is also a goal in integrating diverse workforces.

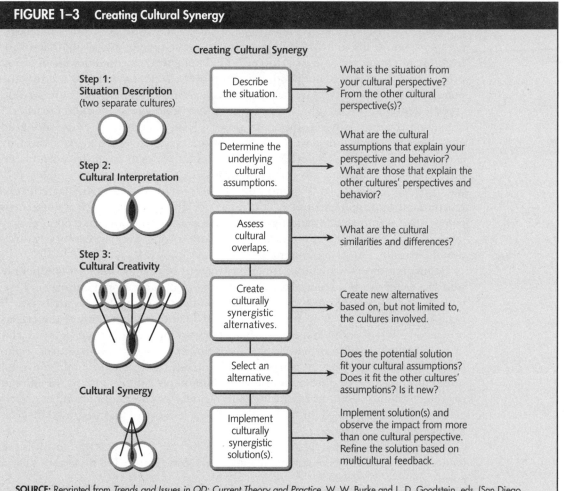

**FIGURE 1–3    Creating Cultural Synergy**

Creating Cultural Synergy

**Step 1:**
**Situation Description**
(two separate cultures)

Describe the situation.

What is the situation from your cultural perspective? From the other cultural perspective(s)?

**Step 2:**
**Cultural Interpretation**

Determine the underlying cultural assumptions.

What are the cultural assumptions that explain your perspective and behavior? What are those that explain the other cultures' perspectives and behavior?

Assess cultural overlaps.

What are the cultural similarities and differences?

**Step 3:**
**Cultural Creativity**

Create culturally synergistic alternatives.

Create new alternatives based on, but not limited to, the cultures involved.

Select an alternative.

Does the potential solution fit your cultural assumptions? Does it fit the other cultures' assumptions? Is it new?

**Cultural Synergy**

Implement culturally synergistic solution(s).

Implement solution(s) and observe the impact from more than one cultural perspective. Refine the solution based on multicultural feedback.

**SOURCE:** Reprinted from *Trends and Issues in OD: Current Theory and Practice*, W. W. Burke and L. D. Goodstein, eds. (San Diego, Calif: Pfeiffer and Company, 1980). Used with permission.

## *MANAGING WORKFORCE DIVERSITY AS COMPETITIVE ADVANTAGE*

The workforce in the United States is becoming more diverse across several primary and secondary categories.[33] It is important to point out that diversity includes not only cultural or ethnic diversity but also age, gender, sexual orientation, and physical abilities as primary categories of diversity. Secondary categories of diversity include education, work experience, income, marital status, religious beliefs, geographic location, parental status, physical and mental disabilities, and behavioral styles. It is estimated that by the year 2000, developed countries will supply only 21 percent of the world's high school enrollees; four of the next six greatest sources of college graduates are developing countries, including Brazil, China, the Philippines, and South Korea; the average age of the world's workers will climb to about 35; and pressure for workers to emigrate from less to more developed countries will continue to rise.[34] The U.S. workforce will consequently continue to diversify.

Managing diversity means "managing in such a way as to get from a heterogeneous workforce the same productivity, commitment, quality, and profit that we got from the old homogeneous workforce."[35] Managing diversity does not mean giving preferential treatment to nonproductive employees. It does mean fully utilizing the potential of all employees regardless of age, gender, sexual preference, color, creed, national origin, ability, and the other categories identified earlier.[36] Managing diversity is an evolutionary process that assumes that empowering all employees is directly linked with achieving business objectives. To manage diversity is to minimize or remove performance barriers that result from diversity-related problems such as bigotry, any form of harassment, turnover, absenteeism, low productivity, work quality, and group cohesiveness. It is also argued that effective recruitment and management of a diverse workforce can enhance a company's competitive advantage by adding expertise relevant to addressing increasingly diverse markets; expanding creativity in problem solving; and increasing organizational flexibility, goal achievement, and profitability.[37]

"Managing diversity includes the improvement of relationships among people who are different, but recognizes that changes in organizational culture and systems may also be required to create an environment that enables all employees."[38] Becoming aware of our stereotyping of ourselves and of others and of the effects of stereotyping on people's attitudes, behaviors, and work performance is one aim of managing diversity. A broader objective is the creation of a multicultural organization[39] with a culture that values diversity; enables full structural and informal integration of the workforce; minimizes or eliminates cultural bias in the human resource system (of recruiting, hiring, and training people); and minimizes intergroup conflict. Table 1–3 illustrates these characteristics of an integrated diverse, multicultural organization.

Managing diversity can be an organizationwide change process that involves the leadership and includes major management systems. Figure 1–4 illustrates such a comprehensive framework.

**TABLE 1–3    The Characteristics of Multicultural Organizations**

1. A culture that fosters and values cultural difference
2. Pluralism as an acculturation process
3. Full structural integration
4. Full integration of the informal networks
5. An absence of institutionalized cultural bias in human resource management systems and practices
6. A minimum in intergroup conflict due to the proactive management of diversity

SOURCE: T. C. Cox, Jr., *Cultural Diversity in Organizations: Theory, Research & Practice* (San Francisco: Berrett-Koehler, 1993), 229. Used with permission.

**FIGURE 1–4    Organizational Change Framework: Managing and Valuing Cultural Diversity**

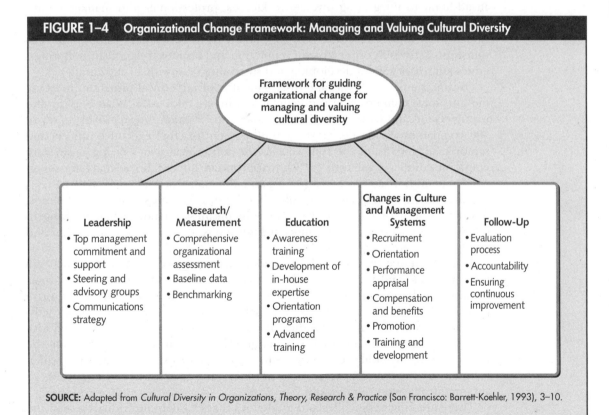

SOURCE: Adapted from *Cultural Diversity in Organizations, Theory, Research & Practice* (San Francisco: Barrett-Koehler, 1993), 3–10.

### Change Agents

Change agents can be designated professionals inside or hired from outside an organization to help create, implement, and manage change, and often are involved from the beginning of this process of assisting organizations to become multicultural. The process begins with the commitment, strategy, and communications from top management. Then, collecting and assessing organizational information follows in establishing a diversity-related baseline with benchmarks (industry high-standard goals). The OB specialists, such as change agents, are particularly involved in the next step, which is education, that is, implementing awareness training programs. Changes in the culture and management systems are then made with follow-up evaluations, accountability, and improvement activities. Many of the implementation tools used in this change process are grounded in OB concepts and skills—for example, mentoring programs, support groups, cultural audits, education and training, orientation programs, and conflict management.

## MANAGING ETHICALLY

In addition to integrating diverse workforces, professionals and managers must meet legal and ethical standards in conducting business. The assets of a professional or an organization are only as valuable as its reputation, image, and relationships. Trust is a cornerstone of reputation and business relationships. Business ethics addresses ways of developing and sustaining trust with all stakeholders.

"Business ethics is the art and discipline of applying ethical principles to examine and solve complex moral dilemmas. Business ethics asks, 'What is right and wrong? Good and bad?' in business transactions."[40] In an international survey of 300 companies worldwide, more than 80 percent of chief executive officers and senior managers listed the following as the top ethical issues facing businesses: employee conflict of interests (91%); inappropriate gifts (91%); sexual harassment (91%); unauthorized payments (85%); and affirmative action issues (84%).[41]

Additionally, a national survey of 1,400 working women showed that the most frequently occurring unethical practices in business include managers lying to employees; expense account abuses at high levels; nepotism and favoritism; and taking credit for others' work.[42]

Managing ethically starts with the leadership of any organization. It is the leaders who direct and model the cultural values, norms, and acceptable (or unacceptable) behaviors in the organization. It is also the leaders who authorize policies, directives, and procedures that define and enforce legal and ethical activity and behavior. However, individual managers and employees are presented with daily situations in which questionable ethical decisions arise. Often, there may be no clear company policy or guidelines to follow. There are also occasions in which company or supervisory pressures to produce cause managers and employees to act unethically and even illegally.

There are ethics principles and guidelines that can help individuals screen the rightness and wrongness of decisions and behaviors before an impulsive or random

## THE CHANGING WORKPLACE

### Diversity Perspectives

Issue: Argue this question: "Can diversity programs really affect a business's bottom line; or are diversity programs just the right thing to do ethically?"

#### Allstate Insurance on Diversity

Allstate made diversity a priority in 1993 after it had tried other sensitivity-training programs. Carlton Yearwood, director of the diversity team said, "... none of it went to the heart of how we're going to grow our business." Allstate's CEO and chairman, Jerry Choate, commented, "Affirmative action [alone] was decisive in some ways because it's not based on what you *think*, it's what you *observe*. That gives feedback that you can see."

Allstate, in Northbrook, Illinois, surveys (with its "diversity index") all 50,000 employees each quarter to find out how the firm is performing with its customers and employees. The survey asks how employees feel about their managers regarding the firm's policy on bias-free service to customers, respect for individuals, and a sensitive workplace. Outcomes on these indexes determine 25 percent of managers' merit bonuses.

Allstate claims that managers' evaluations of their employees' satisfaction helps create a productive environment. Carlton Yearwood stated that in just two years, the company "identified a correlation among sales managers between sales performance and scores on the diversity and leadership indexes. While that doesn't prove a connection to profits, the measurement feat points the way to a better business case for diversity."

Exercise: Answer the questions and then share your responses with your class or in a small group.

1.  Can diversity programs and surveys such as Allstate's affect a company's ways of doing business? How? Why? Why not?

2.  Have you been part of a diversity training program? Has your company offered such a training program? What is your evaluation of the program?

3.  Describe elements of a diversity program that you believe would effectively integrate individuals' backgrounds and talents to create business and work opportunities for the company, customers, and employees.

SOURCE: Adapted from Leon Wynter, "Allstate Rates Managers on Handling Diversity," *The Wall Street Journal*, Oct. 1, 1997, B1.

act causes unforeseen, negative consequences. Table 1–4 lists some classic, long-standing principles that can be used to examine the motives and possible consequences of decisions or actions. When evaluating the ethics of an act, decision, or policy, it is often helpful to frame questions from the perspectives of rights, justice, duty, utilitarianism, and relativism. For example, a rights perspective asks, Whose rights will be violated by whom and toward what end? Equivalent questions can be asked and important discussions instigated from the other perspectives as well. The point here is that all of these perspectives and questions can be used to evaluate ("me-test") a decision or course of action.

| TABLE 1–4 | Ethical Decision-Making Principles | |
| --- | --- | --- |
| Perspective | Frame | Authority |
| Rights | Whose rights are violated by whom for what end? | Based on individual right and entitlements (all individuals are created equal and have the rights to pursue life, liberty, and happiness. |
| Justice | Is the opportunity, wealth, and/or burden fairly explained and distributed? Will harm be compensated—to whom, by whom, and for how much? | Based on the fair distribution of opportunity, wealth, and burden. *Distributive justice* is concerned with the disbursement of opportunity, wealth, and burden to all parties. *Procedural justice* is concerned with fair procedures, practices, agreements. *Compensatory justice* is concerned with compensating someone for a past harm or injustice. |
| Universalism and duty | Are individuals involved valued as human beings, not as means toward an end? | Based on the extent to which the intention of an act treats all persons with respect, as unique human beings, and ends in themselves, not means. |
| Utilitarianism | Will the benefits exceed the costs for the majority? | Based on the determination that the net benefits of the acts, consequences exceed the costs for the greatest number involved. |
| Relativism | Is an action normally acceptable in a particular situation? | Based on individual or cultural specific contexts, self-interest. |

Copyright: Joseph W. Weiss, 1998.

Other ethical approaches and quick tests include the following: Practice the Golden Rule. Do unto others as you would have them do unto you. Get feedback from others before acting. Use the test of "one's best self"—is this action compatible with my concept of myself at its best? Take the public exposure test: Would I take this action if I knew it would be a headline on the front page of my newspaper tomorrow? Ask the following questions: Will this action hurt anyone? Will I regret having taken this action in a week or in a year? What is my motivation in taking this action?

Finally, using a reflective approach before acting impulsively can often prevent an illegal or unethical consequence. These are examples of reflective questions: Did I take time to define the problem objectively? Have I asked how this situation came about? Have I used the who, what, when, where, why, how, and so what tests? Have I asked how others would be affected? What will be the consequences? For whom? What

---

## THE CHANGING WORKPLACE

### Ethical Questions

**Exercise:**

1. Write an ethical dilemma you are now facing or have experienced over the past year.

2. Write a few sentences explaining how you would solve (or solved) the dilemma.

3. Read each of the ethical criteria below and answer the questions in the following exercise.

    - **Golden Rule:** "Do unto others as you would have them do unto you."

    - **"Best Self":** "What action should I take to be compatible with my self-concept at its best?"

    - **Public Exposure Test:** "What action should I take if I knew it would be tomorrow's headline in my city's newspaper?"

- **Harm Test:** "Will the action I take hurt anyone?"

- **Regret Test:** "Will I regret having taken this action tomorrow, in a week, or in a year?"

- **Motive Test:** "What is my motivation and intention in taking this action?"

**Exercise:**

1. Which criteria did your solution violate? Why or how?

2. Which of the criteria did you find the most helpful? The least? Explain.

3. What other ethical principles from this chapter might be helpful in your decision making with this dilemma?

4. What other criteria did you or would you use to help identify an action to solve your problem? Explain.

---

is the worst thing that can happen if I take this action? What if I do nothing—what then? These ethics tests can be used throughout this text and in everyday organizational life as guides to more socially responsible decisions, behaviors, and policies.

## CHANGE AGENT METHODS: THREE DIAGNOSTIC APPROACHES

OB theories, concepts, and methods are action oriented. Some chapters in this book offer concepts and methods that can be applied to change individual, group, and organizational behaviors, policies, and procedures. All these methods require objective judgment and field research. A basic organizational analysis begins with the following eight steps: (1) gather reliable, valid information and define the problem(s), (2) research the causes of the problem, (3) diagnose, analyze, and validate the problem's causes, (4) propose alternative interventions and/or solutions, (5) select an intervention and/or solution(s), (6) implement the intervention and solution, (7) evaluate the implementation effects and readdress the problem, and (8) make changes in the original problem identification and proposed interventions. This is the first step a change agent can use for problem solving in the field of OB.

### A Jump-Start Analysis: Where's the Pain?

A second, related diagnostic approach is the jump-start analysis which can be used separately or as a complementary approach with the eight-step method just discussed. The jump-start analysis examines the organization's dimensions and subsystems at different levels. To determine where the problem is located in the organization, we can use Figure 1–5 to ask "trigger" questions.

For example, is the problem at the leadership level or with an individual(s)? Inside or between teams? Is the problem endemic to the entire organization (e.g., its vision,

---

**FIGURE 1–5   Jump-Start Analysis**

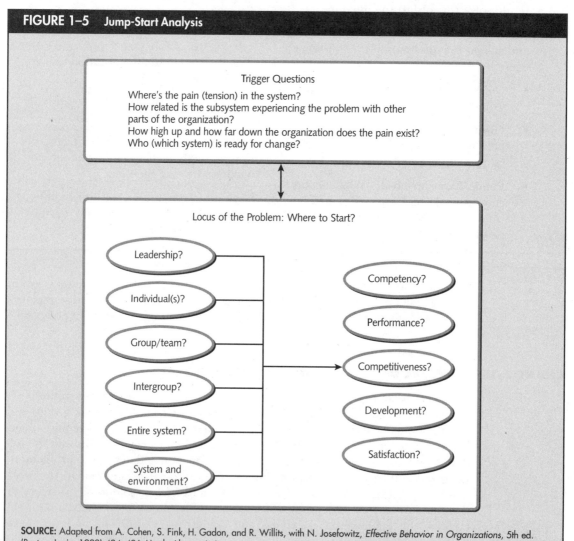

**SOURCE:** Adapted from A. Cohen, S. Fink, H. Gadon, and R. Willits, with N. Josefowitz, *Effective Behavior in Organizations*, 5th ed. (Boston: Irwin, 1992) 424–426. Used with permission.

policies, procedures)? Or is the problem between this organization and another or between this organization and a segment of its environment (e.g., is the organization losing its market niche, a major customer, supplier)? Continuing this process, we may find that one problem is related to and is cause and effect of several dimensions.

Concepts, theories, and tools for diagnosing and addressing organizational behavior problems within these frameworks are the content of each chapter in this book. A final diagnostic model introduced here is a more macro-oriented, organizational systems framework.

### A Diagnostic Contingency Model

The diagnostic contingency model addresses systems-level dimensions of organizations. This method also requires some field and document research. The logic of this model assumes that effective organizations demonstrate a "fit" among the dimensions of the systems shown in Figure 1–6. Also note in this figure the three basic organizational processes (input, transformation, and output) showing the use of resources through the organization. Customers are depicted as primary participants throughout each of these processes. For example, universities and colleges enroll students as customers at the input stage; students are educated at the transformation stage; and students graduate and are awarded their degrees at the output stage.

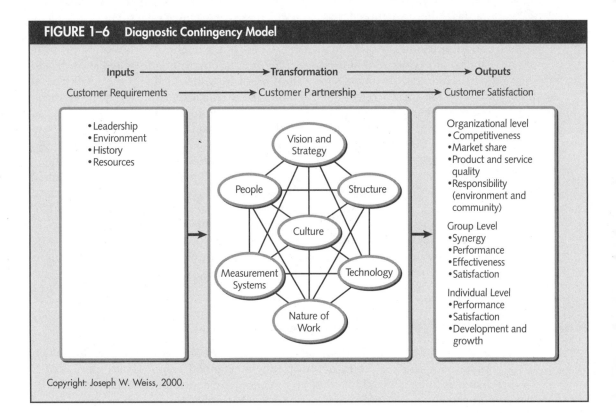

**FIGURE 1–6    Diagnostic Contingency Model**

Copyright: Joseph W. Weiss, 2000.

The model assumes that, at the input stage, organizational leaders both have and use their knowledge of customer requirements, the environment, the history of the organization, and the resources necessary to accomplish work at the transformation stage. For diagnostic purposes, we can ask at the input stage: Do the leaders know and understand customer requirements? Are the leaders capable of orchestrating and leading the delivery of these requirements, given environmental opportunities and threats, the history of the organization, and available resources? Is there a high probability that customers and targeted markets can be satisfied given the answers to the first two questions?

At the transformation stage, the model assumes that there is a "fit" among the organizational dimensions so that work can be profitably, effectively, and efficiently accomplished, according to customer requirements and the vision of the organization. Diagnostically, we can ask: Is there a fit among these dimensions, starting with the vision and strategy? Is the vision too aggressive, not aggressive enough? Can the stated strategy adequately implement the vision? What type of structure, people, culture, measurement systems, and technology are required to best implement the stated vision and strategy of the firm? What kind of culture would enhance the fit among and between these different dimensions? In which dimension(s) or subsystems are there weaknesses and strengths to accomplish the work? What is needed to strengthen the fit within and among the organizational systems? Finally, at the output stage, there are three levels from which we can examine effectiveness, efficiency, and responsibility. At the organizational level, we ask: How competitive is the organization in its industry? Do market share and other financial indicators show profitability and evidence that the organization is accomplishing its stated strategy and goals? Have the customers shown satisfaction with the quality of the product and service? How socially responsible and moral have the leadership and members been toward stockholders and stakeholders in implementing the vision and strategy? At the group and team levels, we ask: Do the groups and teams work with synergy or in fragmented ways? How well did the teams perform? How effective were the teams in meeting their stated goals and objectives? How satisfied were the teams—did members experience personal growth, satisfaction, and development? At the individual level, we ask the same questions as those relating to groups and teams.

The three diagnostic approaches introduced here complement each other. Starting with the eight basic questions, then moving to the jump-start approach, and finally locating any problems in the diagnostic contingency model offer a wide range of organizational, individual, and team diagnostic dimensions and questions that can be used to pinpoint interventions for effectively planned change.

## MAPPING AND CREATING PLANNED CHANGE

Change can be planned or unplanned responses to pressures and forces inside an organization and/or from the environment. Planned responses are preferred if change is to be effected in a desired direction. We conclude this chapter by briefly summarizing two change models. These models serve as reference points to orient and guide the use of OB concepts throughout this text. These models are presented here to help you initially "frame" ways of thinking about mapping and creating change in organizations. The first model, Figure 1–7 describes three types of organizational change: (1) developmental change, improving and/or fine-tuning skills, methods, or conditions to improve what already exists; (2) transitional change, implementing interventions in which changes evolve more slowly toward a new state (e.g., mergers, acquisitions, new systems/services/techniques); and (3) transformational change, introducing new and radically different forms of the organization's mission, culture, and leadership. Transformational change is directed toward what is believed to be possible and necessary for the organization.[43]

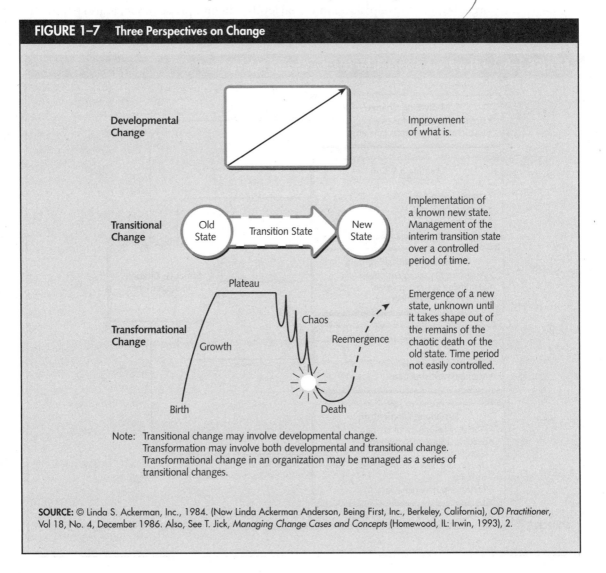

**FIGURE 1–7    Three Perspectives on Change**

Developmental Change — Improvement of what is.

Transitional Change — Old State → Transition State → New State — Implementation of a known new state. Management of the interim transition state over a controlled period of time.

Transformational Change — Birth, Growth, Plateau, Chaos, Death, Reemergence — Emergence of a new state, unknown until it takes shape out of the remains of the chaotic death of the old state. Time period not easily controlled.

Note:  Transitional change may involve developmental change.
Transformation may involve both developmental and transitional change.
Transformational change in an organization may be managed as a series of transitional changes.

**SOURCE:** © Linda S. Ackerman, Inc., 1984. (Now Linda Ackerman Anderson, Being First, Inc., Berkeley, California), *OD Practitioner*, Vol 18, No. 4, December 1986. Also, See T. Jick, *Managing Change Cases and Concepts* (Homewood, IL: Irwin, 1993), 2.

A question to keep in mind while studying organizations is, What is the scope of organizational change planned and how is it intended to affect organizational members? Not all organizations, business units, or branches require transformational change. After identifying the scope of planned change required, the diagnostic models can be used to identify and predict how the different dimensions of the organization would or should change to accommodate the planned state of the change.

The second model, which identifies five activities or phases that can be used to guide a change management program, is illustrated in Figure 1–8 This model is particularly relevant to the field of OB since each activity suggests several behavioral interventions or planned implementation methods to facilitate change at the organizational, group, and individual levels. The five-phase model is also helpful in classifying the level and type of required or planned change.

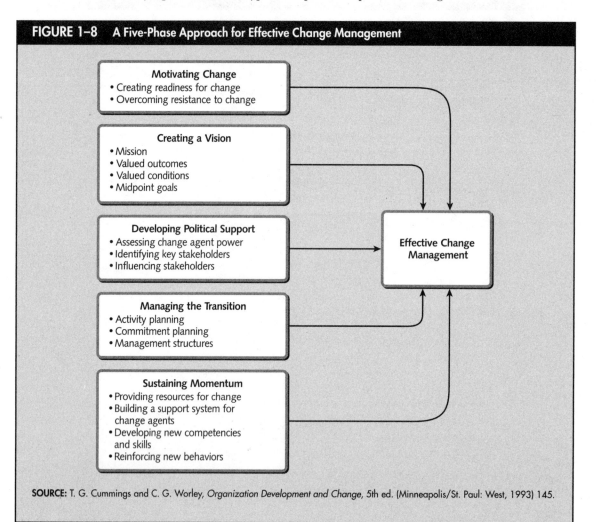

**FIGURE 1–8    A Five-Phase Approach for Effective Change Management**

**Motivating Change**
• Creating readiness for change
• Overcoming resistance to change

**Creating a Vision**
• Mission
• Valued outcomes
• Valued conditions
• Midpoint goals

**Developing Political Support**
• Assessing change agent power
• Identifying key stakeholders
• Influencing stakeholders

**Managing the Transition**
• Activity planning
• Commitment planning
• Management structures

**Sustaining Momentum**
• Providing resources for change
• Building a support system for change agents
• Developing new competencies and skills
• Reinforcing new behaviors

**Effective Change Management**

**SOURCE:** T. G. Cummings and C. G. Worley, *Organization Development and Change,* 5th ed. (Minneapolis/St. Paul: West, 1993) 145.

The three-perspective views of change presented in the previous paragraph and the five-phase model are complementary frameworks and both can be used simultaneously to determine the scope and nature of organizational change to be undertaken.

Referring to Figure 1–8, you can see that the first activity, motivating change, involves creating a readiness for change and overcoming resistance to change. Specific methods and skills relating to these activities are presented in Chapter 4 (Motivation). The second activity, creating a vision, involves defining a mission, valued outcomes and conditions, and midpoint goals. These are activities that involve an organization's leadership. Methods and skills regarding these activities are discussed in Chapter 7 (Leadership and Followership). The third activity, developing political support, deals with assessing change-agent power, identifying key stakeholders, and influencing stakeholders. Skills and tools relating to these activities are described in Chapter 8. The fourth major change-management activity is managing the transition; this involves activity, commitment planning, and managing structures. This topic is discussed in Chapter 11 (Structure). The last major activity is sustaining momentum, which involves providing resources for change, building a support system for change agents, developing new competencies and skills, and reinforcing new behaviors.

## The Game Plan

The plan of this four-part book is based on arranging topics from a micro to macro level of analysis:

### PART I: INTRODUCTION AND OVERVIEW

**Chapter 1, Organizational Behavior in the 21st Century,** sets the agenda for integrating the themes of the text. Emphasis is placed on discussing contemporary organizational settings and challenges; identifying change agent and management frameworks and tools as they relate to OB principles and applications; providing a framework for managing diversity and the international and ethical dimensions of workplace behavior; and using diagnostic models to examine OB issues.

### PART II: INDIVIDUAL PROCESSES

**Chapter 2, Individual Differences and Personality,** focuses on the individual as the "unit" of analysis. The importance of personality and the personal system is emphasized as ways to understand and read individual differences and work effectiveness are examined. Personality characteristics that hinder and facilitate relationships are discussed.

**Chapter 3, Perception and Attribution,** describes perception and attribution theory, with particular reference to workforce diversity and cross-national workforces. How individuals see, avoid stereotyping, and evaluate problems and opportunities is a first step in understanding organizational problems.

**Chapter 4, Motivation, Learning, and Rewards,** deals with classical theory and contemporary issues and guidelines for diagnosing and motivating members of workforce 2000. How to motivate professionals during organizational changes is also discussed.

## PART III: TEAM AND INTERPERSONAL PROCESS

**Chapter 5, High-Performing Teams and Groups,** describes the process of group formation and includes characteristics of high-performance, self-managed, virtual, and international teams. Cross-cultural, diversity perspectives on team performance are also discussed.

**Chapter 6, Communication,** presents models for diagnosing and using effective communication skills in organizations with reference to international and culturally diverse workforces. Interpersonal communication and issues related to effectively managing electronic communication are addressed.

**Chapter 7, Leadership and Followership,** explains the distinctive competencies of organizational leaders and how leaders can be viewed as partners with followers. Organizational behavior at the team and individual levels are greatly affected by the leadership's choice of vision and mobilization around strategy. The role of leadership skills in setting a vision and formulating a strategy for obtaining it is emphasized. Classical studies and approaches to leadership are summarized. The role of **followers** is presented as the "other face and force" of leadership.

**Chapter 8, Power and Politics,** describes models and skills for effectively using and managing power and politics in organizations in socially responsible ways. A change model that incorporates power is also presented.

**Chapter 9, Conflict and Negotiation,** examines sources of conflict and presents conflict resolution and negotiation methods that relate to cross-cultural situations. Ethics principles and negotiation strategies for resolving conflicts are presented.

## PART IV: ORGANIZATIONAL PROCESSES

**Chapter 10, Work, Jobs, and Job Design,** presents contemporary and classical methods for designing and redesigning jobs. Issues regarding meaningfulness, motivation, and relevance of jobs in changing contexts are discussed.

**Chapter 11, Organizational Design and Structure,** explains the challenges that present and future structural arrangements must address. The evolution of structure is presented. Strategies for managing and working in contemporary structures are examined.

**Chapter 12, Organizational Culture,** defines culture and describes symptoms of cultures in trouble and attributes of those that are successful. Methods for diagnosing and changing culture are presented. International perspectives that influence organizational culture are given.

**Chapter 13, Careers and Socialization,** focuses on contemporary forces affecting career and career planning. Models and skills for managing and navigating career development in the twenty-first century are presented.

**Chapter 14, Organizing and Managing Change,** presents additional organizational development (OD) strategies and interventions for managing organization-wide change.

## SCENARIO AND EXERCISE: "THE COMPANY OF THE FUTURE: 6 GLUES FOR FINDING AND KEEPING TALENTED PROFESSIONALS"

Joe Liemandt, 30, founded Trilogy [software] in 1989, after dropping out of Stanford only a few months before graduation. To finance the startup, Liemandt charged up 22 credit cards. [Trilogy is in Austin, Texas, and is on the cutting edge of sale-and-marketing software.] If Trilogy were to go public today, analysts say, it would be valued at more than $1 billion. Four years ago, Trilogy had 100 employees, today it has almost 1,000—and plans to add another 1,000.... But to call Trilogy workers "employees" misses the point. They're all shareholders. They're all managers. They're all partners. That's how Liemandt has chosen to run his company—and that's what makes it successful.

Finding and retaining talented people is, according to Liemandt and other CEOs, the most difficult and pressing challenge of leaders today. In the article just cited, the author discusses six "social glues" of the company of the future that enable leaders to hire and keep talented people in companies of the future, such as Trilogy.

**Step 1.** After reading each of the six "social glues" listed here, rank yourself on a scale of 1 (not relevant to me) to 10 (describes me very well):

1.  "Money makes it mutual." Money and stock options (equity in a company) are very important

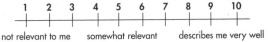

| 1 | 2 | 3 | 4 | 5 | 6 | 7 | 8 | 9 | 10 |

not relevant to me    somewhat relevant    describes me very well

**because** _____.

2.  "Mission makes a difference." People want to be part of a company they can believe in, that confers meaning on their work and lives, that has purpose and motivates

| 1 | 2 | 3 | 4 | 5 | 6 | 7 | 8 | 9 | 10 |

not relevant to me    somewhat relevant    describes me very well

**because** _____.

3.  "Learning makes you grow." People want a company with a culture that values learning, a career that allows growth with responsibilities, and a chance to learn continuously

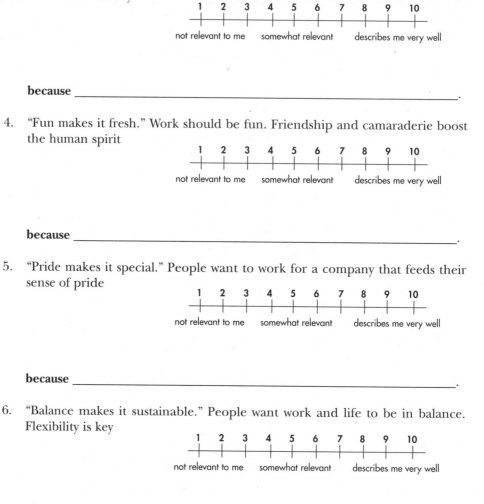

because _____.

4.  "Fun makes it fresh." Work should be fun. Friendship and camaraderie boost the human spirit

because _____.

5.  "Pride makes it special." People want to work for a company that feeds their sense of pride

because _____.

6.  "Balance makes it sustainable." People want work and life to be in balance. Flexibility is key

because _____.

**Step 2.** Write your reason(s) beside each of your rankings.

**Step 3.** Address these questions:

1.  What factors, other than the social glues, motivate you to leave and join another company?

2. Is the company where you are working a "company of the future"? (Interpret this comparing your answer to Trilogy and/or other firms you know.) Why or why not?

3. What incentives would it take to have you join a company where you would "love" to work?

SOURCE: Adapted from Robert Reich, "The Company of the Future," *Fast Company*, November, 1998, 124-150.

## REVIEW QUESTIONS

1. What are the major changes and challenges that corporations are currently experiencing?

2. What is "OB" and what is the aim of this field?

3. What are some of the major OB perspectives that have evolved historically? What different trends characterize the beginning of the twenty-first century? Can you think of another trend?

4. Explain one method to create cross-cultural synergy in a diverse workgroup. How would you use this method?

5. Explain how an understanding of "diversity" in organizations could help you work more effectively with different individuals.

6. Identify some categories that characterize diversity. Which category(ies) describe(s) you?

7. Discuss three ethical principles that you could use to clarify a moral dilemma at work. Which principle, including your own, do you use the most? Explain.

8. Select and describe one of the three diagnostic change approaches presented. Which of the three approaches would you find most helpful to use? Why?

9. After reading this chapter, do you believe that studying OB can be useful to you at work? Explain.

10. What specific part(s) of this chapter do you find most interesting? Explain.

# Individual Processes

**CHAPTER 2**
Individual Differences and Personality

**CHAPTER 3**
Perception and Attribution

**CHAPTER 4**
Motivation, Learning, and Rewards

# 2

# Individual Differences and Personality

---

LEARNING OBJECTIVES

After studying this chapter, you should be able to:

1 Define personality and the "personal system."

2 Present five major trait theories.

3 Identify methods for measuring personality.

4 Describe five personality characteristics.

5 Describe personal mastery and habits of effective people in organizations.

6 Identify managerial issues regarding individual differences in organizations.

7 Present characteristics of ethical behavior and guidelines for evaluating it.

---

A recent study summarized eight characteristics of successful business leaders: (1) integrity, maturity, and energy (the foundation on which the other characteristics were built), (2) business acumen (a solid understanding of the business with a strong profit perspective—an instinctive feel for how the firm makes money), (3) people acumen (evaluating and leading teams, coaching and developing people; cutting unnecessary losses), (4) organizational acumen (engendering trust, sharing information, being decisive and incisive, having excellent listening skills; diagnosing the organization on its full potential; changing the business), (5) curiosity, intellectual capacity, and a global mindset, (6) superior judgment (having an external orientation and a hunger for knowledge of the world; skilled at connecting developments and seeing patterns), (7) an insatiable appetite for accomplishment and results, and (8) powerful motivation to grow and convert learning into practice.[1] It is interesting to note that several of these characteristics are personality related. We argue that this profile applies not only to CEOs and business leaders but also to professionals in organizations who wish to excel. This chapter identifies and describes how personality concepts, characteristics, and individual differences are studied, measured, and applied to organizational behavior to identify and improve individual effectiveness.

## INDIVIDUAL DIFFERENCES IN PERSONALITY

Why do two individuals approach the same job or work assignment in very different ways? Why does one employee insist that a project is too vague and confusing while another believes that the same project is challenging and interesting? Why is the "chemistry" between two employees on a team constantly negative regardless of what others try to say or do? Understanding individuals and individual differences in workstyle involves defining the concepts of "personality" and the "personal system." Personality is the combination of stable physical and mental characteristics that make up an individual's identity and give consistency to a person's behavior. The concept of *emotional intelligence* (EQ) is a concept that complements traditional beliefs that personality is defined only as thinking intelligence (IQ). Goleman defined EQ as being "self-motivated, knowing and controlling one's own emotions, recognizing and being able to control others' emotions (empathy)."[2] To understand differences in individual behavior and to be able to manage oneself is an important part of EQ.

Individuals who refuse or who are unable to understand and control their emotions will endure more stress as organizations continue to undergo historic transformations. Brenda Barlick, a supervisor at Integra Financial, a bank holding company in Pittsburgh with $14 billion in assets, states,

> In a time of radical change like this you have to keep up the momentum, but it's hard because people are so competitive and they're so scared to fail. One thing I've seen is people who are not just participating at all, and you can tell they're thinking, "This is just a passing phase; I'll put my energies elsewhere." Or saying one thing and doing another, not putting their best effort in, going through the motions."[3]

Leading and working during times of rapid technological and organizational growth and hyperchange may require different personal strengths and skills than during more stable times. The following profile is a comparison of personal and professional characteristics of entrepreneurial e-business CEOs[4] (e.g. Michael Dell of Dell, Jeff Bezos of Amazon, Steve Case of AOL, Tim Koogle of Yahoo, Halsey Minor of CNET, John Changers of Cisco, Meg Whitman of eBay) with qualities of traditional CEOs:

| Traditional CEO | e-CEO |
|---|---|
| encouraging | evangelizing |
| alert | paranoid |
| cordial | brutally frank |
| infotech semiliterate (at best) | infotech literate (at least) |
| clearly focused | intensely focused |
| fast moving | faster moving |
| hates ambiguity | likes ambiguity |
| suffers from technology confrontation anxiety | suffers from bandwidth separation anxiety |

| Traditional CEO | e-CEO |
|---|---|
| age: 57 | age: 38 |
| rich | very rich |

Not everyone working in an e-business environment demonstrates this caricature of e-CEOs or e-professionals. This e-profile does indicate that managing a faster growth environment may require different personal and skill orientations. Understanding personality characteristics can help leaders and professionals deal with individual adaptation and resistance to change. Organizational change, including technologically driven change, can be accomplished only through people. Learning to "read people" is a valuable skill in understanding and leading organizational change. Before discussing specific personality theories, we examine the psychological profile of an employee (disguised) excerpted from the book *Psychological Consulting to Management: A Clinician's Perspective* by Lester Tobias.[5] This profile offers us insight into how trained psychological consultants describe, use, and make recommendations about employees and performance, based on several personality measurement methods and observations that we describe in this chapter. Think of yourself being described as you read this profile. (What characteristics would best portray you?)

*Ms. X is . . . a relatively expansive thinker with a very strongly analytical mind and a capacity for comprehensiveness. She is analytically reflective, resourceful, alert, decisive, and incisive in her thinking. Logical and rational in style, she nevertheless appreciates shades of gray and can operate fluidly with intangibles as well as facts and figures. She emphasizes the tangible, however, and tends to make less use of her intuitions than she could. She is willing to take intellectual risks and can handle ambiguity, although she prefers putting a structure on it. . . .*

*She is characterized by intellectual integrity and is basically open-minded and receptive. Yet there is a dogged, persistent quality to her thinking that sometimes leads to a kind of stubbornness despite her overall breadth and openness. She can force an issue into a framework or toward a conclusion; and it is the forced or relentless quality of her approach that can lead to some diminution of her ability to get outside herself in her own thinking, or outside the facts at hand. She is a self-scrutinizing thinker who tries to filter and reflect but, on occasion, her inner intensity is so powerful as to obscure the dimmer shadows. She is, then, much stronger where the acuteness of a laser beam is the requirement than where the need is for night vision. . . .*

*Deep down, her self-concept remains somewhat underdeveloped, and there is a part that never feels content, that doubts her successes and her inherent legitimacy, that drives her to overcompensate. She tends to take herself for granted and to fail to grant herself acceptance, making her satisfactions transitory and leaving her with a feeling of being unquenched, of something still missing. As a result, she has too great a need to win, to press her will, and, as the tensions this creates build, her mood and temper get the better of her. . . .*

*She is receptive to criticism, does not externalize blame, and is basically a nondefensive, honest, open, sincere, deep, and self-accountable person, although she could pay better attention to her feelings. Her ability to benefit from criticism is facilitated by her growth orientation as well as her capacity to conceptualize.*

*Socially, she is forceful, dominant, aggressive, dynamic, unpretentious, and intense. She can lack diplomacy, tact, and subtlety, and is somehow "rough around the edges" and occasionally overbearing. Nevertheless, she does tend to wear well owing to her dedication, energy, and the fact that her good intentions usually surface one way or the other. . . . She is concerned about developing subordinates, but can allow it to take second place, and she tends to have to "work at" being a manager. Her subordinates would see her as well meaning, fair, demanding, very goal oriented, and usually—but not always—respectful. She is most effective when her manager challenges her, but allows her freedom and latitude in meeting objectives. . . .*

This report offered the following prognosis. Again, think of your own personal profile and what your prognosis would state.

### Conclusions and Prognosis

*Ms. X is a strategic business thinker and analyzer with high intellectual capacity. She is a goal-oriented achiever with a strong sense of accuracy, a willingness to create change, and a dedication to a sense of purpose. She is self-reliant and self-determined.*

*Were she able to mobilize the courage she employs in facing the outer world in the service of accepting herself as is, she would go a long way toward quenching the inner thirst that drives her to be too relentless, too impatient, too driven, and too prone at having to prove. She would benefit from learning better to distinguish between introspective reflection and cross-examination of self. Growth here would help her to flow better with rather than against adversities and obstacles. . . . "*

These observations and generalizations provide a basis for feedback and dialogue between Ms. X and her evaluator. Some companies provide comprehensive tests and interview feedback, as in this example, to help managers assess a potential employee's fit with a workgroup or company. Constructive feedback can also help Ms. X develop professionally and personally. You may want to draft a sketch of your own personal style, using the "personal system" diagram in Figure 2.1. You might ask yourself, How would an objective observer using the concepts in this chapter describe and evaluate me? A goal of this chapter is to enable you to begin to understand and evaluate personal differences, yours and those of others who work and interact with you. In organizational settings, this skill can be used to enhance working relationships, help make more objective decisions, and understand your own personal style relative to others.

We begin this chapter by presenting the framework of the **personal system**, and then go on to explain major personality theories. Methods for measuring personality are summarized, and personality characteristics that managers and employees can observe and address in organizational settings are discussed. The ethical dimensions of personality are then presented. The characteristics of personal mastery and effective habits are examined; these are benchmark processes that individuals can use to enhance motivation. Finally, we present general guidelines for understanding and managing individual differences in the workplace.

## The "Personal System"

Joy Covey, former chief financial officer at Delta Airlines, is Amazon.com's chief strategy officer, where she has a $150 million stake. She is described as "unconventional, expansive, high risk, with a pitch that goes something like this: 'It may not seem logical, but trust me. I know where I'm going. And it's far.'"[6] Covey is the younger of two daughters of a doctor and nurse from Northern California. Her parents "had a complete and utter disregard for social expectations," Covey noted. She dropped out of high school her freshman year from boredom. She said her parents did not criticize her. "They know it wouldn't do any good. I thought, They won't beat me or throw me out. If I don't obey, what can they do? I decided, there's no more following the rules." However, she did return for a year before passing the California high school-equivalency exam. (She has a 173 IQ). At 19, she graduated from California State University at Fresno and passed the CPA exam (with the second best score in the country that year). Before joining Jeff Bezos at Amazon.com, she worked at Arthur Young and then took an MBA from Harvard. She's a sports fanatic (rock-climbing and wakeboarding—like snowboarding only done behind a boat). Bezos notes, "Joy is really good at figuring out what's going to be important six months from now, which, in Internet companies, is very hard to do."

How would you describe yourself? How would others describe you? What makes you unique from others? What are your distinctive competencies and traits? Where are you going and why? The "personal system" construct, described in this section, and the concepts in this chapter identify personality and personal dimensions that can help you address these questions.

Managers and organizational members are interested in personal dynamics as they affect behavior and therefore performance. Performance is, after all, based on behavior. Kurt Lewin, a noted psychologist, asserted that behavior is a function of the person and environment. Lewin expressed this idea in the following equation, $B = f(P * E)$[7] where B is behavior, P is the person, and E is the environment. Interactional psychologists have extended Lewin's ideas by stating that human behavior can best be understood by explaining the person, the situation, and how the two interact. The following assumptions outline this logic.[8]

1. Behavior is a function of a continuous, multidirectional interaction between the person and the situation.

2. The person is active in this process, and both are changed by situations and changes in situations.

3. People vary in many characteristics, including cognitive, affective, motivational, and ability factors.

4. Two interpretations of situations are important: the objective situation and the person's subjective view of the situation.[9]

A dynamic model that embodies Lewin's interactional logic and that can be used to understand individual personality differences is the "personal system." At the core of the personal system are the "personality" and the "self-concept," as illustrated in Figure 2–1. The individual personality and self-concept are the sum of the factors identified in this figure: the person's genetics; background and environment; values, attitudes, beliefs, and ethics; current environment; and personal goals and competencies. These factors serve as both objective dimensions that

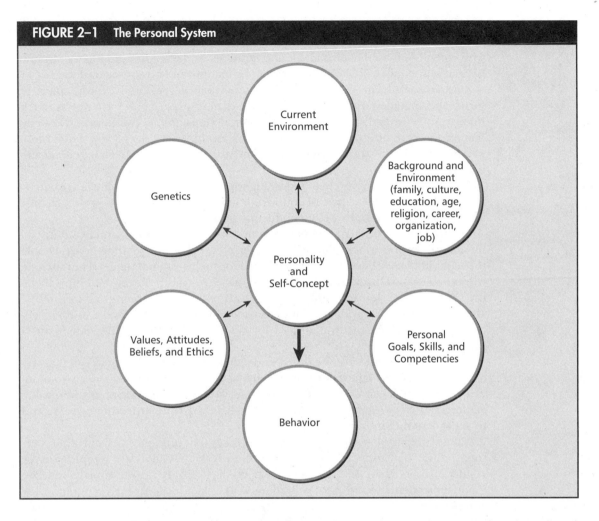

FIGURE 2–1    The Personal System

influence individuals and subjective factors that are interpreted and mediated through an individual's self-concept. The self-concept in turn influences the person's behavior. In the view of the personal system, individuals are holistic, intentional actors who consciously affect their attitudes, beliefs, and behaviors.

At the core of the personal system is the self-concept—that is, the person's self-understanding, the way the individual sees and interprets the world, others, and himself or herself.[10] The importance of the self-concept in understanding human behavior cannot be underestimated. How people perceive and view themselves determines to a large extent their self-worth and self-esteem, their manner of communication and their level of performance, the roles they choose and refuse to play, and the career choices they take and don't take.

An underlying assumption of this system is that individuals will most likely behave in situations that are consistent with, and that will maintain and enhance, their self-concept.[11] In other words, individuals tend to act in ways that "fit" and are congruent with their self-concepts. An entrepreneur who sees herself as a risk taker, who embodies these beliefs, values, and attitudes, and who grew up in an entrepreneurial household will likely act or react to situations in entrepreneurial ways.

Certain background environmental factors (such as age, family culture, place of birth, upbringing, early socialization, and learning experiences) are not as much under an individual's control as are other dimensions in the personal system. Values, the core of a person's character, for example, are deeply embedded in a person's socialization and early learning and are more difficult to change than attitudes or beliefs.

Values are broad preferences regarding what is right or wrong. Values are enduring beliefs that a specific type of conduct or end state of existence is preferred over an opposite or different type of conduct or state of existence.[12]

M. Rokeach argues that a person's value system consists of terminal and instrumental values. Terminal values are long-term end states or lifetime goals. People throughout history have died and sacrificed for their terminal values. They include wisdom (a mature understanding of life), salvation (desire for eternal life), pleasure (desire for leisure, enjoyment), and happiness (being contented).[13] Understanding an individual's values provides an important indicator of their self-concept. You can begin to identify your values by completing the statement, "I value. . . . "

Instrumental values are means to ends; these values enable behaviors that will achieve the desired end states. A particular set of terminal values is likely to motivate a compatible set of instrumental values. For example, individuals who value achievement as a terminal value are likely to have a driving instrumental value and to act with ambition.

Values are part of people's internal compasses that influence not only their personal ethics but also their skills and attitudes. Values motivate people. Survey results of more than 350 managers and human resource professionals and 200 graduate students found nine prevailing work-related values: (1) recognition for competence and accomplishments, (2) respect and dignity, (3) personal choice and freedom, (4) involvement at work, (5) pride in one's work, (6) lifestyle quality, (7) financial security, (8) self-development, and (9) health and wellness.[14]

### Contemporary American Values

Results from a recent *New York Times* survey[15] found a swing back to individualism. Early American individualism was described as "utilitarian individualism" (i.e., values such as self-reliance and achievement prevailed). This survey identified an "expressive individualism" (i.e., values based on emotional gratification, self-help, getting in touch with feelings, personal needs). This type of individualism is influenced by economic prosperity. Results from the survey also showed an ambivalence about both styles of individualism, that is, a dominant (utilitarian value) "being responsible for your own actions" received the highest rating from respondents (95 percent) in every major category (white, black, Hispanic, women, men, poor, rich, liberal and conservative). On the other hand, only 17 percent say they are overly

## THE CHANGING WORKPLACE

**Your Personal System Exercise**

**Step 1:** After reading and studying this chapter, use Figure 2–1 to describe yourself by sketching a self-profile using each dimension in this figure. You may want to use results from any assessments and personality, values, or other tests you have taken to help with this sketch.

**Step 2:** Answer these questions after you complete this assignment:

1.   How would I describe myself to others?
2.   What did I learn about myself?

3.   What are three areas in which I can develop personal improvement?

**Step 3:** Team up with a classmate and share your sketches by interviewing each other, using these questions to help.

1.   Briefly describe your background.
2.   What are your personal goals, skills, and competencies?
3.   What are your dominant personal and professional values?
4.   How would you describe your ethics?

concerned about themselves; 60 percent believe that most people are overly concerned with themselves. Only 12 percent say that the people they know personally would take advantage of others; 37 percent think that most people would do so. Andrew Cherlin, professor of public policy at Johns Hopkins University, commented on these results: "In other words, there are lots of self-centered people in America, but nobody seems to know them." The survey had Americans across diverse categories rank ("What is most important" to you) the following 15 values: (1) being responsible for your own actions—97 percent; (2) being in good health—91 percent; (3) being able to stand up for yourself—89 percent; (4) being able to communicate your feelings—78 percent; (5) having faith in God—75 percent; (6) having children—71 percent; (7) having a fulfilling job—70 percent; (8) being a good neighbor—68 percent; (9) being financially secure—65 percent; (10) being married—62 percent; (11) being religious—56 percent; (12) having enough time for yourself—52 percent; (13) being involved in the community—35 percent; (14) having a lot of friends—28 percent; (15) being physically attractive —18 percent. To what extent do these value profiles reflect your own? How does your profile differ from these?

### Gender and Generational Value Differences

"Stop the Fight!" is the title of an article in *Fast Company* magazine.[16] "The battle of the generations: 20 somethings vs 40 somethings, can this fight be stopped?" the headline continues. The scenario of this so-called generational divide reads as follows: "Senior executives who are utterly clueless about technology and dangerously out of touch with markets . . . kiddie corps: know-it-alls who can't run their own lives, let alone a company." Mixing experienced and many times older managerial talent with younger technically capable employees is likely to be a continuing trend in the Internet-driven workforce. While generational and value differences are real, honest feedback and mutual mentoring are keys to integrating generational and skill differences.

Parker and Chusmir's study[17] found that people's values do differ on the basis of generation and gender. "Preboomers" rank accomplishment and self-respect as their most important values; salvation, beauty, and national security are ranked as least important. "Baby boomers" rank a comfortable and exciting life, mature love, and social recognition at work higher than preboomers, who give higher values to inner harmony at work. One can see how differing personal values can be a source of tension and conflict in organizations.

From the perspective of gender, women from both generations value equality at work more than men. Preboomer men value comfortable and exciting work life; preboomer women value peace and wisdom more than all other groups. Do these profiles fit you?

## Value Conflicts and Conformity

Individual values play a major role in the conflicts that can arise within a person (intrapersonal), between individuals (interpersonal), and between individuals and organizations.[18] Intrapersonal value conflict can arise when individuals experience a gap between the values they believe to be important and the conflicting values held by friends, co-workers, or managers. For example, a religious person may not believe that working on a particular day of the year is right, but the person's supervisor demands work on that day. Ethical intrapersonal value conflicts can arise: think of the person who ranks honesty high as an instrumental value and is asked to cover up a serious mistake made by a co-worker. Tension and behavioral difficulties (e.g., absenteeism, or even sabotage) can result from intrapersonal value conflicts.

Interpersonal value conflicts arise when individuals within the organization find themselves at odds. An employee who believes in achievement at all costs may have problems working with a co-worker who values family above individual or even organizational achievement. The former will think nothing of working weekends, and the latter may refuse to work weekends. The ensuing resentment and tension could result in infighting, arguments, lowered effort, motivation, and/or poor performance.

Individual-organizational value conflicts arise when an employee's values and beliefs do not "fit" an organization's or a work unit's vision or mission. Understanding the fit (or misfit) of the individual's values with those of the organization is essential to an effectively functioning company culture. What, then, is the best fit between an individual's values and an organization's values? Some organizations, for example, do not tolerate rebels or mavericks. Other organizations encourage and even reward mavericks and rebels to channel their creative energies productively. Microsoft is considered by many to have a maverick culture, which has obviously worked for it. Casual dress and task-related group schedules have promoted a highly creative organization that reigns supreme in its industry. Some people would find Microsoft's culture intimidating and even scary. These people would not fit Microsoft; however, other (just as successful) organizations have just as viable but less intimidating and more traditional cultures. The answer then is, it depends—on the individual's personal system and on the organization's values as reflected in its culture.

## Beliefs and Attitudes

Beliefs and attitudes are also an integral part of an individual's self-concept. Beliefs and attitudes are difficult to change but less so than values. Beliefs are learned ideas that people have about the world and how it operates. As noted in Chapter 1, Theories X and Y are beliefs managers hold about human nature. Theory X managers believe that employees are lazy and must be forced to work to be productive. Theory Y managers believe that employees are interested, willing, and desire work and productivity.[19] So-called generation X individuals often hold beliefs that reflect a Theory Y orientation since individual initiative, motivation, and accountability are required in the workplace.

Individuals see the world, including themselves and others, through learned belief systems. Goals, skills, and abilities are also, to a certain extent, seen through beliefs and attitudes. Individuals tend to develop goals and skills not only to meet market demand and opportunity but also to reflect their self-concept. For example, many older employees are having to learn computer skills to maintain their productivity. Many of these individuals are not technically trained, and they do not see themselves as technology users. They had to change their beliefs about themselves and their attitudes toward technology.

Attitudes are positive or negative feelings and learned mental states that influence one's responses to the world. Attitudes can be both enduring and short lived. They define one's predispositions, provide an emotional basis for relationships, and serve as screens for interpreting events and people.[20]

Attitudes are composed of three components: affect (the emotional or feeling component that is learned in families, at school or work, and from peers); cognition (the thought processes based on rational logic, which also includes perceptions and opinions); and a behavioral component that refers to an individual's tendency to act in a certain way, for example, aggressively, submissively, coldly, or friendly.[21]

## Ego Ideal and Self Image

Harry Levinson, the distinguished organizational psychologist, argued that the psychological distance between an individual's "ego ideal" (i.e., his desired self-concept) and "self-image" (current self-definition) can explain that person's attitudes and behaviors toward himself and toward his work and life in general.[22] For example, a person whose ego ideal is to be a vice president in the company but whose current self-image is that of an average performing supervisor will most likely experience tensions that can result in low self-esteem and negative attitudes about the present job and that may even lead to lowered productivity. The psychological stretch between the ego ideal and the current self-image can therefore have significant effects on attitudes and actions. On the other hand, individuals whose self-image and ego ideal are in sync experience less tension and self-imposed pressure and pain.

## THE CHANGING WORKPLACE

### You're the Change Consultant

You have just been assigned to mentor members of a new team. You have established rapport. One member, Bill, asks to have lunch with you to get perspective and advice based on your OB expertise. He confides in you:

*I do have some issues. First, things are moving too slowly here. If we're going to make a difference in this industry, we've got to challenge ourselves continuously and come to work each day believing we could lose our jobs. Management here is "old school." I may get fired for my beliefs, but I want to deliver on results,*

*and I can't do it working in this "post office" environment.*

### Discussion Questions:

1. Using this chapter, describe a "briefing" session you will have with Bill.
2. What kind of questions would you ask?
3. Share and compare your responses with a team in the class.
4. What insights did you gather from this exercise? Did you identify with Bill's statement or disagree with it? Explain.

---

### Cognitive Dissonance

Related to Levinson's reasoning is the concept of "cognitive dissonance." This term refers to any uncomfortable inconsistency or incompatibility an individual perceives or experiences between two or more of her attitudes or behaviors.[23] When this discrepancy is experienced by an individual, he may seek to restore consistency by modifying the cognitive part of the attitude, modifying future behavior, and/or rationalizing or explaining the discrepancies. Festinger argued that individuals would seek to reduce cognitive dissonance based on the (1) *importance* of the particulars that created the discrepancy, (2) *influence* the person believes she has over the particulars, and (3) *rewards* involved in the inconsistency. For example, most individuals will not try to reduce the dissonance if the elements creating it are not believed to be important, if they believe their influence or power is too low to make any changes, and if the rewards are seen as significant enough to decrease or eliminate the dissonance.

This concept is useful in understanding employees' performance and satisfaction with work. For example, suppose a manager (Mr. X) has been missing work days to care for important family matters that can be handled only during the week since his wife also works full-time. His vice president has informed him that if he misses any more days, he will lose his annual vacation time. Cognitive dissonance results. Several scenarios can result in Mr. X's thinking. If he believes his vice president's warning is important and that his own influence in making any difference in the situation is low, he can change his behavior and stop missing days. He can also change his attitude to reduce the discomforting dissonance; he may think, for example, I don't need my vacation days this year anyway. Or he may think that the rewards for having a vacation outweigh results for getting personal business done and seek to rationalize and justify his behavior and thinking: I shouldn't have to do these chores during the week, my vacation is more important than getting personal business done. Another way to decrease the dissonance would be for Mr. X to search for more consonant reasons to offset the inconsistent ones; for example, he may think and decide, My family business is more important to my long-term welfare than a vacation. Whatever decision Mr. X actually makes, according to this theory, it will be based on his perception of the importance of the elements of the dissonance, his influence in changing the elements, and the rewards involved.

Cognitive dissonance theory has important implications for managers and employees. For managers, the nature and way that policies, procedures, and decisions are articulated and communicated can affect the ways employees perceive and resolve any experienced cognitive dissonance. For professionals, understanding cognitive dissonance theory can help identify rationalizations, selective perceptions, and other biases in thinking and decision making that could affect their work and working relationships in undesired or unintended ways.

### Competencies, Skills, and Goals

Competencies, skills, and goals are an important part of an individual's personal system, as shown in Figure 2–1. These dimensions also define who one is and what one chooses to become and do in an organization, a job, and a career. Theoretically, the better the fit between work and one's goals, competencies, and skills, the more satisfied and productive one will be. We know, however, that other organizational processes (rewards, leadership, technology, power/politics, and culture) intervene to affect individual goals, skill development, and behavior. Many corporations and organizations are experiencing a paradigm shift in skills and competencies required to perform at industry competitive levels regionally, nationally, and globally. Use of technologies at organizational systems as well as individual levels is taken for granted. At the organizational level, intranets and extranets (internally secured online systems that enable organizational members to communicate directly with suppliers, vendors, each other, and sometimes with their customers) also require employees to understand and use Internet and software applications. Skill training using new software applications has become a given. Understanding an individual's skills, goals, and abilities is a starting point not only for retraining people but also for diagnosing organizational commitment, satisfaction, and performance.

Goals are consciously chosen milestones or end points that direct and guide a person's organizational affiliation, commitment, and satisfaction. Competencies are learned and practiced skills that enable individuals to succeed in organizations and their lives. Competencies and skills are not limited to technical knowledge and practices. Having good interpersonal, communication, and problem-solving skills will be a competitive advantage in the twenty-first-century workforce. Balancing the ability to work independently and yet be a cooperative team member is becoming a requirement in many companies.

Matching a job and career to a person's preferred goals, competencies, and skills can be a major source of satisfaction and work commitment for the individual and can produce positive results in work performance. The Westin Hotel chain, for example, has reduced both employee turnover and the need for supervision by identifying critical skill standards all employees must have. To this end, the hotel redesigned its recruiting process to identify these skill standards in job candidates. Among the standards are technical competence, a capacity to demonstrate initiative, an ability to communicate clearly, and a commitment to quality.

Job satisfaction and personal commitment to the organization are related to an individual's goals, skills, and sense of personal worth and to her belief in her ability to contribute. Job satisfaction and commitment influence absenteeism and turnover and are important indicators of an individual's job and organization fit, performance, and work quality.

The Job Descriptive Index (JDI) and the Minnesota Satisfaction Questionnaire (MSQ) are two popular job satisfaction questionnaires. The JDI measures satisfaction with the work itself, quality of supervision, relationships with co-workers, promotion opportunities, and pay. In the JDI, a respondent is asked to rate attitudes about such topics as "work on your present job" as "routine, satisfying, or good." The JDI respondents evaluate co-workers as "boring, responsible, or intelligent."

The Minnesota Satisfaction Questionnaire asks respondents to evaluate statements about their jobs. The statements indicate the degree of job satisfaction regarding a person's independence, advancement, authority, recognition, and compensation.[24] These surveys combined with one-on-one interviews and selected focus groups can assist individuals and managers in evaluating job satisfaction and organizational commitment and performance; the evaluations, in turn, can be used to customize training and skill development.

### Using the Personal System Diagnostically

The components of the personal system become a conceptual map that enables individuals and managers to begin to address such questions and issues as, Is there a fit between the individual and the organization or work unit? In what skills and competency areas does an individual need training and/or development? Does the individual need more orientation to the organization? Is career, job, or individual counseling and/or mentoring needed?

Identifying issues leads to a diagnosis of the underlying fit and eventually to a solution. Then concrete steps can be taken in whatever areas have been diagnosed as problematic, be they recruiting, selection, and job assignments, or in job design, communication, motivation, and reward systems.

In the following section, we look at various personality theories. The purpose here is to enable current and potential managers, employees, and students of OB to understand personality dynamics and differences.

## PERSONALITY THEORIES

**Personality** is a stable set of distinctive characteristics influenced by hereditary, cultural, societal, and environmental factors. A person's perceptions, emotions, feelings, values, and attitudes are part of his personality. Personality affects the ways in which a person acts and interacts. Few supervisors or managers would state that personality is not an important determinant of employee behavior, yet most cannot explain what personality is.

It should be noted that there is not an ideal personality type or profile for an organization, a job, or an assignment. Because of the diversity of the workforce, the complexity of work environments, and innovative, changing ways of doing business, the search for ideal personality types is senseless.[25] There are, however, good matches between individuals, organizations, and assignments that can be optimized by using qualitative and quantitative evaluations. This section presents major theories that explain personality and personality dynamics, including trait theories, pschodynamic and humanistic theories, and an integrative approach. The aim here is to provide information for better understanding of self and others to increase the success of choice in assignment, job, organization, and working relationship matches.

### Trait Theories: The "Big 5"

Trait theory classifies observable psychological and physical traits—general guides that give consistency to behavior. Recent research has suggested that all personality traits can be reduced to what is referred to as the "Big 5": (1) extroversion, (2) agreeableness, (3) openness to experience, (4) conscientiousness, and (5) emotional stability.

These traits can also be understood as dimensions on a continuum: Extroversion-introversion is a dimension that ranges from outgoing, sociable, active, and talkative at one end to cautious, reserved, and retiring at the other. Agreeableness ranges from cooperative, good-natured, and hopeful to uncooperative, ruthless, and inflexible. Openness to experience ranges from sensitive, imaginative, and polished to insensitive, narrow minded, and crude. Conscientiousness ranges from careful, responsible, self-disciplined, and organized to irresponsible, disorganized, and lacking in self-control. Emotional stability ranges from excitable, angry, insecure, and depressed to calm, poised, secure, and enthusiastic.[26]

Studies relating these personality dimensions to organizational behavior[27] have found first that conscientiousness is a reliable predictor of performance for all types of jobs. More conscientious employees are more productive than those who are less conscientious. People in sales and managerial positions who rank high on extroversion are more successful in their jobs. Conscientiousness and extroversion positively correlate with job performance, but these relationships are qualified by perceptions of job autonomy; that is, people who feel a certain amount of independence in their jobs tend to express themselves in responsible ways.

It has also been found that emotional stability and agreeableness are not related to job performance. A word of caution on these findings: The sample in these studies could be skewed because those who were less conscientious, agreeable, and emotionally stable were presumably more likely to leave, quit, or be let go.

These findings suggest that linking personality dimensions to organizational behavior is complex and that making generalizations about the fit between organization and personality traits must be done cautiously. Nevertheless, trait theory is a useful preliminary diagnostic tool for evaluating individual differences in work settings.

## Psychodynamic Theory

Sigmund Freud is the founder of the psychodynamic school of thought, which accounts for individual differences by arguing that people deal with their unconscious, fundamental drives differently.[28] Freud described an ongoing battle between the id (the primitive, unconscious storehouse of basic drives in the personality that functions irrationally and impulsively), the superego (where parental and societal values are internalized at the unconscious level), and the moderating ego (the arbitrator and filter between the id and superego). Terms from Freud's theory—ego, ego involvement, and defense mechanisms—are household words today.

## Ego Defense Mechanisms: Resistance to Change

An understanding of major ego defense mechanisms is especially useful in understanding individual resistance to change and other workplace problems. An awareness of defense mechanisms can also help us see ourselves and others more realistically. For example, **rationalization** is the justification of one's actions when behavior may not be justifiable: I tell co-workers that I was demoted because my manager has problems understanding my expertise when, in fact, my performance was poor. **Denial of reality** is a self-protective defense that causes people to avoid or escape reality as it is: I've been informed that I will be laid off, but I continue putting even more effort into routine tasks. **Compensation** is the process of covering up weaknesses in one area by emphasizing desirable strengths in another: I perform poorly as a general manager, but I make myself available during the workday to discuss highly technical problems that are unrelated to my job.

Once the major force in psychoanalytic theory, Freud's theory has been subject to numerous criticisms which have gained credence. First, Freud's assumptions and major arguments cannot be tested or proven. They are subjective and philosophic without empirical support. Second, Freud's theory is a product of his times. For example, he proposed that love and work are the two essentials for well-being. Twentieth-century, Western, non-Victorian society has shown that recreation is also essential. Still, Freud's concepts and insights have become part of our contemporary society and remain a mainstay in current psychoanalytic practice. As the preceding discussion of defense mechanisms shows, these concepts apply to the organizational setting.

## Humanistic Theory

Humanistic theorists focus on self-actualization, human growth, and the way individuals perceive the world. The basic approach is people centered, and the thrust is self-fulfillment.

Carl Rogers[29] is the founder of the humanistic school of psychoanalytic theory. He focused on "nondirective listening" to individuals, which facilitates their listening to themselves. Once individuals learn to hear and get in touch with their feelings and potential, they can begin to "self-actualize." Humanistic practitioners endeavor to be sounding boards so as to reflect back what individuals usually do not hear in their own logic.

Critics of this theory list the lack of explanations for the origin of self-actualization mechanisms and the fact that complex work environments are not conducive for individual self-actualization as its major weaknesses. Critics say that after employees get in touch with their feelings, they must return to the workplace, which may not be receptive to this type of behavior.

## Integrative Approach

More recently, research has taken a wider, integrated approach to the study of personality. Personality is explained here as a combination of psychological processes and dispositions that include fantasies, attitudes, moods, expectancies, and emotions.[30] The focus is on the interaction of person (dispositions) and situation (as behavioral influences). For example, moods influence whether people feel good or bad at work. Moods can shift and develop into patterns that affect attitudes, emotional states, and behavior and therefore performance.

Positive and negative affectivity are two important concepts of the integrative approach. Positive affectivity is a personality characteristic that is more stable and enduring than moods; it is manifested in people who tend to be upbeat and who see the world, work, and others in a positive light. Negative affectivity, on the other hand, is manifested in people who generally view themselves, others, and work negatively, in overly cautious or critical ways.[31]

Studies relating positive and negative affectivity to organizational behavior[32] found that salespeople who worked in groups with positive affectivity offered more assistance to customers than did those in groups with negative affectivity. Moreover, people in groups with similar personalities (in this case, affectivity characteristics) tended to be attracted to, selected by, and retained in those groups. These findings apply to selection, hiring, forming teams, and training. Namely, managers must be aware of the personality characteristics of those responsible for selecting, hiring, and evaluating people since "like attracts like."

## Jung's Personality Theory

One of the most influential theories on organizational management was developed by Carl Jung, a pioneer in the field of psychoanalytic theory. Jung argued that there were two basic personality types: introverts and extroverts.[33] He also held that there were two types of perception, sensing and intuiting, and two types of judgment, thinking and feeling. Perception and judgment are the basic mental functions that everyone uses. Individual differences can be understood, Jung argued, by combining these different preferences.

The extroversion/introversion preference refers to the source of the person's energy. Extroverts are energized by interacting with other people—that is, with the outside world. Introverts are energized from internal sources. Extroverts like variety in their work settings. Interruptions from others are welcome. Introverts like quiet and privacy for thinking and for solving problems.

The sensing/intuiting preference refers to how people prefer to get information. The sensor uses her five senses and is reality based. The intuitor uses the sixth sense of intuition and is attuned to possibility over reality.[34] Sensors prefer specific solutions to problems and are frustrated with fuzzy instructions. Intuitors prefer working on new problems and are restless with details and routine.

The thinking/feeling preference refers to decision-making styles. Thinkers are logical and objective. Feelers are personal and value oriented in their decision processes. At work, thinkers show little emotion and become uncomfortable with emotional people. Feelers show emotion at work.

The judging/perceiving preference represents one's approach to the external environment. Judgers are organized, structured, and like to plan and make decisions. Perceivers are flexible and spontaneous. They prefer to see more alternatives before making a decision.

Critics of Jung's theory point to whether his sources of the archetypes are valid. However, because of the current widespread and successful applications of this theory in organizations, it has commonsense appeal. We expand our discussion of Jung's theory in Chapter 3 on methods for measuring personality.

### Measuring Personality

Managers benefit from personality theories that can be measured, tested, and used for feedback to improve, adjust, train, and make decisions about employee behavior. Personality assessments are most commonly made through self-report questionnaires, projective tests, and behavioral measures. Projective tests ask individuals to describe what they see in a drawing or photo or to relate a story to the images. It is supposed that unique personality differences will surface and can then be interpreted by a skilled analyst. Projective tests, however, have low reliability because the results are subjective. In fact, personality tests and results should be approached with the following cautions: First, personality tests do *not* predict job performance. In fact, most such tests are poor predictors of job performance.[35] Secondly, there is an on-going controversy regarding the "differential validity" of personality tests (i.e., the question of whether or not such tests measure races differently). There are presently too few studies to answer this very relevant question.[36] Personality tests are not used by all, or even most, companies for screening and hiring. For example, Microsoft uses demanding interviews. Personality test results are only one tool to help managers interpret employees' "fit" with an organization's culture and required skills.

Personality tests and results should be administered and interpreted by reputable and licensed psychologists. Personality tests should be used along with other methods of assessing abilities, such as job-related skills tests.[37] Managers who use personality tests should be sensitive and alert to any discriminatory interpretations resulting from such tests.

Behavioral measures involve direct observation of a person's behavior in a controlled environment. Expert analysts then record, for example, the frequency of particular actions on an index of personality characteristics. The necessarily small sample of behavior can render this measure low in reliability.

The self-report method is most commonly used for assessing personality. Individuals respond to questions in a simple format. One of the easiest to use and interpret and one that is preferred by many managers is the Myers-Briggs Type Indicator (MBTI) (Table 2–1). This test measures the dimensions of extroversion-introversion, sensing-intuiting, thinking-feeling, and judging-perceiving. Results

## TABLE 2–1    Personality Profiles

Using the following personality preference descriptions, place a check beside each description that best characterizes you. This is not a valid instrument sample of your personality profile. It is an example. According to the most checks under each pair, you are either an E or I, S or N, T or F, and J or P. Then go to Table 2–2 and, according to the four letters identified here, decide if this Myers–Brigg related profile accurately describes you.

### E or I

| (E) Extroversion | (I) Introversion |
|---|---|
| _____Outgoing | _____Quiet |
| _____Publicly expressive | _____Reserved |
| _____Interacting | _____Concentrating |
| _____Speaks, then thinks | _____Thinks, then speaks |
| _____Gregarious | _____Reflective |

### S or N

| (S) Sensing | (N) Intuiting |
|---|---|
| _____Practical | _____General |
| _____Specific | _____Abstract |
| _____Feet on the ground | _____Head in the clouds |
| _____Details | _____Possibilities |
| _____Concrete | _____Theoretical |

### T or F

| (T) Thinking | (F) Feeling |
|---|---|
| _____Analytical | _____Subjective |
| _____Clarity | _____Harmony |
| _____Head | _____Heart |
| _____Justice | _____Mercy |
| _____Rules | _____Circumstances |

### J or P

| (J) Judging | (P) Perceiving |
|---|---|
| _____Structured | _____Flexible |
| _____Time oriented | _____Open ended |
| _____Decisive | _____Exploring |
| _____Makes lists/uses them | _____Makes lists/loses them |
| _____Organized | _____Spontaneous |

**SOURCE:** Based on O. Kroeger and J. Theusen, *Typewatching Training Workshop* (Fairfax, VA: Otto Kroeger Associates, 1981).

from this test can be used in coaching employees, improving team building, conflict management, job assignments, assessing management styles, and career counseling.[38] After reading this section, identify your basic personality type in Table 2–1; then turn to Table 2–2, which explains the dimensions of the basic personality types in the MBTI.

The MBTI has 16 combinations of types. The acronyms for using the types are I, introvert; E, extrovert; S, sensor; N, intuitor; T, thinker; F, feeler; P, perceiver; J, judger. The ESTJ (extrovert, sensor, thinker, judger) is a common profile for managers.[39] These are known as "life's administrators." Their profile is summarized in the following way: orderly and structured, sociable, opinionated, results driven, producer, traditional. They are viewed as dependable, practical, and results oriented. They work well in a chain-of-command structure and can implement goals well within the context of following rules and procedures. They have a high need for control and cannot tolerate disorganized settings. Turn to Table 2–1 and systematically check only those characteristics under each pair of categories that best describes your personality. Record only one letter from each of the four paired categories to describe your personality (e.g., write either E or I in the first paired category, depending on how many checks you marked under E or I and so on). You will have four letters after you complete this exercise. (It is possible to have both in some cases, which means you are on the borderline of the two dimensions). This is a superficial rendering of your Myers-Briggs profile. If you have taken the MBTI profile, bring it to class to discuss.

Although the Myers-Briggs test results are not unquestionably scientifically valid, the test itself is easy to administer and score. With informed feedback, test results can give insight into career planning, job analysis, work satisfaction, and performance. These tests are being widely used to evaluate individual fit with the organization.

We now turn to five personality characteristics that can be observed more readily in organizational behavior and that complement the broader theories and dimensions presented earlier. There are many such characteristics, but these have been selected because of their pertinence to current organizational settings.

## ORGANIZATION-BASED PERSONALITY CHARACTERISTICS

### Locus of Control

Locus of control[40] is a personality characteristic manifested in individuals who attribute causes of their behavior to either external (environmental) or internal (themselves) sources. "Externals" have an "external locus of control" orientation and tend to focus their attention to "other-oriented" causes and effects of activities. "Internals" have an "internal locus of control" and look within themselves for the causes and effects of activities. Internalizers tend to believe that they control their decisions and lives; externalizers believe that outside forces and events control their decisions and lives. Blame and praise (attributing causes) are also associated with these two personality characteristics. Internalizers tend to blame and praise

## TABLE 2–2    Personality Profile Types

| ISTJ | ISFJ | INFJ | INTJ |
|---|---|---|---|
| "Doing what should be done" Organizer, compulsive, private, trustworthy, rules and regulations, practical | "A high sense of duty" Amiable, works behind the scenes, ready to sacrifice, accountable, prefers "doing" | "An inspiration to others" Reflective/introspective, quietly caring, creative, linguistically gifted, psychic | "Everything has room for improvement" Theory based, skeptical, "my way," high need for competency, sees world as a chessboard |
| Most responsible | Most loyal | Most contemplative | Most independent |

| ISTP | ISFP | INFP | INTP |
|---|---|---|---|
| "Ready to try anything once" Very observant, cool and aloof, hands-on practicality, unpretentious, ready for what happens. | "Sees much but shares little" Warm, sensitive, unassuming, short-range planner, good team member, in touch with self and nature | "Performing noble service to aid society" Strict personal values, seeks inner order/peace, creative, nondirective, reserved | "A love of problem solving" Challenges others to think, absentminded professor, competency needs, socially cautious |
| Most pragmatic | Most artistic | Most idealistic | Most conceptual |

| ESTP | ESFP | ENFP | ENTP |
|---|---|---|---|
| "The ultimate realist" Unconventional approach, fun, gregarious, lives for here and now, good at problem solving | "You only go around once in life" Sociable, spontaneous, loves surprises, cuts red tape, juggles multiple projects/events, quip master | "Giving life an extra squeeze" People oriented, creative, seeks harmony, life of party, more starts than finishes | "One exciting challenge after another" Argues both sides of a to learn, brinksmanship, tests the limits, enthusiastic, new ideas |
| Most spontaneous | Most generous | Most optimistic | Most inventive |

| ESTJ | ESFJ | ENFJ | ENTJ |
|---|---|---|---|
| "Life's administrators" Order and structure, sociable, opinionated, results driven, producer, traditional | "Hosts and hostesses of the world" Gracious, good interpersonal skills, thoughtful, appropriate, eager to please | "Smooth-talking persuaders" Charismatic, compassionate, possibilities for people, ignores the unpleasant, idealistic | "Life's natural leaders" Visionary, gregarious, argumentative, systems planner, take charge, low tolerance for incompetence |
| Most hard charging | Most harmonizing | Most persuasive | Most commanding |

SOURCE: from *Report Form for the Myers-Briggs Type Indicator* by Isabel Briggs Myers. Copyright 1987 by Consulting Psychologists Press, Inc. All rights reserved. Myers-Briggs Type Indicator and MBTI are registered trademarks of Consulting Psychologists Press, Inc. Further reproduction is prohibited without the publisher's written consent.

outcomes to their own actions. *Externalizers* tend to attribute outcomes to outside environmental factors (such as luck, fate, others.) For example, a student who tends toward the internal locus of control would attribute his A on an exam to the type of test, the weather, or luck. An internalizer would say that her study habits, change in attitudes, and determination were the cause of the A grade.

*Internals* are also generally more motivated in, and satisfied with, their work, and they perform higher on tasks that require learning or problem solving and that lead to rewards that are valued. Externals tend to be more anxious than internals.[41] Note that these are generalizations. Some individuals may not be on one extreme dimension of this spectrum. There are degrees of internal and external control orientation, as some of the other personality tests described in this chapter. For purposes of this discussion, you may want to ask to what extent the patterns of your behaviors and actions indicate an internalizer or externalizer orientation. The locus of control activity is a shortened and simplified evaluation form that is proposed to stimulate your own self-reflection rather than to present valid results of your orientation to these dimensions.

Since internals have and exert a greater sense of control over their work environment, managers can draw on these characteristics through job placement and task assignments that require initiative and low compliance. Internals also do well with rewards such as commissions and merit pay. For externals, the reverse is suggested; managers need to place them in structured work situations that require more participation and compliance. Externals may not need rewards that link directly to perceived value.[42]

Highly creative people generally tend to have an internal locus of control. Managing creative individuals requires allowing them greater autonomy and flexibility.[43] Such individuals have mental habits (self-motivation) and a devotion to their work that is similar to people with an internal locus of control. Go to the Changing Workplace box that identifies your Locus of Control orientation and complete the 10 question profile.

Identifying and understanding this personality characteristic is helpful for managers and employees in the following ways. First, assignments and positions that require close supervision suggest that internals are less likely to perform optimally. Internals work best in jobs and assignments that require high initiative and low compliance. Externals may work well in structured jobs with high compliance. Second, reward and incentive systems that respond directly and straightforwardly to effort suit internals since this orientation has a belief system that links effort to performance.[44] Again, these are generalizations. Knowing these theories provides information that individuals in specific situations can use to better predict and discuss strengths and weaknesses of the fit between people and tasks.

### Type A and Type B Characteristics

In contrast to the locus of control characteristic, which addresses why a person is behaving in a certain manner, the well-known type A/B classification describes how a person behaves in his life and work. *Type A* individuals are characterized as compulsive and obsessive, impatient and irritable, high achievers, perfectionists, very

## THE CHANGING WORKPLACE

**Locus of Control**

Answer "yes" or "no" to each of the following questions to identify your Locus of Control Orientation.

1. Do you believe that opportunities and problems solve themselves if you leave them alone? _____
2. Do you feel that trying hard doesn't really pay off most of the time anyway? _____
3. Most people are born lucky. _____
4. Hoping and wishing can make things turn out right. _____
5. People tend to blame you for things you really didn't do. _____
6. Do you believe it's better to be highly intelligent than lucky? _____
7. Hard work, not random chance, leads to good things for you. _____
8. People like you regardless of how you act. _____
9. Hard and focused study leads to passing any subject. _____
10. You have a lot of choice in selecting who your friends are. _____

If you answered yes to questions 1–5, you are more likely to be an externalizer. If you answered yes to questions 6–10, you are more likely to be an internalizer.

**SOURCE:** Based on questions from R. Aero and E. Weiner, *The Mind Test* (New York: William Morrow, 1981), 20–23.

competitive, quick movers, and very time conscious. *Type B* individuals, on the other hand, are more methodical in getting tasks accomplished, more relaxed and laid back, and more patient with others.[45] Type A personalities, when carried to extremes, can lead to overcontrolling and conflict-oriented behavior.

A higher incidence of cardiovascular disease has also been linked to type A personalities. In a recent study,[46] researchers found a positive correlation between type A behavior and cardiovascular disease among police and fire department personnel. Job complexity was shown to bring out "time-urgent" stress responses from type A personalities. Still, the type A individuals rated their jobs as very satisfying. Type B individuals did not show this type of behavior in response to the same stimulus.

Identifying where an individual is on the spectrum between Type A and Type B enables managers to effectively build teams with specific styles, for example, more aggressive and time-conscious or more laid back and analytic teams.

### Self-Esteem and Self-Efficacy

Self-esteem, a widely used concept in contemporary U.S. society, describes a person's general feeling of self-worth.[47] Self-esteem and self-efficacy are related to the self-concept dimension of the personal system discussed earlier. Individuals with high self-esteem tend to be confident and thus act more confidently. They value their strengths over their weaknesses. Individuals and teams with high self-esteem tend to be higher performers and are more satisfied with their work. However, research has shown that individuals who have very high self-esteem and are in stressful situations may brag and thus be viewed as egotistical by co-workers.[48]

Individuals with low self-esteem emphasize their weaknesses over their strengths, perceive themselves negatively, and are more concerned about how others view and feel about them. People with low self-esteem usually cannot tolerate criticism well and are apt to criticize people who attempt to offer them constructive feedback.

Self-efficacy is related to self-esteem; it is a person's belief about the likelihood of successfully completing a task. Even individuals with high self-esteem can exhibit feelings of low self-efficacy about particular tasks. Sources of self-efficacy include previous experiences, one's assessment of present physical and emotional abilities, comparing one's competency with others' competency, and the level of one's acceptance of others' evaluations of one's abilities.[49]

Supervisors and managers can assist in developing self-efficacy by first giving reliable and constructive feedback. Managers also can share power with employees and model empowering attitudes. Third, managers can reinforce performance attitudes and self-worth by offering job coaching and counseling and by rewarding accomplishments.[50]

### Organization-Based Self-Esteem

The values, attitudes, and beliefs of the individuals working in an organization are important indicators of what has been termed *organization-based self-esteem* (OBSE); that is, "the self-perceived value that individuals have of themselves as organization members acting within an organizational context."[51] Individuals with high self-esteem tend to feel good about themselves and generally act more confidently and capably; they are also more readily accepted by their peers. Self-esteem is also an important ingredient in the cognitive link between personal system and organizational productivity. The opposite tends to hold for persons with low self-esteem. The OBSE model has been extensively tested and validated. High scorers see themselves as effective, important, worthwhile, and meaningful in their organization.

Determinants of OBSE include managerial respect, organizational structure, and job complexity.[52] Employees' self-esteem increases when they believe their supervisors respect them and are concerned about their welfare. Moreover, organic, flexible organizational structures tend to positively influence OBSE more than mechanistic, rigid structures. Challenging, rich, and complex jobs can also positively influence OBSE, in comparison with boring, repetitious, and simple jobs. Factors that are positively related to high OBSE and negatively related to low OBSE include global self-esteem, job performance, organizational commitment and satisfaction, general satisfaction, intrinsic motivation (personal feelings of individual accomplishment), and citizenship behavior (performing helpful tasks for the organization).

Managerial and self-designed strategies for building high OBSE include having faith in oneself and in the self-management abilities of employees; providing work that has autonomy and variety and that challenges employees' values, abilities, and competencies; building trust; creating management-employee cohesiveness; showing support and concern for one's own and others' personal interests, problems, and contributions.[53]

## THE CHANGING WORKPLACE

### Diversity Perspectives

Louise Smith was shocked as one of her eager young employees announced he was quitting. Smith, 46, is chairwoman and CEO of one of the Web's fastest-growing online communities. Eight months earlier, she had promoted the 24-year-old to an important job at the company, director of marketing, with an agreement that he would stay at least 15 months. "You made a deal!" she said. He disregarded her comment. "It wasn't written down. We never had a legal contract. I told you I would help out to add value. I helped out and added value. Now I've got another opportunity. Don't take it personally. It's just a job."

Louise was shocked. She felt betrayed. She tried to help out a "young person," but discovered he had another agenda.

### Discussion Questions:

1. What are the problems or issues here?
2. Are there any value differences? If so, whose and what?
3. Are there any ethical questions here? Explain.
4. Outline a diagnosis of the issues here, using this chapter.
5. Propose a solution.
6. Share your responses to questions 1–5 with a classmate. What differences in your responses (if any) did you find? What are some insights you gained from sharing this exercise?

### Authoritarian Traits and Workforce Diversity

Research has shown that authoritarian personalities have a lower tolerance for ambiguity, but no studies have directly tested ambiguity tolerance and authoritarianism in working with diverse workgroups.[54] Budner argued that individuals who are intolerant of ambiguity perceive ambiguous situations as threatening, whereas persons more tolerant of ambiguity do not perceive or experience such situations as threatening.[55] Moreover, research has also shown that individuals with authoritarian personalities (i.e., traits showing aggressiveness, power orientation, political conservatism, cynicism, and a conforming commitment to the dominant authority system) have a lower tolerance toward minority group members than other individuals.[56]

T. Cox argues that the logic of connecting authoritarian personality traits and low tolerance for ambiguity to ineffectiveness in working with diverse workgroups seems straightforward. He states:

> Cultural differences create uncertainty about human behavior. When the cultural systems driving behavior are unknown, the behavior of others becomes less predictable. According to the ambiguity tolerance concept, a person with high tolerance for ambiguity should not experience cultural difference as threatening and may even prefer it, while a low-tolerance person would feel threatened by the difference and therefore react negatively. Thus people may welcome or resist diversity in workgroups partly as a function of the levels of tolerance for ambiguity in their individual personalities.[57]

Cox has also suggested that since personality is to some extent changeable, organizations desiring to integrate diverse workgroups would do well to invest in development programs that increase individuals' tolerance for ambiguity and lessen their authoritarian orientation.

Managers must be continually alert for individuals who demonstrate consistent intolerance and inflexibility in their attitudes and behavior when working with culturally diverse people and teams. After determining that such attitudes and behaviors exist and/or that they negatively affect performance, managers should provide coaching, training, and education programs for the individuals.

## DIAGNOSTIC QUESTIONS FOR MANAGING INDIVIDUAL DIFFERENCES

The following questions are useful in identifying issues of fit and productivity based on individual differences and in determining a plan for change:

- Is there an understanding of the dominant personality style of the individual(s)?

- Does the individual have a basic understanding of how her personality characteristics (locus of control, self-esteem, self-efficacy, type A/B, authoritarian level) affect her productivity?

- Is there a fit between the individual and his team, work group, the organization?

- Does the individual understand her values, beliefs, attitudes, and goals in relation to the organization's values, vision, and goals?

- Do performance and development appraisals and evaluations use individual characteristics to assess and guide employees' progress and potential? To address individual/organizational problem areas?

- Are there specialists who can provide individual evaluations, feedback, and counseling for interested employees?

Now that we have examined some concepts that we can use to evaluate and characterize differences in personal motivation and styles of operating, we are ready to look at what makes people effective.

## PERSONAL MASTERY AND HABITS OF HIGHLY EFFECTIVE PEOPLE

"Organizations learn [and grow] only through individuals who learn [and grow]. Individual learning does not guarantee organizational learning. But without it no organizational learning occurs."[58]

What do highly successful and effective individuals have in common? What do they do that is different from what the rest of us do? As we shall see, these people practice certain disciplines and have certain habits that enhance their perspectives on work and life in general. Acquiring such disciplines and habits can only benefit individuals and organizations.

### Personal Mastery

Senge describes the discipline of "personal mastery" as a continuous learning process that enhances individual wholeness. He states that personal mastery is more than competence and skills: "It means approaching one's life as a creative work, living life from a creative as opposed to reactive viewpoint."[59] Senge identifies two underlying movements of personal mastery: "The first is continually clarifying what is important to us. . . . The second is continually learning to see current reality more clearly." Senge identifies the first movement as having a personal vision (i.e., "what we want"); the second is keeping a clear picture of current reality (i.e., "where we are relative to what we want").

Senge states that a sense of purpose and vision go together: "Nothing happens until there is vision. But it is equally true that a vision with no underlying sense of purpose, no calling, is just a good idea. . . . "[60] Personal vision is not the same as purpose. Purpose is a direction; it is more abstract. "Vision is a specific destination, a picture of a desired future." It is concrete. Purpose is advancing an individual's "capability to explore the heavens. Vision is 'a man on the moon by the end of the 1960s.' Purpose is 'being the best I can be,' 'excellence.' Vision is breaking four minutes in the mile." [61]

"Creative tension" is the juxtaposition of one's personal vision with a clear picture of reality; it is "a force to bring them together, caused by the natural tendency of tension to seek resolution." Thus, "the essence of personal mastery is learning how to generate and sustain creative tension in our lives."

Creative tension is not to be confused with emotional tension. *Emotional tension* involves dealing with feelings associated with anxiety, discouragement, hopelessness, happiness, and so on. Creative tension involves deciding on and sustaining a focus on reality with commitment to one's personal vision in order to achieve that vision. Creative tension prevents one from lowering the goals of his vision or from abandoning it.

Personal mastery—a lifelong discipline—means gaining a level of personal and professional proficiency. People who have a high level of personal mastery share the following characteristics: (1) they have a strong sense of purpose, a calling, underlying their goals; (2) they see reality not as an enemy but as an ally, and they work with, not against, the forces of change; (3) they are inquisitive and insist on seeing reality, not illusion; (4) they feel connected to others, to life, and to a larger creative process and, at the same time, feel unique and that they can influence but not control the creative process; (5) they live in a continual learning mode, are self-confident while being aware of their ignorance, incompetence, and growth potential; and (6) they accomplish complex tasks with grace and ease.

Why strive to maintain the discipline of personal mastery?

> *People with high levels of personal mastery are more committed. They take more initiative. They have a broader and deeper sense of responsibility in their work. They learn faster. A great many organizations espouse a commitment to fostering personal growth among their employees because they believe it will make the organization stronger."*[62]

Senge also argues that we want personal mastery because "we want it." That is, it is an end in itself, comparable to a terminal value, which is, as we discussed at the beginning of the chapter, not just a means toward an end, like an "instrumental value." Personal mastery involves a commitment to truth, to integrating reason with intuition, to seeing our connectness to the world.

Organizational leaders and managers can foster personal mastery by creating a climate and culture that strengthen and value personal growth and that provide experience and on-the-job training for developing the disciplines of personal mastery. Companies benefit from energized and empowered employees. A certainty exists: If organizational leaders and employees are not aligned and do not have shared common visions, the organization's effectiveness will be diminished.

### Seven Habits of Highly Effective People

A book on individual wholeness and effectiveness that is widely read by individuals in corporations is Stephen Covey's *The 7 Habits of Highly Effective People.* He defines a *habit* as "the intersection of knowledge, skill, and desire."[63] Knowledge is "what to, why to," skills are "how to," and desire is "want to." The seven habits, Covey explains, provide an integrated approach to personal and interpersonal effectiveness along a "maturity continuum" from dependence ("you take care of me") to independence ("I am responsible and self-reliant") to interdependence ("we can do it"). Figure 2–2 illustrates the clustering of these habits within each of the dimensions of the maturity continuum. Each habit builds on the previous ones.

The first three habits deal with self-mastery and move an individual from dependence to independence. These habits represent "private victories" and character growth: (1) be proactive, (2) begin with the end in mind, and (3) put first things first.

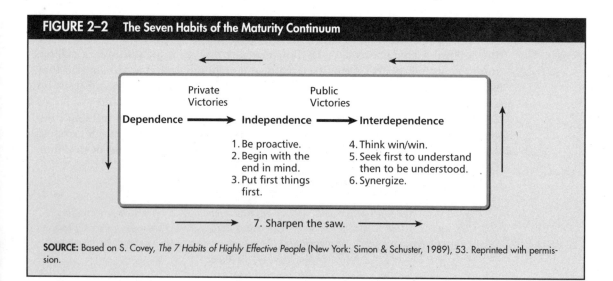

**FIGURE 2–2    The Seven Habits of the Maturity Continuum**

**SOURCE:** Based on S. Covey, *The 7 Habits of Highly Effective People* (New York: Simon & Schuster, 1989), 53. Reprinted with permission.

"Being proactive" involves taking initiative and responsibility ("response-ability") for one's life at work and away from work in other spheres. "Begin with the end in mind" is based on the principle that "all things are created twice"; first there is a mental creation and then there is a physical creation. One's "first creation" is deciding on a personal vision, mission, and goals based on selected principles. Moving proactively through each day with this principle-centered visualization process focuses one's life and increases personal effectiveness. "Put first things first" involves implementing the first two principles on a daily basis. It involves managing and organizing one's time around priorities and preferred values. Putting first things first involves accomplishing results by focusing on managing relationships, not just checklists of activities.

Moving from independence (self-mastery and self-discipline) to interdependence (productive relationships with others) involves developing open communication, effective interaction, and synergy with others. Creating and caring for relationships to achieve common results are the characteristics of what Covey calls "public victory."

Before explaining the habits that lead from independence to interdependence, Covey discusses six major "deposits" in what he terms "the emotional bank account," which is a metaphor describing "the amount of trust that is built up in a relationship."[64] These include (1) understanding the individual, (2) attending to little things, (3) keeping commitments, (4) clarifying expectations, (5) showing personal integrity, and (6) apologizing sincerely when you make a "withdrawal" (from the emotional bank account). Attending to these six deposits in one's interpersonal relationships prepares a person for creating and sustaining effective relations at work and elsewhere.

The fourth habit, "think win/win," is "frame of mind and heart that constantly seeks mutual benefit in all human interactions. Win/win means that agreements or solutions are mutually beneficial, mutually satisfying."[65] The win/win approach and mentality are based on the interdependent dimensions of our life; character (integrity, maturity, and an abundance mentality), relationships (trust, mutual learning, and communication and creativity), agreements (performance and partnership understanding), supportive systems (organizationally aligned mission, goals, values, structure, and control systems), and processes (high-trust relationships and agreements that "effectively clarify management expectations as well as accomplishments"). Entering relationships with close attention to these dimensions enables mutual win/win outcomes.

The fifth habit, "seek first to understand, then to be understood," first involves empathic (nonjudgmental) listening, diagnosing before prescribing, and understanding through perceiving. Then seeking to be understood involves giving careful attention to the following sequenced processes: ethos (the trust you inspire, your personal credibility), pathos (your alignment with the emotional trust of another's communication), and logos (the reasoning of your representation). These three processes taken together and in the mentioned order determine the extent to which the other party will understand you, your character, your relationship, and your logic.

The sixth habit, "synergize," involves "opening your mind and heart and expressions to new possibilities, new alternatives, new options."[66] Synergy is the highest level of communication and relationship between trust and cooperation; it is a win/win approach to interpersonal relationships. Defensiveness (win/lose or lose/win) is the lowest level of communication and relationship between trust and cooperation. Covey states, "When you see only two alternatives—yours and the 'wrong' one—you can look for a synergistic third alternative. There's almost always a third alternative. . . ."[67]

Finally, the seventh habit, "sharpen the saw," involves embodying a continual, holistic renewal process in which an individual enhances the four dimensions of her nature: the physical (through exercise, nutrition, stress management), the social and emotional (through service, empathy, synergy, intrinsic security), the mental (through reading, visualizing, planning, writing), and the spiritual (through value clarification and commitment, study, and meditation).[68]

Taken together, both Senge's and Covey's works represent a trend toward understanding individuals not only as organizational workers but also as human beings from a holistic context: spiritually, emotionally, physically, mentally, and socially. These authors believe that individual effectiveness is a result of a fully functioning and integrated person—fully integrated with self, family, friends, co-workers, organization, community, and society.

## PERSONALITY AND ETHICAL BEHAVIOR

Why is it that one person in a situation chooses to lie, cheat, or steal while another person in the same situation acts honestly and with moral integrity? Researchers have attempted to answer this question by using personality measures with two large samples of people; one sample included federal prison inmates who were convicted of white-collar crimes (such as fraud and embezzlement), and a second sample included people who were employed in white-collar positions of authority (such as presidents and senior managers).[69] The results showed that white-collar criminals scored lower on the following personality characteristics than did their corporate counterparts:

- Socialization (the extent to which individuals follow social norms, such as behaving honestly and dependably instead of lying, cheating, and stealing)

- Responsibility (the degree to which individuals endorse moral and criminal values instead of antisocial values)

- Performance (the degree to which individuals are motivated to produce on jobs by following work rules, acting reliably and responsibly)

- Tolerance (the extent to which individuals are tolerant and trusting and show patience instead of acting judgmentally, compulsively, and suspiciously)

The white-collar criminal sample also showed a lack of concern with others, even though these respondents were extroverts and were socially popular and involved in group activities. As extroverts, the criminals possibly had more "people skills" and chose to use these as weapons to con others. The criminals were also found to be self-indulgent and lacking in tolerance, reliability, honesty, self-control, and social responsibility. Poor socialization to such norms as behaving in dependable, honest, and responsible ways could also explain the opportunistic and manipulative tendencies of criminal behaviors. These findings indicate that early socialization can affect whether or not someone commits an illegal or immoral act.

### Guidelines for Evaluating Ethical Behavior

Managers and employees can use the following questions for deciding whether an individual is ethical:

* Does the individual follow values, social norms, and beliefs that indicate and promote honesty and dependability or unethical conduct?

* Does the individual's behavior indicate maturity, independence, and responsibility toward self, others, and the organization, or does the behavior indicate immaturity, dependence (or co-dependence), and irresponsible actions?

* Do the individual's decision making and judgments reflect conscientiousness and an ability to follow organizational values and rules, or self-indulgence, limited self-interests, and intolerance?

Managers must also ask to what extent the leadership, strategy, culture, reward, and control systems of the organization influence individual employee values, beliefs, and behaviors. Immorality tends to "breed" immorality, and morality tends to bread morality.

## CONCLUDING COMMENTS

The workplace and the workforce are rapidly changing as are group and individual values regarding the nature of work, organizations, and careers. Understanding individual personality characteristics and one's personal system is an important first step in managing oneself and others effectively. Personality is a combination of stable physical and mental characteristics that make up an individual's identity. Individual differences affect recruiting, selection, training, communicating, and motivating activities in organizations. Managers are, or should be, interested in behavior that results in effective performance. Behavior is a function of the interaction between personality and environment. To understand behavior, we must understand the interaction between personality and environment.

The "personal system" is an integrative framework that includes an individual's self-concept and personality, values, beliefs, skills, and competencies. The concept of values was discussed in detail, since values are a central part of the "personal system." Beliefs (i.e., the learned ideas that people have about the world and how it operates) and attitudes (i.e., the positive or negative feelings and mental states that influence individuals' actions) are an integral part of an individual's personality and self-concept. The concept of cognitive dissonance (i.e., the psychological distance between a person's values and beliefs and an opposing threat, demand, or request) can be used to explain behavioral issues in the workplace.

Job satisfaction and organizational commitment are also affected by one's values, beliefs, and attitudes. Satisfaction and commitment are important indicators of an individual's job and organizational fit, performance, and work quality.

Personality theories presented include trait theories, psychodynamic theories, humanistic theories, and an integrative approach. Trait theory classifies personality characteristics that give consistency to behavior. Psychodynamic theory accounts for individual differences by arguing that people deal with their unconscious and fundamental drives differently. Humanistic theories focus on self-actualization, human growth, and ways individuals perceive the world. The integrated approach focuses on the interaction of person (moods) and situation as behavioral influencers.

Other personality characteristics that are more observable in organizational behavior include Carl Jung's theory of traits: extrovert/introvert, the locus of control dimension, type A/B personalities, self-esteem, and self-efficacy.

Most commonly used personality assessment methods include self-report questionnaires, projective tests, and behavioral measures. The Myers-Briggs test is a method used by organizations to identify and evaluate personality characteristics.

Personal mastery techniques were described as a continuous learning process that enhances individual wholeness and enables individuals to cope with continuous change in the working environment. Stephen Covey's *The 7 Habits of Highly Effective People* provides an integrated approach to personal and interpersonal effectiveness along a maturity continuum from dependence to independence to interdependence.

To be an effective manager and employee, a person will find an understanding of individual differences and personality styles helpful in assessing the fit between the person and the organization. Both ethical and general guidelines for using a knowledge of personality styles to diagnose organizational behavior were presented.

## SCENARIO AND EXERCISE: TACKLING PERSONALITY DIFFERENCES

**Step 1:** Read the following scenario:

Semitechx.com is a three-year-old software applications company that has 100 employees. Louise, the manager, is 42, at mid-career, and the oldest of the employees—most of whom are in their 20s. Louise is an ENFJ, according to the Myers-Briggs Personality Inventory. She is also the most experienced manager in the company. She cares about people but does not allow herself to be pushed around. Ricardo, a senior programmer, is 36, originally from a Latin American country, is very "high strung," and is an ESFP on the Myers-Briggs. He loves detail, likes to delve into the process of technical programming, and doesn't care much for being managed. An incident between Louise and Bill showed the tensions of their personality differences and of this fast-paced firm. Last Saturday, Louise asked Bill to attend a meeting with some of the programmers and sales staff to discuss customer dissatisfaction and recommendations regarding some of the products. It was a heated meeting; two salespeople—noted for wanting quick answers—started shouting at the programmers—noted for being perfectionists in their work—for not "hearing" what the salespeople or the customers were saying about the products. Frank, a leading sales rep, told Lou (lead programmer), "If you guys weren't so buried in your own heads playing technical games, you'd hear about features our customers want, not what you want."

Bill jumped in and responded to Frank, "What do you guys know about technical features? If you weren't so concerned about your commissions, you would understand how much time and effort we put into these applications." Louise couldn't restrain herself, "Bill, stop pulling that technical superiority stuff. Frank is right. Go on, Frank."

By this time, no one was really paying attention. Several of the programmers put their heads down. One salesperson left the meeting. Louise adjourned the meeting until the next day. She and Bill went for coffee.

"What went wrong with the meeting, Bill?" Louise asked.

Bill responded, "Louise, I don't think you or the salespeople understand who the programmers are or how they operate. We're focused, get the 'real work' done, and don't like all the gab and dumb gesturing the salespeople do. Salespeople don't have a clue about our work." Louise stopped him, "Bill, everyone has to learn to work together or we're finished. We're on Internet time here. Put personal differences aside and tell me how to pull this team together!"

Bill replied in a quiet voice, "Easy for you to say, Louise. I've got to work with these people on all the details."

Louise looked at Bill and said, "Ok, ok . . . got any suggestions for tomorrow's meetings? I don't want a repeat performance."

**Step 2:** Identify the problems and issues here. How can or do the chapter concepts apply?

**Step 3:** Write suggestions to present to Louise to diagnose the situation. Also offer some ways she might bring the salespeople and programmers, as well as herself and Bill, together despite their individual differences.

## REVIEW QUESTIONS

1. What is the "personal system?" How can understanding your own personal system assist in leading, managing, and adapting to organizational change?

2. Describe your *personality*. How does the concept of emotional intelligence (EQ) contribute to an understanding of personal competencies? Describe your EQ.

3. Characterize some contemporary U.S. values. How would these differ from your values?

4. What are some gender and generational value differences which are described in this chapter? Do you agree that these differences exist? What are your dominant values? Explain.

5. What is cognitive dissonance? Give an example from your experience.

6. What are the "Big 5" (trait theory)? How would you describe your dominant traits? Are traits important in discussing one's personality? Explain.

7. What is the Myers-Briggs Personality Inventory? What is your profile? Do you agree with your profile? Explain.

8. Describe your organization-based self-esteem (OBSE). What are strategies for building your own OBSE?

9. Explain Senge's "personal mastery" concept. Apply this concept to yourself.

10. Which of Covey's seven habits of highly effective people do you find helpful for yourself? Explain.

11. Describe one relationship between your personality and your ethical behavior.

12. What are some of your guidelines for evaluating your behavior? Do you see any correlations or influences between your personality and ethical behavior? Explain.

13. Explain a relationship between authoritarian traits and effectively managing workforce diversity. How do authoritarian traits hinder effective diversity management? Give an example.

# 3 Perception and Attribution

## LEARNING OBJECTIVES

After studying this chapter, you should be able to:

1 Define *perception* and explain the perception process.

2 Explain prejudice and discrimination.

3 Identify perceptual distortions and barriers.

4 Explain attribution and the attribution process.

5 Discuss the relationship between perception, prejudice, discrimination, and stereotyping.

6 Discuss effective ways to prevent and manage perceptual and attributional distortions.

7 Discuss ethical dimensions of perception and attribution.

8 Present a managerial checklist for diagnosing perceptual biases.

## THE PERCEPTION PROCESS

Why do several individuals see an opportunity when entertaining an idea or a possibility or observing an event, while others respond to the same phenomenon as a problem or potential crisis, or perhaps others find it of little interest? Consider the coming of the Internet, for example.

> When we try to comprehend something as vast, amorphous, and downright scary as the Internet, it's no wonder we grope for familiar historical precedents—the railroads, the interstate highway system, the telephone network. But none of those really captures the Internet's earthshaking impact on the business world.... In the Cambrian period, 550 million years ago, something snapped. In the space of less than 10 million years—a geologic instant—there was an explosion of multicelled organisms. Strange new life forms appeared . . . the world's first predators. . . . That burst of new life both wondrous and dangerous is precisely what's happening in business today. Out of this primordial technological swamp called the Internet are emerging new companies, business models, corporate structures—even new industries. . . . In the five years since the World Wide Web made the Internet usable by mere mortals, everything we thought we knew about business seems questionable. . . . The Center for Research in Electronic Commerce at the University of Texas figures the Internet economy already amounts to $301 billion if you include online sales of industrial and consumer goods and services as well as the equipment and software to support e-commerce.[1]

It is interesting to observe that many stock market analysts and financial news reporters initially did not take Internet stocks or funds seriously. Initial public offerings (IPOs) of new Internet start-ups were seen as almost incidental happenings that serious investors should not take seriously. Commentators on television shows such as those on CNBC's financial programs observed and noted that Internet companies were a bubble waiting to burst. Many investors and early start-up entrepreneurs who saw the Internet as an opportunity that would transform most, if not all, forms of business perceived the opportunity accurately.

Travel back in time. Why did Sears's executives in the 1950s see that their business would grow and flourish in the suburbs while Montgomery Ward executives decided that growth would remain inside cities? Sears expanded; Montgomery Ward retrenched. Why was Sam Walton of Wal-Mart a pioneer envisioning retail stores as giant discount centers to be built in suburbs coast to coast? Why did U.S. automakers wait years before perceiving and responding to Japanese competitors whose four-cylinder cars created a new market niche? Why did administrators at Morton-Thiokol disagree with the judgment of their project engineers and not question the safety and readiness of the space shuttle *Challenger* to launch? Top-level administrators gave a "go" to what became a historic human disaster. These are questions about the perceptions, attributions, and judgments of individuals and groups. Executives and owners as well as managers and employees who are not aware of how they perceive and make judgments have a higher probability of making poor—sometimes costly—errors. Furthermore, as with the case of the Internet, seeing opportunities and moving as early entrants into new business opportunities can have substantial competitive advantages. In this chapter, we continue our discussion from Chapter 2 and examine how individuals perceive and attribute cause and effect to people and events. Later we will discuss how to prevent and correct perception and judgment biases.

*Perception* is the process by which individuals view reality and make sense of it. Perception precedes and affects decision making, planning, individual productivity, listening, and understanding customers. Perceived quality, for example, is based as much on inferences about service and product quality from sources such as advertising, brand image, and company reputation as it is on the product itself. These influences are subjective and are based on individual customer perception. Organizational marketing and design strategists who understand customer perceptions of quality have a competitive market advantage.

Perception determines how we see ourselves and others. A process termed *360 (degree) feedback* allows us to see ourselves "from the outside." This evaluation tool enables managers, in particular, to see how their perceptions of their own behavior differ from the perceptions of the same behavior held by bosses, co-workers, and subordinates. For Joe Malik, the manager of a team of engineers at AT&T, the feedback confirmed what he already knew, that his temper affected the team. However, it also pointed out that engineers around him felt he was evasive while he thought he was only trying to come up with answers. These were employee perceptions that Joe needed to know but did not before the 360(degree) feedback session.[2]

The process of perception explains how strategists and organizational members understand their firms' environments. How organizational leaders and strategists perceive their environments can be as important as what the numeric indicators say about those same environments. A recent study developed a theoretical framework to explain the causes and consequences of using archival data and perceptual data to measure the environment.[3] Archival data are information that is gathered, published, and stored; an example is statistical information. On the other hand, perceptual data are the information gathered through interactions with other people; they are obtained and stored only by the gatherer. Archival data, the study proposed, are best used for measuring external constraints and firm outcomes. Perceptual data, which include perceptual and numeric indicators, are best used for studying firm actions. Using both types of data concurrently is recommended for investigating the match between an organization and its environment. This study determined that perceptual factors are important in examining and explaining external environments.

Our purpose here is to define and illustrate the perception process so that we may become more aware of how we perceive (or do not perceive) in order to control our biases and those of others and to see organizational situations more objectively.

### Perception as a Social Information Process: Five Steps

*Perceiving* is a mental and cognitive (i.e., information-based) process. While the perception process focuses on both objects and people, in this book we emphasize social perception and people since this topic is relevant to organizational behavior. Social cognition, as viewed from the perspective of the social information process, addresses how individuals interpret the behaviors of other people—how the "others" think and behave. The field of cognitive psychology, social cognition, and perception analyzes how individuals perceive themselves and their relationships with others.[4] This topic is relevant to the study of behavior in organizations since performance evaluations, productivity, quality, and customer service are all based on individual, team, and organizational perceptions.

Perception, as a social information process, includes at least five steps.[5] **First**, we as individuals observe and sense (i.e., select and screen out) external stimuli through internal factors, which include, among other things, our personality traits and our personal systems. **Second**, this information is interpreted; **third**, it is categorized (i.e., encoded and simplified) and **fourth**, information is stored and retained in our memory. **Fifth**, our judgments and decisions are made by retrieving and responding to this stored information.

At the first step, our initial perception—i.e. how we sense and see the world in any given situation—is affected by our personality, previous learning, level of motivation, moods, attitudes, and cultural conditioning. We do not select information from the environment in a totally objective way. For example, as discussed in Chapter 2, research indicates that authoritarian personality types with a low tolerance for ambiguity screen reality differently than do egalitarian personalities. The former act more directly, taking less note of nuances and differences in the social environment from their perceptions; the latter are more inclusive and participative.[6]

Research regarding internal factors has found that family members of respondents interfered with work when unpleasant moods generated in the familial environment spilled over from family to work; and that unpleasant moods at work also were carried from work to home.[7] Although this is counterintuitive, the study found, however, that pleasant moods had little spillover. Task demands, personal control, and goal progress were found to be related to an individual's moods at home and at work. The study concluded that juggling work and family roles affected a person's mood and end-of-workday family conflict.

To what and whom we initially give our attention is partly a function of the properties of external stimuli (e.g., size, intensity, contrast, motion, repetition, familiarity, and novelty). A person who appears dominant in the immediate visual field—for example, one who wears bright colors—tends to draw our attention more readily, whether it is positive or negative. In organizational settings, such people can catch and hold our attention.

Our goals, objectives, and agenda influence our selection process. For example, an anxious production manager may view his employees' efforts only in terms of his production quotas, and exclude other information about the process, which could be relevant to his goals.

The second and third steps in the process of social information perception are our encoding and simplifying, interpreting, and translating of the raw data into our own cognitive categories or schemata (i.e., mental images and summaries of stimuli and events).[8] It is during these steps that several perceptual distortions and barriers can enter the process. A point to keep in mind here is that we never store data in its first-observed, original form. We frame it through our schemata.[9]

**Schemata** help us to make sense of incoming information. Four general types of schemata include self-schema, other-person schema, script schema, and person-in-situation schema. Self-schemata refers to the interpretation of information about our behavior, appearance, and personality. That is, we categorize what we determine to be our best and most effective ways of behaving and presenting ourselves, as well as ways that we view as unacceptable. The term other-person schemata refers to interpretations of information we have on others' behaviors and modes of thinking. For example, we may form an initial prototype of what constitutes an exceptional performer or a poor performer. Thereafter, we use stereotypes—positive and/or negative—to identify exceptional and poor performers from our prototypical schemata. A third type, script schemata, is used to describe what we consider appropriate steps or sequences of events (i.e., cognitive memory structures that consist of objects, events, roles, conditions, sentiments, and outcomes that happen in sequential patterns in known or familiar tasks and situations). We understand that certain steps should be taken or certain sequences should occur; script schemata enable us to decide whether this is happening and thereby to develop reasonable expectations. Finally, person-in-situation schemata refers to combining categories of self, person, and script schemata. For example, we tend to categorize how meetings, encounters, and interactions should proceed and terminate.

The fourth step in the perception process is the storage and retention of observed information in our long-term memory. Long-term memory consists of schemata in which we store information on events, people, and networks of detailed traits and behaviors.[10] How accurately we perceive the information before we store it is always questionable because it is, by definition, subjective. The point here is that research suggests that we store our perceptions in categories and schemata, as just discussed. For instance, physical appearance of people, the topics they speak about, their tone of voice, and even their accent as well as eye contact, facial expressions, body movements, and posture are detailed ways we categorize others to use as interpretative mental references later.

Finally, we retrieve information from our long- and short-term memories in response to questions, problems, events, and issues. Again, the appropriateness of our response depends in large part on the accuracy of our perceptions and the particular construction of our schemata.

One study looked into the ways employees use prior experiences stored in memory to handle current issues.[11] The study results provide insight into how employees handle crises in their jobs. For minor issues, employees or professionals use the most quickly available information, and, when faced with very difficult problems, they use and adapt all available information, including information that is less easily retrieved. For example, imagine that a manager is in her office and an employee rushes in and recounts a story he heard about something in the company. In this case, the manager is more likely to react immediately to the story, which may be true or untrue, than to consult a lengthy report to determine whether the story has any foundation. This example demonstrates the difference in using perceptual and archival data. This study concluded that the more cognitively complex employees access more script tracks (schemata). Also, the script tract that is most easily accessed in a person's short-term memory will most likely be selected for solving a job problem.

### The Perceiver, the Perceived (Target), and the Setting

A related way to summarize the perception process is to view the key factors as (1) the perceiver, (2) the perceived or target, and (3) the setting (Figure 3-1). All three dimensions are inextricably linked. When individuals discuss their plans, decisions, and evaluations about other people and events, they usually assume that their assessments are objective and mostly accurate. However, understanding the process of perception must include the perceiver's subjectivity and therefore requires that the perceiver's most basic assumptions (or her "lens") be understood. First, the perceiver tends to view people, events, and objects from the vantage point of her own personality, needs, moods, desires, and attitudes. These internal factors of the perceiver serve as the perceptual schemata we previously discussed. Perception begins with the perceiver, but we would do well to recall the adage, "When Peter talks about Paul, he is also talking about Peter."

The perceived or the target—that is, the object, event, person—is the second element in the perception process. The target of our perceptions contributes the information or factors mentioned earlier—that is, contrast, intensity, size, motion,

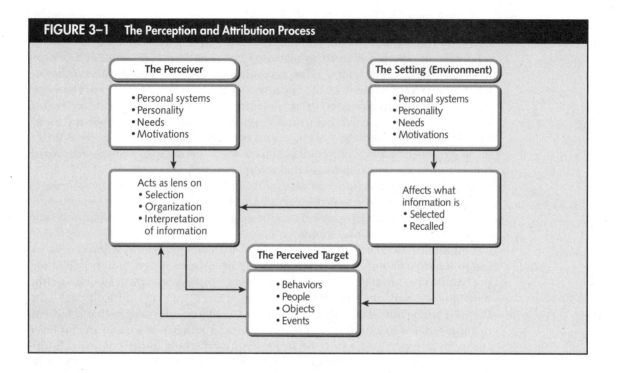

**FIGURE 3–1    The Perception and Attribution Process**

repetition, and novelty. What we tend to select out in the way of objects, people, or detail from the target is often characterized by how bright a color is or how often something is repeated; whether it is new, fast, or slow; and by how much something or someone contrasts or blends into the environment.

Finally, the setting and situation affect what and how much information we will choose to select and the amount that we can recall. Meetings in noisy hallways as compared to those in quiet restaurants with pleasant decors affect what, whom, and how much we perceive and remember. Meetings with 10 people present or 5 present may change what we see, sense, hear, feel, say, and perceive.

These three factors (the perceiver, the perceived, and the setting) help us to understand the process in which these elements interact to influence the information we select, store, and act on later. We next turn to attitudes and resultant actions that underlie perceptual distortions of the perceiver.

### Prejudice and Discrimination

*Prejudice* refers to a person's predetermined negative attitudes toward people based on some group identity.[12] When an individual acts on his negative prejudicial attitudes, discrimination occurs. *Discrimination* is the result of prejudicial attitudes. Prejudices are generally deeply ingrained, learned beliefs and attitudes passed on by family, regional, and peer cultures. Negative prejudicial attitudes are not based on objective facts or reality but on biased belief systems. Such negative attitudes are often grounded in fear and hatred and are the sources of sexual harassment, homophobia (an irrational fear and hatred of homosexuals and homosexuality), racism, and other irrational biases about individuals and groups. Diversity programs are designed to change negative prejudicial attitudes by raising awareness, enabling individuals to identify and see their biases in safe environments. Such change programs involve reading, sharing perceptions on cases, role-playing, and participating in games that reveal individuals' ways of perceiving differences in people and groups.

It is against the federal law for employers to discriminate against employees. Actions of employers that are based on race, color, ability, religion, gender, and national origin (Title VII of the Civil Rights Acts of 1964 and 1991) are defined as discriminatory. Discrimination can be found in practices related to hiring, selection, promotion, and benefits. If negative prejudices can lead to discriminatory behaviors and practices, understanding perceptual distortions is a first step in gaining awareness of how we see ourselves, our team members, our colleagues, and newcomers to our organization.

## THE CHANGING WORKPLACE

### Stereotyping Exercise

**Step 1:** As an individual, use the following list and identify stereotypes generally associated with each of the groups (use a word or phrase):

1. Freshmen in college
2. Lesbians and gays
3. Arab people
4. Jewish people
5. Italian people
6. Ph.D.s
7. Physicists
8. Presidents of the United States
9. The Christian Coalition
10. Caucasian women executives
11. Middle-aged male congressmen
12. National Rifle Association members

**Step 2:** As a group,

1. Share your written stereotypes from Step 1 and discuss the source(s) of these stereotypes.

2. Count the number of positive versus negative stereotypes from each person's list. Discuss why you think the positive stereotypes were labeled as positive and the negative ones as negative.

**Step 3:** Each group now summarizes its findings and reports its findings to the class. Discuss the following:

1. What did people learn from this exercise about stereotyping?
2. What is the source of these stereotypes? (TV? folklore? families? communities? friends? regional culture?)
3. How did this exercise make people feel? Why?
4. What steps can be taken to reduce stereotypes in the culture, family, communities, and workplace?

**SOURCE:** Adapted from T. Cox and R. Beale, *Developing Competency to Manage Diversity*, (San Francisco: Berrett-Koehler, 1997), 86–88.

## Perceptual Distortions and Barriers

Pogo, the cartoon character, said, "We have met the Enemy, and it is us!" Since perception involves subjective and individual interpretations of information, perceptual "distortion" can affect the accuracy of these interpretations. These distortions can be likened to "noise." Some of the more common and perceptual distortions include stereotyping, the halo effect, selective perception, projection, and self-fulfilling prophecies. These distortions (summarized in Table 3–1) are, in effect, barriers to seeing events, people, and actions objectively.

**Stereotyping** is a tendency to make generalizations, positive and/or negative, about a group or category of people. Stereotyping involves applying these generalizations to an individual. Not all generalizations are false or harmful. Stereotyping is useful when an initial structure must be constructed and when the amount of incoming data must be reduced to make sense of the information. Stereotyping is dysfunctional when it hinders working relationships, team effectiveness, and productivity.

Stereotypes can present barriers to seeing, communicating, and acting effectively when they are based on erroneous or hurtful misinformation. Stereotypes are often applied to social and cultural groups. Age, gender, social class, and regional origin are reasons for stereotyping. For example, not all older workers are less skilled in computer technology; not all Arabs support Islamic principles; not all Asians are mathematically skilled; not all African-Americans are athletic; not all Caucasian middle-aged men are angry and prejudiced against different races; and not all women are more nurturing than men, although stereotypes indicate that they are.

| TABLE 3–1 Perceptual Distortions | |
|---|---|
| Stereotyping | Making positive or negative generalizations about a group or category of people, usually based on inaccurate assumptions and beliefs. |
| Halo effect | Developing one's overall impression of an individual or situation from a single characteristic about that individual or based on one situation. |
| Selective perception | Screening out information on objects, people, or events that is inconsistent with one's beliefs, values, and moods. |
| Projection | Attributing one's own feelings, attitudes, or perceptions to others. |
| Self-fulfilling prophecy | Having expectations about other's behaviors and justifying behavioral outcomes based on those expectations, regardless of the actual behaviors. |

Stereotyping is a process. As mentioned, individuals are first grouped into categories based, for example, on race, gender, sex, education, or occupation. Second, inferences are made that all individuals within the assigned category have the same characteristics (e.g., men are more thinking than feeling, women are more nurturing than men, African-American men are better skilled athletes than Caucasian men, all physics majors are intelligent). Third, expectations based on these stereotypes are made to interpret the behavior of the stereotyped individuals. Then we maintain the stereotypes by exaggerating the frequency of stereotypic behaviors the others show, inaccurately explaining the behaviors of those stereotyped, and separating the stereotyped from ourselves.[13]

Three common stereotypes include *race, age,* and *sex-role stereotypes.* Cox and Beale report that race stereotypes—like all stereotypes—(1) are frequently based on false assumptions and anecdotal evidence or even impressions without direct experience with the specific group, (2) ascribe negative traits to individuals in a particular group, and (3) assume that characteristics believed to be common to a cultural group apply to every member.[14] Corporate firms and organizations are frequently found to discriminate against individuals based on race, not performance. Denny's restaurant chain settled a federal law suit in 1993 for discriminating against African-American customers in California. The company then implemented a successful cultural diversity program. *Fortune* magazine surveys corporations and publishes those that are exemplars in diversity programs by instituting and promoting real-time diversity measures; for example, such practices surveyed include how many managers' bonuses are tied to meeting departmental diversity goals and the number of minorities on boards of directors and among corporate officers. Recently, the top five companies using exemplary diversity programs for African-Americans included Fannie Mae, Advantica, Allstate, Shoney's, and Sempra Energy; for Asians, the companies were Union Bank of California, Toyota Motor Sales, Applied Materials, Texas Instruments, and Computer Associates.[15] Employers can and should focus on developing sensitivity programs for the entire workforce that identify employees' race stereotypes, present evidence that demonstrates the inaccuracy of race stereotypes, and provide role-playing and training that build a collegial, performance-based culture that has zero tolerance for race stereotypes.

Age stereotypes also can lead to discrimination and dysfunctional consequences for individuals and organizations. With the preeminent role that technologies are playing in work globally, the assumption that older employees cannot or will not perform well in this changing environment can lead to age stereotyping. Some studies show that job experience had a higher relationship with performance than age and that age and experience predicted higher performance for more complex jobs.[16] Studies generally show a positive relationship between increasing age, job satisfaction, job involvement, work motivation, and commitment. Also, the stereotype that older workers are more accident prone is unsubstantiated.[17] Employers should institute mentoring programs in which workers of different ages, skills, and experience can share and learn from each other. "Radical mentoring" programs allow older, senior executives (radical mentors) to "move [younger] people along faster than they want to go."[18] The assumption behind this model of using senior executives' mentoring to grow younger employees is that "real-time feedback—direct, honest, public"—cuts through red tape and provides direct communication. Commitment, time, and intellectual honesty are ingredients of these relationships. "People have much greater capacity for growth than they get credit for. Once you get your first taste of being really challenged, you want to be challenged more."[19] Radical mentoring programs provide one way to alleviate problems that arise from age stereotypes.

Sex-role stereotypes are based on the belief that men and women are best suited to different roles based on differing traits, characteristics, and abilities. Are men best suited for certain jobs instead of women? Do men think more logically than women? Are women more caring and emotionally intelligent than men? Yes answers to these questions indicate that you have stereotyped ideas about both men and women. Research shows that men and women do not systematically differ on these dimensions.[20] However, gender stereotypes do exist. A cross-cultural study that compared sex-role stereotypes held by women and men from Japan, Germany, China, England, and the United States found that men in all these countries believed that effective managers had traits attributed more to men than women. Among women, the same results were found with the exception of the female sample in the U.S., who perceived that males and females equally possessed traits necessary for managerial effectiveness.[21] Women are rapidly accounting for half of the U.S. workforce. Two-thirds of the new entrants between 1985 and 2000 were female.

Organizations that condone stereotyping that often leads to discrimination in selection, hiring, promoting, and distributing benefits are violating the Equal Employment Opportunity Act and the Civil Rights Act, Title VII in the United States.[22] Employers must establish companywide corporate policies, procedures, and training programs that enable employees to identify, understand, and change their perceptual biases based on sex, race, gender, national origin, age, and sexual identity and preference.

Workforce diversity training programs focus on identifying different group and individual stereotypes as a process of developing our awareness of hidden assumptions and prejudices.

The **halo effect** is another perceptual distortion that occurs when a dominant feature of a person being observed overwhelms the observer's evaluation of the person being observed, resulting in bias. The observer's overall impression of the person or situation is skewed by a single characteristic of the person or situation. First impressions can involve the halo effect; for example, an initial meeting at work with a newcomer who moves slowly and speaks softly might lead one to judge that person as being lethargic and easygoing. In reality, the newcomer may be recuperating from an illness or may be a highly productive and intense worker who simply thinks carefully before acting.

**Selective perception** is a common distortion by which people unconsciously focus on aspects of individuals, events, or situations that are consistent with, or

## THE CHANGING WORKPLACE

### Diversity Exercises

**Exercise 1:** (Individually)
**Step 1:** Make a list of at least three groups that are often the object of negative prejudice and discrimination by society.

**Step 2:** Identify several negative and positive stereotypes for each group you identified in Step 1.

(As a small group or team)
**Step 3:** Share your findings with the group. Discuss issues related to the stereotypes for each group. How do these stereotypes affect members of these groups in their jobs and work? What could companies and supervisors do to overcome such stereotypes?

(As a class)
**Step 4:** Each group should share its findings with the class. What are the insights gained?

**Exercise 2:** (Individually)
**Step 5:** Write a detailed experience in which you were stereotyped as a member of a category (group). Identify the group, the stereotype, the what, when, where, who, how, and why in your experience. Describe the consequence(s) of the effects of your experience. How did you feel? How did the experience affect you? What did you think? What were your emotions (anger, hurt, sadness, disappointment...)?

(As a small group or team)
**Step 6:** Share your experiences. Describe the experience, the consequences, and your feelings. How did it feel to be stereotyped as part of a group?

(As groups first and then as a class)
**Step 7:** Each group should select one incident reported by its members from which it prepares a role-play of the incident to the class.

**Step 8:** Select groups or all groups (depending on time) should present their role-plays.

(As a class)
**Step 9:** Discuss the following: (1) What thoughts and feeling did you have doing the role-play and observing the role-plays? (2) What did you learn from this exercise?

**SOURCE**: Adapted from A. McKee and S. Schor, "Confronting Prejudice and Stereotypes: A Teaching Model," *Journal of Management Education*, November 1994.

reinforce, their preexisting attitudes, moods, values, needs, or schemata even as they screen out other, relevant information as inconsistent with the preheld beliefs. For example, a software development manager who values creativity more than productivity may evaluate a lower-level, creative but average software developer positively even though the employee had an unusual number of unexplained absences and poor product designs during the quarter. The manager is screening out the absences and rewarding the average creativity as a result of selective perception.

Studies on selective perception indicate that employees perceive and select from situations the important elements of their own work unit's goals and activities. This is especially the case when stimuli are ambiguous, in which case employees depend on their own interests, attitudes, and backgrounds for interpretation of situations.[23] These results suggest that, in general, specialists in organizations selectively perceive and assign more importance to situations that meet their particular interests. Sales professionals tend to select and give more importance to organizational activities that relate to sales and commissions. The same selective perception also applies to marketing, production, research and development, finance, legal, and other organizational units.

**Projection** refers to individuals' attribution of their own feelings, attitudes, or perceptions to other people. Projections, as defense mechanisms, are often emotional and can be applied to others in positive or negative ways. Individuals can project their fears, hatreds, anxieties, and resentment onto others whom they view as less powerful. Projections can serve as defense mechanisms or as scapegoating, a means to shift blame or hurtful feelings onto the target. Projection can also involve attributing unrealistic demands and positive or exaggerated attitudes, feelings, and judgments to others. For example, an employee who is laid off might project feelings of blame and mistrust of the company, its owners, and senior management onto the immediate supervisor. In reality, the supervisor may not have been responsible or even in favor of the layoff. Still, the employee's emotional bias, fear, and blame are transferred to the supervisor. Projection affects perception and can lead to other biases discussed in this section (e.g., stereotyping, self-fulfilling prophecy, and acting out biases through discriminatory actions). Being aware of one's fears, concerns, blame, and other strong emotions before projecting them onto others is a first step in preventing projection. In an increasingly diverse workforce, it is easy to project one's biases onto people who are different. Being aware and mindful of our thinking, perceiving, and assigning causes to behavior is essential in preventing dysfunctional behaviors.

Finally, **self-fulfilling prophecies** are the results of expectations that people will *behave* in certain ways, regardless of whether or not they actually do. Individuals act out their expectations, which become self-fulfilling prophecies. We often find ourselves and others living up to (or down to) such expectations. This happens because we unconsciously strive to fulfill expectations as ways, for example, to resolve conflict, to secure our self-esteem, and to gain approval. We are more likely to try harder in our actions for a supervisor who shows respect for us as professionals and expresses high expectations for our work than we are for a supervisor who views us as just another cog in the machine and expresses low expectations. We may even work down to the level of that supervisor's expectations. Expectations become self-fulfilling because we tend to see only what we want to see. In self-fulfilling prophecies, the expectations I have for you are manifested in my behavior toward you. The way I interact with you elicits and develops the behaviors I expected from you.

## Perceptual Biases: Hiring, Selecting, and Appraising

Perceptual biases can be especially problematic and counterproductive in the human resource practices of hiring, screening, and selecting qualified candidates and in appraising people's performances. Predetermined attitudes, perceptions, and opinions can blind interviewers to valuable qualities in candidates and to their shortcomings.

Selecting candidates based on biased judgments is all too common in organizations. Why? According to the attraction-selection-attrition concept, people select and retain candidates who are similar in personality to themselves ("like attracts like"). Managers tend, therefore, to look for, evaluate, and reward people not necessarily on their merit but on the fact that they meet the managers' expectations and match the managers' own personalities.

Corrective measures that can prevent or at least minimize perceptual biases in the selection, hiring, and appraisal processes include the following:

- Use criterion-based written standards and expectations.

- Use job-based and performance-based criteria that apply objective measures to identical or similar positions.

- Include a wide range of job criteria.

- Use a process that systematically involves others. Use group-based decision steps as well as one-on-one subjectively based judgments.

- Include the participant's written feedback and participation as part of the process. This feedback can be part of an iterative loop that allows the participant to respond to potential employer bias.

## ATTRIBUTION AND THE ATTRIBUTION PROCESS

*Perception* refers to seeing, selecting, and recalling information. *Attributions* are causes and effects assigned to observed behavior. Attributions are inferred causes; that is, the cause-and-effect connections are not necessarily based on actual behaviors. A broad outline of the attribution process is shown in Figure 3–2. We focus on the attribution part of the process here. Note that the attribution process cannot start without certain perceptions occurring first. Attribution is, in effect, part of the perception process.

Kelley, an attribution theorist, explains the attribution process by describing how perceivers determine another's behavior from internal (personality, feelings, capabilities) or external causes (situational factors)[24] (Figure 3–3). People make attributions about others from perceived information based on three factors: consensus (the extent to which others in the same situation behave the same way), consistency (the frequency of a person's behavior over time), and distinctiveness (the degree to which the person behaves the same way in other situations).

Attributions are assigned to other's behavior based on whether these three factors are high or low in the perceiver's judgment—not necessarily in fact or reality. For example, a perceiver who determines the conditions of the target's behavior as having high consensus, low consistency, and high distinctiveness, most likely attributes the target's behavior to external causes. A perceiver who determines that the conditions of the target's behavior are low consensus, low distinctiveness, and high consistency, attributes the behavior to internal causes, as Figure 3–3 illustrates.

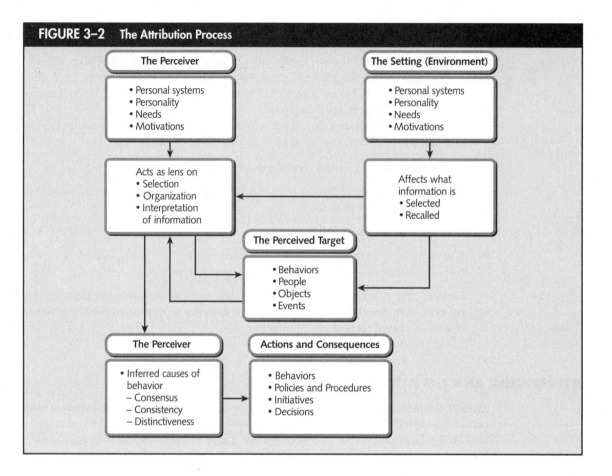

**FIGURE 3–2   The Attribution Process**

Suppose that as a manager you observe that Jackie, a software designer, is behind schedule on new product development. However, upon investigation, you find that the other six members of her group are also behind (high consensus) and that Jackie is ahead of schedule on another demanding job task of debugging software (high distinctiveness). Also, on further examination, you discover that over the previous year she and others of the group were behind schedule on new software development when time pressures increased (high consistency). With this information in mind, you attribute Jackie's poor performance on this assignment to external factors. Corrective action therefore would not involve counseling or other interventions related to personal issues but would focus instead on adjusting external variables in the situation.

Attributing causes to another's behavior is not always a clearcut and easy process. Notably, when a person does not always behave the same way in a situation (low consistency), the cause can be attributed to either internal or external factors or to a combination of the two. Kelley's model is helpful as a screening tool to

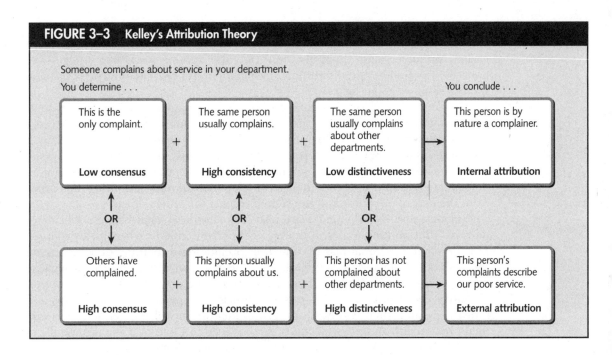

**FIGURE 3–3    Kelley's Attribution Theory**

Someone complains about service in your department.

You determine . . .                                                                                          You conclude . . .

| This is the only complaint.  **Low consensus** | + | The same person usually complains.  **High consistency** | + | The same person usually complains about other departments.  **Low distinctiveness** | → | This person is by nature a complainer.  **Internal attribution** |

OR                              OR                              OR

| Others have complained.  **High consensus** | + | This person usually complains about us.  **High consistency** | + | This person has not complained about other departments.  **High distinctiveness** | → | This person's complaints describe our poor service.  **External attribution** |

check different informational cues before assigning a cause to the target behavior. Discussing problems and issues with the person, as well as with others involved in the situation, can validate attributions.

### Other Attributional Errors

A common general attributional error is the tendency to assign cause to internal factors when assessing another's behavior. That is, people tend to assess both the success and the failure of another's efforts to such factors as ability, intelligence, motive, and emotions rather than situation, luck, chance, or other external factors. This bias is known as the *fundamental attribution error.*[25]

Individuals generally assign their own successes to internal factors (ability, effort, creativity) and their failures to external conditions (luck, task difficulty, others). This attribution process is termed *self-serving bias.*[26] This bias involves the use of blaming, defensive behaviors and other perceptual distortions discussed earlier.

## PERCEPTION, ATTRIBUTION, AND WORKFORCE DIVERSITY

Managing a diverse workforce is not easy. "Organizational experts and experienced managers agree that managing diversity and working with people who are different is more complex than working with people who share the same attitudes, values, and work behaviors."[27] Effectively integrating diverse workforces can produce a competitive advantage by using individual and group differences to enhance creativity and synergy. In addition to the perceptual distortions and barriers discussed earlier, prejudice and discrimination can also inhibit workforce integration. Sources of prejudice and discrimination include intrapersonal, interpersonal, and societal reinforcement factors.[28]

We discussed authoritarianism and intolerance of ambiguity as personality traits in Chapter 2. These tendencies are especially important in the workplace because they prevent individuals from working effectively in diverse groups. Individuals with authoritarian personality profiles often "shut out" another's ideas and opinions if the do not fit the authoritarian's beliefs. Authoritarians also tend to have little patience or ability to allow others to develop their thoughts. Conflict then arises from the lack of openness and the lack of respect for others' ideas.

Prejudice and discrimination are also major intrapersonal barriers that deter persons from working well with diverse groups. As defined earlier in this chapter, *prejudice* is an attitudinal bias that involves prejudging something or someone on the basis of a characteristic.[29] Prejudice can be based on either positive or negative predispositions toward others. It is considered to be negative when perceptions, emotions, feelings, and attributions are directed at specific cultural groups and individuals, and when it is based on group identities involving gender, race, ethnicity, nationality, and physical ability. As discussed in Chapter 2, an argument can be made that negative prejudices often stem from authoritarian personality traits and a low tolerance for ambiguity.

Negative prejudices are a major source of the perceptual distortions and barriers discussed earlier. Stereotyping is one example. Stating stereotypes openly and publicly can result in the person seeing how irrational and absurd the logic is. Examples of stereotypes of particular cultural groups include the following: Jews (rich, miserly, supporters of Israel, well educated, run New York City); African-Americans (athletes, underqualified, poor, lazy, uneducated, oversexed, on welfare); Caucasian men (competitive, intelligent, domineering, powerhungry, elitists); Caucasian women (bad at math and science, passive, trusting, flaky, shallow, timid); Japanese men (meticulous, workaholics, racists, sexist, deferring to authority); French men (good lovers, frank, egotistical, individualistic, unfaithful).[30] Stereotypes are usually spotted when someone uses the words "all, everyone, always" when relating cause and effect or attributing a characteristic, trait, or practice to a group or individual.

Discussed earlier in the Chapter, *discrimination* refers to negative and unfair behaviors toward individuals and groups and is based on a target cultural group identity. Negative prejudices, when actually manifested against members of different groups, involve discrimination. We all have prejudices, but not all of us actually show them in word or action against others. Sources of prejudice and discrimination not only are individually derived, but also are historically rooted and socially reinforced. Racism, for example, is part of U.S. history and is perpetuated in institutional practices. Therefore, encouraging understanding and awareness of individual and institutional prejudices can prevent discrimination; this involves not only increasing awareness on the individual and group levels but also educating everyone involved on the historical and societal sources of prejudices and the accompanying discriminatory practices.

### Perception and Attribution Across International Settings

Perceiving is a "mind-set," that is, a pattern of seeing and interpreting reality. A *mind-set* has been described as "a predisposition to see the world in a particular way that sets boundaries and provides explanations for why things are the way they are . . . a filter through which we look at the world. . . . A 'global' mind-set means that we scan the world from a broad perspective, always looking for unexpected trends and opportunities to achieve our personal, professional, or organizational objectives."[31] People with global mind-sets generally tend to strive for the larger, broader perspective as they constantly look for contexts from which to understand opportunities. They value workforce diversity and multicultural teamwork as the basic form within which to achieve their objectives. They show sensitivity and flexibility in meeting the needs of diverse individuals while attaining project and organizational objectives. They accept life and its complexities as a balance of contradictory forces. They trust organizational processes more than organizational structure as a way to manage the unexpected. Individuals with a global mind-set also flow with change and see ambiguity as an opportunity; they continuously search for improvement while being open to others. Global mind-sets tend to be inclusive, not exclusive, and people with such mind-sets show personality characteristics related to Jung's intuitive and feeling types, discussed in Chapter 2.[32]

Unfortunately, not all organization leaders and members have global mind-sets. A major source of individual and group cross-cultural misunderstandings and conflicts begins with different cognitive systems and styles. Such differences can lead to synergy and creativity in organizations, or they can lead to mistrust and conflicts. A recent study comparing Japanese and U.S. employees identified a major influence in their respective cognitive systems.[33] One is the difference in social interactions. Japanese employees have a category of "company friends," with whom socializing extends beyond the workplace. This is seen as necessary to meet both the individual's needs and the organization's goals. Employees in the United States have a concept of "well-being" from which they view socializing with co-workers within the "social environment" of the workplace as important for meeting only the individual's needs, not the organization's goals. Frequent and extended socializing after working hours is considered normal for Japanese employees, but not in general for Americans—especially those with families.

The Japanese see supervisors as "company friends" with whom they socialize on a frequent and continual basis. American respondents in this study placed supervisors in the category of "authority figures," with whom socializing is not common. This finding does not mean that Americans do not socialize with their supervisors, but that this practice is more frequent and acceptable—even expected—in the Japanese culture than the U.S. culture.

A study of Canadian and Japanese cognitive styles also found significant differences.[34] On the judging/perceiving cognitive style dimension, the Canadians in the study preferred making fast decisions and rushed to closure on collecting data, whereas the Japanese resisted quick decision making and had a need to obtain more data. The Canadians also tended to minimize relationship building in contrast to the Japanese. The Canadians displayed a cognitive style favoring analytical, impersonal, and national factors. The authors of this study concluded, "the more different the culture into which people are venturing, the more specific and rigorous the training needs to be."[35]

Finally, at the opposite pole from the global mind-set described earlier is the mind-set of parochialism and ethnocentrism. *Parochialism* is the state of thinking and acting in narrow-minded or limited local ways. Quotes that characterize parochialism are, "this is the way we do things here," and "it's our way or the highway." Parochial attitudes can lead to biased and closed ways of seeing and treating others. *Ethnocentrism* is "a proclivity for viewing members of one's own group (in-group) as the center of the universe, for interpreting other groups (out-groups) from the perspective of one's own group, and for evaluating beliefs, behaviors, and values of one's own group somewhat more positively than those of out-groups."[36] This perceptual bias is evident within as well as across cultural groups. Some research suggests that, in the business domain, Anglo-American managers, for example, are more ethnocentric than managers in mainland Europe, Britain, and Australia.[37]

Sources of ethnocentrism are found in the personality (high-authoritarian, low-morale development, and low tolerance toward out-group members)[38] and in attributions. Causal attributions, research suggests, are negatively influenced by ethnocentrism.[39] For example, individuals who judge in-group members make internal attributions for positive outcomes (i.e., they credit success to individuals in the in-group). When judging the out-groups, the same individuals make external attributions for positive outcomes (i.e., they credit success to external factors, not to the individuals in the out-group). When applied to career progression, performance appraisals, and customer relations, ethnocentric attitudes and behavior can be harmful. Training and coaching in cognitive styles and personality assessments can increase an individual's awareness of his attitudes and behaviors toward cultural differences.

## Preventing and Managing Perceptual Distortions and Attributional Errors

Understanding the processes of perception and attribution and the various biases associated with perceiving behaviors and assigning cause to them is a first step in damage control—that is, in developing a cognitive awareness of perception and attribution as systems that can be influenced, managed, and changed. In this regard, impression management has become an important trend in organizational behavior.[40]

*Impression management* is the deliberate attempt to influence and control another's impressions, evaluations, and responses to our presence and behavior. Research has focused on the human resource area of employment interviews. Results indicate that those who use impression management techniques do better on performance evaluations than those who do not try to influence evaluators and that those who use impression management techniques are more likely to obtain jobs.[41]

Impression management techniques involve wearing appropriate clothing, projecting a desired appearance, attending to verbal and nonverbal cues, and communicating skillfully. Interpersonal coaching skills and job interviewing techniques include many such impression management techniques. Caution should be taken not to overuse such techniques; if a person is perceived to be manipulative, inappropriate, and/or not authentic, negative perceiver reactions can result.

Impression management strategies can and do influence another's perceptions. High self-monitors (those who are highly sensitive to social cues) actively gather and use such information as to who is friends with whom. Low self-monitors (those who rely on their internal attitudes and feelings) do not focus much on others' social activities or on gaining influence through them.

Other ways to prevent and manage perceptual biases and attributional errors at the individual level are depicted in Table 3–2. These include the following approaches:

1. Becoming emotionally as well as cognitively aware of our own biases is helpful. This may involve keeping a diary or log of our perceptions and the attributions of others within the organization. Also, being conscious of biases in past decisions can affect our perception and attribution process in such a way to prevent the biases from recurring in our future decisions.

2. Getting feedback from others and validating our perceptions also can be used to check biases. Perceptions are validated by checking and questioning assumptions. What may be believed to be a "fact" could, for example, be a projection. Also, it is important to critically compare evaluations and judgments. Many individual biases and attributional errors can be corrected when others objectively share their perceptions and views

3. Attending diversity and interpersonal skills training programs can increase our awareness of individual, institutional, and historical sources of prejudice, discrimination, perceptual biases, and attributional errors.

Managers can also encourage employees to increase their awareness of goal-performance discrepancies and to develop and test new action strategies.[42] Task forces and problem-solving meetings can be used to raise awareness of perceptual

---

**TABLE 3–2    Impression Management Techniques**

1. Become emotionally and cognitively aware of personal predispositions.
2. Keep a diary or log of perceptual distortions and attributional errors.
3. Get feedback on perceptions before making organizational decisions.
4. Question and compare perceptions and assumptions.
5. Validate judgments by obtaining and evaluating information.
6. Attend diversity and interpersonal skills training programs.
7. Organize diverse task forces for decision-making activities.

differences and to develop and encourage the implementation of organizational changes.

Training that incorporates lessons from attributional research can be offered and encouraged. To this end,

> *Training will be more effective when employees are taught to engage in interpretation, sense-making, and understanding processes. The understanding of employee cognitive processes may also aid managers in other areas such as task and job design, motivation, job satisfaction, leadership, and communication. The results also suggest that managers should attempt to hire or promote cognitively complex employees for jobs that are complex and that require the use of a large number of script tracks [schemata].*[43]

The techniques and strategies presented throughout this text relate directly or indirectly to increasing perceptual awareness in organizations. Diagnostic skills and behavioral change methods are also techniques that can enhance our ability to perceive objectively and to make attributions based on accurate interpretations of fellow employees and their activities.

### Perception, Attribution, and Ethics

Do perception and attribution affect ethical decision making in organizations? The relationship among perception, attribution, and business ethics is an important but undeveloped research area; however, the effects of cognitive styles (the distinctive ways in which people see and approach the world) on ethical reasoning in business have been recently explored.[44] In particular, Jung's four psychological types,[45] which were discussed in Chapter 2, are used in the study cited here to indicate cognitive styles: sensory thinkers (whose goal is "to do it right"), intuitive thinkers (whose goal is "to think things through"), intuitive feelers (whose goal is "to make things beautiful"), and sensory feelers (whose goal is "to be helpful").

The following hypothesis was tested in this study: Individuals of different cognitive styles will vary in their perceptions of whether various actions represent ethical issues. Results indicated that what might be a question of ethics for some organization members may have no ethical relevance for others. In other words, a person's particular cognitive style appears to influence her perception of whether an action or question is ethical. For example, the study found that intuitive feelers were more likely to perceive issues as ethical than were either sensory or intuitive thinkers. Intuitive feelers tend to focus on morality, whereas sensory thinkers tend to accept things that are not specifically forbidden. Intuitive feelers also process information in a personal, value-laden manner, whereas intuitive and sensory thinkers process information in an impersonal, value-free way, focusing more on economics than ethics. The study showed no differences between sensory feelers and the other styles.[46]

Findings from this and related studies suggest that gaining an awareness of our cognitive styles can provide information and insight into determining whether we even detect or identify business situations as ethical. Personality and cognitive style assessments discussed in Chapter 2 can be used to gain such awareness.

## A MANAGERIAL CHECKLIST FOR DIAGNOSING PERCEPTUAL BIASES

Managers can use the following checklist to help prevent perceptual biases. The use of the results from this checklist can also alert individual employees to their biases in decision making.

- What current state of mind and moods generally bias our objectivity?
- What biases generally influence our perceptions and attributions regarding particular types of decisions?
- What additional information is needed to correct and/or change our potential biases (stereotyping, halo effect, selective perception, projection, self-fulfilling prophecy) in our decisions?
- What written policies and/or procedures can be designed and used to decrease individual and group biases?
- Are we thinking and acting parochially and/or ethnocentrically in our decisions, or do we think and act globally?
- How do our personality styles influence how ethically or unethically we perceive and assign fair and just causes to events and behaviors?

## CONCLUDING COMMENTS

*Perception* is the process we use to screen and interpret reality. Perception involves selecting external stimuli and then interpreting and categorizing the information, storing and retaining it in our memory, and finally retrieving and responding to external stimuli. External stimuli are screened through an individual's personal system—that is, his needs, desires, mood, and personality, as well as the physical setting in which the stimuli occur. This process involves distortions and bias. Some of the most common distortions are stereotyping, the halo effect, selective perception, projection, and the self-fulfilling prophecy.

*Attribution* is the inferred cause and effect that is assigned (attributed) to events. The cause and effect can be attributed to internal factors (i.e., personality, feelings, or abilities) or to external factors (the situation, others, or chance). Intrapersonal biases can act as a negative screen when perceiving external stimuli. The results can be attributed, incorrectly, to perceived differences, that is, race, creed, culture, or gender. The most extreme biases manifest themselves in prejudice and discrimination. Individuals with global mind-sets, on the other hand, are described as people who view reality with broader, less parochial perspectives.

*Ethnocentrism* is described as a parochial way to view one's own cultural group as being superior to that of others. Differences in national cognitive styles (as between Japanese, Americans, and Canadians) can lead to perceptual and attributional differences that may result in miscommunication and conflict if not recognized and managed.

## THE CHANGING WORKPLACE

### You're the Change Management Consultant

You have been asked to help ANC.com company ease tensions that are occurring with its 10-member team. The company has been operating for a year and, since day one, several members of this software applications start-up have been arguing and feuding. The 25-year-old MIT engineering graduate and founder is worried that she will not be able to hold the team together to reach the next round of venture capital infusion to really lift off. The company has three customers but needs more. The founder offered you the following information as a start: "We have four, very young technical programmers who like to keep to themselves. They are very bright but don't communicate well. They know they are the engines of the company, but they don't seem to understand that they can't do it all. There is a marketing person and two salespeople in their 40s. They tend to see the world as one big target market that needs to be segmented and sold. They have no technical experience and often can't get the product information from the programmers. They tell me 'the techies' should be separated and told to cooperate . . . or else. Two of the technical staff told me to get rid of one of "the old timers" in sales or she will quit. I also have a technical writer who is a liberal arts major, a talented person who tells me she is 'fed up' with the technical guys' introverted jokes and lack of cooperation with her. She also doesn't get along with one of the sales guys who has, she claims, 'come on twice to me in blatant sexual ways.' I have talked to the salesperson about the incident. Another marketing person is 41 and originally from Pakistan. He feels the technical writer is racist and will not cooperate with her until she can accept him as an equal."

**Exercise**: Complete the following:

**Step 1** (as an individual): Using the information, (1) list what may be the present problems and issues, (2) outline the steps you would take to diagnose these problems and issues, and (3) identify the concepts from this chapter that might help you interpret what is going on.

**Step 2** (as a team or small group): Share your information from Step 1 and come up with a shared plan using chapter concepts for diagnosing this company.

**Step 3** (as a class): Each team/group should report its shared diagnostic outline. Discuss these questions as a class: (1) What were your thoughts and feelings about this situation as you read it? (2) Would you take on this consulting assignment? Why or why not? Explain.

Ideally, having a global mind-set is a preferred way to perceive diversity and change in the workplace. Perceiving the inclusive, instead of exclusive, nature of people, events, and possibilities opens opportunities for relating and working productively.

Perceptual distortions and attributional errors can, in general, be prevented and managed by understanding and being aware of the perception and attribution process. Impression management is one such prevention technique in which individuals deliberately attempt to influence and control others' impressions.

Preventing negative attributions can be accomplished by becoming cognitively aware of our own biases.

Finally, we addressed the issue of how perception and attribution can affect ethical decision making. Certain psychological profiles or types (intuitive feelers) perceive ethical dimensions in situations in which others (sensory thinkers and intuitive thinkers) do not.

We have described our understanding of the perception and attribution processes as three-dimensional: involving the perceiver, the perceived, and the setting. Using this framework as a paradigm, we should be able to consciously include our own assumptions when questioning the accuracy or relevance of another's perceptions and judgments. We also presented a checklist for diagnosing perceptual biases.

## SCENARIO AND EXERCISE:
## PERCEPTION AND ATTRIBUTION IN THE WORKPLACE

**Step 1:** Read the following scenario and identify the major problems and issues. Then respond to Steps 2 and 3.

Samir had been working as a marketing analyst for a year after graduating from college. He had changed from a CIS to e-marketing major during his junior year. He was achievement oriented and valued money as an indicator of his success. He had perceived e-business—and marketing in particular—as "his path to gold," as he said. He thought marketing would give him exposure to more product lines and perhaps get him involved in the strategy of the company. None of this was happening.

He found his job dull and too research oriented and began to feel that he was moving further away from many of his technical skills, which he was beginning to value. At his annual evaluation, his supervisor told him, "You've been doing good work, but several of us have noticed you leaving early and that you're not getting excited about the projects." Samir said he felt "pigeon holed" in his job: "I don't feel the time and effort I'm putting into this research is really leading to anything. I thought this was an Internet company that offered opportunity to really go somewhere. I'm bored." Samir blamed the company, his supervisor, and his bad luck for his discomfort. His supervisor suggested he take a brief vacation and come back "renewed." Samir told a friend, "The e-business revolution is happening and I'm going nowhere fast. How is it so many people our age are becoming millionaires and I'm working an 8-to-7 job with the salary of an entry-level market analyst?"

**Step 2**: Use concepts on perception and attribution from the chapter to explain Samir's situation.

**Step 3**: What should Samir do now? Why? Explain.

1. Use the coming of the Internet to discuss what the perception process is and how it works (i.e., how are professionals—people you work with—perceiving the Internet and the effect it is having or will have on work, organization, and jobs?).

2. Why is perception a social information process? Explain.

3. Using Figure 3–1, give an example of how you as "the perceiver" are affected by your personality, needs, and motivations in mistakingly seeing and/or interpreting an event in your work group or organization.

4. Explain how the following perceptual distortions operate in the perception process: (a) stereotyping, (b) halo effect, (c) selective perception, (d) projection, and (e) self-fulfilling prophecy. To which one(s) of these distortions do you find yourself most vulnerable? Why?

5. What is the *attraction-selection-attrition* concept? Do you find it valid in your experiences? Explain.

6. Explain *attribution* and *the attribution process* and *fundamental attribution error* in your own words. Discuss how understanding these concepts can help a manager and an employee in their decision-making processes. Give an example of how knowing these concepts could have helped you in a previous work or personal situations.

7. Define *prejudice* and *discrimination*. How do these concepts differ? How are they related? Give an example from your own experience of how a prejudice led to a discriminatory behavior or act. What was the consequence?

8. Define *parochialism* and *ethnocentrism* and offer an example of how to prevent them.

9. What is *impression management*? Is it an important concept for managers and employees to understand? Explain.

10. Explain how perception and attribution affect ethical decision making in organizations according to your own experience.

# 4

## Motivation, Learning, and Rewards

---

### LEARNING OBJECTIVES

After studying this chapter, you should be able to:

**1** Define *motivation*.

**2** Explain and compare Maslow's, Alderfer's, Herzberg's, and McClelland's theories of motivation.

**3** Explain equity, expectancy, learning, and goal-setting theories.

**4** Discuss relationships between motivation and reward systems.

**5** Discuss cross-cultural perspectives on motivation.

**6** Explain motivational issues in managing diverse workforces.

**7** Present guidelines for managing motivation ethically.

**8** Identify issues for managing motivation in organizations.

## *MOTIVATION IN THE ORGANIZATIONAL CONTEXT*

Motivation, from the Latin word *movere*, literally means "to move." Motivation is a process of arousing, directing, and sustaining goal-directed behavior. Motivation is related to a person's needs, learning, performance, and rewards.

A key question that everyone must address regarding motivation, especially work motivation, is, How much is enough? One survey(cross-indexed by gender, age, and income) addressed this question. The findings from the survey follow: (1) balance is a choice: you can have it if you want it; (2) the outside world makes balance hard to achieve (77 percent said that if money were not an issue, they would either quit work or reduce their work hours); (3) sooner or later, it all comes down to money (86 percent identified "making more money" as a factor that would help them obtain balance in their lives); (4) enough is never enough; (5) too much is no good (family should not be sacrificed at the expense of money).[1]

From the perspectives of both the manager and the employee, key issues regarding motivation include effectively motivating others and oneself to reach higher performance levels and to create and sustain a motivating, high-performance environment. Underlying these issues are more basic ones, such as What is motivation and how can it be diagnosed and changed?

Individual and team motivation does not occur in isolation from the organizational context. Motivation depends, as Figure 4–1 illustrates, on a number of interdependencies both internal and external to the organization. For example, motivation is related to the organization's mission, goals, culture, history, and values. A fast-paced, e-commerce company competing for brand name will most likely have different expectations, motivations, appraisal, and reward systems than will a large steel manufacturing company. High-tech companies such as Intel, Cisco Systems, Silicon Graphics, and Genentech follow different business norms and principles. For example, motivation, performance, appraisal, and reward systems' norms might operate around these practices:

*(1) Organize work around tasks and accept constant reorganization as a way of life. (2) Promote e-mail and other forms of electronic communication. (3) Put extraordinary emphasis on the recruiting process. (4) Break the company into small teams; eight people is probably best. (5) Cultivate the most demanding customer. (6) Don't make critical decisions until you really have to. (7) Glorify the people who create the product. (8) Practice "coopetition," i.e., "Often a company's enlightened self-interest says it should cooperate enthusiastically with the same hated rivals it confronts daily in a range of markets." (9) Help your people become world-renowned experts in their fields. (10) Foster an egalitarian culture but don't get carried away. (11) Look to profit by selling a unique service or customized products capable of incessant, incremental improvement. (12) Eat your own lunch before someone else does (i.e., "cannibalize your business by competing against your own products"). (13) Spread information widely through the ranks. (14) Accelerate! (15) Abandon the notion that salaries and status depend on age. (16) Institute a policy of frequent sabbaticals.*[2]

Figure 4–1 illustrates how individual and team motivation can be viewed in an organizational context. Note that our discussion from Chapter 2 regarding personality

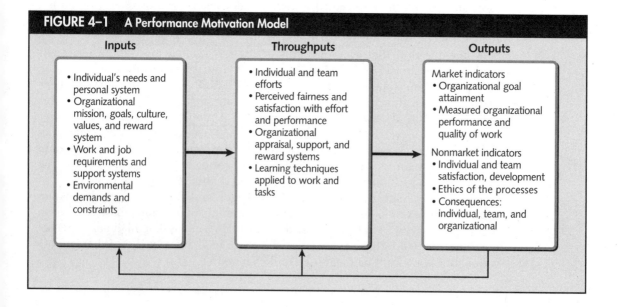

**FIGURE 4–1    A Performance Motivation Model**

| Inputs | Throughputs | Outputs |
|---|---|---|
| • Individual's needs and personal system<br>• Organizational mission, goals, culture, values, and reward system<br>• Work and job requirements and support systems<br>• Environmental demands and constraints | • Individual and team efforts<br>• Perceived fairness and satisfaction with effort and performance<br>• Organizational appraisal, support, and reward systems<br>• Learning techniques applied to work and tasks | Market indicators<br>• Organizational goal attainment<br>• Measured organizational performance and quality of work<br><br>Nonmarket indicators<br>• Individual and team satisfaction, development<br>• Ethics of the processes<br>• Consequences: individual, team, and organizational |

and personal systems applies at the individual level. For example, individuals with high self-efficacy and self-esteem will generally be more motivated than those who suffer from low self-esteem or "learned helplessness." Also, from Chapter 3 we know that how a person perceives a task, rewards, and her importance in the organization affects her level of motivation.

Finally, as Figure 4–1 depicts, the effects of motivation are demonstrated by a number of market and nonmarket indicators. Organizational goal attainment is an obvious measure of effectiveness, as is the quality of the work, products, and services. In contemporary organizational settings, nonmarket outputs are very important indicators of motivational effectiveness, for example, the satisfaction, development, and growth of employees; how ethically (e.g., procedurally just) the appraisal and reward systems are applied; and the effect that the performance evaluation system has on individuals and teams.

*The Wall Street Journal* article title "What Job Candidates Want to Know: Will I Have a Life?"[3] is telling. In that article, Intel's college recruiting director is quoted: "Students today don't hesitate to ask questions around 'How long do you typically work in a day? How long do you work in a week?'" The director of recruiting at Eli Lilly said recruits wanted to know "how do people work together, how are people treated, and is the work environment friendly and supportive?" Dupont's staffing director said students will "point-blank ask, 'How much pressure do you have to achieve your projects, and how much freedom is there to extend a deadline?'" Motivation operates inside and outside the workplace. The following theories of motivation are useful methods for helping professionals understand the perceived (internal) and experienced (external) forces that affect motivation, effort, satisfaction, and performance.

## CONTENT THEORIES OF MOTIVATION

Motivation theories can be divided into two approaches: content and process. **Content** (or static) **theories** focus on internal or intrapersonal factors that energize, direct, sustain, and/or prohibit behaviors. These theories explain sources of motivation by focusing on individual needs. **Process theories**, on the other hand, attempt to identify factors that motivate, energize, sustain, and/or stop behaviors. For example, process theories focus on expectations about effort and performance that affect motivation, expectancies and reinforcements, goals, and perceived equity. We begin by explaining the content need theories of Maslow, Alderfer, Herzberg, and McClelland.

### Maslow's Needs Hierarchy Model

Abraham Maslow developed one of the most popular need theories in 1935.[4] His hierarchy of needs, shown in Figure 4–2, argues that individuals have five needs, which are arranged from the most basic to the highest level. Physiological needs, from an organizational perspective, are the most primary. These would include housing and pay. Safety and security needs, the second level, are self-evident but organizationally might include such needs as job seniority, physical safety at work, and health care. Belonging and love include such social needs as friendship, inter-action, and affiliation. In organizational settings, certain positions and jobs that require interaction, teamwork, and positive feedback might also satisfy this need. Esteem involves the need for self-esteem, a feeling of self-worth and value, and recognition from others. Organizationally, this can mean taking pride in one's work and achievements or holding a prestigious position in which one is publicly recognized and valued. Finally, self-actualization is the need to achieve one's fullest creative and productive potential. Self-actualization in organizations can involve taking charge and taking initiative, being autonomous, assuming responsibility, seeking challenges, and pushing for peak performance. Note that not everyone has the need to self-actualize according to Maslow's scheme.

Maslow's needs hierarchy assumes that the lowest unsatisfied need becomes the most dominant one; this need requires fulfillment before one seeks to satisfy the next

**FIGURE 4–2    Maslow's Needs Hierarchy**

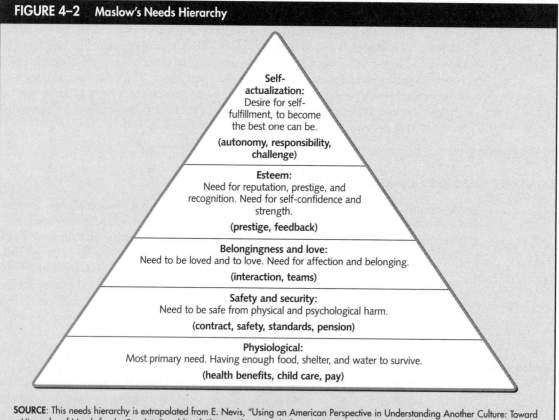

**Self-actualization:**
Desire for self-fulfillment, to become the best one can be.
**(autonomy, responsibility, challenge)**

**Esteem:**
Need for reputation, prestige, and recognition. Need for self-confidence and strength.
**(prestige, feedback)**

**Belongingness and love:**
Need to be loved and to love. Need for affection and belonging.
**(interaction, teams)**

**Safety and security:**
Need to be safe from physical and psychological harm.
**(contract, safety, standards, pension)**

**Physiological:**
Most primary need. Having enough food, shelter, and water to survive.
**(health benefits, child care, pay)**

SOURCE: This needs hierarchy is extrapolated from E. Nevis, "Using an American Perspective in Understanding Another Culture: Toward a Hierarchy of Needs for the People's Republic of China," *The Journal of Applied Behavior Science*, Vol. 19, No. 3 (1983): 249–294.

level of the need hierarchy. The idea here is that satisfied needs do not energize or motivate individuals; unsatisfied needs do. Everyone must, for example, satisfy physiological needs before safety and security needs become important. Maslow called the *lowest unsatisfied need* the **prepotent need**. Organizationally, the prepotency of needs could translate this way: Individuals will not strive toward self-actualization if they feel insecure. For example, if individuals are not sufficiently paid or do not receive resources that help them to satisfy safety, belonging, and esteem needs, they will likely not take risks that may enable them to perform their work more effectively.

Although Maslow's theory is intuitively appealing, it is not supported by empirical studies. Maslow, it should be noted, recognized and admitted that the concept of self-actualization needed to take into account other factors such as the good of others and the organization in its entirety.[5] There is also no universal evidence that there are five levels of needs as Maslow claimed. In fact, later needs theorists reduced the number to three. Maslow's theory does not apply universally across national cultures, which we shall discuss later. What people in the United States strive toward (say, self-actualization), for example, may not be the same as what the Chinese or other Asians strive toward. The theory, then, has little proven predictive value; nevertheless, it remains popular and continues to be taught and used in management training programs. Bolman and Deal state. . . .

> *Maslow's influential hierarchy of motivation suggests that, as people satisfy lower level needs for food and physical safety, they move to higher level needs for self-esteem and self-actualization. Human resource theorists such as Argyris and McGregor note that traditional managers often treat employees like children, satisfying only their lower level needs. Techniques such as participative management can satisfy higher level needs and tap higher levels of employee motivation and capacity."* [6]

### Theory X and Theory Y: Management Assumptions About Motivation

Douglas McGregor added a key dimension to Maslow's needs theory, namely that the lens through which managers view other people influences how they respond to them.[7] Managers in the United States for much of the twentieth century have practiced McGregor's Theory X, a short-term, profit-driven management style in which managers see people through a Theory X lens; that is, people are basically lazy, untrustworthy, resistant to change, and need to be led. Theory X is a carrot-and-stick approach: Do good and be rewarded, do poorly and get punished. Some have noted that Theory X management practices range between "hard" and "soft" dimensions:

> *Hard Theory X emphasizes coercion, tight controls, threats, and punishments . . . it results in low productivity, antagonism, militant unions, and subtle sabotage. In contrast, soft Theory X is a permissive style that tries to avoid conflict and satisfy everyone's needs. It may produce superficial harmony but leads to apathy and indifference and causes people to expect more and more while giving less and less. Either way—hard or soft—Theory X creates self-fulfilling prophesies."*[8]

McGregor's Theory Y management practices and assumptions about human nature are the opposite of Theory X. In Theory Y, employees are viewed as having and desiring autonomy, creativity, recognition, commitment, and responsiveness. Theory Y is based on participative management practices: "the essential task of management is to arrange organizational conditions so that people can achieve their own goals best by directing their efforts toward organizational rewards."[9] Theory Y relies on self-management techniques while Theory X focuses on management-directed practices.

It is interesting to note that Rich Teerlink, CEO of Harley-Davidson, referred to the downside of management needs and empowerment theories by stating, "If you empower dummies, you get bad decisions faster."[10] We might also add from Lee Bolman that "Theory X treats people like children, whereas Theory Y treats them like adults."[11] Although Theory X and Theory Y are powerful in their straightforward and practical appeal, human behavior and beliefs are more complex than these theories suggest. Still, the theories have currency and relevance in instructional and training applications. It is also helpful to think about Theory X and Theory Y along a continuum, not as an "either-or" dichotomy. One can then determine to what extent a manager or professional is responding to others on the Theory X, Theory Y continuum.

### Alderfer's ERG Theory

The third content theory is C. P. Alderfer's ERG theory.[12] Alderfer collapsed Maslow's needs into three categories as Figure 4–3 shows: (1) **existence**, which includes the most basic survival needs (comparable to Maslow's physiological and safety needs); (2) **relatedness**, which is the need for meaningful interaction and relationships

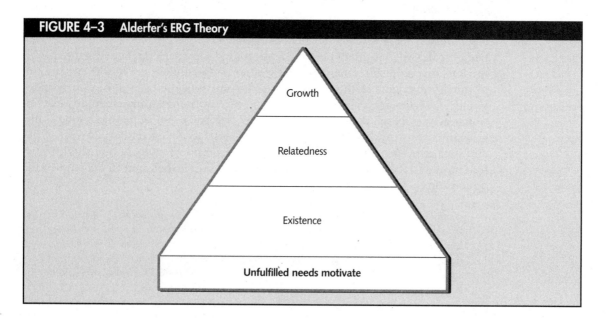

**FIGURE 4–3    Alderfer's ERG Theory**

Growth

Relatedness

Existence

**Unfulfilled needs motivate**

(comparable to Maslow's belonging and love); and (3) **growth**, which includes the need for creativity and productivity (comparable to Maslow's self-actualization). Alderfer later attributed an individual's needs to his developmental level as well as to the organizational context. For example, people in the early adult stage of development (ages 18–28) generally have more existence needs than people in mid-life transition (ages 40–45), who may have more growth or relatedness needs.

There are *six diagnostic questions* in Alderfer's theory: What needs do individuals presently have? What needs have been satisfied? Which is the lowest unsatisfied need in the hierarchy? Have some higher-level needs not been satisfied, and if so, why? Has the individual regressed on a lower-order need? How can the unsatisfied needs be fulfilled?[13]

Alderfer's theory agrees with Maslow's in that a **satisfaction-progression process** occurs; that is, people progress to the next higher level of needs only after the lower-level ones have been satisfied, although Alderfer places less emphasis on the hierarchy of needs than Maslow does. Alderfer also differs from Maslow by proposing that a **frustration-regression process** also occurs; that is, individuals who continue to be frustrated in satisfying their growth needs regress to relatedness needs, which then become a powerful motivating force. Alderfer's theory holds that higher-level needs increase in importance as they are met. For example, increased job responsibility might also lead an employee to need and desire increased autonomy and job challenge. If these needs are not met, the employee may regress to looking for a job that offers more interaction and a sense of belonging.

Much research has been generated using Alderfer's theory, but the results are mixed and offer weak support for the validity of the theory, although Alderfer's theory has more support than does Maslow's.[14] Nevertheless, like Maslow's theory, Alderfer's model is straightforward, easy to understand, and appeals to common sense.

### Herzberg's Two-Factor Theory

F. Herzberg's two-factor theory explains factors that affect work satisfaction instead of needs.[15] Based on research in which 200 accountants and engineers were interviewed, Herzberg asked such questions as these: "Can you describe, in detail, when you felt exceptionally bad about your job? Can you describe, in detail, when you felt exceptionally good about your job?" Responses generally indicated that similar experiences were categorized and polarized as good and bad. Two types of factors that affect job satisfaction emerged from the research, as shown in Table 4–1. The two factors are as follows: (1) **Hygiene factors** (dissatisfiers) are the broad dimensions of working conditions that include the social environment of work, safety and pay, procedures, status of work, and quality of supervision. Hygiene factors are based on extrinsic conditions. When these factors are present, employee satisfaction is not necessarily motivated; however, without these factors, dissatisfaction can be expected. Hygiene factors are, therefore, minimal requirements and are needed to maintain a "no-dissatisfaction" level of motivation. (2) **Motivators** (satisfiers) are the categories related to work performance, for example, achievement,

| TABLE 4–1    The Virtues of a Pluralistic Society | |
| --- | --- |
| Job Dissatisfaction ←→ No Job Dissatisfaction | No Job Satisfaction ←→ Job Satisfaction |
| Job security<br>Pay<br>Working conditions<br>Interpersonal relations<br>Supervision<br>Fringe benefits<br>Company policies | Achievement<br>Meaningful work<br>Responsibility<br>Growth and advancement<br>Recognition |

autonomy, responsibility, recognition for quality of work performance, the work, and possibility of growth. Motivators are based on intrinsic conditions. Without these conditions, people are not necessarily dissatisfied with their work, but when satisfiers are present, motivation is strengthened as is the possibility of higher job performance.

Herzberg's theory and subsequent research changed the one-dimensional concept from understanding job satisfaction as either satisfied or dissatisfied to viewing job satisfaction along two continuums: (1) low to high job dissatisfaction (hygiene) and (2) low to high job satisfaction (motivators), as indicated in Table 4–1.

Criticisms of Herzberg's two-factor theory center on the following: (1) the limited research sample and the inherent bias in the self-report method he used, (2) the ambiguous classification of factors, using pay as both a hygiene and a motivator factor, (3) the collapsing of individual differences into arbitrary categories, and (4) the overemphasis on pleasure as a desired outcome.[16] Nevertheless, Herzberg's theory contributes to a more complete understanding of the nature of job satisfaction and, along with the previously discussed theories, continues to serve as a useful corporate training and heuristic concept in management classes.

### McClelland's Trichotomy of Needs

David McClelland developed three types of learned, acquired needs in the 1940s.[17] He believed these needs were culturally acquired and could be changed through training. McClelland's theory has no notion of hierarchy or of progression or regression among needs as do the previous theories. Unlike Maslow or Alderfer, McClelland is not concerned with satisfying needs but with creating and developing appropriate needs that increase productivity (e.g., power and achievement). The three types of needs are discussed here.

One type of need, for **achievement** (designated by McClelland as *nAch*), is the need to demonstrate high performance levels and mastery over difficult and complex tasks. Individuals who have high achievement needs are generally goal oriented and set realistic goals that require risk but that are not impossible to achieve.

These individuals like to have control over individual (preferably challenging) tasks. They have high energy levels and work hard. They desire immediate and concrete feedback on their performance.

McClelland argues that high need achievers perform better than those with low or moderate levels of need achievement. His research also shows that individuals with high achievement needs account for about 10 percent of the U.S. population. People with high achievement needs are likely to excel in work and jobs characterized as entrepreneurial, high energy, and autonomous such as sales, marketing, and advertising.

A second type of need is for **power** (*nPower*) to take charge, assume responsibility and influence, and make an impact. Individuals with a high need for power are concerned with getting, using, and keeping power to influence others. They enjoy constructive confrontation and engage in competitive situations in which they stand a chance of winning.

McClelland distinguishes between *socialized power* (i.e., power that is used to benefit others and the organization) and *personalized power* (i.e., power that is used only or mainly for one's own personal gain or benefit and many times at the expense of others' needs). Managers who rated the highest or "best" in McClelland's research were those who had a high need for socialized power.[18] Examples of contemporary business leaders who seem to show a high need for personalized power include Bill Gates of Microsoft; Frank Lorenzo, former CEO of Eastern Airlines; Ross Perot, formerly with EDP; and Donald Trump, an independent entrepreneur. Examples of business leaders who seem to show a high need for socialized power include Sam Walton of Wal-Mart, Ben Cohen and Jerry Greenfield (founders of Ben and Jerry's ice creams), and Dave Packard and Bill Hewlett of Hewlett-Packard.

The third type of need, for **affiliation** (*nAff*), is the need to interact socially with others, to make and sustain friendly relationships. Individuals with a high need for affiliation have a desire for belonging and for giving and receiving affection. They have a need to be liked and seek close emotional relationships and communication. They shun conflict.

Individuals who have low to moderate affiliation needs generally require low to moderate levels of interaction. They can also work well alone for long time spans. People with high affiliation needs seek closeness with others and desire more interpersonal interaction.

All individuals have varying degrees of all three models. Usually one of these needs predominates. To discover which of a person's needs is predominant, McClelland used the Thematic Apperception Test (TAT). This test requires a person to project her needs by observing a series of pictures of people in different settings. The person taking the test describes what she believes is happening in the picture. For example, perceiving and describing a social event indicates a need for affiliation. Observing and describing one person controlling or dominating a situation indicates a need for power.

McClelland tested his theory in Kakinda, India, where he trained business professionals to practice high-achieving roles and methods (e.g., setting and meeting challenging goals). After two years, results from the study showed that new jobs had doubled because of the activities of those who had been trained compared with those who had received no training.[19] These findings present a strong argument for cross-cultural applications for the achievement dimension of this theory, with particular reference to a developing country. However, a word of caution is in order. McClelland's TAT method may not have accurately discerned achievement as it is expressed or experienced in the Indian culture.

Other studies indicated that national culture makes a difference in the emphasis placed on need achievement. For example, Anglo-American countries whose cultures emphasize high productivity and risk taking—for example, the United States, Canada, and Great Britain—are characterized as achievement oriented and follow high-need achievement patterns of behavior. Countries such as Portugal and Chile, whose cultures are high in uncertainty avoidance and place less emphasis on productivity, follow a low-need achievement pattern.[20] These are, of course, generalizations that may not apply to every member of the culture.

McClelland's theory has been widely applied to management and leadership training across cultures. From his studies, McClelland has found that a "leadership motive pattern" exists: a moderate to high need for power combined with a low need for affiliation leads to effective leadership profiles in organizations.[21] While this relationship may be true for low- and middle-level managers, the higher an individual goes in an organization, the more important it is for that person to emphasize managing interpersonal relationships and being competent in doing so. At higher organizational levels, a person with both a high need for power and a high need for affiliation generally has a higher probability of success.

High socialized power needs enable leaders and managers to exert influence on others; low affiliative needs enable leaders and managers to implement tough decisions without being too concerned about being liked.[22]

McClelland's theory also can be used to match people with high power, affiliation, and achievement need profiles with work, positions, and assignments that fit them well. For example, entrepreneurial people with high achievement needs can be matched with highly challenging, realistic goals; they can be given responsibilities that encourage their drive and can be given concrete feedback on performance-based achievements. Bonuses and other entrepreneurial rewards should be linked to their performance. People showing a high need for power can be assigned work and positions in which they exert legitimate, socialized influence over others in performance-based task relationships; they can also be considered for assignments requiring leadership and control and in which they receive recognition for their accomplishments. People with high affiliative needs can be assigned positions and work that provide interaction and a sense of belonging. As always, care must be taken in making these assessments and assignments to ensure that perceptual biases and attributional errors are not part of the assessment process.

Critics of McClelland's theory focus (1) on the validity of his use of the TAT projection test as a means of identifying needs (whether this or other tests are more valid for determining a person's needs requires further attention), (2) on whether the needs are acquired and learned or whether they are innate; and (3) on the question of whether needs can be changed and whether training can accomplish change. If so, how long does the change last? These questions and issues have not adequately been resolved.[23]

## THE CHANGING WORKPLACE: MY NEEDS PROFILE

### Personal Needs Questionnaire

**Exercise**: The following set of 13 statements reflects different priorities that people have. There are no right or wrong answers. Read each item carefully and then select the response that most closely fits *your* preference.

1. In general, I would rather work
   a. by myself.
   b. on a team.

2. When working on a school-related project, I usually
   a. spend a great deal of time on it to ensure it is well done.
   b. try to make it acceptable.

3. On a team,
   a. I really try to be the leader.
   b. I let others take the lead.

4. When I'm working on a project, I prefer to
   a. do it my way.
   b. see how others have done it or want to do it.

5. My goals at work or at school are usually to
   a. be good enough to get by.
   b. outperform others.

6. When I am involved in a disagreement, I usually
   a. don't say too much if people I really like are arguing against my opinion.
   b. speak my mind.

7. On a team, I
   a. let ideas or recommendations develop naturally from team discussion.
   b. try to influence my teammates with my opinion.

8. At work, I pretty much
   a. keep to myself and get the job done.
   b. enjoy chatting with my co-workers.

9. At work or school, I usually
   a. avoid risks.
   b. "stick my neck out" and take moderate risks to get ahead.

10. When I'm involved in sports or other games, I usually play to
    a. have a good time.
    b. win or least do better than I have previously.

11. When working on a project, I like to
    a. have a direct influence in its outcome.
    b. be accepted as a "team player."

12. When I am working with other people, I usually want to
    a. do better than they do.
    b. organize and direct the activities of others.

13. In my work and school life, I often
    a. make certain I give adequate time to my personal life (friends, family, etc.).
    b. get so overscheduled that I have less time for my personal life.

*(continued on next page)*

## THE CHANGING WORKPLACE (continued)

### Personal Needs Scoring Sheet

Score one point in the following if you marked the appropriate letter:

| N Pow | N Ach | N Aff |
|-------|-------|-------|
| 3a    | 2a    | 1b    |
| 4a    | 8a    | 4b    |
| 5b    | 9b    | 6a    |
| 7b    | 10b   | 8b    |
| 11a   | 12a   | 11b   |
| 12b   | 13b   | 13a   |

Total ___          ___          ___

**Interpretation**: In this chapter, you read about David McClelland's theory of socially acquired needs. McClelland's research suggested that people's higher-order needs were not arranged in the hierarchical fashion suggested by Maslow but were shaped by socialization processes and life experiences. He identified three basic needs: the need for power ($N Pow$), the need for achievement ($N Ach$), and the need for affiliation ($N Aff$).

According to McClelland, these three needs coexist in each person, but to varying degrees. $N Pow$ relates to the desire to be in charge, in control, to influence and direct others. $N Ach$ reflects the desire to excel and to set and fulfill demanding goals. Finally, $N Aff$ is related to the need to be included, accepted, and liked, to be part of a group.

This brief questionnaire reflects your needs in these three areas. This exercise, of course, is not a rigorous, scientific measurement of your needs; rather, the results are intended to provide you with a general sense of your needs.

Each area has a total of six points. The area in which you have the highest number of points reflects your dominant need. There are no "good" or "bad" scores. In fact, depending on your career orientation and desires, any combination of need levels can work for you. Someone with a low need for power, for example, might not be attracted to leadership positions, while an individual with a high need for affiliation might be drawn to people-intensive type of work environments.

What do *you* think? Do your scores reflect what you feel are your basis needs?

**Source**: Adapted from Dorothy Marcic, "Manifest Needs," in *Organizational Behavior*, 5th ed., D. Marcic & J. Seltzer (Cincinnati, Ohio: South Western College Publishing, 1995), 69–71.

### Content Theories in Perspective

The five content theories of motivation we have discussed are summarized in Table 4–2. Taken together, these theories challenge leaders, managers, and organizational members to the following:

- Gain an understanding of their own needs and the needs of those with whom they work and manage regarding the nature of the work

- Learn how to best match organizational jobs, positions, and assignments to professional needs

- Create learning environments that motivate the needs of individuals and teams to perform more effectively and with quality

| TABLE 4–2   Needs Theories: A Comparison | | | |
|---|---|---|---|
| Maslow's Need Hierarchy | Alderfer's ERG Theory | Herzberg's Two-Factor Theory | McClelland's Trichotomy |
| Physiological safety and security | Existence | Hygiene | |
| Belongingness and love | Relatedness | | Affiliation |
| Self-esteem Self-actualization | Growth | Motivators | Achievement Power |

Managers can use the theories to develop questions for feedback and guidelines for performance appraisals so that employees can identify their job-related needs, their sources of job satisfaction and dissatisfaction, and their needs for power, affiliation, and achievement. Such exercises can enhance performance and development.

Some of the commonalities of the four theories include a recognition of the role that human needs play in organizational satisfaction, performance, and growth, and the distinction between lower- and higher-level needs. Higher-level needs for Maslow include self-actualization, esteem, and belonging; for Alderfer they are growth and relatedness; for Herzberg motivational factors, and for McClelland they are achievement and power. There are important distinctions in the four theories. Maslow held to a hierarchy of five needs; Alderfer constructed a hierarchy of three needs with much more flexibility; Herzberg used two factors that collapsed the needs of Maslow and Alderfer. Herzberg also looked at factors that did and did not motivate employees (e.g., dissatisfiers). McClelland found there to be three major needs common to all cultures; he viewed all people as learned and capable of being taught.

Most of these theories lack sufficient empirical validation, especially from a cross-cultural perspective, but they are a starting point for discussing the role of human needs and motivation in the workplace. They can also be used to discover the effects of organizational change on individuals' needs and motivations. Managers can use the vocabulary and concepts of the content theories in employee interviews and dialogues to identify development and training areas in which employee motivation can be improved.

## PROCESS THEORIES OF MOTIVATION

*Process theories* use external variables to identify individual sources of motivation. Whereas content theories deal with intrapersonal, internal sources (i.e., needs) for motivation, process theories include perceived and actual exogenous, workplace dimensions, for example, performance, goals, and tasks.

## Equity Theory

*Equity theory* argues that people compare their efforts (inputs) and rewards (outcomes) with others to determine the fairness of the outcomes. Inequity is based on perception as well as situation-specific, objective observations. Perceived inequity can motivate individuals to take action to remedy the felt inequity.

J. Stacey Adams first extended the logic and application of equity theory to work settings.[24] Adams noted the following elements in equity theory: the individual, who perceives equity or inequity in a situation; the *comparison other* or group, whom the person uses as a reference; the inputs, which are the characteristics an individual brings to the work situation (e.g., gender, age, education, skills, experiences, seniority, time, effort); and outcomes, which are what the individual receives from the work (pay, bonus, fringe benefits, recognition, status symbols, job security, working environment).

Felt or perceived inequities exist when individuals perceive that their efforts (inputs) are greater or lesser than their rewards (outcomes) when compared to those of others. Specifically, individuals compare two ratios in determining equity or inequity; that is, they compare the ratio of their rewards to their efforts and the ratio of another's rewards to efforts. Perceived or felt equity exists when people feel they receive as much as the "comparison other."

### Reducing Inequities

Equity theory states that individuals are motivated to reduce perceived inequities to make the outcomes to inputs (O/I) ratios equal. The theory argues that people will react to inequities in proportion to their perceived inequity. For example, individuals who perceive that they receive too much for the work they have done will also seek to "equalize" the inequity; that is, they may work longer hours or contribute more to the job. This is known as the *overjustification effect*. Research has questioned whether this effect happens.[25] However, some researchers argue that overcompensating employees improves performance.[26]

Three types of individuals who have different preferences for equity include entitleds, benevolents, and equity sensitives.[27] *Entitleds* are comfortable when their equity ratio is higher than that of their comparison other. *Benevolents* are willing to accept that their equity ratio may be lower than that of the comparison other, and *equity sensitives* desire ratios that are equal.

Individuals who believe that negative inequities exist between themselves and their comparison others can take a number of actions to change the ratios: they can try to change the outcomes or rewards (e.g., ask for more or different kinds of rewards or pay); change the inputs (reduce their efforts or the quality or the nature of contributions); quit or change their comparisons (use a different comparison other); rationalize or distort the comparisons (tell themselves that the inequities will change or are invalid); or try to change the comparison other's ratio (persuade the other to contribute more or accept fewer rewards). Table 4–3 compares inequity

| TABLE 4–3 | Inequity Reduction Conditions and Strategies |
|---|---|

$$\frac{O_A}{I_A} < \frac{O_B}{I_B}$$

*Person B*
> Requests reduced outcomes
> Enhances inputs

*Person A*
> Reduces inputs
> Requests increased outcomes

*Person A or B*
> Changes comparison other
> States that equity exists when it does not
> Quits or exits the situation

$$\frac{O_A}{I_A} > \frac{O_B}{I_B}$$

*Person A*
> Requests reduced outcomes
> Enhances inputs

*Person B*
> Requests enhanced outcomes
> Reduces inputs

*Person A or B*
> Changes comparison other
> States that equity exists when it does not
> Quits or exits the situation

reduction conditions and strategies. Note the conditions where $O_A$ is the outcome for person A (as the receiver); $I_A$ is the input of person A; $O_B$ is the outcome for person B (the comparison other); $I_B$ is the input of person B.

Owners and managers can reduce and minimize inequities by establishing different wage and incentive systems, for example, two-tier wage systems, which clearly specify rules and procedures for pay and performance based on different levels of experience and expertise; skill-based pay, which calculates and bases wages on specific job skills; and gainsharing, which uses a formula-based group incentive plan to allow employees to share in the organization's financial gain due to the improved performance. Whatever pay and performance system is adopted, managers must ensure that procedural justice guides the design, implementation, and follow-through of the system. That is, clear policies must state the conditions of the situation and what *equitable distribution* means. Fair due process grievance procedures for those who perceive they have been mistreated should be made known and followed at all levels of the organization.

Equity theory is intuitively appealing and seems commonsensical. However, the theory has limitations. First, most research focuses on pay as the outcome. Other variables can also affect outcome. One study, for example, suggests that employees assigned to higher status offices increase their performance while those assigned to lower status offices reduce their performance.[28] More research is needed to identify all the types of motivating rewards and inputs. Second, most research on equity is limited to short-term comparisons. Longitudinal studies that examine different individual responses over time are needed.[29] Also, equity theory research should focus on issues other than the distribution of rewards. For example, one study in a manufacturing plant found that employees expressed concern about the injustice of decision-making procedures.[30] It thus appears that personal ethics and issues regarding procedural justice can be a motivator or a dissatisfier.

## Expectancy Theory

Victor Vroom developed *expectancy theory* to explain and predict behavior and motivation.[31] Expectancy theory goes beyond equity theory in addressing a major question, What determines the willingness of a person to exert effort to work on tasks that contribute to work unit performance in the organization? Vroom argues that motivation is a function of expectancy, valence, and instrumentality; that is,

*Motivation = E × V × I (Expectancy × Valence × Instrumentality)*

Think of motivation as a perceived process in which a person makes the following linkages in his thinking:

1. *Effort* leads to *performance* (expectancy): the individual perceives that exerting a certain amount of effort will lead to performance.

2. *Performance* leads to *reward* (instrumentality): the individual believes that performing at a given level leads to a certain reward or outcome.

3. *Rewards* lead to *personal goals* (valency): the individual perceives that certain rewards motivate his needs and goals.

Motivation, in effect, is determined by a person's beliefs concerning the relationships between effort and performance and desirabilities about rewards and performance. Stated simply, people will do what they can do when they want to.[32]

The three components in this formulation of motivation explain the relationships between perceived effort, performance, and reward. Each set of relationships can range from negative to zero to positive, depending on a person's perceptions. Expectancy (*E*) refers to an individual's perception about the probability that effort leads to performance (effort —> performance). These expected probabilities range from 0 to 1.0. Individuals who perceive or expect no link between their effort and performance thus have zero expectancy. These are *low expectancy* individuals; they perceive that their efforts will not lead directly to higher performance. *High expectancy* (a probability of 1.0) individuals perceive direct links between their effort and performance. Employees' expectancy perceptions are influenced not only by the nature of the task but also by factors such as self-esteem, past history of success at completing similar tasks, available resources, information, and assistance.

Valence (V) refers to the value (positive or negative) individuals attach to outcomes (value —> outcome). People subjectively assign valences based on their personal preferences and needs to outcomes from their work. Probabilities range between 0 and 1.0, 0 being low and 1.0 being high.

Instrumentality (I) refers to an individual's perceptions of the likelihood that particular negative or positive outcomes will be attached to performance (performance —> outcome). A *high instrumentality* person perceives that there will be more pay or rewards for harder work or greater contributions. Individuals who perceive no link between pay and performance have *zero instrumentality.*

Although we do not carry around a calculator to assign numerical values to our own or others' perceived expectancies, valences, and instrumentalities to determine motivational levels, Vroom's early version of this theory does provide for such measurement. For example, when all elements of the theory are positive—that is E —> P = 1.0 (expectancy leads to performance), P —> O = 1.0 (performance leads to outcome), and V = 1.0 (value placed on outcomes)—motivation is high (1.0 × 1.0 × 1.0 = 1.0). However, if an employee does not believe that her performance will lead to more pay, the resulting motivation will also be low.

Vroom's early version of expectancy theory was later revised and extended by Lyman Porter and Edward Lawler III.[33] Their version identifies the source of an individual's expectancies and valences and links effort to performance and job satisfaction. In Figure 4–4, effort is viewed as a valence (the perceived value of a

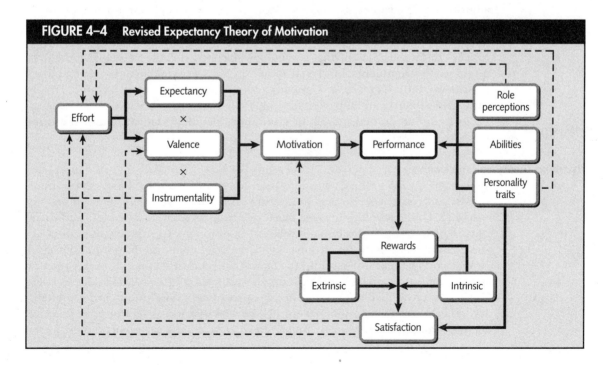

**FIGURE 4–4    Revised Expectancy Theory of Motivation**

reward) and an expectancy (that effort will lead to a reward). Performance, how-ever, is influenced not only by effort but also by an employee's role perceptions, abilities, and personality traits. Employees who are more able and have a better understanding of their roles, so this model suggests, will reach higher performance levels.

Satisfaction in this model is a function of both *extrinsic* (tangibles such as pay and bonuses) and *intrinsic* (intangibles such as a sense of accomplishment and gratification) *performance rewards*. Satisfaction is also determined by employees' per-ceptions of having been equitably rewarded; thus, satisfaction loops back to valence in the figure. It also loops back to effort because increased satisfaction generally brings about more and better effort. Research is mixed on the validity of this the-ory. Some studies validate some of the predictions made by the expectancy theory, such as job satisfaction, occupational and organizational choice, and retirement decisions.[34] The research problem has been not studying the same individuals under different circumstances as the theory proposes. Instead, replication studies have examined different individuals in different situations.

### Managerial Uses of Expectancy Theory

Organizational leaders and managers can apply expectancy theory to diagnose, create, and direct employee motivation in the following ways. The first is to ensure that the "right" rewards are linked to the desired performance standards and behaviors. Steven Kerr's classic article, "On the Folly of Rewarding A, While Hoping for B,"[35] applies here. Managers must effectively communicate and ensure that the employee values organizationally appropriate rewards. If not, further adjustments or changes are needed. Second, accurate, valid, and reliable perform-ance ratings, rankings, and comparative evaluation procedures must be in place. Otherwise, perceived inequities and undesirable consequences are likely to occur. Third, continuously clarifying psychological contracts and comparing them to actual work assignments and rewards will provide an understanding of employee motivation and increase a company's options in motivating people. Finally, expectancy theory can help explain why people perform at low levels doing certain projects and assignments. Lack of motivation may be found in one of the three linkages discussed here.

### Learning Theory and Motivation

*Learning* is an integral part of motivation for several reasons. First, expectations, needs, and responses that are motivating and demotivating are learned (or not learned). Understanding how we learn can assist organization leaders and mem-bers in diagnosing motivational levels and finding ways to enhance them Second, since rewards and punishments are a vital part of human motivation, understand-ing how people learn to respond to rewards and punishments can assist organiza-tion leaders and managers in allocating rewards more effectively. Finally, learning has taken on added importance in the process of "continuous improvement." Influenced by the Japanese concept of *kaizen* (translated as "continuous improve-ment") which focuses not on "quick fixes" to problems or opportunities but on transformational, incremental, and organizationwide learning processes that enhance product and service quality, many successful corporations practice kaizen. Learning how we learn is important to enable self-improvement.

The three major learning theories we summarize here include *classical conditioning* (which is discussed here as a basis for understanding later developments in learning theory), behavior modification, and goal setting. *Classical conditioning* was introduced by the Russian physiologist Ivan Pavlov. His experiments with dogs (subjects) showed that ringing a bell (conditional stimulus) and giving a dog food (unconditional stimulus) later became linked in the dog's memory so that the dog salivated (a learned or conditioned response) whenever the bell was rung. Controlled learning was born.

In contrast to classical conditioning in which the response to be learned is present in the subject, *operant conditioning* is about learning a response that is not innate in the subject. The desired response must be planned and conscientiously delivered to produce the desired results (not a necessary condition in the classical theory). The A-B-C operant sequence, now used by many organization trainees, was developed from this theory. The A-B-C sequence indicates that antecedent A stimuli (which can also refer to our assumptions that drive behavior) precede and influence our choice of behaviors B, which in turn result in consequences C, either desired or undesired. Understanding this sequence on how and what we learn can assist planning and implementation activities.

*Reinforcement theory*, which has had tremendous impact on learning in almost all institutions, emerged from operant conditioning. Behavior modification is one type of reinforcement learning, and we shall discuss it later. Reinforcement theory holds that motivation is an internal cause of behavior and that reinforcements are external causes. Feedback and rewards, when appropriately and systematically applied through positive and negative reinforcement, punishment, and extinction, can direct learning and motivation toward defined outcomes.

*Positive reinforcement* is defined by the type of outcome used and the action taken by the influence agent. The behavior is encouraged, conditioned, and reinforced by positive feedback. For example, as a manager, you want a sales professional to use computer projections and report on variances of actual sales against projected monthly figures. To accomplish this, you meet with him at the beginning of the month and explain to him that 10 percent of his commission is linked to using and completing the monthly report. You meet again at the end of the month, praise and encourage him and pay his commissions, showing that the 10 percent is a result of his using the data.

*Negative reinforcement* refers to an increase in the frequency of a response after the removal or termination of a negative reinforcer immediately after the response occurs. For example, exerting a lot of energy to finish an assignment ahead of schedule may be negatively reinforced by not having to be overly controlled by an authoritarian boss. Finishing the assignment early by giving more effort reduces the likelihood of having to be subjected to unnecessary control (negative reinforcer) from the boss.

*Punishment* in reinforcement theory refers to applying an uncomfortable reinforcer to an undesired behavior to stop it. Punishment is a risky method when used to stop undesired behaviors for several reasons. First, punishment often has short-term effects, and undesired behaviors tend to recur. Second, punishment can have unintended and undesirable consequences—for example, sabotage, withdrawal, and other defensive or revenging actions. Punishment may be effective in last-resort situations and when the advantages clearly exceed the costs, as when an employee continues to intentionally disrupt the operation of a unit after being repeatedly reprimanded.

*Extinction* refers to the continued withholding of a positive reinforcement until an undesired behavior is eliminated. Nonreinforcement of the behavior is the key here. This is passive elimination when ignoring, avoiding, and using other nonreinforcers extinguish the undesirable behavior.

## Behavior Modification

The basic tenet in the behavior modification approach to learning is that to effect change, behaviors must be addressed, rather than their psychological inferences or causes. Behavioral modification specialists, therefore, approach human problems in organizations by focusing on specific behaviors. A five-step behavioral modification model addresses change[36] as follows:

1. Identify and define specific behavior(s). Can these be seen? Can they be measured?

2. Establish a baseline. Before attempting to change the behavior, determine its strength in the present by measuring or counting the occurrences of the behavior.

3. Analyze the A-B-Cs (antecedents, behaviors, consequences) of the behavior to determine the source of the problem.

4. Develop and implement an action plan using operant conditioning; strengthen the desirable behaviors, and weaken or extinguish the undesirable one through conditioning techniques.

5. Evaluate the effects of the changes using different measurements.

Reinforcement theory and techniques have been used in a number of organizations, including B. F. Goodrich, General Electric, Michigan Bell Telephone, and Connecticut General Life Insurance. By identifying and rewarding specific desired performance behaviors, companies have increased productivity. Research also suggests that behavior modification techniques have contributed to desired organizational behavior changes.[37]

Critics of behavior modification, in particular, attack the technique on the grounds that self-reinforcement is the real change agent, not the other techniques discussed previously—that is, individuals actually motivate their own behavior changes and they do so without the reward systems in behavior modification.[38]

Also, employees may not truly change their behaviors; that is, they may only pretend to change their behavior to get the short-term award. Finally, behavior modification techniques are sometimes implemented poorly; therefore, desired results cannot be accurately assessed since the techniques were not properly applied.

Behavior modification and other reinforcement theories and techniques have become an integral part of organizational behavior literature and tools. Although the preceding criticisms have value, the practice and use of these theories remain part of the expanding repertoire of management interventions.

## Managerial Implications

Learning is the acquisition of skills, knowledge, abilities, and attitudes. The behavioral approach to learning emphasizes external influences and the power of reward reinforcement. The *cognitive approach* (as in the content theories) emphasizes the internal mental processes that result from combining environmental cues into mental maps. Managers need to ensure that proper and adequate (preferably optimal) conditions are present for learning. Managers must provide stimuli to encourage the acquisition of skills, knowledge, and/or attitudes and then must reinforce the desired behaviors. It is important that the organization have individuals who can model the appropriate behavior for followers.

## Motivation and Goal Setting

Goal setting is an application of motivation and learning theory. Goal-setting activities benefit individuals and organizations because goals direct and guide attention, regulate and shape effort, increase commitment and persistence, and encourage strategies and action planning.[39] Goal setting leads to performance and is practiced cross-culturally—for example, in such widely varying places as Japan, the Caribbean Islands, West Germany, Malaysia, Canada, and India.[40]

## SMART GOALS AND OBJECTIVES

Goals motivate individuals and organizations if the goals are SMART. (i.e., specific, measurable, assignable, realistic, and time related).[41] To motivate individual behavior as well as organizational behavior, goals must target specific and identifiable areas for improvement. For example, an organizational goal "to gain market share" is not specific. However, "to gain a 15 percent market share in each of three business segments" is. Goals must also be measurable. To be implemented, goals must be assignable and then must be assigned to an individual or group. Goals are assignable if they are understood, capable of being implemented, and acceptable to those implementing them. Goals must be realistic; that is, there must be sufficient resources and time, given other contingencies, to ensure proper implementation. Finally, goals must be time related: completion times must specify when the goal is to be accomplished. In the preceding example, it might be specified that gaining 15 percent market share should occur by a given quarter in a particular year.

The following example clarifies the setting of a SMART goal. A colleague who is the manager of the Program of Project Managers (PPM), an organization of which you are a member, approaches you and asks you to help her develop a goal and some objectives to get the PPM back on track. Membership has dropped over the past four years, and the life of the organization is at stake. You meet with her and decide to conduct an annual conference. After working together for a morning, you come up with a SMART goal and set of objectives that you both believe can help gain support of others to implement.

The goal and objectives must be specific, measurable, assignable (i.e., can someone else execute them), realistic, and have time parameters. After getting mem-

## THE CHANGING WORKPLACE

### Setting SMART Goals and Objectives

**Goal**: Plan and implement the next PPM annual conference, August 15-20, 2001, in Las Vegas. Plan on 4 percent of the 23,000 membership attending; aggressively recruit another 500 new members to attend, realizing a new profit of $35,000. These target membership and profit goals will reverse the downward trend.

**Objectives:**
1. Conduct the PPM annual conference at an attendance level 15 percent above that of last year.

2. Offer three concurrent tracks in the program, highlighting nationally known experts who will draw existing and new members.

3. Realize a net profit of $35,000 and 500 new members based on an aggressive networking and mailing campaign.

4. Recruit a planning and implementation team by November 5 (in one month) who are committed, energetic, an empowered to mobilize resources to execute these goals and objectives.

**Note:** This is the first phase of SMART goal and objective setting. You still need to plan specific activities and assign individuals and resources to meet the goal.

**Exercise:** First as individuals and than as dyads, complete the following: Write a SMART goal and at least three objectives (objectives are also milestones that break the goal down further) for an important event that you need to achieve and that is related to your career, work/job, education, or studies.

1. Start with the questions, What is the need, problem, or opportunity I have that, if completed, would result in positive returns for me? What problem would I solve or opportunity would I accomplish by achieving this goal? Draft what the *outcome(s)* would look like (which will help you write your goal). Go over your goal statement(s). Is your goal SMART?

2. Now break the goal down into smaller milestones (end states). Ask this question: What major steps do I have to accomplish to reach this goal? Do not write small tasks. Break the large goal into smaller ones (these are the objectives.) Number

*continued on next page*

---

**THE CHANGING WORKPLACE (continued)**

at least three objectives. After you write these, ask: Is each objective SMART? If I achieve these objectives, will I have achieved my goal? If you answered yes, you're on the right track.

3. Meet with a member of the class and share your written goal and objectives with each other. Determine whether the other person's goal is SMART. Interview each other, asking Could you plan and implement my goal starting with these objectives? What would you need (information, resources) to feel comfortable starting with my goal and objectives?

**Class Exercise**: Report the answers to these questions to the class from your teams of two:

1. What did you learn from this exercise?

2. What did you learn from having someone interview you about your goal and objectives using the SMART criteria?

3. What observations do you have?

**SOURCE**: Adopted from J. Weiss and R. Wysocki, *5-Phase Project Management, A Practical Planning and Implementation Guide* (Perseus Books, 1992).

---

bership information, facts, and relevant data on PPM and then brainstorming, you produce the information presented in the accompanying box.

Research on goal setting has shown the following.

1. Difficult goals can lead to higher performance levels. *Goal difficulty* refers to the amount of effort and level of proficiency needed to achieve a goal. Studies show that difficult goals lead to higher performance than do easy, moderate, do-your-best, or no goals, but there is a threshold at which goals are perceived to be impossible to reach.[42]

2. *Specific* goals generally lead to improved performance. However, the positive effects of specificity can be diminished when new interdependent tasks are introduced if other conditions are not met.

3. *Feedback* increases positive effects of setting difficult, specific goals. Employees who must implement difficult goals do so more successfully if they have feedback that provides information and support. Such feedback enables them to understand resource availability, to learn to adjust their direction and effort, and to bring their expectations in line with those of the organization.

4. Goals *jointly* set by managers and subordinates lead to increased goal acceptance and commitment.[43] Participation in goal setting is a necessary and important condition for goal attainment. Other conditions that affect goal performance include goal-related organizational values, rewards and incentives, competitive peer pressure, and the presence of self-administered rewards.

5. *High expectancy* (the belief that efforts leads to performance) and *high self-efficacy* (the belief in one's ability to obtain a goal) enhance goal commitment and lead

to goal performance.[44] These findings support the expectancy theory of motivation discussed earlier. The point here is that goal achievement is not only or even necessarily a property of the goal itself.

Finally, research shows that employees increase goal-setting activities after successful achievements and reduce such activities after failures.[45] Moreover, in complex tasks, the strategies used in goal achievement have proved to be an important link between goals and their attainment.

## MOTIVATION AND REWARD SYSTEMS

Individuals generally value the rewards they receive in organizations in relation to their own motivation and satisfaction. Since people value and are motivated by different rewards for different reasons, reward systems must be diverse to accommodate different and changing employee needs. Reward systems must be comprehensive and based on realistic analyses of employee needs and work situations. Reward systems also must be consistent to demonstrate fairness.

Edward Lawler III argued that satisfaction with rewards is influenced by at least five factors.

1. The actual reward and the amount should agree with what the person believes he should have received. In general, the greater the award, intrinsic or extrinsic, the more the satisfaction. However, if an individual perceives the size of a reward as being unjustifiable (e.g., if the reward appears to be too large given the effort exerted), the motivation and therefore the effort may level off or even decrease.

2. People compare the rewards they receive with awards that others receive. This influences their level of motivation. Employees who believe they are under- or overawarded in comparison to others may not feel motivated or satisfied.

3. Intrinsic and extrinsic awards influence an individual's motivation and job satisfaction. A common fallacy is the assumption that only extrinsic awards such as money motivate.

4. There is a wide variation in the rewards people value. Some people value pay more than vacation or flextime; others value day care and other benefits as much as pay.

5. Some extrinsic awards are valued because they lead to other rewards. For example, increased pay may be valued by an employee because it leads to mobility in her chosen career path.[46]

Rewards and reward systems, then, must serve several purposes to effectively motivate employees and to meet the needs of the organization. Relative to the organization, reward systems also must fit the organization's vision, mission, and value statements and must be congruent with other systems in the organization, as shown in Chapter 14, Figure 14–1. That is, reward systems should fit the culture, the people, the structure, the strategy, the technology and the work. Reward systems also must be competitive with the market environment and with competitors' reward systems. Reward systems must accommodate the quality of work life rather than meeting only minimal requirements. For example, allowing flextime and providing other intrinsic rewards reinforce an organization's quality of worklife by putting its philosophy into practice. At the same time, reward systems must be based on performance and quality of work product or service. In the current, highly competitive business environment, it is product and service quality and speed to market that meet customer demands and, to this end, rewards must reflect performance-based criteria. The following section outlines in more detail general requirements of reward systems.

### Requirements of Effective Reward Systems

Effective reward systems link performance and effort. Criteria for allocating rewards should, at a minimum, include the following:

1. Rewards should be clearly defined and consistent with other rewards for comparable work and expertise.

2. Employees should be informed about what exactly they are being rewarded for. Is level and/or quality of performance, effort, attendance, innovation, or creativity being rewarded?

3. Not all employees should be rewarded the same since not all employees perform at the same level.

4. Management must ensure that employees perceive the rewards to be distributed equitably. This requires that the criteria for giving rewards be accurately and comprehensively communicated across the organization.

5. Management must ensure that its organization's rewards are comparable to those of its competitors. In addition to these criteria, Table 4-4 presents criteria that an effective reward system should address.

## CROSS-CULTURAL PERSPECTIVES ON MOTIVATION

Motivation is, to a large extent, culturally conditioned and learned. Since most motivation theories have been developed in North America and the West, it is not surprising that these concepts reflect western assumptions about human nature. However, not all western cultures view motivation the same way, as we shall see. In this section, we critique the theories presented earlier from a cross-cultural perspective and discuss how certain other cultures view motivation.[47]

Maslow's needs hierarchy has been criticized from a cross-cultural perspective. For example, K. Hofstede, a leading international cultural expert, argues that in

**TABLE 4–4    Reward System Criteria**

1.   Rewards must fit individual needs.
2.   Rewards must be perceived to be distributed equitably.
3.   Rewards must be equal to or greater than those in comparable organizations.
4.   Rewards must be high enough to provide personal satisfaction.
5.   Rewards must satisfy high performers.
6.   Rewards must be related to job satisfaction.
7.   Rewards must be related to performance.
8.   Rewards must fit other organizational system requirements
     (e.g., management style, strategy, structure).

SOURCE: Based on E. Lawler III, "Reward Systems," in *Improving Life at Work: Behavioral Science Approaches to Organizational Change*, ch. 3, ed. J. Hackman and J. Suttle (Santa Monica, Calif.: Goodyear Publishing, 1977).

countries with cultures that value uncertainty avoidance (e.g., Japan and Greece), job security and lifelong employment are stronger motivators than is self-actualization.[48] Moreover, in certain European countries that value and reward quality of life as much as—if not more than—productivity (e.g., Denmark, Sweden, Norway), social needs are stronger motivators than self-esteem or self-actualization needs (which are higher-order needs in Maslow's hierarchy).

In countries that value collectivist and community practices over individualistic achievements, belonging and security are higher-order needs (again, in contrast to Maslow's hierarchy). For example, one study found that China's hierarchy of needs differs significantly from that of Maslow.[49] Figure 4–5 compares the differences. The need hierarchy for China is based on the following cultural assumptions underlying Chinese management practices:

- The nation has priority over everything; loyalty to the country is of the utmost importance.

- Consideration for the family is very important.

- Personnel selection (leadership) is based on ideological contributions.

- One should have great respect for age.

- Equity is more important than wealth.

- Saving and conserving (money, resources, etc.) are to be valued, as is high respect for traditional ways.

- It is considered unhealthy for individuals to stand out or to take personal credit for their accomplishments.

- Every decision must take ideology into account.

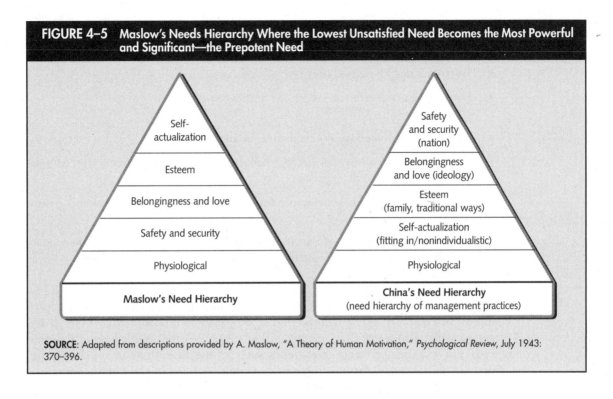

FIGURE 4–5   Maslow's Needs Hierarchy Where the Lowest Unsatisfied Need Becomes the Most Powerful and Significant—the Prepotent Need

SOURCE: Adapted from descriptions provided by A. Maslow, "A Theory of Human Motivation," *Psychological Review*, July 1943: 370–396.

- Communal property is more important than private possessions; collectivism is the best economic mechanism.

- Emphasis is placed on group forces for motivational purposes.

- Central planning and the powerful state are continually emphasized.[50]

It will be interesting to observe whether or not and to what extent these cultural assumptions change as China integrates into the global economy.

Maslow's needs hierarchy is based on the following cultural assumptions underlying North American management practices:

- People believe that they can substantially influence the future; people believe in self-determinism, that they are masters of their own fates.

- Freedom of expression and opinion is generally valued; individualism is encouraged.

- "To get ahead" is taken for granted; all should have equal opportunity to do this.

- Independent enterprises are the most effective instruments; competition is the most effective mechanism.

- The emphasis is on private property and a limited state.

- Personnel selection is based on merit.

- Decisions must be based on objective analysis.

- One makes a continual quest for improvement; a pragmatic approach to change exists.

- High value is placed on specialization in all fields.

- One views the country as having virtually unlimited resources; the "streets paved with gold" myth persists.

- "Fairness" is the guiding principle for the integration of individual and group needs.[51]

The point here is that need hierarchies differ with culture. Maslow's needs may thus be universal, but the logic or the sequence of the hierarchy is likely to differ from culture to culture.

Herzberg's two-factor theory also fails to hold up across cultures. One study showed that interpersonal relationships and supervision in New Zealand act as motivators, not as hygiene factors; that is, they reduce dissatisfaction.[52] Hofstede, cited earlier, also notes that cultures influence factors that motivate and demotivate. For example, collectivist societies such as the Scandinavian countries use organizational restructuring strategies (forming work groups to enhance interaction) to increase quality of work life; more individualistic societies such as the United States focus on job enrichment to increase the productivity of individuals. Other studies also show that what acts as a hygiene factor or dissatisfier in the United States may act as a motivator in other countries.[53]

Similarly, Vroom's expectancy theory is also subject to cross-cultural influences. "Expectancy theories depend on the extent to which employees believe they have control over the outcomes of their efforts as well as the manager's ability to identify desired rewards, both of which vary across cultures."[54] Vroom's expectancy theory works best in individualistic cultures in which people are viewed as "rational maximizers of personal utility" and in which need fulfillment and expectancies of future achievement are determinants of performance and satisfaction. However, in collectivist societies, individuals have different types of commitments and links to their organization, work, and to what influences success and satisfaction. For example, in many collectivist societies in the Middle East and Asia, individuals are rewarded not primarily on the nature of the job or achievements but on relationships with supervisors, owners, and co-owners. The accompanying rewards are less likely to be individual incentives such as pay or promotion but are more likely to be job security. Expectancy theory is still applicable to different types of societies; the types of rewards, motivations, and expectancies simply differ from those in many western societies.

McClelland's motivation theory holds up better under the test of cross-cultural analysis than any of the other theories we have discussed. Even so, his methods can be questioned as to whether they actually identify and "detect" achievement and power as defined by other peoples and other cultural business practices. Some societies, such as Tahiti, do not follow McClelland's logic.[55]

Individual organization members working in and/or with those from different cultures should, for starters, not assume when the topic is motivation—whether it be needs, expectancies, or satisfiers. These individuals should learn what the basic cultural orientation is: collectivist, individualist, productivity, or quality of life oriented, uncertainty avoidance, or comfort with ambiguity, dimensions that are discussed in more detail in Chapter 8. Not everyone in a culture shares all of its basic societal values, but these values can certainly influence unspoken beliefs, attitudes, and motivations. Individuals working in and/or with those from other cultures should not use their own values or motivational assumptions and standards as absolute standards. Instead, they should be open to discovery through others' motivating values and ideas. Synergistic sharing can lead to innovation. Finally, these individuals should obtain information on basic cultural and motivating values and practices before starting to work with people from other cultures. We provide such basic maps throughout this book.

## MOTIVATION AND WORKFORCE DIVERSITY

The changing, ever-more diverse workforce in the United States suggests that managing motivation will be challenging and difficult. The average worker before the 1970s was Caucasian, male, 29 years old; had less than a high school education; was married to a woman who was a homemaker; raised two or more children; and usually worked in the same geographic area in which he was raised. In contrast, and as was discussed in the first chapter, Workforce 2000 has been characterized as multicultural and aging with an influx of "baby busters"; more than half are women; dual-career families and single parents with children prevail; and more people with disabilities are entering the workforce. The gap between the very educated and the undereducated is widening, and workers have values that are as diverse as the workforce itself.

Many younger workers entering the workforce have different values and outlooks. A *Fortune* article, "What 25-Year-Olds Want," characterizes the younger knowledge worker in the United States in the following way:[56]

> *These are the employees who can say no, a novel breed that won't be easily manipulated into workaholism by the traditional lures—money, title, security, and ladder climbing. Let's call them yiffies, for young, individualistic, freedom-minded, and few.*
>
> *The busters insist on getting satisfaction from their jobs but refuse to make personal sacrifices for the sake of the corporation. Their attitude and other interests—leisure, family, lifestyle, the pursuit of experience—are as important as work. It's hard to figure out what they think is most important. They don't seem to have much sense of themselves as a distinct generation, and they certainly aren't impassioned about political or social issues. Nobody would describe them as a bunch of activists.*

*Sure, you might want to laugh derisively the first time one of your youngest subordinates tells you he intends to work a mere 40 hour week so he can go scuba diving and learn a non-Indo-European tongue. But don't complain, then, when you can't seem to find another competent molecular biologist or quality-control specialist.*

Welcome to the new generation gap. Margaret Regan, a consultant at Towers Perrin, holds focus groups at Fortune 500 companies, bringing together employees of all ages. "It's amazing to see how puzzled the different generations are by each other," she says. "There's a real clash of values in the workplace right now. The older managers think that if the shoe doesn't fit, you should wear it and walk funny. The baby-busters say to throw it out and get a new shoe. Their attitude says that they are going to make the choices."

Jamieson and O'Mara wrote in *Managing Workforce 2000* that middle-aged and older workers will also be the core of the workforce.[57] This projection will also have many implications for motivation; for example, they note that "the increasing number of over-forty workers will mean that motivations for working will change. What seems motivating, challenging, or stimulating to people in their twenties may look different to them in their forties or fifties."[58]

The motivational challenge for owners, managers, and organizational members will be to seek ways to integrate, not assimilate, these diverse individuals. Integrating and motivating such a diverse workforce involves understanding and consciously addressing value differences. Table 4–5 shows Gallup Poll results indicating that the percentage of U.S. workers who identify certain job characteristics as very important and the percentage who are "completely satisfied" with those aspects in their current job. Note the disparities between what workers identify as important and what they experience as missing in their current jobs.

Built into integrating and motivating a diverse workforce are certain learning opportunities for organizational managers and managers, including the following:

- They will learn how to deal with the frustrations of encountering differences.

- They will increase cultural awareness training.

- They will rethink communication techniques to account for some employees' unfamiliarity with the English language.

- They will emphasize training for service jobs that require verbal skills.

- They will provide remedial education for those groups that were previously disadvantaged.

- They will design jobs and utilize new technology in which a command of the English language is not critical.

- They will rethink what is meant by participative management and what the participation mores are for each culture represented in the organization.

- They will establish rewards that are valued by different cultural groups and will be flexible about holidays, time off, and leaves.

**TABLE 4–5**    What's Important: Workers Say that Good Health Insurance is More Important Than a High Income

| Job Characteristic | Percentage of Workers Stating | |
| --- | --- | --- |
| | Very Important | Completely Satisfied |
| Good health insurance and other benefits | 81 | 27 |
| Interesting work | 78 | 41 |
| Job security | 78 | 35 |
| The opportunity to learn new skills | 68 | 31 |
| Annual vacations of a week or more | 66 | 35 |
| Being able to work independently | 64 | 42 |
| Recognition from co-workers | 62 | 24 |
| Having a job in which you can help others | 58 | 34 |
| Limited job stress | 58 | 18 |
| Regular hours, no nights or weekends | 58 | 40 |
| High income | 56 | 13 |
| Working close to home | 55 | 46 |
| Work that is important to society | 53 | 34 |
| Chances for promotion | 53 | 20 |
| Contact with a lot of people | 52 | 45 |

SOURCE: Cited with permission from the Gallup Poll, 1991.

- They will create special career development programs to better match people with jobs that fit their skills, wants, needs, and values.

- They will reward managers for successfully blending a diverse workforce."[59]

Managing and motivating an increasingly diverse workforce involve addressing issues that are included throughout this text. Some of these issues, which Jamieson and O'Mara also discuss, include understanding an individual's needs and skill levels; matching people with flexible and challenging jobs; aligning rewards with employee values and performance; mentoring and developing people in their careers; educating as well as training people in their deficiencies; involving and informing people through shared responsibilities and decision-making participation; and supporting changing personal needs and lifestyles through flextime benefits and services. This is a big agenda for organizations given their imperative to continue to streamline and reorganize to successfully compete in a global marketplace. However, if people and brainpower are primary competitive advantages in this quest, then valuing and motivating diverse workforces are organizational priorities.

### Effects of Prejudice and Discrimination on Motivation in Diverse Workforces

Discriminatory attributions and actions are based on negative prejudices toward certain individuals and groups, as we discussed in Chapter 3. Discrimination can be found in all areas of organizational life: screening candidates, hiring employees, preparing performance appraisals, giving formal and informal feedback, offering reward systems (extrinsic and intrinsic), and, ultimately, firing, demoting, or promoting people. Motivation depends on all of these processes and in all of these organizational arenas—not only for members of minority and diverse groups (whether it be diversity by age, race, gender, religious belief, disability, or national origin), but also for Caucasian males in the working population. When discriminatory attributions and concrete actions are taken in motivation-related organizational activities (such as performance feedback, appraisal interviews, and rewards), the stakes can be significant for the individual and the organization. For the individual, such actions can erode trust, hurt performance, and jeopardize careers. For the organization, these actions can lose or decrease valued talent, decrease—if not destroy—the effectiveness of motivational systems, and result in lawsuits.

Negative attributions and discrimination are applicable concepts in motivation theories. For example, recall Vroom's expectancy theory, which states that motivation is linked to (1) the perceived probability that an effort leads to the desired performance, (2) the perceived probability that a performance-based activity leads to a given outcome, and (3) the value given to an outcome. Cox states, "To the extent that group-based discrimination exists, individuals may not believe that performance ratings will adequately reflect effort and therefore motivation may suffer. . . . If the impact of prejudice on the evaluation process is perceived as severe, the lower expectancy probabilities may collectively account for a large motivational loss."[60]

Understanding how prejudice and discrimination as well as the other perceptual distortions operate on individual motivation is a first step in addressing and preventing motivational loss. Moreover, attending to the communication of leader expectations of followers—particularly in performance appraisals and feedback sessions—is another concrete step to take to prevent negative prejudices and discrimination from affecting motivation. As Cox noted, leaders communicate their expectations to followers in at least four ways: "(1) the overall climate set (favorable tone, positive responses, and so on), (2) amount of input given (information relevant to getting the job done), (3) goals are challenging and confidence is shown in the individual's ability to achieve high results."[61]

## ETHICS AND MOTIVATION: MANAGERIAL GUIDELINES

Ethics as a discipline not only is a private or individual affair, but also is an organizational and managerial responsibility because legal, contractual, and moral obligations to stakeholders must be met.[62] In the context of individual motivation, the subject of ethics is relevant from both the individual and the stakeholders' perspectives. At the heart of any motivational and reward system is the psychological contract between employer and employee—that is, the unwritten, agreed-upon, and binding understanding of mutual obligations, roles, and responsibilities, as well as the rewards each party receives for the amount of effort and level of performance given in return for the benefits and rewards. This contract is grounded in trust and respect. A manager has a responsibility for initiating meetings and following through on the understandings reached with employees to ensure that the elements in the psychological contract are articulated, shared, and agreed upon as part of the employees' performance evaluations. If these foundations are jarred or broken, motivation is at risk. Ethics, to a large extent, is the glue that creates mutual trust and respect between the organization and the employee.

From the individual's perspective, personal ethics serves as a strong motivating force, both in terms of how people perceive job tasks, assignments, and rewards as "good or bad," "right or wrong," "fair or unfair." Personal ethics (as we will refer to this subject) goes hand in hand with the perceptually based motivational theories discussed earlier. In other words, perceptions and attributions are partly grounded in an individual's values and beliefs—whether these are learned, conditioned by family or religious experiences and teachings, or acquired in other ways.

From a more prescriptive ethical perspective, we might ask as managers and organization members, What are our obligations to the organization, customers, team, and ourselves in maintaining a high level of motivation to produce quality products and services that are competitive? How fair and equitable are our contributions to our work effort and to the results of our efforts? The ethical test here is to determine the extent to which we are responsibly and fairly meeting our organizational and contractual (including the psychological contract) obligations in our effort and performance.

From the organization's perspective, basic ethical questions include the following: Do we have a mutually desirable and acceptable psychological contract with our employees? Do we share similar ethical principles regarding the required amount of effort and levels of performance, and for types and levels of rewards offered for outputs? Managers and organizational leaders also can ask themselves more specific ethical questions that they can use as guidelines for making policies, procedures, and programs that reflect ethical principles.

- Are our values and practices aimed at serving our customers with the highest-quality products and services? Or do we have an internally focused ethic that is self-serving?

- To what extent does the extrinsic reward system fairly, equitably, and comparably recognize employees' efforts and outcomes?

- Are the policies and procedures for evaluating and rewarding employees effectively communicated, understood, and accepted by employees?

- Is the process for evaluating performance and giving feedback to employees written and available for employee review? Is the process fair, just, and equitable for all individuals and groups?

- Is a grievance system and process in place for employees to respond to the outcomes of the pay, rewards, and feedback received? Is employee involvement part of this system and process?

- Is a specific training and development program in place to upgrade employee skills and learning to enable them to be promoted and increase their base pay and/or bonuses?

- Do employees have a venue in which to discuss and offer input on work goals, processes, performance evaluations, and pay/rewards?

## MANAGING MOTIVATION AND CHANGE

The scope, radical nature, and fast rate of planned organizational change has, as stated earlier, been unprecedented in recent times. Mergers, acquisitions, strategic alliances, reengineering, and downsizing activities have significantly taken off. The extent to which these levels of organizational change will continue is uncertain; however, it has been predicted that organizational change will become a constant—that is, change will no longer be a single event. Because information technologies are also changing the very nature of work and expertise requirements, employee motivation takes on an even greater importance.

The following questions and issues have been raised by scholars in the field of motivation and reward systems.[63] Posing the right and relevant questions is often a first step toward solving a problem.

- As organizations undergo frequent changes through downsizing, mergers, and acquisitions, what can replace old-fashioned loyalty and identification as sources of commitment for employees?

- What will substitute for a sense of long-term continuity and security in their careers?

- How can the postindustrial society satisfy the newer generation of workers who increasingly value actualization and self-expression relative to traditional bread-and-butter rewards and who seem to be seeking a better balance between their work and nonwork lives?

- What are the implications of high technology—computers, robots, telecommunications—for the design of jobs and teams and for the selection, training, and careers of workers and managers?

- What are the implications of changes in gender roles and family patterns for the connections between work and nonwork?

- How can employers adapt their motivational policies and practices to a work-force that is increasingly diverse in terms of gender, age, ethnicity, and culture?[64]

These global issues translate to the microlevel through the following questions relating to motivation in organizations:

*What can be done to increase the attractiveness of and commitment to work goals? How can job involvement be increased? Some methods may involve changing the characteristics of work and its context, whereas others may have to address the personal dispositions of workers. How can sociotechnical systems be designed that include motivational imperatives in orchestrated combination with the technical requirements of work? How can policy makers be convinced of the desirability and feasibility of applying those motivational imperatives? How can barriers to their adoption be removed?"[65]*

Several practices to enhance motivation in the contemporary workplace have been suggested:

- Ensure that employees' motives and values are appropriate and "fit" the jobs on which they are placed.

- Ensure that jobs, roles, and responsibilities are attractive and consistent with employees' values, beliefs, and motives.

- Assist employees and ensure that work goals are clear, challenging, attractive, and attainable.

- Provide employees with required personal and material resources that enhance their effectiveness.

- Create and sustain supportive social and working environments.

- Recognize and reinforce performance.

- Ensure that the elements are harmonized and fit into a consistent sociotechnical organizational system.[66]

Managing motivation in rapidly and continuously changing organizational settings will require flexibility, focus, experimentation, the skill of balancing paradoxes, openly communicating and testing assumptions, and being open to and skilled in implementing planned change.

## CONCLUDING COMMENTS

Motivation is a process of directing and sustaining goal-directed behavior. It is related to a person's needs and learning, an organization's mission and requirements, and performance and rewards. Individual motivation and team motivation do not occur in isolation from the organizational context. They depend on a number of interdependencies, both internal and external to the organization. The effects of motivation are demonstrated by a number of market and nonmarket indicators. Organizational goal attainment and the quality of products and services are obvious measures. Nonmarket (but market-related) outputs are also important indicators of motivational effectiveness—that is, employee satisfaction and development of the economic, political, technical, and social consequences of the motivation performance system.

Motivation theories have been explained from two approaches: content and process. Content (or static) theories focus on internal or intrapersonal factors that energize, direct, sustain, and/or prohibit behaviors. These theories (by Maslow, Alderfer, Herzberg, and McClelland) focus on individual needs to explain sources of motivation. Process theories (equity, expectancy, learning, and goal setting), on the other hand, attempt to identify factors that motivate, energize, sustain, and/or stop behaviors that are not limited to an individual's needs or personality.

Learning is an integral part of motivation because understanding how we learn can assist organization leaders and members to diagnose and find ways to enhance motivation. Understanding how people learn to respond to different types of rewards can assist organization leaders and managers in allocating rewards more effectively. Learning has taken on added importance in the process of "continuous improvement" in organization literature and practice.

Learning is the acquisition of skills, knowledge, ability, and attitudes. The behavioral approach to learning emphasizes external influences and the power of reward reinforcement. The cognitive approach emphasizes the internal mental processes that result from combining cues in the environment into mental maps.

Goal setting is an application of motivation and learning theory. Goal-setting activities benefit individuals and organizations because goals direct and guide attention, regulate and shape effort, increase commitment and persistence, and encourage strategies and action planning. Goals motivate individuals and organizations only if the goals are SMART (i.e., specific, measurable, assignable, realistic, and time related). Research on goal setting has shown that difficult goals and specificity can lead to higher performance levels; goal specificity may not lead to higher performance under certain conditions; feedback increases the positive effects of setting difficult, specific goals; goals set jointly by managers and subordinates lead to greater goal acceptance and commitment; and high expectancy (belief that effort leads to performance) and high self-efficacy (belief in ability to obtain a goal) enhance goal commitment and lead to goal performance.

Motivation is, to a large extent, culturally conditioned and learned. Individual organization members working with those from different cultures should not assume when the topic is motivation, whether it be needs, expectancies, or satisfiers. These individuals should find out what the basic cultural orientation is—that is, whether it is collectivist, individualist, productivity or quality of life oriented, uncertainty avoidance or comfort with ambiguity. Not everyone from a culture shares all of its basic societal values, but these values can and do influence unspoken beliefs, attitudes, and motivations. A person's own values or motivational assumptions and standards should not be accepted as absolute.

The characteristics of a changing, ever-more diverse workforce in the United States suggests that managing motivation will be challenging and difficult. The challenge for owners, managers, and organization members will be to find ways to integrate, not assimilate, the diverse individuals and to address their motivational needs. Integrating and motivating a diverse workforce involves understanding and addressing value differences. Valuing and motivating diverse workforces must be organizational priorities.

The scope, radical nature, and fast rate of planned organizational change in recent times have been unprecedented. Several practices have been suggested to enhance motivation in the contemporary workplace. These include ensuring that employees' motives and values are appropriate and fit the jobs in which they are placed; that jobs, roles, and responsibilities are attractive and consistent with employees' values, beliefs, and motives; and that work goals are clear, challenging, attractive, and attainable. Other ways to enhance motivation include providing employees with required personal and material resources that enhance their effectiveness; creating and sustaining supportive social and working environments; recognizing and reinforcing performance; and ensuring that these elements are harmonized and fit into a consistent sociotechnical organizational system. Managing motivation in rapidly and continuously changing organizational settings will require flexibility, focus, experimentation, the skill of balancing paradoxes, openly communicating and testing assumptions, and being open to and skilled in implementing planned change.

## SCENARIO AND EXERCISE:
## MANAGING DIVERSITY IN THE WORKPLACE—YOU'RE THE CHANGE CONSULTANT

**Exercise:** Read the following scenario. You have been hired as a change management consultant to assist a top-level team in a mid-sized high-tech computer applications company to address diversity needs regarding pay, promotion, and rewards. Almost half of the newly hired workforce consists of young women and minorities (most are in their early 20s). The present CEO is a computer engineer who is an expert in his technical field but has had problems understanding the motivations of his workforce. He knows that several of the new hires are very talented technically but believes they have unrealistic demands for equity (stock), vacation time, and personal leave. He, his chief operating officer, and chief information officer are Caucasian Americans and in their 50s. They came from large, bureaucratic organizations where they had to "earn" their way. A few conflicts have already erupted between the CEO's top officers and some of the younger programmers and marketing staff. These employees want more flex time to "balance" their work and private lives. Some want their business school tuition paid. There are problems in communicating their needs to management. The younger employees believe the managers are "out of touch" with the "new generation." The CEO wants to satisfy his employees but not at the expense of "giving the store away." He knows competition for talent is strong and encourages you to give him advice he can use. He is confused but wants some direction.

Step 1: In small teams, diagnose the problems in this scenario using motivation and rewards concepts from the chapter. Your plan should have a problem(s) statement, concepts that help explain the problems and opportunities to be addressed, and a few options that the CEO can use to address these problems (e.g., reward systems consideration, motivational issues, diversity training).

Step 2: Present your plan to the class.

Step 3: As a class, answer the following questions:

1. What elements from the plans would help the CEO address motivational and diversity issues and opportunities in the scenario? Why?

2. What concerns should the consulting team be aware of before entering the organization to plan and implement interventions?

## REVIEW QUESTIONS

1. What does *motivation* mean to you? Explain.

2. Briefly explain Maslow's theory of motivation. What are a weakness and a strength of this theory? Apply this theory to your motivation needs. What is your predominant need according to this theory? What do you like and dislike about this theory? Why?

3. How does Maslow's needs theory differ from Alderfer's need theory? From Herzberg's need theory? Which theory would you prefer to use if you had to support only one of these three theories? Explain.

4. How would Maslow's theory apply in China? To another country with whose culture you are familiar?

5. Describe McClelland's three needs categories. What are a strength and a weakness of McClelland' theory? Where do you place your predominant motivational need in this theory? Why?

6. Is McClelland's theory cross-culturally applicable? Explain.

7. Briefly describe expectancy theory. How can you use expectancy theory with your needs? Apply this theory to explain your own motivation for performing or not performing a particular task.

8. Briefly explain equity theory. Give an example of how equity theory would apply to a job or assignment you recently had. What are some strengths and weaknesses of this theory?

9. Apply one concept from learning theory to a recent assignment, project, or work situation you experienced (reinforcement—positive or negative; punishment, extinction, behavior modification). Describe the situation and what happened. What behavior(s) were involved? What learning occurred?

10. What are SMART goals? What is the relationship(s) between goal setting and motivation?

11. Identify some of the requirements of effective reward systems. With which of these reward system criteria can you relate best? Explain.

12. What are some effects of prejudice and discrimination on motivation in diverse workforces? Offer an example of how a discriminatory act or stereotyping affected your motivation.

13. What are some ethical criteria that can be applied to reward systems and to motivation practices in the workplace?

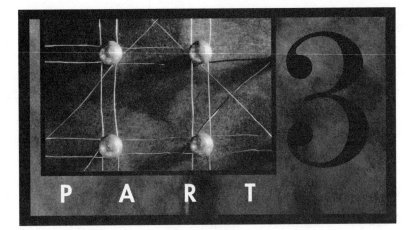

# Team and Interpersonal Process

# 5

# High-Performance Teams and Groups

---

## LEARNING OBJECTIVES

After studying this chapter, you should be able to:

**1** Define *team*, *extreme teams*, and *groups*.

**2** Identify characteristics of virtual teams.

**3** Describe developmental phases of groups and teams.

**4** Identify characteristics of high-performance teams.

**5** Discuss criteria for leading teams.

**6** Discuss relationships between quality management and teamwork.

**7** Identify effective and ineffective team roles.

**8** Discuss effective ways to facilitate teams.

**9** Describe strategies for managing cross-cultural diversity in teams.

**10** Identify criteria for preventing and dealing with ethical conflicts.

**11** Describe group decision-making techniques.

---

## TEAMS, EXTREME TEAMS, AND GROUPS

Why do some teams fly while others crash? Harold Leavitt and Jean Lipman-Blumen spent 20 years exploring this question. In a recent book, *Hot Groups*, they summarized their findings to this question by characterizing what is also referred to as "extreme teams." These authors stated that

> *You don't go out and create hot groups. They grow themselves. Look at organizations, and you'll see the beginnings of hot groups almost everywhere. They're like weeds. But organizations that are bureaucratic and orderly don't like the idea of hot groups, so they go around and spray weed killer on those groups. The issue is not how you create hot groups but how you keep them from being stamped out.[1]*

The *extreme team* is an interesting concept because it suggests that empowered individuals (that is, people who seek meaning and self-motivation in their work) join from common interests to make a difference in organizations. This is especially true for cases in which projects and work are demanding with high stakes. Some extreme teams work in organizations without a formal title, others are adopted by the organization—as is the case with NASA's Academy of Program and Project Leadership. The following are some points about extreme teams: (1) work matters, (2) titles don't matter, (3) people bond in the heat of battle, (4) teams take care of their own, and (5) teams develop extreme goals, deadlines, and pressure. *Work matters* for extreme teams because people look for meaning in their tasks and projects. People want to do something that counts. *Titles don't matter* for these teams since status is secondary to the democratic, informal way of sharing expertise. Traditional parts of bureaucratic organizations may show resentment and even animosity to extreme teams. Still, *people bond in the heat of battle* in these teams. People want to make a task happen. Groups grow around their tasks, as the author Lipman-Blumen states. Long-term relationships form around bonding with tasks throughout a project. Respect grows as people stay with the tasks. *Teams take care of their own* in extreme teams. Instead of working in an isolated, individualistic group or environment, extreme teams create a safe place for individuals to experiment, fail, and still be supported, especially when deadlines and pressures are heightened. If your team loses, you lose. In some of these emerging types of teams, decisions are made by consensus. At NASA's Academy of Program and Project Leadership, extreme teams reject many classical ways of working together. Engineers working on innovative projects from years of experience prefer the close bonding, sharing ideas openly, and developing *extreme goals* (i.e., "never-been-done" project goals that may require decisions without perfect knowledge).

Not all teams can or should be *extreme teams* or *hot groups*. But teams are different than groups. "A team is a small number of people with complementary skills who are committed to a common purpose, set of performance goals, and approach for which they hold themselves mutually accountable."[2] A group is two or more persons who interact in such ways that each person influences and is influenced by the other.[3] Teams differ from work groups in the following ways: (1) teams have shared leadership roles; groups usually have a strong, focused leader; (2) teams have individual and mutual accountability; group members have mostly individual accountability; (3) teams work toward a specific purpose; a work group's purpose is mostly identical to the organization's mission; (4) groups usually deliver individual work products; teams deliver collective work products; (5) teams encourage open-ended discussion and active problem-solving meetings; groups try to run efficient meetings; (6) groups measure effectiveness indirectly by their influence on others (e.g., financial performance indicators); teams measure performance by directly assessing their collective work products; and (7) groups discuss, decide, and delegate and then go do the work individually, whereas teams discuss, decide, and delegate but then do the "real work" together.[4] These definitions may blur, depending on the assignment and specific team or work group, but a major characteristic that distinguishes groups from teams is that teams focus on a specific output, and teams generally are held accountable for the completion of their output.

Work in organizations is increasingly being performed in teams. A recent survey found that 8 out of 10 U.S. organizations with 100 or more employees have assigned people to some type of working team (i.e., "a permanent work team, a temporary project team, or a permanent or long-term cross functional team").[5] The following findings were also reported. In the average organization that uses teams (including health care and public administration), more than half of all employees are members of a team; 45 percent of members belong to a permanent work team; 42 percent belong to a self-directed, semiautonomous, or similar type of team. According to the same study, self-directed teams perform at least one of four roles: they "manage their own work schedules, deal directly with the organization's customers, set production quotas or performance targets, train other team members." Finally, the study reported that "at least 80 percent of those organizations with any firsthand experience report that work teams have improved quality, customer service, productivity, and profits." More than three-fourths of the respondents reported that teams improve employee morale. Says Boeing President Philip Condit, "Your competitiveness is your ability to use the skills and knowledge of people most effectively, and teams are the best way to do that."[6]

## Virtual Teams

Dispersed teams that must communicate electronically across different time zones and geographies are called *virtual teams*. They are increasing because of the global nature of businesses and the increasing mobility of companies and customers who are aligning to compete. The seamless nature of companies and customers also requires teams to be formed quickly, travel frequently, and communicate wherever they are. These teams are usually cross-functional and vary by nature, length, and types of assignments.[7] Common features of virtual teams include the following:

- Fluidity with membership changing and expanding

- Communication primarily by electronic means

- Leadership roles both assigned and emergent

- Team united by shared set of work objectives and responsibilities

- Team driven by a results orientation[8]

Many problems and challenges that virtual teams face are similar to those of other groups and teams. However, the following areas appear to be heightened in virtual teams: (1) primary issues relate to exposure and trust more than to belonging and place, (2) accountability is more open and transparent, (3) team members can legitimately disappear on short notice, given assignments, (4) assignment and deadline pressures increase because of compressed space, time, and nature of electronic communications, and (5) information hoarding is less tolerated because of the dependent nature of teams on information.[9]

In effect, the *success factors* of virtual teams depend on (1) support and involvement of management and the sponsoring organization, (2) clear goals and objectives understood by all members, (3) culture and norms based on trust and clearly defined methods of communicating electronically, (4) detailed protocols (methods) for sending, receiving, and signing off on electronic messages, assignments, and final "products," (5) a robust state-of-the-art technical infrastructure and electronic technologies, continually serviced and maintained by respectful, responsive technicians, and (6) training in state-of-the-art electronic technologies for all members.[10] In one study on virtual teams, a project member told the author in an interview,

> *I enjoy being on this team; what I find most challenging is that I am and become what I send on-line. Some of these people don't know and haven't even met me. I prove myself, my value each time I complete a piece of work I send to others. Sure, I can explain myself and joke about stuff on e-mails, but the real work is done on my laptop.*

It is interesting to note that even in virtual teams, experts agree that occasional face-to-face meetings are still essential in clarifying complex and high-stakes decisions.

## GETTING STARTED: LIFE CYCLE OF A TEAM

Team formation and development focus first on the purpose of the team: why form this team? Then several questions must be addressed. What is the nature of work to be done? What are the requirements of team members to do the work? What are the organization's vision and mission? What are the team's vision and mission? Who leads? How should these visions link together? Who is sponsoring the team (i.e., who funds and supports us)? What is our mission and critical goal? What are our objectives and responsibilities? What are the organization's and our own expectations of this team and of each other? How will we measure progress toward our goal and individual and team performance? What are our team norms (i.e., rules for continuously working and achieving together)? Who will enforce these norms, and how? After these questions are addressed, it is important to develop SMART goals and objectives, which were discussed in Chapter 4. Creating a psychological contract will then help define the team's culture and norms; the psychological contract is a team-developed, and agreed-upon statement of its purpose for existing, its goal and objectives, and its norms.

In practice, not all teams develop in the same way, go through the same stages, or get to completion in the same time spans. Wellins, Byham, and Wilson, who studied self-managed teams, observe that highly effective teams pass through at least four stages of development: **(1) getting started, (2) going in circles, (3) getting on course, and (4) full speed ahead.**[11] This is a flexible process that reflects actual adjustment thresholds that high-performance teams usually reach and pass through. These authors also observe that high-performance teams deal with six factors in their developmental process:

1. *Commitment*—team members see themselves as belonging to a team rather than acting as autonomous individuals.

2. *Trust*—team members have faith in each other to honor commitments, sustain confidence, show support, and behave in consistent and predictably acceptable ways.

## THE CHANGING WORKPLACE

### Creating a Team Psychological Contract

**Exercise**: A team's psychological contract is a written set of assumptions, expectations, and agreed-upon norms (rules of acceptable principle for operating and performing work) with accompanying behaviors. These consensually agreed on expectations serve as the basis for team members to monitor and hold themselves and teammates accountable for performance. The four steps of this exercise can be used by teams at the "forming" stage to define their psychological contract. This contract can serve as the basis for future meetings to address accountability, productivity, and team satisfaction/development issues and opportunities.

**Step 1**: Write a brief sketch of yourself and your views using the following outline:

- Personal background
- Work history and assignments
- Experience in teams/groups
- Goals for this team
- Time constraints/commitments
- Questions and concerns about final team project and work product

Share this information with your team.

**Step 2**: As a team, brainstorm and finalize the team vision. This should read "Our vision for our team is. . . ." Remember that a vision is how you define and see yourselves as a team performing a project(s). The vision should be expressed in a few sentences to a paragraph.

In the same manner, brainstorm and finalize a team goal. This should read "Our goal is . . ." You may also use the SMART goal method discussed in Chapter 4.

**Step 3**: Discuss your expectations for the team itself, other members of the team, and the team assignments and projects you will be working on. After the discussion, write the agreed-upon group expectations.

**Step 4**: Identify specific steps the team will follow to deal with any member(s) who violates the norms in Step 2. For example one norm is to be at every meeting unless an emergency occurs, and the member who misses must inform all other team members five hours in advance. If a member misses a meeting without a valid reason and does not notify anyone on the team before the absence, that member will perform extra work (to be determined by the team) on an upcoming assignment.

3. *Purpose*—team members understand how their roles and mission fit into the organization's overall business; they feel a sense of ownership and understand how they can make a difference.

4. *Communication*—team members learn to interact effectively among themselves and others outside the team; they learn how to handle conflict, make decisions effectively, and communicate on a daily basis.

5. *Involvement*—team members learn to feel a sense of partnership with each other, to respect contributions, and to develop consensus before committing the team to action.

6.  *Process orientation*—the team has a clear sense of purpose; this enables it to develop a process that includes problem-solving tools, planning techniques, regular meetings and agendas.

Another team and group development process includes the five stages (forming-storming-norming-performing-adjourning) shown in Table 5–1. The underlying theory here is that a team or group must resolve each of the stages before it becomes effective. However, the team or group may loop back to previous stages of development because of changes in goals, the environment, and/or membership. If a group or team has the necessary skills to address the issues at each stage and uses its skills appropriately, then fundamental challenges will likely find resolution, and successful development of the team will be ensured.

During the first and shortest stage, orientation, the group is **forming**. Members meet, are introduced to the task and the conditions, and perceive interpersonal and task behaviors of the group. At the same time, members are "getting in"; that is, they are beginning the socialization process of becoming a member. They sense and set expectations and determine the match of newcomers.

During the second stage, redefinition, members **storm**; that is, members act and react to the task, objectives, strategy, structure, and other requirements of the group. Disagreement and conflict normally ensue over such issues as prioritizing tasks and discussing the aspects of task requirements that are liked and disliked. The socialization component of this stage is breaking in or accommodating relationships and organizational and group systems. If issues that started and led to normal conflict are not dealt with and addressed adequately during this phase, conflicts will likely increase and the group or team may not pass beyond this stage, or it may return to the same issues.

The third and longest state is coordination. This is the **norming** phase in which data are collected and interpreted, alternative actions are discussed and debated, and members come to understand that different responses to problems are legitimate. A single leader usually emerges, group cohesion develops, and standards and roles are identified and accepted. Members settle in—they understand and accept their fit with the organization. Conflict must be managed effectively for this step to be completed successfully.

The fourth stage, formalization, is characterized as the **performing** phase. All issues—task and social/emotional—from previous stages are solved. Functional roles take hold during this phase of problem solving. Assigned roles meet group leadership and expertise needs.

The fifth stage, termination, involves the group's breaking up (i.e., **adjourning** or redirecting itself to other tasks). During this stage, feedback from team members and the leader is sought to improve performance. Members' contributions are recognized and appreciated. Mechanisms for ongoing self-assessment are developed. New opportunities may or may not be sought. As teams work on more temporary and geographically dispersed projects, these phases are compressed, and much communication is done electronically.

| TABLE 5-1    Stages of Group Development and Socialization |||
| Stage | Group Development* | Organizational Socialization† |
| --- | --- | --- |
| 1. Orientation | *Forming*<br>Establish interpersonal relationships<br>Conform to organizational traditions and standards<br>Test boundary relationships and and task behaviors | *Getting In*<br>(Anticipatory socialization)<br>Setting realistic expectations<br>Determining match with the newcomer |
| 2. Redefinition | *Storming*<br>Conflicts arise because of interpersonal behaviors<br>Resistance to group influence and task requirements | *Breaking In*<br>(Accommodation)<br>Initiation on the job<br>Establishing interpersonal relationships<br>Congruence between self and organizational performance appraisal |
| 3. Coordination | *Norming*<br>Single leader emerges<br>Group cohesion established<br>New group standards and roles formed for members | *Settling In*<br>(Role management)<br>The degree of fit between one's life interests outside of work and the demands of the organization<br>Resolution of conflicts at the workplace itself |
| 4. Formalization | *Performing*<br>Members perform tasks together<br>Members establish role clarity<br>Teamwork is the norm | |
| 5. Termination | *Adjourning*<br>Members break up or redirect themselves as a group to another assignment<br>Contribution is recognized<br>Feedback on performance is obtained | |

**SOURCE:** Adapted from J. P. Wanous, A. E. Reichers, and S. D. Malik, "Organizational Socialization and Group Development Toward an Integrative Perspective." *Academy of Management Review,* 9, (1984), 670–683.
*Based on B. Tuchman, "Developmental Sequence in Small Groups," *Psychological Bulletin* 63, (1965), 384–899.
† Based on D. C. Feldman, "A Contingency Theory of Socialization," *Administrative Science Quarterly,* 21 (1976), 433–454; D. C. Feldman, "A Practical Program for Employee Socialization," *Organizational Dynamics,* 7 (1976), 64–80.

Not all teams progress systematically or linearly through these or any particular sequence of stages or phases.[12] As stated earlier, groups circle and loop back to certain phases, repeat processes, and get stuck, while others speed ahead. Team members, leaders, and managers can use these models to validate and diagnose developmental issues and concerns of members as well as to evaluate how the team as a whole is progressing.

## HIGH-PERFORMANCE, SELF-MANAGING TEAMS

High-performance, self-managing teams are often self-designed and self-directed. A study by Wilson Learning Corporation asked managers nationwide to define a high-performance team. Eight attributes were given:

---

### THE CHANGING WORKPLACE

#### Building Team Relationships

**Exercise**: Use your experience on a team in your class or work (current or past) as a basis for responding. Please be as specific as possible.

1. What I like(d) most about this team is/was:

2. On this team I have/had the most difficulty:

3. Things that my teammates do/did that I like are:

4. Things that my teammates do/did that bother me are:

5. On this team I would like to change:

6. I wish/wished [insert teammate's name] would:

7. I would like to ask [insert teammate's name] why he or she [insert a specific behavior] during our last or a previous meeting.

8. The individual I have/had the strongest relationship with on the team is [insert teammate's name]. The main reason(s) this strong relationship exists/existed is (are):

9. The individual I have the weakest relationship with on the team is [insert teammate's name]. The main reason(s) this weak relationship exists/existed is (are):

10. I think I can improve/could have improved this relationship by:

11. I can be/could have been a better team member by:

After completing these questions, share your answers with a classmate and answer the following questions:

1. What insights about yourself and this team did you gain?

2. What additional questions would you add to these?

**SOURCE:** Adapted from Dorothy Marcic and Joe Seltzer, "Feedback: Interpersonal Relationships in Groups," in *Organizational Behavior*, 5th ed. (Cincinnati, Ohio: South-Western College Publishing, 1995), 207–209.

1. *Participative leadership*—members are empowered, interdependent, freed up, and willing to serve others.

2. *Shared responsibility*—an environment is developed in which all members feel responsible for the team's performance.

3. *Alignment on purpose*—there is a sense of common purpose regarding the team's existence and its function.

4. *High levels of communication*—a climate of trust, openness, and honest communication is created and maintained.

5. *Focus on the future*—change is seen as an opportunity for growth.

6. *Focus on task*—meetings are centered on results.

7. *Creative talents*—individual talents and creativity are applied to the task.

8. *Rapid response*—opportunities are identified and acted on.[13]

High-performance teams are generally composed of 6 to 12 people who have administrative oversight and ownership for their task domains and "whole" work processes; that is, they can plan, schedule, monitor, and staff their own activities.[14] There is usually a "leader" or "spokesperson"—who is either assigned by management or selected by the team who assumes coordination and administrative responsibilities in addition to overseeing the workload and delivery process.

These teams are formed and used in contemporary organizations for the following reasons. The nature of work is becoming increasingly cross-functional, complex, and demanding. Autonomous and technically capable people work together on large and sometimes temporary projects. Teams rely more on each other's skills, educational and training mix, and knowledge to get work done. Innovations occur as a result of the need for shared technical leadership and followership. Moreover, as organizations are consolidated and work is performed through business processes, independent and integrated teams are required to "do more with less"— that is, assume more control and responsibility over a product's work process with fewer people. Also, as discussed earlier, virtual teams that depend on electronic communication are by definition more autonomous and self-managing.

To meet the challenges of new forms of team development, colleges now require graduate and undergraduate students in management and business courses to complete papers, assignments, and projects in self-managing teams. Teams are given a topic area with some specifications, and it is the team's task to call and coordinate meetings, assign (if members choose) a leader, carry out the work, and deliver a finished product(which team members design and produce) on time.

## EMPOWERED TEAMS

People work better when they have a purpose, are excited, and have control over their work. *Empowered* team members have these characteristics and have the freedom to perform work successfully as they *want* and *are capable of doing*, not as managers and supervisors want. Managers empower employees by removing barriers, controls, and constraints to a team's creativity. In empowered, capable teams, managers become cheerleaders, coaches, and motivators. Managers use a "pull" strategy (i.e., offer incentives and influence as a means to motivate) instead of "push" strategies (i.e., to encourage and support creativity in teams).[15] Empowered teams also have the characteristics of *trust, self-efficacy* (sense of competence, as discussed earlier), *self-determination* (choice in doing their work), *meaningfulness* (a sense of purpose about their work), and *impact* (belief that their work makes a difference). Extreme teams, described earlier, often have these characteristics.

Self-managing teams are also empowered to share various management and leadership functions. They plan, control, and improve their own work processes. They set their own goals and inspect their own work. They often create their own schedules and review their performance as a group. They may prepare their own budgets and coordinate their work with other departments. They usually order materials, keep inventories, and deal with suppliers. They are frequently responsible for acquiring any new training they might need. They may hire their own replacements or assume responsibility for disciplining their own members. They, not others outside the team, take responsibility for the quality of their products or services.

## LEADERSHIP ON TEAMS

In self-managing teams, everyone assumes a leadership role at one time or another, even if there is a designated leader. However, some teams have leaders assigned or hired by the organization. Project managers are usually such leaders. How do team leaders lead in contemporary organizations that are seamless and short-term project oriented? Consider this example.

> In 1989, J. D. Bryant was perfectly content overseeing a staff of 15 circuit board assemblers at Texas Instruments' Forest Lane defense plant in Dallas. "Then one day I heard the company was moving to teams and that I was going to become a facilitator," Bryant recalls [thinking], "I'm supposed to teach the teams everything I know and then let them make their own decisions."[16]

Leading and facilitating high-performance teams is not the same as managing people in a group or a traditional, functional structure. The shift in mind-set from supervisor to manager to team leader involves removing people from traditional structural and often career-tract arrangements and placing them in a riskier environment, because their performance is then based on the team's performance. Also, facilitating high-performance teams requires skills that are different from those of the command-and-control management approach. Brainstorming, listening, and giving and receiving feedback; knowing when to lead and when to follow; learning as well as instructing; orchestrating as well as telling—these skills are demanding, and often the only way to learn them is by doing.

The following five "Tips from Leaders"[17] are derived from those "who have been there." First, "don't be afraid to admit ignorance." After becoming a leader of technically more competent people, Eric Doremus of Honeywell's defense avionics division in Albuquerque stated that "my most important task was not trying to figure out everybody's job, it was to help this team feel as if they owned the project by getting them whatever information, financial or otherwise, they needed. I knew that if we could all charge up the hill together, we would be successful." He was successful in his first project. Second, "know when to intervene." Reed Breland became a team facilitator at Hewlett-Packard two years ago. Having been on the job for some months, he noticed a personality conflict between two people. Nine months later, the team was still squabbling. Instead of trying to resolve the personality conflict, he dissolved the team and placed its members elsewhere. Says Breland, "If the chemistry isn't right, it doesn't matter how good or bad the players are. It's not going to work. As a team leader you have to know when it's reached that point. It's more an art than a science, but that's what makes the job so interesting." Third, "learn to truly share power." J. D. Bryant, quoted earlier, learned to share power as a team leader. He states, "I knew [the teams'] frustrations and fears because I had been in their shoes. So I would meet with them and say, 'Okay, what can you transfer to the team today? What can you transfer in the next couple of months? . . . I was also telling them that they now had more time to go out and get new contracts and new business—or time to train themselves to do something else." Fourth, "worry about what you take on, not what you give up." James Malone, a controller at Dunn & Bradstreet, became a believer in self-directed teams after working and coordinating reengineering and consolidating work with such teams. One of his tasks was recruiting team leaders. In the beginning, he noted that people were more concerned about having an office and a title. After assigning people to self-directed teams, he found that these issues became irrelevant. Fifth, "get used to learning on the job." Barbara Brockett, an engineer at Honeywell who develops pilotless aircraft, stated after becoming a self-directed team leader there, "although more training would have been helpful, it's hard to teach someone to be a team leader. You really learn how to do it by doing it every day, by making decisions with people, not by yourself. . . . I'm getting more comfortable with the fact that I don't need to know everything. But I need to know where to get the answers."

David Nadler, chairman of the Delta Consulting Group, which is now part of the Mercer Consulting Company in New York City, states: "Probably 15 percent of managers are natural team leaders; another 15 percent could never lead a team because it runs counter to their personality. Then there's that huge group in the middle: Team leadership doesn't come naturally to them, but they can learn it."[18]

Given these challenges to leadership, effective team leaders generally must demonstrate the following competencies, in addition to having necessary technical and subject matter expertise: ability to (1) facilitate the identification of a vision, mission, and values of the team, (2) set goals and priorities, (3) provide support and obtain resources,(4) inspire confidence and trust, (5) plan, schedule, and monitor work progress to meet deadlines, (6) provide information and effectively communicate, and (7) foster a results-driven environment while providing competent processes to meet goals. Managing quality is everyone's responsibility.

### Quality Management and Teams

The quality management philosophy embodies responses to competitive industry changes. In many organizations, quality management has provided a context for developing and sustaining high-performance teams. This philosophy refers to

> *an organization-wide performance system that emphasizes continuous improvement in processes and products. In its most pervasive form, it escorts products and people from organizational cradle to grave, providing attentive leaders and trained workers with capabilities to effectively gather and use data and measurements based on a guiding vision and operating values.*[19]

Focused quality programs rely on high-performance teams to provide quality in all phases of work. Such programs tend to flatten vertical organizational structures and distribute power. Because work is carried out mainly in teams, quality management programs can have a transforming effect on organizational culture. This is especially true since, as a philosophy, quality management embraces a belief system that all improvements will follow when quality is emphasized. Grounded on the principle of continuous improvement, quality management programs hold that before anything is done in the workplace, two questions must be continuously answered by all employees and teams: Is it necessary? and if so, Can it be done better? Eight "rules" govern the total quality management (TQM) technique process and now serve as benchmarks for many teams, including those that practice TQM principles: (1) quality is everyone's job; (2) quality comes from prevention, not inspection; (3) quality means meeting the needs of customers; (4) quality demands teamwork; (5) quality requires continuous improvement; (6) quality involves strategic planning; (7) quality means results; and (8) quality requires clear measures of success.[20]

Teams that implement quality management principles are often required to use statistical information, as well as other measurement tools and techniques with process controls in all operational areas (depending on the industry and company) such as purchasing, inventory, inspection, and testing. Training in the use of these tools, as they relate to the TQM principles, is a requirement if the work teams and programs are to succeed.

Related to the implementation of quality management programs is ISO 9000 and subsequent series in the 9000 designation. This is a set of quality standards created by the International Standards Organization in Geneva, Switzerland, to serve as a general framework for quality assurance in the European Union. More than 50 countries have endorsed these standards, including the United States, Canada, and Mexico. To pass certification, a company's entire operation must undergo a thorough assessment of its quality processes and practices from product or service design to customer delivery.[21] Once a company is certified by these standards, customers know that its quality standards will be monitored by an independent group. Many ISO 9000-certified companies have also implemented some form of TQM principles and team work. Many companies prefer not to become ISO 9000 certified because of the costs and time involved.

The implementation of TQM principles and techniques has not proven to be universally successful. When TQM has appeared to fail, its slogans have been used without top-level commitment and follow-through. Adequate systemwide, integrated technology and training support are essential, and without them, TQM does not work. Firms that are unwilling to change their culture to embody TQM principles often find TQM to be unsatisfactory. TQM programs and principles cannot be implemented and/or used in disorganized, uncoordinated ways. However, when organizations set up TQM teams that are led and supported by competent top-level leaders, when the teams are trained and aligned to produce planned TQM work products and programs, and when organizationwide cultural changes are undertaken, the results can be significant.

Organizational cultures that foster team development and effectiveness and that indicate a favorable environment for TQM programs embody the following characteristics. There is a tolerance in the company for ambiguity, uncertainty, and flexibility of structure. It is a company norm to show interest in each member's development and achievement. The company encourages giving and accepting feedback in nondefensive ways. There is a companywide openness to change, innovation, and creative problem solving. The company consciously creates a learning environment for team development that leads to performance; that environment is informal, relaxed, goal committed, comfortable, performance oriented, and nonjudgmental. There is a capacity to establish intense, short-term relationships among members and to disconnect for the next project.[22]

## EFFECTIVE AND INEFFECTIVE TEAM AND GROUP ROLES

Ideally, all team and group members can play a wide range of effective, high-performance roles. However, this is not always the case, even in high-performance teams. Table 5–2 lists three classifications of group and team roles that members can assume: task oriented, relations oriented, and self-oriented.[23] Task-oriented roles, such as initiators, information seekers and givers, coordinators, and evaluators, can enhance team performance and effectiveness. In addition, relations-oriented roles, such as encouragers, harmonizers, gatekeepers, standard setters, and group observers, promote useful team interaction and communication. However, self-oriented roles—blockers, recognition seekers, dominators, and avoiders—can disrupt effective communications and decision-making processes in teams and groups.

Becoming aware of these roles is important because they are useful in evaluating and monitoring individual, team, and group effectiveness. Observing the dysfunctional roles of certain members enables other members and managers to move quickly in giving corrective feedback to get the team, as well as individual members, back on track.

## TABLE 5–2    Roles of Group and Team Members

### Task-Oriented Roles

The task-oriented role facilitates and coordinates decision-making activities. It can be broken down into the following subroles:

1. *Initiators* offer new ideas or modified ways of considering group problems or goals as well as suggest solutions to group difficulties, including new group procedures or a new group organization.
2. *Information seekers* try to clarify suggestions and obtain authoritative information and pertinent facts.
3. *Information givers* offer facts or generalizations that are authoritative or relate experiences that are pertinent to the group problem.
4. *Coordinators* clarify relationships among ideas and suggestions, pull ideas and suggestions together, and try to coordinate activities of members of subgroups.
5. *Evaluators* assess the group's functioning; they may evaluate or question the practicality, logic, or facts of suggestions by other members.

### Relations-Oriented Roles

The relations-oriented role builds group-centered activities, sentiments, and viewpoints. It may be broken down into the following subroles:

1. *Encouragers* praise, agree with, and accept the ideas of others; they indicate warmth and solidarity toward other members.
2. *Harmonizers* mediate intragroup conflicts and relieve tension.
3. *Gatekeepers* encourage participation of others by using such expressions as, "Let's hear from Sue," "Why not limit the length of the contributions so all can react to the problem?" and "Bill, do you agree?"
4. *Standards setters* express standards for the group to achieve or apply in evaluating the quality of group processes, raise questions of group goals and purpose, and assess group movement in light of these objectives.
5. *Followers* go along passively and serve as friendly members.
6. *Group observers* tend to stay out of the group process and give feedback on the group as if they were detached evaluators.

### Self-Oriented Roles

The self-oriented role focuses only a member's individual needs, often at the expense of the group. This role may be broken into the following subroles:

1. *Blockers* are negative, stubborn, and unreasoningly resistant; they may try to bring back an issue the group intentionally rejected or bypassed.
2. *Recognition seekers* try to call attention to themselves. They may boast, report on personal achievements, and, in unusual ways, struggle to avoid being placed in an inferior position.
3. *Dominators* try to assert authority by manipulating the group or certain individuals in the group; they may use flattery or assertion of their superior status or right to attention; and they may interrupt contributions of others.
4. *Avoiders* maintain distance from others; these passive resisters try to remain insulated from interaction.

The dimensions listed in Table 5–3 have been observed in high-performance teams, in particular. Note that these dimensions are not the same as the roles previously identified. We include these dimensions here since they address the specifics of what makes teams self-managed and high performing.

Applied learning is important to the team for "multiskilling" and job rotation purposes; this includes the ability to learn and demonstrate technical and/or professional proficiency. Members who are able to learn new skills can fill other jobs more readily and thereby continue to add value to the team. Other dimensions of successful teams include: *problem identification*—being competent in problem analysis to help the team solve its own problems; *attention to detail*—being able to focus on continuous improvement monitoring of a product, process, or service; *influence*—being able to persuade and negotiate team needs and demands inside and

---

### TABLE 5–3    Critical Team Member Dimensions

| Dimension | Importance to Teams |
|---|---|
| Ability to learn (applied learning) | Multiskilling/job rotation |
| Analysis (problem identification) | Team solves its own problems |
| Attention to detail | Focus on continuous improvement |
| Influence | Persuades others inside and outside the organization |
| Initiative | Emphasis on continual improvement |
| Job fit (motivation to work in an empowered setting) | Job satisfaction, reduction of turnover, team "owns" decisions quality/productivity/ team issues |
| Judgment (problem solution) | |
| Oral Communication | Presents ideas to others |
| Planning and organizing (work management) | Team determines work/ production scheduling |
| Teamwork (cooperation) | Team members work with others on their own work team and on other teams |
| Technical/professional proficiency | Job rotation/multiskilling |
| Tolerance for stress | Handles ambiguity/stress related to new demands and roles |
| Training and coaching | Team members teach and train each other |
| Work standards | Quality/productivity focus |

SOURCE: R. S. Wellins, W. C. Byham, and J. M. Wilson, *Empowered Teams* (San Francisco: Jossey-Bass, 1991), 61. Copyright © 1991 Jossey-Bass. Reprinted by permission of Jossey-Bass, Inc., a subsidiary of John Wiley & Sons, Inc.

outside the organization; *initiative*—noticing and emphasizing the need for continual improvements in products, services, or processes; *job fit or motivation to work in an empowered setting*—being able to own a decision both as an individual and as a team; *judgment or problem solution*—being able to evaluate and solve quality, productivity, or interpersonal issues that evolve in teams; *oral communication*—being able to present and argue ideas effectively with others; *planning, organizing and work management*—being able to identify and determine work and production schedules enables independence and autonomy of the team; *teamwork, cooperation and tolerance for stress*—being able to handle ambiguity and stress related to new tasks and demands, one of the most valuable interpersonal dimensions a member can have; *training and coaching*—being able to teach and to train, as important as being "teachable" and "trainable."

## MANAGING CROSS-CULTURAL DIVERSITY IN TEAMS

Organizations and companies that must increasingly integrate multicultural people face the challenge of achieving and maintaining synergy in teams that are diverse with regard to race, gender, age, ethnicity, culture, and national origin. Table 5–4 compares the potential advantages and disadvantages of culturally diverse teams.

Culturally diverse teams can result in an organization's gaining competitive advantage if the teams are able to use the strengths of diversity (i.e., multiple perspectives and interpretations) to solve problems. The effective use of a team's diversity can add creativity, and flexibility and can widen the range of available alternatives. Moreover, multicultural representation on teams can facilitate understanding and problem solving, thereby reducing miscommunication, potential conflict, and stereotyping.

Disadvantages that culturally diverse teams present center on coordination and results, not of the presence or absence of diversity, but of how effectively or poorly those teams are led and facilitated to show productivity.[24] Barriers to effectively facilitating diversity in teams include (1) leaders who are unable to tolerate and channel the ambiguity, complexity, and confusion that arise over multiple meanings and miscommunication among members, (2) organizational costs that escalate because more time and effort may be spent to obtain synergy (through increased training and creating policies and procedures to integrate peoples), and (3) decreased morale, because of the presence of team members who are unable to channel diverse energies into focused action.

A multicultural team's effectiveness depends on a number of factors: "Diversity becomes most valuable when the need for agreement (cohesion) remains low relative to the need for invention (creativity), and when creativity and agreement can be balanced. A team leader must accurately assess each situation and emphasize those aspects that best fit the group's current function and structure."[25] Culturally diverse teams tend to be more effective in performing innovative tasks as compared to routine tasks. In addition, trust and consensus building, which are necessary during early

## TABLE 5–4    CULTURAL DIVERSITY IN TEAMS: PROS AND CONS

| Advantages | Disadvantages |
|---|---|
| **Organizational Benefits** | **Organizational Costs** |
| • Expanding meanings<br>   Multiple perspectives<br>   Greater openness to new ideas<br>   Multiple interpretations | • Increases in<br>   Ambiguity<br>   Complexity<br>   Confusion |
| • Expanding alternatives<br>   Increasing creativity<br>   Increasing flexibility<br>   Increasing problem-solving skills | • Difficulty converging meanings<br>   Miscommunication<br>   Hard to reach a single<br>   agreement |
| | • Difficulty converging actions<br>   Hard to agree on specific<br>   actions |
| **Culture-Specific Benefits** | **Culture-Specific Costs** |
| • Better understanding of foreign<br>   employees | • Overgeneralizing<br>   Organization policies<br>   Organization practices<br>   Organization procedures |
| • Ability to work more effectively with<br>   particular foreign clients | • Ethnocentrism |
| • Ability to market more effectively<br>   to specific foreign customers | |
| • Increased understanding of political,<br>   social, legal, economic, and<br>   cultural environment of<br>   foreign countries | |

SOURCE: From *International Dimensions of Organizational Behavior*, 3rd edition, by N.J. Adler. © 1997. Reprinted with permission of South-Western College Publishing, a Division of Thomson Learning.

stages of team development, are more difficult with culturally diverse groups, but during the middle and later developmental stages, diversity can facilitate idea generation and problem solving.[26] Understanding the values and norms of the employees' cultures can enhance the facilitation of diverse teams.

### Getting to Synergy

Getting to synergy is a major goal for any team, especially for those that are culturally diverse. The following guidelines can assist leaders and team members in enhancing synergy: (1) be flexible on others' viewpoints and be open to change, (2) exercise patience, perseverance, and professional security, (3) think in multidimensional terms and consider different sides of issues, (4) find ways to deal with ambiguity, role shifts, and differences in personal and professional styles or social and political systems, (5) manage stress and tension and schedule tasks systematically, (6) be sensitive to cross-cultural communication and demonstrate empathy for language problems among colleagues, (7) anticipate the consequences of your own behavior, (8) deal with unfamiliar situations and lifestyle changes sensitively, (9) stress clarity and consistency when dealing with different organizational structures and policies, and (10) learn from your experience and take notes for future projects.[27]

When working on or leading an international team, it is important first to understand the cultural characteristics and assumptions of the team members. These assumptions underlie each member's management and following style. With this information, you can then seek ways to continuously cope (i.e., seek and offer clarity in communicating). It is also important to observe what is happening, to use power appropriately, and to evaluate your own actions and those of others before responding.[28] This is a mind-set as well as a continuous improvement process.

Working closely with international team members on time-limited tasks is not easy. Cultural differences can translate into workforce tensions. For example, Eastern cultures emphasize groups and collaboration, whereas Western cultures emphasize individualism and competition. Western management practices stress team cohesiveness but continue to reflect individualistic tendencies. Strategic and operational information is rarely shared with employees. In Japan, by contrast, employees are kept well informed about their company and share information routinely.

Leadership style, organizational culture and structure, and the different types of rewards are related to cultural norms. Global teamwork, therefore, requires both an understanding of cultural differences and an array of flexible work styles that value diversity. Moreover, team members and managers must practice active listening and assertiveness and must cultivate the ability to seek synergy in problem solving that is not deterred by conflicting or silent assumptions and expectations. Selecting team members who show promise when it comes to working well together and selecting assignments that match a team's expertise can reduce many cultural and communication barriers.

### Ethics, Trust, and Ten Team Decision-Making Criteria

Ethics is every team member's responsibility. The ethics of a team is often embodied in the written norms of behavior in its charter, mission and values statement, or contract. Social loafing (i.e., when members of the team do not contribute their fair share of time, effort, ideas, and resources to the team) is a form of unethical behavior since it violates the principle that most teams have of fairness and equity of work effort.[29]

Teams and team members must also respect the rights of other members, of the stakeholders, and of the organization, and they must fulfill their obligations toward those groups in an ethical manner. This is the responsibility of each team member. How these obligations and rights are fulfilled or violated are often reflected in a team's goals, resource allocation processes, decision-making styles, and outcomes.

Trust is also a key ethical ingredient of a team's cohesiveness (the glue that holds a team together). Studies show that trust is based on five dimensions:

1. Integrity

2. Competence

3. Consistency

4. Loyalty

5. Openness[30]

Integrity is rated as the most important element that people look for in trusting someone, followed by competence. If someone is not perceived as having integrity—moral character and "basic honesty—the other dimensions of trust would not matter."[31]

Since many ethical conflicts can result from poor decisions and decision-making processes in teams, the following guidelines can assist individuals and teams in clarifying motivations and tensions before decisions are made:

- Have you defined the problem accurately?

- How would you define the problem if you stood on the other side of the fence?

- How did this situation occur in the first place?

- To whom and to what do you give your loyalty as a person and as a member of the corporation?

- What is your intention in making this decision?

- How does this intention compare with the probable results?

- Whom could your decision or action injure?

- Can you discuss the problem with the affected parties before you make your decision?

- Are you confident that your decision will be as valid over a long period of time as it seems now?

- Could you disclose without qualm your decision or action to your boss, your chief executive officer, the board of directors, your family, or society as a whole?

- What is the symbolic potential of your action?

- Under what conditions would you allow exceptions to your stand?[32]

## THE CHANGING WORKPLACE

**Ethical Questions**

**Exercise**: Complete the following:

**Step 1**: Answer the following questions individually first.

1. Recall a **team** you have been on in which there was a member whom you did not *trust*. Now write why or what it was about that person, your relationship, and the situation that led to the distrust.

2. Now write briefly what it would have taken, then or now, for you to *change* your lack of trust toward that person. Be specific. (*Note:* for this exercise, you are asked to change your lack of trust in that situation in Step 1.)

3. Did the person in Step 1 trust or not trust you? Write what you know or believe about that person trusting or not trusting you.

4. What do you believe it would take or would have taken (e.g., actions, a conversation) for that person to change—or have changed—his or her lack of trust in you?

**Step 2**: In dyads, share your answers to the questions in Step 1.

**Step 3**: In dyads, answer these questions:

1. What is required in a team to build trust? (Use this chapter as a reference.)

2. How do you evaluate yourself (your communication, style of interacting, values, beliefs, relationship-building skills) in terms of how well you inspire or discourage teammates' trust in you? Explain.

3. Explain your expectations and requirements of team members as to trust.

**Step 4**: The dyads share their answers to Step 3 with the class. Then, as a class, discuss these questions.

1. How can teams at the forming stage of development facilitate an environment for all members to develop and sustain trust in each other in their working relationships?

2. What can be done when one or more members are observed developing or showing mistrust of someone or others in the team?

3. What did you learn about yourself and teams from this exercise?

## *GROUPTHINK AS A DECISION-MAKING PROCESS*

A dysfunctional syndrome that teams and group members sometimes experience and practice and that can lead to unethical consequences is called groupthink. This is the tendency of members in highly cohesive groups to lose their critical evaluative capabilities.[33] Groupthink demands conformity at the expense of critical thinking. Members become unwilling to criticize one another. The goal becomes that of holding the group together at almost any cost. Pressures to conform overwhelm the search for alternative courses of action to maintain the "we" feeling.

Resultant decisions and outcomes can have serious ethical consequences for a team and those affected by team decisions. Poor quality or dangerous products or services can result from groupthink. Some telling symptoms that indicate groupthink is occurring include the following:

- *The illusion of group invulnerability*—that is, members believe the group is beyond criticism or attack.

- *Rationalizing unpleasant data*—members refuse to accept or thoroughly consider contradictory data or new information.

- *Belief in inherent group morality*—members believe the group is right and above reproach by outsiders.

- *Negative stereotyping of outsiders*—members refuse to look realistically at other groups; they may view competitors as weak, evil, or stupid.

- *Applying pressure to deviants*—members refuse to tolerate anyone who suggests that the group may be wrong; every attempt is made to get conformity to group wishes.

- *Self-censorship by members*—members are unwilling to communicate personal concerns or alternative points of view to the group as a whole.

- *Illusions of unanimity*—members are quick to accept consensus; they do so prematurely and without testing its completeness.

- *Mind guarding*—members of the group keep outsiders away and try to protect the group from hearing disturbing ideas or viewpoints.[34]

Janis, who developed the concept of groupthink, suggests following these guidelines to avoid groupthink and to deal effectively with its symptoms:

- Assign the role of critical evaluator to each group member.

- Encourage a sharing of objections.

- Insist that the leader avoid seeming partial to one course of action.

- Create subgroups that operate under different leaders but work on the same problem.

- Have group members discuss issues with subordinates and report back on their reactions.

- Invite outside experts to observe group activities and react to group processes and decisions.

- Assign one member of the group to play a "devil's advocate" role at each meeting.

- Write alternative scenarios for the intentions of competing groups.

- Hold "second-chance" meetings on key issues after consensus has apparently been achieved.[35]

Had administrators and engineers from Morton Thiokol company consciously avoided groupthink symptoms, the *Challenger* space disaster probably would not have occurred.

## EFFECTIVE DECISION-MAKING TECHNIQUES FOR TEAMS AND GROUPS

Several decision-making techniques can enhance team problem-solving capabilities. We summarize three of them here.[36]

### Brainstorming

*Brainstorming* is a common team and group practice. This technique requires group members to generate as many ideas and alternatives as possible, quickly and without inhibitions. Brainstorming is most useful for simple, well-defined problems. For brainstorming to work effectively, all members must agree to and deliberately follow four rules:

1. *All criticism is ruled out.* No one is allowed to judge or evaluate any ideas until the idea-generation process has been completed.

2. *"Freewheeling"* is welcomed. The emphasis is on creativity and imagination; the wilder or more radical the ideas, the better.

3. *Quantity is wanted.* The more ideas, the more likely that a superior idea will appear.

4. *Piggybacking is good.* Everyone is encouraged to suggest how others' ideas can be turned into new ideas or how two or more ideas can be joined into a new idea.

Brainstorming can be disrupted when members try to dominate the process, or when they argue and get stuck on one point or refuse to contribute openly to the process, or when they attack others.

Effective facilitation ensures that all viewpoints are written for all to see and build on, that members listen to each other, and that the focus of the subject is kept on track. Brainstorming is a first-step technique; the refining and selection processes follow.

### Nominal Group Technique

Another useful group and team decision-making technique is the nominal group technique (NGT).[37] This technique attempts to solicit as much valuable information and perspective as possible from as many members as possible. The NGT works when the team or group is so large that free discussion is difficult or when the members disagree and consensus cannot be reached. In this technique, members get to consensus by following this sequence:

1. *Members generate the ideas.* Participants are assigned to groups of five to seven members and are then given a "nominal" question (e.g., what should be done to improve the effectiveness of this work unit?). Usually, this question is stated in writing as part of an individual worksheet. Group participants work silently and independently and respond in writing to the nominal question; they are encouraged to list as many alternatives or ideas as they can.

2. *They record the ideas.* With the assistance of a recorder, participants read their responses to the nominal question aloud in round-robin fashion. The recorder writes each response as it is offered; no criticism or discussion of the ideas is allowed.

3. *They clarify the ideas.* The recorder asks for questions on each response. This is done in round-robin fashion again, and questions are allowed for clarification only.

4. *They vote on the ideas.* Participants are asked to rank the five or seven responses they consider most valuable. The balloting is tallied to rank order each response on the master list.

5. *They refine the ideas.* Steps 3 and 4 are repeated as needed to refine the list to identify the most preferred response or set of responses.

The ranked lists are collected by the facilitator and used to make additional assignments or refinements in the decision process.

### Delphi Technique

The Delphi technique also seeks to gather expert information and perspectives from a wide range of outside resources.[38] This is a group decision-making technique that uses questionnaires to reach consensus. It is most effective when geographically dispersed members need to reach a decision and cannot meet in person or when expert information is needed from people outside the organization. The Delphi technique has four phases: (1) exploration of the subject by the individual members, (2) reaching understanding of the group's view of the issues, (3) discussion and evaluation of any reasons for differences, and (4) final evaluation of all information. In practical terms, the initial questionnaire is sent to all group members who formulate and send in their responses. The initial alternatives are summarized by the leader and copied to all group members. A follow-up questionnaire based on the initial responses (which are revised to reflect the first round of suggestions) is sent, and the process of reiteration and refinement of suggestions is repeated until consensus is reached.

Effectively leading and participating in high-performance teams involves giving attention to the process, as well as to the results, of any decision-making method. Understanding the culture of a team and the organization and also how to take corrective action to keep the team on track is a step toward meaningful and socially responsible participation and productivity. Brainstorming, the NGT, and the Delphi technique are three proven methods for reaching team consensus.

## *PROJECT MANAGEMENT: MIND-SET AND METHODS*

Project management thinking and methods are increasingly being used in cross-functional work team settings. Projects are defined as any work that "involves multiple priorities, complex and numerous tasks, deadlines, constant communication across organizational boundaries, limited resources."[39] Defining work in a project

---

### THE CHANGING WORKPLACE

**You're the Change Consultant**

**Exercise**: Read the following scenario. You have been assigned to work with a virtual team on a two-month project. The results of your team's work on this project can either win you a rewarding promotion or leave you in a dull job. You have the following facts about he assignment and team. First, you will be part of the 10-member international team whose mission is to assist a highly visible and valued customer create a world-class database of prospective global clients. You will meet face-to-face only once with your team in London, two weeks before the "kick off." Second, you will have three training sessions on how to use your primary groupware (software) before you start. Third, you have heard that one team member is a bigot and stereotypes nontechnical people as "dummies." Another member does not write well. A third member is not proficient in writing but is "fun to work with." Finally, since you are taking an organizational behavior course, you have been asked to help organize the first meeting (i.e., provide some ideas for structuring the meeting to maximize the team's process and chances of succeeding).

**Step 1** (individually):

1. List questions and issues you have about this assignment.

2. List "success factors" you believe should be put in place to ensure the team's success.

3. Make a bulleted agenda for the first meeting. (Remember that only one meeting is scheduled before launching the team.)

**Step 2** (in teams of 2 to 4):

1. Share your responses to the three preceding items.

2. Use a flip chart to combine the best of your team's suggestions and prepare to share your final answers to the three exercise items with the class.

**Optional** (as a class):

1. Each team should summarize its agreed-on responses to the Step 1 exercises.

2. After all teams have presented their summaries, discuss these questions as a class:

What were some common themes in each of the three items?

What particular concerns and issues did individuals express?

Would your team's answers have been different if the assignment had not been for a virtual team? Why? Discuss what you learned from this exercise. What did you learn about yourself assuming you will be (or already are) part of a virtual team?

management framework can facilitate decision making and organizing teams around a common set of objectives and timeframe. Moreover, the decision making methods discussed earlier can also be incorporated into a project management methodology.

A project management mind-set involves seeing complex work from a "big picture" perspective, planned and implemented systematically, often in phases with a beginning and end point.

Projects begin by forming teams to identify project goals, objectives, and resource requirements. Work is then divided into discrete activities and tasks with time, labor, and material costs developed for each activity. Status and monitoring reports are developed to show variances between planned and actual costs and time of each activity. Budgets are planned around all activities, and the total number of activities is sequenced into flow diagrams that show the beginning and end of the entire project and for each activity. An entire project can be estimated in time, costs, and completion date. Team synergy and creativity are facilitated in disciplined but flexible ways using project management methodologies that keep accountability for results in continual focus.[40]

## CONCLUDING COMMENTS

Work is increasingly being performed in teams. Extreme teams, or hot groups, represent a contemporary type of team that can be formed voluntarily or by an organization. Quality management and restructuring initiatives have organized work around value-added business processes that use high-performance teams to do more with less.

Teams differ from groups in that teams are small numbers of people (usually 6 to 12 individuals) with complementary skills who are committed to a common purpose and set of performance goals and who are held accountable for reaching those goals. Groups also may share common goals but usually include large numbers of people who are loosely connected, who communicate indirectly, and who share work tasks less frequently.

High-performance teams are defined as self-managing, self-designed, and self-directed. Such teams are characterized as independent and aligned around a common purpose. They have a high sense of empowerment, communication, and shared responsibility. They are task focused and can generate rapid responses around time-based assignments.

Virtual teams are separated by time and space and must operate primarily by electronic collaborative groupware. These teams are usually fluid with membership shifting and expanding, shared leadership roles emerging, work being result driven, and the team being united by its mission, work objectives, and responsibilities. Issues of exposure and trust are more prominent than belonging and place. Hoarding information can be a major issue for these teams. Clear goals, a culture built on trust, management support, robust technology, training, and detailed protocol for communicating are some of the success factors for virtual teams.

The way a team is formed depends on the required expertise, the type of outcome expected, and the nature and structure of the work to be done. Teams proceed through at least five stages of development in completing the job assignment: forming, storming, norming, performing, and adjourning. A team can at any point move through these stages, skip a stage, or repeat one. Being aware of stages can help teams recognize barriers that block performance.

Characteristics of effective teams include the ability to learn, technical and process problem solving, proficiency, attention to detail, influence, initiative, and a results-oriented track record. Effective team roles are task and relationship oriented; ineffective team roles are self-oriented (i.e., blockers, recognition seekers, dominators, and avoiders).

A multicultural team can have a competitive advantage because of the role diversity plays in stimulating creativity and generating a wide range of alternatives/solutions. Reaching synergy is a major challenge for multicultural and international teams. A process was explained for problem solving with synergy: (1) describe the situation from different cultural perspectives, (2) determine the underlying cultural assumptions from each perspective, and (3) assess the overlap of similarities and differences and then select an alternative that draws on the optimal alternatives.

The following group and team decision-making processes were discussed: brainstorming, the nominal group technique, and the Delphi technique. Symptoms of groupthink (a forced consensus, noncritical decision process) also were identified and discussed. These include rationalization, belief in the group's invulnerability, belief in the inherent morality of the group, negative stereotyping, applying pressure to deviants, self-censorship, illusion of the group's unanimity, and mindguarding. Methods for preventing groupthink and criteria for preventing unethical behavior and for resolving ethical dilemmas in the workplace were also summarized.

Ethics plays an integral part of teams through the trust between members that is earned or broken. Integrity is a key ingredient in trusting. Cohesiveness of team members (how well they operate together) depends on the degree to which members have trust. Ten decision-making criteria were presented; if they are used, they can help prevent conflict and potential ethical dilemmas among members.

Project management was introduced as a way of thinking, planning, and implementing team decisions. Seeing complex work in project terms enables teams to manage and control decisions and plans according to specifications, budgets and results.

## SCENARIO AND EXERCISE: TEAMS IN TROUBLE

**Step 1:** Read the scenario.

An eight-month-old start-up dot-com company is having difficulty coordinating activities, people, and moving forward on schedule to the next round of venture capital. The two founders, both programmers, were clear when they started about their vision, their product and their market. They moved quickly to write a convincing business plan, which landed them $500,000 matching funds with the $200,000 they raised on their own. One of the programmers is CEO; the other is president. Two Fortune 500 technology companies sponsored them. They hired four additional programmers, a marketing professional, and an office manager, and then proceeded to launch their Web site. Now they're floundering. The office manager is threatening to quit because the programmers control the office. The marketing professional doesn't know who to turn to for direction since the founders—even though they're the president and CEO—both spend their time programming. If they can't show that they are a high-performing, focused team that is still on track with their business plan and schedule, the entire endeavor will collapse.

**Step 2:**

You have been invited to diagnose the problems here and make recommendations to "Get a high performance, cohesive team in place. . . fast!" Identify the key issues and obstacles presently facing the company that are preventing a cohesive team to take shape.

**Step 3:**

Use concepts from the chapter, as well as any other ideas you may have, to help the company form a team and get on track.

## REVIEW QUESTIONS

1. Define *team?* What are some differences between teams and groups?

2. What is an *extreme team?* Would you rather be a member of an extreme team or a loose-knit group to complete a project? Explain.

3. Identify characteristics of high-performance, self-managing teams.

4. What is empowerment? How can one determine whether a team is empowered? What are some signs of empowerment? Have you been empowered as a team member? Why or why not?

5. How do virtual teams differ from other teams? Have you been a virtual team member? What difficulties or challenges would you experience as a member of one of these teams? Why?

6. Identify popular life cycle or developmental stages of teams.

7. Identify some qualifications for leading a team. What are some difficulties a person might experience in leading a team? Why?

8. What is the quality management (or total quality management) philosophy? Do you believe it is an important consideration for teams? Why or why not?

9. Are principles from the quality management philosophy important for Internet companies and products? Explain your point of view.

10. What is a team psychological contract? Is it important, why or why not?

11. Identify some effective and ineffective team roles. Which roles do you feel most qualified in performing on a team? Why? Which roles do you feel least qualified in performing? Why?

12. What are some pros and cons of managing diversity in teams? Do you believe diversity is a competitive advantage for team composition, in the final analysis, or just a complicating factor? Argue your viewpoint.

13. What is synergy? Why is it important for teams?

14. Discuss ethical criteria for team decision making that can prevent dysfunctional conflict.

15. What is groupthink? Give an example of groupthink symptoms you observed in a team in which you were a member.

16. Which of the decision-making techniques (brainstorming, nominal group technique, delphi technique) for teams and groups did you find most helpful that you would and could use?

# 6 Communication

---

## LEARNING OBJECTIVES

After studying this chapter, you should be able to:

1 Define the communication process.

2 Identify barriers to effective interpersonal communication.

3 Describe interpersonal communication skills for managers.

4 Discuss communication processes in organizations.

5 Identify strategies for effective electronic communication.

6 Describe cross-cultural communication differences and managerial strategies.

7 Present a communication checklist of ethical guidelines for managers.

---

## COMMUNICATION DEFINED

The sender of a message seeks to achieve a common understanding of that message by every receiver. The aim of communication, therefore, is to achieve coordinated action between the sender and the receiver of a message. When professionals are asked to identify major problems in their organization, a frequent answer is poor communication. Even with increasing business communication over the Internet and other forms of electronic media, face-to-face interaction remains the richest, i.e. most complete and well understood, type of information exchange.

Virtual teams working in separate spaces and time zones rely on sophisticated groupware technologies (such as desktop and real-time conferencing and electronic meeting systems) to approximate face-to-face meetings.[1] It is interesting to note that, given the increasing use of electronic exchanges, interpersonal communication still remains one of the most important, yet difficult to master, forms of relating. This chapter addresses specific methods to enhance face-to-face communication since verbal communication consumes the bulk of professionals' time.[2] For this reason, companies such as Polaroid have established systems to facilitate communication.

Polaroid's What's Happening system of interpersonal communication was started at R-Z, a facility located in Waltham, Massachusetts. The program seeks to increase the quality and efficiency of teamwork by providing a system for sharing knowledge of all aspects of Polaroid's products and manufacturing processes. The plant manager at the time, Harvey Greenberg, stated, "Successful communication depends on good information and continued dialogue and, most importantly, on responsiveness."[3] Polaroid's What's Happening program involves attacking the "three dragons" that endangered communication at the plant (i.e., fear of relinquishing absolute control, the muddle in the middle, and information filtering). The program required each frontline supervisor—with an assigned secretary who took notes and prepared agendas—to hold monthly shift meetings with hourly and management staff to share strategic and operations information. Packets of information were distributed to update staff and keep them current about plant and company issues. There has been consensus in the organization that the program has worked.

### Two-Way Communication

The lessons learned from the What's Happening program at Polaroid identified a number of facts about two-way communication:

- Information disseminated by management must be timely, clear, and useful.

- The significance of data is not always self-evident, nor are management's priorities.

- Participation in a communication system is not a given: people need to be invited to participate, encouraged to speak up, and made to feel valued.

- Good presenters are not born; coaching and practice make a difference.

- Two-way communication is the lifeblood of a communication system; without it, the system becomes malnourished and frail.

Perhaps the most important lesson to be learned from Polaroid's program is that good communication is never easy. Installing a powerful two-way communication system requires enormous amounts of attention, flexibility, and patience. Greenberg puts it succinctly: "In real estate they say it's 'location, location, location'; in today's manufacturing organizations, I believe it's communication, communication, communication."[4]

In this chapter we address why communication in organizations fails as well as why it succeeds. We begin by discussing the interpersonal process of communication and then the organizational process in which the goals, stakes, technologies, and players multiply. This chapter also discusses barriers and facilitators to effective communication. We also examine the complexity of cross-cultural communication and present strategies and skills for effective and ethical communication.

## THE COMMUNICATION PROCESS

As a process, *communication* involves sending and receiving information (messages) through symbols—that is, words, nonverbal cues, attitudes, and moods. Simply stated, communication involves Who . . . says what, . . . in which way . . . , to

## THE CHANGING WORKPLACE

### Skill Assessment
### Communication Exercise

Answer either YES or NO to the following questions.

1. I sometimes intentionally and unintentionally criticize people in conversations.
   Yes___          No___

2. I frequently am quiet when listening to people until I understand what they mean.
   Yes___          No___

3. I usually ask a lot of questions while someone is talking to me.
   Yes___          No___

4. I tend to offer a lot of support to someone in conversations.
   Yes___          No___

5. I respond very quickly to someone, even before he or she finishes talking.
   Yes___          No___

6. I like to logically evaluate what someone is saying before he or she goes on to the next point.
   Yes___          No___

7. People feel I understand their point of view in a discussion.
   Yes___          No___

8. I usually keep good eye contact with someone in a conversation.
   Yes___          No___

9. I almost never interrupt people while they are expressing themselves.
   Yes___          No___

10. I like talking more than listening.
    Yes___          No___

11. If I get bored with listening, I change the topic, or try to.
    Yes___          No___

12. I like to give advice to people in a helping way.
    Yes___          No___

13. I like to solve people's problems for them during a conversation.
    Yes___          No___

14. I try to think about what to say when someone is still talking.
    Yes___          No___

15. I often complete people's sentences for them if they pause while talking.
    Yes___          No___

Scoring: Based on literature and studies in listening, the accurate answers of an attentive listener are 1. No, 2. Yes, 3. No, 4. No, 5. No, 6. No, 7. Yes, 8. Yes, 9. Yes, 10. No, 11. No, 12. No, 13. No, 14. No, 15. No

If you scored 12–15 correct, consider yourself a very good listener. A score of 8–12 indicates that you need to practice listening skills in this chapter. A score below 8 indicates poor listening skills. Work on understanding and practicing listening skills. Consider taking a class on listening.

whom , . . . with what effect?[5] A simplified model of the communication process is presented in Figure 6–1. Note, however, that sending and receiving a message is rarely a straightforward data exchange because of our ever-present perceptual screens.

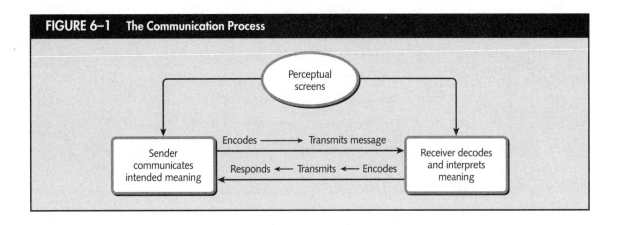

**FIGURE 6–1    The Communication Process**

Perceptual screens

Sender communicates intended meaning

Encodes ⟶ Transmits message

Responds ⟵ Transmits ⟵ Encodes

Receiver decodes and interprets meaning

Interpersonal communication involves a process that is defined by at least four factors:

1. Feelings about oneself

2. Feelings about the other

3. Feelings about the content of what is to be discussed

4. Feelings about the subject being discussed[6]

These four factors can also be defined as the perceptual screens of Figure 6–2. *Perceptual screens* are conditioned not only by immediate, situational variables but also by one's culture, personal system (self-concepts, personality factors, moods, esteem), and by the organizational context. For example, a manager who is feeling insecure about himself or negatively toward a receiver will likely send a message differently than a manager who is self-confident and trusts the receiver.

As Figure 6–1 indicates, a sender first encodes (i.e., translates mental images into language and gestures) the message. How the message is formulated is influenced by the sender's feelings—that is, her perceptual screens. The message is transmitted to the intended receiver via language and gestures. The receiver of the message also views it through his own perceptual screens and uses those same screens to formulate and encode a response. A sender who has recently been demoted will probably not communicate an announcement regarding more planned personnel cutbacks the same way as would a recently promoted sender. Likewise, a receiver who is being courted by an outside firm will probably respond differently than a receiver who has no outside job prospects.

Managers and employees can improve their effectiveness and objectivity in sending and receiving messages (face-to-face and electronically) by noting the process model in Figure 6-1 and by consciously reflecting on their own and others' perceptual screens. More specifically, organizational members can use the

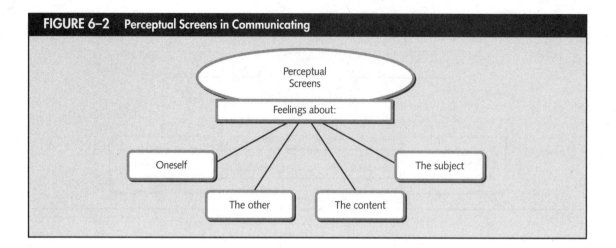

**FIGURE 6–2 Perceptual Screens in Communicating**

following four factors as a practical checklist or to help prepare for a coaching or feedback session:

1. What is my frame of mind? How objective can I be now?

2. How do I feel about X (sender/receiver) of the information? What are my biases toward her?

3. How do I feel about the specific content of the message? What are my biases?

4. How do I feel about the subject of this message?

  The choice of medium through which we send and receive messages also affects the quality of our communication. A first step then, might be to determine the most effective way to send this type of message.


## THE COMMUNICATION MEDIUM AND INFORMATION RICHNESS

Table 6–1 compares the different media through which we communicate. These media are important when considering the effectiveness (sending the right message) and efficiency (saving transmission costs). These media range from highest information richness (i.e., the information capacity of data; some information provides a deeper understanding than other information) and lowest capacity (face-to-face exchanges) to lowest information richness and highest data capacity (formal numeric reports). Selecting the proper medium significantly impacts the receiver's perception and acceptance of the message. Since, for example, messages can carry emotional and mixed meanings as well as hidden and ambiguous ones, an appropriate medium is an essential part of the communication.

**TABLE 6–1    What Different Mediums Communicate**

| Communication Medium | Information Richness | Data Capacity |
|---|---|---|
| Face-to-face discussion | Highest | Lowest |
| Telephone | High | Low |
| Electronic mail | Moderate | Moderate |
| Individualized letter | Moderate | Moderate |
| Personalized note or memo | Moderate | Moderate |
| Formal written report | Low | High |
| Flyer or bulletin | Low | High |
| Formal numeric report | Lowest | Highest |

SOURCE: Based on R. L. Daft and R. H. Lengel, "Information Richness: A New Approach to Managerial Behavior and Organizational Design," in B. Staw and L. Cummings, ed., *Research in Organization Behavior*, vol. 6 (Greenwich, Conn.: JAI Press, 1984), 191–233.

In addition to the exchanges in Figure 6–1, virtual teams depend on electronic exchanges to accomplish work. Two common forms of electronic communication include *synchronous* groupware (those that enable team members to engage at the same time) and *asynchronous* applications (those that facilitate delayed interaction). Synchronous groupware is used for more complex tasks and attempts to approximate face-to-face interactions through desktop and real-time data conferencing, including electronic meeting systems and video and audio conferencing. Asynchronous groupware is lower on the scale of information richness and is related to one-way communication; it includes e-mail, bulletin boards, Web pages, databases. Sending a fax or an e-mail to inform a person that a family member had suddenly died would not be appropriate, nor would announcing a major reorganization through a voice mail to all employees be an effective medium, although some companies have chosen to communicate this type of announcement in just this way. On the other hand, stock reports and statistical analyses may best be communicated in report form by fax or e-mail. As simple as this point sounds, it is continually violated in the workplace, compounding problems in relationships and in performance. *How* the information is transmitted can be as important, if not more important, than *what* is communicated.

A major goal of communication is that an intended message be understood and accepted by the receiver and that necessary action be taken as requested. Understanding and reducing noise (i.e., whatever interferes with the understanding and acceptance of a message) must therefore be a necessary consideration of senders.

Table 6–1 shows that face-to-face communication has the lowest data capacity but the highest information richness. Information that is highly personal, ambiguous, or complex and that requires persuasion as well as explanation is best transmitted face-to-face. For sending information of this nature, the telephone is the next best medium, followed by electronic mail. Formal reports contain the highest data capacity but are lowest in transmitting information richness. Managers and employees can ask certain questions before sending messages inside and outside the organization. They are as follows:

- What is the nature of the information/message being sent?

- What medium is most appropriate for acceptance of this message?

- What are the likely consequences if the message is transmitted through an inappropriate medium?

In the information age, in which speed and timed competition are criteria for doing business, effective communication still depends on the extent to which information is accurately—and emotionally—received, accepted, and acted upon. Selecting the right medium is a first step in effectively communicating interpersonally, between groups, and interorganizationally.

## BARRIERS TO EFFECTIVE INTERPERSONAL COMMUNICATION

Barriers to effective interpersonal communication originate in the *perceptual screens* of both the senders and the receivers of information. By *information* we mean body language and gestures as well as words. One general way to understand and identify barriers to effectively sending and receiving messages is the "fight-or-flight" syndrome[7] shown in Figure 6–3.

Humans seem to be born knowing how to effectively fight or escape from situations that threaten their space, time, needs, and values. Aggressive (fighting) and submissive (fleeing) behaviors come naturally and are the source of most other barriers to interpersonal communication. These behaviors readily manifest themselves in abrasive or escapist words, nonverbal gestures, and actions. Both aggressive and submissive communication behaviors are based on a lack of respect for self

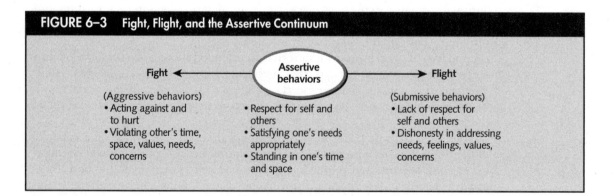

**FIGURE 6–3    Fight, Flight, and the Assertive Continuum**

Fight ← → Flight

Assertive behaviors

(Aggressive behaviors)
- Acting against and to hurt
- Violating other's time, space, values, needs, concerns

- Respect for self and others
- Satisfying one's needs appropriately
- Standing in one's time and space

(Submissive behaviors)
- Lack of respect for self and others
- Dishonesty in addressing needs, feelings, values, concerns

and others. Moreover, the results of aggressive and submissive behaviors and communications are often nonproductive and even destructive.

*Aggressive* communication behaviors entail moving against others. Most of us have experienced employees who communicate in an "attack" mode. Such behaviors can take the form of glaring eye contact, moving too close to people, pointing fingers, clenching fists, cursing and using abusive language, using sexist and/or racist terms, making explicit threats, and using put-downs.[8] Submissive behaviors entail moving away others. These communication clues and behaviors are self-denying and inhibited. Employees who send messages in hesitating ways are acting submissively. Submissive behaviors include nonverbal communication, such as showing little eye contact, staring down, slumping, and speaking in a weak or whiny tone of voice. Verbally, submissiveness involves using qualifiers ("maybe," "kind of"), filters ("uh," "you know what I mean," "well, uh"), and negators ("it's not really that important"; "never mind"; "I'm not sure"; "you wouldn't do it anyway"). Recognizing aggression and submissiveness in our own and in others' communication is a first step toward managing and changing such behaviors.

The alternative to the aggressive response is *assertiveness*. Assertive communication behaviors must be learned. Being and acting assertively involves "pushing back" without attacking. Assertiveness also means protecting one's space, time, and integrity by allowing others to influence outcomes without taking advantage of or abusing others. Employees who communicate honestly, straightforwardly, and with confidence and enthusiasm are usually acting assertively. Good eye contact, upright body posture, and a strong and self-assured voice and facial expressions are all important assertive nonverbals. Verbally, assertiveness means speaking directly and unambiguously; it means using I and we statements instead of you statements. ("You" statements tend to threaten, blame, and accuse.) There are no blaming, threatening, or punishing behaviors as with aggressive communication, nor are there escapist, withdrawing, or fear-based behaviors as with submissiveness. Assertiveness involves being open to change but not at your own or the other's expense. Keeping the fight/flight/assertive continuum in mind can help move your verbal and nonverbal communication toward assertiveness.

### Roadblocks to Effective Communication

Any hindrance to effectively sending and receiving an intended message can serve as a roadblock. There are numerous roadblocks to effective communicating; we discuss 12 major barriers, or high-risk responses, that add noise to interpersonal communicating.[9] These roadblocks are listed in Table 6–2, which can serve as a checklist for diagnosing our own and others' communication in organizations. When a person is stressed, over/underworked, or is in a rushed or uneasy state of mind, one or more of these roadblocks is likely to appear. The 12 barriers are categorized under the classifications judging, sending solutions, and avoiding the other's concerns. The aim here is to be able to recognize these communication roadblocks in our own and others' behaviors and practice changing our behaviors toward assertiveness. We explain the three types of barriers and then briefly comment on some of the more subtle types.

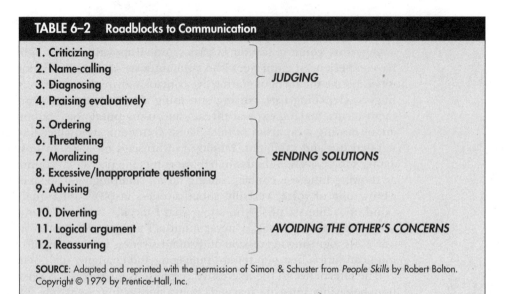

**TABLE 6–2    Roadblocks to Communication**

1. Criticizing
2. Name-calling
3. Diagnosing       } *JUDGING*
4. Praising evaluatively

5. Ordering
6. Threatening
7. Moralizing       } *SENDING SOLUTIONS*
8. Excessive/Inappropriate questioning
9. Advising

10. Diverting
11. Logical argument } *AVOIDING THE OTHER'S CONCERNS*
12. Reassuring

SOURCE: Adapted and reprinted with the permission of Simon & Schuster from *People Skills* by Robert Bolton. Copyright © 1979 by Prentice-Hall, Inc.

**Judging** can be a roadblock to effective communication when "sitting in judgment" is meant. Judging occurs (e.g., when a manager states, "I can't believe you gave a 'go' to that shipment. How dumb.") There is no evidence presented, only a judgment. Many of these situations are obvious and understandable. Criticizing unconstructively and calling people names are forms of judging. Less obvious ways of judging include excessive praising, evaluating, and diagnosing. These are often subtle but destructive ways to send a person a message that he is being graded or ranked by some criteria that may not be relevant to the situation or to him. Moreover, judging removes the other's feeling and ability to control or change a situation.

**Sending solutions** when solutions are not requested or desired is another barrier to interpersonal communication. Ordering a person to do something and/or threatening her are obvious ways to send solutions. Moralizing is also a method of sending a solution under the guise of help. Some of the less obvious types in this category include excessive and inappropriate questioning and advising. Unsolicited questions and advice that, in our minds, may seem like a generous or helpful gesture can easily be interpreted by others as offensive. People generally are best able to solve their own problems only when they recognize the problem.

**Avoiding the other's concerns** also can block effective interpersonal communication. Avoiding includes diverting the conversation with unnecessary comments; using logical arguments and facts to neglect or escape a person's emotional concerns; and reassuring. On the surface, some of these tactics appear helpful. In practice, they can create emotional distancing between people. Only the other person knows his core issues and concerns. Misguided logic and reassurance do not assist the person to discover the important issues.

## Other Communication Barriers

Other barriers to effective communication include such factors as *frame of mind* and *moods, timing, information overload, unclear semantics, information filtering, expectations, lack of trust and openness,* and *gender and cultural differences.*

A person's *frame of mind*, emotional disposition, and mood can have a significant effect on her ability and willingness to listen and respond effectively. Anger, disappointment, or overexcitement can blur objectivity. Being able to read nonverbal clues and listen to others to understand their frame of mind is a necessity in communicating effectively.

*Timing* is a key ingredient to effective communicating. Timing is deciding when to send a message only after considering whether or not the receiver is ready to listen. Informing a person in the hallway in front of his friends that he is being relocated is not the best timing.

Assigning tasks to someone who is experiencing *information overload* is not an effective means of communicating. Presenting people with more information than they already have, can understand, or act on is a significant barrier, especially in the current "do more with less" work environments. Observing, listening and inquiring before sending new or different messages is a first step in meaningfully relating.

*Unclear semantics* (word meanings) is another commonplace communication barrier. Using words and phrases with multiple meanings can cause confusion and even lead to conflict. For example, telling a person to get a task done ASAP (as soon as possible) may confuse her. You may mean in the next five minutes; she may interpret ASAP as sometime during the same day.

*Information filtering distorts communications.* This involves changing, reducing, and/or adding data to a message as it moves from one person or organizational layer to another. The very process of exchanging information between more than two individuals usually involves some filtering. Information filtering can be intentional or unintentional. A result of this process is inaccuracy in the intended meaning once the final message is received. Miscommunication, misperceptions, and inaccurate—sometimes harmful—attributions of intent can result. Information filtering occurs in all organizations but more frequently in large bureaucracies.

*Expectation* is another major cause of communication problems. Unspoken expectations that later go unrealized can be sources of misunderstanding, unfair attributions, and resentment. For example, an individual expecting to be assigned to a highly visible project may communicate his enthusiasm to peers. Should this person not get the assignment, disappointment and negative attributions may negatively affect subsequent communication with supervisors and peers.

*Gender differences* can affect interpersonal communications. Some studies suggest that men act in more authoritative, action-oriented, direct, and informational ways and as controlling communicators; women tend to act in more intimate, collaborative, facilitative, and accommodating ways and as inquiring communicators.[10] Effective communication skills and capabilities cut across gender differences.

Understanding underlying meanings to an individual's words and body language can overcome this barrier to effective communication.

*Cultural differences*, as we discuss later in more detail, also affect communications. Perceptions of time, space, and business practices can disrupt effective communications. In the Middle East, for example, being kept waiting for extended periods of time before seeing a client is not uncommon. Time, in Egypt, does not mean money as it does in New York City. Relationships come first, business second in the Middle East. Also, in Latin American countries, physical closeness in public spaces is not avoided as it is the United States. Physical friendliness and showing emotional warmth are part of doing business in Latin America. Being alert and sensitive to cultural cues and contexts before speaking is a first step in overcoming cultural communication barriers.

## THE CHANGING WORKPLACE

**Diversity Perspectives**
**"Does Gender Matter When Communicating?"**

**Step 1**: Briefly describe in writing your reactions to the following statements:

In general:

1. Men tend to control greater territory and personal space, a characteristic associated with status and dominance. Women tend to occupy less space. Women's bodily behavior is generally more restricted and restrained than men's.

2. Women generally establish more eye contact, that is, look more at the other person when communicating, than do men. Women also tend to sustain more woman-to-woman eye contact.

3. Women are more effective communicators than men since women are more nurturing.

4. Men are better at giving orders and getting things done in their communications, since men are socialized as "doers."

**Step 2**: Form dyads, male and female. First read your written reactions to the preceding statements in turn. Then respond individually to the other's reactions to the four statements.

**Step 3:** Report what occurred in your dyad to the class. Use the following four questions as a guide:

1. What, if any, patterns of responses and communication occurred in the dyad?

2. How did individuals feel after sharing their responses in the dyad?

3. Were there any differences in the ways males versus females responded to the questions? Identify the differences and explain why you believe these differences occurred.

4. What lessons did people take away from this exercise?

Copyright © Joseph W. Weiss, 2000

**SOURCES**: For questions 1 and 2 see T. Zorn and M. Violanti, "Communication Abilities and Individual Achievement in Organizations." *Management Communication Quarterly*, 1993, 181–208; and D. Hellriegel et. al. *Organizational Behavior*, 8th ed. (Cincinnati, Ohio: South-Western College Publishing, 1998).

Finally, *lack of trust and openness* is as much a cause as it is a result of ineffective interpersonal communication. Assertive communication based on sharing authentic feelings and beliefs is the basis of building trust and openness in interpersonal relating.

### Johari's Window

Understanding and obtaining as much information as possible about others and ourselves is a major step toward effectively communicating in professional and personal relationships. Being unaware of important information about individuals in a team or about oneself can prevent trust and therefore collaboration. The Johari window, illustrated in Figure 6–4, is an analytic method that individuals and teams can use to identify information that is available and known or unknown by all relevant parties.[11]

Figure 6–4 shows how information about someone is presented in two dimensions: across the horizontal axis (1) information is known and unknown by A (i.e., a person, or oneself); down the vertical axis (2) information is known and unknown by B (others). When we combine these cells, we have four possibilities of communication in a team or between/among individuals:

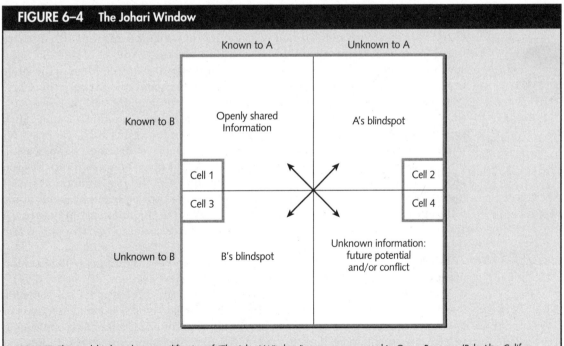

**FIGURE 6–4    The Johari Window**

Known to A | Unknown to A

Known to B — Openly shared Information | A's blindspot

Cell 1 | Cell 2

Cell 3 | Cell 4

Unknown to B — B's blindspot | Unknown information: future potential and/or conflict

**SOURCE:** This model is based on a modification of "The Johari Window," a concept presented in *Group Processes* (Palo Alto, Calif.: National Press Books, 1970).

1.  *Openly shared information:* information known to A (self) and B (others). This is the desired situation for trust and open dialogue to occur.

2.  *A's (self's) blind spot:* information unknown to or concealed from A (self) but known to B (others). This information could be attitudes and perceptions as well as data.

3.  *B's (other's) blind spot:* information known by A (self) but unknown by or concealed from others.

4.  *Unknown information:* information unknown to A (self) and B (others). This situation has potential for conflict as well as for stagnation. Knowing that we do not know is a key element for moving out of this situation.

Figure 6–4 illustrates how blind spots can knowingly or unknowingly lead to lack of trust and openness. Ideally, two or more individuals would strive to be in cell 1, where information is openly shared between self and others. In this situation there are no hidden agendas or concealed information. One person is not "setting up" or excluding others, intentionally or unintentionally.

In theory, openness leads to trust, which in turn can enhance constructive working relationships and result in higher productivity. The opposite, cell 4, is to be avoided or at least corrected; that is, when neither A nor B shares a common base of information about a problem, opportunity, or each other, there is potential for conflict. Cell 2 shows A's blind spot; that is, B knows information that A does not know; A is therefore uninformed. Correcting this situation suggests that B share information to increase openness, trust, and productivity. And, of course, B's blind spot, cell 3, indicates that A knows more than B about a subject. Moving the situation to cell 1 increases the likelihood of creating trust and openness.

It should be noted, however, that some situations actually call for not openly sharing all information with all people in an organization at a particular time. Such situations may be justified under the following conditions: (1) B has betrayed A's trust in the recent past and there may be reason to believe this could happen again if the relationship has not been renewed ; (2) A and B are in a temporary or even legitimate adversarial or competitive relationship; (3) the organization's culture punishes or does not reward openness; or (4) status, power, or other professional differences legitimately characterize and differentiate the relationship between A and B. Judgment (discernment) is required in the decision to openly express and self-disclose.[12]

Johari's window is a tool that individuals, dyads, and teams can use to discuss informational needs and to problem solve. In effect, Johari's window can be used as an opportunity to discuss and apply most of the concepts in this chapter, such as the following: (1) the barriers preventing information exchange between self and others or between two specific parties or groups; (2) the communication methods applying to two parties, or self and others, to bridge gaps that create and sustain blind spots; (3) the stereotypes and other perceptual biases preventing open communication in any of these situations in Figure 6–4; and (4) the methods for opening new ideas and channels of communicating if information is unknown to all individuals in a team or group, as in cell 4.

## EFFECTIVE INTERPERSONAL COMMUNICATION SKILLS

In this section, we extend our presentation of major methods for communicating effectively by addressing specific strategies, active and reflective listening skills, and giving and receiving feedback. These techniques are based on assertive attitudes and behaviors and seek to prevent many of the barriers and roadblocks identified earlier.

Classic strategies for effective interpersonal communication include the following:

- Understand your intent, goal, and expectations. What exactly do you expect and want to achieve from this exchange?

- Understand with whom you are communicating. What are the other person's background, expectations, feelings about the subject matter? About you?

- Examine the environment and organizational climate. Are the physical and political climate and time, space, and setting conducive for the exchange?

- Practice the message before sending it. Listen to yourself on tape or video. Evaluate the message objectively. Listen for your tone. Is the message assertive, submissive, understandable?

- Ensure that organizational systems (e.g., reward systems) support and do not detract from communication efforts.

- Check with the receiver for understanding your message. Ask for clarity checks. Clarify words and meanings if necessary.

- Ask for verification. If you desire a specific outcome, ask if that outcome is possible. If not, start over.

These general strategies acknowledge the importance of the sender/receiver model of communicating that we presented early in the chapter. As a sender, you are checking your assumptions, perceptions, accuracy of intent, and nonverbal means of communication before you engage your receiver. You are also checking your knowledge and feelings about the receiver.

Understanding the effect that personality (from Chapter 2) has on communications in organizations can enable you to create strategies for dealing with people in general and leaders in particular. A field study of registered nurses and their supervisors specified certain variables that relate to attributions in leader-follower communications. The study found that the leader's perceptions were related to the quality of leader-follower transactions.[13] The researchers compared four attributes that they felt related to leader-follower exchanges: leader-follower attitude similarity (i.e., the more similar the attitudes, the higher the quality of leader-follower communication exchanges); follower introversion/extroversion (i.e., extroverts were more likely to seek out interaction with leaders); follower locus of control (i.e., internals may attempt to exert more influence over leaders than externals); and follower growth-need strength (i.e., individuals with high growth need may be more willing to take on extra challenges when they see the activities as leading to desired outcomes or rewards). Attitude has the strongest correlation to leader-follower exchanges. Follower extroversion is second in its effect on leader-follower transactions. That is, followers who are perceived by leaders as extroverts and who share similar attitudes with leaders tend to interact more and have higher-quality communications with leaders. The point here is that personality and perceptions play an important role in interpersonal communications.

### Active and Reflective Listening

The idea that there is more power in talking than listening is not always true. Active and reflective listening (illustrated in Figure 6–5) enables receivers to more

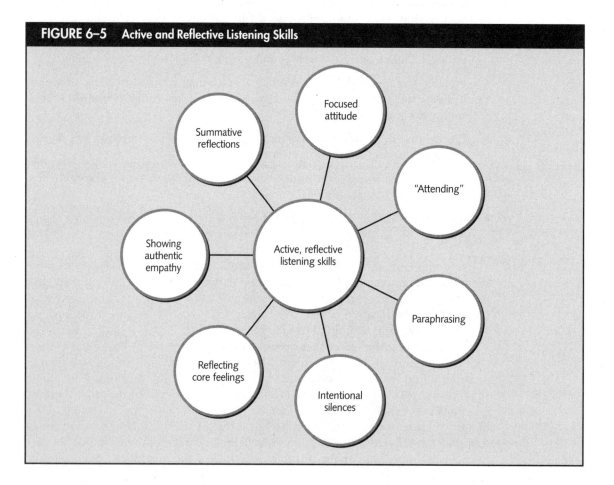

**FIGURE 6–5    Active and Reflective Listening Skills**

accurately understand a sender. All manner of business activities are enhanced by active and reflective listening, including effectively initiating and managing large accounts in sales; participating in or running customer focus groups to identify buying and source needs, and identifying and monitoring continuous process and quality improvements with fellow employees and customers.

Active and reflective listening begins by focusing one's attitude and attention on the sender and by being empathetic to the sender's intended but perhaps not explicitly expressed meaning. Since a person's meaning is found not only in the spoken word, reflective listening attempts to understand the full verbal and non-verbal, cognitive, and emotional—sometimes hidden—levels of meaning in the sender's message.

A focused attitude requires having a desire to understand the message. One must intentionally strive to understand and then "reflect back" both the sender's implicit message and her explicit message. To reflect back a sender's meaning involves the receiver providing a "mirror" for the sender. This ensures that the sender understands her own message and meaning. In other words, this is a chance for the sender to verify and, if necessary, clarify the message.

The basic skills of active and reflective listening include, as Figure 6–5 shows, "attending," paraphrasing, keeping eye contact, maintaining intentional silences, showing empathy, reflecting core feelings and meanings, and clarifying and providing summative (additive or cumulative) reflections.

*"Attending"* involves following the speaker attentively and authentically using, when appropriate, such phrases as "uh-huh," "I see," "yes, OK." Attending involves both verbal and nonverbal involvement.

*Paraphrasing* the sender is done mainly to ensure that the receiver understands the sender's meaning. Paraphrasing requires skill in being precise and in choosing words and phrases that carry the essential or core meaning of the sender's message. The reflective listener is reflecting back the sender's own meanings to clarify the sender's expressed meaning. As with attending, paraphrasing must focus on words and phrases that carry essential but unexpressed meaning. Receivers must authentically show that they are connecting with the sender as well as understanding him or her.

*Using intentional silences* gives senders time and space to hear and feel themselves. They can sort out confusions in their thinking without time or other situational pressures. Intentional silence also gives the listener time to understand and follow the sender's message. Silences must be felt as essential and not create tension for the speaker. Maintaining eye contact and showing interest are necessary and appropriate.

*Reflecting core feelings* and meaning empathetically is also part of the paraphrasing skill, only here the receiver is going beyond literal words and phrases to reach (without overextending) and assist the sender in expressing the intended core meaning. This requires skillful listening. For example, a speaker may say, "I'm always running in a thousand directions and getting nowhere fast." A listener might reflect back, if appropriate in that situation, "You feel frustrated and unfocused because you see no results from your efforts?" The listener can quickly tell if he has overextended or missed the core feeling or meaning of the speaker by the speaker's reaction. The speaker may deny the reflection or say "no, that's not it at all." Sometimes, the reflected meaning may be accurate but not acceptable for the speaker at the time. Again, the listener's goal is not to prove how skillful he is as a listener but to enable the speaker to hear, understand, and begin to solve the problem. If the speaker continues to express and develop the meaning and message, the reflective listening skills are working.

It is important to note that reflecting back core meanings and feelings by showing *authentic empathy* in a caring manner is a process that starts at the beginning of (or before) the discussion and continues throughout. Therefore, the listener must keep in mind the "thread" of the meanings in the context of the entire dialogue. The listener must not derail or distract the sender's train of thought and expression until the emotion and content of the message have been delivered, heard, and accepted by the sender.

Finally, *summative reflections* are offered by the listener near, or at the end of, the dialogue. These are reflections that try to identify the main themes, concerns, feelings, and message of the speaker. The purpose is to reflect back information that may have been unclear and unspoken at the beginning of the dialogue. This information can serve as a basis for problem solving. For example, the listener may reflect back a following summative set of comments, "So you are feeling angry with your supervisor because she has not fully informed you of her reasons for your demotion. You are considering quitting but would like to express your feelings to your supervisor constructively before taking any immediate action." If the sender agrees with, or adds to, that message and expresses relief or the need to start problem solving, the summative comments were effective.

### Giving and Receiving Feedback

Another major interpersonal communication skill is *feedback*. Giving and receiving feedback effectively involves using the principles of communication that we have just discussed. Since communication should be a two-way process, our discussion here takes on added importance because we need guidelines for keeping the exchange two-way. Major problems arise in the workplace when individuals assume that giving and receiving feedback is a quick-fix form of communication that can be done in the hallway. Of course, many informational and data exchanges can be made quickly; however, depending on the nature of the information, who is involved, and what the consequences will be, it is best to treat most feedback as important.

Guidelines for giving feedback include the following:

- Before offering feedback, understand your motivation. Are your reasons clear and justifiable to the recipient? Is more clarification or information needed?

- Examine your frame of mind, disposition, and timing. Being angry, tired, or overwhelmed can interfere with the process and result. Make sure that your timing is appropriate. Not allowing adequate time can be a problem; giving feedback during a stressful event can be counterproductive.

- Ensure that your feedback is intended to help the recipient.

- Give your feedback directly to the recipient with real feeling; base it on a foundation of trust you have established between yourself and the receiver.

- Make your feedback descriptive rather than evaluative. In other words, "should," "must," and "ought to" can be replaced with precise, less judgment-laden language.

- Be specific rather than general; use clear and recent examples.

- Give your feedback at a time when the receiver appears to be ready to accept it.

- When appropriate, check the intended feedback with others in the group to be sure they support its validity. Make sure that you are not merely transmitting rumor and gossip.

- Include only those areas that the receiver would be expected to have control over.

- Do not talk about more than the receiver can handle. Information overload is not helpful.[14]

These guidelines can serve as a useful checklist, whether you are a leader or a follower. Your goal in giving feedback must be to help the receiver, your work group, and your organization meet the stated goals.

We have all been in the position of receiving feedback and no doubt will be in this position in the future. It is no exaggeration to say that how we receive feedback can affect our standing in an organization, work group, and career. Think about the following guidelines carefully and practice them when you can.

- Make a sincere effort not to be defensive. You can accomplish this by listening as a third-party observer, that is, by making your attitude that of a neutral, objective, uninvolved bystander. Your aim should be to hear and understand before you react or evaluate.

- If you are having difficulty understanding what the sender is trying to tell you and the sender is unable to provide clarifying examples, seek and gather examples from informed others.

- To be sure that you understand, briefly summarize what you believe the sender is saying. Reflective listening skills, discussed earlier, can help you as the recipient of feedback.

- Share your feelings about the specific behaviors at issue. This enables you to validate your information, feelings, and understanding of the subject.

- Remember that you have the right to evaluate what you hear, to decide what you believe about the feedback, and to decide in what respect, if any, you feel it is personally and professionally worth the effort to change.[15]

Note that it is also useful for the sender to review these guidelines before offering feedback. Since giving feedback usually requires some action on the part of the receiver, the sender should understand the rights and needs the receiver has in formulating her response.

## COMMUNICATION PROCESSES IN ORGANIZATIONS

The preceding principles of interpersonal communication apply for the most part to exchanges between two individuals; when we add groups, multiple roles, technology, the goals of superiors, and structure and authority to the process, communication becomes more complicated. The changing marketplace demands that organizations communicate faster, more flexibly, and in more focused ways so the communication process must be continually examined. Also, since organizations are increasingly forming and reinforcing strategic alliances and networked partnerships, it is important for organizational members to effectively communicate with external stakeholders, including current competitors who may become future partners.

We begin by posing key questions that leaders and followers can ask from an information-gathering perspective. We then distinguish among five basic formal and informal communication networks that facilitate information flows.

### Key Communication Questions

The following questions can alert organization managers and members to a range of issues regarding the effectiveness of their information and communication exchanges:

- What information do I need to perform and complete my work successfully? What information is routine (programmed) and what is critical (unprogrammed) to my work and to the organization's work?

- What are the sources of the information I receive and transmit? What am I expected to do with the information I receive and process?

- Where am I in the configuration and structure of information flow? From whom do I get information? To whom do I give?

- How fast and in what form must the information be interpreted and transmitted? Does the organization structure and technology help or hinder this process?

- What actions and results are expected of me relative to the information I receive and transmit? What effect does the information I handle have on the final product or service of the organization?

Answers to these questions provide a wide range of clues regarding the effectiveness or inadequacy of the organization's structure, the employee's roles and responsibilities, available technologies, and the quality and forms of communication used to accomplish the work. Much of this text can be used to address these questions. For our purposes here, we focus these questions on the roles that information and communication play regarding the appropriate forms of communication that can be used; the direction of information through the organization (e.g. wheel, circle, or all channel); the nature of information and communication (formal versus informal); and the implications of electronic communication.

### High-Tech and High-Touch Communication

Earlier we discussed the different characteristics of communication, that is, the medium, information richness, and data capacity. Recall Table 6–1: the more rich, ambiguous, and nonroutine the information, the more intense the medium needed. Thus, "high-touch" interactions are required to interpret information that, for example, contains confidential strategic plans. Ambiguous situations that require more flexibility are also indicative of the need for high-touch interactions. There is also the following paradox: "The more dispersed a work group, the more important it is to meet face to face."[16]

High-tech informational exchanges will continue to increase in the twenty-first century. Everyone will be using e-mail, voice mail, cellular phones, the Internet, group software, faxes, teleconferencing, and wireless systems not yet invented. These electronic forms of communication speed the rate at which information is transmitted and connect users up, down, across, inside, and outside organizational boundaries as never before. Such high-tech forms of communication and information sharing are increasingly in use as timed competition and outsourced organizational resources (i.e., bought, rented, or leased from other sources)are emphasized. The rate at which Hewlett-Packard generates information today will be the norm for the organization of tomorrow. "Every month Hewlett-Packard's 97,000 employees exchange 20 million e-mail messages (and 70,000 more outside the company); nearly 3 trillion characters of data, such as engineering specifications; and execute more than a quarter of a million electronic transactions with customers and suppliers."[17]

With ever larger volumes of information transmitted electronically, it has become increasingly important for employees to be able to differentiate the types of information they receive and to correctly decide the appropriateness of the communication form, with whom the message should be shared, and the occasion on which it should be transmitted. Being able to manage the flow, the appropriateness, the quantity, and the cost of information is a necessary part of the communication structure in and between organizations.

### Wheel, Y, Chain, Circle, or All Channel?

Managers and work groups need to know how to organize people to communicate information effectively in teams, groups, and work units. How best to organize people to exchange information, to accomplish the work and solve the problems depends on a number of variables: the nature of the work, the resources available, the expertise needed, and so on. Table 6–3 compares five network configurations for organizing and facilitating communication. In practice, many teams and groups use all of these configurations. However, one or two of these configurations is probably sufficient for the information exchange needs in any given group. These configurations allow groups to identify bottlenecks, barriers, and opportunities for facilitating communication.

As Table 6–3 illustrates, the **all-channel network** enhances participative involvement and cross-functional information flow more than do the other models. However, the speed of information exchange is variable. Leadership and centralization (i.e., the degree of single-person responsibility in decision making) are not important factors here. Note also that saturation (the point when an equal amount of information goes to all members) is high in the all-channel network, and information overload can thus be a potential downside in this configuration.

More organizations are using this model to reconfigure themselves, with cross-functional teams and decentralized restructurings the notable results. Total quality management initiatives generally encourage an all-channel communication network, particularly with tasks that require integration among different levels of expertise across the organization. Moreover, teleconferencing technologies also encourage the all-channel communication network.

**TABLE 6–3    Communication Network Configurations**

| | Wheel | Y | Chain | Circle | All-Channel |
|---|---|---|---|---|---|
| **Characteristics of Information Exchange** | | | | | |
| Speed | Fast | Slow | Slow | Slow | Fast-Slow |
| Accuracy* | Good | Fair | Fair | Poor | Good |
| Saturation | Low | Low | Moderate | High | High |
| **Responses of Members** | | | | | |
| Overall satisfaction | Low | Low | Low | High | High |
| Leadership emergence | Yes | Yes | Yes | No | No |
| Centralization | Yes | Yes | Moderate | No | No |

SOURCE: Based on A. Bavelas, "Communication Patterns in Task-Oriented Groups," *Journal of Acoustical Society of America* 22, 1950, 725–730.

*These accuracy estimates can change depending on the nature and complexity of the task.

Companies that are increasingly "wired" through a host of technologies resemble a dispersed electronic all-channel configuration.

> *Businesses around the world will spend three and a quarter billion dollars this year to buy 'intelligent hubs,' hardware-and-software devices that sit at the center of computer networks. . . . Networks connect people to people and people to data. They allow information that once flowed through hierarchies—from me up to my boss and then hers, then down to your boss and to you—to pass directly between us. . . . In a wired world, fundamental management jobs such as planning, budgeting, and supervising must be done differently. Tools like e-mail, teleconferencing, and groupware let people work together despite distance and time, almost regardless of departmental or corporate boundaries, which networks fuzz up or even obliterate.*[18]

On the other hand, the all-channel network may not be the most desirable form of organizing group communications if focused leadership, a single decision-making person, and speed are major criteria in the dissemination and use of information. (In certain military situations where a final decision checkpoint is required, for example, an all-channel form may not be effective.) The wheel may then be a more desirable form. Again, the point here is to decide which form is most appropriate given the nature of the task, the people and work unit involved, the technologies available, the desired results, and the time and resources at stake.

### Communication in the Informal Organization

Informal organizational networks (*friendship circles, grapevines, rumor mills*) and emergent relationships are major factors in how and with whom information is discovered, passed on, and finally acted upon, and they will continue to play this role.[19] Because formal structures and decision making are often slow, ineffective, and inefficient in transmitting critical information, informal social linkages and networks emerge. These linkages are not identified on a formal chart. Asking people how and with whom they talk to obtain answers to their questions is one method for constructing a grapevine and an informal social network. *Sociograms* were an early method used to identify frequent communication patterns and linkages among members and groups in organizations and are still used for this purpose. Sociograms are constructed by drawing circles around individuals and groups and then drawing arrows pointing to and from these parties to indicate whom they communicate with and who communicates with them and how frequently.[20]

Informal networks and linkages not only speed up and facilitate critical decision making within and between organizations, but also offer other social functions. They provide a release for tension and stress; convey a sense of belonging, security, recognition, and interaction; and so on. In the downside of information communication networks, dysfunctional group norms and rumor mills can be created and sustained; loyalties can begin to conflict with the larger, official organization; and coalition building can occur that resists planned organizational changes.

With the use of electronic communications, especially with the Internet, informal communications and linkages are increasing. Organizations must learn to accommodate and institutionalize the effective aspects of informal communicating while coping with and managing the dysfunctional elements. Professionals should be aware of the boundaries between their private and public spaces in informal communications, especially in their use of e-mails and where they "surf" on the Web. Many employers can and do track employees' use of the Internet. The boundaries between formal and informal spaces between employees are sometimes a blurred area. However, since computers and software are the property of the company, care and discretion should be taken as to the language and content of e-mails, especially since such messages are usually stored.

## Electronic Communication

Regardless of what form of organizational arrangement management or a work-group chooses to implement, electronic networking appears to be an evolutionary fact in most companies. Benefits of "wired" companies include the savings in time and money that accrue across geographic locations; easy access and short circuits that cut through and integrate functional department boundaries; and accessing markets that without the bureaucratic filtering process, can be more easily seen and penetrated.[21]

Electronic communication are disrupting old ways of managing business. Formerly closed bureaucracies and command and control systems are being pressured to open up. It is important for leaders and followers to remain focused on the aim of all communication: coordinated action that achieves the organization's goals and mission. The following guidelines are offered to people either entering or already participating in the wired environments of companies today:

- *Don't fight the net.* Information networks are here. Avoiding or escaping the use of increased speeds in information exchange causes reactions and more delays.

- *Create a climate of trust.* Networks open up information and force the sharing of resources across functions. Trust becomes a key ingredient for doing business inside firms.

- *Manage people, not work.* With information networks, less synergism of work content is needed, and more attention can be given to overall performance and careers. Professionalism and commitment in employees replaces direct supervisory controls.

- *Press the flesh.* Paradoxically, people need more, not less, face-to-face interaction in electronic communication environments.

- *Build and support teams.* Teams do more of the "real work" of the entire enterprise in integrated, wired companies. Teams must therefore be trained, rewarded, and supported in their work.

- *Do the things leaders do.* Work in wired companies also emphasizes the need for leadership—at all levels. A study of more than 170 teams of knowledge workers found that teams "are most successful in an environment where decisions spring from rigorous evaluation of costs and benefits, corporate strategy is firmly laid out, and the company has a clear view of its market. All [of this] depends on leaders."[22]

Managing and working in wired environments can also create problems. Leading is often more difficult in environments with diffused accountability. Following up on dispersed commitments requires time, energy, and money. Information overload confuses and overwhelms individuals and teams. Around-the-clock information flow can lead to emotional and physical stress and burnout, and without clear strategic objectives, decisions and outcomes can become chaotic.

It is clear that with new information technologies, individuals and teams must assume more responsibility for their work, support, and training needs. Interpersonal (high-touch) and high-tech skills will be emphasized in future work. Learning environments and cultures that encourage and facilitate change are required. Stephen Rutherford, human resource analysis manager at Federal Express, has made integrating new information technologies a priority. Under his leadership, Federal Express has implemented a Survey-Feedback-Action (SFA) process that uses climate surveys, subordinate reviews of management, and workplace problem-solving initiatives. Rutherford states, "You truly have to understand your organization, its values, strategies, and philosophy. And you have to have your own program for effectiveness. But even more important, you have to surround yourself with the best staff you can find and let them take you to places you've never been."[23]

## CROSS-CULTURAL COMMUNICATION APPROACHES

"Cross-cultural communication occurs when a person from one culture sends a message to a person from another culture. Cross-cultural miscommunication occurs when the person from the second culture does not receive the sender's intended message. The greater the differences between the sender's and the receiver's cultures, the greater the chances for cross-cultural miscommunication."[24]

To communicate effectively with culturally diverse individuals and groups, you must have an understanding of your own culture and then of the other culture's assumptions and differences. Answering the following questions can assist you in preparing to communicate more effectively in multicultural environments:

- What must I know about the social and business customs of country X?

- What skills do I need to be effective as a negotiator in country Y?

- What prejudices and stereotypes do I have about the people in country Z?

- How will these influence my interaction?[25]

Cultures have what Edward Hall has called a "silent language."[26] This language includes the language of time, space, things, and contracts. The *language of time* is related to present, past, and future orientations. Past-oriented cultures evaluate

## THE CHANGING WORKPLACE

### Ethical Questions

Louise Johnson is a sales professional at a large high-tech computer manufacturing firm. She is on the road a lot and gives as much time to the company as to her personal life. When she is in the office on Fridays, she catches up on correspondence with customers and other company sites across the country. At the same time, she takes the occasion to e-mail her friends and set up meeting times and places on the weekend. She also purchases essential items such as home-delivered groceries on the Internet. On one occasion the week before, she had a long on-line argument with the person she was dating. She and her friend had used some highly charged language and content in their lengthy cyber dispute.

She has been with the firm for a year and has few friends in what is mostly a male-dominated environment—especially in sales. She met the president of the company only once and has heard about his conservative views and controlling personality. The general manager to whom she reported is a friend of the president and also shares a conservative view of how the internal operation should be run.

On Monday morning, she stopped in the office to check some e-mails before heading to the airport. A flashing e-mail on her screen caught her attention: "SEE ME, NOW," the message from the general manager stated. She didn't have much time at this point, so she took her suitcase with her to his office. He opened the door, said in a low somber tone, "Have a seat, Louise. We have a problem." He proceeded to inform her that her and other employees' e-mails in the facility had been randomly "screened" on instruction by his assistant. She and two other employees had, he told her, been using "company time and property" for very personal matters. One of her e-mails in particular caught his attention. He handed her a printout of the argument. Enraged, Louise blurted out, "You have no right to read my personal correspondence!" He retorted, "Your correspondence is on company property and time. And I'd say, you have some explaining to do."

### Questions

1. What would you do and say at this point if you were Louise?

2. What, if any, are the ethical issues in this scenario?

3. Advise Louise on what she might do and say.

new policies, change, and innovation in terms of their fit with customs and tradition. China and the Middle East are examples of past-oriented cultures. American culture is generally present and future oriented. Of course, not all people in these cultures share the same time orientations. We are speaking about the context of the culture. For Hall, cultural context "directs the organization of the psyche, which in turn has a profound effect upon the ways people look at things, behave politically, make decisions, order priorities, organize their likes...how they think."[27] Relating to people with past-oriented time perspectives requires a knowledge of their historical beliefs and values and of how to properly demonstrate respect for these beliefs and values.

The meaning and use of space is the subject of proxemics. *Proxemics*, which is the study of the nature and effect of the spatial separation individuals naturally maintain, is an integral part of nonverbal communication. Cultures value and treat public and private space differently. As stated earlier, Latin Americans and Middle Easterners generally tolerate smaller space separation in public, both with acquaintances and with strangers, than do Americans, who value privacy and therefore larger space separations.

The silent language of things can speak loudly. Status symbols such as business cards and a person's clothing, watch, and shoes are very important and can signal credibility for a person doing business in Japan, China, and other Asian countries. In the United States, although things are important, informality is usually more the norm.

The silent language of contracts is also important in business communications. In the United States, written contracts are final agreements that are long standing and legally binding. This is not so, for example, in China where a contract may simply be the beginning of negotiations and is expected to be changed and modified. Understanding the underlying cultural values and unspoken context is a first step in doing business in a global and cross-cultural environment: culture first, business second.

### *High-Context/Low-Context Cultural Communications*

Edward Hall also distinguishes between high- and low-context cultures.[28] *Context* here refers to how communication and negotiations vary according to the context of the culture. High-context cultures include China, Japan, Korea, Vietnam, Arab countries, Greece, and Spain. Low-context countries include Germany, Switzerland, Scandinavian and North American countries, England, and Italy. Figure 6–6 illustrates the differences between high- and low-context cultures; for example, high-context cultures establish social trust before getting down to business. High-context cultures also value personal relations and goodwill before expertise and performance. They base contracts on trust, not on specific, legally written contracts, and negotiate slowly and ceremoniously, not quickly and efficiently. These characteristics contrast to those of low-context cultures. It is easy to see that these differences can create conflict and how understanding and respecting them can facilitate cooperation.

Excerpts from a study of U.S. corporate expatriates returning from China illustrates differences in the dimensions of silent language and how a high-context culture compares to the low-context U.S. culture:

> *Communication difficulties were observed and attributed in large part to language barriers . . . the role and structure of organizations in China, effects of the Communist Party system in the workplace, and cultural differences in relating. These recurring themes are also exemplified in the following survey excerpts: "Generally there exists no level of organizational hierarchy regarding communication flow. A factory employee walks into a general manager's office without the knowledge of his immediate supervisor." Another respondent said, "Cross-communication within and between divisions and departments is poor; I'm not sure organizational divisions really exist." Meetings were noted as too frequent and often political in*

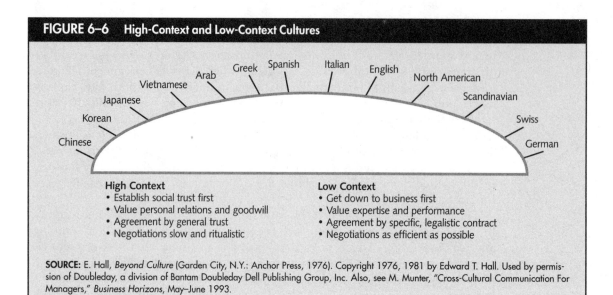

**FIGURE 6–6**   High-Context and Low-Context Cultures

Chinese, Korean, Japanese, Vietnamese, Arab, Greek, Spanish, Italian, English, North American, Scandinavian, Swiss, German

**High Context**
- Establish social trust first
- Value personal relations and goodwill
- Agreement by general trust
- Negotiations slow and ritualistic

**Low Context**
- Get down to business first
- Value expertise and performance
- Agreement by specific, legalistic contract
- Negotiations as efficient as possible

**SOURCE:** E. Hall, *Beyond Culture* (Garden City, N.Y.: Anchor Press, 1976). Copyright 1976, 1981 by Edward T. Hall. Used by permission of Doubleday, a division of Bantam Doubleday Dell Publishing Group, Inc. Also, see M. Munter, "Cross-Cultural Communication For Managers," *Business Horizons*, May–June 1993.

nature; for example, this quote reflects general consensus in the survey: "There are too many weekly meetings, and communication usually takes the form of political as well as technical concerns. There are two groups of employees: the Communist [elite] and the non-Communist [less-privileged]." Several respondents expressed frustration over their not being kept informed by the Chinese: "We were not kept as informed as we would have liked. They would leave the meetings they had with political groups and that was that." The following observations that reflected communication differences were repeatedly made: the Chinese were sensitive to non-verbal communications; they tend to speak subtly, leaving many messages to interpretation; they engaged in a lot of "small talk, gossip," and "Chinese seem to argue constantly in very high tones, irrespective of position." Several respondents told us that their lack of preparation for understanding the interaction between China's political and work situations left them initially disadvantaged in their jobs. Because so many organizations in China are part of the governmental system, overlap between public and private interests occurs in the workplace. This was a reality to which respondents found it difficult to adjust.[29]

## COMMUNICATION AND ETHICS: GUIDELINES FOR MANAGERS

Effective communication is built and sustained on the trust between managers and employees. "Doing what is right" and having employees follow this principle also requires initiating and sustaining mutually trusting relationships. Open and trusting communication between managers and employees enables the former to learn about tensions and pressures that can lead to unethical behavior. Setting ethical standards is based on knowing and communicating relevant, moral principles of behavior. Managers who wish to communicate ethically in organizations would do well to consider this checklist:

- Set and communicate high standards in public and private. Do not tolerate double standards.

- Act quickly and firmly when the standards are violated.

- Communicate with openness and candor to all members. Expect and give honest, direct feedback.

- Keep in touch with employees. Remember that communication happens all the time in organizations.

- Listen to the spoken and silent concerns of employees. Show concern.

- Take responsible, swift action to correct any illegal or immoral activities in the workplace.

- Survey employees on their concerns and issues in the work environment.

- Follow up with action steps to correct problems discovered through legitimate feedback.

- Design and implement peer reviews of supervisory, management, and employee positions. Use the results as a basis to communicate openly with members and to create an open organizational culture.

- Educate and train people on other cultures' communication practices.

- Educate and reward effective multicultural communication.[30]

Following these recommendations can create opportunities for developing a climate of honest, straightforward, and open communication and dialogue in which moral behavior can be seen, modeled, and reinforced.

## CONCLUDING COMMENTS

Communication is the vehicle through which we negotiate, resolve conflicts, and improve productivity. It is how we express our thinking, problems, decisions, and our understanding of others and ourselves. It is how a sender of a message seeks to achieve a common understanding with a receiver. It also is the vehicle professionals must use to transmit large amounts of increasingly more complex information to stakeholders inside and outside the organization.

Communication involves sending and receiving information (messages) through symbols—that is, words and nonverbal cues. The message is filtered

## THE CHANGING WORKPLACE

### You're The Change Consultant

"You're going to enjoy working in China," Alice said to Lou on his last day in the Chicago office. "Remember, you're not going to be in Beijing...what is the name of that city?" Lou laughed nervously but was beginning to wonder how he was going to adjust. He had been to Europe only on assignments and wasn't sure what to expect. He was from New York City and was used to a fast-paced, fast-talking, thinking, acting lifestyle. His friends often teased him about not only talking for them, but also helping them do their thinking. He was known in the company as an aggressive go-getter who spoke his mind whenever to whomever. He took his assignment to show the president he was a risk taker (nobody else had volunteered). If he succeeds in negotiating only a few government contracts with the help of a local partner, he will have succeeded.

Turning back to Alice, he replied, "Look, I don't plan on being there very long. Once you hear about the size of my first contract from Bill (the president), you'll be asking for my opinions on international affairs!"

### Questions

1. What problems, including communication problems, is Lou likely to encounter on this assignment?

2. What coaching would you offer Bill to prepare him for this assignment? (Refer to this chapter for references.)

through the perceptual screens of both sender and receiver; such screens certainly slant and can even alter the meaning of the communication. Perceptual screens are conditioned not only by immediate, situational variables but also by one's culture, personal system (self-concepts, personality factors, moods, esteem), and organizational context. Since messages can carry emotional and mixed meanings and hidden and ambiguous meanings, choosing an appropriate medium for a message is an essential part of communication. Mediums include the fax, e-mail, the telephone, face-to-face communication, and the written report.

Communication styles and strategies were discussed. Aggressive (fighting) and submissive (fleeing) behaviors are the source of most barriers to interpersonal communication. Assertive communication behaviors were described as options to the fight-or-flight syndrome.

The role of information technology was emphasized as playing an increasingly important role in organizational communication. High-tech as well as high-touch informational exchanges were described. Ideas on how best to organize people to exchange information, to accomplish work, and to solve problems also were presented by evaluating the all-channel configuration as a communication channel. Guidelines for determining how to organize and facilitate communication were presented.

Cross-cultural communication differences and negotiation strategies were described through the perspectives of high- and low-context cultures. Finally, ethical considerations—that is, the motives and motivation in communicating—were summarized. A list of strategic questions to use when entering new alliances and partnerships to use was also presented.

## SCENARIO AND EXERCISES: COMMUNICATION CHALLENGES

*Step 1*: Read the following scenario and list the major issues and opportunities you observe.

Donna, 29, is from Mountain View in Silicon Valley (California). She is a new hire to this $2 billion global manufacturing firm located in the Midwest. She is an E-business specialist who has five years of experience in a consulting firm that automates business processes through intranets and extranets. She has assisted Fortune 500 firms in developing Web-based systems to streamline operations and connect suppliers, customers, and vendors. She is an extrovert, "Get-it-done-now" person who has a B.S. in computer science and marketing. She loves moving from project to project, eliminating unnecessary paper-heavy tasks. Her former employer noted that "she likes flattening organizations and authority structures." Her responsibility is to examine each of the major functions of the firm's headquarters by forming a core team "to help move operations into the New Economy" and to present a change plan for automating operations in one month. She will have to work with the following three people as a start.

Andrea, 25, is from Greece. She has a B.S. from a U.S. university. An information specialist, she is quiet and soft spoken, and very detail and results oriented. She works best alone and with small groups in which she can feel comfortable. She does not like change. She is excellent at her work, and her skills are very marketable. Hans, 43, is German and has been with the company as a finance professional for 10 years. He is an extrovert, also detail oriented but likes to know the "big picture" as well. He is a "by-the-book," rules-based person. He is also very logical and systematic in his work. His motto is "The best predictor of the future is past performance." He has built a loyal following in the company and enjoys being a leader and mentor. George is 58, has been with the company 15 years, is very energetic, does not like to think about retiring, and has difficulty using computers. He believes in change as long as it doesn't affect him. He also has difficulty working with some of the "newcomers" since, he has said, "some of them know more about technology than I do, but I know more about our business."

*Step 2*: Identify the communication and "people" challenges Donna faces in forming the team to carry out her task. Use chapter concepts.

*Step 3*: Write Donna brief memo offering your informed observations and advice regarding some ideas and insights she can expect to encounter with her three new team members.

*Step 4:* What should Donna do to proceed? (List your observations and advice.)

## REVIEW QUESTIONS

1. Describe the communication process between a sender and receiver. What are the four perceptual screens involved in sending a message?

2. Give an example of a recent conversation in which one of these perceptual screens blurred your intended message and prevented you from being understood.

3. Give an example of how you recently miscommunicated a message by using an inappropriate communication medium (for example sent an e-mail when you should have delivered the message in person or vice-versa). Explain why the medium you used was not effective.

4. Describe your predominant response mode on the fight-assertive-flight continuum. What (from whom) do you believe is the source of your most frequently used mode on this continuum?

5. Which of the roadblocks to effective communication most aggravates you when someone uses this barrier(s) in relating to you? Why? Which of these roadblocks do you most frequently use?

6. Briefly explain a situation in which you had a blind spot that hindered communicating within a work situation (using Johari's window). What happened? Was the blind spot discovered? If so how? If not, why not?

7. Give an example of how you would use active and reflective listening. What situation would be helped by these skills? Why?

8. Give an example of your effective use of giving feedback skills. Did you use any of the guidelines listed in this chapter? Did you do anything else effectively that is not listed here?

9. Which is more difficult for you, giving or receiving feedback? Explain. Discuss how skills and tips in this chapter can help you in these situations.

10. If you were placed in an international cultural setting somewhat unfamiliar to you and you were asked to join an all-channel multicultural team to complete an assignment, how would your knowledge of high- and low- context cultures assist you? What other communication practices would you want to be aware of?

11. Does gender play a difference in your daily communications? How? Do you believe that being sensitive to gender differences can make your interpersonal communication more effective? Explain.

12. How does ethics fit into the communication process in the workplace? Which of the guidelines offered in this chapter do you find relevant or helpful in your workplace for creating more effective, ethical communication between people?

# 7

# Leadership and Followership

---

After studying this chapter, you should be able to:

**1** Define *leadership* and *followership*.

**2** Identify differences between leaders and managers.

**3** Explain contemporary leadership competencies.

**4** Explain transformational leadership and strategic change.

**5** Describe traditional and modern leadership theories.

**6** Identify international dimensions of leadership.

**7** Identify effective leadership for managing cultural diversity.

**8** Describe ways to lead ethically.

---

## LEADERSHIP IN THE TWENTY-FIRST CENTURY

Leadership in the Information Age is changing. As speed, customer involvement, and innovation begin to drive business, leaders must lead or get out of the way. "The old model of technology was based on the mainframe; all intelligence was in the host computer. Similarly, the old model of leadership was focused in a single, powerful individual. Great leaders were often those with the biggest brain or brain/mouth combination . . . . In the Age of Networked Intelligence, leadership is internetworked. This approach to leadership is the antithesis of the old-style, brilliant-visionary, take-charge, rally-the-troops type . . . . Today, the leader is a collective, networked, virtual force with powers flowing from a jointly created and shared vision."[1]

Internetworked leadership includes six elements: "(1) Achieving internetworked leadership is your opportunity and responsibility, (2) Leadership in the new economy is leadership for learning, (3) Internetworked leadership is collective leadership, (4) Internetworked leadership can be digital, (5) Internetworked leadership is incomplete without the CEO and, (6) Personal use of the technology creates leaders."[2] Leaders do not have to be technologists to lead, but they will have to use electronic communications and understand how technology enhances business transactions to lead effectively.

*A Quick Story: Netscape*

The meteoric rise of the Mosaic Communications Corporation—later named Netscape—illustrates how internetworked leadership built and scaled a phenomenal new business on Internet time. Navigator, the company's browser, captured more than 60 percent of the market in less than two months after its release. "Despite a fierce battle with Microsoft, Netscape built Navigator's installed base to more than 38 million users, making it the world's most popular personal computer application."[3] Netscape earned $80 million in sales its first year and, more than $500 million after three years. (It took Microsoft 14 years to earn this amount). The four principles that characterized Netscape's quick rise to success follow: "(1) Create a compelling, living vision of products, technologies, and markets that is tightly linked to action. (2) Hire and acquire managerial experience, in addition to technical expertise. (3) Build the internal resources for a big company, while organizing like a small one. (4) Build external relationships to compensate for limited internal resources."[4] Netscape's leaders (Jim Barksdale and Marc Andreessen) succeeded in part because they were able to create a shared innovative and lucrative vision and strategy. They then collaboratively implemented their plan through a technically capable team.

In this chapter, we define leadership and its complement, followership. Current and past leadership approaches are presented. We start with contemporary perspectives of leadership, followed by earlier theories. Recent directions in leadership thinking include the topics of self-leaders, superleaders, transformational and charismatic leadership, servant-leadership, and leading culturally diverse workforces.

## LEADERSHIP DEFINED

**Leadership** is the ability to effectively use strategic competencies and influence to accomplish organizational goals. To be effective, leaders must enable their core team and followers in a desired direction, quickly. "Internet time" and the race for on-line presence and innovation have created a Darwinian race for survival of industry and company niches. CEOs, in particular, must lead with boldness, courage, and insight into the projected future of their organizations. At the same time, leaders are also responsible for setting the moral climate and culture of the organizations. Their strategies, policies, and decisions reflect the integrity and image of the organizations, which are also an integral part of their economic and social capital.

In a global, deregulated, and information-based environment, leaders cannot lead effectively without the cooperation and expertise of their managers, followers, and external constituencies For this reason, effective leadership is a partnership. Leaders face two major tasks: first, to develop and articulate exactly what the company aims to accomplish; and second, to create an environment where employees can determine what needs to be done and then carry out the work.

A recent global study by Andersen Consulting, "The Evolving Role of Executive Leadership," created a 14-dimension profile of the global future leader.[5] The key competencies of this profile present a leader who

- Thinks globally
- Anticipates opportunity
- Creates a shared vision
- Develops and empowers people
- Appreciates cultural diversity
- Builds teamwork and partnerships
- Shows technological savvy

- Encourages constructive challenge
- Ensures customer satisfaction
- Achieves a competitive advantage
- Demonstrates personal mastery
- Shares leadership
- Lives the values
- Embraces change

This study also asked leaders to rank the 14 leadership dimensions and an additional 82 subcharacteristics. The top three ranked dimensions included *self-confidence, vision,* and *personal excellence.* New attributes that emerged included these: (1) leaders view business from customers' perspectives and ensure that commitments to these perspectives are met; (2) leaders create effective teams; (3) leaders genuinely listen; (4) leaders inspire people to commit to the organization's vision; (5) leaders build alliances with other organizations, making decisions that reflect global considerations, and (6) leaders treat people with respect and dignity. As we show throughout this chapter, there is no one "best way," philosophy, set of dimensions, or style of leading. Effective leadership depends on the characteristics of the individual, on the context and contingencies of the environment and situations at hand, and on the team, followers, and managers.

## LEADERSHIP VERSUS MANAGEMENT:  ARE YOU READY FOR LEADERSHIP?

Is there a difference between organizational leadership and management? This is an important distinction since large scale successful change is 70 percent to 90 percent leadership and about 10 percent to 30 percent management.[6] Also, selecting, hiring, and training leaders versus managers requires an understanding of the differences between the two.[7] **Leaders** focus more on *enterprisewide, strategic, long-term, eventful, and value-added* roles and competencies. **Managers**, on the other hand, are concerned more with *implementation-oriented, routine, short- to mid-term predictable tasks, and technical detail.* Managers and followers certainly add value in their work, but at a hands-on level. Take the test on page 228 to determine your leadership readiness.

Kotter's comparison between leaders and managers illustrates four different dimensions.[8] Table 7–1 compares these dimensions: (1) agenda creation: *leaders* establish direction; *managers* plan and budget; (2) network development for agenda achievement: *leaders* align people; *managers* organize and staff; (3) execution: *leaders* motivate and inspire; *managers* control and problem solve; (4) outcomes: *leaders* produce often dramatic and useful change; *managers* produce predictable (on-time, within budget) ordered results that are expected of stakeholders. The following section defines followership and the relation of follower to leaders.

| TABLE 7–1    Kotter's Comparison of Leadership and Management | | |
|---|---|---|
| **Dimension** | **Leader** | **Manager** |
| Agenda creation | **Establish direction**<br>1. Develop future vision (often very distant)<br>2. Develop change strategies to achieve vision | **Plan and budget**<br>1. Develop detailed steps and and timetables for results<br>2. Allocate necessary resources |
| Network development for agenda achievement | **Align people**<br>1. Communicate directly by words and deeds to those whose cooperation is needed<br>2. Influence creation of coalition and teams that understand and accept vision and strategies | **Organize and staff**<br>1. Develop necessary planning, staffing, delegation structures<br>2. Provide policies and procedures for guidance and methods and systems for monitoring |
| Execution | **Motivate and inspire**<br>1. Energy to overcome barriers (e.g., political, resource, bureaucratic) to change by satisfying basic needs | **Control and problem solve**<br>1. Monitor results vs. plan in detail<br>2. Identify results and plan deviations and plan and organize to correct |
| Outcomes | **Tend to produce**<br>1. Change, often dramatic<br>2. Provide potential for very useful change (e.g., new products, etc.) | **Tend to produce**<br>1. Order and predictability<br>2. Key results expected by stakeholders (e.g., on time, within budget) |

SOURCE: Adapted with the permission of The Free Press, a Division of Simon & Schuster, Inc. from *A Force For Change: How Leadership Differs from Management* by John P. Kotter. Copyright 1990 by John P. Kotter, Inc.

## EFFECTIVE FOLLOWERSHIP DEFINED

**Leadership** is not achieved only by individuals and managers. In fact, without followers, leaders cannot lead. Effective followers are team players who partner with organization leaders to create the organization's vision and to implement goals and strategies. Effective followers have some similar characteristics to leaders, as Table 7–2 shows. A major difference between high-performance followers and leaders is their role perception and enactment.[9]

## THE CHANGING WORKPLACE

### Are You a Manager or a Leader?

**Exercise**: Answer T (true) or F (false) for each item. Then check the scoring key at the end with discussion questions.

T  F    1. I would rather carry out a well defined plan than create one.

T  F    2. I am more a hands-on, get-it-done person than a visionary.

T  F    3. I like to create the "big picture" and help carry out the plan.

T  F    4. I prefer *not* to get involved in the implementation of a plan once I help create it.

T  F    5. I find it easier to delegate than to do tasks.

T  F    6. I like to plan, delegate, and carry out tasks.

T  F    7. I would rather be given structured directions for an assignment than design an assignment.

T  F    8. I like to set meeting agendas and then take charge of meetings.

T  F    9. I like to set the agenda, run the meeting, and proceed to implement some detail work.

**Scoring**: If you answered *true* to questions 7, 2, 1, you prefer managerial roles. If you answered *true* to questions 3, 4, 5, and 8, you prefer leadership roles. If you answered *true* to questions 3, 6, and 9, you prefer managerial and leadership roles.

**Discussion**: After reading how you scored on the overall questionnaire, answer these questions:

1. After reflecting on how you answered these questions, what do you believe your preferred style is: leader, manager, some of both, more leader than manager, more manager than leader? Explain.

2. Is it possible for you to learn and assume leadership roles if you found you are more of a manager? Or is it possible for you to learn and assume managerial roles if you found you are more a leader? Explain your reasoning.

3. If you found you are a mix between manager and leader, how comfortable are you having to take one role over another when the situation requires? Explain.

*People who are effective in the follower role also have a vision to see both the forest and the trees, the social capacity to work well with others, the strength of character to flourish without heroic status, the moral and psychological balance to pursue personal and corporate goals at no cost to either, and above all, the desire to participate in a team effort for the accomplishment of some greater common purpose.[10] Successful followership characteristics include commitment to the organization's vision and goals; ability to self-manage; a sense of integrity and honesty; credibility, competence, and focus; versatility; work and task ownership; critical problem-solving skills; and the ability to be team players and energetic, empowered individuals.[11] Effective followers, then, are less the creators of the organizational vision and strategy and more the implementors of it.*

| TABLE 7–2    Effective Followership Competencies |
| --- |
| 1.   Ability to self-manage |
| 2.   Organizational commitment |
| 3.   Integrity, credibility, and honesty |
| 4.   Competence and focus |
| 5.   Versatility |
| 6.   Job and task ownership |
| 7.   Critical problem-solving skills |
| 8.   Team player |
| 9.   Energetic and empowered |

As effective self-managers, followers give a cost advantage to their organizations by eliminating the need for supervisory levels. They work as empowered, self-motivated coleaders who do not always wait to be told what to do. Effective followers are committed to organizational goals. However, they balance their personal needs with their loyalty. They are not "yes" people. High-performance followers have high standards in the areas of integrity and honesty. "Followers expect high consistency between what leaders say and what they do. Likewise, leaders expect agreement between followers' expressed values and values observed."[12] High-performance followers demonstrate competence and focus. They search for problems to solve, take initiative in enforcing quality and performance standards, and ensure that work is aligned with organizational goals. They also take ownership and responsibility for organizational tasks and their work. "Owning the territory . . . means knowing your job very well and taking pride in that expertise. It means working constantly to help your piece and fit into the larger puzzle."[13] Finally, effective followers are versatile and critical problem solvers. "Versatility involves being able to deal with ambiguity."[14] Followers are able to communicate effectively and keep information flowing. As critical problem solvers, high-performance followers seek to understand assumptions and causes of problems. They are not satisfied with symptoms and quick fixes. They strive for organization wide achievement: "One for all, and all for one."

Effective followers are independent, critical thinkers and are active in the organization. The manager of a Levi's sewing plant, Tommy Jo Daves, has discovered that

> you can't lead a team by just barking orders, and you have to have a vision in your head of what you're trying to do. . . . It's real hard for me not to push back and say, "You do this, you do that, and you do this." Now I have to say, "How do you want to do this?" I have to realize that their ideas may not be the way to go, but I have to let them learn that for themselves."[15]

Daves has encouraged her team to develop into a group of effective followers. As a result, flawed jeans have been reduced by a third, time between an order and shipment has fallen by 10 days, and the time a pair of jeans spends in processing has shrunk from 5 days to 1 day. Thus, effective leadership involves cultivating, empowering, and managing high-performance followers.

### Ineffective Followers

Not all followers are effective. The other classifications of followership as seen in Table 7–3 have been identified according to the criteria of "passive vs. active, and independent, critical thinking vs. dependent, uncritical thinking."[16]

**Alienated followers** are independent, critical thinkers who are passive. They remove themselves from the leaders and can become disruptive to the organization. **Sheep** are dependent, uncritical thinkers. They do as they are told; they are slaves to the system. **"Yes" people** are active in the organization but are also dependent, uncritical thinkers. They reinforce leaders' ideas and thinking enthusiastically without challenge or criticism. They are often dangerous to a leader because they will react positively even as a crisis or disaster is revealing itself, thus creating the false impression that nothing is wrong. More than a few leaders have been ambushed by a crisis because their closest followers were yes people. Sheep and "Yes" people create fertile conditions for groupthink, a state in which a group shows uncritical acquiescence to a leader's demands. **Survivors** are midway between independent, critical and dependent, uncritical thinking, as well as the passive, active dimension. They are cautious, "better safe than sorry" low risk takers. Survivors are the least disruptive to the organization. They test the waters before asserting themselves in word or deed. They neither take extra risks nor allow themselves to fall completely behind those who are succeeding. They manage to stay hired.

We return next to contemporary descriptions of leadership competencies. You may wonder as you read this section, how these competencies and skills differ for managers and followers.

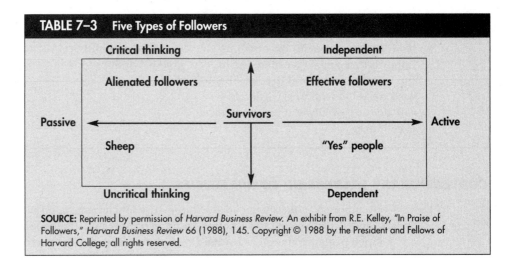

**TABLE 7–3     Five Types of Followers**

|  | Critical thinking | | Independent |
|---|---|---|---|
|  | Alienated followers | | Effective followers |
| Passive ← | | Survivors | → Active |
|  | Sheep | | "Yes" people |
|  | Uncritical thinking | | Dependent |

## THE CHANGING WORKPLACE

### What Kind of Follower Are You?

**Exercise**: Circle T (true) or F (false) for each question. Read the scoring key after you complete all the items.

T F    1. I like doing things my own way and in my own time; teams and I don't mix well.

T F    2. I don't like coming up with ideas or being creative on a team. I usually go along with the majority position if the members have thought out the problems and solutions.

T F    3. A main concern of mine when working on a team is to have the work done on time and with the least amount of conflict and unnecessary risks. I mainly try to meet the requirements for just getting a project done.

T F    4. Even though I actively do my share of the work, I usually follow a strong leader or other persuasive person's directions in a team if he or she has good ideas. I "go with the flow."

T F    5. I like to examine everything and include most people's ideas in a team before agreeing on anything important. I am concerned about the quality and standards of the work as well as the work product. I will go out of my way to ensure excellence.

**Scoring**: These questions and your responses are designed more for your reflection and inquiry into your style as a follower on a team. The following indicate your style if you said true: 4 ("yes" people), 3 (survivors), 1 (alienated), 2 (sheep), and 5 (effective follower). Consult the text under Followership to further examine these styles. It is possible to have more than one followership style, but it is not likely to be an effective follower and have the characteristics of ineffective followers.

**Discussion Questions:** After observing which style best characterizes you on a team as a follower, answer these questions:

1. What is your predominate followership style(s)? Why? Explain.

2. Under what conditions would you adopt or be able to adopt a different style? Explain.

Join *your team* if you have been assigned one, or with three or four classmates, and address these questions:

1. Share your answers to Questions 1 and 2 above.

2. Discuss ways that your group as members of a team could help others become more effective followers.

## CONTEMPORARY LEADERSHIP COMPETENCIES

Contemporary and strategic leadership competencies are based on capabilities that are linked to the new information-based economy and the transition to it. These competencies are viewed as leader directed, not manager or follower directed.

Leaders are increasingly called on to lead and direct—not cope or adjust to—change. Figure 1–4 in Chapter 1 illustrates the large-scale dimensions of change management that organizational leaders are called to initiate and orchestrate—especially as industries and companies transition to on-line and Web-based operations and sales, downsize, expand, and merge. These change tasks include creating a dynamic and competitive vision, developing political support, managing the transition, and sustaining momentum for the vision. Change competencies also include envisioning and creating trust through empowerment, self-understanding through positive self-concept, and meaning through communication.[17]

Vision creates focus for an organization. As Figure 7–1 illustrates, creating a vision is a process that begins by asking four questions: What business are we in? What is our product or service? Who is our customer? What are our core competencies? Note at the beginning of this chapter that Netscape's leaders used similar principles to those posed in Figure 7–1.

Once a vision is articulated, organizational leaders often work with staff to identify the mission and values of the company before developing a strategy. Several years ago, Apple Computer went through the following—still relevant and used—strategic process to develop a vision:

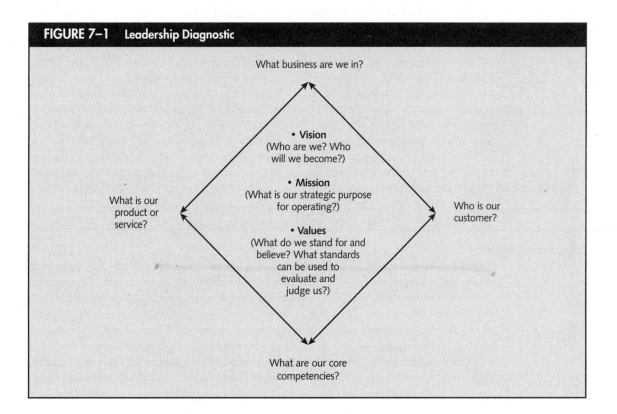

**FIGURE 7–1    Leadership Diagnostic**

What business are we in?

• **Vision**
(Who are we? Who will we become?)

• **Mission**
(What is our strategic purpose for operating?)

• **Values**
(What do we stand for and believe? What standards can be used to evaluate and judge us?)

What is our product or service?

Who is our customer?

What are our core competencies?

1. Generate broad scenarios of possible futures.

2. Conduct a competitive analysis of the industry and its strategic segments.

3. Analyze the company's and the competition's core capabilities.

4. Develop a strategic vision and identify the strategic options.[18]

Apple's vision then became to be a company that offers innovative but affordable computers for individuals. It will provide the most user-friendly operating system and software available. Apple will continue to be a major player in the business segment, emphasizing people rather than machines. However, the overall strategy was to implement a consumer-oriented electronics company focused on communication and information-processing products.[19] Apple's turnaround at the turn of the new century seems to be working. Steve Jobs as CEO has returned Apple to its core competencies with new marketing energy and innovations.

Leaders must create meaning for their followers through communication. They must capture the imagination of their vital stakeholders and effectively communicate the vision of the organization. Leaders must motivate and create a readiness for change. They are challenged to inspire a shared vision by actively enlisting others. This is accomplished when leaders appeal to a common purpose, communicate expressively, and show sincere belief in what they say.[20] The new breed of Internet CEOs and leaders exemplify these characteristics and competencies. For example, Jeff Bezos, CEO of Amazon.com, has inspired venture capitalists and Wall Street to believe (at least for the near term) in his vision "to create the online place where people can find anything they want to buy—not just books and music CDs." Stephen Case, CEO of America Online Inc., also keeps his vision and enthusiasm links to the marketplace's support. His vision is "to make AOL the gateway to e-commerce and one of the world's most valuable companies." Margaret Whitman, president and CEO of eBay Inc., has created one of the most popular on-line business models, auctioning goods and services. Her ambition is "to make eBay an international phenomenon where all sorts of things are auctioned—including big-ticket items such as collectible autos." Not all e-commerce companies will succeed. Those leaders who embody the leadership characteristics and competencies described here, time the market right, and manage to move smoothly with strategic partners have a higher probability of succeeding.

### Empowering Others

Leaders, then, are challenged to trust and empower others. Building trust and enabling others requires sharing power and information, fostering cooperation over competition by example, developing cooperative goals, and being open and even vulnerable in searching for innovative solutions.[21] Effectiveness and productivity are built on trust and empowerment. Leaders who encourage and rely on trusting relationships build comfort, open communication, and sharing into the work groups surrounding them. Their subordinates respond with the same kind of open sharing of information. On the other hand, subordinates of untrusting leaders and managers tend to distort and withhold information.[22] Effective leaders develop and nurture self-understanding through a positive, realistic self-concept. The "creative deployment of self"[23] is a continuous process of self-understanding and self-management that involves recognizing strengths and compensating for weaknesses, nurturing skills and discipline (i.e., working on and developing one's talents), and developing the capacity to discern the fit between one's perceived skills and those that the job requires.

### Superleadership and Self-Leadership

Additional key competencies are found in the perspectives of super- and self-leadership. **Superleadership** is "leading others to lead themselves."[24] Superleader-ship "empowers others to stand on their own two feet and to feel ownership of their job."[25] In this sense, superleadership begins with **self-leadership**: "the influence we exert on ourselves to achieve the self-motivation and self-direction we need to perform."[26]

Superleadership involves a seven-step process, which is illustrated in Figure 7–2. We state the process in an action mode, quoting the authors of the model:[27]

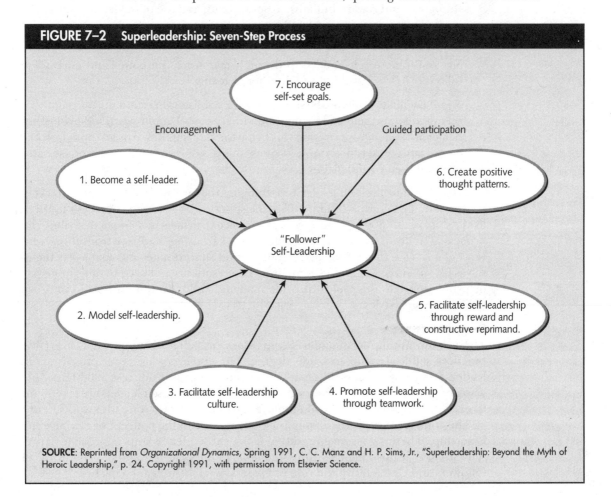

**FIGURE 7–2    Superleadership: Seven-Step Process**

**SOURCE**: Reprinted from *Organizational Dynamics*, Spring 1991, C. C. Manz and H. P. Sims, Jr., "Superleadership: Beyond the Myth of Heroic Leadership," p. 24. Copyright 1991, with permission from Elsevier Science.

*Step 1*: Become a self-leader. Set specific, challenging, achievable, and rewarding goals for yourself; redesign your job to motivate yourself; think constructively to seek opportunities over obstacles; examine and challenge your beliefs, assumptions, and mental images.

*Step 2*: Model self-leadership. After mastering Step 1 strategies, demonstrate your self-leadership strategies to followers and give them a chance to adapt these methods to their needs.

*Step 3*: Encourage followers to set their own goals. Help followers set their own goals by modeling goal-setting skills and behaviors.

*Step 4*: Create positive thought patterns. Help followers realize their own potential by encouraging their own belief in themselves and by helping them find opportunities in problems.

*Step 5*: Facilitate self-leadership through reward and constructive reprimand. Recognize and reward initiative, responsibility, and use of self-leadership; make feedback constructive, and followers will, over time, provide their own constructive feedback.

*Step 6*: Promote self-leadership through teamwork. Empower and encourage followers to work and help each other as teams.

*Step 7*: Facilitate a self-leadership culture. Establish values and norms that focus on initiative and self-leadership. Encourage, model, and reward self-leadership behavior while demonstrating this behavior yourself. Rewards are both task oriented and centered around responsibility, self-recognition, self-praise, and increased self-confidence.[28]

Table 7–4 illustrates self-leadership strategies that are alluded to in the seven-step process. Finally, Figure 7–3 summarizes the superleader approach. A recent trend in leadership is the 360 degree feedback. A recent article in *Fortune* describes the process as a means of improving leaders' styles by using feedback from those who work closest with them. Colleagues, bosses, and subordinates and managers themselves fill out anonymous questionnaires. The results are not used to determine pay or promotion but as a tool to provide managers information on how to improve their leadership styles.[29]

### Everyone a Leader

These basic assumptions underlie our ideas on self-leadership. First, everyone practices self-leadership to some degree, but not everyone is an effective self-leader. Second, self-leadership can be learned and thus is not restricted to people who are "born" to be self-starters or self-motivated. Third, self-leadership is relevant to executives, managers, and all employees—that is, to everyone who works.

The concept of superleadership is closely related to the concept of effective followership. These two concepts differ from earlier leadership approaches (presented later in this chapter) since these views endorse the empowerment of all followers and characterize the role of leaders as facilitators and coaches.

| TABLE 7–4    Self-Leadership Strategies |
|---|

**Behavior-Focused Strategies**

1. *Self-Observation*—observing and gathering information about specific behaviors that you have targeted for change
2. *Self-Set Goals*—setting goals for your own work efforts
3. *Management of Cues*—arranging and altering cues in the work environment to facilitate your desired personal behaviors
4. *Rehearsal*—physical or mental practice of work activities before you actually perform them
5. *Self-Reward*—providing yourself with personally valued rewards for completing desirable behaviors
6. *Self-Punishment/Criticism*—administering punishments to yourself for behaving in undesirable ways

**Cognitive-Focused Strategies**

1. *Building Natural Rewards into Tasks*—self-redesign of where and how you do your work to increase the level of natural rewards in your job. Natural rewards that are part of rather than separate from the work (i.e., the work, like a hobby, becomes the reward) result from activities that cause you to feel
   - a sense of competence
   - a sense of self-control
   - a sense of purpose
2. *Focusing Thinking on Natural Rewards*—purposely focusing your thinking on the naturally rewarding features of your work
3. *Establishment of Effective Thought Patterns*—establishing constructive and effective habits or patterns in your thinking (e.g., a tendency to search for opportunities rather than obstacles embedded in challenges) by managing your
   - beliefs and assumptions
   - mental imagery
   - internal self-talk

SOURCE: Reprinted from *Organizational Dynamics*, Spring 1991, C.C. Manz and H.P. Sims, Jr., "Superleadership: Beyond the Myth of Heroic Leadership," p. 24. Copyright 1991, with permission from Elsevier Science.

## TRANSFORMATIONAL LEADERSHIP AND STRATEGIC CHANGE

Transformational leadership is an important contemporary theory of leadership.[30] Linked to this model is the role of leader as guiding and implementing large-scale strategic change. Multinational corporations worldwide are experiencing tremendous transformational changes. Moving from "bricks and mortar" to "clicks and mortar" requires visionary leadership. General Electric, Boeing, Chrysler, General

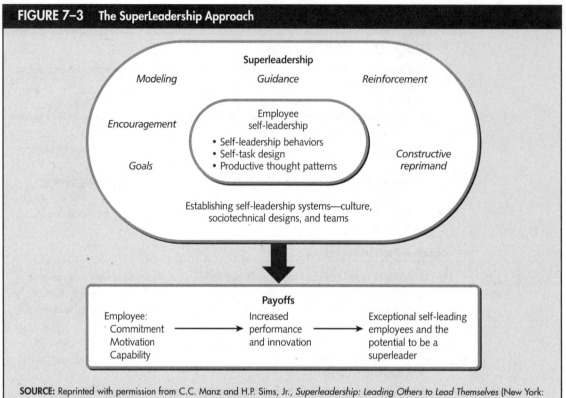

**FIGURE 7–3   The SuperLeadership Approach**

Superleadership

Modeling                    Guidance                  Reinforcement

Encouragement

Employee
self-leadership
• Self-leadership behaviors
• Self-task design
• Productive thought patterns

Goals                                                Constructive
reprimand

Establishing self-leadership systems—culture,
sociotechnical designs, and teams

Payoffs

Employee:                   Increased                 Exceptional self-leading
Commitment        →        performance      →        employees and the
Motivation                  and innovation            potential to be a
Capability                                            superleader

Motors, AT&T, to name just a few corporations, have led and are leading the way in dramatic information-based, on-line transformations.

Transformational leaders guide organizations through dramatic political, technical, and cultural changes in response to environmental, market, and competitive threats and opportunities. Figure 7–4 represents a strategic-change model that is relevant to large-scale changes. We recommend that you read this section of the chapter to understand the stages and steps of major organizational changes. Compare the leadership and change models, and identify the overlaps and similarities. Get a "big picture" view of a transformational change process. You might ask, If I were a member of a strategic change team, which models or parts of these models would I want to use to help my strategic team plan and implement a large scale change?

### Stages of Organizational Change

Figure 7–4 shows five stages of organizational change that transformational leaders can use to determine strategies and interventions necessary to move members

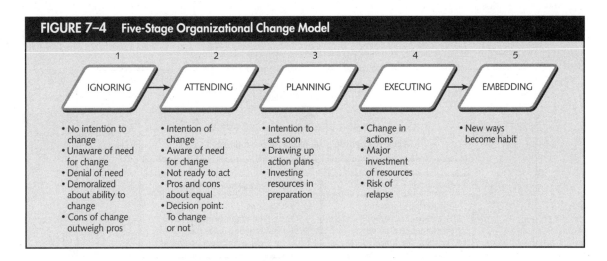

**FIGURE 7–4    Five-Stage Organizational Change Model**

| 1 | 2 | 3 | 4 | 5 |
|---|---|---|---|---|
| **IGNORING** | **ATTENDING** | **PLANNING** | **EXECUTING** | **EMBEDDING** |
| • No intention to change<br>• Unaware of need for change<br>• Denial of need<br>• Demoralized about ability to change<br>• Cons of change outweigh pros | • Intention of change<br>• Aware of need for change<br>• Not ready to act<br>• Pros and cons about equal<br>• Decision point: To change or not | • Intention to act soon<br>• Drawing up action plans<br>• Investing resources in preparation | • Change in actions<br>• Major investment of resources<br>• Risk of relapse | • New ways become habit |

from stages 1 (ignoring) and 2 (attending) to planning, executing, and embedding planned changes. This figure illustrates a planned cycle of change in organizations. Figure 7–5 illustrates the strategic work of transformational leaders, which involves guiding their organizations through three acts: **Act I** is recognizing the need for revitalization. During this stage, the leader assists subordinates in recognizing and developing a felt need for change. The goal is to overcome the organization's resistance to change and to avoid quick-fix responses to change. Leaders assist their organizations through this stage of change by helping subordinates play the devil's advocate role, building networks external to the organization, and benchmarking excellence standards and management practices from other organizations. The value-added leadership role during this stage is in helping organization members to disengage from, and "dis-identify" with, the past and deal with their disenchantment and resistance to change.

During **Act II**, creating a new vision, the leader's strategic task is to create a vision for the organization and to mobilize commitment around it. The leader accomplishes this task by assisting in the planning and education of organization members and by building trust through modeling personal competence, self-confidence, and commitment. The leader can use his sources of power discussed earlier to form and guide change-management teams.

**Act III**, the third stage of change—institutionalizing change—is characterized by creative destruction of old ways of viewing and doing business and by reweaving the social fabric. The major task of the leader is to "recognize these mixed feelings, act to help people move from negative to positive emotions, and mobilize the energy needed for individual renewal."[31] Aligning people with new "scripts" and "charging" them with enough energy to institutionalize the new changes is the transformational leader's desired outcome from this phase.

Transformational leaders guide and motivate subordinates during the organizational change process in the following ways.[32] They inspire people to look beyond fixed expectations toward new outcomes. They encourage people to obtain new

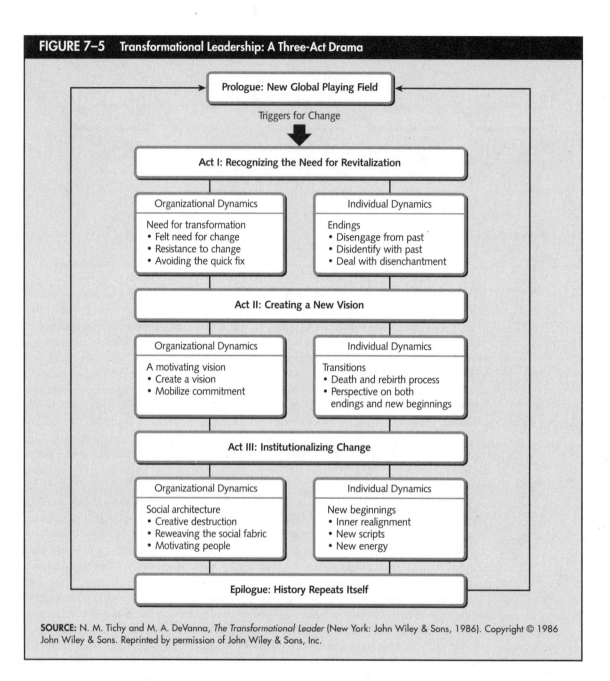

**FIGURE 7–5    Transformational Leadership: A Three-Act Drama**

Prologue: New Global Playing Field

Triggers for Change

**Act I: Recognizing the Need for Revitalization**

Organizational Dynamics

Need for transformation
• Felt need for change
• Resistance to change
• Avoiding the quick fix

Individual Dynamics

Endings
• Disengage from past
• Disidentify with past
• Deal with disenchantment

**Act II: Creating a New Vision**

Organizational Dynamics

A motivating vision
• Create a vision
• Mobilize commitment

Individual Dynamics

Transitions
• Death and rebirth process
• Perspective on both
  endings and new beginnings

**Act III: Institutionalizing Change**

Organizational Dynamics

Social architecture
• Creative destruction
• Reweaving the social fabric
• Motivating people

Individual Dynamics

New beginnings
• Inner realignment
• New scripts
• New energy

Epilogue: History Repeats Itself

SOURCE: N. M. Tichy and M. A. DeVanna, *The Transformational Leader* (New York: John Wiley & Sons, 1986). Copyright © 1986 John Wiley & Sons. Reprinted by permission of John Wiley & Sons, Inc.

outcomes and to look for means for achieving new goals. Leaders expand the needs of others beyond their own self-interests to those of the team, organization, and society. They raise the consciousness of followers toward new possibilities and outcomes. Transformational leaders challenge the values and belief systems of followers and thus groom their workforce for a new and different growth potential. Finally, they create and share strategic vision and strategies that guide and pave the way to change.

### Charismatic Leadership and Organizational Change

Literature on the subject of charismatic leadership offers similar descriptions of transformational leadership and strategic-change management. Figure 7–6 outlines four stages of charismatic leadership that resemble points in the preceding discussion.[33] In **Stage 1**, charismatic leaders detect unexploited opportunities, diagnose deficiencies in the present situation, show sensitivity to stakeholders' needs, and formulate a strategic vision. In **Stage 2**, the leaders communicate and motivate followers around the new vision. In **Stage 3**, the leader builds trust, and in **Stage 4**, the leader demonstrates how to achieve the vision through modeling and empowering followers.

Others have offered behavioral commitments and practices that effective leaders can use to achieve desired results.[34] We summarize these commitments here to reinforce the preceding discussion regarding strategic activities and transformational leadership competencies:

1. *Challenge the process*: search for opportunities; experiment and take risks

2. *Inspire a shared vision*: envision the future; enlist others.

3. *Enable others to act*: foster collaboration; strengthen others.

4. *Model the way*: set the example; plan small wins.

5. *Encourage the heart*: recognize individual contributions; celebrate accomplishments.

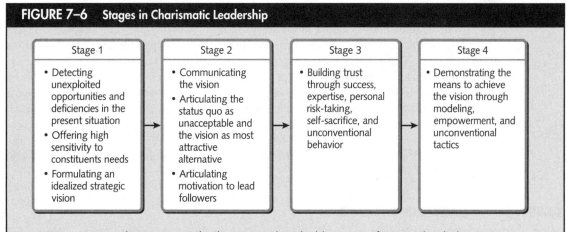

**FIGURE 7–6    Stages in Charismatic Leadership**

| Stage 1 | Stage 2 | Stage 3 | Stage 4 |
|---------|---------|---------|---------|
| • Detecting unexploited opportunities and deficiencies in the present situation<br>• Offering high sensitivity to constituents needs<br>• Formulating an idealized strategic vision | • Communicating the vision<br>• Articulating the status quo as unacceptable and the vision as most attractive alternative<br>• Articulating motivation to lead followers | • Building trust through success, expertise, personal risk-taking, self-sacrifice, and unconventional behavior | • Demonstrating the means to achieve the vision through modeling, empowerment, and unconventional tactics |

**SOURCE:** J. A. Conger and R. N. Kanungo, *The Charismatic Leader: Behind the Mystique of Exceptional Leadership* (San Francisco: Jossey-Bass, 1989), 27. Copyright © 1989 Jossey-Bass. Reprinted by permission of Jossey-Bass, Inc., a subsidiary of John Wiley & Sons, Inc.

Transformational leaders need not be heroes. Nevertheless, they do have certain value-added competencies and characteristics, as explained earlier, that help them move their organizations and followers to renewal. In this regard, such leaders have been characterized as follows:[35]

- They identify themselves as change agents.

- They are courageous individuals.

- They believe in people.

- They are value driven.

- They are life-long learners.

- They have the ability to deal with complexity, ambiguity, and uncertainty.

- They are visionaries.[35]

Change is very personal and starts from the top of the organization. It must begin with leaders who practice what they preach by transforming themselves.[36]

### The Downside of Charismatic Leadership

Transformational and charismatic leaders are human. Major limitations of this leadership style include political and arbitrary misuse of power and unethical leadership practices. Charismatic leaders and administrators often accrue substantial power in their strategic roles and stakeholder relationships. The influence and use of power by the leader over the organization's vision, mission, strategies, and resources can sometimes be to the leader's—and not to the organization's—best interest. Transformational leaders' strategic "logics of action" (i.e., their underlying strategic rationales) may include self-survival, prestige, career advancement, or greed, to name a few undesirable motives.[37] Certain transformational leaders have destroyed their companies by creating and executing an ineffective personal vision.[38]

Charismatic leaders can also censure and overwhelm opposing or critical opinions and ideas. Leaders such as those have imposed their narrow, untested, and even unethical views over an entire enterprise.[39] Involvement of strong boards of directors in selecting leaders, instituting frequent organizational audits and control systems managed by independent auditors, and maintaining an integrated approach in all strategic planning and implementation are ways to guard against these very real downsides of charismatic leadership. In the following section, we examined traditional leadership theories, many of which are applicable to managers and followers.

## CLASSICAL LEADERSHIP THEORIES

In this section we summarize traditional leadership theories, many of which are widely used. In practice, many of these theories apply to managers, supervisors, and top-level organizational officers and leaders. Since leadership style and effectiveness depend on their environment, followers, tasks, and other contextual variables, this section presents the evolution of leadership studies and illustrates how leadership styles are contingent on other dimensions, as Figure 1–7 in Chapter 1 illustrates. You may wish to refer to Chapter 1 and review the historical context and overview of management thought as you read about the evolution of these leadership theories. It is interesting to note how changing environment, competition, and business practices influence management theory.

Classical leadership theories summarized here include (1) the trait approach, (2) behavioral theory: the managerial grid, (3) contingency theory: Fiedler's model, (4) the path-goal theory, (5) the Vroom-Yetton-Jago model, and (6) the life-cycle model.

## The Trait Approach

The early trait approach (known as the "great man" theory) attempted to select leaders from nonleaders and to identify effective leaders based on personal traits associated with success. Physical, mental, and psychological characteristics were the main criteria used in identifying successful leaders. Such traits as intelligence, self-confidence, charisma, and courage were used as arbitrary benchmarks and indicators of leadership.[40] These studies proved unsuccessful in selecting universal leadership traits as early as the 1940s. Methods and measurements were inadequate to provide a general theory of leadership traits. Also, such contingencies as type of organization, situation, and definitions of what constitutes effective leadership proved problematic.

### Recent Trait Theory Research

Trait theory laid the foundation for theorizing about leadership traits and behaviors associated with effective leaders. A recent study of more than 20,000 respondents world wide identified four major values and personal traits they admired most in their superiors: *honesty, forward-looking, inspiring, and competent.* The researchers suggested from this study that people wanted their leaders to be "credible."[41]

## Behavioral Theories

Behavioral theorists later turned their attention to identifying effective leadership behaviors. Early trait theory assumed great leaders were born, not made; behavioral theories assumed that leadership behavior, once identified, could be taught and trained. A new avenue of research took hold. Researchers began to plot leadership effectiveness along two axes: people and production capabilities. The managerial grid exemplifies this thinking.

## The Managerial Grid®

One of the most well-known and practical managerial grids for evaluating self-reported leadership behavior was created by Blake, Mouton, and their associates. Figure 7–7 illustrates their managerial grid. Leadership behavior is plotted along two dimensions, concern for production (task-centered leadership) and concern for people (socioemotional leadership). The grid has nine positions along each

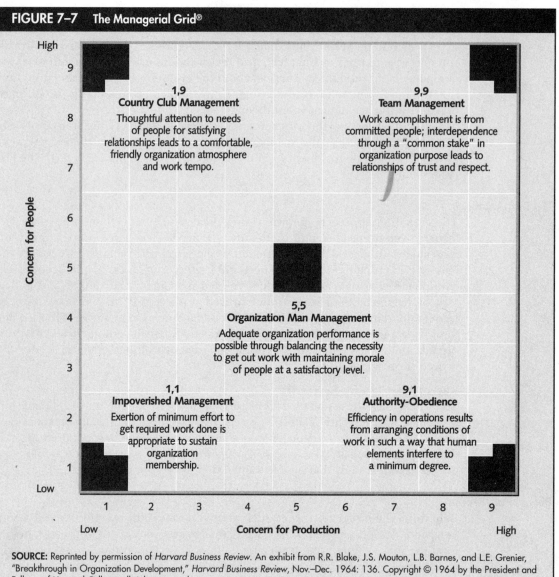

FIGURE 7–7    The Managerial Grid®

**1,9**
**Country Club Management**
Thoughtful attention to needs
of people for satisfying
relationships leads to a comfortable,
friendly organization atmosphere
and work tempo.

**9,9**
**Team Management**
Work accomplishment is from
committed people; interdependence
through a "common stake" in
organization purpose leads to
relationships of trust and respect.

**5,5**
**Organization Man Management**
Adequate organization performance is
possible through balancing the necessity
to get out work with maintaining morale
of people at a satisfactory level.

**1,1**
**Impoverished Management**
Exertion of minimum effort to
get required work done is
appropriate to sustain
organization
membership.

**9,1**
**Authority-Obedience**
Efficiency in operations results
from arranging conditions of
work in such a way that human
elements interfere to
a minimum degree.

Concern for People (vertical axis: Low 1 to High 9)

Concern for Production (horizontal axis: Low 1 to High 9)

axis in which a leader's style can be diagnosed—81 positions in all. According to this model, the (9,9) position—team management—is the style that results in the best leadership performance. The country club management (1,9) position, impoverished management (1,1) position, and authority management (9,1) position, are less desirable styles or behavioral leader profiles to have.

This has been a very lucrative consulting tool, but the results from the self-diagnoses indicate less information about leadership results, performance, or effectiveness, and more about what an individual thinks or believes about her leadership style. There is little empirical evidence to establish any relationship between these styles and productivity, absenteeism, and turnover.[42] However, the same criticism can be applied to many of the leadership theories presented here. Nevertheless, this application has proven to be a popular evaluation tool. It is interesting to note the combination of people and production capabilities in the "Five Signs of Failure: A Self-Test for CEOs" reported in *Fortune*: "(1) How's your performance—and your performance credibility? (2) Are you focused on the basics of execution? (3) Is bad news coming to you regularly? (4) Is your board doing what it should? (5) Is your own team discontented?"[43]

## CONTINGENCY THEORY

### Fiedler's LPC Contingency Model

Fiedler developed the first contingency model of leadership[44] that differed from behavioral and situational models previously discussed. His contingency approach proposed that effective group performance depends on a leader's style of interacting with followers and on the degree of influence and control that a situation offers a leader. Group performance can therefore be evaluated according to the situation and the leader's style. Change occurs, therefore, when a mismatch between the leader and the situation occurs. Training, coaching, and other interventions can be used when appropriate. Although Fiedler assumes that leadership styles are not changeable, some consultative applications of Fiedler's model do not make this assumption.

What constitutes the fit between leader and work situation? Leaders can choose a style in Fiedler's model that is either task oriented, relations oriented, or both. One problem in Fiedler's model is the arbitrary and fixed nature of leadership style.

Fiedler argues that leadership style depends on three major contingency variables: task structure, leader-member relations, and the leader's position power. **Task structure** refers to the extent to which the task is routine or nonroutine. Routine tasks have well-defined goals and procedures. The outcomes are verifiable, and the means of performing the work is specific. Nonroutine tasks have the opposite characteristics. **Leader-member relations** refer to the extent to which a group accepts a leader. Acceptance leads to commitment and loyalty, nonacceptance leads to friction and tension. **Leader position power** refers to the extent to which a leader can hire, fire, reward, and discipline subordinates. Organizations, Fiedler claims, should match tasks and work environments with an individual's leadership style to ensure high group performance.

A leadership style is determined by giving respondents a 16-item questionnaire (called the least-preferred co-worker, LPC). Respondents describe the person they are *least* able to work with in either favorable or unfavorable terms. The leadership style of the person is judged relationship oriented if the person is favorably evaluated and task oriented if unfavorably judged. After a leader's style is determined through the LPC, a match can be determined through the other major contingency variables: leader-member relations, task structure, and position power.

The most effective leadership style depends on the control and power the leader has in the position. Low-control situations require a task-oriented leadership style that requires the leader to exert power and influence. Moderate control situations require relationship-oriented leadership because the leader needs the help of his followers. High-control situations also permit the leader to be relationship oriented since good relations exist with followers.

Although Fiedler's theory has been tested, questions remain as to the cross-cultural reliability of the theory and of the selection and measurement of the major variables. Still, his model has advanced our understanding and evaluation of leadership effectiveness.

### Path-Goal Theory

A promising approach for determining leadership effectiveness is House's path-goal theory.[45] Essentially, this approach proposes that leaders can help followers by showing them how their performance directly relates to the organization's goals and to obtaining rewards. Effective follower performance occurs if the leader clearly defines the employee's job and the path to reach his work goals. The leader can assist by providing training, coaching, and guidance and by removing obstacles to goal attainment.

According to House, leaders are effective when their styles enable employees to accomplish their work goals and thus achieve the organization's aims. This happens when the appropriate leadership style matches and complements follower characteristics, taking other environmental factors into consideration. When leadership style fits with these other factors, followers' perceptions of the leader are likely to be positive, and followers are likely to be motivated, reach their work goals, perform well, and be satisfied.

House proposes and defines four leadership styles, which he believes could be adapted (any or all) by leaders, depending on the situation:

1. *Directive.* Leaders inform followers of what to do and when to do it. This is a telling style.

2. *Supportive.* Leaders are friendly with followers and show them what to do. This is more a sharing style.

3. *Participative.* Leaders consult with followers and solicit their ideas and suggestions. This is a consultative style.

4. *Achievement oriented.* Leaders set challenging goals and show confidence in employee performance. This is a delegating style.

The environmental factors that moderate leadership behavior and style include tasks, formal authority of the organization, and the work group. The contingency factors that also affect a leader's choice of style are the characteristics of the followers: locus of control (internal or external) and their experience and ability. Environmental factors can influence followers' motivation.

Many hypotheses can be derived and tested using the path-goal approach. For example, a directive leadership style is more appropriate when the task is unstructured, the goals are ambiguous, followers are unskilled and do not have high social needs, and formal authority is limited. Also, when the work group is strongly networked and the organizational culture is not participative, this leadership style is more adaptable. A supportive leadership style is more appropriate when the task is structured, there are clear goals, followers are skilled and have high social needs, there is not a strong social or collaborative work group, and the organizational culture does not support participation. An achievement leadership style is more appropriate when goals are unclear and ambiguous, there are high achievement needs but low social needs, there is a strong social but collaboratively inexperienced workgroup, and the organizational culture supports achievement but not participation. A participative leadership style is appropriate when there is a strong social work group experienced in collaborating and there are high social needs and low achievement needs.

One study found that middle managers and other employees who receive a directive from senior management to change a tactical process or procedure expect to be included in the planning and implementation of the change.[46] However, if the change is strategic, they expect little or no participation.

Research results regarding the validity of the path-goal theory are mixed. However, House's contribution to contingency leadership theory includes his approach's practicality and conceptually appealing diagnostic method.

### Path-Goal Theory and Cross-Cultural Leadership

How does the path-goal leadership model apply to other cultures? Studies indicate that a leader's preferred style in her own culture may not work well in a different setting. For example, the participative leadership style in the path-goal model is more culturally appropriate (not necessarily the best) and has the widest applicability across an 18-country study: Australia, Brazil, Canada, France, former West Germany, Great Britain, Hong Kong, India, Italy, Japan, Korea, Netherlands, New Zealand, Pakistan, Philippines, Sweden, Taiwan, and the United States.

The directive leadership style is culturally inappropriate in North America (the United States and Canada), Europe (Great Britain, and West Germany—France being the exception), Australia, and Northern Europe (Sweden, New Zealand, and the Netherlands). In Hong Kong and the Philippines, greater leadership versatility (i.e., all four leadership styles, directive, supportive, participative, and achievement) is required.

### *The Vroom-Yetton-Jago Leadership Model*

The original Vroom-Yetton leadership model was developed in 1973 and expanded by Vroom and Jago in 1988.[47] Similar to the path-goal model, this model prescribes a leadership style that fits a particular situation. It assumes that a leader can and should change styles, given the requirements of the situation. It also assumes that the leader (or a group) can adapt to a style ranging from very autocratic to highly participative.

The purpose and intent of the model are to provide a quality decision while ensuring the followers' acceptance of the decision. The major concern of the model centers on followers' participation in, and acceptance of, the decision. The model also proposes that different situations require different decision-making processes and leadership styles and that followers' participation in, and acceptance of, decisions depend on situational characteristics.

A leader can select among five approaches that range from individual to joint problem solving to delegating problem-solving responsibility to others. Appropriate choice of the decision process depends on the evaluation of these six factors: (1) the quality requirements of the problem, (2) the source of information regarding the problem, (3) the structure of the problem, (4) the probability of acceptance by those most affected, (5) the commonality of organizational goals, and (6) the probable conflict among possible solutions.

The Vroom-Yetton-Jago model has been praised for its scientific validity and practical usefulness,[48] but some of the shortcomings include the complexity of its use, the oversimplification of its inquiry process, and the narrow focus regarding the extent of subordinate involvement in decision making.[49] The model continues to be used, however, as a popular diagnostic management tool.

## The Life-Cycle Model of Situational Leadership

Paul Hersey and Kenneth Blanchard are authors of a situational leadership theory based on the premise that effective leadership styles depend on two factors: the followers' level of readiness or maturity and situational demands. According to the life-cycle mode of situational leadership,[50] a leader should be able to adapt his or her style to meet these contingencies. Follower readiness indicates the extent to which subordinates have the ability and willingness to perform a task. Leadership style (situational leadership) centers around task and relationship behaviors. Task behavior signals the giving of instruction and direction; relationship behavior indicates the giving of emotional and human support. The leader offers the type of behavior that suits the followers' readiness to perform tasks.

Figure 7–8 illustrates Hersey and Blanchard's model. Note at the bottom of the model the four dominant leadership styles:

- *Telling* (S1): Providing specific instructions; closely supervised performance

- *Selling* (S2): Explaining decisions and providing opportunities for clarification

- *Participating* (S3): Sharing ideas and facilitating in making decisions

- *Delegating* (S4): Assigning responsibility for decisions and implementation

You can see that a leader should use a telling style (S1, lower right quadrant of the leadership style square) when followers are unable and unwilling to perform a task. A leader should use a selling style (S2) when followers have low ability and are moderately willing to perform tasks. A participating style (S3) should be used when followers have moderate to high ability and readiness. A delegating style (S4) should be used when followers show a high ability and readiness to perform.

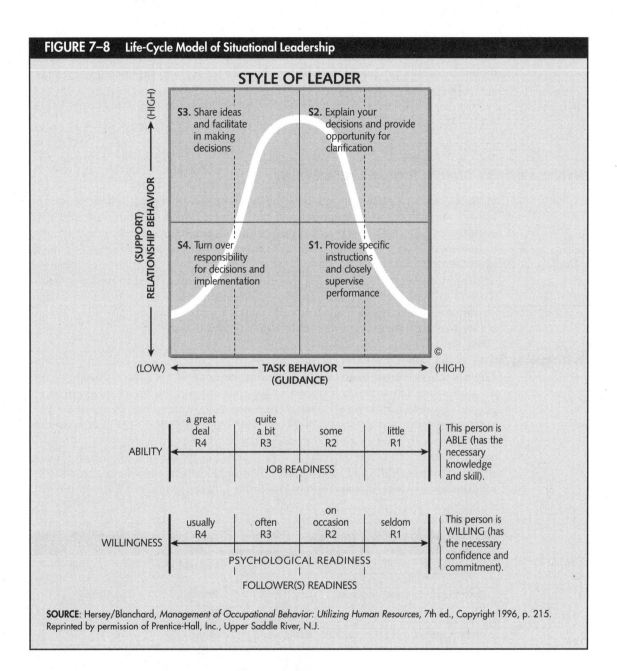

**FIGURE 7–8    Life-Cycle Model of Situational Leadership**

SOURCE: Hersey/Blanchard, *Management of Occupational Behavior: Utilizing Human Resources*, 7th ed., Copyright 1996, p. 215. Reprinted by permission of Prentice-Hall, Inc., Upper Saddle River, N.J.

Research is mixed on the empirical validity of this model. Some critics challenge the validity and usefulness of the model; others claim it is a valuable diagnostic tool.

The enduring contribution of the contingency theory model is its message that there is no one best leadership style for all situations. Leadership style depends on the situation and the followers. Effective leaders can and do change and adapt their style to accommodate follower readiness and situational contingencies. This model can also supplement the followership, self-leader, and superleader literature at the beginning of the chapter.

We turn next to the international dimensions of leadership before discussing ways to lead culturally diverse workforces and then to ethical leadership.

## INTERNATIONAL DIMENSIONS OF LEADERSHIP

Effective organizational leaders have been described as cosmopolitan, cross-cultural communicators and negotiators; creators of cultural collaboration and synergy; leaders and influencers of cultural change.[51] Since some students are already in leadership roles, or will, at some point, be required to lead, manage, or work with cross-cultural professionals (if not in different countries, then in their own organizations), it is important for these students to understand underlying international cultural differences. Regarding leadership and followership, we follow this assumption: We must first understand our own cultural orientation and biases before we can appreciate, understand, and manage those of others.

### Understanding Cross-Cultural Value Differences

The Kluckhohn-Strodtbeck model illustrated in Table 7–5 is a basic starting point for understanding how leaders and followers perceive and value differences in people. Values are our most fundamental internal guides; they direct and filter out perceptions and actions. Understanding cultural differences that underlie basic values can inform leaders, managers, and followers working with culturally diverse workforces. It is important to note that not everyone in each culture shares all the dominant values of that culture. National cultural values are contexts in which we each share to some extent. In Table 7–5, we have circled the dominant

---

### TABLE 7–5    CROSS-CULTURAL VALUE DIMENSIONS

| Value | Variations | | |
|---|---|---|---|
| Relationship to the environment | (Domination) | Harmony | Subjugation |
| Time | Past | (Present) | Future |
| Human nature | Good | (Mixed) | Evil |
| Activity | Being | Controlling | (Doing) |
| Locus of responsibility | (Individualistic) | Group | Hierarchical |
| Space | (Private) | Mixed | Public |

SOURCE: F. Kluckhohn and I. Strodibeck, *Variations in Value Operations* (Evanston, Ill.: Row, Peterson, 1961).

U.S. values. Americans typically value dominating and controlling the environment, whereas people in Far Eastern and Middle Eastern cultures value harmony. The domination orientation of Americans reveals itself in our use of aggressive planning and implementation as a means to assert control over problems—whether the problem is in agriculture, disease, natural disaster, or space exploration. Rational goal planning and proactive problem resolution also characterize this value dimension in U.S. culture. In contrast, in the harmonious orientation of Far Eastern and Middle Eastern societies, religion is an active and accepted approach to problem solving—that is, God's help and will are sought. This value orientation is really even more subtle than we have described: In these cultures, if God's help is not forthcoming, people may view the problem as not having a solution or may even view it as no problem at all, that this is the way things are. Contemporary U.S. business professionals may be more ready to assert control over physical places and spaces than would those in China, the Middle East, or India in the same situation since all responses are culturally conditioned. Value and perceptual conflicts may very likely arise over such expressed attitudes, which can also affect business and work relationships. Americans, for example, never seem to have enough time, have little sense of history, and often take a short-term view when it comes to business, the bottom line, and future development. The U.S. stock market and business investing practices embody and symbolize this short-term time horizon. Quarterly quotes are used to determine the health of companies. In contrast, the Chinese, Japanese, and other Asians take a long-term view of time. They are keenly aware of how they have done things, tend to revere these past ways of doing things more than Americans do, and so may be less open to change. They also view the present as just a small part of the continuum of time. That is, there is plenty of time to solve a problem, so long-term solutions are not so easily dismissed in favor of the short-term "fix." The Japanese, in particular, take a long-term perspective. Negotiating a licensing agreement, for example, may take three years, but once concluded, the Japanese may be ready to go into production within a few weeks. This cultural view of time can have significant consequences for leaders and followers. Americans leading and working in China, Japan, the Middle East, and Latin America would do well to understand that their constant sense of immediacy is a cultural orientation and that valuing future and past orientations to time can be productive.

Human nature can be valued as inherently good, evil, or mixed. Americans tend to have a mixed view of human nature; people are seen as "evil" if a pattern in their actions so indicates or "good" if their deeds evidence goodness. Chinese traditions can go either way: extreme good and evil. In the Chinese cultural view, peasants are generally viewed more as "good" than are wealthier citizens. Societies that take an evil view of human nature are more likely to encourage authoritarian styles of leadership than participative. American leaders view leadership on a continuum between participative and autocratic.

Different cultures emphasize activity from "doing" and "being" orientations. Americans, originating from a young, pragmatic, frontier context, emphasize a "doing" orientation with the locus of responsibility centering on the individual.

That is, in the American orientation, you as an individual are who you are because of what you do—not necessarily because of who your family is or what it does. It is not uncommon, for example, for two Americans who meet for the first time to discuss their professions and work before sharing names and personal information. Malaysians, Mexicans, Latin Americans, Middle Easterners, and Far Easterners, however, value "being" over doing. In these cultures, the group is valued over the individual as the basic locus of responsibility. Thus, who you are is defined much more by who your family is and what it does. One's family name locates that person in the society and cultural milieu. Since many of these countries lack a social security system, families take care of their elderly and retired members. Having time to be with family and friends in these cultures is a must. Working to live, not living to work, is more characteristic of "being" cultures. Japanese, Chinese, and Mexicans, for example, value the group as the basic social unit of responsibility over the individual.

Cultural-value orientations of activity and the locus of responsibility have significant consequences for effectively leading. Japanese managers in Mexico, for example, have found that not allowing local employees sufficient time with their families results in poor performance and motivation. Also, although Mexicans have a group orientation, they do not generally, as do Japanese, extend that identification to the company or country. Japanese tend to believe that what is good for the company is good for the country and is therefore also good for the individual.

Space can be valued culturally as private, mixed, or public. In Japan, working without walls or cubicles is commonplace. Protecting one's private space over shared space is uncommon in Mexico and Latin and South American companies. North Americans, on the other hand, value space and expect others to respect each person's private space. Leaders who understand this value difference can enhance productivity and morale by not isolating workers in cultures that value a public sense of space, for example.

### Hofstede's Cross-Cultural Map

A second comprehensive model that serves as a context from which to interpret leadership theories and applications is the cross-cultural map of Geert Hofstede.[52] Hofstede's 60-country study included more than 160,000 managers and workers from IBM. He found that national culture explained more work-related values and attitudes than did gender, age, profession, or company position. The four national cultural dimensions used to explain work values were individualism and collectivism, power distance, uncertainty avoidance, and masculinity versus femininity.

- *Individualism* indicates loosely knit frameworks in which people are supposed to take care of themselves and their families only. In contrast, *collectivism* indicates tightly knit social frameworks in which people take care of, and are protected by, extended family members, clans, and relatives. Individualist cultures reflect a concern of what's best for me; collectivist cultures reflect a concern of what is best for the group, family, and even social class. Examples of individualist cultures include Australia, Canada, England, France, Italy, Sweden, and the United States. Examples of collectivist cultures include Greece, Japan, Mexico, Singapore, and Venezuela.

- *Power distance* is a measure of the extent to which followers accept their boss's influence over them. It also measures the extent to which less powerful members of society accept the unequal distribution of resources and power in society. High power-distance societies and members believe the boss is right because she is the boss. People respect the status, rank, and individual position holders. Low power-distance societies and members believe the society or the boss is right only when she knows the correct way or answer. Rank, title, organizational, or official positions are not respected mainly for their stated authority. High power-distance cultures include France, Greece, Mexico, Singapore, and Venezuela. Low power-distance cultures include Australia, England, Sweden, and the United States. Moderate power-distance cultures include Canada, Italy, and Japan.

- *Uncertainty avoidance* is a measure of the extent to which risk or ambiguity is avoided. People in cultures or organizations that avoid risk try to protect themselves by adding rules, structure or hierarchy, and procedures; rejecting threatening or new ideas; and seeking security. High uncertainty-avoidance cultures include France, Greece, Italy, Japan, Mexico, and Venezuela. Low uncertainty-avoidance cultures include Canada, Singapore, Sweden, and the United States. Moderate uncertainty-avoidance cultures include Australia and England.

- *Masculinity/femininity* is a measure of the extent to which cultures emphasize a set of values that have traditionally been characterized as "masculine" (e.g., assertiveness, seeking material gain and money, and not emphasizing nurturing, caring for others, intimacy) and "feminine" (valuing relationships, quality of life, concern for others, and not emphasizing material things and aggressiveness). Japan ranked the highest on masculinity, followed by Australia, England, Italy, Mexico, the United States, and Venezuela. The Scandinavian countries ranked the highest on femininity, along with France, Canada, Greece, and Singapore were moderately ranked countries (between masculinity and femininity).

## LEADERSHIP AND CULTURAL DIVERSITY

Integrating cultural diversity throughout an enterprise's workforce is a strategic role of top management. As regional and global markets have grown, integrating culturally diverse groups has become an important part of leaders' major change mandates. Performance is linked to cohesive workforces; such workforces succeed through synergy in planning and performing together. Individuals and groups are able to be effective when their cultural differences are valued in a multicultural organization that, as stated in Chapter 1, relies on diversity as a competitive advantage. Diversity can add creativity and depth to a company's problem-solving capabilities and therefore to its performance. We present an overview of the leader's strategic role in this process: "Leadership refers to the need for champions of the cause of diversity who will take strong personal stands on the need for change, role-model the behaviors required for change, and assist with the work of moving the organization forward."[53]

A framework for leading organizational change to value and manage diversity was summarized in Chapter 1. Figure 1–4 outlines major leadership areas suggested for integrating organizations. These areas include leadership, research and measurement, education, changes in culture and management systems, and follow-up.[54]

### Demonstrate Commitment to Diversity

The leader's initial role in this change effort is personally modeling and showing commitment to diversity. Diversity applies to race, gender, creed, national origin, (dis)ability, age, and sexual preference. The areas of leadership responsibility[55] required here include committing resources to the change effort; including diversity management as part of the organization's business strategy, demonstrating the willingness to change human resource management of the company (e.g., through performance appraisal and compensation systems), showing a willingness to focus mental energy and financial support on management diversity over the long term, establishing the value of diversity as a high priority, core value along with total quality, safety, and integrity.

Through commitment, an organization's leaders need to create and guide a communications strategy for implementing cultural diversity programs. This strategy creates awareness and motivation and explains diversity to the company. A communications strategy defines the importance of integrating diversity among other initiatives into the corporation and defines a process for implementing the effort. Linking diversity to the total quality process sends the message that diversity is an integral part of the company.

### Create Milestones of Change, Measure Progress, and Raise Awareness

Leadership is required to support planned research and measurement activities. Information on diversity-related topics such as *raising awareness of negative stereotypes, using diversity as a marketplace competitive advantage, and developing integrated mentoring programs* should be planned and implemented. Research on attitudes and practices in the workforce must be collected to create and assess a baseline of data and to benchmark milestones for change. Topics needed to create the baseline include measures of organizational culture, equal-opportunity profiles, employee attitudes and perceptions, and cross-cultural career experiences from different groups to describe how promotions and compensation vary by age, gender, nationality, and race. This information can help identify and plan change and training areas in management practices, organizational culture, and interpersonal relations.

## THE CHANGING WORKPLACE

### Leading Diversity: You're the CEO; Draft Your Philosophy Statement

**Exercise**: Draft a "philosophy statement" for the company you are leading as the CEO. Write only half to one page. Assume that (1) "What we believe and value or do not believe or value ultimately determines our behavior." (2) We can effectively manage only what we can measure. Use the chapter and the following four points to help you think through and draft your own originally stated philosophy statement with suggested measurements:

### Philosophy

1. **Valuing diversity**

Diversity is a competitive advantage. It is also a reality. Diversity affects individual and group performance and satisfaction. Legally meeting diversity requirements may be necessary but not sufficient in today's heterogeneous workforce.

2. **Ignoring diversity**

Diversity is important but not essential. In our organization, gender, race, nationality, age, and sexual preferences are private and individual matters. Productivity is more important. People are more concerned with work than with each other.

3. **Acknowledging and accommodating diversity**

To avoid discrimination, we must take proactive steps to recognize and ensure equal opportunity in our selection, hiring, promotion, reward, and other systems. We need to educate and train our managers and employees about understanding and accepting individual and group differences.

4. **Discouraging and minimizing diversity.**

Diversity is too costly and irrelevant a topic to even try to recognize or legislate in our organization. The payoffs do not affect our bottom line, and it is a wasteful activity.

### Behavioral Implications?

**Hints:** What are the behavioral implications of these statements? What program or standards would you create to implement your idea?

What behavioral implications would these statements have on individuals, groups, the company if the CEO endorsed them?

What measurements could you suggest in these systems to encourage fairness and acknowledge the value of a diverse workforce?

What problems and situations among employees and different groups might arise if this became company policy? What statement, policy, program would you want to have? How would you measure these?

**SOURCE**: Based on and adapted from T. Cox, Jr. and R. Beale, *Developing Competency to Manage Diversity* (San Francisco: Koehler-Berrett, 1997), 307–310.

Guiding and supporting employee education programs and workshops that focus on increasing awareness and sensitivity to diversity issues is also part of the leader's role. Top-level executives participate in these programs for their benefit and to model the way for other employees.

### Audit the Culture for Biases

Leaders must be involved in overseeing audits of the organization's culture and management systems. Audits of management systems should investigate areas such as fairness of access by different groups (i.e., gender, race, creed, national origin, sexual preference, age) in recruitment, training, appraising performance, compensating, and offering benefits. The objective here is to identify subtle sources of *harmful* and *negative biases* that are or can become discriminatory in management practices and procedures and therefore hinder recognition, performance, and promotion of certain groups and individuals. The results of the audit should be translated into change programs that revise and/or remake policies, procedures, and management practices in the areas discussed earlier.

### Oversee Accountability and Follow-Up

Leaders must oversee the establishment of accountability for creating mechanisms to follow up and evaluate the results of the performance on the achievement of diversity-related goals and to assess the impact of managing diversity on other performance indicators. There should be zero tolerance for *negative* and *harmful stereotyping* based on age, gender, race, disability, sexual preference, nationality, or other differences an individual has rights to under the Constitution. The aim is to ensure the institutionalization of programs that create a multicultural organization, as described in Chapter 1. "The ultimate goal must be zero correlation of sociocultural identity with opportunity, motivation, and achievement as well as full capitalization on the potential benefits of a diverse workforce."[56]

### "Ways Women Lead"

*Fortune* magazine's second annual ranking of its 50 Most Powerful Women[57] is based on the amount of revenues and profits a woman controls, her influence within a company, and the importance of her business in the global economy and effect of technological firm's leadership on the larger American economy. It is instructive to note some of the leadership abilities of these women. More than half of the newcomers to the list are technology stars (Meg Whitman, CEO eBay, Judith Estrin, Chief Technology Officer of Cisco Systems, Jan Brandt, president of marketing of America Online). A new superhighway to their success is the Internet. Second, "generalists win." Versatility, not functional expertise, is common in their leadership success. Third, the ability to make decisions quickly is also a value added in climbing to the top. Fourth, flexibility is key in the new "rapid-fire" economy. "Many women developed that trait from their mothers . . . and developed it early on."[58] Fifth, these women thrive on being different. Some dropped out of school for a time (Joy Covey, chief strategy officer at Amazon.com and Andrea Zuberti, BGI's head of global risk management) to develop themselves and expand their experience. Sixth, most of the women "see advantages to being female in a man's world." Cynthia Trudell (chair and president of Saturn) noted, "Competing in a man's world is what I want to do. I'm very much in touch with my male side. I'm really competitive. . . . But I keep those qualities in check. I use my feminine traits—empathy, collaboration."[59]

Judy Rosener, a faculty member at the University of California, Irvine, has written that a "second wave" of women is coming into top management. These women represent different styles of leading than their male counterparts. In a study sponsored by the International Women's Forum, 31 percent of respondents answered questions about their organizations, leadership styles, family issues, and personal characteristics. The following is a selected summary of those findings.[60]

*First*, the study showed that women earn the same annual salary as their male counterparts—$136,510 for men and $140,573 for women. *Second*, men's household income is lower than that of women—$166,454 for men and $300,892 for women; 39 percent of men have full-time employed spouses compared to 71 percent of the women. *Third*, both men and women leaders pay female followers about $12,000 less than male counterparts with similar titles and positions. *Fourth*, women are more likely to use power based on charisma, work record, and contacts, compared to men, who use power based on organizational position, title, and ability to reward and punish. *Fifth*, women who characterize themselves as predominately "feminine," or "gender neutral" report a higher level of followership from their female followers than do women who report themselves as "masculine." *Sixth*, most men and women characterize themselves as having an equal mix of traits that are "masculine" (dominant, aggressive, tough, assertive, autocratic, analytical, competitive, independent), "feminine" (excitable, gentle, emotional, submissive, sentimental, understanding, compassionate, sensitive, dependent), and "gender neutral" (adaptive, tactful, sincere, conscientious, conventional, reliable, predictable, systematic, efficient). *Finally*, married men and women experience moderate levels of conflict between work and family areas. With children at home, women experience slightly higher levels of conflict than men, with the observation that women carry 61 percent of the child care load.

## LEADING ETHICALLY AND FOR ORGANIZATIONAL INTEGRITY

Organizational leaders are responsible for the design, implementation, and monitoring of organizational moral environments (including strategies and policies). Lynn Paine has summarized this process as a way of developing an effective "integrity strategy" with the following features.[61] **First**, "the guiding values and commitments make sense and are clearly communicated." This is a leadership responsibility. Organizational obligations and values should appeal to and be shared by employees at all levels. **Second**, "company leaders are personally committed, credible, and willing to take action on the values they espouse." Consistency is the key. Embodying values and following through on the tough calls is a requirement of leaders. **Third**, "the espoused values are integrated into the normal channels of management decision making and are reflected in the organization's critical activities. . . . " **Fourth**, "the company's systems and structures support and reinforce its values." **Finally**, "managers throughout the company have the decision-making skills, knowledge, and competencies needed to make ethically sound decisions on a day to day basis." Ethical decision making should be part of an organization's training.

# THE CHANGING WORKPLACE

## Do You Lead and Manage Ethically?

### Step 1

Answer true or false to the following questions. Rely on your first response after reading the question. Answer what you really would do, not what you think you should or ought to do.

T F    1. I generally tend to listen carefully to all sides of an issue or problem with my work group or colleagues with the intent of ensuring a "win-win" situation for all parties involved.

T F    2. I am more concerned about getting the "job" done at almost any costs as long as no one gets seriously hurt.

T F    3. If a member of my work group or team falls behind on a project or assignment, even after two meetings, I am ready to drop him or her, cut our losses, and move on.

T F    4. Values are important but the bottom line is what really counts in any organization. I work mainly to meet the bottom-line requirements, even if it means violating some of my—or others'—basic values.

T F    5. Society is too abstract a concept for me to take seriously when or if I'm working on a project and my grade, promotion, or job is on the line. If there's a conflict between my grade, promotion, or job and doing what's right for society, I choose what's best for me.

T F    6. I usually "go the extra mile" to help someone on my team or work group, even if it means hurting myself in some way.

T F    7. For me, integrity and honesty are more important than monetary gain.

T F    8. I will not cut corners when it comes to producing a report, an assignment or work product, even it means coming in late and risking competitiveness for my team and company.

T F    9. For me, everything is relative to the situation at hand. I do not believe in or use standards of truth, justice, or fairness in the abstract. I act pragmatically to get the most for the effort I put in to something.

T F   10. I believe in "an eye for an eye" If someone hurts me at work, I believe he or she deserves to be hurt. If someone treats me well, I'll treat him or her likewise. But I generally will not go out of my way to do good or help someone just to do "what is right."

### Step 2

Before scoring your answers to Step 1, answer the 10 questions again, only this time answer the questions as they pertain TO YOUR SUPERVISOR OR A LEADER IN YOUR COMPANY, not for yourself.

### Step 3

Answer these questions after you score Steps 1 and 2:

1. What, if any, differences did you observe in your answers in Steps 1 and 2?

*continued on next page*

The head of executive training at AT&T was quoted in *Fortune* as saying, "This company is not going to be successful unless we have people who can learn from experience. We need our people to act independently, to be accountable and responsible for managing their own piece of the business. It takes a certain amount of reflection to do that successfully."[62] In other words, leaders must know their own values, be able to communicate them, and then must act on them.

**Servant-Leadership**

Leading ethically also involves the role of leader as "servant." Robert Greenleaf originated the term "servant-leadership" in 1970. As servant-leaders, exemplary leaders place the needs of customers, community, and employees as priorities.[63] Characteristics of servant-leaders include the following:

- Listening
- Empathy
- Conceptualizing
- Foresight
- Awareness

- Building community
- Developing people
- Healing
- Stewardship
- Persuasion

This view of leadership expands the traditional notion of leadership beyond a purely profit-oriented dimension to include characteristics of striving to be aware of others as whole persons, especially when facing situations involving crisis and suffering. Spiritual growth and development of people are also part of this leadership perspective. Leaders can and should care for and build communities with their resources. They are citizens of the environment, not only of their organization. The idea of stewardship means serving and helping people to help themselves in a context of caring not just directing and managing. Leadership from this perspective incorporates a long-term, holistic approach.

## THE CHANGING WORKPLACE

### How Ready Are You for Leadership?
### Scoring and Interpretation

Since leaders must assume multiple roles and interact with others in a variety of ways, it is important for potential leaders to consider whether they are ready for leadership positions. Because roles carry expectations from people with whom we work, mismatches in expectations or skills can readily undermine a leader's effectiveness. This exercise is intended to assess your readiness to assume a leadership position.

Please indicate the extent to which you agree or disagree with the following 20 statements. There are no right or wrong answers. Please be as candid as possible and respond to each item individually, circling the responses that reflect your opinion.

|  |  | Strongly Disagree | Disagree | Neutral | Agree | Strongly Agree |
|---|---|---|---|---|---|---|
| 1. | I enjoy having people count on me for ideas and suggestions. | 1 | 2 | 3 | 4 | 5 |
| 2. | If you asked my friends, they would tell you that I inspire others. | 1 | 2 | 3 | 4 | 5 |
| 3. | It's a good practice to ask people provocative questions about their work. | 1 | 2 | 3 | 4 | 5 |
| 4. | It is easy for me to compliment others. | 1 | 2 | 3 | 4 | 5 |
| 5. | I like to be cheerful around others, even when my own spirits are down. | 1 | 2 | 3 | 4 | 5 |
| 6. | My personal accomplishment is less important to me than what my team accomplishes. | 1 | 2 | 3 | 4 | 5 |
| 7. | People often imitate my ideas. | 1 | 2 | 3 | 4 | 5 |
| 8. | Building team spirit is important to me. | 1 | 2 | 3 | 4 | 5 |
| 9. | I enjoy coaching other members of my team. | 1 | 2 | 3 | 4 | 5 |

*continued on next page*

## THE CHANGING WORKPLACE, cont.

| | Strongly Disagree | Disagree | Neutral | Agree | Strongly Agree |
|---|---|---|---|---|---|
| 10. It is important to recognize others for their accomplishments. | 1 | 2 | 3 | 4 | 5 |
| 11. I would enjoy spending time with visitors to my company even if it interfered with completing a report. | 1 | 2 | 3 | 4 | 5 |
| 12. I like to represent my team in gatherings outside my department. | 1 | 2 | 3 | 4 | 5 |
| 13. My teammates' problems are my problems. | 1 | 2 | 3 | 4 | 5 |
| 14. I enjoy resolving conflict. | 1 | 2 | 3 | 4 | 5 |
| 15. I would cooperate with another team in my organization even if I disagreed with the position taken by its members. | 1 | 2 | 3 | 4 | 5 |
| 16. I am an idea generator in my team. | 1 | 2 | 3 | 4 | 5 |
| 17. My teammates listen to me when I speak. | 1 | 2 | 3 | 4 | 5 |
| 18. I like to negotiate with others. | 1 | 2 | 3 | 4 | 5 |
| 19. People have asked me to take the lead on an activity several times in my life. | 1 | 2 | 3 | 4 | 5 |
| 20. While I am willing to listen, I am able to convince others of my views. | 1 | 2 | 3 | 4 | 5 |

*continued on next page*

## THE CHANGING WORKPLACE, cont.

### SCORING

Total your score for the 20-item questionnaire.

| | |
|---|---|
| 90–100 | High readiness for a leadership role |
| 60–89 | Moderate readiness for a leadership role |
| 40–59 | Some uneasiness about assuming a leadership role |
| 39 or Less | Low readiness for a leadership role |

### DISCUSSION QUESTIONS

1. Do you agree with the interpretation of your readiness to assume a leadership role?

2. If you scored 59 or less, how might you attempt to increase your readiness to lead? Using the 20 items in the questionnaire, how might you enhance your leadership readiness?

3. What types of problems occur when you exert leadership in a group? What specific leadership actions and/or behaviors might help to resolve these problems? What is your underlying rationale? Why would these actions/behaviors resolve the problem?

**SOURCE:** This exercise was adapted from A.J. DuBrin, *Leadership: Research Findings, Practice, and Skills* (Houghton Mifflin Co., 1995), 10–11; and R. Kreitner and A. Kinicki, *Organizational Behavior*, 4th ed. (Irwin McGraw-Hill, 1998), 521–52.

## CONCLUDING COMMENTS

In the evolving information-based workplace, traditional methods and styles of leadership must change to be successful and sustain competitiveness. Leadership styles must be flexible and adaptable to the situation at hand. Leadership is the ability to use strategic competencies and influence to accomplish organizational objectives. This includes managing cross-cultural differences. Leaders must also responsibly guide the design, implementation, and monitoring of the organization's moral environment. Leaders are also stewards of people and resources; they differ from managers in terms of developing vision, setting agendas, innovating, working from a long-term view, and inspiring people.

Recent directions in leadership thinking include the topics of followership, self-leaders, superleaders, and transformational and charismatic leaders. Effective followers, in fact, act like leaders by performing as team players who partner with organization leaders to create a vision and to implement goals and strategies. Ineffective followers slow down leaders. Superleadership is leading others to lead themselves and allowing others to own their jobs. Superleaders must be self-leaders first. Self-leaders are internally motivated and driven. Superleaders, after mastering self-leadership, must then model self-leadership, encourage others to set their own goals, create positive thought patterns, facilitate self-leadership through reward systems, promote self-leadership through teamwork, and facilitate a self-leadership culture.

As a result of market forces, leaders in the role of transformational or charismatic leaders are being called upon to lead and direct change, whether that change is a result of political, technical, or cultural attributes. These change tasks include motivating change, creating a vision, developing political support, managing the transition, and sustaining momentum for the vision.

Traditional leadership theories summarized include the trait approach, the managerial grid, Fiedler's contingency model, the path-goal theory, the Vroom-Yetton-Jago model, and the life-cycle model.

## SCENARIO AND EXERCISE: CHANGE MANAGEMENT MAVERICK

Nick Earle, a 42-year-old marketing executive, has been charged by Carly Fiorina, CEO of Hewlett-Packard (HP), to become a maverick for the company. He has been at HP since 1982. His mission is to start as many new Internet businesses within the company as he can! Earle is now running what is called the "e-services.solutions group" at HP. It is one of only two groups that cuts across all of HP's operating units. "This lets Earle wreak havoc—of the good sort—in all of HP's business units. Earle's primary job is to get HP's businesses to work in innovative ways with other companies to create Web services. He's also charged with building a *keiretsu*, or ecosystem, of Internet companies around HP." Earle is known to be charismatic and to have marketing savvy. He has already negotiated a deal with Qwest Communications (a Denver-based firm) in return for a share of the unit's revenues. He has also made a deal with the watchmaker Swatch to create an Internet-ready watch. Now Earle is charged—with a $150 million investment budget—with making a deal a week. Carly wants everyone at HP to start thinking this way.

Source: Eric Nee, "Hewlett-Packard's New E-vangelist," *Fortune*, 10 January 2000, 166–167.

### Questions

1. What are some problems and challenges Earle is likely to experience in his new maverick role? Explain.

2. Would you enjoy taking on this role? Explain.

3. Draft a memo to Earle offering some change management leadership advice.

### Optional

4. Share your questions and memo with an assigned member from the class. What commonalities and differences did you discover in your answers to questions 1 and 2 and the memos?

5. Have a spokesperson from your group share your group discussion with the class.

## REVIEW QUESTIONS

1. Identify a list of competencies needed to successfully lead a mid- to large-size contemporary organization. Would these competencies change for leading a start up? Explain.

2. What are some differences between managers and leaders? Are you ready for leadership? (Discuss your score on the assessment.)

3. Give some examples of effective and ineffective followers. Characterize yourself as a follower.

4. What are *superleadership* and *self-leadership*?

5. Identify a change model that a leader might use to guide a large-scale organizational transformation effort.

6. Describe the characteristics of a charismatic leader. Do you have these characteristics?

7. Identify three relevant contemporary traits of effective leaders. Which trait(s) best describe you?

8. How can the managerial grid be used to describe the effectiveness of an organizational team?

9. Of the traditional earlier theories do you find (a) Fiedler's contingency model, (b) the path-goal theory, or (c) the life-cycle model to be most useful? Why?

10. Briefly explain the four dimensions of Hofstede's cross-cultural map. Which dimension(s) best describe your mode of operating? Why?

11. Identify some of a leader's suggested roles regarding diversity in an organization.

12. Comment on the section Ways Women Lead. Do you agree/disagree with the descriptions and findings in this section? Explain.

13. Describe ways identified in the chapter for leading ethically in an organization.

14. Do you believe the servant-leadership view is possible and/or helpful in an organization? Explain.

# 8

# Power and Politics

---

After studying this chapter, you should be able to:

1 Define *power* and *politics* in organizations.

2 Identify sources of power and politics.

3 Use power dependency analysis to diagnose power.

4 Present a planned political change model.

5 Discuss tactics for using and increasing power bases.

6 Describe the empowerment process.

7 Identify cultural and international differences in managing power.

8 Present guidelines for ethical uses of power.

---

## POWER AND POLITICS IN AND AROUND ORGANIZATIONS

Doug Ivester, former chairman and CEO of Coca-Cola, resigned under fire in December 1999, illustrating both the complexity and straightforwardness of power in and around corporations. "Ivester's sudden fall from one of the world's premier corporate jobs is more than just a tale of bad luck or plans gone wrong. It is a management story full of leadership lessons. It features colossal arrogance and insecurity. Its main character was blind to his own weaknesses and unwilling to take advice. He became increasingly isolated and obsessed with controlling the tiniest details."[1] At the age of 52, Ivester was let go after serving only two years as CEO. He had worked under the respected Roberto Goizueta (former CEO) for over two decades. Goizueta's untimely death put Ivester in charge. After two years of declining earnings and the dismal prediction of continued shareholder equity loss (35 percent in 1999, 41 percent in 1998, and 56.5 percent in 1997), Warren Buffett—a major stockholder who owns 31 percent or 200 million company shares—and Herbert Allen, who owns more than 8 percent, or nine million shares, apparently lost confidence in Ivester as CEO. Shortly after a meeting in Chicago, which included Buffet and Allen, on December 1, 1999, Ivester resigned his position. What happened?

*the ultimate measure of a CEO is how he handles crises, and again and again, in the view of certain directors and powerful bottling executives, Ivester was a day late and a dollar short. "It's a little like mountain climbing," says a source close to the board. "Anyone can get to a certain level. But very few can function well in the really rare air. Doug [Ivester] was simply unable to give people a sense of purpose or direction." Almost from day one it was apparent that Ivester lacked political skills.[2] He took pride in being a substance-over-style guy—but that translated into taking no heed of image and perception issues, which are merely all-important to a company like Coke. He took pride in managing for the long haul—but that made him unyielding in the face of immediate circumstances. And while he was in command of a vast number of details, he seemed to lose sight of the big picture.[3]*

Company veterans should have foreseen Ivester's problems from a speech ("Be Different or Be Damned") he gave in 1994. He described himself as a wolf—highly independent, nomadic, territorial. He told the audience, "I want your customers. I want your space on the shelves. . . . I want every single bit of beverage growth potential that exists out there." Ivester lost sight of his responsibility of managing power and stakeholders in and around the company. His ability to manage perception, impression, and confidence finally impaired his power to influence and lead.

Leading and participating in organizations, especially those involved in change, require the effective use of power, empowerment, and the management of politics. The lessons in the excerpt apply to everyone working in organizations as well as to CEOs. Understanding the effects we have on others, our ways of influencing, and the sources and uses of our power all determine our effectiveness. We begin this chapter by defining power, influence, and politics. Sources of individual and departmental power are then identified, followed by methods for diagnosing power. A planned change model that considers the role of politics is presented. Tactics for increasing legitimate power are discussed. An empowerment process is described, followed by suggestions for managing cultural differences regarding power. Finally, guidelines for managing power ethically are identified.

## Power Defined

Everyone in an organization has varying degrees of power. Without power, people cannot plan and achieve goals; they cannot motivate themselves or others, manage their careers effectively, mobilize resources, or protect their rights. Without power, organizations cannot compete effectively in national and global markets. Power in and of itself is neither bad nor evil. The motivations underlying power and its uses determine how functional or dysfunctional, moral or immoral power and its consequences are.

**Power**, at the individual level in an organization, is the ability of A to influence B to do something that A desires. At the organizational level, power is the ability of a leader or a dominant coalition to use resources to achieve stated goals. McClelland, as mentioned in Chapter 4, identifies "two faces of power": socialized power and personalized power.[4] Inherent in socialized power is a concern for the interests of others and of the organization; personalized power is about the self and seeks individual aggrandizement. Effective leadership involves the use of socialized power.

## THE CHANGING WORKPLACE

### Women's Uses of Power:  Breaking the Glass Ceiling

**Exercise**: Research by B.R. Ragins and E. Sundstrom suggests that female managers show greater need for institutional power than for personal power compared to their male counterparts. Ragins, Townsend, and Mattis in another study surveyed female executives and identified 13 career strategies, 9 of which were believed by respondents to be central in their career advancement.

**Step 1**. Rank order from 1 (most important) to 13 (least important) the following strategies that you believe to be most important for yourself in climbing a career ladder. If you are male, rank order this list according to what you believe would help women climb a career ladder.

_____ Change companies.
_____ Upgrade educational credentials.
_____ Consistently exceed performance expectations.
_____ Develop style that men are comfortable with.
_____ Gain international experience.
_____ Develop leadership outside the office.
_____ Network with influential colleagues.
_____ Be able to relocate.

_____ Seek difficult or high visibility assignments.
_____ Initiate discussion regarding career aspirations.
_____ Move from one functional area to another.
_____ Gain line management experience.
_____ Have an influential mentor.

**Step 2.** Pair with a member of the opposite sex in the class. Share your rankings and explain your reasons for them. What factors influenced your ranking? Observe the differences between your rankings. Identify why each of you believes the rankings differed, if they did. Do you believe your gender influenced your rankings? Explain.

**Step 3.** Turn to the end of this chapter (page 259) for the results of how female executives in the study rated dimensions in this list. After you compare your rankings with results from the study, what did you discover? Were yours similar, different?

SOURCES: B.R. Ragins and E. Sundstrom, "Gender and Power in Organizations: A Longitudinal Perspective," *Psychological Bulletin*, 1989, 70, 105, B.R. Ragins, B. Townsend, and M. Mattis, "Gender Gap in the Executive Suite: CEOs and Female Executives Report on Breaking the Glass Ceiling," *The Academy of Management Executive*, February 1998, 28–42,

Copyright Joseph W. Weiss, 2000.

### Five Sources of Interpersonal Power

Five sources of interpersonal power in organizations include (1) reward power, (2) expert power, (3) referent power, (4) position or legitimate power, and (5) coercive power.[5] *Reward power* is the ability of a person to influence another by assigning pay, promotions, or other incentives for desired behavior. Managers or supervisors usually have reward power through their use of extrinsic motivators; however, individuals in an organization can reward others through powerful intrinsic means (e.g. praise, a pat on the back, and expressions of gratitude and trust for behaviors). *Expert power* is a person's ability to influence others through specialized skills, knowledge, and other talents. Expert power is part of an individual's training and experience in a particular area such as accounting, computer information technology, finance, or marketing. With the advent of the Internet, programmers and professionals with e-business skills and experience have market power—these skills are in demand. Expert power also can be exerted in areas such as interpersonal communication ("people skills"), the ability to speak powerfully and effectively,[6] and the ability to listen, empathize, and offer constructive support and understanding to others ("emotional intelligence"). *Referent power* is an individual's ability to influence others because she is liked, admired, and/or respected. People usually identify with and seek out a person who has referent power. Sources of referent power can include personality characteristics, charisma, or certain abilities. Individuals are usually attracted to and identify with people who have referent power. Media, movie, sports, political, and other well-known figures often have referent power in the general population (i.e., people identify and are attracted to them). *Position or legitimate power* resides in an individual's job or position in an organization. Company officers, managers, and supervisors have power and the legitimate authority to influence from their organizational position and title. Organizational leaders, for example, can define a company's vision, mission, and strategies. Often part of position power includes reward, expert, and/or coercive power that are defined in the position. Position power, however, can be tenuous (i.e., a person can lose legitimacy if his followers lose confidence in his ability or perceived authority to influence effectively, ethically, or legally as the opening excerpt indicated). *Coercive power* is the ability of a person to influence others through the use of punishment for undesired behaviors. Coercive power is manifest in actions such as reprimands, demotions, less than desired assignments, transfers, suspensions, micromanagement, and dismissal. Coercive power must be carefully considered since actions taken can have negative reactions from affected employees (e.g., sabotage, lowered productivity, increased sick days, and spreading rumors).

### Authority, Influence, and Politics

Power differs from authority and social influence. Authority is the right vested in organizational positions and the chain of command to influence others; authority may—or may not have—the legitimate acceptance of followers.[7] *Social influence* refers to the means and ways of the changing the attitudes and behaviors of others. Individuals can have position power without authority and thus have no social influence. Think, for example, of U.S. presidents who lost authority (legitimacy) such as President Nixon, who could not effectively influence the populace during the latter part of his presidency; he was finally forced to resign. Former President Carter stayed in office (position power) until his term ended, but his influence was weakened in the eyes of the public because he was unable to obtain release of the U.S. hostages in Iran. Bill Clinton managed his influence and power with the public well enough to avoid impeachment and to serve out his term, despite pressures from so many stakeholders. To effectively manage and lead in organizations, individuals, like presidents, must have appropriate authority and be able to influence others. While power, authority and influence are, to a certain extent, invested in positions, there are also other sources and tactics for gaining power and exerting influence; we discuss these later in this chapter.

### Organizational Politics

Politics in organizational life has until recently had negative connotations and has thus been viewed as something to avoid or eradicate. However, politics does have positive connotations and thus is not necessarily bad. Organizational politics (the use of power and influence) happens all the time: individuals and groups strive to exert their interpretations and preferences over organizational goals; groups compete over resources, rewards, and recognition; ambiguous information is used for strategic ends; "facts" are used for different interests.[8] *Politics*, defined as the need and ability to have and use power, is a natural phenomenon.

Politics, like power, can become dysfunctional, destructive, and even immoral when individuals or groups use power to supersede organizational goals for their own private ends. Self-interests and organizational interests must always be weighed and balanced. Political behavior works against the organization when self-interests are not aligned with those of the organization. As the opening story illustrated, Doug Ivester, former Coca-Cola CEO, alienated the company's executives, customers, shareholders, board of directors, and employees with his apparent arrogance, obsession with detail, and inability to inspire confidence and purpose from these stakeholders. He seemed to have maintained his own interests and personal wealth accumulation at the expense of Coca-Cola's direction.

Global competitiveness can even be threatened by divided organizational interests if enough companies experience the dark side of politics. One of the reasons that companies fail can be attributed to the enemies within.

"Why is it that I always get a whole person when what I really want is a pair of hands?" Henry Ford lamented. Understandably hostile workers rip apart and sink many a company whose top managers, whatever their public declarations, take that sort of narrow view of their employees. Strikes or hostilities are the obvious signs that a firm has waited way too long to address this problem. During the final days of Eastern Air Lines, senior executives regularly received death threats in the mail; they posted security guards to watch their cars in the company lot. When a new general manager at Mack Truck was touring a plant in Pennsylvania a few years back, a disgruntled worker threw a bolt at him. "Morale was an absolute disaster—everyone self-protective, people trying to keep false pride,"[9] says Mack Chief Executive Elios Pascual. Less blatant but no less fatal are the cynicism and resentments that build when management preaches one doctrine and practices another. An all-too-common example is corporate leaders who can scuttle a reengineering effort quite quickly if they pump up their own bonuses and order a new fleet of company jets while telling the troops to tighten their belts. This brand of managerial hypocrisy goes well beyond pay and perks. Scott Morgan of Arthur D. Little says far too may managers ignore the human dimension of day-to-day operations, taking actions that violate unwritten rules as well as their stated intentions. They preach the importance of teamwork—then reward individuals who work at standing out from the crowd. They announce a preference for workers with broad experience—then denounce job jumpers within the organization. They encourage risk taking—then punish good-faith failures. Says Morgan: "It really is tantamount to managerial malpractice."[10]

## Understanding and Managing Politics and Power

Harold Leavitt, a noted Harvard marketing professor and consultant, offers these thoughtful insightful guidelines for understanding and managing politics and power to prevent the dysfunctional results we have just seen.

> What does it mean to manage with power? First, it means recognizing that in almost every organization, there are varying interests. This suggests that one of the first things we need to do is to diagnose the political landscape and figure out what the relevant interests are, and what important political subdivisions characterize the organization. It is essential that we do not assume that everyone necessarily is going to be our friend, or agree with us, or even that preferences are uniformly distributed. There are clusters of interest within organizations, and we need to understand where these are and to whom they belong.
>
> Next, it means figuring out what point of view these various individuals and subunits have on issues of concern to us. It also means understanding why they have the perspective they do. It is all too easy to assume that those with a different perspective are somehow not as smart as we are, not as informed, not as perceptive. If that is our belief, we are likely to do several things, each of which is disastrous. First, we may act contemptuously toward those who disagree with us—after all, if they aren't as competent or insightful as we are, why should we take them seriously? It is rarely difficult to get along with those who resemble us in character and opinions. The real secret of success in organizations is the ability to get along with those who differ from us, whom we don't necessarily like, to do what needs to be done. Second, if we think people are misinformed, we are likely to try to "inform" them, or to try to convince them with facts and analysis. Sometimes this will work, but often it will not, for their disagreement may not be based on a lack of information; it may, instead, arise from a different perspective on what our information means. Diagnosing the point of view of interest groups as well as the basis for their positions will assist us in negotiating with them and in predicting their response to various initiatives.
>
> Third, managing with power means understanding how to get things done, you need power—more power than those whose opposition you must overcome—and thus it is imperative to know where power comes from and how these sources of power can be developed. We are sometimes reluctant to think very purposely or strategically about acquiring and using power. We are prone to believe that if we do our best, work hard, be nice, and so forth, things will work out for the best. I don't mean to imply that one should not, in general, work hard, try to make good decisions, and be nice, but that these and similar platitudes are often not very useful in helping to get things done in our organizations. We need to understand power and how to get it. We must be willing to do things to build our sources of power, or else we will be less effective than we might wish to be.
>
> Fourth, managing with power means understanding the strategies and tactics through which power is developed and used in organizations, including the importance of timing,

*the use of structure, the social psychology of commitment and other forms of interpersonal influence. If nothing else, such an understanding will help us become astute observers of the behavior of others. The more we understand power and its manifestations, the better will be our clinical skills. More fundamentally, we need to understand strategies and tactics of using power so that we can consider the range of approaches available to us. . . .and use what is likely to be effective. Again, as in the case of building sources of power, we often try not to think about these things, and we avoid being strategic or purposeful about employing our power. This is a mistake. Although we may have various qualms, there will be others who do not. Knowledge without power is of remarkably little use. And power without the skill to employ it effectively is likely to be wasted.*[11]

Bill Gates has effectively understood and used his knowledge as power to build what may be the world's most successful software technology company.

*Gates self-consciously tries to sustain the company's image as dauntingly capable and his own as a youthful genius. He has become so identified with his company that in the public mind he is Microsoft. From a marketing standpoint, a bunch of faceless corporations are competing against a superhuman billionaire. . . . "Microsoft's greatest strength is perception," says Bill Raduchel, chief strategist for Sun Microsystems. "Our customers get lots of pressure from end users in their organizations to go with Microsoft."*[11]

However, Gates' ability to use his political power responsibly is controversial. He was found by the U.S. Department of Justice to have created a monopoly illegally and unethically. Gates' supporters contend that he used his power shrewdly to compete in a hypercompetitive, imperfect technology environment.

## SOURCES OF POWER AND POLITICS

Corporate sources of power are found in the quality of its management, the quality of its products and services, and the degree of its innovation. Whether it views value as a long-term investment; maintains financial soundness; actively cultivates the ability to attract, develop, and keep talented people; manages community and environmental responsibilities—these are responsible and productive uses of corporation's assets, and these are its power base.[13] Obviously, not all firms that rank high on these indicators use power responsibility or effectively, but these dimensions serve as benchmarks for "scoring" a company's market and nonmarket effectiveness and, we may add, its uses of power.

Within an organization, individual sources of power for top- and mid-level managers and lower-level employees come from different areas.[14] Top management's vertical power sources are found in the following areas. The structure of the organization—the positioning of individual—defines the degree of control, authority, and governance responsibilities formally given them as well as their control over information and other positions. (Many CEOs have, and would prefer to have the title chair of the board combined with their CEO title to add to their

## THE CHANGING WORKPLACE

### Your Political Tendencies

**Exercise**: Check only True or False to the following statements that best generally represent your belief or behavior.

T F 1. You should make others feel important through an open appreciation of their ideas and work.

T F 2. Because people tend to judge you when they first meet you, always try to make a good first impression.

T F 3. Try to let others do most of the talking, be sympathetic to their problems, and resist telling people that they are totally wrong.

T F 4. Praise the good traits of the people you meet and always give people an opportunity to save face if they are wrong or make a mistake.

T F 5. Spreading false rumors, planting misleading information, and back-stabbing are necessary, if somewhat unpleasant, methods to deal with your enemies.

T F 6. Sometimes it is necessary to make promises that you know you will not or cannot keep.

T F 7. It is important to get along with everybody, even with those who are generally recognized as windbags, abrasive, or constant complainers.

T F 8. It is vital to do favors for others so that you can call in those IOUs at times when they will do you the most good.

T F 9. Be willing to compromise, particularly on issues that are minor to you, but major to others.

T F 10. On controversial issues, it is important to delay or avoid your involvement if possible.

**Scoring Key:** If you answered "true" to all the questions, your tendencies indicate those of an organizational politician. If you answered "false" to all or most of the questions, your tendencies see political activities such as hoarding information, manipulation, and self-oriented behavior as unacceptable. If you answered "false" to questions 5 and 6, but "true" to most of the other questions, you are a politician with some fundamental ethical standards.

**SOURCE:** J. Byrnes, "The Political Behavior Inventory." Permission granted for reprint here.

power). Top-level managers also have: (1) initial access to, and control of, strategic information and decisions; (2) network centrality—top administrators position themselves at the center of an organization's critical and strategic information flow. They can therefore build and expand their power base to build alliances through the information and people they control.

### Middle Managers' Power Sources

Mid-level managers are influenced by organizational design and network interactions since people at mid-levels need information and task control to enhance their productivity. Rosabeth Moss Kanter identifies the following task activities and network interactions that accrue power to mid-level managers in organizations:

1. Task activities

2. Network interactions

3. Few rules, precedents, and established routines in the job

4. Central physical location

5. High task variety and flexibility

6. High publicity about job activities and contact with senior officials

7. Many rewards for unusual performance and innovation

8. High participation in programs, conferences, meetings

9. Few approvals needed for nonroutine decisions

10. High participation in problem-solving task forces

11. Central relation of tasks to current problem areas[15]

Note that the opposite for each of the dimensions can generate powerlessness; for example, too many rules and precedents can indicate powerlessness. Low task variety, distant physical location, and low publicity about job activities with senior officials can all generate powerlessness.

### Lower-Level Participants' Power Sources

Employees who work below managerial, supervisory, and team leader positions have less power but can and do exert influence through personal sources and, to a more limited extent, through position sources. Personal sources of power include an individual's expertise, effort, and ability to persuade and manipulate. For example, employees who gain high proficiency over limited but technical activities and information can become indispensable to others. People who take charge, put forth great effort, and show interest can increase their power: they make themselves available for advancement and for assignments on critical tasks. Finally, the ability to persuade upper management through direct and assertive appeal and by manipulating information effectively (not inaccurately or in a deceiving manner) can accrue power to an individual. For example, an employee who started her career as an executive secretary at a pharmaceutical firm positioned herself as a strategic interpreter of her boss's memos and incoming mail. She became his assistant and an advisor on two teams.

Position power is also available to lower-level participants. By having a central physical location, information access and flow, and access to powerful people, lower-level employees can gain power. (In the information age, in particular, status and, to some extent, position are being leveled through electronic access to information and, therefore, to powerful people. The use of e-mail, fax, and Internet as well as other software server programs open communication channels and thus disperse power to a wider range of people in and around organizations.)

## THE CHANGING WORKPLACE

### How Well Do You Manage Your Boss?

**Exercise**: Answer only "yes" or "no" to the following questions based on your work experiences. (If you have not worked under or for anyone, answer the questions based on what you would do.)

|  | Yes | No |
|---|---|---|
| 1. I make sure I understand my boss's expectations of me and my assignments by asking for clarification and sometimes getting the expected outcomes in writing. | ____ | ____ |
| 2. I keep my boss updated on my progress and on any problems or opportunities that surface during my work. | ____ | ____ |
| 3. I believe in maintaining an honest and open relationship with my boss to avoid unnecessary crises and to ensure taking advantage of opportunities. | ____ | ____ |
| 4. I believe in sharing the glory and success, as well as problems and mishaps, with my boss. | ____ | ____ |
| 5. I make sure I understand my boss's goals and objectives. | ____ | ____ |
| 6. I share the pressures I experience. | ____ | ____ |
| 7. I inquire about my boss's preferred work style. | ____ | ____ |
| 8. I try to understand my boss's weaknesses, strengths, and blind spots. | ____ | ____ |
| 9. I assess and understand my own strengths and weaknesses. | ____ | ____ |
| 10. I assess my own personal work style. | ____ | ____ |
| 11. I evaluate and understand my predisposition toward dependence on authority figures. | ____ | ____ |
| 12. I try to develop and maintain a relationship my boss that ...fits both our styles and needs. | ____ | ____ |

*continued on next page*

---

**THE CHANGING WORKPLACE, cont.**

13. . . . is characterized by mutual expectations.                         ____   ____

14. . . . selectively uses his or her time and resources wisely.           ____   ____

15. . . . is based on honesty and dependability.                           ____ .  ____

**Scoring Key:** If you answered "yes" to most or all the questions, you probably manage, have managed, or can manage your boss or supervisor very well. If you answered "no" to most or all questions, you would most likely have or had difficulty managing her or him. Questions 1–3 indicate how well you manage your boss's expectations. Questions 5–8 indicate how well you understand your boss and his or her situation. Questions 9–11 indicate how well you assess and understand your own needs, which is often a first step to managing your boss. Questions 12–16 indicate how well you develop and maintain a relationship with your boss.

SOURCE: Adapted from J. Gabarro and J. Kotter, "Managing Your Boss," *Harvard Business Review,* January–February, 1980, 92–100.

---

### Organizational Sources of Power

An organizational unit (whether it is a department, division, strategic business unit, cluster, or team) has power to the extent that it can respond to "strategic contingencies" that is, activities and events needed to obtain an organization's critical mission goals.[16]

The power sources that indicate an organizational unit's ability to respond to strategic contingencies include the following dimensions: dependency creation, ability to decrease uncertainty, nonsubstitutability, fiscal resources, and central activities. The unit's power is based on the extent to which it can create dependency; that is, other units depend on its products or services. A department of information and finance, for example, may create such dependencies since it controls critical data and financial information needed by all organizational units. An R&D unit may be more "upstream" (i.e., at the beginning of the product or service creation process) and could therefore create dependencies of units—such as production, marketing, and sales—on it. Ideally, all departments and units should be working as integrated teams, sharing resources and talent. However, the reality is that as for individuals, some units and departments are able to gain more power than others by using these power sources.

An organizational unit's ability to decrease uncertainty is another indicator of its power in the enterprise. A unit need not solve strategic uncertainties to gain power; it can help other units cope with and decrease uncertainty. For example, forecasting, marketing, and other boundary-spanning and information-gathering functions can add power to an organizational unit.[17]

A department, team, or unit is also powerful to the extent that it is nonsubstitutable; that is, it cannot be replaced by another unit.[18] Units that perform highly specialized tasks or that have professionals who are skilled and proficient at such tasks become more nonsubstitutable. There was a time when computer programmers held such positions; now this function is dispersed throughout organizations. What organizational units or departments will be viewed as nonsubstitutable in the twenty-first century?

Control over fiscal resources adds power to an organizational unit.[19] Whether the unit is sales, production, R&D, or finance, the one that controls incoming financial revenue and resources will have a source of power. (The Golden Rule has been restated as "Those who have the gold rule.")

Finally, the degree to which a unit's activities are central—that is, critical to the product, services, or final output of the organization—will add power. Again, since information has become an invaluable resource, units that can access, interpret, and use information to positively affect an organization's outputs accrue power.

### Sources of Politics and Political Behavior

Uncertainty is usually a source for political activity as well as for an opportunity to accrue power; Certain situations provide especially fertile growing ground for uncertainty, which provides opportunities for individuals and units to define their interests. These include lack of an organizational vision and mission, unclear organizational goals and objectives, poorly defined performance metrics and measures, poorly coordinated teams and units, or major change programs that are poorly planned.[20] Unproductive and even destructive political behavior and competition between groups and individuals can occur when leaders do not see and correct these sources of uncertainty. On the other hand, organizational members and groups who seek to constructively define areas of uncertainty for the good of the organization can accrue power in politically responsible ways.

A summary of a research project involving managers from a Southern California electronics company provides an insight into the general nature of the sources of organizational politics:

- Sixty percent of the managers said organizational politics was a frequent occurrence.

- The larger the organization, the greater the perceived political activity.

- Ambiguous roles and goals and increased conflict were associated with increased political activity.

- Marketing staffs and members of corporate boards of directors were rated as the most political, while production, accounting, and finance personnel were viewed as the least political.

- Reorganizations and personnel changes prompted the most political activity.[21]

### Managing Politics in Organizational Change

A Cranfield School of Business survey of 50 senior managers in England who were involved in significant change programs found that in more than half the cases, the executives were resistant to change ideas. In 44 percent of the cases, the senior executives disapproved of many of their managers' ideas by pulling rank ("I'm the boss") as the rationale. After six months of implementing certain changes, 95 percent of the managers saw managing political behavior as central to managing change. The same managers observed that their senior executives relied on their position rather than their leadership in making change decisions and that they were more concerned with their own image than business reasons for taking action. Executives were also observed as being less collaborative than their staff. The following are the lessons from this survey:

> *the control and management of personal self-interest is critical to the success of any change program. The key is to recognize and balance one's own motivations with those of others. Executives [Directors] who are good politicians must be aware of the hidden agendas both of their peers and the managers who report to them. They must be able to work the formal and informal decision-making processes, and decipher the subtext of what is said and not said.*[22]

Another study of change agents' roles in organizations concluded that "organizational political behavior thus presents both positive and negative, 'nice and nasty' faces to the observer and to recipients or victims. . . . a reappraisal and further investigation of the multifaceted political dimension of change agency, and the complex and tacit nature of the skills involved, seem appropriate."[23]

### Preventing and Controlling Dysfunctional Politics

Each organization differs in the specific nature of its politics. The dimensions offered here are broad categories that can be used to mitigate unconstructive political activity. Strategies for reducing, preventing, and managing dysfunctional aspects of organizational politics include the following actions.

**To Reduce System Uncertainty**

1. Make clear what the bases for evaluation are.

2. Differentiate rewards among high and low performers.

3. Make sure the rewards are as immediately and directly related to performance as possible.

**To Reduce Competition**

1. Try to minimize resource competition among managers.

2. Replace resource competition with externally oriented goals and objectives.

**To Break Existing Political Fifedoms**

1. When highly cohesive political empires exist, break them apart by removing or splitting the most dysfunctional subgroups.

2. If you are an executive, be keenly sensitive to managers whose mode of operation is the personalization of political patronage. First, approach these persons

with a directive to "stop the political maneuvering." If it continues, remove them from the positions and, preferably, the company.

**To Prevent Future Fiefdoms**

1.  Make one of the most important criteria for promotion an apolitical attitude that puts organization ends ahead of personal power ends.[24]

Finally, there are strategies for managing the politics and paradoxes of transformation in planned organizational change programs. The following should be kept in mind as an organization steers its way through transformation.

1.  Everyone must have a voice, but cynics must be silenced. Those individuals with the most to lose from change will be the loudest opponents. Diffusing their arguments will help keep the change moving forward.

2.  Without taking their eyes off the horizon, leaders must watch where they step. In order to achieve an organization's vision, the leaders must ensure that all actions taken by their followers are necessary to achieve desired results.

3.  Change is scary, but people volunteer for dangerous tasks only when they feel safe. People will feel safe when they know their future. By giving them responsibility for the implementation and results of the transformation, the new way becomes their future.[25]

## Sexual Harassment as Abuse of Power

Working women experience and are increasingly reporting sexual harassment in and related to the workplace. Employers continue to face the problem of women being harassed by men. In this context, *sexual harassment* has been defined as "unsolicited non-reciprocal male behavior that asserts a woman's sex role over her function as a worker."[26] The Supreme Court ruled in 1986 that sexual harassment is illegal under Title VII of the 1964 Civil Rights Act when a "hostile environment" is created, thereby interfering with an employee's performance. Later court rulings have further identified sexual harassment as "unwelcome sexual advances, coercion, favoritism, visual harassment, physical conduct."[27] Sexual harassment is about the abuse of power; in many cases, sexual harassment involves a male's use of position power in an *organization* over a female's. Sexual harassment is about coercion: do what I say, or lose your job; be demoted; be transferred; be given an undesirable assignment. Recent sexual harassment cases at Mitsubishi, Astra (a Swedish pharmaceutical firm), and the U.S. Navy involved the abuse of power of superiors over lower-ranking women within the context of a culturally hostile environment. EEOC (Equal Employment Opportunity Commission) guidelines place absolute liability on employers for actions and violations of the law by their managers and supervisors. The uses and abuses of power in organizations are the responsibility of the organization's owners, its leaders, managers, and its supervisors. An organization's vision, mission, values, leadership, policies, training programs, and enforcement of rules must spell out for all parties expectations, conduct, and consequences of violating policies.

## POWER DEPENDENCY ANALYSIS

How much power do you have or have you had in your organization? How can or could you find out? The power/dependency analysis[28] can be used by individuals as well as by groups.[29]

The power dependency analysis also involves a mapping of major players between a focal person and or others in an organization—as well as for the entire organization. Figure 8–1 is an example of a power dependency map for a hospital manager. The major difference between this analysis and the stakeholder analysis is that the focus here centers on identifying major dependencies between the focal person or organization and the other groups. An assessment (high, medium, or low) of the nature of the dependencies is then made. Influence strategies can then be identified to decrease the dependency on each player regarding an issue or plan and thereby increase options for gaining power.

For example, Figure 8–1 shows that this hospital administrator is highly dependent on the smaller unions and employee associations to accomplish the hospital's goals. The administrator must communicate frequently and keep aligned with the mayor's office, accreditation agencies, the affiliated medical school, and civil service agencies. These are all ranked high as the administrator's power sources.

John Kotter states the following:

*Considerable evidence, accumulated by observing and talking with managers, suggests that successful managers cope with their dependence on others by being sensitive to it, by eliminating or avoiding unnecessary dependence, and by establishing countervailing power over those others. Good managers then use that power to help them plan, organize, staff, budget, motivate, and evaluate. Without the skillful acquisition and use of power, managers are seldom able to cope effectively with their dependence on others; the dependence in their jobs is just too great, and their automatic control over it is far too little. They need additional power and ability to use it so as to influence others to cooperate. In other words, the primary reason power dynamics emerge and play an important role in organizations is not necessarily because managers are power hungry, or because they want desperately to get ahead, or because there is an inherent conflict between managers who have authority and workers who do not. It is because the dependence inherent in managerial jobs is greater than the power or control given to the people in those jobs.[29]*

This observation reinforces the point made earlier; that is, managers should ensure that organizational systems are appropriate and fit together. Alignment among systems minimizes dysfunctional politics and power-seeking behavior.

The power dependency analyses can assist managers and organizational members in identifying, planning, and implementing strategies to enhance their power base.

**FIGURE 8–1    A Power Dependency Map**

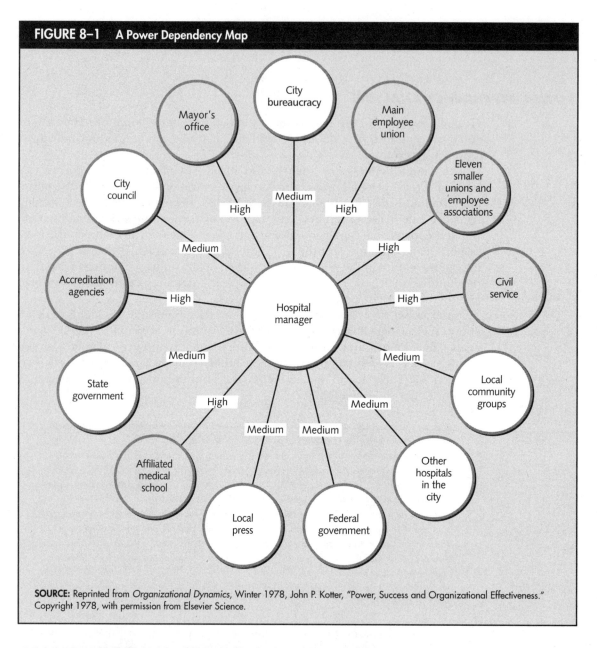

SOURCE: Reprinted from *Organizational Dynamics*, Winter 1978, John P. Kotter, "Power, Success and Organizational Effectiveness." Copyright 1978, with permission from Elsevier Science.

## ORGANIZATIONAL POLITICS AND PLANNED CHANGE

If you were assigned to a task force to plan an organizational transformation initiative in a company, how would you view the politics that could arise? Organizational development (OD) researchers and practitioners have long recognized the reality of politics in the process of planned organizational change;

## THE CHANGING WORKPLACE

### Your Power Dependency Map

**Exercise:** Refer to the section on power dependency in the chapter. On the following map, select a situation at a current or previous job or in your role as a student at your university or college. You may want to select a particular project you are working on.

1.  On the map, fill in the persons or groups on whom you depend most to successfully accomplish your work, assignment, or tasks.

2.  Place on the lines from "you" in the center circle to each of your other stakeholders a "high," "medium," or "low" power dependency rating.

3.  Answer this question for each of your dependency relations: What is the nature of this dependency: why are you dependent on this person or group? Why is this relationship a high, medium, or low rating?

4.  What tactics or strategies (check the influence tactics in the chapter) do you plan to use or did you use to decrease your dependency or increase your success of using the support of each person's or group's resources?

5.  What is the probability your tactic or strategy will or will not, did or did not, work? Why? What did you learn from this exercise? What strategies, tactics, ways you viewed this situation changed after having done this exercise? Why?

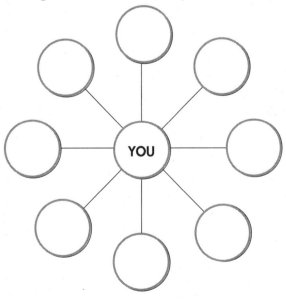

however, some have avoided the topic, but most have been at best cautious in articulating political approaches to help implement the changes. One model that acknowledges and suggests the use of legitimate political strategies in assisting planned organizational change is illustrated in Table 8–1.[30] In this approach, politics is seen as a given and is part of the planning effort.

Planned organization change is presented through three levels of change in Figure 8–2 on page 256. Notice that each level is explained as affecting the following dimensions of the change process: intended outcomes and change targets, extent of political involvement, and basic political strategies. The higher the level of change attempted, the more widespread the change effects in the organization and the greater the political involvement of change agents is required. For example, at the third and highest level of change effort, the intended outcome is what we have referred to as *transformational*, that is, an organizationwide change of values and systems. The extent of political involvement required from agents in this type of change is termed *political intervention* as compared with *political awareness*, which is required at the first level of maintaining status quo.

| TABLE 8–1 | Political Involvement Framework for Implementing Planned Organizational Change | | |
|---|---|---|---|
| *Level of Change* | *Intended Outcomes and Change Targets* | *Extent of Political Involvement* | *Basic Political Strategies* |
| First level | • Maintain status quo<br>• Enhance effectiveness of subsystem/unit/department. | Political awareness | • Awareness of values, beliefs, and power dependencies.<br>• Tacitly supporting them.<br>• Create impetus for change. |
| Second level | • Introduce new perspectives and changes within subsystem/s. | Political facilitation | • Assume the role of influencer.<br>• Harmonize divergent interests.<br>• Ensure smooth transitions. |
| Third level | • Organizationwide changes in values.<br>• Create self-renewing capacity. | Political intervention | • Question and debate.<br>• Gain support of dominant coalition.<br>• Manipulate if required to operationalize changes. |

SOURCE: K. Kumar and M. Thibodeaux, "Organizational Politics and Planned Organizational Change," Sage Publications, Inc., *Group and Organizational Studies*, Vol. 15, No. 4 (1990), 357–365. Reprinted by permission of Sage Publications, Inc.

Political intervention requires the active use of strategies and tactics to implement the change goals. The basic political strategies of change agents at the third level of change include questioning and debating, gaining support of the dominant coalition, and, if necessary, manipulating and leveraging resistant stakeholders to operationalize the changes. Again, this model does not shy away from advocating the responsible use of political skills and interventions in assisting change programs in organizations. One of your possible task force assignments at this level might be to identify the new changes and power shifts required of a stakeholder and then to develop ways to negotiate these changes with this individual or group.

*Political facilitation* is required at the second level for introducing new perspectives within a subsystem. Political facilitation can involve assisting new managers in the design and implementation of sensitive strategies and programs. A possible role for you at this level might be to form a focus group with an agenda that includes changing, even confronting, attitudes and responsibilities of organizational members to the planned changes.

This change model recognizes the political realities that exist in organizations, especially when planned change is implemented. Political maneuvering may be required of change agents.

Matching political involvement to the level of desired change makes conceptual as well as practical sense. Although the benefits of matching political maneuvers with the degree of change sought are somewhat obvious, such an approach also advocates occasional use of such tactics and behaviors that may be considered ethically objectionable. We have not tried to make an exclusive argument for ends justifying the means; however, organizational politics is an organizational reality, and ensuring success of a change program may occasionally require tactical confrontation with this reality. Baritz argues that industrial psychologists [change agents] should concern themselves with means only, not with goals, aims, or ends. The debate on this issue continues. In a pragmatic sense, although some of the behaviors that change agents may have to apply occasionally to ensure the success of a change program could be initially distasteful to them, these behaviors in the long term may also provide an effective approach to achieving the organizational goals.[31]

In other words, politics is a reality, especially during organizational change programs. Managers and consultants alike require political skills in understanding and effectively negotiating and using power sources and tactics to obtain organizational goals.

## INFLUENCE TACTICS FOR INCREASING POWER

More than a decade of research, testing, and refinement of Davis Kipnis's influence method and strategies has resulted in identifying eight generic influence tactics.[32] Kipnis and his colleagues identified these influence tactics by asking employees how they manage their bosses, co-workers, and followers. The tactics are as follows:

- *Consultation.* Gaining the participation of others in decisions and changes.

- *Rational persuasion.* Convincing others with reason, logic, or facts.

- *Inspirational appeals.* Building enthusiasm by appealing to others' emotions, ideals, or values.

- *Ingratiating tactics.* Getting someone in a good mood prior to making a request.

- *Coalition tactics.* Gaining the support of others in your effort to persuade someone.

- *Pressure tactics.* Soliciting compliance or using intimidation and threats.

- *Upward appeals.* Persuading someone on the basis of express or implied support from superiors.

- *Exchange tactics.* Making express or implied promises and trading favors.

Obviously, certain tactics would be more effective and appropriate under some circumstances than others. For example, U.S. business professionals must be flexible in negotiating internationally. Rational persuasion alone may not work effectively with certain international business negotiators. Exchange and ingratiating tactics must also be used in cultures that are "high context," as discussed in the chapter on communication.

Other influence strategies[33] that also identify potential outcomes include the following:

| **Influence Strategies** | **Outcome** |
| --- | --- |
| Involve the person in the decision process. | Identifies with and accepts the decision. |
| Control the information. Be the expert. | Needs your direction. |
| Engineer the situation. Control tasks, schedules, where people work, and so on. | Does what you want without knowing you wanted it. |
| Make formal requests within your realm of authority. | Complies with your request if it is seen as legitimate. |
| Use rational persuasion. Show people that it is in their best interest. | Complies because request leads to accomplishment. |
| Offer desired rewards. | Complies to get a particular resource. |
| Generate hope of a better future; higher show a good is being accomplished. | Complies because it is "morally right." |
| Increase your dependence on the other person. | Responds to informal expectations because of growing trust. |

Additional influence and political tactics for increasing power that apply to individuals and organizational units[34] include the following: entering high-uncertainty areas, building coalitions, expanding networks; controlling decision premises, and enhancing legitimacy and expertise.

*Entering areas of high uncertainty* can increase power, especially if such areas are critical to the mission of the organization and provide payoff if uncertainty is decreased or solutions are provided. For example, in the software industry, areas of high uncertainty but with profit potential include groupware and networking and enabling cross-team online communications. Some risk is involved in pursuing this strategy; for example, if the individual or unit attains a level of visibility while working with the uncertainty and is unable to effectively deal with the area, loss of status or credibility could follow.

*Building coalitions* involves enlisting others to form a group to pursue strategy interests.[35] Coalition building requires interpersonal skills, trust, and possibly resource sharing. This strategy enhances power since goal achievement may not be possible without group strength and support. For example, hospitals and health care providers have been building coalitions, merging, and forming strategic alliances to cut costs and gain expanded access to clients.

Similarly, *expanding networks* can build power through either of two approaches. First, initiating contact with organizational members (preferably powerful and influential ones) and aligning interests to meet common objectives increase the likelihood of gaining support to sell or implement strategies or initiatives. Secondly, co-opting dissenters into your network increases your power by decreasing that of your opponents.

*Controlling decision premises* refers to gaining control over decision processes. With this control, the premises for decisions can be manipulated in any one of the following ways: limiting access of information to other managers or members; adding items to an agenda; and emphasizing particular problems or alternatives at meetings.

*Enhancing legitimacy and expertise* refers to the fact that those who have or gain expertise are more likely to be seen as legitimate and can therefore exert more influence and power. Hiring outside experts for their opinions or informed judgments on decisions can add legitimacy and expertise in organizational situations.

Finally, keeping power implicit—that is, unspoken—safeguards it. The powerless usually "show and tell"; the powerful have no need to make claims. They have the means to act.[36]

These tactics and strategies for enhancing individual and organizational unit power in organizations are not intended to advocate selfishness or unethical uses of power. Organizational activities, as discussed earlier, are by nature political. When power is used wisely and for organizational ends, it is functional and constructive and even adds value.

## THE CHANGING WORKPLACE

### Your Empowerment Profile

**Exercise**: Check either a or b to indicate how you usually are in these situations:

1. If someone disagrees with me in a class or a meeting, I   .
   a. immediately back down.
   b. explain my position further.

2. When I have an idea for a project, I
   a. typically take a great deal of time to start it.
   b. get going on it fairly quickly.

3. If my boss or teacher tells me to do something which I think is wrong, I
   a. do it anyway, telling myself he or she is "the boss."
   b. ask for clarification and explain my position.

4. When a complicated problem arises, I usually tell myself
   a. I can take care of it.
   b. I will not be able to solve it.

5. When I am around people of higher authority, I often
   a. feel intimidated and defer to them.
   b. enjoy meeting important people.

6. As I awake in the morning, I usually feel
   a. alert and ready to conquer almost anything.
   b. tired and have a hard time getting myself motivated.

7. During an argument, I
   a. put a great deal of energy into "winning."
   b. try to listen to the other side and see if we have any points of agreement.

8. When I meet new people, I
   a. always wonder what they are "really" up to.
   b. try to learn what they are about and give them the benefit of a doubt until they prove otherwise.

9. During the day, I often
   a. criticize myself on what I am doing or thinking.
   b. think positive thoughts about myself.

10. When someone else does a great job, I
    a. find myself picking apart that person and looking for faults.
    b. often give a sincere compliment.

11. When I am working in a group, I try to
    a. do a better job than the others.
    b. help the group function more effectively.

12. If someone pays me a compliment, I typically
    a. try not to appear boastful and downplay the compliment.
    b. respond with a positive "thank you" or similar response.

13. I like to be around people who
    a. challenge me and make me question what I do.
    b. give me respect.

14. In love relationships, I prefer the other person
    a. have his/her own selected interests.
    b. do pretty much what I do.

15. During a crisis, I try to
    a. resolve the problem.
    b. find someone to blame.

16. After seeing a movie with friends, I
    a. wait to see what they say before I decide whether I liked it.
    b. am ready to talk about my reactions right away.

*continued on next page*

## THE CHANGING WORKPLACE, cont.

17. When work deadlines are approaching, I typically
    a. get flustered and worry about completion
    b. buckle down and work until the job is done.

18. If a job comes up I am interested in, I
    a. go for it an apply.
    b. tell myself I am not qualified enough.

19. When someone treats me unkindly or unfairly, I
    a. try to rectify the situation.
    b. tell other people about the injustice.

20. If a difficult conflict situation or problem arises, I
    a. try not to think about it, hoping it will resolve itself.
    b. look at various options and may ask others for advance before I figure out what to do.

**Scoring**: Score one point for each of the following circled: 1b, 2b, 3b, 4a, 5b, 6a, 7b, 8b, 9b, 10b,11b, 12b, 13a, 14a, 15a, 16b, 17b, 18a, 19a, 20b.

**Analysis of Scoring**

16–20  You are a take-charge person and generally make the most of opportunities. When others tell you something cannot be done, you may take this as a challenge and do it anyway. You see the world as an oyster with many pearls to harvest.

11–15  You try hard, but sometimes your negative attitude prevents you from getting involved in productive projects. Many times you take responsibility, but there are situations in which you look to others to take care of problems.

0–10    You complain too much and are usually focused on the "worst case scenario." To you the world is controlled by fate and no matter what you do, it seems to get you nowhere, so you let other people develop opportunities. You need to start seeing the positive qualities in yourself and in others and see yourself as the "master of your fate."

## THE EMPOWERMENT PROCESS

*Empowerment* is the process of sharing power with others through decentralizing structures, roles, and responsibilities and through delegating work that has inherent authority.[37] As discussed in Chapter 7, the process of empowerment centers on involving people and enabling them to take ownership of their work process and outcomes. Empowered individuals have a sense of trust, energy, commitment, responsibility, and pride in their work and its product or service.

Empowering people is essential in contemporary organizations that are flatter, more dispersed, outsourced, virtual, and networked. And, because workforces are so diverse, one size of motivation does not fit all. Empowering individuals of different cultural, religious, socioeconomic, age, racial, and educational backgrounds requires organizational behavioral skills that we have discussed throughout this book: communication, leadership, delegation, and understanding how to motivate.

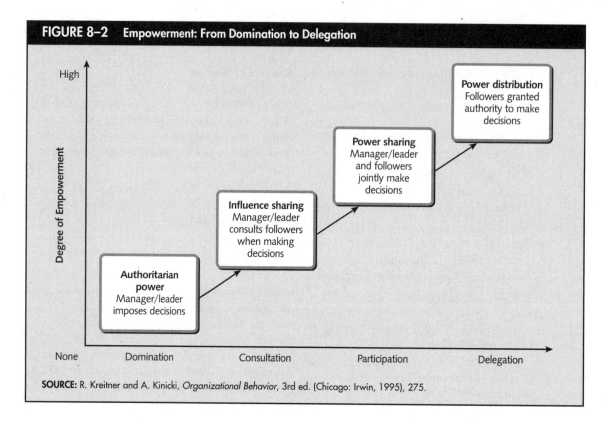

**FIGURE 8–2    Empowerment: From Domination to Delegation**

High

Degree of Empowerment

**Power distribution**
Followers granted
authority to make
decisions

**Power sharing**
Manager/leader
and followers
jointly make
decisions

**Influence sharing**
Manager/leader
consults followers
when making
decisions

**Authoritarian
power**
Manager/leader
imposes decisions

None          Domination          Consultation          Participation          Delegation

**SOURCE:** R. Kreitner and A. Kinicki, *Organizational Behavior*, 3rd ed. (Chicago: Irwin, 1995), 275.

Empowerment, therefore, involves managerial involvement on an individual and team basis.

Empowerment is a process. As Figure 8–2 illustrates, the degree of empowerment corresponds with the degree of delegation.[38] This is a useful figure to keep in mind in gauging the extent or lack of delegation of who's empowering whom or, conversely, who's not empowering whom at meetings, planning sessions, and in conversations in which assignments are given and negotiated.

Leaders empower followers through a number of processes and means: by providing direction through ideals, vision, and superordinate goals; by stimulating with ideas and proposals; by rewarding formally through incentive systems and informally through personal and peer recognition; by using inspiration, involvement, and feedback sessions to further a follower's development; and by appealing to the needs for autonomy and independence of followers.[39]

## CULTURAL DIFFERENCES IN MANAGING AND USING POWER

The meaning of empowering and the management of power differ across national cultures. As discussed earlier, Hofstede, an international expert on cultures, studied the dimension of power distance. He defines and measures power distance as

> *the extent to which less powerful members of organizations accept the unequal distribution of power. In high power-distance countries, such as the Philippines, Venezuela, and India, superiors and subordinates consider bypassing authority to be insubordination; whereas, in low power-distance countries, such as Israel and Denmark, employees expect to bypass the boss frequently in order to get their work done. When negotiating in high power-distance countries, companies find it important to send representatives with titles equivalent to or higher than those of their bargaining partners. Titles, status, and formality command less importance in low-power countries.[40]*

Andre Laurent studied managerial styles in Western Europe, the United States, Indonesia, and Japan.[41] He asked managers whether they agreed with the statement, "The main reason for a hierarchical structure is so that everybody knows who has authority over whom." What he found was that 86 percent of the Indonesian respondents, 52 percent of Japanese, 50 percent of the Italians, and 45 percent of the French agreed with this statement. Only 38 percent of respondents in the Netherlands and Great Britain agreed, and only 24 percent of the German managers and 18 percent of the Americans agreed with the statement. Laurent's study showed that Americans, in particular as compared with managers in Indonesia, Japan, Italy, and France, believe that organizations operate better with less hierarchy and that employees work more effectively as colleagues than in boss-subordinate relationships. Formal authority means less to American managers than to other nationals.

Nancy Adler points out the following:

> *Americans typically approach a project by outlining the overall goal and each of the major steps and then addressing staffing needs. Indonesians, on the other hand, first need to know who will manage the project and who will work on it. Once they know the hierarchy of people involved, they can assess the project's feasibility. Both cultures need to understand the project's goals and staffing arrangements, but the importance of each is reversed. An American would rarely discuss who will be the project director before at least broadly defining the project, while an Indonesian would rarely discuss the feasibility of a project before knowing who will be its leader.[42]*

As stated earlier, understanding one's own cultural perspective is a first step toward working effectively in other cultural contexts and with other peoples. Not all peoples respond to power and authority in the same way.

## ETHICS AND POWER

Ethical problems and issues often arise because of the misuse of power by those who are in a position to exert power over others. Sexual harassment is a contemporary example of the unethical use of power. Whether it is deliberate or not, sexual harassment occurs from a position of power. Conversely, the targets of the harassment are usually those who have less power in their position, rank, or status than the perpetrator.

Another aspect of the misuse of power is that whistleblowing is one of the last options for those who have no power to assert their rights. Grievance procedures and use of due process mechanisms are preferred avenues for effective resolution of issues arising from powerlessness because whistleblowing, is a high-risk choice for everyone.

Managers can use power ethically by observing the following guidelines:

- Know the stakeholders and, their power and claims involved in each organizational activity, initiative, and proposal.

- Understand employees' rights and the organization's obligations to employees.

- Use ethical principles of fairness, justice, rights, and respect for individuals in dealing with people and situations involving power imbalances and conflicts. The following questions can help guide ethical uses of power.

  - What is the motivation and reason for your own and others' use(s) of power?

  - Whose interests are served by an action? At whose costs? For whose benefit?

  - Is it right? Whose rights are or may be violated?

  - Is it just? Who must suffer undue burden? Who will receive unfair benefits?

  - Do the means justify the ends?

  - Is human dignity respected from those involved and affected?

- Assume a proactive role in ensuring that organizational members understand the vision, mission, values, principles, and procedures for hearing and solving grievances. This can be accomplished by dispersing information at informal and formal meetings and in newsletters, having officers speak to groups, and through seminars, and other forms of instruction.

- Ensure that grievance procedures are in place in the organization and that employees understand the process of these procedures.

Managers can also prevent misuses of power by ensuring that clear organizational goals, plans, and individual roles and responsibilities are understood and followed. Maintaining open and continuous communication with employees is a requirement for managing power ethically.

## CONCLUDING COMMENTS

Leading and participating in organizational change requires the effective use of power and the careful management of politics. Power, for an individual, is the ability to influence someone else to do something that he or she wants. At the

## THE CHANGING WORKPLACE

### Answer Key for Women's Uses of Power: Breaking the Glass Ceiling

| Strategy | Percent Ranked as Critical | Fairly Important | Not Important | Did Not Use |
|---|---|---|---|---|
| 1. Consistently exceed performance expectations | 77% | 22 | 1 | 0 |
| 2. Develop style that men are comfortable with | 61% | 35 | 3 | 1 |
| 3. Seek difficult or high visibility assignments | 50% | 44 | 2 | 4 |
| 4. Have an influential mentor | 37% | 44 | 9 | 9 |
| 5. Network with influential colleagues | 28% | 56 | 9 | 6 |
| 6. Gain line management experience | 25% | 29 | 11 | 33 |
| 7. Move from one functional area to another | 23% | 34 | 20 | 22 |
| 8. Initiate discussion regarding career aspirations | 15% | 47 | 25 | 12 |
| 9. Be able to relocate | 14% | 22 | 17 | 45 |
| 10. Upgrade educational credentials | 12% | 33 | 24 | 29 |
| 11. Change companies | 12% | 24 | 23 | 39 |
| 12. Develop leadership outside office | 11% | 41 | 29 | 18 |
| 13. Gain international experience | 5% | 19 | 24 | 51 |

**SOURCE**: Republished with permission of the Academy of Management from B.R. Ragins, B. Townsend, M. Mattis, "Gender Gap in the Executive Suite: CEOs and Female Executives on Breaking the Glass Ceiling," *The Academy of Management Executive*, 12, 1, 1998, Table 1, 41; permission conveyed through Copyright Clearance Center.

organizational level, power is the ability of those in control over resources to impact stated goals. McClelland has identified two faces of power: socialized power and personalized power. *Socialized power* includes concern for the interests of others and the interests of the organization; *personalized power* is about the self and seeks individual aggrandizement.

Authority is the right vested in organizational positions and chain of command to influence others. *Social influence* refers to the means and ways to change attitudes and behaviors of others. Politics in organizations is the use of power and influence.

Five sources of interpersonal power include expert power, reward power, position or legitimate power, coercive power, and referent power.

Sexual harassment is an abuse of power, particularly between males who use position power over females who are lower ranking in an organizational structure. Sexual harassment results when a hostile environment is created in which an organization's leaders, managers, supervisors, and/or colleagues make unwelcomed gestures, take unwelcomed actions, and speak inappropriate words to employees (more often females). The EEOC and court rulings have held owners, managers, and supervisors liable for all illegal and unethical actions taken in demonstrated sexual harassment cases.

Corporate sources of power may be found in the following dimensions: quality of management; quality of product or service; innovativeness; value as a long-term investment; financial soundness; ability to attract, develop, and keep talented people; community and environmental responsibilities; and use of corporate assets. Within an organization, the sources of power differ for top- and mid-level managers and lower-level employees. An organizational unit has power to the extent that it can respond to strategic contingencies; this is related to the extent to which other units depend on it. An organizational unit's ability to decrease and solve uncertainty is another indicator of its power in the enterprise.

Major sources of uncertainty for organizations are usually sources for dysfunctional politics as well. These include lack of a vision and mission, unclear goals and objectives, poorly defined performance metrics and measures, poorly coordinated teams and units, and major change that is poorly implemented or unplanned.

Planned organizational change was presented through three levels of change: intended outcomes and change targets, extent of political involvement, and basic political strategies. This change model recognizes the political realities that exist in organizations, especially when planned change is being implemented.

The power dependency analysis is a method for diagnosing power in organizations. The power dependency analysis involves mapping the major players between the individual and/or an organization and its constituencies. It focuses on identifying major dependencies between the focal person or organization and the other groups.

Eight influence tactics for increasing power were presented. They are consultation, rational persuasion, inspirational appeals, ingratiating tactics, coalition tactics, pressure tactics, upward appeals, and exchange tactics.

Empowerment is the process of sharing power with others through decentralizing structures, roles and responsibilities and through delegating work with authority. The process of empowerment involves people and enables them to take ownership in their work process and outcomes.

The meaning of empowerment and the management of power differs across national cultures. As stated throughout the book, understanding one's own cultural perspective—on such topics as power—is a first step toward working effectively in other cultural contexts and with other peoples.

Ethical guidelines for managing power were offered. Setting realistic goals, knowing the stakeholders, using fairness criteria in situations involving conflict and uses of power, and communicating ethical standards to employees are all essential steps in managing power responsibly.

## SCENARIO AND EXERCISE

You've just been hired to work in an Internet start-up company that is planning an initial public offering (IPO) if all goes well. The company is based on an auction model of getting customers connected with technical professionals. The customers present their technical problems; professionals bid on the opportunity to answer customers' questions and get paid to do so. You're excited about this opportunity because of the possible monetary reward in cashing in on the favorable stock options you negotiated. You also can learn new e-business skills. However, you face some challenges: first, you are hired to work with a team of 10 professionals—2 marketing, 5 programmers, 1 sales, and 2 database people who do not get along well. Second, there is no "manager" or person in charge. Third, you and your group are charged with taking the company "to the next level"—before the IPO. You will work with these people to assist them in developing a revised, more aggressive strategy to attract more customers, enlarge and enhance the Web site, do some focus groups with outside people, and ensure that the team stays pumped up and productively focused. You have about five months to accomplish this—in Internet time. After a week on the job, you get the picture that no one is going to give you a blueprint on how to make all this happen. You realize that without a lot of authority but plenty of responsibility, you have some quick thinking to do. You also have learned that the programmers get restless with too much talk and not enough action—they're also not socially oriented but are extremely task oriented. The marketing people are frustrated because the programming people are too pushy and feel superior to them and everyone else. The database people want more direction on how to do their jobs but don't know whom to ask. The salesperson is the oldest in the group and feels he should be in charge. He has said he is not getting enough information or cooperation from anyone. You feel closest to the marketing people but know you must cooperate with everyone to get a revised business plan up and running. You are wondering if you have any power here. You are wishing you knew how to influence people. You want the great promised experience and rewards but, in reality, you're frustrated.

1. What are the major issues here?

2. What method(s) could you use to size up this situation?

3. What influence strategies could you use with the different people here?

4. What tactics could you use to empower yourself and others?

5. Should you cut your losses and find another job, or do you believe your analysis of the situation with a good strategy(ies) could work? Explain.

## REVIEW QUESTIONS

1. What is "power" in organizations and how do you get it?

2. Rank in order (1 = best describes, 5 = least describes) the five sources of interpersonal power that best describe your power. Give an example from your work or other group experiences.

3. Give an example of a functional and a dysfunctional use of politics in an organization. Explain a difference between the two examples.

4. Identify three of the influence strategies in the chapter that you have used (or read or seen in the media) in an organization or group setting. Did they work? Explain.

5. Refer to Figure 8–2. Give an example from your own experience or an example with which are aware of a leader, manager, or yourself showing how an action(s), conversation, or assignment moved someone (yourself) up or down the degrees of empowerment. What happened? What was the reason(s) for the empowerment or lack of empowerment?

6. Why is or isn't sexual harassment related to power in organizations? Explain. Are women or men more often than not the victims of sexual harassment? Explain.

7. Is power seen and experienced the same way in organizations across cultures? What are some cultural differences in this chapter or that you have experienced or read about regarding organizational power or perceptions of power? Explain.

8. Give an example of how you were unethically treated regarding a misuse of power in a group or organization. What happened?

9. Name a few ways to prevent or control dysfunctional politics in organizations. Would any of these ways discussed in the chapter have worked for you in a situation in which you were involved or are familiar? Explain.

10. What method(s) in this chapter would you find useful to diagnose power in an organization? Why?

# 9
# Conflict and Negotiation

---

## LEARNING OBJECTIVES

After studying this chapter, you should be able to:

1 Define *conflict*.

2 Identify sources of conflict in organizations.

3 Describe conflict-resolution approaches.

4 Identify strategies for dealing with "difficult people."

5 Discuss a diagnostic checklist for identifying conflict.

6 Define *negotiation*.

7 Explain the negotiation approach of *Getting to Yes*.

8 Describe a cross-cultural negotiation approach.

9 Discuss guidelines for managing conflict and negotiating ethically.

---

## CONFLICT DEFINED

Conflict is an integral part of organizational life. It occurs because of disagreements or incompatibilities between, among, and within individuals, groups, and organizations.[1] Conflict also results from perceived or experienced differences over substantive or emotional issues. Such issues can be related to values, beliefs, goals, policies, procedures, rewards, work assignments, and competencies.

Conflict can be functional (i.e., it can contribute to performance) or dysfunctional and even destructive. The consequences of functional conflict can bring about a greater awareness of problems, it can enhance the search for solutions, and it can motivate employees to change and adapt to new solutions. The consequences of dysfunctional conflict, on the other hand, can create distortions in perception, negative stereotyping, poor communication, absenteeism, decreases in productivity, and even sabotage.

Conflict can be viewed as a bell curve, as Figure 9–1 illustrates. A moderate level of healthy conflict, like stress, (also called "eustress") can enhance achievement. Too much or too little conflict, on the other hand, can lead to negative and even unethical and destructive behaviors, especially if unreasonable pressures and tensions are present.[2] One responsibility of managers and individual employees is to observe and decide how much functional conflict is needed to motivate, enhance,

**FIGURE 9–1** Conflict Continuum

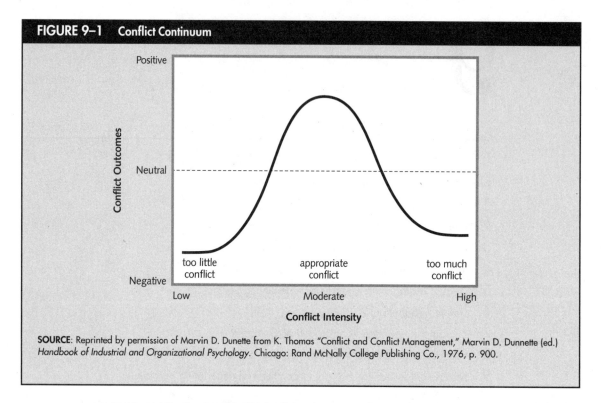

SOURCE: Reprinted by permission of Marvin D. Dunette from K. Thomas "Conflict and Conflict Management," Marvin D. Dunnette (ed.) *Handbook of Industrial and Organizational Psychology.* Chicago: Rand McNally College Publishing Co., 1976, p. 900.

and sustain the productivity of employees and to make sure that it does not degenerate into dysfunctional conflict.

### "She Stands on Common Ground": One Negotiator's Methods

"Where there are organizations, there are people. And where there are people, there are conflicting interests. One of the most basic and most difficult jobs of a leader is sorting through conflicting interests to make choices and achieve common ground."[3] Susan Podziba is a career negotiator and conflict resolution expert. A faculty associate with the Program on Negotiation at Harvard Law School, she has facilitated dialogue between Israelis and Palestinians, environmentalists and fishermen, and prochoice and prolife activists. She expressed her beliefs and principles on negotiating: "Life isn't fair," she says. "The reality is that people everywhere have hard choices to make. My job is to challenge people to see the complexity of a situation and to encourage them to take an active part in making those hard choices." She begins a negotiation by talking with each party separately, untangling issues, perceptions, emotions, and dynamics in a dispute before deciding whether mediation can work. "Mediation is a particular kind of tool that works only when appropriately applied. . . . It won't work unless everybody agrees that some resolution is better than no resolution." She begins a negotiation between two disagreeing parties by designing a mission statement, ground rules for deliberations, and a consensus process in which everyone agrees to participate. For example, answers to these questions must be agreed on: What's an achievable goal? What's the deadline? What are the roles and responsibilities of the mediators? Then Podziba explores worst-case scenarios as well as the best aspirations of the parties. She helps bring the fears and hopes of the parties to the surface so that issues can be analyzed in realistic ways. Following this process, she guides detailed discussions, helping the parties frame the situation and develop proposals. She uses listening exercises to model good communication. Finally, Podziba develops a "universe of options" in which the parties can brainstorm the situation to satisfy everyone's basic needs. "When the process is successful, people force themselves to think in a new way, and they reach a new level of creativity. . . . They start to work in a problem-solving mode."

In this chapter, we identify sources of conflict, describe major conflict-resolution approaches, and present a checklist for diagnosing conflict. We then turn to the related topic of negotiation and discuss cross-cultural and ethical perspectives of negotiating. Our goal here is to enhance the ability of managers, organization members, and students of management to diagnose conflict and to use resolution and negotiation techniques effectively just as Susan Podziba does.

## Sources and Types of Conflict

There are at least five types of conflict in organizations: **structural**, **intrapersonal**, **interpersonal**, **intergroup**, and **interorganizational**. **Structural conflict** occurs because of cross-functional departmental differences over goals, time horizons, rewards, authority, line and staff activities, status, and resources. In classic organization arrangements, experts are organized by functional areas and departments: marketing and sales, research and development (R&D), production, finance, legal, and human resources. These groups have different goals, cultures, approaches, and resources, and conflicts can be expected to arise between and among them.

Sales personnel, for example, may be rewarded on a quota system that depends on how much they sell. Time horizons for selling are often short. Salespeople often have high status in companies because they command high incomes and relate directly with customers. They generally receive enviable resources to do their demanding work, as well as perks and benefits that other groups do not.

R&D personnel, on the other hand, have goals based on product innovation, extension, and modification. They need longer time horizons to develop new products and ample resources to perform their work. They often are seen as creators and inventors, another high-status group. Their work is specialized, and their rewards can be significant.

Production personnel have traditionally clashed with R&D people because R&D sometimes gives new but untested product designs to production. If the design is faulty, both production and salespeople later feel the "heat" from customers, and conflict ensues.

The legal, finance, and human resources departments are classified as "staff" positions; that is, they are not related directly to production operations. The upper-level managers usually appoint staff positions. Staff professionals' rewards, resources, status, authority, goals, and specialization are usually not directly linked to market performance as are line positions (jobs which have direct impact on the production or delivery of a product or service.) Conflict can occur between staff and line positions over status and authority differences.

Because of increased competition, continuous innovations, shortened product life cycles, and the pressure to increase product quality, these different functional areas have begun to work more in cross-functional teams and less in "stovepipes" or traditional departments. Although structural conflict occurs between members of cross-functional teams, today this conflict has more to do with production deadlines, demand for product innovations, meeting customer demands, and having to do more with less than it does with status and frustration levels, which was the case in the past when teams were rare.

**Intrapersonal conflict** occurs within an individual. When this happens, conflict often results over a person's role in the organization—that is, conflict over differences in the expectations of others versus those of the person. An individual can experience three types of role conflict: intrarole, interrole, and person-role.[4] *Intrarole conflict* refers to a person's receiving conflicting information from others concerning a particular role. For example, a salesperson receives a bonus from her supervisor for her quarterly sales productivity report. Two hours later, however, she is called into the CEO's office and is told that one of the company's largest clients is complaining about the aggressiveness of her approach. She believes her approach is appropriate. Who is right? Conflicting expectations can lead to confusion and conflict. The individual in this example may begin to question whether she understands and can effectively perform in her sales role.

**Interrole conflict** occurs when an individual experiences pressure over several roles in a job or in life. For example, a working mother (who may also be single) may experience conflict over providing for the needs of her children. At the same time, she must also meet the same work standards as her counterparts who have no family responsibilities. Such conflict has become increasingly common.[5]

**Person-role conflict** occurs when an individual finds his values clashing with job requirements. For example, an R&D professional who is a perfectionist is required to speed up new product design and to overlook the zero-based defect policy. This person may experience conflict over being pressured to follow standards other than his own.

Such role conflicts can cause considerable strain and stress on individuals. Learning to manage intrapersonal conflict involves first identifying the nature and extent of the conflict and then selecting an appropriate conflict-management approach.[6]

**Interpersonal conflict** occurs between two or more individuals. The nature of interpersonal conflict in organizations can be emotional or content based and can be caused by many factors: differences in personalities, values, judgments, perceptions, competencies, and management styles. Solving and managing interpersonal conflict requires knowledge about the nature of the conflict, skills for dealing with the conflict, and practice.

**Intergroup conflict** occurs as a result of disagreements over any number of turf or substantive issues. Basic differences in group structure, i.e., how centralized or decentralized a group is, can often be sources of pressure between groups. Techniques for managing and resolving intergroup conflicts include:

- developing superordinate goals (i.e., enterprise goals that may include but ultimately override separate group goals).

- altering structures and roles (collapsing groups, creating integrated teams, and assigning "linking pin"—i.e., project liaisons and cross-functional team leaders who integrate and enhance group communication across organizational boundaries).

- enlarging and/or reallocating resources (when and where necessary, adding or reallocating resources to reduce or eliminate conflict)

- changing personnel (replacing, adding, or transferring people across selected groups, teams, and geographies).

- encouraging negotiations between groups (with assigned integrators and liaisons who can move a conflict from a zero-sum perceived or actual situation to a range of creative, pragmatic solutions).

The fifth type of conflict, **interorganizational**, occurs between enterprises and external stakeholders. Mergers and acquisitions often create interorganizational disaccord. Situations that pit unions or employees against management also lead to significant hostility. Examples include the Caterpillar and Major League Baseball strikes. Such conflicts usually require the help of outside professional negotiators. Sometimes interorganizational conflict can be resolved only through litigation. This was the situation when Microsoft's competitors (e.g., Sun Microsystems, Sybase, Apple, and America Online) accused it of practicing what they claimed were monopolist practices. The resolution of this situation had not been determined when this book went to press.

Understanding the sources of conflict inside organizations and among and between them is a first step toward resolution. Organizations, groups, and individuals can use effective conflict-resolution techniques. We discuss these in the following section.

## CONFLICT-RESOLUTION APPROACHES

The goals of conflict management are, first and foremost, to prevent negative or dysfunctional conflict from occurring while encouraging healthy conflict that stimulates innovation and performance. If prevention does not work, eliminating the dysfunctional conflict is a second goal; if it fails, minimizing or decreasing the conflict becomes the fallback position.

We discussed indirect conflict-management techniques that can be applied to situations which are structurally related to an organization, for example, the development of superordinate goals (i.e., larger, inclusive goals); expanding resources when necessary and desirable; redesigning work units; changing, reassigning, and transferring personnel; and assigning integrating and linking pin roles.[7] We add to this list identifying a common enemy (e.g., a competitor) as another technique for regrouping troops and focusing energy and resources on a target. Once the role of IBM (the Big Blue target), Microsoft recently has served as the common enemy for technology firms to strategize against. Use of a common enemy is a technique widely accepted in our culture by groups as varied as high school football teams and national economic policy makers.

The approaches we discuss next attempt to manage conflict directly. They are especially appropriate for stimulating functional conflict in organizations and for systematically structuring debate so consensus can be reached. The first approach is aimed at directing attention and solutions to the emotional and substantive causes of a conflict. Attention to process as well as to the outcomes must be part of any conflict-resolution approach.[8]

### Thomas's Conflict-Resolution Approach

The Thomas's conflict-resolution approach, illustrated in Figure 9–2 and Table 9–1 identifies five resolution styles along two dimensions for preventing or resolving conflict.[9] The first dimension indicates the extent to which a party (individual, group, or organization) is willing to satisfy its own needs and concerns (assertiveness). The second dimension represents the extent to which a party is willing to meet the needs and concerns of another individual or group (cooperativeness). The five

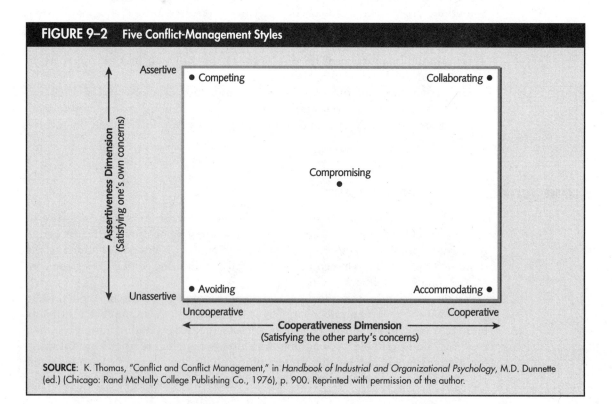

**FIGURE 9–2    Five Conflict-Management Styles**

SOURCE: K. Thomas, "Conflict and Conflict Management," in *Handbook of Industrial and Organizational Psychology*, M.D. Dunnette (ed.) (Chicago: Rand McNally College Publishing Co., 1976), p. 900. Reprinted with permission of the author.

| TABLE 9–1    Five Styles of Conflict Management | |
| --- | --- |
| *Conflict-Handling Style* | *Appropriate Conditions* |
| Competing | 1. When quick, decisive action is vital (e.g., emergencies). <br> 2. On important issues when unpopular actions need implementing (cost cutting, enforcing unpopular rules, discipline). <br> 3. On issues vital to company welfare when you know you are right. <br> 4. Against people who take advantage of noncompetitive behavior. |
| Collaborating | 1. To find an integrative solution when both sets of concerns are too important to be compromised. <br> 2. When your objective is to learn. <br> 3. To merge insights from people with different perspectives. <br> 4. To gain commitment by incorporating concerns into a consensus. <br> 5. To work through feelings that have interfered with a relationship. |
| Compromising | 1. When goals are important but not worth the effort or potential disruption of more assertive modes. <br> 2. When opponents with equal power are committed to mutually exclusive goals. <br> 3. To achieve temporary settlements to complex issues. <br> 4. To arrive at expedient solutions under time pressure. <br> 5. As a backup when collaboration or competition is unsuccessful. |
| Avoiding | 1. When an issue is trivial or more important issues are pressing. <br> 2. When you perceive no chance of satisfying your concerns. <br> 3. When potential disruption outweighs the benefits of resolution. <br> 4. To let people cool down and regain perspective. <br> 5. When gathering information supersedes immediate decision. <br> 6. When others can resolve the conflict more effectively. <br> 7. When issues seem tangential or symptomatic of other issues. |
| Accommodating | 1. When you find you are wrong—to allow a better position to be heard, to learn, and to show your reasonableness. <br> 2. When issues are more important to others than to yourself—to satisfy others and maintain cooperation. <br> 3. To build social credits for later issues. <br> 4. To minimize loss when you are outmatched and losing. <br> 5. When harmony and stability are especially important. <br> 6. To allow employees to develop by learning from mistakes. |

**SOURCE**: K. W. Thomas "Toward Multi-Dimensional Values in Teaching: The Example of Conflict Behaviors," *Academy of Management Review* 2(1977), 484-490.

conflict-resolution styles include avoiding, competing, compromising, collaborating, and accommodating.

Figure 9–2 shows that avoiding and accommodating styles are nonconfrontational approaches. The competing style is a control approach, and the collaborating and compromising styles are solution oriented.[10] Table 9–2 lists the appropriate conditions for using the different styles.

No one style is always appropriate. A competing style may be necessary in emergencies or when individuals take advantage of noncompetitive behavior. Avoiding is an unassertive style and strategy that may be necessary when disruption outweighs the gains of resolution or to allow people to calm down. Collaborative approaches are generally the most effective approaches for stimulating new, creative ideas and getting positive outcomes associated with high productivity and performance.[11]

### Cosier and Schwank's Model

A major goal of managers is to channel potential conflict into positive, functional frameworks that lead to productive outcomes. Programmed conflict is "conflict that raises different opinions regardless of the personal feelings of the managers."[12] Encouraging open dialogue and constructive debate among potentially conflicting parties is the aim of programming and channeling conflict for productive uses.

Cosier and Schwank's method provides two approaches for simulating functional conflict. Figure 9–3 illustrates a **devil's advocate** decision program and a **dialectic decision** model. Both approaches require that the participants engage in structured role-playing and submit proposals for debate and selection. A laboratory study comparing the effectiveness of the two approaches found that neither appears to be more advantageous.

As Figure 9–3 indicates, Steps 2–4 distinguish the two approaches. In the devil's advocate approach, the proposal is critiqued in Step 2 and the proposal critique is presented in Step 3. Devil's advocates can be rotated (i.e., different people can and should assume this role).

The dialectical approach involves a win-lose debate over competing proposals. However, the process is designed to ensure an open and fair debate about assumptions as well as proposed actions in each proposal. Moreover, a different proposal than the two presented may be adopted. This approach requires more preparation to defend the proposal.

Anheuser-Busch's corporate policy committee has successfully used the dialectic approach, as the following describes:

> When the policy committee . . . considers a major move—getting into or out of a business, or making a big capital expenditure—it sometimes assigns teams to make the case for each side of the question. There may be two or three teams. Each is knowledgeable about the subject; each has access to the same information. Occasionally someone in favor of the project is chosen to lead the dissent, and an opponent to argue for it. Pat Stokes, who heads the company's beer empire, describes the result: "We end up with decisions and alternatives we

## FIGURE 9–3    Channeling Conflict: Two Methods

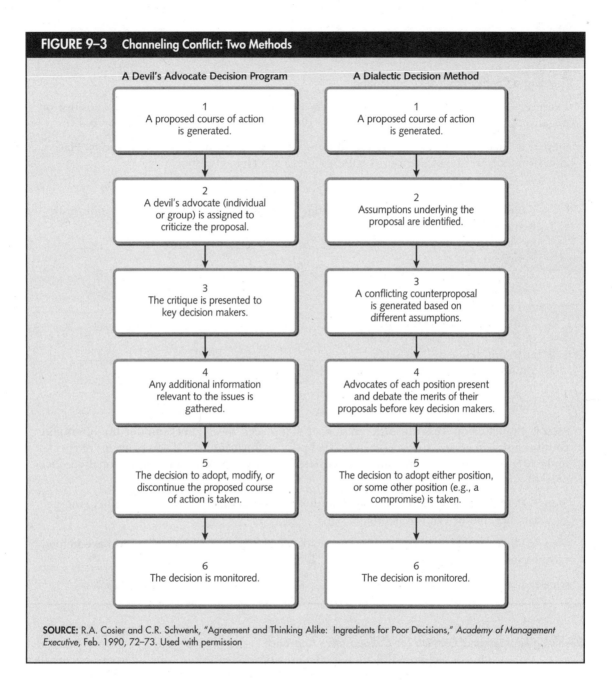

**A Devil's Advocate Decision Program**

1
A proposed course of action
is generated.

2
A devil's advocate (individual
or group) is assigned to
criticize the proposal.

3
The critique is presented to
key decision makers.

4
Any additional information
relevant to the issues is
gathered.

5
The decision to adopt, modify, or
discontinue the proposed course
of action is taken.

6
The decision is monitored.

**A Dialectic Decision Method**

1
A proposed course of action
is generated.

2
Assumptions underlying the
proposal are identified.

3
A conflicting counterproposal
is generated based on
different assumptions.

4
Advocates of each position present
and debate the merits of their
proposals before key decision makers.

5
The decision to adopt either position,
or some other position (e.g., a
compromise) is taken.

6
The decision is monitored.

**SOURCE:** R.A. Cosier and C.R. Schwenk, "Agreement and Thinking Alike: Ingredients for Poor Decisions," *Academy of Management Executive*, Feb. 1990, 72–73. Used with permission

*hadn't thought of previously," sometimes representing a synthesis of the opposing views. "You become a lot more anticipatory, better able to see what might happen, because you have thought through the process."*[13]

## THE CHANGING WORKPLACE

### Creating a Conflict-Positive Organization

**Exercise**: The characteristics below represent organizations that view conflict as positive or negative. Conflict-positive organizations have the four characteristics listed below.

**Step 1**: Evaluate your previous organization or work team on these four dimensions. Place a check under only one of the four categories after each characteristic.

| Characteristics | Very Little | Sometimes | Often | Continuously |
|---|---|---|---|---|
| 1. Rewards success; learns from mistakes; plans for improvements | ____ | ____ | ____ | ____ |
| 2. Shares cooperative goals; rewards teams and individuals for goal completion | ____ | ____ | ____ | ____ |
| 3. Empowers employees; helps people have a sense of control and confidence in their skills | ____ | ____ | ____ | ____ |
| 4. Values diversity, innovation, honest and open confrontation | ____ | ____ | ____ | ____ |
| Sum | ____ | ____ | ____ | ____ |

**Step 2**: Evaluate your team or organization. If you placed more checks under the often and continuously categories, you work in a conflict-positive environment. If you place more checks under the very little and sometimes categories, your environment has dysfunctional conflict present.

**Step 3**: Describe how it felt/feels to work in this environment. What types of conflict emerge? How are they handled or not handled? Why?

**Step 4**: What specific changes in the organization or team would help or would have helped create a more conflict-positive environment? Explain.

**SOURCE**: Adapted from D. Tjosvold. *The Conflict-Positive Organization*. Copyright © Addison-Wesley Publishing Company, Inc.

### Resolving Interpersonal Conflict: The Collaborative Approach

One of the most difficult but effective approaches to resolving interpersonal conflict is the collaborative approach.[14] Interpersonal conflict and disagreements often involve and may center on emotions, complaints, and criticisms. Whetten and Cameron (1998) state that defining the problem and generating solutions are the most difficult steps to manage in the collaborative approach. This approach usually involves a dyadic confrontation: two actors (an *initiator* and a *responder*) are faced with the challenge of turning a complaint into a problem-solving dialogue. If the two actors cannot succeed, a third actor (a *mediator*) may be required.[15] The following sections present the roles of these individuals. Many individuals in organizations have probably occupied one or more of these roles in conflict situations.

## The Initiator

The *initiator* is the person who bring attention to a complaint or problem. Initiators usually accuse or blame someone for having done something to her. Initiators who are aware of the following six guidelines can act more effectively to help define and solve the problem: (1) take ownership of the problem; (2) describe the problem in terms of behaviors, feelings, and consequences; (3) do not jump to conclusions or attribute blame; (4) maintain two-way communication; (5) repeat your concerns until they are acknowledged; and (6) address the issues incrementally.

By personally *taking ownership* of the problem, the initiator avoids becoming defensive and threatening and is able to focus on needs that are not being recognized. Using "I" statements instead of "you" statements can help the initiator assume personal responsibility and accountability and begin to communicate with the other(s) involved in the situation. Second, the initiator can *describe his problem in terms of behaviors, feelings, and consequences* instead of making accusations. An approach to identifying a problem in terms of behaviors, feelings, and consequences defuses the emotions surrounding the issue and focuses on the effects of the problem on the initiator. This approach involves defining the problem in a specific way. "[Person's name], when you [behavior], I feel [initiator's feelings about the behavior] because [consequences of behavior on initiator]." For example, the initiator can say, "John, do you have a minute? Yesterday, when you forwarded my e-mail on to the work group before responding to me [behavior], I felt confused and somewhat hurt [feelings about behavior] because I still didn't have your own feedback on the system breakdown. The system is still down and I've lost three important files that backed my work up [consequences]." The third step is *not to jump to conclusions or assign blame*. In heated situations, it is important not to start blaming or assigning blame to individuals when the initiator has little or incomplete information regarding the causes of the conflict. Again, the initiator can avoid the use of you statements with the responder and maintain *two-way open communication* (the fourth step). Two-way communication again involves the initiator's use of I statements to identify the problem in terms of behaviors, feelings, and consequences on the initiator. Fifth, the initiator can *repeat his concerns* in nonevaluative, nonthreatening ways until the responder hears and acknowledges the message. The point here is not to enlarge the issues but to repeat the behaviors, feelings, and consequences of the problem until the responder hears the complaint. Sixth, *address the issues incrementally*. Approaching complex issues in an incremental, fact-finding way opens the possibility of dialogue and prevents further misunderstandings. Finally, *direct attention to what the initiator and responder have in common*. When the problem is defined, the next step is to problem solve. This is an opportunity to use "we" statements regarding what all parties have in common in terms of work goals, schedule deadlines, interests, rewards, and the like. For example, "We know the product has to be shipped on May 2 or none of us get our bonuses. Getting the system up and running as early as possible benefits us all. What are some tactics we can do to make this happen?"

### The Responder

The **responder** is assumed to be the cause of the problem, complaint, or issue. Responders who are familiar with the following steps also can help identify and resolve the conflict instead of avoiding, defending, or attacking the initiator. These guidelines, according to Whetten and Cameron (1998), help the responder shape the initiator's behavior to move the problem-solving process forward.[16] The four steps the responder can use include (1) creating a *climate* for joint problem solving; (2) obtaining more *information* regarding the problem; (3) agreeing *with part of the complaint or issue*; and (4) seeking *acceptable options* to the problem. The responder also can use the guidelines discussed for the initiator, especially using the behaviors/feelings/consequences approach and I instead of you statements when communicating.

### The Mediator

The **mediator** can be a manager, another professional inside an organization, or someone from the outside.[17] The mediator's role is ideally to assist both the initiator and the responder resolve the conflict. A mediator, like an arbitrator, might use these procedures. (1) *Listen* to both parties until the mediator acknowledges that there is a conflict. (2) Understand the level of *awareness and motivation* of both parties regarding the nature of the problem or complaint. (3) Get an *understanding of the views and relationship* between the parties while remaining impartial, which involves understanding the issues, causes of the problem, commonalties and differences of perception, and values of both parties regarding the problem. (4) Remain *fair* by keeping the discussion fact and issue oriented—by not involving personalities—maintaining balance in the discussion with and between both parties, and asking direct questions in nonthreatening ways. (5) Explore solution paths and options. Avoid assigning responsibility for causes of the problem. Since interpersonal problems often involve differences in perspective rather than right or wrong answers, it is important for the mediator to remain open to different problem solutions. (6) Focus on the *interests* of the parties, not their *positions* or *stances*. Ask open-ended questions. When a mediator senses that both parties recognize areas of agreement, seeking a solution is the next step. (7) Identify an agreed on *solution* from Step 5 and determine a *plan* of action with *follow-up* steps.

### *"Learning Organization" Tools for Dialoguing*

Peter Senge's book, *The Fifth Discipline*, is a source of tools and techniques that can assist individuals and teams in creating a learning organization. Such tools model effective listening and dialogue skills and can be particularly useful in preventing and managing dysfunctional conflict. Ford, Motorola, Federal Express, and Intel are a few of the companies that have used Senge's techniques.

In this section we summarize the *left-hand, right-hand column technique, and the ladder of inference technique, and the container technique*; these methods are effective in preventing and managing conflict.[18] Senge places special emphasis on dialogue, which he believes creates opportunities for sharing information and creating joint solutions; it differs from discussion and argument. Senge states that

> In dialogue, individuals gain insights that could not be achieved individually. A new kind of mind begins to come into being which is based on development of common meaning. . . . People are no longer primarily in opposition, nor can they be said to be interacting, rather they are participating in this pool, of common meaning, which is capable of constant development and change.[19]

Individual dialogue can be improved through the use of the *left-hand, right-hand column technique.* This is an exercise in which Senge has individuals in meetings write what they really think (in the left-hand column of a paper) and what they actually said (in the corresponding right-hand column of the same paper). For example, one may be sitting at a meeting thinking, "I wish this boring futility would end." However, when the presenter asks the person to reflect on the meeting at its conclusion, he might say, "I thought we really accomplished our goal." The aim of this exercise is for people to get in touch with the biases and feelings that hinder constructive dialogue. An honest dialogue can begin only when each person says what he or she really thinks. However, dialogue is most effective in a learning environment in which trust and sharing are valued.

Two other of Senge's techniques that focus on defusing distractions and on initiating and maintaining dialogue can be used to create a learning environment. The *ladder of inference* helps people understand and admit that their conclusions, logic, claims, and behaviors are based on subjective processes. By learning to admit and see one's reasoning as a process, a person can then feel free to change her conclusions and adopt others' ideas. *Climbing down the ladder* involves acknowledging and owning one's reasoning as just that—reasoning, not an eternal truth. Use of the ladder of inference enables a person to understand and admit his statements, behavior, and positions; it involves moving through these steps:

- I take **ACTIONS** based in my beliefs.

- I adopt **BELIEFS** about the world.

- I draw **CONCLUSIONS**.

- I make **ASSUMPTIONS**.

- I add **MEANINGS** (cultural and personal).

- I select **DATA** from what I observe.

- I **OBSERVE** data and experiences (as a videotape recorder might capture them).

In this situation, dialogue begins when participants learn to perceive their conclusions as "beliefs" or "assumptions" instead of as nonnegotiable truths. Teams trained in these methods can help each other question meaning and strive for open problem solving and joint solutions.

Senge's container technique has members of a team in a meeting imagine a container sitting in the center of the room in which they can put their fears, biases, anger, prejudices, and blame. This method enables members to disassociate their own biases and emotional roadblocks from their search for common solutions.

Taken together, these methods encourage systems thinking by opening up opportunities to share information, experiences, and ideas from different perspectives. These are systems of thought and action that require joint collaborative understanding and actions.

## Tactics for Dealing With Difficult People

Resolving some conflicts can be complicated because they involve problematic individuals. Interpersonal conflicts can easily arise when so-called difficult individuals are involved. Bramson has written about seven types of difficult people and how to cope with them in organizational settings.[20] Everyone is difficult to communicate with at times. Bramson discusses difficult people as individuals who consistently demonstrate predictable patterns of dysfunctional communication and behaviors. These profiles elucidate how such problematic behaviors can create interpersonal conflict. Table 9–2 offers tactics for dealing with each type.

*Hostile-aggressives* surprise and attack people at emotional and substantive levels. This type works with "guerilla" warfare tactics. They attack when you are not expecting attack. Being assertive with hostile-aggressives is necessary. You should avoid direct confrontation but, at the same time, stand up for yourself.

*Complainers* complain but rarely act. They feel powerless and are persistently flagging problems. Problem solve with them but do not oversympathize. Keep the complainer focused on taking concrete actions.

*Clams* are silent and indirect, they avoid open conflict. Bring clams out by encouraging and supporting open dialogue.

*Superagreeables* are nice on the surface but do not follow through. They say yes to everything but do nothing. Understanding what they really mean and gaining their realistic commitment on a task or item is the challenge. You must be ready to compromise and negotiate, but you should not accept unrealistic commitments or bluffs.

*Negatives* are pessimistic, and their attitude is contagious. Keep an objective, action-oriented stance as you explore concrete alternatives to a problem. Instead of suggesting solutions, encourage the negatives to problem solve even if you have some solutions available in the wings.

*Know-it-alls* are classified as bulldozers that is, people who do know a subject competently but use their competency to bully others—and balloons—people who do not know a subject well and bluff instead. With bulldozers, prepare carefully; know at least something about the subject and ask questions to gain information and commitments. Balloons can be confronted (only in private to help them save face) when they state perceptions as facts. Offer factual evidence in a neutral, objective manner.

**TABLE 9–2    Tactics for Managing Interpersonal Conflicts with Difficult People**

*Hostile-Aggressive*

1. Stand up for yourself.
2. Give them time to run down.
3. Use self-assertive language.
4. Avoid a direct confrontation.

*Complainers*

1. Listen attentively.
2. Acknowledge their feelings.
3. Avoid complaining with them.
4. State the facts without apology.
5. Use a problem-solving mode.

*Clams*

1. Ask open-ended questions.
2. Be patient in waiting for a response.
3. Ask more open-ended questions.
4. If no response occurs, tell clams what you plan to do because no discussion has taken place.

*Superagreeables*

1. In a nonthreatening manner, work hard to find out why they will not take action.
2. Let them know you value them as people.
3. Be ready to compromise and negotiate, and do not allow them to make unrealistic commitments.
4. Try to discern the hidden meaning in their humor.

*Negativists*

1. Do not be dragged into their despair.
2. Do not try to cajole them out of their negativism.
3. Discuss the problem thoroughly, without offering solutions.
4. When alternatives are discussed, bring up the negative side yourself.
5. Be ready to take action alone, without agreement.

*Know-It-Alls*

*Bulldozers:*
1. Prepare yourself.
2. Listen and paraphrase their main points.
3. Use the questioning form to raise problems.

*Balloons:*
1. State facts or opinions as your own perceptions of reality.
2. Find a way for balloons to save face.
3. Confront balloons alone, not in public.

*Indecisive Stallers*

1. Raise the issue of why they are hesitant.
2. If you are the problem, ask for help.
3. Keep the action steps in your own hands.
4. Possibly remove the staller from the situation.

**SOURCE:** From "Coping with Difficult People," R.M. Bramson, Copyright © 1981 by Robert M. Bramson. Used by permission of Doubleday, a division of Random House, Inc.

Finally, *indecisive stallers* may want to resolve a conflict or solve a problem but cannot do so because of their inability to move to decision or for fear of hurting someone in the process. Raise the issue of their hesitancy; acknowledge their indecisiveness. If you are the source of their fear, get outside assistance but stay in control of the situation. If the stallers are disruptive, remove them from the situation; otherwise, control the decision process and insist on their follow through.

## A DIAGNOSTIC CHECKLIST

A checklist can help organization members and managers diagnose the sources and causes of conflict. The jump-start framework illustrated in Chapter 1 (Figure 1–5) is presented here as a starting point. Key questions from this figure are restated to apply to conflict:

- Where is the conflict in the system? At the leadership, individual, group/team, intergroup, organizational, or organization-environment level?

- What is the nature of the conflict?

- Is the conflict functional or dysfunctional? For whom?

- What are the causes of the conflict?

- To what degree is the subsystem experiencing the conflict related to other parts of the organization?

- How high up and how far down the organization does the conflict extend?

- Who (which system) experiencing the conflict is ready for change?

- Do we have an agreed-upon conflict-resolution method for solving the problem?

Interventions that address and attempt to solve organizational problems related to conflict are found throughout this text. The following section on negotiation presents methods that also can be used to resolve organizational conflict and to seek solutions to conflict that involve both material and emotional solutions.

## NEGOTIATING DEFINED

"Negotiation is . . . a process in which two or more entities come together to discuss common and conflicting interests in order to reach an agreement of mutual benefit."[21] Negotiation involves two or more parties with common interests and conflicting interests who enter a process of interaction with the goal of reaching an agreement.[22] Negotiation is also a decision-making process that involves people and parties with different preferences.[23]

Two types of negotiation include distributive and integrative. *Distributive* negotiation involves a single issue, win-lose strategy with a "fixed pie" at stake.[24] This type of negotiation can be appropriate when an issue is not complex and can be resolved with straightforward bargaining. *Integrative* negotiation, on the other hand, usually involves unclear interests, needs, and several viable options for resolving issues. Negotiators need skill and training to reach win-win solutions, as we discuss here.[25]

Knowledge of negotiation techniques for managers and employees increases in importance as workforces with competing interests become more diverse. Negotiation also becomes essential in global and cross-cultural situations, especially in cases of mergers, acquisitions, and strategic alliances. The following classical technique, *Getting to Yes*, illustrates an example of negotiating that involves techniques from both distributive and integrative bargaining methods.

### Getting to Yes

*Getting to Yes*, the book by Roger Fisher and William Ury, is a consultative negotiation approach that illustrates four principles for reaching win-win solutions:

1. Separate the people from the problem.

2. Focus on interests, not positions.

3. Generate a variety of possibilities before deciding what to do.

4. Insist that the result be based upon some objective standard.[26]

When separating the people from the problem, it is important to determine how the other party sees the situation. This can be accomplished by active listening and questioning to determine whether your perceptions are accurate. It may be necessary to develop an affinity with the other person that allows you as a negotiator to focus on the problem, not on the personality—this will prevent your being swayed by emotional outbursts. By focusing on interests, not on positions, the problem can be thought out in detail and the needs and concerns behind the positions taken by each party identified.

Focusing on goals and principles separates the desired outcome from the people involved and allows you to find other solutions. Taking attention from specific positions removes personal claims and attachments to fixed ideas. Generating a variety of possible outcomes uncovers solutions that give each party a bigger slice of the pie. The zero-sum game (i.e., a win-lose situation with perceived and/or actual limited resources) is opened up to many possibilities.

Before arriving at commonly accepted solutions, it may be helpful for the parties involved to discuss and agree on an objective standard to guide their choice(s) of solution. The agreed-on outcome should minimize costs and still provide high benefit to the other party.

Fisher and Ury cite the following example of Tom Griffith, who is negotiating a settlement with an insurance adjuster. This example illustrates the four principles discussed. Tom remains unemotional, focuses on his interests, separates people from the problem, insists on an objective standard, and generates possibilities:

*Adjuster:* We have studied your case and have decided the policy applies. This means you are entitled to a settlement of $3,300.00.

*Tom:* I see. How did you reach that figure?

*Adjuster:* That was how much we decided the car was worth.

*Tom:* I understand, but what standard did you use to determine that amount? Do you know where I can buy a comparable car for that amount?

*Adjuster:* How much are you asking?

*Tom:* Whatever I am entitled to under the policy. I found a second-hand car just like mine for about $3,850. Adding sales and excise tax it would come to about $4,000.

*Adjuster:* $4,000! That's too much!

*Tom:* I'm not asking for $4,000, or 3 or 5; I'm asking for fair compensation. Do you agree it's only fair I get enough to replace the car?

*Adjuster:* Okay, I'll offer you $3,500. That's the highest I can go. Company policy.

*Tom:* How does the company figure that?

*Adjuster:* Look, $3,500 is all you get. Take it or leave it.

*Tom:* $3,500 may be fair. I don't know. I certainly understand your position if you're bound to company policy, but unless you can state objectively why that amount is what I'm entitled to, I think I'll do better in court. Why don't we study the matter and talk again?

*Adjuster:* Okay, Mr. Griffith, I've got an ad here for a 1978 Fiesta for $3,400.

*Tom:* I see. What does it say about the mileage?

*Adjuster:* It says 49,000, why?

*Tom:* Because mine had only 25,000 miles. How much does that increase the value in your book?

*Adjuster:* Let me see, $150.

**Tom**: Assuming the $3,400 as possible base, that brings the figure to $3,550. Does that ad say anything about a radio?

*Adjuster:* No.

*Tom:* How much extra in your book?

*Adjuster:* That's $125.

*Tom:* What about air conditioning?

Thirty minutes later, Tom took home a check for $4,100.

### Mediating Conflict

There may be occasions in which you, as a manager or employee, must mediate between other parties. In addition to the mediator roles discussed in the section on conflict resolution, the following are six principles from *Getting to Yes* that can guide you in this mediation role:

1. Acknowledge to your people that you know a conflict exists and propose an approach for resolving it.

2.  In studying the positions of both parties, maintain a neutral position regarding the disputants—if not the issues.

3.  Keep the discussion issue oriented, not personality oriented. Focus on the impact the conflict is having on performance.

4.  Help your people put things in perspective by focusing first on areas about which they might agree. Try to deal with one issue at a time.

5.  Remember that you are a facilitator, not a judge. Judges deal with problems, facilitators deal with solutions.

6.  Make sure your people fully support the solution they agree upon. If you notice any hesitation, ask for clarification and don't stop the process until all parties have a specific plan.[27]

Insisting on an objective standard will prevent the negotiation from turning into a battle of wills. The negotiation process should be based on principles, not pressure. To do this, you must identify the theories and assumptions of each party that underlie the positions.

Finally, the authors of *Getting to Yes* suggest that a person should always develop and articulate her the best alternative to a negotiated agreement (BATNA) before negotiating a position. The BATNA is a standard that protects the negotiators' interests and power and sets parameters around what one will or can afford to give up. The BATNA is also a minimally acceptable agreement. For example, if you are selling a car, you might set your BATNA at $5,000, as the lowest price at which you would sell it. It may be possible that a buyer could offer you $4,000 for the car with a year's subscription to theater performances. You might decide to accept this offer after calculating the costs and benefits. You can select an alternative solution because you have a standard against which to measure alternatives.

## PERSONALITY TRAITS AND GENDER IN NEGOTIATIONS

Research shows that personality traits have no noticeable effect on either the process or outcomes of negotiations.[28] Attempting to gain advantage over another by shaping tactics to fit a personality style is seemingly futile. Staying with principled negotiating procedures as those discussed earlier would be more productive.

Research suggests that there are no differences in negotiating tactics or success according to gender.[29] There do appear to be differences regarding negotiations in the power held by managers. Managers with low power, whether male or female, use soft persuasive strategies, avoiding confrontational tactics. However, the attitudes of women toward themselves as negotiators and negotiations are not the same as men's. Women who are managers showed less performance satisfaction with and confidence toward negotiations than do men—regardless of whether the women managers' results and performance were similar to that of men. From this research, one generalization indicates that women tend to have a lower view of their negotiation performance and confidence than the actual results support.

## NEGOTIATING ACROSS CULTURES

Effectively negotiating across cultures requires an understanding of different countries' characteristics. For example, Table 1–1 in Chapter 1, listed cultural differences in persuasion styles for North Americans, Arabs, and Russians. North Americans tend to rely on logic, facts, short-term relationships, and emphasize deadlines in persuasion. Arabs, on the other hand, tend to appeal to emotions, argue with subjective feelings, take a long-term view, and be casual about deadlines. Russians tend to appeal to and argue ideals, make few concessions, do not consider continuing relationships a necessary interest, and ignore deadlines. The initial position taken by these three national negotiating styles include a moderate approach by North Americans and extreme approaches by both Arabs and Russians. Refer to Chapter 1, Table 1–2 for the negotiation styles of Japanese, and Latin Americans, and North Americans. Understanding these different national profiles is a starting point toward reaching cross-cultural conflict resolution and effective negotiating. Strategies built on these differing cultural styles are more effective. It is also interesting to note that the French tend to favor conflict and gain recognition by taking aggressive approaches toward their adversaries.[30] The Chinese can continue negotiations endlessly, emphasizing and reemphasizing details. Like Japanese, Chinese emphasize relationships at the core of negotiations. Americans, by contrast, are noted for their impatient, bottom-line approach.

Copeland and Briggs offer the following applied approach to negotiation that has practical rules for international negotiators in cross-cultural differences.[31] **Before the negotiation**, it is necessary to adequately prepare to ensure both tactical and cultural awareness. A strategy should be in place, and everyone should be comfortable with it. Send a winning team—nothing but your best—to the negotiation. Allow time for relationship building. Whether you take a competitive or cooperative stance should be decided in advance and should be part of your strategy. Following the approach by Copeland and Briggs, the team must decide how competitive or cooperative to be in the opening sessions.

During the remaining stages (beginning the negotiation, hard bargaining, and beyond the contract), an extensive knowledge of the cultural perspective of the other side is crucial. **Beginning the negotiation**, you should make the opening scene work for you. Focus on the agenda, pay attention to the physical arrangements, and be sure to open with cultural awareness of the other party. **Hard bargaining** requires being in control of information, language, and timing. Going behind the scenes to get information is a must. In cross-cultural situations, it is imperative to be conscious of saving face (yours and theirs) while not appearing to be browbeaten. (A note of caution: Allow enough time to practice these stances—they must appear natural to be successful.) Get your agreement signed before you leave. Make sure both sides agree on the significance of what is being signed. Be willing to give up cherished notions of the proper contract. At the **beyond the contract** stage of cross-cultural negotiation, it is important to remember that discussions are always preferable to court settlements and that without a relationship, there is no deal.

## NEGOTIATING STRATEGIC ORGANIZATIONAL ALLIANCES: EIGHT TACTICS

Business assignments increasingly involve negotiating or participating in strategic alliances, deals, and partnerships across national borders. In addition to the background and strategies previously discussed, clues for successfully negotiating the early phases of strategic alliances are summarized here.

The failure of intercompany alliances has been attributed to poor communication, especially in the early phases of a negotiation. Initial discussions must always involve gathering relevant information. This is in preparation for developing the initial, flexible plan that will present your company's interests and thinking on the topic. Attending to both partners' interests is essential in the early stages of negotiating alliances. The following eight strategies build on the tactics offered earlier:

1. Compensate your partner with a benefit if they must make an uncomfortable concession. Provide a rationale that does not incur debt.

2. Express disagreements in terms of difficulties—such as time constraints, limited resources, or policy—rather than refusals.

3. Return to agreed-upon objectives as reasons for your proposal or for your inability to accept your partner's proposal.

4. Seek your partner's perspective often and check to see whether your reasons are understood.

5. Be prepared to offer alternatives that meet your partner's concerns.

6. Avoid value judgments and personalizing.

7. Pause to reflect on proposals, positions, tones, and style changes.

8. Back up proposals with evidence of their feasibility.[32]

Negotiating cross-cultural alliances involves gaining knowledge of and sensitivity to your own and the other party's cultural context, values, and business practices. Being prepared is a necessary precondition for all types of negotiating. The early and initial phases are especially important in cross-cultural settings since it is there that the tone and understanding of both parties are set. Causing (or being perceived as causing) the other party to lose face can in many cultural situations be the end to a formal and/or informal relationship.

## ETHICS AND NEGOTIATION: MANAGERIAL IMPLICATIONS

Managing conflict and effectively negotiating in moral ways depends on a number of factors. First, organizations, managers, and members must consider their motives in resolving conflicts and in negotiating with other stakeholders. This knowledge requires that each party understand the explicit and implicit obligations in the situation. Make sure that expectations, whenever possible, are known.

Hidden agendas can lead to backstabbing and other unethical actions. Second, understand your and the other party's methods of communicating and negotiating. Miscommunications based on inaccurate cultural assumptions and attributions can lead to actions that inadvertently violate values and rights. What adjustments need to be made in your approach that still protect your rights and values? Third, consider the nature, costs, and benefits of the outcomes for different stakeholders. Prioritize both the harm and rewards that estimated outcomes will

## THE CHANGING WORKPLACE

### Ethical Conflicts of Interest in Organizations

One source of employee conflicts in organizations is a conflict of interest (i.e., when an individual must choose between his or her personal interests or those of the organization). This is often a fuzzy area. There are some rules and policies, but there are often few specific guidelines to help employees. For example, managers often face making decisions that would promote their own individual professional power, prestige, or monetary interests over the interests of the organization, shareholders, or work unit. Managers can, for example, manipulate financial and productivity data, expense reports and other statements to hide their mistakes or protect their individual advantage. Employees can pad expense reports, take unnecessary time off, steal, accept bribes, or lie to protect their own interest over the organizations.

**Exercise:**

1.  Describe an incident in your present or previous work or study environment in which you observed a colleague, boss, or officer violate the interest of a team, work unit, or organization by promoting a "hidden agenda" or the individual's own interests.

2.  What did you do or not do? Why?

3.  Where would you draw the line; what guidelines would you use in your team or

organization regarding the prevention of violating the organization's or team's interests over your own? Explain your rationale.

4.  Describe the "ethical principle" you used in question 3. Was it, for example, one of the following:
    a.  "Rights" principle? I do/do not have the right to violate the organization's interest.
    b.  "Fairness" principle? It is not fair for me or others to violate the employer's interest.
    c.  "Cost/benefits" principle? I have to weigh the costs against the benefits to decide whether to violate the organization's interests.
    d.  "Relativism" principle? It's all relative to the situation, circumstances, and to my best interests. I would violate the organization's interests if others were and not getting caught if I really needed something and believed it was right for me.
    e.  Other principles?

5.  Share your responses with another member of the class. What similarities and differences did you find?

6.  What did you learn from this exercise?

have on different parties. How responsible and socially moral do you want the outcomes to be for the different stakeholders?

### Core Human Rights Across Cultures

Freedom from torture, physical harm, discrimination, freedom of speech, and the right to political participation have been identified as core human rights that should not be sacrificed or compromised unless to preserve other rights of equal or higher value.[33] Ethical dilemmas occur when two parties are both right in their divergent values, interests, actions, and/or outcomes. Core human rights and ethical principles apply in the absence, as well as in the presence, of legal principles and laws.

In Chapter 1, we introduced a number of ethical principles that can be used to examine a party's motives and motivation, methods, and outcomes in taking a certain course of action: rights, duty, fairness, and justice are among them. Should one communicate or negotiate a particular action if someone's core rights will be violated? If an unjust burden or benefit will be distributed to a particular party, especially a less advantaged person or group? If one's sense of duty is violated? If the action is unfair for the other party? Ethical reasoning can help individuals, groups, and organizations evaluate and examine their thinking and potential actions. Examining the ethics—that is, the rightness and wrongness—of potential negotiated outcomes from a stakeholder framework can clarify who may get hurt at whose and at what expense.[34]

---

## THE CHANGING WORKPLACE

**Your Conflict Resolution Style**

**Exercise**: Think of specific incidents and situations in which you experienced significant differences with someone. On the following 30 items, recall those situations and answer only A or B to each of the paired statements with this question in mind, "How do you generally respond to situations involving differences of opinion, choice, or action?" Even if you may not respond as an A or B statement indicates, select the choice that is most similar to how you would typically respond.

1.  a. There are times when I let others take responsibility for solving the problem.

    b. Rather than negotiate the things on which we disagree, I try to stress those things upon which we both agree.

2.  a. I try to find a compromise solution.

    b. I attempt to deal with all of his and my concerns.

3.  a. I am usually firm in pursuing my goals.

    b. I might try to soothe the other's feelings and preserve our relationship.

4.  a. I try to find a compromise solution.

    b. I sometimes sacrifice my own wishes for the wishes of the other person.

5.  a. I consistently seek the other's help in working out a solution.

    b. I try to do what is necessary to avoid useless tensions.

6.  a. I try to avoid creating unpleasantness for myself.

    b. I try to win my position.

*continued on next page*

## THE CHANGING WORKPLACE, cont.

7. a. I try to postpone the issue until I have had some time to think it over.
   b. I give up some points in exchange for others.

8. a. I am usually firm in pursuing my goals.
   b. I attempt to get all concerns and issues immediately out in the open.

9. a. I feel that differences are not always worth worrying about.
   b. I make some effort to get my way.

10. a. I am firm in pursuing my goals.
    b. I try to find a compromise solution.

11. a. I attempt to get all concerns and issues immediately in the open.
    b. I might try to smooth the other's feelings and preserve our relationship.

12. a. I sometimes avoid taking positions that would create controversy.
    b. I will let him have some of his positions if he lets me have some of mine.

13. a. I propose a middle ground.
    b. I press to get my points made.

14. a. I tell him my ideas and ask him for his.
    b. I try to show him the logic and benefits of my position.

15. a. I might try to soothe the other's feelings and preserve our relationship.
    b. I try to do what is necessary to avoid tensions.

16. a. I try not to hurt the other's feelings.
    b. I try to convince the other person of the merits of my position.

17. a. I am usually firm in pursuing my goals.
    b. I try to do what is necessary to avoid useless tensions.

18. a. If it makes the other person happy, I might let him maintain his views.
    b. I will let him have some of his positions if he lets me have some of mine.

19. a. I attempt to get all concerns and issues immediately out in the open.
    b. I try to postpone the issue until I have had time to think it over.

20. a. I attempt to immediately work through our differences.
    b. I try to find a fair combination of gains and losses for both of us.

21. a. In approaching negotiations, I try to be considerate of the other person's wishes.
    b. I always lean toward a direct discussion of the problem.

22. a. I try to find a position that is intermediate between his and mine.
    b. I assert my wishes.

23. a. I am very often concerned with satisfying all our wishes.
    b. There are times when I let others take responsibility for solving the problem.

24. a. If the other's position seems very important to him, I would try to meet his wishes.
    b. I am concerned to work out the best agreed-upon course of action.

25. a. I try to show him the logic and benefits of my position.
    b. In approaching negotiations, I try to be considerate of the other person's wishes.

*continued on next page*

## THE CHANGING WORKPLACE, cont.

26. a. I propose a middle ground.
    b. I am nearly always concerned with satisfying all our wishes.

27. a. I sometimes avoid taking positions which would create controversy.
    b. If it makes the other person happy, I might let him maintain his views.

28. a. I am usually firm in pursuing my goals.

29. a. I propose a middle ground.
    b. I feel that differences are not always worth worrying about.

29. a. I propose a middle ground.
    b. I feel that differences are not always worth worrying about.

30. a. I try not to hurt the other's feelings.
    b. I always share the problem with the other person so that we can work it out.

**Step 1:** Circle the letters below that you selected on each item of the questionnaire.

**Step 2**: Complete the scoring in each column by adding up the number of As and Bs listed in each column, and then place that sum on the underlined space under each column.

| Item Number | Competition (Forcing) | Collaboration (Problem Solving) | Sharing (Compromise) | Avoiding (Withdrawal) | Accommodation (Smoothing) |
|---|---|---|---|---|---|
| 1. | | | | A | B |
| 2. | | B | A | | |
| 3. | A | | | | B |
| 4. | | | A | | B |
| 5. | | A | | B | |
| 6. | B | | | A | |
| 7. | | | B | A | |
| 8. | A | B | | | |
| 9. | B | | | A | |
| 10. | A | | B | | |
| 11. | | A | | | B |
| 12. | | | B | A | |
| 13. | B | | A | | |
| 14. | B | A | | | |
| 15. | | | | B | A |
| 16. | B | | | | A |
| 17. | A | | | B | |
| 18. | | | B | | A |
| 19. | | A | | B | |
| 20. | | A | B | | |
| 21. | | B | | | A |
| 22. | B | | A | | |

*continued on next page*

## THE CHANGING WORKPLACE, cont.

| Item Number | Competition (Forcing) | Collaboration (Problem Solving) | Sharing (Compromise) | Avoiding (Withdrawal) | Accommodation (Smoothing) |
|---|---|---|---|---|---|
| 23. | | A | | B | |
| 24. | | | B | | A |
| 25. | A | | | | B |
| 26. | | B | A | | |
| 27. | | | | A | B |
| 28. | A | B | | | |
| 29. | | | A | B | |
| 30. | | B | | | A |

Total number of items circled in each column:

    ____       ____          ____        ____       ____

   Competition  Collaboration    Sharing      Avoiding   Accommodation

**Step 3**: With one or more members in your class, answer these questions:

1. On which of the conflict resolution styles did you score highest? Lowest?

2. Do these styles reflect a pattern that represents how you manage conflict? Explain.

3. Which style works best for you in effectively solving conflicts? Least well? Why?

4. Which styles would you like to learn to use more than you do now or have in the past? Why?

5. How do your patterns differ from members in your group? What are the sources those differences do you believe? Discuss.

**SOURCE:** Reprinted with permission, Randolph Flynn and David Elloy, *Conflict Management*. (Washing., D.C.: National Institute for Dispute Resolution, Working Paper, 1987).

## CONCLUDING COMMENTS

Conflict is an integral part of organizational life. Understanding the sources of conflict and the different resolution methods enhances both communication skills and management ability in contemporary organizations. Conflict can be both functional and dysfunctional. There are at least five types of conflict in organizations: structural, intrapersonal, interpersonal, intergroup, and interorganizational. The goal of conflict management in organizations is to prevent negative or dysfunctional conflict while encouraging healthy conflict that stimulates innovation and performance.

Four conflict management approaches were discussed: Thomas's conflict-resolution method, Cosier and Schwank's devil's advocate/dialectic decision model, the collaborative approach (which includes an initiator, a responder, and a mediator), and Senge's dialoguing methods. Thomas describes styles for resolving conflict; Cosier and Schwank provide approaches for channeling healthy, functional conflict toward innovation; and Senge's methods uncover assumptions and biases that prevent openly sharing information.

Negotiation was defined. Two types of negotiations are distributive (win-lose) and integrative (win-win). The classic technique discussed in *Getting to Yes* shows how an integrative approach is used. Cross-cultural negotiation differences and strategies relating to Japanese, North American, Arab, Russian, and Latin American cultures were described.

Finally, managerial implications for negotiating ethically were summarized: Managers should understand the motives and motivations of all parties negotiating, understand the obligations and rights of all involved and affected parties, and be aware of methods of negotiating parties since cross-cultural differences can lead to misperceived judgments and later to possible hidden agendas and unethical activities. Managers should also estimate the nature, costs, and benefits of the outcomes for different stakeholders and determine whether the outcomes are just, fair, and respectful of human rights for all parties affected.

## THE CHANGING WORKPLACE

### Conflict in the Workplace

**Step 1**: Read the following scenario and write down the problems and issues that you observe.

Lois a newly appointed plant manager at Z-Corp., a small manufacturing and distribution company located in the Southwest. She was hired to start bringing in professionals with new ideas and energy. She oversees research and development, manufacturing, sales, marketing, finance, and the IT group. After being introduced to the supervisors of each of these divisions and given the "go" to start "sizing up" the plant, Lois began by sending an e-mail to the functional area supervisors in which she introduced herself and asked everyone to e-mail her regarding any outstanding issues or opportunities they wish to discuss at their first staff meeting in a week. Here is a summary of the e-mails:

### Bill in Marketing Communications, February 15

"Lois, welcome aboard. We can't wait to start working with you. We need to get our Intranet cranked up immediately to get our

*continued on next page*

## THE CHANGING WORKPLACE, cont.

major customers connected with us so we can get their immediate input and feedback on our products and services. (I would also like to get them involved in our R&D planning cycle, but you're going to have to talk to Jeff in R&D about that. He thinks we should wait on that idea. I personally think he's hoarding power and is afraid of direct customer involvement in product design decisions. You're going to have to really kick him to bring him into the 21st century.)

See you at the meeting."

### Al in IT, February 14

"Hi, Lois. Thanks for getting the information flowing. We're a friendly group. I think you'll enjoy working here. My biggest gripe is not getting everyone trained and involved in our Intranet. Jeff (R&D) is dragging his feet, but so is Bill in marketing. Bill talks a good talk, but he hasn't come to any training sessions and spends most of his time on the Web looking at competitors. He's smart but lazy. We should have all our distributors linked to his laptop as we talk. I'd also like to encourage you to help me get Mr. Rosen, our president, to back up our IT efforts to go fully online with all our operations. He still doesn't believe we can increase efficiency and effectiveness by multiples if we go online. I know it's a sensitive issue to approach, but you'd be great at convincing him."

### Janice in Finance, February 16

"Lois, I'm so happy you've come. You're an added light in this male-dominated environment. (We'll talk more later, but you should know that we had a big sexual discrimination suit last year between one of our male supervisors and a female employee. We settled out of court.) In case everyone's been telling you what's in their "shopping cart," let me say that none of the department supervisors keep close tabs on their spending or their budgets. Bill in Marketing and Jeff in R&D are the worst. They are constantly blaming me for watching their expenditures. Jeff thinks R&D has an unlimited spending account and Bill believes he should wine and dine our top customers once a month. Mr. Rosen sides with Bill and Jeff when I reject some of their invoices. (The truth is, we're really in a mess here with our information flow and our expenditures.) Help!"

### Jeff in R&D, February 17

"Joe Rosen asked me to especially welcome you and to introduce you to our new product lines. If you can come down tomorrow morning, I'll show you around. I certainly want to talk to you before Bill, Al, and Janice color your picture of the place. Without R&D, we're through as a company. I especially need your help in getting approval of a $1.5 million project that will put us in front of our closest competitor. In the meantime, I need an assistant to get us online with the new Intranet.

See you tomorrow!"

### Joe Rosen, president, February 17

"Lois, it's a pleasure having you on board. Welcome from all of us. I hope you've had a chance to meet all the supervisors and some of our champion employees. We run a tight ship here and we're proud of our R&D record of new product launches. A small problem we're facing is that we're running behind our return on investment targets for the last two quarters. I'll need your help on determining

*continued on next page*

---

**THE CHANGING WORKPLACE, cont.**

what's going on there. But I do hope you'll get everyone together and give me a full report on your take of our company."

**Step 2:** What types of conflict do you believe are occurring here? What concepts from the chapter are relevant to exploring the potential problems here?

**Step 3:** Write an outline for your meeting with the supervisors. What are your goals, strategies, and tactics for dealing with the supervisors?

**Step 4:** When do you plan on meeting with Joe Rosen, the president? What will you say? Outline your discussion.

---

## REVIEW QUESTIONS

1. Give one example of dysfunctional and functional conflict in an organization.

2. Which source(s) of conflict have you experienced recently? How did the conflict arise? How can Figure 1–5 in Chapter 1 help identify the source of a conflict in an organization?

3. Which style of conflict resolution (using Thomas's approach) do you find most difficult to use? Easiest to use? Explain.

4. Give one example when (in a team, group, or at work) you experienced the roles of initiator, responder, and mediator in conflicts, as explained in the chapter. Which role was the most difficult to use in the collaborative approach? The easiest to use? Explain.

5. Who is or was the best example you have known of a mediator (as explained in this chapter) in settling a conflict? What were this person's characteristics as a mediator?

6. Give an example of left-hand, right-hand column exercise. Use yourself. What were you really thinking when someone was talking? What did you actually say? If you had been in a "learning" organization team, what would you have said differently in a supportive environment? Do you believe it could work well in a team?

7. Which "difficult person" profile would best characterize you on occasions? Explain. Which profile would best characterize someone with whom you have had to deal? Did you use the suggested techniques in this chapter for dealing with that person? Would that technique have worked in communicating more effectively with that person? Explain.

8. What is the difference between distributive and integrative negotiations?

9. Which technique could you use more effectively in a conflict situation? Explain.

10. Give a current situation in which you could use *Getting to Yes* negotiating techniques. Explain why and how you would use the four steps in your situation.

11. Do you agree that personality and gender do not make a difference in negotiations? Explain.

12. Briefly interview someone from another national culture. Ask questions that would enable you to determine whether the discussion in this chapter applies to the person's cultural negotiating style.

13. Do the characteristics of the North American negotiation styles fit you if you are a North American? Explain. If you are Asian, Arab, Latin American, Chinese, or Russian, do the characteristics described in Table 1–1 fit your negotiation style? Explain.

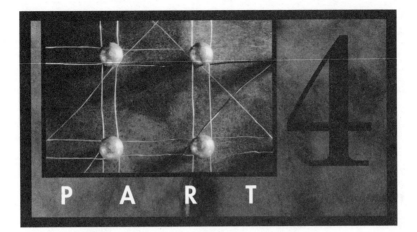

# Organizational Processes

# 10

## Work, Jobs and Job Design: Present, Past, and Future

---

### LEARNING OBJECTIVES

After studying this chapter, you should be able to:

**1** Understand work in the Information and Internet Age.

**2** Define *job* and *job design*.

**3** Describe the transformation of work and jobs.

**4** Explain the traditional approach to job design: "Fitting people to jobs."

**5** Identify job enlargement and enrichment strategies.

**6** Describe the job characteristics model.

**7** Explain contemporary approaches to work and job design.

**8** Discuss a flex-management model to address diversity issues.

**9** Understand the diagnostic checklist for evaluating and redesigning jobs.

**10** Discuss ethical issues for managing jobs.

---

## WORK IN THE INFORMATION AND INTERNET AGE

The nature of work and jobs is changing. As information technologies integrate and speed business transactions, work and jobs will become even more decentralized, project oriented, and dependent on technologies.

> *"The lone corporate soldiers ... have been replaced by teams of people with the autonomy of small-business owners. Internet Age companies rely on the initiative and intelligence of individual employees to foster decisions that are closer to the customer and therefore more responsive to the market. The ultimate goal, says CEO Jorma Ollila of Finland's telecom giant Nokia, is "flexibility, an open mind, and transparency of organization."*[1]

The following excerpts characterize the nature of these changes. Consider Planet-Intra.com Ltd., a year-old software company that is nominally based in Mountain View, Calif. Alan J. McMillan, the 37-year-old founder and CEO, is a Canadian who had been working in Hong Kong. A software team in Croatia wrote the company's product. The vice-president for technology is Russian, while the VP of international sales is a German living in Tokyo. They use the Internet—in fact, their own product, to collaborate across borders. "We live and breathe the Internet," says McMillan.[2]

> *In this new environment, the most successful companies are endowing entry-level employees with the reverence once accorded only to customers. . . . And they are paying generously for performance, not only with cash, but with ownership. As Cisco Systems Inc. CEO John Chambers puts it: "The New Economy is heavy on intellectual capital. The sharing of knowledge is what really makes it go. In the New Economy, you expect not necessarily lifelong employment. . . . In the New Economy, people work for ownership. Security comes from the stock. Labor fought management in the Old Economy. Today, teamwork and empowerment are crucial to success.[3]*

In the New Economy, work is structured around innovation and results that require creativity and marketable skills. For example, FedEx allocates 3 percent of total expenses to training, six times the proportion of most companies.

> *The world is going through a seismic shift to intellectual capital from capital investment. . . . Executives worldwide who rank human performance ahead of productivity and technology in strategic importance: 75 percent. Those who say that by 2010 attracting and retaining people will be the No. 1 force in strategy: 80 percent.[4]*

## JOBS AND JOB DESIGN DEFINED

We begin this chapter by providing basic definitions as a starting point of understanding: *Jobs* refer to specific work assignments and activities that are defined in job descriptions, assignments, and experiences. Jobs serve as the building blocks with which we differentiate individual roles and responsibilities in organizations. Jobs are intended to give direction, boundaries, and meaning to work. Defined in terms of "positions," jobs have traditionally located individuals in organizational structures and have defined the status of employees. Cumulative job experiences shape the careers of individuals. As with work and organizational structures, the nature of jobs, especially in knowledge-based industries, is changing as we will explain.

*Job design* refers to "the study of jobs, tasks, and constellations of tasks that encompass properties, perceptions, and responses to properties and/or perceptions. It . . . includes job enrichment, job enlargement, job characteristics models, and social information processing perspectives."[5] Job design also refers to methods and interventions for changing jobs to improve the fit between the individual jobholder's skills and competencies with the job. The subject of jobs and job design are considered core topics in the field of organizational behavior, along with the study of individual differences, motivation, groups and teams, and perception.

In this chapter, we discuss the forces in and around organizations that are transforming work and jobs. We then explain the traditional approach to job design and identify relevant strategies for evaluating and designing jobs. Contemporary approaches to job design are presented, including a flex-management model that addresses diversity issues in organizing jobs. A diagnostic checklist for evaluating and designing jobs is presented. We conclude by discussing how ethical issues relate to job design.

## Transformation of Jobs

Consider the work environment of a major U.S. corporation. It's 9 a.m., and the revolutionary workplace of the future is awfully quiet. On one side of the converted warehouse, beneath orange girders and massive yellow ducts, perhaps 50 of 220 desks are occupied. Employees tap laptop computers or whisper into phones; some meet in small groups or venture across "Main Street" to confer with administrators and managers. A low roar from the air conditioning blankets the cavernous space in antiseptic stillness. Beneath the remarkable austerity at IBM's new Cranford, New Jersey, sales office, though, is something of a revolution. The 600 representatives based here have no offices; one day each week, or less often, they come in to pick up mail and see associates, and a computer assigns them a spot with little accouterment save one chair, a telephone, and a jack for a laptop. Most of the time, they're on the road. Software marketer Lynn M. Fox gets most administrative work done by modem from home or spare offices at customer sites. Her time with customers is better spent: Because all of the product, the pricing, and technical data she needs are available via her laptop, a bid takes minutes, not days, to work up. No approvals are needed from the office bureaucracy. She's home by 6 p.m., allowing her a few hours with Matthew, her three-year-old, before she checks in again for electronic messages. It's still a 10–12 hour work day, "but a lot more productive and I feel I have more control," she says.[6]

The same external forces that are affecting organizations—the Internet's immediateness in creating global markets, shrinking organizational layers, and giving customers instant access to products and services—are affecting the nature of jobs. Consider the following reasons for the diminishing importance and even the disappearance of many traditional jobs:

For most of human history, nobody held what we now call a job. People worked, of course, but in different ways. They were farmers, home workers, craftspeople. They did whatever needed to be done on a schedule set by the sun or the seasons.

Then came the Industrial Revolution and the bizarre idea that a person should show up at the same place and time every day and do what someone else said to do, over and over—presto: the birth of the job. By the middle of the twentieth century, holding a job had come to carry all kinds of extra social meaning. A job implied security. It implied an occupation, a career, and an identity. So are these industrial-style jobs really disappearing? The answer is yes and no—or rather, no and yes.

No, they are not disappearing. For the foreseeable future, the vast majority of Americans in industrial-style jobs will continue to go to work in the morning and come home at night and perform some discrete collection of tasks in between.

Right now having a job is no guarantee that you'll have the same job tomorrow, let alone next year. If you go looking for a new one, the old rules—send out resumes, answer and fill out applications—no longer seem to apply. Job descriptions are more fluid than they used to be. Job titles and ranks are less important than they used to be (unless you work for the federal government). Quit thinking that what you have to do is "get" or "keep" a job. Start looking for customers—that is, people whose wants or needs you can help satisfy.

It is only a change in mind-set, maybe, but it is a big one. Old-style employees define themselves by what they are (lathe operator, nurse) and say to employers, "Hire me." New-style employees see themselves as entrepreneurs in a marketplace and say to employers, "Here's how I can help you." Like any entrepreneur, they've always got an eye out for new market niches.

Smart, confident individuals will learn to cope with these new demands. But will we as a society be able to cope? Old-style industrial jobs, once we got used to them, offered a level of stability and predictability that some people need and a lot of people want. Now that stability and predictability are disappearing.[7]

Work, organizations, structures, and, therefore, jobs are changing. Consider how it feels to work inside a cluster-oriented team structure, which we will discuss in Chapter 11.

> *Monica James heard about a rapidly growing firm that was looking for additional people. She already had a sales position in a large company but was bored, so she decided to investigate. A meeting with some personnel representatives followed, then a meeting with the president of the interested firm. There were several other interviews and finally a call with an offer of employment, which she accepted.*
>
> *On her first day, James met a second time with the company president. "We hired you," he told her, "because we are impressed with your experience and your abilities. Now, what would you like to do here?"*
>
> *In an instant, the question crystallized a number of concerns James had about the interviewing process she had been through. There had been many questions about her background, skills, and interests, but she had never been told what she was being hired to do—apparently because the company did not have a specific spot for her. She became anxious about the situation.*
>
> *"I don't know," she answered. "Don't you know what job I'm supposed to have?" The president smiled. "Not yet," he answered. "Why don't you hang around the company for a few weeks? Get to know our people. Find out what's going on. Decide where you can make a contribution. Then come back and we'll talk about it. Meanwhile, I'd like you to meet the staff person who will be your sponsor. He'll help you to meet people and show you the ropes. Just call on him whenever you want to know something or get an introduction, or need something."[8]*

Rapid change in technologies, business practices, and decision-making processes influence the nature of work and jobs. It is still useful to understand traditional methods and strategies for evaluating and designing jobs since many of these techniques persist and are guidelines in job evaluation and design. In the following section, we review traditional approaches to job design before presenting newer, future-oriented perspectives.

### Job Design: Traditional Approach, "Fitting People to Jobs"

Job design "refers to any set of activities that involves the alteration of specific jobs or interdependent systems of jobs with the intent of improving the quality of employee job experience and their on-the-job productivity."[9] The traditional approach involved fitting people to jobs. The focus was on the job, not on the people. Based on the scientific management school of thought (recall our discussion of historical management development in Chapter 1), this approach emphasized economic efficiency and optimization of piecework. Work simplification was the principle used to reduce a job to its component parts and then redesign the components into a maximally efficient work process. When work was routine and technology could be standardized to accomplish planned optimal results by jobs, these principles applied. The efficiency perspective paved the way for modern methods of business process engineering when work in specialized jobs required standardized procedures and economies of scale.

Questions related to job redesign that contemporary business process engineers might use in designing or redesigning a job include the following:

- Should all the work activities now included in the job actually be part of it?

- Does the jobholder currently perform some of the work activities in the job in a random fashion when order and consistency might promote greater efficiency?

- Can some of the work activities be batched—that is, performed in groups for several transactions rather than separately for each one?

- Can instructions for managing work activities be standardized?

- Does the layout of the workplace (including equipment and supplies) facilitate the completion of the work activities?

- Are the time and effort consumed by a particular work activity so great that it should be broken into a sequence of smaller activities?

- Can some of these smaller work activities be eliminated by physical rearrangement of the workplace or by the use of different equipment (calculators rather than adding machines, word processors instead of typewriters)?

- If some of the smaller work activities were performed in a different sequence, could any of them be eliminated or combined?

- Could overall productivity be increased by redistributing work activities among a group of workers?

Problems that have resulted in the efficiency-based fitting-people-to-jobs approach center around the issue of treating human beings in machinelike ways, assuming that individuals' motivations, feelings, and need for interaction are less important than their capability and willingness to perform tasks optimally. The traditional job design approach—especially when combined with the nature of routine, simple, and boring work, low wages, and lack of advancement—can contribute to high levels of turnover, absenteeism, and problems relating to mental health, alcoholism, drug abuse, depression, and alienation.[10] For these reasons, as the nature and complexity of work, technology and the environment evolved, so did job design. And, just as important, as employees became more educated and sophisticated, the increasing complexity of their needs, aspirations, and motivation demanded consideration in the design of jobs.

## THE CHANGING WORKPLACE

### My Best Job–My Worst Job

**Step 1**: Briefly describe the best job you can remember. List five characteristics of the job itself that you specifically liked. Then briefly list what each characteristic meant to you. For example, you may say that you liked your boss's style (a characteristics). Then you might say because she gave me freedom to express myself.

### Best Job

| Characteristics | Because . . . |
| --- | --- |
| 1. | 1. |
| 2. | 2. |
| 3. | 3. |
| 4. | 4. |
| 5. | 5. |

**Step 2**: Now identify five characteristics of the worst job you had; and then explain each characteristic.

### Worst Job

| Characteristics | Because . . . |
| --- | --- |
| 1. | 1. |
| 2. | 2. |
| 3. | 3. |
| 4. | 4. |
| 5. | 5. |

**Step 3**: Refer to Figure 10–2 *The Job Characteristics Model.* Use the following job characteristics referring to your responses in Step 1 and then in Step 2. Beside each characteristic, place a check under the dimension that best explains that characteristic. You may check more than one dimension for each characteristic. For example, if you said a characteristic in Step 1 was that you like your boss because she provided you will a lot of freedom to do your work, you would place a check under D for that characteristic. (If you found another dimension that described your characteristic, write it down under *Other.*)

*Dimensions* of Job Motivation, Satisfaction, and Work Effectiveness

**A.**  **Skill variety**:        "This job did or did not challenge many of my skills and abilities. I was unchallenged and bored."

**B.**  **Task identity**:       "This job did or did not enable me to see and complete enough of the entire product, service, or activity from start to outcome to motivate or satisfy me to perform at a high-quality level."

## THE CHANGING WORKPLACE, Cont.

**C.    Task significance:**  "I didn't see this job as having meaningful impact on others to moti-vate or satisfy me to perform at a high-quality level."

**D.    Autonomy:**        "This job did or did not empower me by allowing me to schedule time, tasks, and procedures to perform at a high-quality level."

**E.    Job Feedback:**    "I did or did not receive clear and direct information and feedback about how effectively I was performing."

### From Step 1: Best Job

| Characteristic/ Because | A Skill variety | B Task identity | C Task significance | D Autonomy | E Feedback | (F) Other? |
|---|---|---|---|---|---|---|
| 1. | | | | | | |
| 2. | | | | | | |
| 3. | | | | | | |
| 4. | | | | | | |
| 5. | | | | | | |

### From Step 2:  Worst Job

| Characteristic/ Because | A Skill variety | B Task identity | C Task significance | D Autonomy | E Feedback | (F) Other? |
|---|---|---|---|---|---|---|
| 1. | | | | | | |
| 2. | | | | | | |
| 3. | | | | | | |
| 4. | | | | | | |
| 5. | | | | | | |

### Step 4:

1.   What observations and patterns do you see by comparing your checks from Best Job with Worst Job in Step 3?  Did you have more checks under any one dimension?  Did your Best Job and Worst Job dimension checks match?

2.   What did you learn about factors that motivate you to perform well from this analysis?

3.   How would you describe your "ideal job" (and its characteristics) now?

4.   Share your results with a classmate or group and compare your insights.

### Job Design: A Modern Approach

A more recent approach to designing jobs incorporates both objectively gathered descriptions of the jobs and the perceived requirements and relationships of jobholders. The first step in such a job design involves performing a functional job analysis (FJA)—that is, objectively describing a job by gathering information on the job's content, requirements, and context.

As illustrated in Figure 10–1, an FJA identifies specific activities, methods, and required outcomes of the job. Analyzing a job includes identifying its requirements (i.e., what information, relationships, skills, experience, and education are required to perform the job), its content (the physical conditions, environment, and external factors that affect the job; as well as, the supervision, accountability, and responsibility required to perform the job), and its context (the location and setting of the job in the physical environment and in the organization).

The result of the job analysis is the preliminary job design. The initial job design considers the perceived as well as objective content of the job. Former jobholders of identical or similar jobs are interviewed to obtain information. Managers are also interviewed to identify reporting relationships required with the job (i.e., who supervises whom and how many a person supervises—the span of control).

The performance evaluation of the jobholder is made possible and facilitated by the job design. Both objective and perceived criteria can be used from job descriptions for evaluation purposes.

### Job Enlargement and Job Enrichment: Redesign Strategies

Job designs change as jobholder needs and work requirements change. Job redesign strategies seek to address these changes. Job redesign approaches aimed at enhancing productivity and employee motivation include job enlargement and job enrichment. *Job enlargement*, the opposite of work simplification, increases the horizontal scope of the job, variety of activities, number of processes, and required skills to accomplish work. *Job extension*, doing more of the same work, is

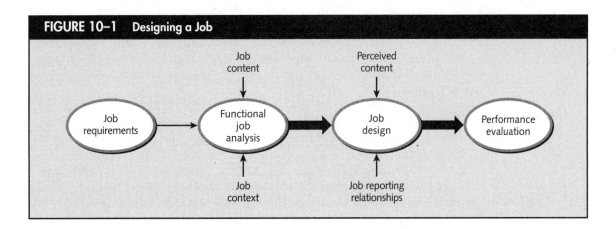

**FIGURE 10–1    Designing a Job**

a form of job enlargement. With *job rotation*, another form of job enlargement, employees learn and perform more and different or new tasks and activities. Japanese companies practice and reward horizontal job rotation. Individual workers learn a company's broader work processes. The United States has traditionally rewarded and used a narrower, more vertical job-specialization focus with mobility tracks. As discussed earlier, this practice is changing, especially in the high end of knowledge industries.

*Job enrichment* attempts to enhance employee motivation by changing work both horizontally (the number and variety of activities) and vertically (responsibility and recognition). Herzberg's motivation-hygiene approach (recall Chapter 4 on motivation) provides the basis for enrichment strategies. Herzberg showed that jobs could be enriched by increasing motivators (e.g., responsibility, growth, challenge, and autonomy).[11] Examples of enrichment programs include giving workers more control over decisions regarding their work context, offering flextime scheduling, giving and receiving systematic feedback over mutually set work goals and objectives, combining activities, and enabling customer contact. These strategies will increase in importance as workforces become more diverse, as work becomes more varied and outsourced, and as technologies enable employees to perform outside conventional offices.

### Jobs Characteristics Model

Another approach for designing jobs is the jobs characteristics model, created in the 1960s. Instead of representing a one-size-fits-all approach, this model attempts to fit individuals (considering their psychological as well as skill differences) with jobs.[12]

Figure 10–2 illustrates a later version of this model. According to this model, five core characteristics of a job—skill variety, task identity, task significance, autonomy, and feedback—influence employee attitudes and behaviors and the extent to which the job is experienced as meaningful. *Skill variety* describes the extent to which a job's activities challenge a person's skills and abilities. *Task identity* refers to the extent a job requires beginning-to-end completion activities. *Task significance* identifies the extent to which a job is perceived and objectively has a significant impact on the lives of other people. *Autonomy* is the degree to which a job offers an employee freedom, independence, and discretion in scheduling work and determining how the work will be performed. *Feedback* represents the degree to which an employee obtains direct information about the effectiveness of her performance.

The moderating variables and processes that link the core job characteristics in Figure 10–2 with the critical psychological states and then to the outcomes include a person's skill, knowledge, and competencies; strength of his growth needs for personal accomplishment, development, and learning; and his satisfaction with the work context. The underlying logic of this model is that people with higher-level competencies, growth needs, and desire for learning will, in effect, perform more effectively in enriched jobs that offer more variety, autonomy, and feedback. (It is an interesting exercise to review your current job or a previous one against these criteria.)

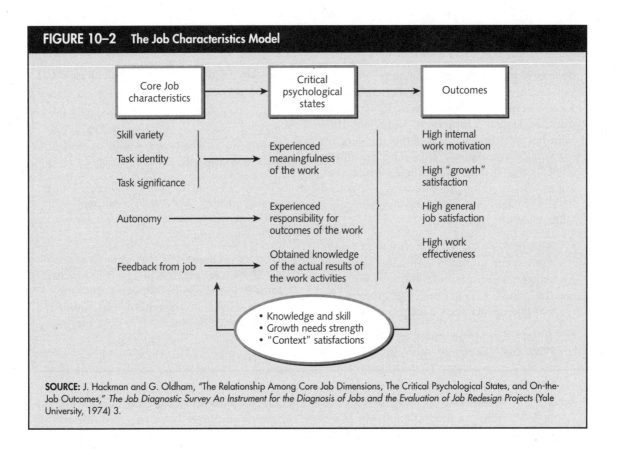

FIGURE 10–2   The Job Characteristics Model

SOURCE: J. Hackman and G. Oldham, "The Relationship Among Core Job Dimensions, The Critical Psychological States, and On-the-Job Outcomes," *The Job Diagnostic Survey An Instrument for the Diagnosis of Jobs and the Evaluation of Job Redesign Projects* (Yale University, 1974) 3.

## CONTEMPORARY JOB DESIGN APPROACHES AND PRACTICES

The social information processing model (SIPM)[13] is a modern job redesign approach. It argues that the social cues and feedback of co-workers and managers influence individuals' perceptions and responses to jobs. Moreover, according to this perspective, employees' perceptions of their jobs may be more influenced by subjective social cues and others' perceptions than by objective information and facts. This approach contributes to the field of work redesign in that managers and employees must take seriously other people's perceptions and communication about the nature of the work and jobs.

### Total Quality Management

Total Quality Management (TQM) is both a philosophy of management and a set of specific approaches and methods. There is no one best TQM approach but many. We discussed TQM principles in Chapter 1; here we discuss the philosophy of TQM as it relates to modern and contemporary job design.

Rooted in the concept of continuous improvements in quality throughout an organization's processes of planning, organizing, designing, delivering, and servicing

## THE CHANGING WORKPLACE

### How to Work at a dot-com Company

Bill Schaffer, author of *High-Tech Careers for Low-Tech People* (Ten Speed Press, 1999), began work at Digital Equipment Corp. in 1984 knowing only how to type before moving on to Sun Microsystems, Inc. The following advice, offered for nontechnical people wishing to work in a dot-com company, is adapted from and based on a *Fast Company* (November 1999, 234) interview:

- *Understand what the job actually involves.* Find someone in a company who can answer these questions for you: Who are the people who get jobs like the one you want? What are their backgrounds?

- *Just get the employee badge that allows you to enter daily.* Don't go after the ideal job quickly. Find out about technical aspects of the job.

- *Once in, keep your mouth shut and listen.* Pick up the company culture. Then ask questions to find out about technical aspects of the job.

- *To keep up with the pace of change, identify trends,* predict how your company will respond, then *position yourself for success* with your company.

- *Be able to work amid total chaos in the dot-com world.* Be a self-starter. Be ready to discard knowledge daily (it becomes obsolete). There's little management and training in dot-coms. Be ready.

products, TQM begins with the vision of a company and works through the embedding or institutionalizing of that vision. Every employee has a role and responsibility in implementing quality standards adapted to the organization's products and services. Focusing on customer satisfaction and requirements, most TQM initiatives are planned and implemented through teams.

Autonomous work teams, quality circles, and quality of work life programs are job design strategies related to TQM. TQM, which is both an old and new philosophy, really serves as an integrating logic and set of criteria for job design methods and approaches. The central question focuses on job design for what and for whom. Ultimately, the purpose of job and work redesign is to position organizations competitively in their respective industries through productive and responsible partnering of managers with employees to realize a joint vision: better quality and service to customers.

### Quality Circles

*Quality circles* (QC) is another modern approach to job redesign. This concept was invented in the United States and taken to Japan by W. Edwards Deming (the late guru of total quality management). QCs are groups of employees ranging in size from 4 to 30 members. The groups meet during work hours to identify and problem solve job-related issues such as reduction of production errors, improvement of communication and decision-making capacity, promotion of leadership, and development among nonmanagerial employees.[14] During the 1980s, more than 90 percent of the Fortune 500 companies had some form of quality circles.[15]

Experience with quality circles has been mixed. The results include increased job safety and better health care as well as higher morale and interest, increased commitment, expanded individual growth, and improved communication and respect between management and workers. The downside includes such issues as management's emphasizes on profits over employee development, failure to inform management of QC activities and developments, and overestimation of the benefits of quality circles.[16]

Various forms of QCs will probably continue in organizations where TQM programs thrive. The effectiveness of QCs depends in large part on the extent to which they add value to a corporation's profitability, productivity, and to employees, as well as management's openness to legitimizing the processes and recommendations of quality circles, which is essential. Employees' desire and ability to participate in and manage this activity while keeping management and owners informed and involved is another success factor.

*Quality of work life* (QWL) programs include and incorporate some of the approaches discussed earlier. Specifically, QWL programs emphasize teamwork and employee participation in making decisions that influence workers' satisfaction and productivity. For example, GM was an innovator and a leader in using QWL teams in 1970. Later, Saturn, a GM division, organized union representatives into planning groups. Issues in which management and employees have a shared interest include problem-solving in areas such as cost and quality control, innovation, pay, employee involvement, training and development, job redesign, absenteeism, turnover, and retention of high performers. The QWL initiatives also include such policies as flextime working schedules, work at home and off site, child care for employees, and autonomous work teams.[17] It is interesting to note that many of these job redesign approaches that date back to the 1970s and 1980s have reemerged in both TQM and workforce diversity initiatives.

### Contemporary Work and Job Options

Ask employees in start-ups, virtual teams, and even large corporations that have been restructured around customers about their work week and they will usually say something that resembles "7-24-365" (i.e., on call 7 days a week, 24 hours a day, and 365 days a year.) Changes in the context and ways work is performed have affected work schedule arrangements. Because of the uses of the Internet, information and wireless technologies, physical space and time constraints affecting work have also changed. The following types of virtual employment represent ways that work is being (re)scheduled: compressed and shorter workweeks(e.g. allowing employees to work the same number of hours in four days instead of five), telecommuting (using electronic communications to perform work away from an organization), flextime (i.e., giving employees choice in scheduling tasks), job sharing and splitting (i.e., dividing the job by tasks or skills rather than time or schedule). While most of these practices are known and have been widely used for some time, we will discuss telecommuting in particular since it facilitates the other flexible schedules.

### Telecommuting

*Telecommuting,* the driver of virtual employment, enables employees to use their computers and other electronic devices to work at home or away from their physical workspaces.[18] Sales professionals have always used some form of telecommuting. The U.S. workforce is expected to exceed 60 million telecommuters this year.[19] While the advantages of telecommuting are obvious (flexibility, opportunity to work at home and be with family members, cost savings on travel and expenses), the downside of telecommuting includes social isolation and possible negative effects on career advancement opportunities as a result of being removed from the action.[20] From the employers' perspective, the advantages of telecommuting exceed the costs, particularly in terms of (1) productivity: companies' efficiency increased while productivity jumped 2.5 percent in 1999; (2) longer hours: workers are putting in 260 hours more a year than a decade ago, many without overtime pay; (3) variable pay: 70 percent of companies offer stock option and bonuses, which enable them to lure and keep talent without locking in large salaries; and (4) temporary workers: The Bureau of Labor Statistics predicts that the number of temporary workers will increase 50 percent between 1996 and 2006; (5) immigrant workers: they can work as telecommuters, enabling many businesses to be able to operate—but against unions' complaints; and (6) the ability to layoff more costly senior staff who can be replaced by less expensive, younger, outsourced labor who telecommute.[21] Professionals should weigh these advantages and disadvantages on their careers and performance evaluations before committing to telecommuting.

## Workforce Diversity and Job Design

Until fairly recently, organizing principles did not specifically consider workforce diversity or individual and group characteristics. The U.S. experience of job design dealt mainly with a homogeneous workforce (diversity was invisibly present) and management mind-set (i.e., one size fits all). This mind-set reflected the following profile regarding organizing:

- Narrow and tightly defined jobs

- Narrow spans of control (i.e., number of people a manager supervises)

- Layers in management for approval and monitoring

- Rigid demarcations between functions

- One-way communication systems

- Evaluation, promotion, planning, and decision-making systems controlled at the top

- Policies that tightly monitored work hours, time off, good behavior, disciplinary processes, and work rules.[22]

Because of the increasing elements of cultural diversity in the workforce, newer organizing paradigms such as the flex-management model shown in Figure 10–3, are being implemented. This model represents a contemporary trend in organizations that are individualizing systems, policies, and practices to more directly use and connect people and resources to performance. IBM and its Lotus Development operation, Nynex, AT&T, and Motorola are a few examples of large corporations that have implemented some form of a flex-management model.

In this model, broader policies are adapted to focus on intent and contain more options and less specific parameters regarding individuals. For example, one such policy guideline might read, "Performance planning and management discussions are valuable to improve and maintain productivity and performance" instead of

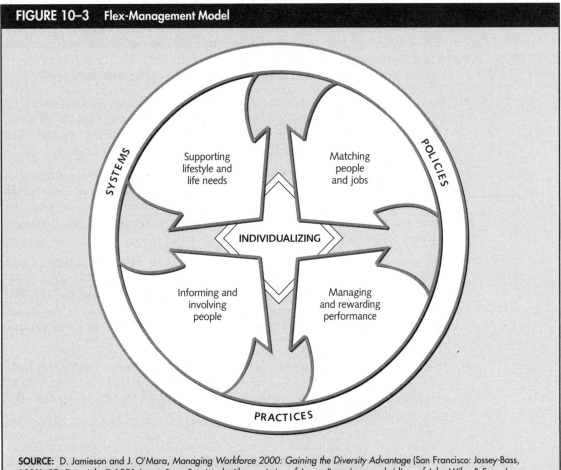

**FIGURE 10–3    Flex-Management Model**

SYSTEMS — POLICIES — PRACTICES

Supporting lifestyle and life needs

Matching people and jobs

INDIVIDUALIZING

Informing and involving people

Managing and rewarding performance

**SOURCE:** D. Jamieson and J. O'Mara, *Managing Workforce 2000: Gaining the Diversity Advantage* (San Francisco: Jossey-Bass, 1991), 37. Copyright © 1991 Jossey-Bass. Reprinted with permission of Jossey-Bass, Inc., a subsidiary of John Wiley & Sons, Inc.

"The corporatewide standard performance appraisal forms shall be completed twice each year in April and October for each employee."[23]

Other flexible policies are designed to individualize procedures related to holidays, transfers, and rotations, for example. The key is to keep information-sharing policies open, complete, and regular instead of being restrictive and not informing or involving employees.

Systems in the flex-management model are characterized by versatility, a less prescriptive focus, and an emphasis on flexibility to customize the fit between employee and organization regarding compensation and classification, benefits, rewards, job evaluation and design, job descriptions, and training. A results orientation that respects and rewards individual effort and productivity should be reflected in the policies, systems, and organization practices.

Finally, the practices in a flex-management model require managers to manage by questioning, listening to employees, negotiating, arbitrating, and facilitating organizational requirements with individual differences and demands. Some employees may need and request more control, structure, and direction than others. Few overall corporate or work unit prescriptions can address individual differences in a highly diverse workforce.

The four basic strategies that guide a flex-management model include:

- *Matching people with jobs based on individuals skills, and work preferences with job characteristics and requirements.* Objective and subjective dimensions of work must be considered. Human resource infrastructure policies, systems, and practices must be coordinated and in sync to implement this strategy.

- *Managing and rewarding individual and team performance.* Implementing this strategy requires performance coaching, mentoring, feedback, and the use of both monetary and intrinsic rewards. A flexible approach must be taken in using and varying structured and unstructured procedures and practices with different individuals.

- *Informing and involving people.* Some people need more information and feedback than others. This strategy requires that organizations provide flexible arrangements to direct information to and accommodate the involvement of employees. For example, ongoing and temporary groups can be set up; suggestion systems established; and attitude surveys and focus groups arranged.

- *Finally, supporting life-style and life needs.* This requires companies to identify individuals' needs and interests to create and respond to needs for options such as child care, substance abuse counseling, flexible time schedules, remedial education, and leave options.

If higher-level work is indeed becoming less routine and less predictable and requires more individual skills, the organizational structure, jobs, policies, systems, and practices must respond to attract, retain, and develop skilled people.

### From Job-Based to Competency- and Skill-Based Organizations

As stated at the beginning of the chapter, a paradigm shift is occurring in work and jobs—from job-based organizations to competency- and skill-based models and practices.[24] This shift will most likely occur in organizations performing knowledge work that is highly interdependent and changing and that is accomplished both individually and in teams. Fast-growing knowledge-based firms such as Microsoft and Lotus Development Corporation use some form of competency-based job design.

As competency-based organizations seek competitive advantage in their industry and marketplace, they must fit work and skills to performance requirements. The change can be characterized as follows: "The alternative to job-based organizing is designing organizational systems in which the capabilities of individuals are the primary focus and which cause them to be managed in a way that facilitates the development of organizational capabilities that provide competitive advantage."[25] Instead of fitting people to organizations, organizations are aligning people with particular work. In other words, a skill-based approach will replace detailed job descriptions with the "skill and person descriptions" required to accomplish work in a particular area. The focus will be on what individuals need to be able to do in order to make the work processes operate effectively.

This paradigm shift has implications in a number of human resource areas. The following is an overview of the issues that such changes presents.

- *Selection*: Instead of fitting individuals to jobs, competency-based organizations fit individuals to learning environments through realistic job previews and skill-based assessments.

- *Retention*: A competency-based organization attracts those individuals who are interested in and capable of learning or who already have the skills required. Rewards will be skill based; therefore, retaining individuals who are successful should suit the organization's and individual's needs.

- *Pay for performance*: Individuals will be rewarded for the degree to which they fill the blocks of skills needed by organizations, not for jobs or positions held. The focus will require an evaluation, measurement, and marketplace pricing of skills.

- *Training and career development*: Instead of hierarchical and vertical mobility training and career paths, individuals will be continuously trained on multiple-skills acquisition tracks. Managers might advance by learning how the organization operates as an enterprise and through training.

Although many organizations may not—or perhaps should not, given their particular environment, goals, and type of work and outputs—shift to this paradigm, many companies will need to do so to stay competitive.

Obstacles and issues involved in the change from job-based to competency and skill-based systems include the following. First economies of scale are lost. That is, when many individuals hold the same job, costs increase when individuals are targeted and paid for skills and work they do as individuals. If individual skill-based competencies do not add value to the organization's product and return on investment, costs can exceed benefits. Second, significant change is required to make the transition from a traditional job-based system to a competency- and skill-based approach. The human resource infrastructure must be altered or recreated. Employee involvement programs that emphasize skill-based work, training, rewards, and promotions must be implemented. The competitive environment, the changing nature of work, and the increasing role of technologies will, to a large extent, determine whether and to what extent organizations will change or reinvent their definitions of work and jobs. Again, these descriptions and new types of job design may occur incrementally and in unplanned ways in organizations. The point here is that we must be aware of the changes so that we can evaluate the strengths and weaknesses of each job design approach.

A systematic way of evaluating and designing jobs to fit individual skills and motivation to work requirements is presented next.

## EVALUATING AND DESIGNING JOBS: A DIAGNOSTIC JOB CHECKLIST

Jobs will to a large extent depend on the nature of the transformation an organization undergoes. Business process engineering (and reengineering) can dramatically reduce the nature and number of jobs in a company.

A realistic evaluation for assessing job design readiness should be undertaken by management, employees, supervisors, and outside observers. Hackman, Oldman, Janson, and Purdy[26] offer the following steps as diagnostic questions to use as a starting point:

**Step 1.** Are motivation and satisfaction central to the problem? If the answer is no, other aspects of the work situation would be examined to identify the real problem. Otherwise, proceed to Step 2.

**Step 2.** Is the job low in motivating potential? If so, we go to the next step; if not, other dimensions of the work—supervision, pay system, and so on—would be reviewed.

**Step 3.** What specific aspects of the job are causing the difficulty? The five dimensions of the job characteristic model are used to answer this question—that is, skill variety, task identity, task significance, autonomy, and feedback from the job. Once a profile of high- and low-motivational potential is identified, we proceed to the next step.

**Step 4.** How "ready" are the employees for change? Once the need for job improvement is documented, using a job diagnostic survey instrument can identify the "growth-need strength" of employees. This instrument can help determine how fast or gradually planned changes should be implemented and with whom to begin.

Then, specific action steps are considered. Some of the implementing concepts for changing and enriching jobs include forming natural work units, combining tasks, establishing client relationships, vertical loading (i.e., adding or giving responsibilities and controls of a job to the jobholder), and opening feedback channels.

### Beginning a Large-Scale Job Design Program

The following 12-point procedure has been used to begin a large-scale job design program.[27] This provides a broader, macro-level picture of how management with the help of outside consultants might begin such a change program:

1. *Define the system's goals.* After selecting the organization, system, or subsystem to be studied, specific group(s) who will be involved are identified. The goals of the organization (or group targeted for change) are identified, the structure of the organization is examined, and the job classification structure is also reviewed.

2. *Define the relevant tasks and activities.* This step identifies the work tasks that accomplish the organization's objectives, pertinent managerial and personal skills, and the needs and aspirations of the jobholders under review. A balance between social and technical requirements of the organization must be considered during this step.

3. *Obtain an overview.* Information is gathered under direct observation, on-the-job experience, interviews with job incumbents and their supervisors, meetings with management, questionnaires, tests, and ratings, and analysis of job and training manuals. The aim here is to obtain a comprehensive overview of the jobs under study.

4. *Develop the unique characteristics or constraints.* The work setting, age of the workforce, job classification plan, and other characteristics are reviewed to determine what characteristics of the job are unique and what outside or internal constraints influence the design of the jobs.

5. *Develop a clustering of tasks.* Work tasks and personal skills are clustered on the basis of similar behaviors and common requirements to determine what tasks should be meaningfully grouped together.

6. *Develop a list of intervention techniques,* for example, focus groups.

7. *Relate techniques to requirements and assumptions.* Managers brainstorm to identify a list of techniques and principles appropriate for the job clusters.

8. *Define the appropriate level of implementation.*

9. *Pull it together in a picture.* Portray and summarize the findings from the preceding steps.

10. *Screen generalities.* Eliminate vague statements that do not specify implementation plans.

11. *Develop an implementation process.* Show a force field analysis related to an implementation plan. Screen the design techniques that can and cannot be implemented without changing the job classification plan. A separate implementation plan is required for job classification changes.

12. *Adapt the job description and design process.* The job description design process should be reviewed and changed as the organization's requirements evolve.

Taken together, the diagnostic job checklist and the macro-level job design program offer a practical and comprehensive picture of the steps involved in reviewing and designing jobs and clusters of work tasks assigned to jobs. It should be remembered that the extent to which organizations can benefit from the job diagnosis and design depends to a large extent on who carries out the analysis and implementation of planned changes and how they are carried out. Specifically, the competency, objectivity, and experience of the planners and those who implement the plans determines the success or failure of the outcome.

## ETHICAL ISSUES AND JOBS

Managers have a responsibility to employees to establish and maintain a social and psychological contract—as well as to ensure that job descriptions and obligations are met. Inherent in this psychological contract is the mutual trust—that each will respect the other's legal and ethical rights—that must exist between employer and employee.

Managers are responsible for ensuring that employers' obligations to employees are met. This means that fair wages are paid and that safe working conditions and meaningful work are provided. It also means that employees' rights to know about harmful workplace or job conditions are protected, as are their rights to privacy, to organize and strike, to be given 60 days' notice before a closing (if the company has more than 100 employees), and to due process over grievances.

Employees must also fulfill their contractual and job description responsibilities. This entails following organizational and job goals and objectives, performing procedural rules, offering competence commensurate with the work and job to which employees are assigned, and performing productively according to required job tasks.

At the heart of the social and psychological contract are the practice of sharing information honestly and, of course, mutual respect and trust between manager and employee. These are the building blocks of productivity, and they cannot be had by force. Only by empowering people, delegating responsibility, and openly sharing praise and constructive criticism through dialogue can job and work obligations optimally be achieved.

## THE CHANGING WORKPLACE

### Every Business Delivers a *Value Proposition*: What's Yours?

**Exercise**: A *value proposition* is the *entire set of resulting experiences* that an organization causes some customers to have. Examples are speed, fast service, power, leading-edge technology, on-time performance, reliability, durability, and responsiveness. A value proposition can focus on a single or large number of them. A value proposition can be focused on a set of either primary or intermediary customers. A start-up business plan must have a *value proposition* that is persuasive enough to receive funding, convincing enough to beat out existing or new competitors, and realistic enough to launch a business. Existing business must continually reinvent and rejuvenate their value propositions for their products, services, and company. The "de facto value proposition" creates competitive advantage for a product, service, company. Answer these elements to determine a value proposition:

- What customers do business with you?

- What do they buy or use? What actions do they have to take to do so?

- If they did not do business with your organization, what would they do instead?

- What resulting experiences (i.e., end-result consequences for a customer that are superior, equal, or inferior to any alternative experience he or she could receive from doing business with someone else) does he or she get by doing business with you instead of someone else?

To deliver a value proposition, you/your company) must also answer these questions:

- What are the success criteria for your business?

- What is the organizational unit/responsibility that will deliver this value proposition?

- What is the value proposition this business will deliver?

- Will the intended customers perceive this proposition as superior to their alternative?

### Exercise

1. Describe a major value proposition that the company (college/university) you work(ed) for or attend delivers.

2. List the job, roles, and responsibilities that you play(ed) that help(ed) deliver the proposition.

3. Describe elements of that job that you believe could be or should have been more instrumental in helping the company/organization deliver its value proposition.

4. Share your responses with a class member. Describe insights you and your partner had as a result of doing this exercise. (For example, is it possible to have a job that is removed from the major value proposition of a company or organization—i.e., could someone hold a menial or competitive job that could be removed? If you do not know what your organization's value proposition is, can you evaluate the competitiveness and value of your own job? Explain.)

**SOURCE**: M. Lanning, based on *Delivering Profitable Value* (New York: Perseus, 1998).

## CONCLUDING COMMENTS

The traditional approach of job design involved fitting people to jobs. The Internet and information technologies are changing the way work is performed and designed. Emphasis is placed on brainpower and individual and team talent. Work performed online shrinks international boundaries and organizational layers. The evolution of jobs and job design approaches begins with their definitions. Early job redesign approaches (job enlargement and job enrichment) sought to enhance productivity and employee motivation. A modern job design approach, the social information processing model, considers individuals' perceptions and responses to jobs since these factors are influenced by the social cues and feedback of co-workers and managers.

A contemporary skill-based model of organizing was presented and compared to a traditional job-based paradigm. Other modern and contemporary job design methods and practices discussed included autonomous, self-managing work teams used in total quality management programs, quality circles, and quality of work life programs.

A flex-management model designed to individualize systems, policies, and practices in diverse workforces was presented. The model showed how a general approach for describing work can replace traditional job descriptions.

Contemporary job changes include the practices of outsourcing, compressed and shorter workweeks, telecommuting, job sharing, and flextime.

A four-step diagnostic checklist for evaluating jobs based on the job characteristics model was presented, along with action steps to change and enrich jobs. Outcomes based on a job analysis can result in one or more of the following implementation strategies: form natural work units, combine tasks, establish client relationships, vertical loading, and opening feedback channels.

A 12-point macro-level job design program was summarized to show how managers and consultants design jobs to fit an organization's context.

Ethical issues in managing job (re)design approaches were discussed along with recommendations for observing employee rights and obligations. The changing social and psychological contract between employee and management was discussed.

## REVIEW QUESTIONS

1. Describe changes in your work or job that have been influenced by the Internet and information technology. What are some pros and cons of how work and jobs are evolving as a result of the Internet?

2. Apply the steps from the chapter on redesigning a job to your job (as a professional or student). What changes would be made if these steps were carried out? How would you feel about your work/job if the changes were made? Why?

## THE CHANGING WORKPLACE

### XYZ's Employee Complaints

**Step 1:** Read the scenario and list the problems or issues you observe.

Three high-performing members of the XYZ company have just sent e-mails to Eleanor Smith, Human Resource manager.

Kimberly, an award-winning new product designer, has threatened to quit if she isn't given more control over her work process and product design release. In her e-mail, she wrote, "I'm getting tired of being micro managed. I'm the one who's creating new products and bringing money into this company. I don't need Paul [her manager] standing over my shoulder, trying to take credit for my work, and then pulling his macho control act on me. If you can't get him off my back, I'm out of here."

Michael a star sales professional, is also disgruntled. He wrote, "Eleanor, I'm really getting bored here. I've brought in $10 million in sales over the past two years. My bonus isn't great, but that's not the problem. I'm tired of being shut out of key strategy meetings with the presidents and VPs who are mapping out who our new customers will be. I'm the one selling to these people; I want to be involved in targeting them. I'm not just an employee here. They don't seem to get it. I haven't been invited to the last two top-level strategy meetings. If they don't like my $10 million, I know two companies that will."

Finally, Marcie in the IT department has been given three sizable bonuses over the past two years for her remarkable work on integrating new software applications across the firm. "Without Marcie's work," her supervisor wrote, "we would still be pushing pencils and paper here instead of moving forward with strategic information and account sales!" Marcie is upset because she is not being given the maternity leave she requested. She also requested a flex-time schedule to be with the child for the first year. Her e-mail stated, "They like my work but don't respect my life. If I don't get some balance to my life, I can't do my job anyway."

**Step 2**: Diagnose each of the three employees' complaints using concepts from this chapter. Address this question: "Do you believe each of the three employees has a valid complaint?" Explain.

**Step 3**: What recommendation, if any, would you make to this company's management on behalf of each employee?

3. List one or two specific ways in which your job as a student or professional could be changed from (a) job enlargement, (b) job rotation, and (c) job enrichment. How many of the changes could you now make on your own?

4. Now evaluate your job (as student or professional) using each item in the list of mind-sets discussed in the section Workforce Diversity and Job Design. What similarities and differences did you find? How do you believe your satisfaction, development, and growth are influenced by your findings? Explain.

5. Identify an ethical issue you face or faced resulting from the nature of your job, an assignment, or role you played. How did your issue affect your sense of

trust, loyalty, and energy toward your organization? How do you believe that "good ethics" affects work performance and satisfaction? Explain to what extent you believe that this occurs?

6. To what extent do your job and work as a student or professional enable you to participate in each of the following contemporary changes in the workplace: (a) outsourcing, (b) flextime, (c) job sharing, (d) telecommuting, (e) shorter or compressed workweek?

# 11

# Organizational Design and Structure

---

## LEARNING OBJECTIVES

After studying this chapter, you should be able to:

**1** Define *organizational design* and *structure processes*.

**2** Identify environments and forces pressuring structure.

**3** Describe the evolution of organizational structure.

**4** Explain the organizational change approaches: of reengineering, restructuring, rethinking, and real time.

**5** Present a checklist for reorganizing.

**6** Identify ethical issues for managing structural changes.

---

## ORGANIZATIONAL CHANGE AND DESIGN

Speed, scope, and scale are the imperatives driving organizational design strategy and in the Information Age. Organizations are reinventing the ways they do business to work faster and on a larger scale than ever before. Aligning organizational strategies, structures, and processes to markets is "the name of the competitive game."[1] The principles for designing and structuring an organization represent a starting point and basis for evaluating the effectiveness of the organization. This chapter defines and discusses the organizational design and structuring process, the environmental forces pressuring this process, ways that organizations are restructuring, and the ethics related to reorganizing.

> *However you organize your company or motivate your staff, one thing is clear: It is impossible to manage a company totally from the center. It is impossible for a single person or single committee to stay on top of every issue in every business unit or subsidiary. Leaders need to provide strategy and direction and to give employees tools that enable them to gather information and insight from around the world. Leaders shouldn't try to make every decision. Companies that try to "manage down" to direct every action from the center will simply not be able to move fast enough to deal with the tempo of the new economy. . . . Business leaders who succeed will take advantage of a new way of doing business, a way based on the increasing velocity of information. . . . To get the full benefit of technology, business leaders will streamline and modernize their processes and their organization. The goal is to make business reflex nearly instantaneous and to make strategy through an ongoing, iterative process. . . .[2]*

## ORGANIZATIONAL DESIGN AND STRUCTURE DEFINED

**Organizational design** is the process of identifying and configuring an organization's strategy and structure to achieve its mission and goals.

**Organizational structure** identifies and defines jobs and formal reporting relationships. Structure is a vehicle for coordinating and delegating work to help people implement an organization's goals and strategies. Ideally, structure clarifies the roles, responsibilities, and authority of individuals and groups who must collectively implement the vision and mission of the enterprise. Moreover, when systems are effectively organized, integrated, and streamlined—especially with the assistance of Internet technologies—people can be more energized and empowered and can gain a sense of focus and purpose in their work. Customers, suppliers, and vendors are also more likely to be satisfied when they receive product, service, information, and decisions on time, within budget, and by their specifications.

### Key Questions for Designing Organizations: Structure Follows Strategy

The leadership, vision, and strategy of a company set the direction and focus for the culture, the structure and the jobs, the people to be hired, the technology, and the systems that intregrate and process information. The diagnostic contingency model (Figure 1–6) in Chapter 1, repeated here as Figure 11–1, illustrates this configuration.

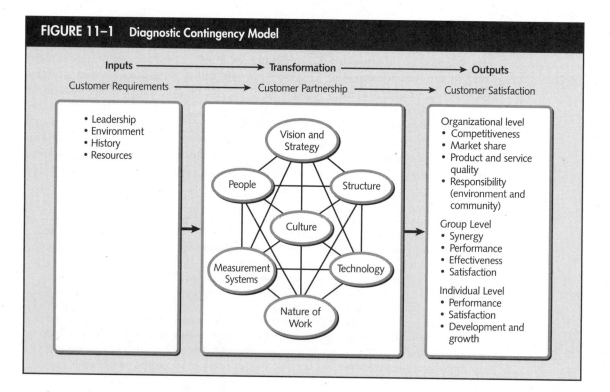

**FIGURE 11–1**    Diagnostic Contingency Model

As companies speed up to transform their business functions and processes by using Web-based technologies, many leaders are discovering that other significant changes may occur. The direction and nature of their business can be altered; relationships with vendors, customers, and suppliers can change; skills and core competencies are often enhanced or substituted by using information systems and electronic networks to perform transactions. For example, IBM and Microsoft have refocused significant areas of their businesses on providing E-business solutions—selling, servicing, and enabling companies to do business online. Dell Computer has almost become a virtual company, selling approximately $4 million in computers a day on the Internet and performing over half its business functions online. Variations of this scenario apply to companies such as GE, Cisco Systems, Xerox, General Motors, and Barnes and Noble. Many companies are making the transition in their businesses from manufacturing products to auctioning products, from being a service provider to being a consulting broker, and so on. As companies change the ways they do business, they also change the way they organize and structure their companies. The **key strategic questions** business leaders address in transforming all or parts of their operations are taken from the Chapter 7 and repeated here and in Figure 11-2:

- What business are we in?

- What is our product or service?

- Who are our customers?

- What are our core competencies?

Addressing these questions involves a process that can and should cascade throughout the organization, as Chapter 14 will show. Analyzing an organization's environment helps address the questions just presented and is necessary in identifying the appropriate design and structure.

## ENVIRONMENTS PRESSURING DESIGN AND STRUCTURE

An organization's environment consists of several components, which we discussed in earlier chapters. These include the (1) technology, (2) economic, (3) political and legal, (4) government/regulatory, and (4) demographic and social environments. Organizations must manage the uncertainties in each of the environmental components in which they operate. Changes in these environments can affect organizations both positively and negatively.

Before briefly discussing each environment, we identify three characteristics that organizational leaders can use to analyze their environments.

### Three Environmental Characteristics
For each environment, organizational leaders and strategic teams need to identify the specific characteristics that affect or will affect their company and the extent to

---

**FIGURE 11–2**    Strategic Questions

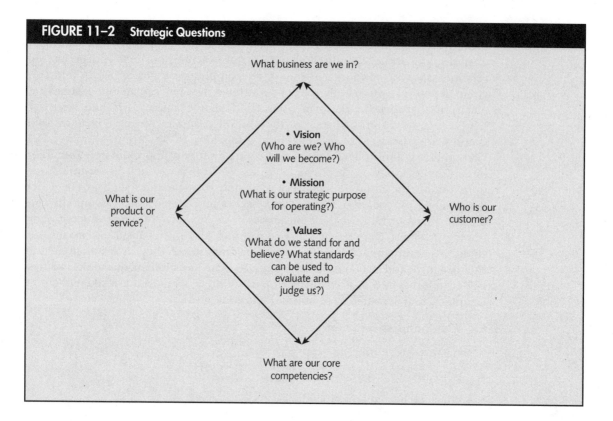

What business are we in?

- **Vision**
  (Who are we? Who
  will we become?)

- **Mission**
  (What is our strategic purpose
  for operating?)

- **Values**
  (What do we stand for and
  believe? What standards
  can be used to
  evaluate and
  judge us?)

What is our
product or
service?

Who is our
customer?

What are our core
competencies?

---

which the firm's strategy, structure, and systems can effectively respond to these forces. The environmental components can be analyzed in terms of (1) complexity, (2) dynamism, and (3) richness.[3] **Environmental complexity** refers to the strength, number, and interconnectedness of the environmental forces that the organization must manage. The more complex and uncertain the environmental characteristics, the more an organization must use resources (e.g., suppliers, products, information, employees) to reduce the uncertainty. The more interconnected the complexity of the environment, the greater the strain on an organization's resources to respond. For example, a new company that started in the late 1980s discovered in the mid-1990s that new competitors were all virtual start-ups, entering the market as Web-based businesses that quickly decided to significantly expand their product offerings by selling other vendors' products on their Web sites. At the same time, these businesses were able to slash their product prices to win volume. These combined interconnected factors increased the complexity that the 1980s firm faced. For example, many brick-and-mortar book stores went out of business after Amazon.com gained a niche in the online book selling market.

    **Environmental dynamism** refers to the degree and rate of change of the forces in an environment. The more stable the environment over time, the easier it is to predict the use of resources to manage in that environment and vice versa. Changing Internet and information technologies have added a permanent degree of dynamism in the environment for most companies. Major financial service firms such as Merrill Lynch had to quickly connect with online trading capability to meet the competitiveness of new start-ups such as E-trade and Ameritrade. Online trading is now institutionalized.

**Environmental richness** refers to the available resources in the environment that an organization can use to succeed. "Rich" environments have an abundance of resources to support an organization's growth. Silicon Valley is rich in venture capital funds for promising technology-related start-ups. However, some of these rich environments may be scarce in other dimensions (e.g., Silicon Valley may be "poorer" in readily available, high level, experienced programmers). An environment can also be rich or poor in terms of the amount and degree of resources required for the specific industry and company to succeed. Each of the three environmental characteristics can be identified and measured using the following general dimensions:

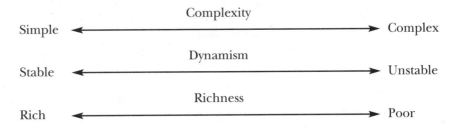

### Four Organizational Environments

The four environments discussed here include the technology environment, the economic environment, the political/legal environment, and the demographic/social environment. Each environment can be analyzed using the three characteristics just described: complexity, dynamism, and richness.

In the **technology environment**, most if not all organizations are pressured by having to incorporate and integrate automation and networked systems in their operations and structures—whether the changes are B to B (business to business transactions) or B to C (business to customers). The Internet and Web-based technologies provide speed, lowered costs, and increased efficiencies and satisfaction to an organization's stakeholders and customers. In the **economic environment**, organizations are pressured by rising interest rates and accompanying side effects: higher prices, costs of doing business and lower consumer confidence and spending. Changes in the global economy also present uncertainties to domestic firms: fluctuating national and regional currencies and interest rates affect increased, or decreased, costs of doing business. The **political and legal environment** impacts companies domestically and internationally. When a computer chip factory in Taiwan or Mexico that ships to the United States is damaged,

U.S. chip manufactures and distributors feel the economic effects. When an insurrection in another country disrupts a stable regime, other regional banks and businesses experience the effects. When a new environmental law is passed, companies may experience loss of—or increase in—markets. When tobacco companies settle lawsuits and begin paying billions to claimants, other companies servicing that industry also pay. The **government/regulatory environment** can create uncertainties for businesses by deregulating industries (e.g., airlines, utilities, and telecommunications). In the short term, companies in these industries can face increased costs in restructuring; in the long term, revenues may increase with lower barriers for gaining clients and increasing the range of services or products.

## MAJOR ORGANIZING DESIGN PRINCIPLES

After the process of identifying and analyzing the dominant organizational environments, designing and structuring organizations to effectively manage in those environments includes the use of two principles: differentiation and integration. **Differentiation** involves dividing and defining goals, tasks, roles, and responsibilities. Without a **division of labor** and tasks, work cannot be accomplished. Once differentiated, an organization must then be integrated; that is, roles and responsibilities must be coordinated and, to some extent, controlled to achieve synergy and economies of scale.[4]

The now classic study by Paul Lawrence and Jay Lorsch showed how companies in different industries differentiate and integrate their structures to successfully fit the characteristics of their industry.[5] They found that the **higher the perceived uncertainty of the environment, the more differentiated and integrated the company in the industry became to compete in that environment**. For example, the plastics industry faced the most uncertain and unstable environment. Companies in this industry were more highly differentiated and integrated to compete (i.e., they were more decentralized in their structures and less formalized in their decision making). Also, **the lower the perceived uncertainty of the environment, the less differentiated and integrated the company in that industry, (i.e., the more standardized, formalized, and centralized the company's structure**). The container industry faced highly stable and predictable environments. The food-processing industry operated in environments that were moderately uncertain and unstable. Companies in this industry, Lawrence and Lorsch found, worked well with more bureaucratic structures and procedures. All executives, corporate teams and managers must face the tasks of determining the degree of uncertainty in their environments and then integrating and differentiating their structures and systems accordingly.

### Organic and Mechanistic Structures and the Environment

A study by Tom Burns and G. Stalker found that organizations require different types of design and structure to respond and adapt to changing environments.[6]

Figure 11–3 illustrates their findings: companies operating in highly unstable, unpredictable environments were likely to succeed with an organic structure and companies operating in very stable, unchanging environments worked more effectively with mechanistic structures. **Organic structures** are characterized by their complexity, decentralized decision making, highly differentiated and integrated systems, and mutual adjustment mechanisms for responding to unprogrammed inputs from the environment. Employees at all levels need to have the authority, ability, and know-how to respond to decisions rapidly in changing environments. Many companies today are facing hypercompetition due in part to the automation of operations and by doing business on line. Speed, flexibility, and the ability to scale up quickly are required. Organic structures meet these requirements. **Mechanistic structures** operate in stable environments and are characterized by simple structures, standardized policies and procedures, centralized decision making, and low differentiation and integration. In the Lawrence and Lorsch 1960s study, the container industry worked best with a mechanistic structure. The U.S. Postal Service used mechanistic structures until it adopted new technologies and adapted organic structural features to compete with the competitive threats of the Internet, UPS, Federal Express, and other delivery services.

### Five Design Dimensions for Organizing

Five additional principles that organizational leaders and managers can use to design a competitive structure to fit their operating environments are presented here.[7]

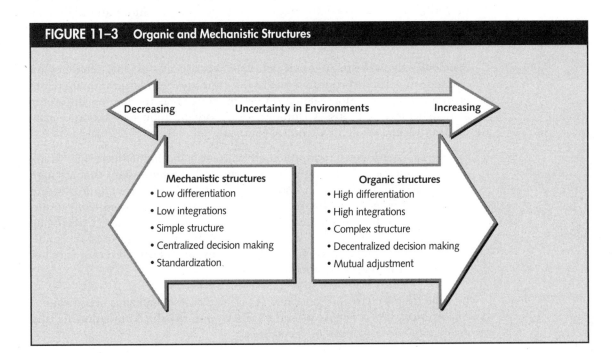

FIGURE 11–3    Organic and Mechanistic Structures

Decreasing    Uncertainty in Environments    Increasing

**Mechanistic structures**
- Low differentiation
- Low integrations
- Simple structure
- Centralized decision making
- Standardization

**Organic structures**
- High differentiation
- High integrations
- Complex structure
- Decentralized decision making
- Mutual adjustment

1. *Hierarchy of authority* refers to the vertical levels of reporting relationships and the "span of control" (i.e., the number of people who report to each manager or supervisor). Some type of reporting structure is necessary to ensure that intended information is given by one group to another. This dimension requires managers to ask how flat or tall, how large or small the structure should be to best accomplish required work and meet market needs. The taller the organization, the more bureaucratic and procedurally oriented it may become. Still, some form of hierarchy and reporting relationships is necessary. Parts of the military may require more hierarchy than a small software company.

2. *Centralization* is the extent to which decisions are made at the top and delegated down the organization. Some degree of centralization is necessary to ensure that work units are implementing the organization's vision. In decentralized organizations, decision making is shared horizontally. Managers must consider how much power and authority to disperse throughout the organization to accomplish customer-required work. The U.S. Postal Service bureaucracy may require more centralization than a mid-sized Internet company servicing clients online and by phone.

3. *Complexity* refers to the number of tasks and work activities in the organization. The degree of complexity depends on the environment; the more activities required from the environment, the more the structure will be affected. Complexity is an indication of how differentiated the structure needs to be to perform the work. Low complexity requires simple structures, and high complexity requires more complex structures. The Pentagon has a higher degree of complexity than a small-town bank.

4. *Standardization* is the degree to which skills, work processes, and outcomes are defined and executed routinely and in the same way. Standardization increases economies of scale. More standard work processes may require less differentiated structures and jobs. A Dunkin Donuts organization may be more standardized than a small architectural company.

5. *Professionalism* is the extent to which specialization and higher-level skills, training, and education are required to perform work. Organizations that are high on professionalism, standardization, centralization, hierarchy of authority, and complexity are more mechanistic and bureaucratic and are more likely to succeed in predictable, unchanging environments. The reverse is also true; organizations that are low on these categories are more likely to succeed in rapidly changing, uncertain environments. A university and a hospital require greater professionalism than a fast-food franchise.

The following section, presents five straightforward organizing classifications that incorporate the concepts presented above and lay the foundation for discussing examples of organization structures.

### "Structure in Fives"

A useful guide for classifying different organizational designs, past, present and future, is illustrated in Table 11–1. These designs represent an evolution as well as a general classification of structure. As we move from simple structure to adhocracy, size and complexity increase, the means of coordination require more flexibility and adjustment, and the degree of control varies. **Simple structures** are centralized with upper-level managers directly supervising employees. Small, private businesses are examples. **Machine bureaucracies** are less centralized but are still hierarchically controlled. Technical staff persons work through well-defined policies and procedures. **Professional bureaucracies** are decentralized and operate through the standardization of professional expert skills. Examples are universities and hospitals. **Divisionalized forms** are more loosely coupled. Each division of an organization can have a different design; for example, one division can be organized by function, one by product, and another as a machine bureaucracy. GM was one of the first divisionalized corporations. Finally, **adhocracies** are just that: ad hoc (i.e., these structures are highly fluid and organic in that they are less rule and procedures based and more

---

**TABLE 11–1    Structure in Fives**

| Structure | Means of Coordination | Types of Departmentation Typically Included |
|---|---|---|
| Simple structure | Mutual adjustment, direct supervision | Functional |
| Machine bureaucracy | Direct supervision, standardization of work processes | Functional |
| Professional bureaucracy | Standardization of skills | Functional |
| Divisionalized form | Standardization of outputs | Product, project, clientele, geographical location |
| Adhocracy | Mutual adjustment | Integrated (matrix and other forms) |

SOURCE: H. Mintzberg. *Structure in Fives: Designing Effective Organizations* (Englewood Cliffs, N.J.: Prentice Hall, 1983).

expert and skill oriented). These structures may be temporary, like project teams. Flexibility, expertise, and control by mutual adjustment are the main characteristics of these forms. High-tech computer firms in Silicon Valley epitomize adhocracies. Online dot com companies also represent adhocracies. These generic types of structures will serve as our reference for the specific designs we discuss next.

Figure 11–4 presents a general classification of major organizational structures. Note that these structures have evolved from mechanistic structures to organic ones and from simple, functional hierarchies to networks.

### Functional Structure

Most organizations begin organizing from a functional perspective. This is the classic chain-of-command structure. Experts are needed in distinct areas; the company

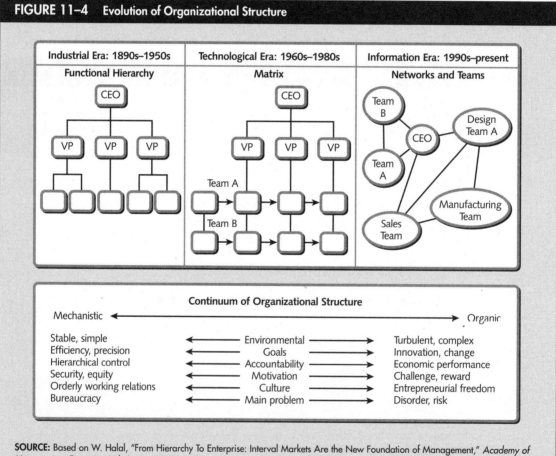

**FIGURE 11–4    Evolution of Organizational Structure**

| Industrial Era: 1890s–1950s | Technological Era: 1960s–1980s | Information Era: 1990s–present |
|---|---|---|
| Functional Hierarchy | Matrix | Networks and Teams |

**Continuum of Organizational Structure**

Mechanistic ← → Organic

| Mechanistic | | Organic |
|---|---|---|
| Stable, simple | Environmental | Turbulent, complex |
| Efficiency, precision | Goals | Innovation, change |
| Hierarchical control | Accountability | Economic performance |
| Security, equity | Motivation | Challenge, reward |
| Orderly working relations | Culture | Entrepreneurial freedom |
| Bureaucracy | Main problem | Disorder, risk |

**SOURCE:** Based on W. Halal, "From Hierarchy To Enterprise: Interval Markets Are the New Foundation of Management," *Academy of Management Executive*, Vol. 8. No. 4 (1994), 70.

organizes around those expert areas, for example, marketing, sales, finance, production. As Table 11–2 shows, these structures are still useful in stable environments characterized by low uncertainty when routine technologies are required and efficiency and economy of scale are emphasized. Small- to medium-size firms with goals of internal efficiency may benefit from functional structures.

Functional structures have recently come under attack in large companies that compete for global markets. The reason, in part, is that these structures are not appropriate for the goals, type of business, size of company, and type of environment of these firms. The functions, or stovepipes, may also have become protected turfs, insulated from competition and customers. Communication across functional areas is hindered, and thus the quality of products and the speed of services with attention to customers have not proven successful.

---

**TABLE 11–2    Functional Structure**

*Context*

Environment: Low uncertainty, stable
Technology: Routine, low interdependence
Size: Small to medium
Goals: Internal efficiency, technical quality

*Internal Systems*

Operative goals: Functional goal emphasis
Planning and budgeting: Cost basis—budget, statistical reports
Formal authority: Functional managers

*Pros*

1. Allows economies of scale within functional departments
2. Enables in-depth skill development
3. Enables organization to accomplish functional goals
4. Is best in small- to medium-size organization
5. Is best with only one or a few products

*Cons*

1. Slow response time to environmental changes
2. May cause decisions to pile on top, hierarchy overload
3. Leads to poor horizontal coordination among departments
4. Results in less innovation
5. Involves restricted view of organizational goals

SOURCE: Adapted from R. Duncan, "What is the Right Organization Structure? Decision Tree Analysis Provides the Answer," *Organizational Dynamics* (New York: AMACOM, a division of American Management Associations, 1979), Winter 1979, 429. Reprinted by permission of Publisher. American Management Associations, New York. All rights reserved. Also quoted in R. Daft, *Organizational Theory and Design*, 4th ed. (Saint Paul, Minn.: West Publishing, 1992), 192.

### Sources of Functional Structure Conflict

Natural conflict has occurred and continues to occur when organizations divide and differentiate by function and specific expertise area. The cause of this is that dimensions normally differ across functions. For example, sales and production personnel usually have a shorter **time horizon** than do research and development (R&D) or planning and finance personnel, as discussed in Chapter 9. People who are technically oriented differ in expertise and training from those who are skilled in relationships or more "fuzzy" specialties. Medical doctors, for example, require years of training and may feel that they deserve more authority and respect than others on their team. In addition, goals may differ. R&D professionals, for example, may be more interested in innovation and creativity than production people who may be more interested in getting a product technically assembled with zero defects. Sales may want customers to be satisfied; finance may want all entries to be accurate. Another source of conflict involves **rewards**. Salespeople are rewarded by meeting customer demand and satisfaction; R&D types are rewarded by getting innovative designs out the door; production personnel are rewarded by getting a product without defects to sales. You can see how problematic integration becomes in organizations that primarily differentiate by function and expertise. The reason that total quality management programs and integrated teams have increased in popularity is that these programs promise integrated structures.

## Product Structure

Product structures related to functional differentiation are organized, staffed, and resourced by products. The major focus becomes product instead of function. This structural focus is chosen because a company's major business and customers are product oriented, not functionally oriented. Responding to customers and markets is accomplished by organizing around products that meet demand. Thus, departments or divisions are grouped by product area (e.g., running shoes, walking shoes, etc.) instead of by function (marketing, sales, finance). Product managers supervise other functional and staff positions such as legal, marketing, manufacturing, and sales.

Table 11–3 lists the benefits and problems of product structures. Again, whatever the reasons for differentiating, reintegrating the different structural units into the superordinate goals and budget always presents problems and challenges.

## Matrix Structure

The matrix structure was introduced in the 1960s to respond to and support U.S. defense industry requirements to speed missile systems productions. As Table 11–4 shows, the matrix is an attempt to integrate functionally differentiated or product-differentiated structures. The matrix was designed to respond to conditions in which time pressures require quick turnaround, the environment is complex and uncertain, and integration across functionally isolated or compartmentalized areas is required.[8]

**TABLE 11–3    Product Structure**

*Context*

Environment: Moderate to high uncertainty, changing
Technology: Nonroutine, high interdependence among departments
Size: Large
Goals: External effectiveness, adaptation, client satisfaction

*Internal Systems*

Operative goals: Product line emphasis
Planning and budgeting: Profit center basis–cost and income
Formal authority: Product managers

*Pros*

1. Suited to fast change in unstable environment
2. Leads to client satisfaction because product responsibility and contact points are clear
3. Involves high coordination across functions
4. Allows units to adapt to differences in products, regions, clients
5. Best in large organizations with several products
6. Decentralizes decision making

*Cons*

1. Eliminates economies of scale in functional departments
2. Leads to poor coordination across product lines
3. Eliminates in-depth competence and technical specialization
4. Makes integration and standardization across product lines difficult

**SOURCE**: Adapted from R. Duncan, "What is the Right Organization Structure? Decision Tree Analysis Provides the Answer," *Organizational Dynamics* (New York: AMACOM, a division of American Management Associations, 1979), Winter 1979, 431; also quoted in R. Daft, *Organizational Theory and Design*, 4th ed. (Saint Paul, Minn.: West Publishing, 1992), 196.

Project managers are recruited from outside or inside organizations to form teams that organize across functional or product areas. Each team can therefore benefit by having a manufacturing, finance, production, and R&D specialist dedicated to a particular team effort. The matrix team has its own budget, team leader or manager, time horizon, and, in effect, project goals, and authority. People working inside the matrix between "two bosses" must manage—as well as be managed by—both. The matrix manager must be managed in terms of a specific project's goals and pressures; the functional area manager must be managed according to the unit's and corporate's goals. Since the functional area manager pays, promotes, disciplines, and dismisses, his authority remains intact.

| TABLE 11–4   Matrix Structure |
|---|
| **Context** |
| Environment:  High uncertainty<br>Technology:  Nonroutine, many interdependencies<br>Size:  Moderate, a few product lines<br>Goals:  Dual—product innovation and technical specialization |
| **Internal Systems** |
| Operative goals:  Equal product and functional emphasis<br>Planning and budgeting:  Dual systems—by function and by product line<br>Formal authority:  Joint between functional and product heads |
| **Pros** |
| 1. Achieves coordination necessary to meet dual demands from environment<br>2. Flexible sharing of human resources across products<br>3. Suited to complex decisions and frequent changes in unstable environment<br>4. Provides opportunity for functional and product skill development<br>5. Best in medium-size organizations with multiple products |
| **Cons** |
| 1. Causes participants to experience dual authority, which can be frustrating and confusing<br>2. Means participants need good interpersonal skills and extensive training<br>3. Is time consuming—frequent meetings and conflict resolution sessions<br>4. Will not work unless participants understand it and adopt collegial rather than vertical-type relationships.<br>5. Requires dual pressure from environment to maintain power balance |
| **SOURCE:** Adapted from R. Duncan, "What Is The Right Organization Structure?  Decision Tree Analysis Provides the Answer," *Organizational Dynamics* (New York: AMACOM, a division of American Management Associations, 1979), 429; also quoted in R. Daft, *Organizational Theory and Design*, 4th ed. (Saint Paul, Minn.: West Publishing, 1992), 206. |

Many companies, especially those servicing the defense industries, still use some variant of the matrix structure, but experience shows that it has not worked well. It has proven too costly in terms of time and the amount of conflict generated between the two bosses. The former Digital Equipment Corporation lived, thrived, and died by a matrix structure.

Matrix structures exist in different forms. For example, global firms (multinationals and transnationals) use different variations of combined divisionalized, product, geographic, and matrix structures. Motorola uses a global matrix structure that organizes its businesses by product group and region.[9]

## Global (Multinational and Transnational) Structures

Global (multinational and transnational) firms such as Xerox, Ford, General Motors, and Procter & Gamble must design organizational structures that integrate products, services, and entire businesses across geographic and regional boundaries.[10] These types of structures are often hybrid, (i.e. mixed) and combine functional, multidivisional, geographical, matrix, and network forms (discussed later) to manage country responsiveness, customer satisfaction, competitiveness, and production and distribution economies of scale.

## Emerging Structures

New forms of organizing that are responding to the external forces are discussed later in this chapter: networks, clusters, and virtual teams. These forms have evolved to address new competitive forces and also because the previous structures have not worked. The critical elements underlying the new structural forms focus on satisfying customer demand, increasing revenue and profit, cutting cycle times (product idea to customer payment), cutting operational costs and wastes, and "leapfrogging" competition. Figure 11–5 is a simplified version of the important features of any organizational design. The idea is to keep the focus on planned results.

There is no one predominant new form of organizational structure; instead, there are several types of adhocracies. A key ingredient in most emerging forms is teams. How the teams are defined, differentiated, and integrated with the core structure (if there is one) is a distinguishing characteristic of changing structures. Examples of new forms—some of which were described in previous chapters and others which are described in this chapter—include the following:

- Network structures

- Mixed flexible arrangements

- Clustered teams

- Decentralized product or service teams

- Virtual teams

- Modified matrix with self-design teams

- Customer, end-user teams networked to the organization

- Outsourced specialized functions

- Strategic alliances sharing functional area and cross-geographical expertise

- Strategic functions by "horizontally sliced" task force

- Joint ventures aligned through licensing agreements

- American *keiretsu* aligned by shared R&D, venture costs, and profit sharing

An impetus for developing new flatter, horizontal organizational firms, especially for large corporations such as Ford, AT&T, Chrysler, GM, IBM, was the

**FIGURE 11–5    Crucial Features of Organizational Design**

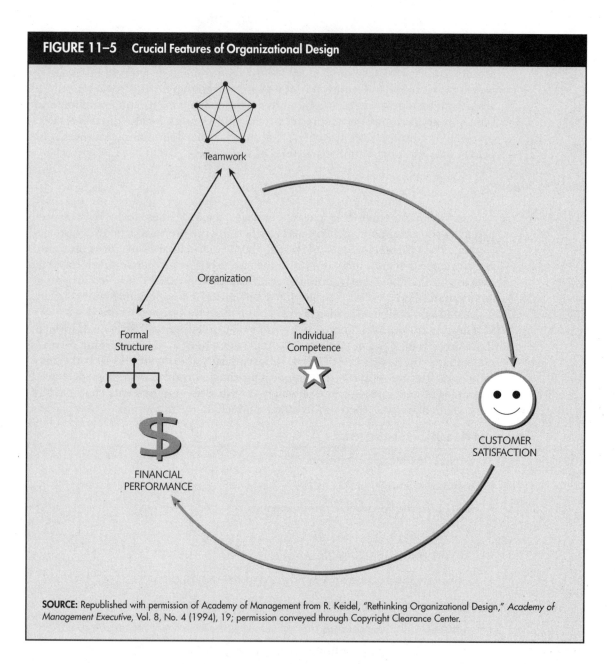

**SOURCE:** Republished with permission of Academy of Management from R. Keidel, "Rethinking Organizational Design," *Academy of Management Executive*, Vol. 8, No. 4 (1994), 19; permission conveyed through Copyright Clearance Center.

competition in the 1970s resulting from the Japanese practice of *keiretsu*. A *keiretsu* is a large cartel, or family of organizations, that has interlocking directorates. These structures have banks for shared economic resources, are closely aligned with government agencies, and are vertically integrated. Mitsubishi, Toyota, NEC, and Sony are examples of successful *keiretsu*. To compete with the

Japanese, U.S. government agencies have sponsored industry consortia in the high-tech field. U.S.-based multinationals have also formed Western-style *keiretsu* through joint ventures and alliances. Companies such as Microsoft, IBM, Motorola, Cisco, Olivetti, Borland, and Hewlett-Packard have successfully formed mutually advantaged working agreements, including alliances with Japanese and European firms.

U.S.-based firms have had to downsize and flatten simply to compete. Information technologies have been a major factor in flattening organizational structures by eliminating layers of middle managers. Large bureaucratic structures are costly in this environment. Networks and clusters are the emergent organizational structures that many companies are using to stay competitive.

## Networks

**Networks** are organizational structures that attempt either to circumvent the problems of previous forms or to recreate organizations to take competitive advantage of markets. Network structures take at least three forms: internal, stable, and dynamic, as shown in Figure 11–6.[11] The internal network is designed to capture entrepreneurial and market benefits without causing the company to outsource. Managers of this network form are encouraged to align prices to markets and innovate accordingly while remaining part of the organization. Internal networks were used by GM early in the 1980s. The **stable network** injects flexibility into the overall value chain of a company. Assets are usually owned by more than one firm but are dedicated to one particular business. "Often, a set of vendors is nestled around a large `core' firm, either providing inputs to the firm or distributing its outputs."[12] BMW, for example, outsources between 55 and 75 percent of total production costs using a stable network structure. The **dynamic network** works in faster-paced or discontinuous competitive environments. These forms provide specialization and flexibility. Fashion, toy, publishing, and biotechnology companies require firms to outsource extensively. A lead firm may, for example, outsource cores skills such as manufacturing (e.g., Motorola); R&D and design (Reebok); or copy editing (most educational publishing firms).

Networks have four characteristics. First, they are independent organizations within a network that perform business functions such as marketing, product design, and manufacturing. This vertical disaggregation saves overhead costs while gathering expertise from different areas. Second, brokers pull together and align business groups through targeting and subcontracting for targeted services. Third, market mechanisms (not contracts, plans, supervisors, or control systems) link and align the networked components. Fourth, full-disclosure information systems align the network groups.

## Clusters

Clusters are another form of adhocracy. They are designed to speed information flow, shorten product cycle time, align companies closer to customers, and increase productivity. Clusters are a way to break up bureaucracies and create focused work teams across internal boundaries. Organizing by cluster begins by thinking about organizing in terms of teams and circles, not boxes and vertical lines.

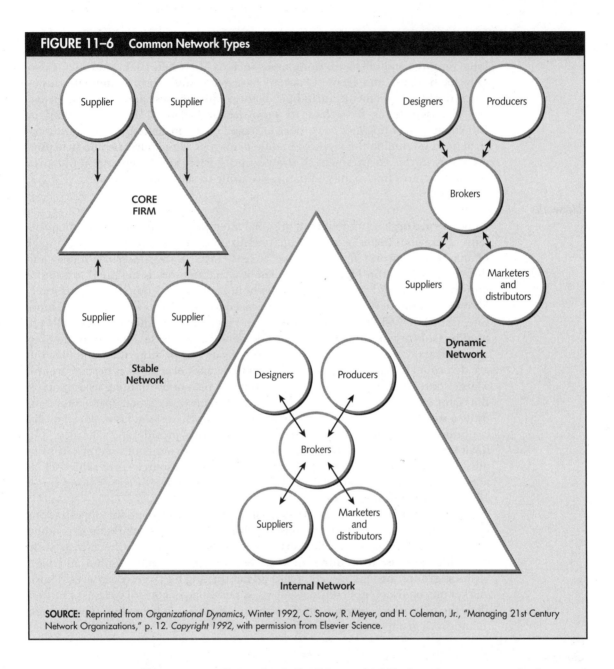

**FIGURE 11–6    Common Network Types**

SOURCE: Reprinted from *Organizational Dynamics*, Winter 1992, C. Snow, R. Meyer, and H. Coleman, Jr., "Managing 21st Century Network Organizations," p. 12. *Copyright 1992*, with permission from Elsevier Science.

**Clusters** are self-contained, flexible, multiskilled work teams organized around key corporate missions, activities, concrete production, or service projects and tasks. Clusters have specialized and general knowledge expertise and shared leadership. They can range from 5 to 7 members or from 30 to 50 persons, depending on the nature of the task and the size of team needed.[13]

Clusters can replace parts or whole divisions and functional units; in fact, entire organizations can become clusters. DuPont, Royal Trust of Canada, GE Canada, British Petroleum Engineering, GM, and Hewlett-Packard among other firms, have successfully adopted different forms of clusters to simplify business processes and link dispersed resources in companies focused on customer needs. An example of British Petroleum Engineering's cluster is illustrated in Figure 11–7.

The clusters in British Petroleum Engineering are free standing, are residually linked (i.e., in an indirect, nonauthoritarian way) to top management, act like business units, and report indirectly to a managing director (who along with three general managers constitute a core team). The managing director links to the senior consultants to coordinate strategic decisions of the dispersed clusters. There is no formal hierarchy in the clusters.

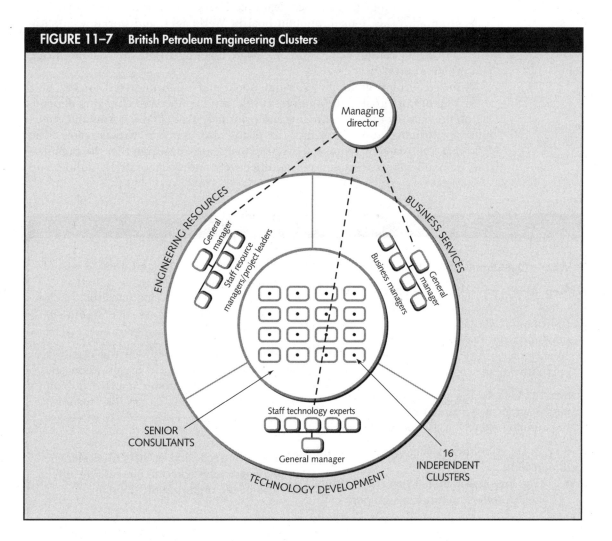

**FIGURE 11–7    British Petroleum Engineering Clusters**

Successful individual requirements for clusters are as follows: each person must know the mission of the company and team, must have the necessary competencies, must have the necessary information—business and administrative—and needs to know that she is trusted. Interestingly, many small companies have a cluster form!

## Virtual Teams

Virtual teams were defined and discussed in Chapter 5. Here we add that virtual and geographically dispersed teams (including clusters and networks) have, to some extent, become part of organizations that do business using cross-functional professionals across geographic boundaries. Consulting companies, high-technology firms, and units of global businesses have long used virtual teams to some degree. What has changed is the sophistication of electronic collaborative communication groupware technologies. Dispersed team members can now use both asynchronous groupware (i.e., e-mail, bulletin boards, Web pages, and workflow applications) and synchronous groupware (i.e., real-time desktop data conferencing, video and audio conferencing, and electronic meeting systems) to communicate and problem solve.[14]

Virtual teams are generally cross-functional and often matrixed, united by a shared set of work goals and work objectives, with membership changing depending on the nature of the assignments and priorities. Many of the norms and guidelines for forming and performing in teams also apply to virtual teams. The following are some key requirements in virtual teams: ensuring that the organization trains members to communicate effectively and collaboratively online, and

### THE CHANGING WORKPLACE

**What's Your Organization's Structure?**

**Step 1**: Form a three-member team and select one organization for this exercise. Information about the organization can be obtained from the business press, a Web site, your college/university, or where one of you currently works.

**Step 2**: Identify the organizational structure and diagram it. Obtain the chart if it is an organization where you are studying or working

**Step 3**: Describe these structure features and dimensions:
- Type of organizational structure (functional, product, network, geographic, etc.)

- Particular strengths and weaknesses of the structure
- Strategy, workforce characteristics, technologies, product(s)/service(s) and culture

**Step 4**: Is there a fit between the organizational dimensions? Is the organization succeeding, struggling, doing poorly? (Obtain some indicators such as profits, turnover, market share, and costs over a three-year period.

**Step 5**: What redesign or structural changes would your team suggest to increase the effectiveness of the organization? Explain.

providing technical infrastructure support and state-of-art equipment and group-ware to members, and ensuring that the team establish norms regarding the hoarding of information, sharing leadership on-line, and developing a culture that supports long-distance problem solving and meeting deadlines.

### Advantages and Disadvantages of New Structures

The advantages of emerging structures include the breakdown of stovepipes (functional organizational departments) and other turfs to speed the flow of information; alignment of company resources to markets and customer needs; decrease of product and service cycle times (get the product out and the income in); survival; accomplishment of work faster and less expensively; and increased profitability.

Disadvantages may involve the loss of control and therefore the inability to maintain quality of products and services, the inability to access some services and skills when immediately needed and on a long-term basis (a company does not completely own its products and services when it brokers, buys, rents, and leases them); and the potential loss of competitive advantage (i.e., since other companies are outsourcing the same or similar services, the service is not necessarily unique and competitors are also enjoying the same advantages).

Cluster organizations must manage problems related to structure, in particular, the following: (1) the coordinator role needs to be more clearly defined, and communication between (and among) the teams and the coordinators must be improved; (2) reward and compensation systems need to reflect expanded job designs and must recognize both team and individual performance based on quality and productivity measures; (3) jobs need to be reexamined in some teams because the work changes significantly; and (4) career planning must recognize that the flatter cluster organization often provides less opportunity for advancement into managerial positions.[15]

Organizations in all industries have undergone and will continue to undergo some type of restructuring activity to survive, increase competitiveness and productivity, and leapfrog over others in their industry. Organizations are using a variety of both classic and new forms of organizational structure to flatten and make authority and reporting relationships more horizontal. Most companies will also utilize forms of virtual teams and online business transactions.

## ORGANIZATIONAL STRUCTURAL CHANGE PROCESSES: REENGINEERING, RESTRUCTURING, RETHINKING, AND REAL TIME ONLINE

Redesigning and changing organizations can be planned and implemented in very different ways, some of which we alluded to in Chapter 7. In this section, we summarize four organizing approaches that enable companies to streamline business processes and begin to move operations on-line.[16] Table 11–5 illustrates three of these approaches—that is, restructuring (organizational units), reengineering (organizational processes), and rethinking (organizational cognition). We also discuss real-time reorganizing in this section.

| TABLE 11–5 | THREE APPROACHES TO ORGANIZATIONAL DESIGN | | |
|---|---|---|---|
| | Restructuring (Organizational Units) | Reengineering (Organizational Processes) | Rethinking (Organizational Cognition) |
| Metaphors | Downsizing Rightsizing Delayering | Process management Process innovation Process redesign | Framing Patterning Learning |
| Target | Organizational units and hierarchical levels | Business functions and work systems | Individual, group, and organizational mindsets |
| Nature | Numerical | Technical | Conceptual |
| Rationale | Survival or repositioning | Tactical competitiveness | Strategic advantage |
| Beneficiaries | Shareholders | Shareholders and customers | Shareholders, customers, and employees |
| Performance criteria | Efficiency | Efficiency and customer satisfaction | Efficiency, customer satisfaction, and employee development |
| Organizational variables addressed | Control | Control and autonomy | Control, autonomy, and cooperation |
| Method | Computing ratios | Flow-charting work processes (interdependencies) | Modeling organization as a balance of multiple perspectives |
| Upside | Reduced costs | Simpler, faster work processes | Richer planning, decision-making, and innovation capabilities |
| Downside | Organizational trauma | Organizational anxiety | Organizational frustration |

SOURCE: Republished with permission of Academy of Management from R. Keidel, "Rethinking Organizational Design," *Academy of Management Executive*, Vol. 8, No. 4 (1994); permission conveyed through Copyright Clearance Center.

**Restructuring**, the most fundamental approach to organizational redesign, focuses on reconfiguring organizational units, which are often large units. The primary technique used in downsizing, rightsizing, and/or delayering units is the computation of ratios (e.g., headcount, sales volume, corporate staff to employees). Benchmarks sometimes are used by companies such as when Digital Equipment Corporation compared revenue per employee with more favorable ratios at Hewlett-Packard. Advantages of restructuring include cost savings and increased operating efficiencies. Most large U.S.-based corporations underwent some form of restructuring in the late 1980s, a trend that continued throughout the 1990s. (Some form of restructuring continues in most companies and is part of an organization's revitalizing process.)

The downside of restructuring is that it may not produce the desired results. One study showed that of 150 companies that downsized, 75 percent were in worse shape after the downsizing.[17] Another issue involves how long successful restructured designs last. We do not know the answer with certainty. In addition, employees who survive restructuring can experience trauma and become demoralized. As an employee in the insurance industry (under attack from many of the forces we have been discussing) said, "I am tired of having to reinvent myself."

**Reengineering** originally focused on dramatically—not incrementally—changing business processes in work systems. However, reengineering has evolved into another change process that can be used as broadly as an organization's leadership determines. This approach requires the sponsorship and involvement of top managers.

A goal of reengineering is to (re)design work processes that focus on simplifying operational processes by eliminating, collapsing, and/or cutting through unnecessary steps, and structure. Reengineering relies on the use of core cross-functional planning teams and information technologies. The aim is to satisfy customers through increased efficiency in the very near term. Michael Hammer and James Champy, original authors of reengineering strategies, cite Hallmark, Taco Bell, Capital Holdings, and Bell Atlantic as examples of successful reengineering efforts.

The downside of reengineering is the anxiety that can result since the human dimension is not an important factor. It is estimated that 50 to 70 percent of large scale reengineering efforts fail to achieve the stated goals.

**Rethinking** focuses on individuals and groups and seeks to redesign thinking and mind-sets. Senge's learning organization and techniques discussed in previous chapters exemplify this approach. Organizational rethinking involves redesign that starts with the ways people think and communicate and refers to "character" (who we are, our purpose and mission), "constituencies" (whose benefits we serve), and "capabilities" (methods we use to satisfy customers). To "rethink" organizational design is to address questions such as these:

- Is the proposed action true to our essential character? Does it fit the kind of organization that we are (want to be)?

- What impact will this action have on our various constituencies? How are the latter likely to respond?

- Will this action exploit and hopefully enhance our distinctive capabilities? In what ways?[18]

The upside of organizational rethinking involves more in-depth and sophisticated decision making and innovation at all organizational levels. The downside of this approach is that individual and collective frustration can result. "Our egos and self-images are closely aligned with the way we perceive and interpret reality. Any criticism of established patterns is bound to provoke discomfort."[19]

**Real-time online** reorganizing can be facilitated by using the three preceding approaches, especially for existing companies entering Internet-based ways of doing business. Bill Gates termed an organization's connected information systems the "digital nervous system"[20] Reorganizing business around online and digital processes involves first recognizing that, "Information flow is the primary differentiator for business in the digital age. Most work in every business is 'information work….'"[21] Gates further defines the "digital nervous systems" of every firm as "the digital processes that closely link every aspect of a company's thoughts and actions. Basic operations such as finance and production, plus feedback from customers, are electronically accessible to a company's knowledge workers, who use digital tools to quickly adapt and respond. The immediate availability of accurate information changes strategic thinking from a separate, stand-alone activity to an ongoing process integrated with regular business activities."[22]

> *The digital nervous system, then, links strategic thinking, basic operations, customer interaction, and business reflexes so that each knowledge worker has instant access to real-time information in each of these areas. Intranets and extranets, discussed earlier, create digital nervous systems that link major live databases in companies that enable professionals to respond to customers, suppliers, vendors, and each other in real time to solve problems quickly and effectively. Organizationally, creating structures and processes that support a digital nervous system could include a combination of basic reengineering, restructuring, and rethinking steps. The speed, interconnectedness, and quality of information decisions are imperative in this change process.*
>
> *Creating a digital network which automates and integrates organizational processes requires a major change effort.*

## NINE ORGANIZATIONAL "THINK-THROUGH" RECOMMENDATIONS: A CHECKLIST

The following recommendations for redesigning organizations focus on minimizing negatives, maximizing positives, and challenging the way redesign is understood.

1. *Minimize negatives.* Think through all cost-reduction alternatives. Buildings, machines, and material cost should be considered before people costs. For example, Hewlett-Packard managed to successfully redesign its organization with no loss of jobs.

2. *Front-end load sizable layoffs.* Downsize first, develop afterward. IBM effectively announced a one-time layoff of 35,000 jobs. This action was a result of force field of analysis, which is used to identify the driving (i.e., positive) and inhibiting (negative) forces for creating change. A desired policy change such as the one IBM implemented can be analyzed to identify the positive and negative forces influencing the implementation with the goal of reducing negatives before increasing positives to avoid confusion.

3. *Spread the pain.* Distributing the pain—for example, of pay cuts, across the organization, especially including upper-level management positions—reduces the negative impact. Fujitsu Ltd. reduced executive compensation by one-third during that company's struggle during the 1990s.

4. *Maximize positives.* Leverage human development. Overinvest in human research and development. The 3M Corporation allows scientists and employees to "bootleg," or spend 15 percent of their paid time researching their own business-oriented projects. Applied Manufacturing and Engineering Technology in Austin, Texas, supports people in inventing their way out of current jobs to more rewarding ones.

5. *Create and reward shared wins.* Use profit-sharing, bonus, and "gain-sharing" programs to connect employees' pay to corporate goals and results.

6. *Keep people informed.* Involve and share the big picture and information about the organization. AT&T involves union officials, especially during critical redesign periods, in its corporate planning and gives union employees the opportunity to compete for offshore jobs.

7. *Challenge the way design is understood.* Beware of quick fixes. Understand the organization's root issue and problem; inquire about alternative approaches, evaluate strengths and weaknesses, and identify long-term consequences and short-term results of different courses of action.

8. *Identify and integrate multiple perspectives.* Nontrivial organizational designs affect shareholders, customers, and employees. Managers should anticipate and be able to resolve difficulties and conflicting interests.

9. *Take time to reflect.* A ready-fire-aim style should be complemented with reflective time-outs since 20 percent of all activities produce 80 percent of the value added.[23]

In addition to these items, two additional questions are related to the real-time approach: First, do you have the information flow that enables you to answer the hard questions about what your customers and partners think about your products and services, what markets you are losing and why, and what your real competitive edge is? Second, do your information systems simply crunch numbers in the back room or help to directly solve customer problems?"[24]

### Ethical Questions and Considerations

Ethical issues that managers and organizational members can address as restructuring and the blurring of organizational boundaries occur include the following:

- What happens to employees' professional identity when a company or parts of an organization are outsourced or networked? Managers can initiate and maintain open communication with employees before, during, and after any major organizational change. Issues relating to fairness often arise when people are not informed about organizational plans to reorganize.

- What happens to trust and loyalty between employee and management when downsizing and streamlining occur, when individuals are required to become more independent and rely less on and expect less from organizations? What happens to the role of duty to the company? Again, openly and authentically seeking and sharing information with employees about organizational plans and initiatives regarding restructuring can instill trust. Organizational restructuring changes require that managers cultivate relationships in meaningful ways.

- Who manages the obligations of the organization to its stakeholders as it becomes more free standing, networked, and dispersed through the use of information technologies? First, managers have the responsibilities of identifying all major stakeholders (including employees as primary ones) involved in structural changes. Second, managers can call meetings and use focus groups to share information and ideas regarding changing roles, responsibilities, and obligations between employer and employee. Often new ideas emerge when managers skillfully facilitate open, nonjudgmental, and nonauthoritarian meetings designed to brainstorm issues and solutions. Obviously, meetings with unionized employees may have to be structured, planned, and facilitated with union representatives.

- How will employee rights and obligations to the company change with the emerging competency-based organizations, work, and jobs? This was discussed in Chapter 10.

There are no easy answers to these questions. We have suggested that leaders and managers initiate and maintain an ongoing dialogue with employees to identify and address these questions and to discover and implement new solutions together. One model for responding to change is that of helping employees "rethink" their responsibilities and work as discussed earlier in Senge's model of the learning organization. (Learning organizations enable employees to share expertise by initiating dialogue and joint problem-solving processes that are required to transform an organization's systems. )

## CONCLUDING COMMENTS

Organizations must design strategies and structures that thrive in hypercompetitive economic, political, social/demographic, and government/regulatory environments. Leaders and teams must determine the complexity, richness, and dynamism of these environments to successfully design appropriate structures. Because of

# THE CHANGING WORKPLACE

## Ethics and the Organization

**Exercise**: Use your experience in your current or previous organization. You may also interview someone you know who works in an organization.

**Step 1**: Answer (or interview someone using) these questions:

1. What pressures and tensions do you experience in your organization role and current responsibilities?

2. To what extent can or do you receive professional work-related support from your immediate supervisor or the person to whom you report? Explain your answer.

3. Do you feel that you're caught in dilemmas in your work which you have little or no control over resolving? Explain.

4. How much freedom and autonomy do you have in making decisions at work?

5. To what extent do you experience people deliberately withholding information or miscommunicating with you? Give an example.

6. Have you experienced, and if so how often, backstabbing at work (i.e., people deliberately misusing information about you without your knowledge to hurt or gain advantage over you)?

7. Do you have a confidential process that you can follow and objective individuals to whom you can report abuses or misuses of power over you and at your expense in your work?

8. Does your organization provide you with specific policies, procedures, and training that help in your professional development and growth?

9. Do the leaders and managers lead by fair and just standards?

10. How often are you praised and rewarded for your accomplishments at work? Explain.

**Step 2**: Summarize your answers to these questions.

**Step 3**: Answer these questions based on your summary.

1. What themes and patterns emerged from the answers to these questions?

2. To what extent is the environment of this company ethical (i.e., shows justice, respects people's rights, and supports fairness)? Explain.

3. To what extent does your place or that of the person interviewed in the organization's structure affect these answers?

4. To what extent do the strategy, culture, nature of the work, and means of getting work done affect the answers?

5. How do the nature of the industry and of the environment affect the answers?

6. Recommend three or four changes to this company's structure, strategy, or other dimensions that would create a more ethical organizational environment.

deregulation, increased global competition, and advances in telecommunications, hierarchical structures in many companies have decreasing value, cost too much, and clog information flow. "Structure follows strategy" is now, more than ever, influenced by customer demand, which translates into requirements for quality, speed, and service satisfaction. Teams are organized into clusters, networks, and virtual teams. New boundaryless organizations have more flattened, horizontal, outsourced, and networked structures.

The innovation and diffusion of digital and network technologies are also transforming work and organizational structures. A useful guide for classifying different organizational designs includes "Structures in Fives": simple structures, machine bureaucracies, professional bureaucracies, divisionalized forms, and adhocracy.

Since a major purpose of organizational structure is to differentiate and integrate jobs, roles, and responsibilities to meet the goals of the company, organizations can be structurally differentiated either horizontally by function or vertically by flat or tall structures, by personnel specialization and expertise, or spatially by geography.

The different types of structures that have evolved were identified and compared: functional, product, matrix, and global. Networks and clusters are emerging forms of organizational structure that attempt either to circumvent the problems of previous hierarchical forms or to recreate organizations to take competitive advantage of markets. Network structures take at least three forms: internal, stable, and dynamic.

Clusters are another form of adhocracy designed to speed information flow, shorten product cycle time, align companies closer to customers, and increase productivity. Clusters are a way to break up bureaucracies and create focused work teams across internal and external organizational boundaries.

Redesigning and changing organizations can be planned and implemented in at least four major ways: restructuring, reengineering, rethinking, and real time. Restructuring focuses on downsizing, rightsizing, and/or delayering organizational units. Reengineering focuses on changing business processes in work systems. Rethinking is redesign that focuses on changing the thinking and mind-sets of individuals and groups. Real time involves networking an organization's strategic thinking, customer information, and business operations to a secure online digital system in which vendors, suppliers, customers, and key employees can jointly problem solve and create mutual opportunities.

Nine recommendations were discussed for redesigning organizations. The recommendations focused on minimizing negatives, maximizing positives, and challenging the way redesign is understood.

Major ethical issues regarding restructuring and networking of global firms were identified. As global firms become leaner, they can also become meaner through networking with each other. Dualistic internal labor markets and unfair incentive systems are also problems that can result by structural networking among major global reorganizations. Managerial considerations regarding ethical issues were raised vis-à-vis restructuring activities. Managers and employees must encourage and support dialogue and openly share information to effectively meet customer demands in the more entrepreneurial organizational arrangements.

### SCENARIO AND EXERCISE: YOU'RE THE CHANGE CONSULTANT

A large independent retail store has invited you to join its strategic management team to offer ideas and suggestions with regard to its major restructuring effort. The CEO has addressed this team stating, "We're getting battered by online start-ups, portals, and other Internet service providers that keep building virtual malls and stores. We are stuck with inventory problems, overpricing, and overhead, and now we have to consider downsizing. We need to start from scratch and figure out who we are again and exactly what we're about. We've been in business for 50 years and our 500 employees have been loyal. So before we start laying people off, let's come up with a framework that can help us figure out how to move forward."

The company organization chart follows:

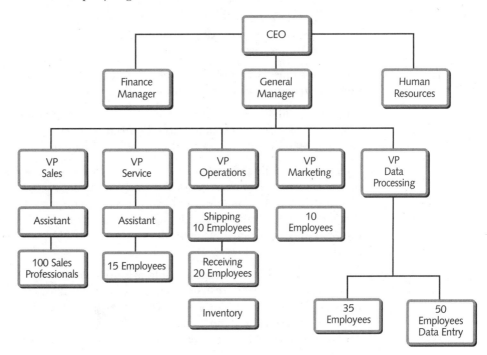

**Step 1**: What major problems and opportunities do you see in this structure? Offer a brief analysis of this company based on this information. What questions would you ask? What information do you need?

**Step 2**: What steps would you recommend to the planning team to begin redesigning the organization?

**Step 3**: Suggest a different structure based on your preliminary analysis.

1. Identify three environmental forces that affect organizational design.

2. Which of these forces affect(ed) an organization, positively or negatively, in which you work or worked or with which you are familiar? Explain.

3. If you begin to design or redesign an organization, what are some key questions from this chapter you would ask? Why?

4. Under what conditions would an organization select an organic versus a mechanistic structure? Explain.

5. Does your college or university have an organic or mechanistic structure? Justify your answer.

6. Evaluate your company's and college or university's environmental characteristics in terms of complexity, dynamism, and richness. Give an example for each of your answers.

7. What are some basic differences between a functional, product, matrix, and network structure? In which structure would you prefer to work? Why?

8. What is one major difference between reengineering, restructuring, rethinking, and real-time approaches to organizational change processes? Which change process would you rather help lead on a team in an organization? Why?

9. What does an online digital nervous system do for a company? Find a company on the Internet or in a newspaper or business magazine that is an example of a company that has its operations and business connected by an intranet or extranet or that uses a "digital nervous system." Describe a technology used in this system. How does that technology affect work? organizational structure? jobs?

10. Identify some ethical issues that could arise before, during, or after an organizational reengineering, restructuring process, rethinking, or real-time change process. Then, identify an ethical issue that you have experienced or been affected by at work or in an organization that is related to organizational structure or processes. How did you respond? What happened?

# 12 Organizational Culture

---

## LEARNING OBJECTIVES

After studying this chapter, you should be able to:

1 Define *organizational culture.*

2 Describe how organizational culture is transmitted.

3 Describe national, regional, and industry determinants of culture.

4 Define strong and weak organizational cultures.

5 Describe high ethics cultures and multicultural organizations.

6 Identify a cultural change process.

7 Discuss a process for leading cultural change.

---

Organizational cultures reflect their national, regional, local, and leaders' influences. Take Silicon Valley as an example.

> *Silicon Valley project teams are driven by people in their twenties and thirties. Great risks and huge budgets, (indeed, "bet the company projects") are staffed by these young people empowered to drive innovation while they are at the peak of their early technical competencies close to the knowledge base of recent major university training. . . . You might also find a dog under the conference table. The notion that the Valley is dominated by a small number of senior executives often visible in the business press is a specious impression. What makes the Valley work is the empowerment of the young technical cadres.*
>
> *As you listen you would sense the group is irreverent toward any existing technology or process. The group's language is both technical and colloquial. There is a high proportion of visual schematics displayed around the room which seem to be the predominant working "documents" rather than carefully constructed prose or algorithms. Silicon Valley is a place that thrives on intuitive symbols. And since the future is being created, in early stages of dialog the intuitive is often captured in imprecise symbols. You would also be impressed by the group's comfort with confrontation. Here is a gathering of youthful, energetic individuals, usually very diverse (in terms of skin coloring, nationality, and gender) engaged in intense confronting dialog with disagreement and differing speculations being "encouraged" as the humus from which will spring forth a new approach. And it is always the "new" which is most reverenced. If an existing approach is seen as efficient and economical, the group searches for ways to incorporate similar features into the "new" as opposed to preferring to stick with the "old."*
>
> *It is this overriding commitment to change, to incorporating the latest, to reaching to new potential designs and approaches which makes Silicon Valley a special place. The Valley sees*

*itself as the "incubator" of the future, and wealth creating in the Valley is associated with those who obsolete the past, doing so more quickly than their competition.*

*So the immediately encountered culture of Silicon Valley you would see and hear if you sat in on a meeting of a typical Silicon Valley project team would include:*

*Youth, always skeptical of solutions their predecessors created. . . .*

*An obsession with speed: work late, work long, work fast, work smart, borrow and acquire technical knowledge at the cutting edge not already possessed, and enter the market place with an elegant solution needed by many with surprising features at a low cost point.*[1]

## *ORGANIZATIONAL CULTURE DEFINED*

**Organizational culture** is the shared values, beliefs, norms, expectations, and assumptions that bind people and systems. Organizational culture gives people a sense of identity; facilitates commitment, initiative, communication; and provides a basis for stability, control, and direction. These elements help members adapt to and integrate internal and external environments.[2]

An organization's culture, like an iceberg, has both visible and invisible elements. The observable aspects include the physical setting, language, stories, legends and myths, heroes and heroines, ceremonies, behaviors, and dress. Figure 12–1 illustrates the visible and invisible aspects of culture. The visible aspects are indications of underlying dimensions such as values, beliefs, and feelings.

The physical setting at Hewlett-Packard Corporation is composed mostly of open spaces with a few closed offices. These arrangements reflect a work culture that has open communication and information sharing. Casual dress and behavior at Microsoft characterize a highly creative, informal culture in which innovation is valued; emphasis is on productivity, not form. The culture can be sensed and felt in the hallways, heard in the conversations, and seen in the mannerisms of teams.

Organizational cultures are started and reinforced by the company's heroes. Examples of cultural heroes include Henry Ford, Ray Kroc (founder of McDonalds), Sam Walton (founder of Wal-Mart), and Jeff Bezos at Amazon.com. Each of them modeled his organization's culture when he took the helm. Those who are gone remain part of the company's culture, becoming its legends, its symbols of success and high standards, and its role models.

An example of a cultural ceremony is the annual sales awards event for Mary Kay Cosmetics when pink Cadillacs are given to outstanding sales professionals. Employees cheer and embrace each other in these celebrations. Hard work—a core value and cultural message—is rewarded by hard play.

The invisible aspects of organizational culture include the underlying values, assumptions, beliefs, attitudes, and feelings of members as well as unwritten rules about the environment, time, space, relationships, and activities. This invisible aspect is sometimes difficult to identify, even though many corporations publish a values statement along with their vision and mission. Value statements offer an indication of the organization's beliefs. Johnson & Johnson, for example, publishes an exemplary document called *Our Credo*, which recognizes its social obligations to

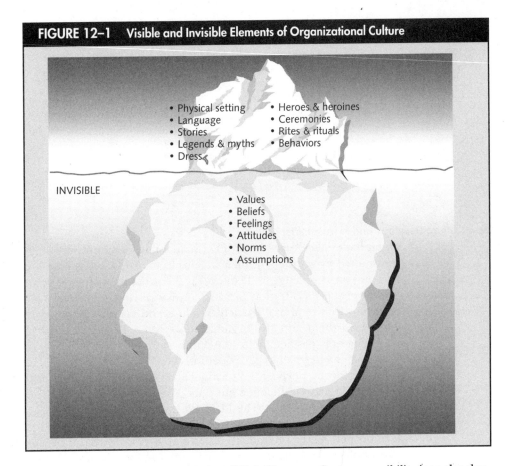

FIGURE 12–1    Visible and Invisible Elements of Organizational Culture

- Physical setting
- Language
- Stories
- Legends & myths
- Dress

- Heroes & heroines
- Ceremonies
- Rites & rituals
- Behaviors

INVISIBLE

- Values
- Beliefs
- Feelings
- Attitudes
- Norms
- Assumptions

stakeholders. The statement begins, "We believe our first responsibility is to the doctors, nurses and patients, to mothers and fathers and all others who use our products and services." It continues, "We are responsible to our employees... to the communities in which we live and work and to the world community as well." The organizational culture at Johnson & Johnson insists that this be put into practice. However, even with published value statements, members of organizations may hold and practice values different than the stated ones. These hidden dimensions of culture can often be identified through interviews, dialogue, and observation.

The following profile of SAP/AG, an innovative German software firm, illustrates many of the cultural characteristics discussed here:

> It's a story that could have happened in Silicon Valley. In 1972, four young employees in the German office of International Business Machines Corp. quit to form their own company. By working nights on borrowed computers, they won their first contract. Twenty-three years and a lot of hard work later, they became Germany's first software billionaires.
>
> But the four founders of SAP AG have done more than just make money for themselves. They have shown that Germans—who often agonize about being complacent, bureaucratic,

*and fearful of change—are sometimes capable of innovation and risk. "We had a vision and we stuck to it," says Hasso Plattner, the company's vice chairman and technology chief. Profits rose 92 percent last year, to 281 million marks ($204.5 million). Sales jumped 66 percent , to 1.83 billion marks. But while the company and stock analysts see many more years of soaring growth, investors have been getting nervous.*

*Though SAP is headquartered in a small town near Heidelberg, a California feel dominates. In contrast to the typical button-down German workplace, employees wear sandals and can choose their own hours. Mr. Plattner spends a third of his time in California, where he keeps a home, a Porsche, and a racing sailboat.*

*Mr. Plattner has long been an iconoclast. Early in his career, he interviewed at Siemens, the huge electronics company, before taking a lesser job with IBM's German subsidiary. "I knew right during the interview that I could never work for Siemens," he says. "It was like the post office."[3]*

### How Culture Develops and Is Transmitted

Organizational cultures, including the invisible elements previously mentioned, are transmitted by a variety of means. Socialization (i.e., ways employees learn, adopt, and pass on knowledge and culture) is the process by which culture is passed on.

Part of the socialization process consists of rites of passage—that is, designated occasions that reinforce particular values and create a bond among and between employees them and the organization.[4] Table 12–1 illustrates such socialization rites. The first, passage, helps the employees transition into new roles and statuses. Universities and colleges have opening ceremonies, picnics, speeches, and initiation meetings for this purpose. Fraternities and sororities have rush, initiation, and other rites and rituals to induct new entrants. The enhancement rite strengthens the bond by acknowledging status. The Mary Kay awards ceremony is such an enhancement rite of passage. Organizations often convene annual meetings to recognize high performers and send a message to other employees: this is one way to succeed and be part of our culture. The renewal rite revitalizes and maintains the employees' identity with the organization. This can be done through retreats, training, and trips: IBM awards trips for high sales performers. GE has the "workout," which is a renewal rite as well as an ongoing training program. Finally, the integration rite continues the process of committing employees to the organization. Events, promotion ceremonies, and other special occasions such as Christmas parties help cement the employees' loyalty to the company.

## SOURCES AND INFLUENCES ON ORGANIZATIONAL CULTURE

An organization's culture does not exist by itself. It is influenced by internal and external factors. In this section, founders, CEOs, and environmental sources that influence organizational culture are discussed.

### Founders and CEOs

The philosophies, examples, and stories of an organization's founders and its CEOs are strong influences on the formation and conditioning of corporate culture. For

| TABLE 12–1 | Organizational Rites of Passage | |
|---|---|---|
| **Type of Rite** | **Example** | **Social Consequences** |
| Passage | Introduction and basic training, U.S. Army | Facilitate transition of persons into social roles and statuses that are new for them |
| Enhancement | Annual awards night | Enhance social identities and increase status of employees |
| Renewal | Organizational development activities | Refurbish social structures and improve organization functioning |
| Integration | Office Christmas party | Encourage and revive common feelings that bind members together and commit them to the organization |

**Source:** Adapted from Harrison M. Trice and J. M. Beyer, "Studying Organizational Cultures Through Rites and Ceremonials," *Academy of Management Review*, 9 (1984), 653-659. Used with permission.

example, Walt Disney's original business philosophy lives on in the company's practices and continues to shape its culture: "Quality will out! Give the people everything you can give them. Keep the place as clean as you can keep it. Keep it friendly. Make it a fun place to be."[5] Heroes such as Tom Watson at IBM, Ed Land at Polaroid, David Packard at Hewlett-Packard, Lee Iacocca at Chrysler, Bill Gates at Microsoft, and Ben Cohen and Jerry Greenfield at Ben and Jerry's are enduring influences on their companies' corporate cultures.

Organizational culture is, however, not always limited to an undivided, homogeneous corporate culture, influenced only by the founder and CEO. Although most organizations have a dominant culture, there may also be subcultures that have their own values, heroes and heroines, and norms. Subcultures may be structured around the localized needs of employees who interact on a daily basis and who are removed from the dominant corporate culture.

Studies of mergers and acquisitions illustrate the importance of recognizing the existence of both subcultures and countercultures (subgroups who strongly reject what the organization stands for or what it is attempting to accomplish).[6] Cultural clashes can and do occur. Subcultural or countercultural resistance can surface during times of vulnerability, especially during merger and acquisition activities. Understanding the visible and invisible aspects of organizational culture is a first step in managing cultural change effectively.

Issues to keep in mind while reading this section are the manner in which and the extent to which national, regional, and industry cultures shape the assumptions, values, and management styles of organizational leaders, managers, and employees and affect its organizational dimensions and systems.

## National Culture

Organizational culture is influenced by **national culture**. "Cultural influence also directly affects the climate for business in general and international business in particular. National ideology determines how members of a culture view the role of business and how strong the culture's identity is."[7] "Every person is socialized into a particular culture, learning the 'right way' of doing things."[8]

National culture influences the extent to which leadership, teams and employee activities are socially valued and meaningfully supported. Studies suggest that directive styles of leadership appear culturally inappropriate in Northern Europe, North America, Australia, and New Zealand. An employee participation program failed in Russia, perhaps the result of that national culture's disbelief and distrust in participative programs. The example of the German software firm SAP indicates that its culture is not representative of more formal aspects of the national German culture. The cultures of Sweden and Japan strongly support employee involvement in organizational activities. The Japanese Union of Scientists and Engineers, for example, promotes quality circles and helps introduce them to private firms. Sweden supports employee involvement programs through the Swedish Employer's Federation. The United States, on the other hand, has no national policy or mechanisms by which to promote teams or employee involvement in private companies. A notable government-supported initiative is the Malcolm Baldrige National Quality Award; this is the exception, not the norm.[9]

## Regional Culture

**Regional cultures** within national contexts influence organizational cultures. A number of reasons for studying regional cultures as influencers of organizational cultures can be given. First, local and regional cultures have direct historical, political, and economical impacts on individual and group values that influence management practices and outcomes. Styles of work, expertise, and working values in companies also are influenced by regional cultures, some of which diverge from the national culture. Some organizations tend to "think globally and act locally." Regional culture may be a strong influence on these organizations. Second, organizations are decentralizing and integrating more into their local and regional environments. Although some R&D and other strategic corporate functions may be centralized, selling and servicing are often done locally.

Organizational members do not have to be born in, or originate from, a region to be affected by regional cultural characteristics. Such influences are part of the environment's value structure and can influence both psychological and physical limits and styles for managing work.

The regional cultural characteristics of California's Silicon Valley have encouraged open and changing entrepreneurial ventures, intense and informal networking, individualism, short-term wealth creation practices, and decentralized structures.

A study comparing economic, statistical, and business outcomes in high-technology firms between Silicon Valley and Massachusetts' Route 95 and 495 concluded that Silicon Valley has succeeded in winning the entrepreneurial high-tech race.[10] Silicon Valley's cultural openness to creative and changing ideas, emphasis on innovation, lack of hierarchical structure, and focus on continuous, informal, and internal networking help explain Silicon Valley's success, which has also changed Internet start-ups and the flow of venture capital funds.

## Industry Determinants of Organizational Culture

Organizational assumptions about an industry's competitive environment, customer requirements, and societal expectations also influence a firm's strategies, structures, work processes, and its performance and even survival.[11] Figure 12–2 presents a model of industry-driven culture formation.

"Culture formation is neither a random event nor an action dependent solely on the personalities of founders or current leaders, but it is, to a significant degree, an internal reaction to external imperatives."[12] Assumptions regarding the industry environment are made and interpreted by an organization's leadership. The point here is that how an organization responds to customer requirements, competition, and societal expectations depends on industry-specific assumptions.

Management assumptions about an industry's competitive environment can range from no competitors (e.g., a public utility) to many competitors (e.g., the office copier business). An industry's competitive environment can be defined by the

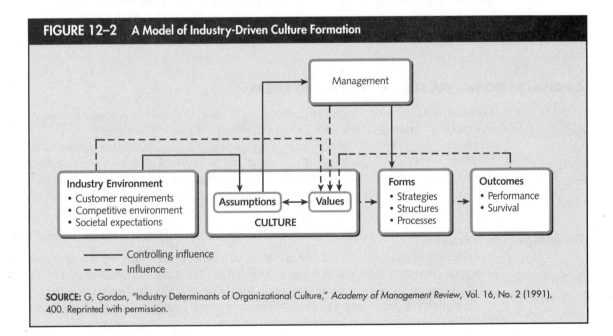

**FIGURE 12–2    A Model of Industry-Driven Culture Formation**

Management

Industry Environment
• Customer requirements
• Competitive environment
• Societal expectations

Assumptions ↔ Values
CULTURE

Forms
• Strategies
• Structures
• Processes

Outcomes
• Performance
• Survival

——— Controlling influence
– – – Influence

**SOURCE:** G. Gordon, "Industry Determinants of Organizational Culture," *Academy of Management Review*, Vol. 16, No. 2 (1991), 400. Reprinted with permission.

number and variability of firms in that environment, the rate of environmental change, and the extent to which the environment can sustain growth.[13] Strategy, type of structure, and the number of risk-taking activities depend on how these competitive factors are interpreted by decision makers.

Assumptions about customer requirements can be placed on a continuum of demands for reliability and novelty; these demands range from highly dynamic (novel) to very static (very reliable). For example, high-technology manufacturers that operate in dynamic environments may emphasize behavioral norms based on risk taking, initiative, and achievement rather than on analyzing problems. At the other extreme, public utility companies that operate in stable environments might base their behavioral norms on interdependence of people and organizational units. They would thus be more likely to focus on retaining and developing people.

Assumptions about societal expectations can significantly affect ways in which an organization does business: "A shift in societal values from the preeminence of property rights to the preeminence of human rights has produced radical changes in [these] expectations, which . . . have taken on the force of law. For instance, health and safety demands for people and the environment have had different, but very profound effects on the chemical, petroleum, food, and cigarette industries."[14] Tobacco companies have experienced a similar shift in societal expectations.

Evidence of the influence of the industry environment on organizations is reflected in managerial beliefs and assumptions about operating forms and outcomes. Taken together, national, regional, and industry influences on organizational culture provide yet another analytic source for identifying members' assumptions, values, beliefs, and norms since these elements are translated into operating decisions and systems (through choice of strategies, technologies, structures, hiring policies, and training).

## ORGANIZATIONAL CULTURE AND EFFECTIVENESS

Given these different sources of cultural influence, the question could be asked: What constitutes an "effective" organizational culture? The answer is that it depends, and the effectiveness is for whom? Organizational effectiveness, whether we are examining culture or other organizational dimensions, is neither a unitary criterion nor a simple concept. Determining organizational and cultural effectiveness is best done by using different approaches and models to diagnose and measure.

### The Strategic Cultural Response

An effective organizational culture adjusts and adapts to its changing internal and external environments. The following four types of cultures, illustrated in Figure 12–3, illustrate an organization's strategic responses to changing environments.

Organizations responding to external environments characterized by change and flexibility would do well to have **adaptability cultures** (i.e., strategic emphasis on flexibility, change, and quick, varied responses to meet customer and environmental

## THE CHANGING WORKPLACE

### Analyze an Organizational Culture

**Step 1**: Choose an organization in which you currently work or have worked and have an understanding of its culture.

**Step 2**: Write answers to the following questions:

a.  What does/did it feel like to work in this organization?

b.  What does/did it take to be very successful in this organization?

c.  What is considered a serious punishment or reprimand in the organization?

d.  What are the unwritten rules (norms) that people are expected to follow?

e.  Who are the heroes here? Why?

f.  What are the rituals, symbols, ceremonies, and folklore that are still talked about, celebrated, and given attention?

g.  Who are the role models? Why are they role models?

h.  If you pretend that this organization were a person, how would you describe him or her?

i.  Is there an influential dominant coalition; that is, does one group exert more power over others in this organization? What are its functions, departments, or fields? What is the base(s) of its power?

j.  How is this organization performing? Is its performance related to its culture? Explain.

**Step 3**: Briefly describe what you learned from doing this exercise. Be prepared to share your observations with class members.

**Note:** Parts of this exercise are adapted from H. Levinson, *Organizational Diagnosis* (Cambridge, Mass.: Harvard University Press, 1972), Appendix A., 519-58; and V. Sathe, *Culture and Related Corporate Realities* (Homewood, Illinois: Richard Irwin, Inc., 1985).

demands). Silicon Valley high-tech firms exemplify this culture. Organizations facing turbulent internal environments should have **involvement cultures** (strategic focus on involving employees, gaining their commitment, and increasing participation, a sense of ownership, and responsiveness to meet changing environmental demands). Japanese auto firms continue to demonstrate this type of culture. Organizations facing stable external environments should place strategic emphasis on a **mission culture** (emphasis on a shared vision and sense of organizational purpose along with clear direction and carefully defined roles and jobs). U.S. firms in most large-scale industries from the period after World War II to the beginning of the 1970s are good examples of this culture. Organizations facing stable internal environments should have a **consistency culture** (strategic focus less on participation and involvement and more on consistency of methods, establishment of systematic policies and procedures, and conformity and membership collaboration). Until the mid-1990s, U.S. governmental administrative agencies were typical of this culture. The extent to which an organization can adapt and align its strategic focus and culture to changing environments will, in part, determine its cultural and organizational effectiveness.

## TWO CULTURAL EFFECTIVENESS APPROACHES

The effectiveness of an organization's culture (i.e., its physical setting, language, behaviors, ceremonies, leaders—heroes and heroines—dominant values, norms, beliefs, and assumptions) can be examined and evaluated from at least three perspectives. These perspectives should be viewed as different but complementary ways to understand cultural effectiveness. No single perspective represents the best or right way. We briefly summarize each approach before discussing these in more detail.

A contingency theory approach identifies effectiveness as the fit of organizational culture with its internal systems and environment. A goal-attainment approach identifies effectiveness as the extent to which stated goals are obtained. A competing values approach is interested in how well leaders and managers adopt effective values and competencies as they respond to changing environments. Ideally, organizational leaders should be able to mobilize organizational culture to meet the demands of all four perspectives.

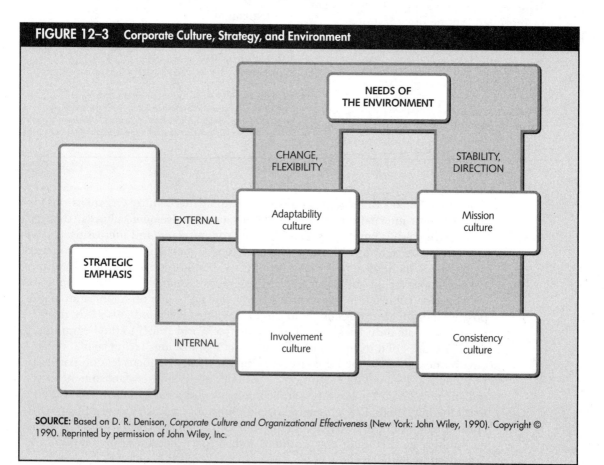

**FIGURE 12–3    Corporate Culture, Strategy, and Environment**

**SOURCE:** Based on D. R. Denison, *Corporate Culture and Organizational Effectiveness* (New York: John Wiley, 1990). Copyright © 1990. Reprinted by permission of John Wiley, Inc.

### Contingency Theory Approach

As Figure 1–6 illustrates, in the **contingency theory approach** organizations and their cultures are effective to the extent that different organizational dimensions are congruent and fit together in responding to environmental contexts and forces. A manufacturing firm may require a different type of leadership, resources, strategy, structure, culture, technology, expertise, and control system to be effective than would either a high-technology computer firm or a university. Add different national and regional contexts to these industry differences, and you can see how complex evaluation of cultural effectiveness can become. For example, SAP, the German software firm discussed at the beginning of this chapter, could develop a Silicon Valley–style culture in part because of the nature of the software business: "Software is about ideas, not production, so the labor agreement and high costs that typically shackle German start-ups were irrelevant."[15] National and industrial cultural contexts would need to be considered in evaluating the effectiveness of SAP as compared to a more mature manufacturing German firm.

Using a contingency approach, we can define and evaluate cultural effectiveness from the following statements:

- "Effectiveness (or lack of it) is a function of the values and beliefs held by the members of an organization." The consistency resulting from shared beliefs provides a basis for coordinated, planned organizational action. Jeff Bezos at Amazon.com modeled that young company's work ethic and empowered entrepreneurial values. Sam Walton of Wal-Mart showed an amazing ability to lead that firm's culture; his personal values shaped the vision and influenced the effectiveness of the company.

- "Effectiveness is a function of how policies and Best Practices are used by an organization." Specific practices (planning, work design, decision making, conflict resolution) affect performance and effectiveness. Organizational strength is a function of the effective implementation of the leadership's vision into consistent and sound policies and practices. If these practices are not sound, ineffectiveness will be built into the very fabric of the company. Culture is a major medium through which management policies and practices are forged. Bill Gates' vision for Microsoft gives strength to that firm's organizational culture and adds to its financial effectiveness.

- "Effectiveness is a function of translating the core values and beliefs into policies and practices in a consistent manner." Consistent, sound practices must be coordinated, accepted, and then used to be effective. Culture often determines the way policies and practices are communicated, understood, and accepted (or resisted).

- "Effectiveness is a function of the interrelation of core values and beliefs, organizational policies and practices, and the business environment of the organization."[16] Statements made about culture and effectiveness incorporate the relationship of the organization's culture to the business environment.

### Goal-Attainment Approach

In the more traditional **goal-attainment** or resource-allocation **approach**, an organization and its culture are effective to the extent that its stated goals are accomplished from input to transformation to output phase. Culture, along with other organizational dimensions, operates to help or hinder goal attainment, which is the central focus of effectiveness. This is a narrower approach than the others described in this section. Still, examining cultures in relation to organizational goal attainment remains an important focus. Viewing goal attainment from three points of view—input, transformation, and output—offers a clear and simple perspective that allows the observer to conceptualize the process discretely and to evaluate culture within each phase.

## OTHER MEASURES OF ORGANIZATIONAL EFFECTIVENESS

### Levels of Organizational Effectiveness

Output criteria can be used to examine effectiveness. The levels of the output dimension—enterprise, group, and individual—can also be used to identify cultural effectiveness. This is based on the premises introduced earlier, namely, that effectiveness is a function of consistently translating and integrating core values and beliefs into constructive policies and practices.

At the **enterprise level**, organizational and cultural effectiveness is gauged by how competitive the organization's performance is—that is, by market share or other industry-accepted criteria. At this level, organizations are also judged effective by the extent to which their products and/or services demonstrate quality as measured by customer or client feedback and by sales revenue.

At the **group** or **team level**, effectiveness is measured by designated performance criteria, by the degree of synergy the team demonstrates. (Is the whole equal to more than the sum of the parts? Is, for example, a team of 10 producing what 15, 20, or more individuals could produce working alone?) Many Internet start-ups begin with teams of 10 or fewer persons and grow at a phenomenal scale, scope, and rate.

At the **individual level**, effectiveness is also indicated by performance, satisfaction, development, and growth. Absenteeism, turnover, and grievances should be low to nonexistent. Organizations that reflect successful outputs at these three levels should also reflect and demonstrate effective cultures.

### Social Responsibility and Effectiveness

The extent to which an organization fulfills its legal and ethical obligations toward its stakeholders is a significant measure of its effectiveness. Among the most valued assets an organization has are its reputation and image in the marketplace. Johnson & Johnson's culture and management practices have consistently demonstrated concern for its employees and customers. The company swiftly removed Tylenol from the market when it was found to have problems to protect its consumers, its image, and profits. Organizational cultures often reflect how ethical, immoral, or amoral will be the actions of its leaders and employees. Thus, organization leaders and owners should not strive to be good to stockholders and stakeholders only for their market image. Leaders, owners, and employees are members of society and the world community as well as the organization. Their families are also affected by the public good and health of society, which is an interconnected system of business, government, and other institutions.

The moral and ethical basis for evaluating an organization's effectiveness can be measured against its contractual (both written and unwritten) agreements between itself and each stakeholder. Organizational obligations to stockholders, employee stakeholders, suppliers, customers, communities, federal/state/local government bodies, and society are thus a basis for assessing how effectively organizations recognize and respond to their legal and moral responsibilities. These responsibilities—creating and delivering quality and safe products and services; offering fair returns on investments; supporting employees and treating them fairly and equitably; competing openly; and returning value to society and its institutions—that make the very existence of organizations possible.

## Strong and Weak Cultures

We stated earlier that there are no universal success characteristics of organizational cultures. Schein stated, "Do not assume that more or stronger culture is better. What is better depends on the stage of evolution of the company and its current state of adaptiveness. Instead of seeking that elusive, possibly nonexistent, and possibly dangerous thing—a strong culture—try to understand and use the strengths of the existing culture."[17] Nevertheless, researchers have long sought to identify the elements of successful, strong organizational cultures and, indeed, successful cultures are usually defined as strong. Although the following generalizations may not necessarily be applicable to all organizations, we present the views of Deal and Kennedy, and Peters and Waterman, here as benchmarks for the ideal organizational culture.

### Strong Cultures

Deal and Kennedy describe strong cultures as having the following elements: a strong, unifying corporate philosophy and mission; trusted and trusting leaders; open communication channels and access to top management; an emphasis on the importance of people and productivity relationships; an emphasis on the customer and on service; a general sense of accomplishment and belonging by all; commonly shared rites, rituals, and ceremonies; an uplifting general feeling about employees' work, the place, and the future; and satisfaction with rewards, performance, and effort.[18]

### Cultures in Trouble

Several signs of weak organizational cultures, or cultures in trouble, can be identified. The heroes of the organization are destructive or disruptive and do not build on any common understanding about what is important in the organization. The rituals of day-to-day life are either disorganized—that is, everyone "does his or her own thing"—or are contradictory—"the left hand and the right hand work at cross purposes." Weak cultures have no clear values or beliefs and cannot agree among themselves on which are most important. At worst, different parts of the company have fundamentally different beliefs about what constitutes success. Weak cultures also tend to have an inward, short-term focus. Fragmentation, inconsistency, and morale problems exist among groups and individuals. Finally, subcultures are ingrown and exclusive, and clashes flare between different groups.

Peters and Waterman's still relevant study focuses on eight characteristics of excellent companies and the organizational cultural characteristics and practices they have in common.[19] While the companies studied have changed, these characteristics offer valuable benchmarks for high-performing cultures and business practices and are still quoted. The first is **bias for action**. Managers have a bias to act even without all the facts. The notion that "too much analysis leads to paralysis" applies here. Second, **stay close to the customer**. Customers provide ideas and information about present and future products, their own needs and expectations, what satisfies them, and what they will buy. The third is **autonomy and entrepreneurship**. Successful firms organize their large companies into smaller units in which they encourage creativity and risk taking that lead to innovations. The fourth characteristic involves **productivity through people**. Excellent companies value their people and believe people are their most valuable asset. The culture is built around commitment, respect, and dignity, all of which lead to high productivity. The fifth characteristic is **hands-on management**. Successful practice management by wandering around and observing. In successful companies, managers stay close to the action, not behind closed office doors. Sixth, **stick to the knitting**. Successful companies value growing and managing the business that the company knows and at which it excels. Too much diversification can dilute business success, especially if talent, knowledge, and experience are not used to build on success. Seventh, develop a **simple form and lean staff**. Small is good. Having too many administrators and too large a corporate staff leads to inefficiency. Performance is not measured by size alone, but also by managers' impact on business. The eighth characteristic is that the firm should be **simultaneously loosely and tightly organized**. Successful companies are tightly organized around core values, but loosely organized in their structures. Bureaucratic and mechanistic structures hinder and choke entrepreneurial risk taking and an action orientation to performing.

## ORGANIZATIONAL CULTURE AND ETHICS

Organizational culture has a pervasive influence on the ethical behavior of all stakeholders.[20] Leaders set the moral tone for what is and is not morally acceptable through the organization's vision, mission, values, strategy, structure, control systems, and activities. Customers, suppliers, regulatory agencies, employees, competitors, financial institutions, and the public all come to understand the moral (and amoral and immoral) boundaries of an organization through these dimensions. "High-ethics" cultures have been identified at Motorola, 3M, Cadbury, Schweppes, Arco, Northern Chemical, and Johnson & Johnson, to name a few. A study of high-ethics organizations yielded four principles that characterize their cultures and practices:

**Principle 1:** High-ethics firms are at ease interacting with diverse internal and external stakeholder groups. The ground rules of these firms make the good of these stakeholder groups part of the firm's own good.

**Principle 2:** High-ethics firms are obsessed with fairness. Their ground rules emphasize that the other person's interests count as much as their own.

**Principle 3:** In high-ethics firms, responsibility is individual rather than collective, with individuals assuming personal responsibility for actions of the firm. Ground rules in such firms mandate that individuals are responsible to themselves.

**Principle 4:** The high-ethics firm sees its activities in terms of a purpose. This purpose is a way of operating that is valued by members of the firm. And purpose ties the firm to its environment.[21]

### Employee Loyalty and Whistle Blowing

Unfortunately, not all organizations create or maintain high-ethics cultures. Employees are expected to show loyalty to their organization of employment, but there may be situations in which managers or supervisors engage in unethical and illegal activities—and pressure employees to do the same. In such instances, employees must decide where organizational loyalty begins and ends and what action, if any, to take to protect themselves and others.

*Whistle blowing* is the attempt by an employee or previous employee to disclose and reveal what the employee believes to be wrongdoing in or by an organization.[22] Whistle blowing is morally justified when an organization threatens to harm the employee and/or the public through a product or policy; all internal procedures and the chain of command have been exhausted with requests to act; when the employee produces accurate, documented evidence that is reviewed and found acceptable by an impartial, credible observer; and when the chance of succeeding equals or exceeds the risk and possible danger the employee incurs by blowing the whistle.[23]

## MULTICULTURAL AND DIVERSE ORGANIZATIONS

Because workforces are becoming increasingly more diverse, organizational cultures must integrate systems effectively to motivate, maintain productivity, and use diversity as a resourceful, competitive advantage. As discussed in Chapter 1, cultural diversity in organizations presents opportunities for advancing creative marketing strategies, decision making, and innovation, especially with a diverse customer base. Companies that have implemented cultural diversity programs include Corning, Avon, Xerox, and Procter & Gamble. The number is growing.

Essentially, a major aim of an organizationwide cultural diversity program is to create a multicultural organization, as discussed in Chapter 1. A multicultural organization not only has a diverse cultural workforce, but also values diversity. Diversity serves as a competitive advantage. A multicultural organization has the characteristics that we identify here (repeating from Table 1–3 in Chapter 1:)

1. A culture that fosters and values cultural differences

2. Pluralism as an acculturation process

3. Full structural integration

4. Full integration of the informal networks

5. An absence of institutionalized cultural bias in human resource management systems and practices

6. A minimum of intergroup conflict due to the proactive management of diversity.[24]

These multicultural characteristics are operationalized and implemented through the efforts of organizational leaders.

### A Culture That Values Diversity: Implementing Multicultural Characteristics

Creating an effective multicultural organization involves creating an environment and climate in which all members can excel.[25] This is done by hiring and promoting people who endorse the organization's values, reinforcing and instilling these values in performance and evaluation systems, and communicating with and educating all employees.

#### Using Pluralism to Acculturate Employees

Using pluralism as an acculturation process involves integrating minority culture perspectives into core organizational values and norms. This is accomplished through programs such as valuing diversity and language training, new member orientation programs (rites of passage), and explicitly managing diversity in mission statements.

#### Instilling Structural Integration and Informal Networks

Creating integration in the corporation means blending the community with the organization. This involves incorporating diversity into major committees, and implementing affirmative action, education, and targeted career-development programs. Mobil Oil, Exxon, IBM, US West, and McDonald's have started special career-development programs that are monitored and measured for members of minority groups.

## THE CHANGING WORKPLACE

### Ethical Weather Report

**Step 1**: Complete the following questionnaire using the organization in which you are working or one in which you have worked. Beside each statement, write the number from the scale that accurately reflects your knowledge and experience with the company.

| Completely False | Mostly False | Somewhat False | Somewhat True | Mostly True | Completely True |
|:---:|:---:|:---:|:---:|:---:|:---:|
| 0 | 1 | 2 | 3 | 4 | 5 |

_____    1.  In this company, people are expected to follow their own personal and moral beliefs.

_____    2.  People are expected to do anything to further the company's interests.

_____    3.  In this company, people look out for each other's good.

_____    4.  It is very important here to follow strictly the company's rules and procedures.

_____    5.  In this company, people protect their own interests above other considerations.

_____    6.  The first consideration is whether a decision violates any law.

_____    7.  Everyone is expected to stick by company rules and procedures.

_____    8.  The most efficient way is always the right way in this company.

_____    9.  Our major consideration is what is best for everyone in the company.

_____    10.  In this company, the law or ethical code of the profession is the major consideration.

_____    11.  It is expected at this company that employees will always do what is right for the customer and the public.

**Step 2**: Score your answers by adding up your responses to 1, 3, 6, 9, 10, and 11. Write the sum under Subtotal 1 below. Now reverse the scores on questions 2, 4, 5, 7, and 8 (5 = 0, 4 = 1, 3 = 2, 2 = 3, 1 = 4, 0 = 5). Add these reverse scores (i.e., number value) and write the sum in Subtotal number 2. Now add Subtotal 1 with Subtotal 2 for your overall score. The total score ranges between 0 and 55. The higher the score, the more the organization supports ethical behavior.

Subtotal 1 \_\_\_\_\_ + Subtotal 2 \_\_\_\_\_ = Overall Score \_\_\_\_\_

**Step 3**: Write a paragraph explaining your organization's ethical profile: Why is it the way it is? Offer specific steps you would recommend in your organization's cultural dimensions, leadership, policies, or procedures that would either enhance its already ethical climate or help change the climate.

**SOURCE**: Reprinted from *Organizational Dynamics*, Autumn 1989, J.B. Cullen, B. Victor, and C. Stephens, "An Ethical Weather Report Assessing the Organization's Ethical Climate." Copyright 1989, with permission from Elsevier Science.

Informal integrating networks are accomplished through company-initiated mentoring programs and social events. Chemical Bank and General Foods have established effective mentoring programs.

### Eradicating Institutional Bias

Changing institutional bias involves auditing reward, appraisal, benefits, and performance systems and changing any inequities identified. Such policies and procedures as hiring, training and retraining, promoting, and offering child care arrangements, work schedules, and parental leave should have no biases in their process or content. Performance regarding the management of diversity goals and processes should be included in the policies and procedures. Baxter Health Care, Coca-Cola, Nations Bank, Levi Strauss, IBM, and Merck have addressed or are addressing such biases in their systems, policies, and processes.

## Managing Intergroup Conflict

A multicultural organization must minimize interpersonal and intergroup conflicts related to group identity and must promote understanding of cultural differences. At Digital Equipment, Corning, and Procter & Gamble, this goal is addressed through conflict management and resolution, adherence to Equal Employment Opportunity guidelines, and managed value diversity training. These training programs focus on identifying and stripping stereotypes and assumptions about out-groups, enhancing relationships, and training awareness and personal empowerment.

Creating and developing multicultural organizations is a major step that companies are taking to integrate the diversity of their workforces as they respond to new and changing markets.

## CHANGING ORGANIZATIONAL CULTURE

Changing organizational culture is not easy; it is an expensive and time-consuming project since it involves changing deep seated values, traditions, and worldviews. Some debate whether changing an organization's culture is even possible.[26] Most who argue that cultural change is difficult but possible advocate trying less difficult and costly solutions first—for example, changing behaviors, strategy, or using teams to manage around the dominant culture.[27]

Still, numerous organizations, including IBM, GM, GE, and AT&T, continue to initiate and undergo transformational changes and adjustments in their culture. Because of combined environmental, industry, and competitive changes, organizations of all sizes must realign—and some even reinvent—their vision, mission, strategy, culture, structure, control systems, and professional expertise to survive and to be competitive. Conditions that signal a need for cultural changes include significant market-share losses, shifting markets, changes in major technologies, growth and downsizing, international expansion, mergers and acquisitions, deregulation, and persistent morale problems.[28]

### Diagnosing Cultural Change: External Adaptation and Internal Integration

Diagnosing whether cultural change is necessary and appropriate involves an external and internal organizational assessment. Problems relating to external adaptation and survival require an examination of the following organizational dimensions to identify the degree to which the organization is effectively managing its relationships to the changing environment.

**Mission and strategy:** Determine the extent to which there exists a shared understanding of core mission, primary task, and manifest and latent functions.

**Goals:** Determine the extent to which there exists consensus on goals as derived from the core mission.

**Means:** Determine the extent to which consensus exists as to the means (such as the organization structure, division of labor, reward system, and authority systems) to be used to attain the goals.

**Measurement:** Determine the extent to which consensus exists regarding the criteria used in measuring how well teams are doing in fulfilling goals.

**Correction:** Determine the degree of consensus on the appropriate remedial or repair strategies to be used if goals are not being met.[29]

Problems relating to internal integration can be assessed by examining the degree to which the following dimensions and integrating mechanisms[30] function to promote internal consensus, cohesiveness, and effectiveness:

- *Common language and conceptual categories.* If members cannot communicate with and understand each other, teams are by definition impossible.

- *Group boundaries and criteria for inclusion and exclusion.* One of the most important areas of organizational culture is the shared consensus as to who is "in" and who is "out" and by what criteria one determines membership.

- *Power and status.* Every organization must work out its pecking order and its criteria and rules for how one gets, maintains, and loses power; consensus in this area is crucial to help members manage feelings of aggression.

- *Intimacy, friendship, and love.* Every organization must work out its rules of the game for peer relationships, relationships between the sexes, and the manner in which openness and intimacy are to be handled in the context of managing the organization's tasks.

- *Rewards and punishments.* Every group must know what its heroic and sinful behaviors are, what gets rewarded with property, status, and power; and what gets punished in the form of withdrawal of the rewards and, ultimately, excommunication.

## THE CHANGING WORKPLACE

### Cultural Diversity Audit

**Step 1**: Select an organization in which you worked or are working or interview someone who is working in an organization.

**Step 2**: To complete the following audit, place a checkmark on the scale between **Always** to **Hardly Ever** based on experiences and observations that you can substantiate and validate (i.e., that are not based on your biases or limited understanding or those of the person you are interviewing). You can be objective by thinking of examples to support your answers. If you are interviewing someone, inform him of his need to be objective and ask for an example to support his answer.

| In this organization, it is generally true that: | 1<br>Always | 2<br>Sometimes | 3<br>Rarely | 4<br>Hardly Ever |
|---|---|---|---|---|
| 1. People respect others' differences of opinion, values, and beliefs. | ____ | ____ | ____ | ____ |
| 2. People are open to emotions being expressed. | ____ | ____ | ____ | ____ |
| 3. Hazing and harassment are disciplined and punished. | ____ | ____ | ____ | ____ |
| 4. Newcomers are welcomed and integrated quickly. | ____ | ____ | ____ | ____ |
| 5. Individuals of different race, color, religious creed, national origin, and physical and mental abilities are readily accepted. | ____ | ____ | ____ | ____ |
| 6. The general feeling one gets here is of an openness to change. | ____ | ____ | ____ | ____ |
| 7. The leaders and managers are role models of openness and inclusion of different professionals. | ____ | ____ | ____ | ____ |
| 8. Barriers between groups are not allowed to develop. | ____ | ____ | ____ | ____ |

*continued on next page*

---

**THE CHANGING WORKPLACE, cont.**

| In this organization, it is generally true that: | 1 Always | 2 Sometimes | 3 Rarely | 4 Hardly Ever |
|---|---|---|---|---|
| 9. There is a fair and just process for settling differences between individuals, groups, and departments or units. | ____ | ____ | ____ | ____ |
| 10. This company is right for anyone who wants to feel a sense of equal opportunity to grow and to develop professionally and personally. | ____ | ____ | ____ | ____ |

**Step 3**: Total the number of responses under each of the four columns. The higher the score in the Always column total, the more open to diversity and accommodation the company, division, or group is.

**Step 4**: What specific recommendations would you or the person interviewed suggest with regard to changing elements in the culture, leadership, policies, and practices?

Copyright © Joseph W. Weiss, 2000.

---

- *Ideology and "religion."* Every organization, like every society, faces unexplainable and inexplicable events, that must be given meaning so that members can cope with them and avoid the anxiety of dealing with the unexplainable and uncontrollable.

If evidence shows a significant lack of external and/or internal integration of the organization with its environment, an argument can be made for cultural change.

Another diagnostic tool, the "jump-start" approach, also can be used to assess whether the corporate culture requires strategic and transformational change or if certain behavioral adjustments can be made instead. This approach was discussed in Chapter 1 and illustrated in Figure 1–5. Briefly, the jump-start approach asks the following "trigger questions": Where's the pain (tension) in the system? How related is the subsystem experiencing the problem with other parts of the organization? How high up and how far down the organization does the pain exist? Who (which system) is ready for change?

### Cultural Change Guidelines

In the competitive information technology environment, gaining new markets and market share through name brand recognition is essential. Who knew what Amazon.com, e-Bay, or AOL were in 1994? However, getting market share and keeping market share are different. Organizational culture is a key ingredient that helps a company remain successful.

Effective cultural change begins first with a clear vision of an organization's new or desired direction.[31] Andrew Grove, who helped turn Intel into a leading company, succeeded in turning the personal computer into the cornerstone of twenty-first century information technology. Grove, although not at the helm of Intel, still embeds his legendry vision at Intel.[32]

Second, cultural change can proceed effectively only if top management is actively committed to the new values and need for change. Top management must have "staying power,"[33] which Jack Welsh at GE has demonstrated. During the first 10 years of his leadership, General Electric was transformed from a sprawling, diversified, unfocused company into a global, world-class competitor.

Third, senior executives must communicate the new culture through their own actions and behaviors—that is, through "symbolic leadership." For example, Stanley Gault at Rubbermaid, Inc., was a devoted open-door manager who listened to all his employees.

Fourth, cultural change must be supported in all of the organization's systems as illustrated in Figure 1–4. The strategy, structure, control systems, and professional expertise must be aligned to the new cultural requirements. PepsiCo's bid to take Coca-Cola head-on for market share has required a cultural change in reward systems and interdepartmental relations. A culture based on aggressive competitiveness necessitates a focused management style and systems approach in the company.

Fifth, effective selection and socialization of newcomers and termination of deviants is required if cultural change is to be successful. This process centers on hiring the best people, including the CEO. Microsoft's Bill Gates has been a leader in announcing that he wants the brightest and most talented to work at Microsoft. The company's innovative record reflects that policy.

Finally, cultural change requires an organization's leadership to exhibit ethical and legal sensitivity toward its internal and external stakeholders. To reduce potential ethical and legal tensions and problems, it is recommended that realistic values be set for cultural change and that no promises be made that the organization cannot deliver, that input from throughout the organization be encouraged in setting cultural values, that mechanisms such as internal review procedures be provided for member dissent and diversity, and that managers be educated about the legal and ethical pitfalls inherent in cultural change and that guidelines be developed for resolving such issues.[34]

## LEADING CULTURAL CHANGE PROCESSES

Changing organizational cultures requires leaders who can lead *transformational* change as compared to *developmental* or *transitional* change. **Transformational change** is distinct in that it represents the emergence of a new, unknown state, although it may require developmental and transitional change. Transformational change can be implemented in a quantum leap, or it can be implemented incrementally. Many large corporations have embarked on quantum leap changes through reengineering (i.e., streamlining work processes by redefining them and then implementing only the essential phases of critical work flow). Transformational change, as discussed in Chapter 7, requires the commitment and involvement of an organization's leaders and top-level managers. In this section, we discuss two organizational change models that involve cultural transformations. These models were introduced in Chapter 1 (Figure 1–8) and Chapter 7 (Figure 7–4). These models are certainly not the only frameworks available on this topic, but they do represent mainstream approaches.

Figure 1–8 consists of five phases that leaders must initiate, oversee, and nurture: motivating change, creating a vision, developing political support, managing the transition, and sustaining the momentum.

In the first phase, *motivating change*, the two key activities required of leaders are to create readiness and to overcome resistance to change. Creating readiness for change requires sensitizing organizational members to the pressures requiring change, for example, increasing competition, costs of doing business, need for quality, employee turnover, and new technology needs. Leaders must assist members in their understanding of the gap and discrepancies between current and desired states of the organization; they must determine strategically where they are now, then where they want to go, where they want and need to be, where they are as a culture and what the gaps are between where they are and where they should be.[35] To address some of these questions, Chairman Lee Kun-Hee of Samsung (a multinational organization with operations in consumer electronics and household appliances) brought his entire top management staff to Los Angeles so they could see how poorly Samsung products were positioned. His main message was that without knowledge of competitors and customers, Samsung could never be able to compete.[36]

In creating a readiness for change, leaders also need to convey credible positive expectations regarding change. Actively informing members of what to expect and the effects that the change will have on the organization and on them personally has been shown to be a more effective strategy than hiding or delaying information.[36] In some cases, the survival of the organization may be at stake.

Overcoming resistance to change involves all of the processes described earlier. Some employees will not stop resisting new and dramatic change. Those who can stop often do so when the leaders present a clear and credible vision, purpose, goals, and realistic means of achieving the goals. Leaders can decrease resistance to change by modeling responsible, planned organizational change, by sharing good and bad news openly, and by identifying examples of life "after the change."

Figure 7–4 identifies the first phase of behavioral stages to change the process. *Ignoring* is the first expected phase. Figure 7–4 assumes that resistance occurs with any organizational or cultural changes. People ignore in the following ways: they have no intention of changing; they are unaware of the need to change; they deny any need to change; they become demoralized about their ability to change;

and/or they rationalize the negatives as outweighing the positives of any change effort. These are expected and predictable behaviors that occur when people are confronted with large-scale organizational change.

Techniques can be used to work through and overcome resistance to change. At the individual and group levels, such techniques include creating empathy and support, actively listening, effectively communicating changes and their likely consequences, and implementing plans that include the participation and involvement of those who will experience the aftermath of the changes.

The aim underlying the complementary change model in Figure 7–4 is to move organizational members from the ignoring stage to the second stage, *attending*, in which there is an awareness for the need to change and the intention to do so, although there still may not be a readiness or willingness to commit to change. It is not until the second phase of the model is addressed (Figure 1–8) that organizational members are willing and ready to plan for changes.

The second phase in Figure 1–8, **creating a vision,** was discussed at some length in Chapter 7. To summarize, creating a vision includes defining the vision. This should involve top management and selected professionals throughout the organization. The organization must determine what its core competencies are, what business it is in, what its product or service is, and who its customers are. From the discussions resulting from determining these factors, a mission statement, a values statement, and a corporate strategy can be developed; they should be based on valued outcomes and conditions as well as the strategic direction and goals of the organization. During this phase, major change initiatives (goals and objectives) can be identified, and the implementation process can be developed.

The third phase of this change approach involves **developing political support**. Because planned changes (whether in technologies, products, administration, structure, or other organizational dimensions) usually produce competition between departments and people over scarce organizational resources, it is necessary to map out and develop political support for cultural change strategies. To make change strategies, the following questions must be answered: What is the problem, issue, or opportunity involved in implementing the planned changes? What are the goals and objectives sought in the change process? Who is the change agent implementing the strategies? What is at stake for each stakeholder? How will each stakeholder be affected by the resulting cultural changes? What result could be planned to resolve the anticipated problems and issues from implementing the desired changes? What stakeholder strategies can be used to achieve a win-win result? What support from whom does the implementing stakeholder need to achieve the desired result with as little disruption as possible?

Addressing these questions can assist the leaders in assessing their power and their strategies to articulate a political implementation plan. The aim in this cultural change process is to succeed in effectively embedding a new organizational culture with minimal costs.

The fourth phase involves **managing the transition**. Active planning, commitment planning, and managing the structures are necessary to create the implementation steps. Active planning entails developing a project plan in which specific objectives, priorities, activities, and tasks are detailed along with projected costs. Commitment planning is related to the stakeholder analysis to develop political support. A specific plan of action with strategies and outcomes is required. Management must create alternative organizational structures and roles to implement new changes that may, at first, lack structure. Creating these alternatives may involve the chief executive or person responsible for managing the change, the project manager, representatives of interested stakeholders, natural leaders who are trusted by employees, a cross-section of people affected by the change, and a cabinet (supported by the chief executive) to manage the change.[37]

The final phase of organizational change involves **sustaining the momentum**. After the initial motivation and energy of the changes wear down, it is necessary to ensure that the changes are embedded in members' values and business practices, as well as the organization's systems. The following requirements and activities are necessary to create and sustain momentum: providing adequate resources for the change; building a support system for the change agents; developing new competencies and skills; and reinforcing new behaviors.

Financial, technical, and human resources and training expertise are among the pertinent support systems. Without adequate support, the new culture cannot be properly embedded. Internal networks of change agents and internal consultants are examples of effective support systems. Building a support system for change agents involves addressing the emotional and psychological as well as the political and organizational needs of those who are responsible for driving the changes. A psychological distance from other employees is often required for change agents to perform their new responsibilities, but it can be an isolating experience.

Developing new competencies and skills is needed to embed the changes. Training, coaching, counseling, and mentoring enable people to execute new technologies, social skills, roles, and responsibilities in the organization. When Digital Equipment Corporation began the shift from an engineering industrial culture to a market-driven, consultative culture, skill training had to be provided in selling nonproprietary products and services. Selling was suddenly required of people who had never sold, and DEC provided the training that enabled them to sell.

Once new behaviors are learned in a large-scale organizational change, it is necessary to reinforce them. If product quality, for example, is a new targeted competitive area, new skills and behaviors required to produce and ensure quality must be reinforced. Behavioral reinforcement can take the *extrinsic forms* of rewards, bonuses, and promotions or the *intrinsic forms* of recognition, praise, and encouragement. Achieving and rewarding early successes are important elements in embedding new and desired behaviors related to the changes.

## CONCLUDING COMMENTS

Organizational culture consists of the shared values, beliefs, norms, and assumptions that bind a group of people together. Culture can help members adapt to their internal and external environments. Culture encompasses both visible (language) and invisible (underlying beliefs) elements. The socialization of culture—that is, the passing on of values, beliefs, and norms—consists of transition rites, enhancement rites, renewal rites, and integration rites. Cultural influences stem from the examples of organizational leaders and from the environmental influences of national, regional, and industrywide cultures.

Two means of evaluating organizational effectiveness were discussed. In a contingency approach, effectiveness was defined as an organizational culture's fit with its internal systems and environments. The goal-attainment approach evaluates whether the resources are used to obtain goals.

Strong cultures were identified as having a unifying corporate philosophy and mission, a results orientation, open communication channels, an emphasis on the importance of people and their productivity, and a focus on customer service. Weak cultures, by contrast, have an inward and short-term focus. Weak cultures experience frequent conflicts between individuals and groups and have leaders who cannot rally members around a vision and purpose.

Leaders of an organization set its ethical culture by defining the firm's mission and strategies.

A multicultural organization creates an environment in which all members can excel, minority cultural perspectives are integrated into organizational values, and inequities in reward and performance systems are changed to eradicate bias. The result is an environment in which interpersonal and intergroup conflicts are minimized.

Changing organizational culture involves altering deep-seated values and traditions. The internal and external integration of the environment must be assessed before a change process can be initiated. Leaders must have a clear vision of the organization's new direction and must be actively committed to the new values. All systems and processes within the organization must be realigned to meet the new strategy.

## SCENARIO AND EXERCISE: YOU'RE THE CHANGE CONSULTANT

ABC.com is a three-month-old start-up software application company that has two founders and six employees. The company has $4 million in venture capital funds to get the product up and out in five months. There is a creative chaos in the firm. The four programmers (20, 22, 23 and 25 years old) like to work from 3 p.m. to 12 midnight. The marketing/office coordinator, a 35-year-old marketing veteran, wants to have meetings at 7:30 a.m. and sometimes at 6 p.m. so she can meet clients and network during "normal" corporate office hours. She needs to touch base with the programmers regularly to give and receive feedback on the product. The Web designer and manager (18 years old) likes to work at home and finds "coming into the office a drag." One of the founders is a program guru, who likes to "hang out" with the programmers on "their time." The other founder is a management major who supports the marketing coordinator and her schedule. The one thing everyone seems to agree on is that they all want to take the company public in two years, get rich, and then who knows what can or will happen. If the stock market crashes, they will have learned how to start a company.

In the meantime, one of the venture capitalists (VCs) has required that the office "get a professional culture while remaining entrepreneurial and results driven." That VC noted, "Every time I call in, I get the feeling I'm calling a college dormitory. You need to get a professional 'face' in the place, especially on the phone."

**Exercise**: You have been called in to analyze the situation and the existing culture and to recommend organizing and initiating a culture that will do what the VC has asked you: "Get a professional culture while remaining entrepreneurial and results driven."

Complete the following:

1. List the elements of the existing culture or cultural situation.

2. Recommend a process for changing and forming a new culture, especially needed since the firm plans on hiring between 25 and 50 people over the next two years.

3. What would a new culture that meets the stated requirements look like?

4. What problems do you expect to encounter in planning and implementing the new culture? Why?

5. What resources and knowledge do you need to carry out this assignment?

6. How do you feel about carrying out this assignment? Explain.

7. Share your answers with members of your class. What similarities and differences in this exercise did you find? What did you learn from your classmates? What did they learn from you?

**REVIEW QUESTIONS**

1. Describe the elements of an organization's culture in which you work(ed) that motivated and empowered you. Now describe the elements of a culture that you did not enjoy. What are the sources of each of the elements you described?

2. Describe how you were or were not "socialized" into a company, (i.e., what were the rites of passage, if any, that you experienced in the company? Were these rites successful or not, in your opinion? Explain.

3. Does national, regional, or local culture affect the company culture in which you work(ed)? Explain.

4. Has a specific industry culture (e.g., engineering, marketing, sales, scientific) affected the organizational culture (norms, attitudes, behaviors, expectations) where you work(ed)? Explain.

5. What determines the effectiveness of an organization's culture in your view? How does your view compare with the discussion on effectiveness in this chapter? Explain.

6. What are some differences between a strong and weak organizational culture? How would you suggest a weak culture become strong? Is it possible for this to happen?

7. Compare an organizational culture with which you are familiar with the eight characteristics of Peters and Waterman's excellent companies.

8. Compare an organization's ethics with the four principles of high-ethics cultures in the chapter. What are some specific similarities and differences? Explain.

9. Comment on your views on the six characteristics of a multicultural organization. How do the characteristics of an organization you are familiar with compare with these listed in the chapter?

10. What would you recommend to begin changing a culture? Compare your suggestions to some of those at the end of this chapter (e.g., see the section on Cultural Change Guidelines). What differences and similarities did you find?

# 13

# Careers and Socialization

---

## LEARNING OBJECTIVES

After studying this chapter, you should be able to:

1  Define *contemporary careers.*

2  Describe contemporary forces influencing careers.

3  Explain the organizational socialization process.

4  Identify individual developmental stages and "passages."

5  Describe career developmental stages.

6  Discuss workforce diversity issues and careers.

7  Present a practical career planning and management model.

---

Boundaryless careers "are the opposite of 'organizational careers'—careers conceived to unfold in a single employment setting . . . the old picture of stable employment, and organizational careers associated with it, has faded, and a new picture of dynamic employment and boundaryless careers calls for our attention."[1] Boundaryless careers are not necessarily limited to one company or one industry for extended periods of time. In addition to starting their own companies—or joining start-ups—individuals are working more in projects and assignments with customers, suppliers, and teams from strategic alliances. The Internet and information technologies have transformed bricks and mortar to "clicks and mortar." More professionals now work in virtual environments with geographically dispersed stakeholders through electronic technologies than ever before. Consider the time we spend in our work lives: "Eleven thousand days of our lives: Roughly speaking that's the amount of time we spend at work between the ages of 21 and 65. It's a staggering amount of time to commit to any single activity."[2]

**Careers** have traditionally been defined as the sequence of jobs, roles, and positions individuals hold during their working lives.[3] **Contemporary careers** can be defined as significant learnings and experiences that identify an individual's professional life, direction, competencies, and accomplishments through positions, jobs, roles, and assignments. Ideally, careers are selected; individuals fit careers to their aims, desires, and competencies. This is a radical change in approach and one to contemplate carefully.

Career opportunities for newcomers to the job market appear riskier, more adventurous, and less defined than a generation ago. Nevertheless, the enduring meaning of career, as compared to a sequence of jobs in one's lifetime, is the idea that one intentionally chooses a field or profession that gives meaning to her professional identity, satisfaction, and growth. Implementing a career choice and path today can involve a struggle. Take the example of 25-year-old Adam Dawes:

> *Returning after graduation (bachelor's degree, visual arts) to his native Palo Alto, jobless and broke, Dawes longed to work as an independent film producer. He quickly lined up two internships with local production companies, one of which paid a pittance, the other nothing. To support himself, he took a flexible office job in a small consulting firm at $12.00 an hour. He saved nearly all his take-home pay during the six months he lived rent-free with his parents, and he maintained his frugal ways after he moved out on his own.*
>
> *Concluding that a career in filmmaking would be a precarious struggle, Dawes decided to explore ways to marry his visual arts training and his competency with computers in the fledgling industry of multi-media computing. He used his free time to haunt trade shows and conferences, read industry magazines, and bone up on prospective employers. Though he was not yet sure where all this would lead, Dawes began to develop what he calls the "fuzzy vision" that he would rely upon to guide him in the future jobs he would take. He was determined not to get sidetracked by economic necessity into taking jobs that didn't fall within his fuzzy parameters.*
>
> *Dawes took a succession of jobs and internships (often two at a time), each nudging him a bit closer to his goal. The frenetic experience, he says, "taught me what it was like to work in the fluid world of high-tech companies." Finally, in August, he learned of an opening in marketing at Smart Valley, a consortium of 60 companies that want to create a regional interactive computer network. Dawes landed the job, again as an intern but with the understanding that it could lead to a salaried position. Last December it did, and at an annual pay of $30,000 plus benefits.*[4]

This chapter identifies contemporary forces that influence career planning and management. A socialization process describes the stages through which individuals go as they enter and settle into organizations. Individual developmental stages are also identified, along with stages of career progression. Workforce diversity issues in career management are discussed. Finally, a practical model for career planning and management in the twenty-first century is described.

## CONTEMPORARY FORCES INFLUENCING CAREERS

Predictions for the changing workplace suggest that these changes will significantly impact individuals and groups.

> *A new, quirky, more democratic U.S. economy is emerging, its information technology-laced networks of services and goods taking the ground once towered over by huge corporate ziggurats of the old industrial system. Millions, perhaps the majority of the population, will be troubled by the change. Those likely to suffer most: young adults without high school diplomas, semiskilled manufacturing workers, people over 40 in the employ of large corporations, and anyone still expecting a 30-year career with the same company.*[5]

## THE CHANGING WORKPLACE

### Hiring Yourself

**Exercise**: Take the role of an employer. You are considering hiring yourself. Complete the following exercise *as the employer* while being yourself (the student, professional).

**Step 1**: Write your answer to these questions which you are asking the person being considered as a hire (yourself).

a.  What are you looking for in a company or organization? What exactly do you really enjoy doing and want to do?

b.  What are your professional goals in terms of employment, a career?

c.  What are your personal goals? What do you want to achieve for yourself?

d.  What specific skills and abilities do you bring that differentiates you from other applicants (technology capabilities, organizational skills, interpersonal skills)?

**Step 2**: Exchange your answers with a classmate. Individually and independently evaluate each other's answers. Each of you write evaluations. Be objective. Answer: Would you hire your classmate? Explain.

**Step 3**: Share what each of you wrote with the other.

**Step 4**: What did each of you learn from this exercise? What were your emotional responses in Step 3? Why?

**Step 5**: Each team shares Step 4 with the class.

Moreover, shifts from national to global markets and from technological to information, service-based economies signal dramatic changes that are also reflected in the nature of work and the way work is performed, as the following excerpt indicates:

> *There are more and different kinds of specialists with different values, career insights, and technical languages, . . . more people are working away from the traditional office setting with more flexible approaches to work (such as flexible hours, job sharing, and part-time employment) . . . employees have decreased loyalty to companies; they will change jobs and careers more often; formal organizational structures are giving way to project teams, task forces, matrix structures, and interdependent units; [there is] an increasing need to train and retrain people at different career stages in order to maintain job security; [there are] changes in how people relate to each other (for instance, communication via computer lacks nonverbal cues and displays no emotions), more collaborative and cooperative work, including involvement in decision making; and pressure to increase job satisfaction by changing job content.*[6]

In a recent *Fortune* article, the following appeared under the heading "What the New Generation Hates": "The best bureaucrats, not the best performers, are most likely to get ahead. It's too easy to get pigeonholed or stuck in a dead-end job with no way out. It takes too long to get enough responsibility, authority, and rewards. There's not enough flexibility about where and when you work. Top managers say they want risk takers, but they don't."[7] The same source stated,

> *The changing attitudes of top business school graduates are particularly revealing. These are people who have choices, who usually boast several years of solid experience and receive multiple job offers in all but the very worst of economic climates. In the past many aspired to corporate power, to hold the reins at some giant company. But now, more and more of them, especially those at or near the top of their classes, want to carve a niche of their own rather than slip into one supplied by a corporation. As recently as 1990, a quarter of Columbia University's new MBAs joined large manufacturers; last year just 13 percent did so. At Stanford nearly 70 percent of the business school's class of '89 joined big companies, defined as those with more than 1,000 employees. In 1994 only about half did so. Also, compare Harvard Business School's class of 1995 with 1999: the 1995 class showed 38 percent of MBA graduates entering consulting—compared to 29 percent in 1999; 17 percent entered investment banking—compared to 12 percent in 1999; 33 percent entered old-line corporate jobs—compared to 30 percent in 1999; and 12 percent went into venture high tech capital jobs—compared to 29 percent in 1999.[8]*

The implications of these trends on careers are far-reaching. As individuals seek employment, they will need to develop new and creative goals. They need to search for different and untraditional ways of achieving job satisfaction and motivation. They must reevaluate the balance between work and family. They must be able to recognize the critical stages of susceptibilities to influence and be aware of periods of transition and stability. They must be resilient—ambiguity and career barriers will be common in their work life. They must know themselves well and understand the current work environment better. They can expect career identity changes over time. They will learn new management behaviors over their careers. They must learn the art of taking calculated risks and be willing to change. They will need to adjust to the new and precarious nature of loyalty to and from organizations. And they will need to find ways to minimize and deal with feelings of discontent and of being locked in.[9]

The New Compass Points of a Manager's Career, shown in Figure 13–1, translates many of the themes discussed earlier into the new career perspectives and requirements. A professional must now be self-reliant, a specialist, a generalist, and a connected team player.[10] The **specialist** has expertise in a particular field or discipline. Professionals are challenged to become more specialized in their particular fields. Traditional administrators and managers who supervise other specialists are and will continue to be in less demand. This is a result of the nature of the complexity and requirements of knowledge-based work, especially as information technologies take over more of the traditional manager's job. The **self-reliant worker** is becoming a networked one-person enterprise. Downsized organizations coupled with integrated computer networks enable specialists to take on multiple business and technical roles, thereby communicating knowledge and solving problems electronically over the skyways. Here is one scenario describing the design of a new car:

> *. . . a bumper designer in one country, a headlamp expert in another forms on the network. As participants exchange information and specifications, one gets an idea for a lighter weight battery, but the battery engineer on the project turns it down. Whereupon an information broker, who knows of another specialist doing interesting work in the field, locates that person electronically and brings her in to develop the new component.[11]*

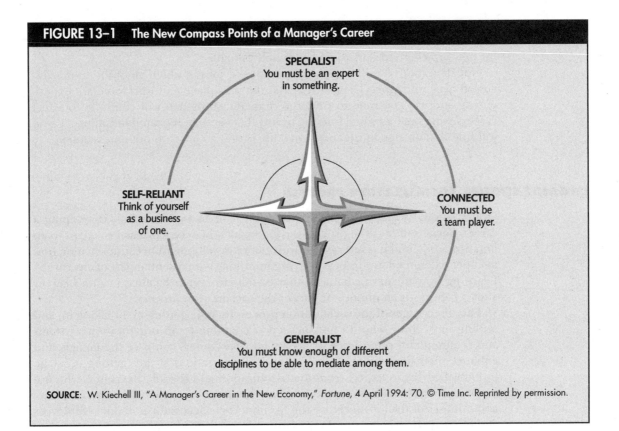

**FIGURE 13–1    The New Compass Points of a Manager's Career**

SPECIALIST
You must be an expert
in something.

SELF-RELIANT
Think of yourself
as a business
of one.

CONNECTED
You must be
a team player.

GENERALIST
You must know enough of different
disciplines to be able to mediate among them.

SOURCE: W. Kiechell III, "A Manager's Career in the New Economy," *Fortune*, 4 April 1994: 70. © Time Inc. Reprinted by permission.

Enhanced self-esteem and independence are personality characteristics that facilitate these types of outsourced and multiple expert roles. The **generalist** knows enough about several disciplines to mediate among them. Employees will also be required to have a broad and general knowledge of multiple jobs and disciplines in addition to their own specialization. This is becoming a requirement for being an effective team member and organizational problem solver. Understanding basics in marketing, finance, engineering, human resources, and strategic perspectives of a project as it relates to the business of the company, for example, is becoming value added in many roles, especially for team leaders. Finally, being a **connected team player** is, as stated earlier, becoming a work requirement. Work will increasingly be accomplished through teams, since mid-level managers will most likely continue to be replaced by management substitutes, such as information technology. Team players must develop "people skills" to connect and effectively communicate with colleagues and external stakeholders.

The specialist is characterized as not liking to be told what to do, especially by less-informed sources, and keeping abreast in a particular field requires continuous learning. For example, an electrical engineer was recently quoted in *Fortune* that, to stay current in his field, he knows he must assume responsibility for his career, find the time to keep up with new trends, and constantly be on the lookout for new projects and ways to make himself valuable.[12]

Not all employees will work in professions or jobs in which all of the trends discussed here will apply. The point is that the workplace and workforce are experiencing and will continue to undergo dramatic shifts that will continue to affect careers, work, and jobs well into the twenty-first century. As stated in Chapter 1, you will find that change in organizational life is now a constant, not an exception.

## *ORGANIZATIONAL SOCIALIZATION PROCESS*

Organizational socialization is a companion process to successfully developing a career. **Socialization** is the process through which newcomers learn to adapt to an organization,[13] and it is interwoven with career development because learning how to cope, accommodate, and excel in organizations is an essential part of any career. Learning how to survive failure—that is, how to regain balance in one's career after a failure—is an important part of the socialization process.

The three stages of the socialization process include getting in, breaking in, and settling in.[14] Those who do not succeed at adapting to an organization's systems and requirements often leave or are let go. Newcomers can ease the anxiety and enhance their probability of succeeding in organizations at the "getting in" stage by knowing what to expect from the organization and the job. Recruiters who use realistic job previews (i.e., an accurate description of the responsibilities and pluses and minuses of the job) increase the likelihood of success for potential employees and decrease the chances of their quitting.[15]

Recruiters and representatives of organizations also can inform applicants of the norms, expectations, and culture of the company and their future job. Potential newcomers can question the recruiter about the actual success factors for various jobs and assignments. Setting mutually agreed on expectations is a crucial part of ensuring a successful getting in phase.

At the **breaking in stage** of socialization, employees enter the organization's culture and are then challenged to adapt to its norms and requirements. This involves learning to effectively interact socially and professionally with colleagues up and down the organization. At this stage, new skills must be tried and mastered. This is the stage where the fit between the organization and the individual is tried and tested.

Individuals who successfully fit their jobs, projects, and organizations move on to the third stage, **settling in**, when they embark on the process of becoming a full member of the organization. Permanent adjustments between the person and the job organization's systems are made at this stage.

Organizations can assist employees in the socialization process in the following ways. First, at the getting-in stage, as already mentioned, every effort should be made to ensure that the job previews are realistic. Moreover, formal and informal orientation programs facilitate an employee's entry into the organization. Expectations, organizational values, and norms should be introduced and discussed. These sessions explain to newcomers what it takes to succeed in the organization.

At the breaking-in stage, employees should be carefully introduced to their roles and given an in-depth job orientation. This is when giving employees technical information and behavioral and normative feedback regarding the extent to which they are meeting work requirements and cultural expectations is crucial. Performance and social feedback enables employees to adjust their own expectations and behaviors to meet organizational expectations. The more questions newcomers ask and the more efforts they make to fit in, the more likely their socialization process will be facilitated.[16] Mentoring programs, formal and informal, can enhance the probability that newcomers will succeed. (We discuss mentoring later in this chapter.)

At the settling-in stage of socialization, it is important for seasoned employees to be able to contribute to the organization. During the first two stages of socialization, the employee and organization focus on the fit; at the third stage, the employee should be given the opportunity to innovate and add value to the organization and its products, services, and practices.

## INDIVIDUAL DEVELOPMENTAL STAGES AND CAREERS

Individuals transition through at least three career stages (defined by biological, social, and family characteristics) after leaving adolescence: early adulthood, midlife, and later adulthood. Table 13–1 illustrates a classical development model by Daniel Levinson.[17] This process is relevant to our discussion here because an individual's needs influence career and job expectations and requirements. The following is a pertinent question: What specific individual needs should the organization and the person address at each developmental stage?

| TABLE 13–1    Individual Developmental Life Cycles | | | |
|---|---|---|---|
| *Age 17-22* | *Age 23-45* | *Age 46-65* | *Age 66+* |
| Early adult transition | Entering the adult world | Entering middle adulthood | Late adulthood |
| | Age 30: Transition | Age 50: Transition | |
| | Settling down | Culmination of middle adulthood | |
| | Mid-life transition | Late adult transition | |

SOURCE: Based on D. J. Levinson et al., *The Seasons of a Man's Life* (New York: Alfred A. Knopf, 1978).

**Young adulthood** is a period in which people finish their education, enter a profession, marry, and become parents. In their early twenties and thirties, people are vital, self-determined, and may work at more than one job. This is a time of experimenting and expending energy to "find oneself" within a profession. Identity development and making one's place in life are key issues that people attempt to solve during this stage.

The late thirties and early forties are characterized as **adulthood and mid-life transition and crisis**. Career, family concerns, and health become major areas of concern in people's lives. Personal and career reevaluation occurs during this time. Anxiety and frustration can set in as children leave for college, expenses accrue, and the disillusioned experience of not meeting lifetime goals occurs. At this developmental stage, single mothers, divorced and single individuals, dual-career couples, and people who return to college struggle to balance career and personal needs. The "sandwich generation"—that is, adults who care for both aging parents and young children—endeavor to strike a balance between job and family demands.

The so-called mid-life crisis usually occurs in relation to, and as a result of, these various demands. At this stage, individuals often question their identity, self-esteem, confidence, and direction in life. The mid-life crisis can be especially problematic if a person has identified more with his work, profession, job, and career than with other supportive but nonwork-related values, principles, interests, and people.[18] The mid-life crisis is exacerbated by the lack of a balanced lifestyle.

**Middle adulthood** usually occurs in one's fifties. Individuals begin to focus on the present and future more than on their past. At this stage, they are very productive. They settle in and attempt to make a significant impact in their work. They consolidate their individual activities and accept their limitations. They seek to mentor and serve as role models. Employees at this stage, however, may face age discrimination and other tensions in the changing workplace: new technology and training requirements, increased travel, and longer working hours. Balancing one's ability to contribute and adjust to new workplace demands can present major challenges during this life phase.

**Late adulthood** is a transition into retirement or another career. With extended life spans for men and women in the United States, individuals at this stage can again explore new personal and work alternatives. Organizational issues can involve exiting and reentry challenges as well as issues regarding how to exit with honor and financial independence.

The point here is that effectively managing self and others in organizations involves understanding both personal and career developmental issues. Working with and managing people (and oneself) in their forties and fifties involves dealing with life issues that are different from those of people in their twenties and thirties.

## New Passages

Gail Sheehy, in her book *New Passages: Mapping Your Life Across Time* (New York: Random House, 1995), reviews the "map of adult life" and argues (page 4) that *there is a revolution in the life cycle . . . . Puberty arrives earlier by several years than it did at the turn of the century. Adolescence is now prolonged for the middle class until the end of the twenties and for blue-collar men and women until the mid-twenties, as more young adults live at home longer. True adulthood doesn't begin until 30. . . . Middle age has already been pushed into the fifties. . . . Fifty is now what 40 used to be."*

Sheehy updates the traditional life cycle as follows:

Provisional Adulthood (18–30)

First Adulthood (30–45)

Age of Mastery (45–65)

Second Adulthood (45–85)

Age of Integrity (65–85+)

An insight that Sheehy's research reveals is that there is a second adulthood for individuals. This "new passage" now requires different attitudes and skills since life has been extended.

In referring to each life stage being prolonged by a decade, Sheehy quotes a psychotherapist she interviewed who suggested the effects of these age shifts (page 13):

- *Do you know how to be 30 and still living with Mom?*

- *Do you know how to be 40 and single and still unfulfilled?*

- *Do you know how to be a forced retiree at 50?*

- *Do you know how to be a cancer survivor who seeks work and a new dream at 60?*

- *Do you know how to be a man today?*

Sheehy's thesis is supported by interviews and existing statistical surveys. Criticism regarding her arguments attack her sample, which was limited mostly to the middle class. Nevertheless, Sheehy's observations and analysis raise challenging career and work questions for each age group. Her book also suggests that entrepreneurial career planning in a rapidly changing society must be an endeavor responsibly managed by participants in each age group.

### Career Stages as Continuous Learning

Another shift in the new careers thinking is that "the career of the 21st century is not measured by chronological age and life stages, but by continuous learning and identity changes. Rather than think of a career as made up of a lifelong series of developmental stages . . . we will regard the 21st century career as a series of short learning stages. . . . "[19] For example, a person will go through *several* developmental phases characterized as exploration-trial-establishment-mastery series of learning experiences. What will be most important is career age (i.e., a professional's work challenges, experiences, and relationships—continuous learning—across organizations).

Traditionally, the chronological age (of the person) has been used to determine developmental turning points in the person's life. Since *learn-how* is becoming as important as *know-how* as a key competency, a person's career age is a more meaningful indicator to organizations and to her professional self-understanding than her chronological age development. Moreover, "The new career contract is not a pact with the organization; it is an agreement with one's self and one's work. The path to the top has been replaced by the path with a heart."[20]

### Career Development and Management

From an individual's perspective, career development requires active planning and managing. Failure to manage a career can lead to negative consequences: stress, unacceptable work attitudes, professional plateauing, and poor quality of life.[21] In this section we begin by explaining career management and career anchors.

In addition to the earlier definition of career, a career is also the pattern of work-related experiences that span the course of a person's life.[22] Effective career planning and management require active and deliberate decision making to direct and enhance the fit between needs, values, and the organizational opportunities, as stated previously. Career management involves planning activities that begin with structured self-assessments (e.g., the Myers-Briggs test) and end with a self-awareness of one's needs and environment. This process, described in detail later in the chapter, requires gathering information, goal setting, exploring career opportunities, and obtaining work and nonwork feedback from expert and experienced sources such as mentors, friends, and associates.[23] A helpful career management and organizing tool is the concept of career anchors.

### Career Anchors

Choosing a career is influenced by an individual's **career anchor**—that is, "the self-image that a person develops around his or her career, which both guides and constrains career decisions."[24] Defining one's career anchor can assist in making one's career choices and decisions regarding how specific career needs fit with family, personal goals, type of industry or company one is interested in, and the nature of the work one should be doing. Ed Shein, of MIT and author of *Career Anchors Concept*, noted, "The concept of career anchor becomes especially applicable in today's turbulent world as more and more people are laid off and have to figure out what to do next in their lives." Table 13–2 lists the different types of career anchors and how preferred work, pay, promotion system, and type of recognition are addressed in each of them.

A well-defined career anchor addresses the following questions: What are my talents, skills, areas of competence? What are my strengths and weaknesses? What are my main motives, drives, and goals in life? What am I after? What are my values, the main criteria by which I judge what I am doing? Am I in the right type of organization or job? How good do I feel about what I am doing?[25]

A person's responses to these questions can assist in identifying his primary career direction, and making this identification can often explain a person's match or mismatch with a profession in an industry and with an organization. It is not

**TABLE 13–2    Features of Career Anchors**

| Career Anchor | Preferred Work | Preferred Pay and Benefits | Preferred Promotion | Preferred Recognition |
|---|---|---|---|---|
| Security, stability | Predictable and stable, concerned about context over content of work | Pay based on years of service, insurance and retirement programs | Seniority | Loyalty and steady performance |
| Autonomy, independence | Contract or project work, low supervision with clearly defined goals | Pay based on performance; cafeteria style choice of benefits | Performance | Medals, awards, testimonials, etc. |
| Technical, functional | Challenging and interesting work, low supervision with clear goals, little or no administrative or managerial work | Skill and education-based pay; in par with peers outside company; cafeteria style benefits | Professional promotional ladder paralleling the managerial ladder | Opportunities for self-development, peer recognition |
| Managerial | High challenge, responsible, varied, and integrative; prefers leadership | Pay on par with peers in the company; bonuses and retirement programs | Performance | Promotions and monetary |
| Entrepreneurial | Creative and variable, with new opportunities | Ownership | Flexible | Personal visibility and public recognition |
| Service orientation | Satisfies personal values, helping people | Fair pay and portable benefits | Performance | Recognition from peers and superiors |
| Challenge | Very competitive, increasing levels of challenges | Rewards winning | Performance | Public recognition |

| | | TABLE 13-2 Features of Career Anchors , cont. | | |
|---|---|---|---|---|
| Career Anchor | Preferred Work | Preferred Pay and Benefits | Preferred Promotion | Preferred Recognition |
| Lifestyle | Balance between personal and professional life; flexibility | Allows integration of personal, family, and professional concerns | Flexible | Consideration for personal and family commitments |

SOURCE: Based on E.H. Schein, "Individuals and Careers," in *Handbook of Organizational Behavior*, ed. J.W. Lorsch (Englewood Cliffs, N.J.: Prentice-Hall, 1987), 155–171.

uncommon, for example, for entrepreneurs to discover their dissatisfaction with traditional, noncreative managerial positions they have taken or to which they have been promoted or for "hands-on" technicians to be promoted to administrators and later discover that they have lost their sense of motivation. Understanding one's career anchor(s) is a starting point for developing and managing one's career.

### Career Anchor Changes

Ed Schein has noted some changes in career anchors. First, *employment security* has changed to *employability security,*(i.e., the shift is from dependence on the organization to oneself.) Second, a person's concern for *lifestyle* to *life system* has changed. Because of a growing number of dual career situations, couples are integrating their lives and careers into a larger life system. As Schein noted, "more individuals will begin dual career situations, they will think, plan, and act more as social units, and organizations will have to consider how to maintain support systems for such units in the form of child care, job sharing opportunities, part-time work, sabbaticals, and other adaptive modifications of the traditional 9 to 5 job."[26] Third, there will always be a need for those who have technical/functional competence as a primary career anchor. However, given the rapid acceleration of new technologies, Schein says that "to remain *technically/functionally competent* will require constant updating and relearning in an organizational world that will not bear the costs in terms of money and time." Individual technical and functional experts will have to negotiate with organizations to obtain necessary continuous training in their fields. Fourth, regarding the *general management competence*," Schein noted, "General management, like leadership, may cease to be a role or a position, and will become more of a process skill that will be needed in kinds of roles and positions." Fifth, individuals with *entrepreneurial creativity* will find matches in new companies. This orientation and competency are presently in great demand. Sixth, an increasing number of individuals have the *service/dedication to a cause* competency as a primary career anchor. Individuals who share this anchor in combination with the entrepreneurial anchor are creating new organizations that address environmental, health, and welfare issues in society. Seventh, a smaller number of individuals who have the *pure challenge* competency as their primary anchor will continue to face the challenge of having to analyze themselves to figure out what kind of job is available or will evolve to satisfy their need. We add that in the Internet Age and the Information Age, which are evolving, technically competent individuals with a pure challenge competency are also in demand, especially as all sizes of companies evolve their operations into some form of E-business transactions.

## Developmental Career Stages and Issues

Individuals often find that they will pass through at least four stages in their careers as Table 13–3 indicates: establishment, advancement, maintenance, and retirement.[27] **Establishment** marks the beginning of one's career. At this stage, an individual obtains a first job, learns the ropes, develops skills and abilities, and initiates contacts and a network. An individual must take charge of her career at this initial stage. Guidance at this stage includes attention to picking a company where one can build a broad range of skills, looking for the employer's toughest problems and making oneself part of the solution, learning how to work in teams, building a network of contacts inside and outside the company, and keeping one's eyes open for opportunities elsewhere."[28] Getting coaching and finding a mentor are helpful during this stage as one navigates through career options. Reading, assessing, and responding to one's fit with an organization are crucial during this phase.

During the **advancement** stage, a person pursues increased independence and responsibility. Advancement through career paths can occur within or across different organizations and jobs as the person seeks opportunities to match and extend his skills and needs. Promotions are important during this period to gain the opportunity to handle more responsibility that, in turn, creates opportunity for further advancement.

The third stage, **maintenance**, is characterized by continued performance, development, and creativity. Stabilizing and self-actualizing oneself and one's accomplishments are characteristics during this stage. However, this stage also corresponds with the mid-life crisis. Increased anxiety and health problems can occur if a person's career plateaus too early, if she is laid off or demoted, or if she decides to leave a secure position to explore new or different career opportunities.

Reaching a *career plateau* is a common obstacle during this maintenance stage.[29] Career plateauing happens when a person can no longer be promoted because fewer, if any, positions are available. Career interventions that may be helpful if and when one reaches a career plateau include organizational and self-assessments, individual counseling, job posting programs, career resource centers, and outplacement programs. Hewlett-Packard, Coca-Cola, CBS, Aetna, AT&T, Exxon, and General Electric use some or all of these types of services.[30] Hewlett-Packard uses a self-assessment system that has employees complete workshops and meet with career counselors. Aetna, CBS, and General Electric offer employees job posting services and career resource centers; AT&T, IBM, Kodak, and Ford provide testing and counseling services to familiarize employees with their skills and aptitudes so as to enhance their placement into prospective positions.

| TABLE 13–3   Career Stages and Issues | | | | |
|---|---|---|---|---|
| Life Stage | Establishment, 17–25 | Advancement, 26–39 | Maintenance, 40–59 | Retirement, 60+ |
| Work-related demands | Obtaining job-related skills and knowledge | Becoming an independent contributor | Developing the skills of others | Sharing work experiences with others |
| Primary psychological needs | Depending on others for rewards | Depending on self for rewards | Depending on others for need satisfaction | Letting go of work identity |
| Primary need fulfillment | Security | Achievement, autonomy | Esteem | Self-neutralization, self-revitalization |

SOURCE: Based on D. T. Hall, *Careers in Organizations* (Santa Monica, Calif.: Goodyear, 1975). See also J. Gibson, J. Ivancevich, and J. Donnelly, Jr., *Organizations, Behavior, Structure, Processes,* 8th ed. (Burr Ridge, Ill.: Irwin, 1994).

During the last career stage, **retirement**, an individual approaches and accepts withdrawal from an organization. The individual may at this stage pursue alternative careers or career activities on a part-time basis. Because of the active and increasing life span, retired and professionally competent individuals often seek ways to contribute knowledge, skills, and wisdom in the marketplace—they will not be alone in this endeavor.

### Workforce Diversity, Careers, and Organizational Responses

Although the list of companies that proactively address diversity as a competitive advantage changes, recent organizations such as Union Bank of California, Fannie Mae, Public Service Company of New Mexico, Sempra Energy, Lucent Technologies, and Wal-Mart are actively responding to the career issues of the changing, more diverse workforce by providing financial rewards and incentives, structured mentoring, flexible work schedules, financial assistance, job sharing, subsidies and grants, child care, additional training and workshops, and leave for parents and people helping elderly family members.[31]

**Career mentoring** has been shown to play an important role in early career promotion and in general work and career satisfaction. It generally can provide emotional support to newcomers, especially to individuals from a different cultural background who may be unfamiliar with a company's environment, by introducing individuals to persons in power and helping the individuals get into professional associations and other career-related networks.

Many new employees or those from different cultures do not seek mentors. Individuals who do (i.e., the protegées) usually have higher needs for power and achievement; one study also indicated that protegées influenced the amount of mentoring received. The following personality characteristics were also found to enhance the initiation of protegées; internal locus of control, high self-monitoring, and high emotional stability.[32] These characteristics also mediated the relationships with the amount of mentoring received. One certainty exists for protegées: they must find mentors and develop relationships; mentors seldom seek protegées.

Some experts do not recommend assigned or formal mentoring,[33] but organizations can enhance the mentoring process and programs with culturally diverse workforces, in particular, in the following ways:

- Select mentors carefully to ensure that they are genuinely committed and good at development.

- Involve protegées in creating matches.

- Provide organizational incentives for being a mentor.

- Provide training for both mentors and protegées.

- Establish some formal mechanism to monitor progress of the relationships and to evaluate their effectiveness.[34]

The various types of planned interventions and programs (i.e., mentoring, flextime, family leave, job sharing, and childcare facilities) can facilitate the integration of culturally diverse people into the workforce.

## CAREER PLANNING IN A CHANGING WORKPLACE: A PRACTICAL APPROACH

Career planning and management are continuous, lifelong individual and organizational processes.[35] As environments and organizations change, individuals must continuously plan and update their goals and planning efforts. It is estimated that people in general people will change careers at least three times during their lives.

Career planning at the organizational level helps companies select, hire, and retain qualified people who will benefit the organization's mission, work, and effectiveness. Career planning for individuals helps people match their professional and emotional needs and abilities with an industry and organization.

Career management also involves the implementation of career plans by both organizations and individuals. Organizations must meet governmental as well as market and industry requirements in implementing human resource hiring and development plans. Individuals manage their careers by searching and interviewing with companies and then by updating and advancing their career development options.

The concept of individual organization fit is a two-way process. From an organization's point of view, this process requires that the human resource staff plan and manage the organization's legal, technical, and work requirements. For example, job skill requirements and recruitment and hiring needs must be identified, affirmative action and diversity programs must be planned and implemented, and

## THE CHANGING WORKPLACE

### Ethical Questions

**Exercise**: Read the following and answer the questions.

**Step 1**: Bill always wants to keep his options open. He spends several hours a week talking to headhunters while at work. He claims there is no real loyalty between employers and employees these days. If downsizing were necessary and he were targeted, he would be laid off—no questions asked. Therefore, he argues, he has to protect his own future interests, even on company time. Do you agree?

**Step 2**: Louise is approaching 60 but performs as well as anyone in her group. A 25-year-old recent graduate with less experience and expertise was recently hired and placed over Louise. Louise believes the vice president she reports to is sending her a message regarding retirement. Louise has no proof of this; however, the pressure and humiliation she feels are affecting her morale and work production. What, if anything, should she do? Whose problem, if there is one, is this?

**Step 3**: You recently went after and received an advertised job you wanted. You did not represent yourself accurately on your resume however. The company is known for its openness and high ethical standing among customers, suppliers, and other firms in the industry. Another person in the company, you have discovered, is familiar with your background. If that person found out about the exaggeration on your resume, you could face some consequences. You're wondering if you should go to the hiring manager and tell the truth, keep quiet and see what happens, or have a confidential talk with your acquaintance. What would you do? Why?

employee reward and compensation benefits must be determined. For individuals, personality and motivational career needs, desires, and requirements must be identified, understood, and matched with organizational opportunities and systems.

### The Changing Workplace and the Worker

We have discussed throughout this book the characteristics of the changing workplace and the changing workforce: the effects of the Internet on E-business and new company start-ups, downsizing and streamlining; professionals having to do more with less; flatter and more geographically dispersed organizational structures; jobs defined as assignments with fewer titles and more cross-functional responsibility; younger individuals, more women, minorities, and culturally diverse people in the workforce; and the growing importance of generalist/specialist knowledge workers. The issue ultimately focuses on the effects these changes have on career planning and management from an organizational and individual perspective.

Gene Dalton, a partner at the Novations Group, a Utah career management consultancy, addresses three changes in career planning and management. He states,

*You no longer have a choice; the old path is gone. Companies used reengineering to jack-hammer out the middle-manager staircase, and now rely on computers to gather and analyze information. Second, businesses have redrawn their boundaries, making them both tight (as they focus on core competencies) and porous (as they outsource noncore work). As a result, work follows a contractor-subcontractor model, not one of vertical integration. The third change is of scale. Project-based (vs. position-based) work has been the norm for decades in industries like construction, Hollywood, and many professional services. . . . Life in the projects has profound implications for careers. "There are basically four levels, and four types of career," says Frank Walker, president of GTW Corp. [a Seattle-based, Microsoft alliance that sells project-management consulting services and software]. . . . In Walker's schematic, the top level sets strategy: It is the land of CEOs, presidents, and executive VPs. Few people live there. Next come resource providers, who develop and supply talent and money; they are the CFOs [chief financial officers] and CIOs [chief information officers], human resources managers, or VPs of marketing or engineering who manage staffs of experts. Third, project managers; they buy or lease money and people from the resource providers and put them to work. Fourth is the talent—chemists, finance guys, candlestick makers—who may report to a functional boss but spend much of their time on project teams.[36]*

John Kotter at Harvard Business School (HBS) describes the lives and careers of 115 members of the HBS whom he tracked for 20 years. This successful group had a median 1994 income of $220,000, a median net worth of $1.2 million, and 85 percent stated that they were satisfied with their family lives. This may not be a representative sample of the United States or world business graduates, but Kotter's findings and lessons can apply to the larger population. Kotter concluded that the successful members of his study followed (consciously or unplanned) the following rules:[37]

- Do not rely on convention; career paths that were winners for most of this century are often no longer providing much success.

- Keep your eyes on globalization and its consequences.

- Move toward the small and entrepreneurial and away from the big and bureaucratic.

- Help big business from the outside as well as on the inside (i.e., you can find opportunity selling services to downsized big companies, but gaining equity is easier in smaller ones).

- Do not just manage; now you must also lead.

- Wheel and deal if you can.

- Increase your competitive drive.

- Never stop trying to grow; lifelong learning is increasingly necessary for success.

Given these trends, the issue becomes how an individual can plan a career in such a changing environment. We present a model for doing this next.

## A Practical Career Planning and Management Model

Classical career planning and management logic suggests a step-by-step process. These steps, revised here to include a change perspective, include the following:

**Step 1.** Obtain individual assessments and feedback: Know your strengths, weaknesses, and what you really want to be and do. Identify your aptitudes and abilities, personality styles and characteristics, work and job preferences, and strengths and weaknesses. Take tests, such as the Myers-Briggs discussed in Chapter 2; seek professional career guidance. Know your needs and what does and does not motivate you. This process must be updated. Your personality will probably not change, but your work and job preferences will.

**Step 2.** Develop a written career plan: Know where you want to go. Based on the information from Step 1, develop long- and short-term goals, objectives, and action steps with a specific industry (or industries) and even company, job, or project in mind. See yourself as a marketable "product." Develop a resume that captures your strengths, competencies, and work experiences. Keep your information on a word processor; you will probably be editing the information to fit positions to your profile. Develop a timeframe to implement your plan. This process must be continuous and updated. You may change careers as well as organizations and jobs. It has been predicted that upwardly mobile individuals may change careers at least three times during their work lives.

**Step 3.** Do a market search of job and project opportunities. Keep current on market opportunities. Survey the environment in the industry (or industries) and companies that match the criteria you developed in Steps 1 and 2. Use databases and implement your network. Search for challenging but temporary projects if you cannot find a permanent job or position. Project excellence can lead to more permanent work.

**Step 4.** Implement your search by getting online! Continue to network by locating, interviewing, and obtaining a desirable position, job, or project assignment. Put your research into action. There are many helpful online job sites: monster.com is currently one of the best. Posting your résumé on the Web is one way to introduce your skills to multitudes. Obtain leads from friends, professors, and people in the industry from your contacts. Find the best fit between the information of Steps 1 and 2 with the results of Step 3. Look for opportunities, assignments, and projects, not a job. People can help you if you are focused but, at the same time, do not pigeonhole yourself. Short-term opportunities can turn into careers. Do not seek perfection or complete congruence with written or official policies; once you get into an organization, things change. You may actually find expanded (or limited) opportunity. Calculated risk is the key in a changing and rapidly shifting environment.

**Step 5.** Continuously update your résumé (online and off); evaluate and monitor your actual job/position/project progress against your plan and current goals. Update and use your network, contacts, and career plan to test your satisfaction, growth, and development against your current employment situation. Look ahead as well as at present conditions. Are you on track with your personal needs and vision? With your salary and compensation growth? With your long-term goals? With the market?

**Step 6**. Make changes and adjustments. Many people stop at this step. Keep current. To grow, change, and progress in any career, you must make changes if the current situation does not meet your needs and goals. You may locate opportunities in the market that are more appropriate. Use professional career counseling services and search capabilities and maintain a network of career contacts; all of these can help in making job/organizational changes.

**Step 7**. Be entrepreneurial. Consider joining or starting a small company or venture with other experts or knowledgeable professionals. Do personal research on fields of interest that excite you and contact experts in those fields. Thinking and acting creatively and responsibly are essential in effective career planning.

### The Acid Test

Use the following new signs of trouble as guidelines to gauge whether a present job, position, or assignment is meeting your near-term and longer-term career needs:

- Are you learning? If you cannot say clearly what you have learned in the last six months or what you expect to learn in the next, you may be stagnating and could be on the road to replacement anyway.

- If your job were open, would you get it? This is a way of benchmarking your skills. Are you current or falling behind on skills that ads require for your type of job?

- Are you being milked? Are you sacrificing your long-term growth for short-term employer demands that use your time and capital without a significant return? If so, it may be time to move on.

- Do you know what you contribute? If you can't answer this question in a concise, two-minute summary, neither can your boss. What are you doing in your work?

- What would you do if your job disappeared? You may have lost your competitive edge if you cannot answer this question. You may try to sell yourself inside your organization. Will your skills sell?

- Are you having fun yet? If your heart is not in your work, you will probably not accept new challenges.

- Are you worried about your job? If not, maybe you should be.[38]

The current market environment in most industries is more dynamic, more competitive, and more uncertain than ever before. Learning to learn, adapt, and change are career survival necessities.

## CONCLUDING COMMENTS

Careers consist of significant experiences and learnings that identify an individual's professional life, direction, competencies, and accomplishments through positions, jobs, roles, and assignments. Because of growing international markets, global competitiveness, changing workplace demographics, and organizational reengineering, careers are reflecting the focus on individuals becoming both specialists and generalists, more self-reliant, and more connected through teams. There is also a trend away from large, bureaucratic organizations toward smaller, entrepreneurial companies.

Career planning and management involve a seven-step process: (1) obtain individual assessments and feedback; (2) develop a written career plan; (3) do a market job and project opportunity search; (4) implement an online search; (5) continuously update your resume and evaluate and monitor actual job/position/project status against current goals; (6) make changes and adjustments; and (7) be entreprenurial.

Organizational socialization is a necessary component of career development. Through the socialization process, people adapt and adjust to organizations. This process includes getting in, breaking in, and settling in. Organizations can assist individuals in this process by explaining realistic job expectations and responsibilities at the outset, by giving and receiving thoughtful feedback on technical and social adaptation—or maladaptation—to the organization, and by providing individuals with opportunities to continue improving their skills to grow professionally.

Individual development stages correspond to career stages. Both types of stages should be considered by individuals in identifying productivity and motivational opportunities and issues throughout their careers. (Organizations should consider these stages as well.) Individual developmental stages include young adulthood, adulthood, middle adulthood, and late adulthood. Career stages include establishment, advancement, maintenance, and retirement or revitalization.

Organizations can integrate culturally diverse workforces through a number of interventions and programs: mentoring, flexible work schedules, job sharing, subsidies and grants, child care, training workshops, and parental leaves.

Each individual must assess his career needs and accomplishments against the fit with the organization. Employed individuals can ask the following questions in addressing career advancement issues: Are you learning? If your job were open, could you get it again? Do you know what you are contributing? What would/could you do if your job disappeared? Are you having fun in your work/projects?

## SCENARIO AND EXERCISE: THE .COM INTERVIEW

**Exercise:** Read the following scenario, which involves you.

You've just introduced yourself to Bill, a staff member at Zip.com, whom you followed to a small room inside the 15-employee, six-month-old software firm that is a spin-off from, and supported by, a Fortune 500 company. You're excited about the possibility of working with this new venture. You want to learn e-business skills and have a chance to obtain stock before the company goes public. Bill seems nice and the place really looks and feels informal; everyone passing by is wearing jeans. You feel prepared since you've read a book on interviewing. After some small talk, Bill hands you a bag of Legos® and informs you that you have eight minutes to build whatever you want, and he'll be back to discuss what you did.

**Step 1:**

(a) Write your initial impressions and reactions to this experience and request.
(b) Think and describe *in detail* here what you would build (hurry; you have only several minutes).

**Step 2:** Bill comes back into the room. Explain to him, as if you were actually talking to him in the interview setting, what you built (write *exactly* what you would say).

**Step 3:** What do you think Bill was looking for from this exercise? (Write a paragraph.) How do you believe you did on this exercise: (a) excellently, (b) OK, (c) average, (d) not well? Why? Write your reasons briefly.

**Step 4:** Consult the **Scenario Key** to gauge your responses to this exercise.

### Scenario Key

A recent article in *The Boston Globe* ("Games, Brainteasers That Can Get You a Job," 9 Jan. 2000) noted that "employers obsessed with teamwork, creativity, say old-fashioned interviews alone just don't cut it." Ravi (a 23-year-old Harvard University graduate) was somewhat shocked when he applied for a job at an Internet solutions firm in Boston. He was initially asked to perform the same exercise described in the exercise you just completed. Ravi constructed an "aerated cognac snifter and then explained its functional and aesthetic qualities." His creativity and ingenuity landed him a consultant's job in the firm's dot-com division.

While traditional interviews are still alive, the article continued, "in the fast-paced world of the Internet, those seeking work as consultants and computer programmers are being asked to solve mathematical equations, brainteasers, or riddles, and to participate in group games and exercises that test a candidate's ability to collaborate and think under pressure." You may find yourself in such an interview, regardless of the position. An employee of a firm that develops recruiting and interviewing strategies for Internet start-ups noted that "many of the CEOs we work for are between 28 and 34; they want to hire clones of themselves. They want people with off-the-shelf energy, wit, and intelligence. They want cowboys—people who don't necessarily follow the rules, who question everything." Because of strong competition, time compression, and the need to think, create, work, and produce in "Internet time," candidates must be able to think and move quickly, effectively, and collaboratively.

Creativity, ingenuity, off-the-shelf and out-of-the-box thinking, leadership ability, ability to work collaboratively in teams, and how you treat and manage people up and down the food chain (from secretaries to the CEO) are some of the indicators new venture owners and CEOs look for in their hires.

### Reflection

**Step 1**: Indicate here, after reading the preceding section, how you believe you performed with your Legos®. Answer on the following dimensions. *Place a checkmark beside each dimension.*

|                          | Excellently | OK  | Average | Poorly |
|--------------------------|-------------|-----|---------|--------|
| 1. Creativity            | ___         | ___ | ___     | ___    |
| 2. Ingenuity             | ___         | ___ | ___     | ___    |
| 3. Off-the-shelf thinking| ___         | ___ | ___     | ___    |

**Step 2**: Return to Step 3 of the earlier exercise and compare your evaluation there to your evaluation here. Any similarities? Differences? Briefly explain why.

**Step 3**: What is your reaction to this entire exercise? Would you like interviewing and then working at a company like this? Explain. What insights about yourself (needs, personality, motivation, and job and type of organization preferences) did you gain from this exercise? Explain.

## REVIEW QUESTIONS

1. Identify a contemporary force in the marketplace that has affected or is affecting your own career thinking and actions.

2. What does a career mean to you? Identify some characteristics of what a satisfying, exciting career would be for you.

3. How would you describe yourself in terms of your present career profile (as a student or professional) regarding the four dimensions in Figure 13–1: specialist, connected, generalist, self-reliant? Explain.

4. Describe a job you have held in which you experienced the socialization processes of getting in, breaking in, and settling in. How (un)successful were

you at each stage? What were the forces that helped or hindered you in each of these phases? What did you learn about your own career process and direction from these phases in your example?

5. How would you characterize the current phase in your individual development life cycle? What issues do you face in this stage?

6. How would you characterize your primary and secondary career anchor?

7. Describe (write or list) the process you are currently using to prepare yourself for employment or job hunting. After you have done this, compare what you wrote to the section in the chapter on A Practical Career Planning and Management Model (7 steps). What did your comparison show? Did you have any ideas or insights?

8. Briefly draft your responses to the last section of the chapter, The Acid Test. Share your responses with a classmate. Record your insights and reactions.

9. Write a paragraph describing the advice that you would offer a friend in her thinking about a career. Assume that she will also want advice on entering the job market. Offer some advice on how she might plan to proceed.

# 14 Organizing and Managing Change

---

## LEARNING OBJECTIVES

After studying this chapter, you should be able to:

**1** Identify the forces for change on organizations.

**2** Describe success factors for organizational change.

**3** Explain resistance factors to change.

**4** Discuss organizational change models.

**5** Identify methods for facilitating change.

**6** Discuss ethical issues involved in organizational change.

---

## *THE TECHNOLOGY REVOLUTION*

Organizations are facing unprecedented competition and change, as the following excerpt shows.

> *Somewhere out there is a bullet with your company's name on it. Somewhere out there is a competitor, unborn and unknown, that will render your business model obsolete. Bill Gates knows that. When he says that Microsoft is always two years away from failure, he's not just blowing smoke at Janet Reno. He knows that competition today is not between products, it's between business models. He knows that irrelevancy is a bigger risk than inefficiency. And what's true for Microsoft is true for just about every other company: The hottest and most dangerous new business models out there are on the Web.[1]*

There is growing consensus that the Internet will change everything: "the Web will fundamentally change customers' expectations about convenience, speed, comparability, price, and service."[2] Essentially, the Internet : (1) has turned many business models into **auctions** as e-Bay pioneered the way, (2) has **ended geography** as we knew it—Amazon.com sells 20 percent of its books to foreign destinations, (3) has made **search (versus distribution) economies** the rule by bundling products together in one location, (4) has made the **customer the focus** with convenience, availability, and speed of delivery the major competitive advantages—"My place, my time" is the mantra of evaluating E-commerce, (5) has toppled monopolies by emphasizing the ubiquity of **innovation, information, and service** in a Net-centric world. Customers are not tied to TV commercials or traditional means of getting information, products, or services. To compete, businesses have to go to customers with the newest, most appealing, and best they have to offer.[3] The E-business revolution is here.

Organizations, consequently, are changing rapidly and dramatically on an international scale. A survey of 12,000 managers in 25 countries stated that international expansion, reduction in employment, mergers, divestitures, acquisitions, and major restructuring characterized the types of changes they have recently experienced. Because information technologies and the Internet are linking customers, suppliers, and vendors to companies and employees, bricks-and-mortar businesses are being transformed by clicks with and without mortar—every industry is affected by this revolution.

## EXTERNAL FORCES AND PRESSURES FOR CHANGE

Other external forces, in addition to technology, influencing change on organization include the following:

- **Globalization**. The fall of the Berlin Wall and many forms of Communism have opened new markets and economies. The formation of the European Union with a common currency has created another new competitive trading group. Japan and Germany continue to bring innovative products and competition to international markets. The global market has influenced the rise of the "boundaryless" organization. Mergers and acquisitions across national regions have made transnational corporations the organizational model of the twenty-first century. In addition, start-ups as well as small, medium, and large companies have immediate access to global customers and partners on the Web.

- **Workforce diversity**. New and diverse entrants to the U.S. workforce, such as women, Hispanic-Americans, African-Americans, and other international professionals, continue to increase, as discussed in earlier chapters. The U.S. workforce also is changing in terms of an aging population, a mix of educational levels (higher and less educated members), and a "braindrain" as the number of needed technical professionals shrinks.[4] Integrating workforce diversity and finding scarce technical "brainpower" present competitive advantages and challenges to organizations in this century.

- **Managing and working legally, responsibly, and ethically**. As organizations evolve, merge, and integrate technologies, acting legally and socially responsible will present more challenges. Problems and lawsuits regarding environmental pollution, sexual harassment, manufacturing and selling dangerous products, engaging in questionable child labor practices, and unfair treatment of employees and community stakeholders pose serious change management problems. Many companies and their leaders have and enforce ethical codes of conduct, but many more do not. The media, government agencies, and local communities are more informed and are working with corporations to expose as well as manage unethical practices.

Taken together, technology, globalization, workforce diversity, and managing ethically pressure organizations to meet their stakeholders' and stockholders' expectations of doing the right thing as well as doing things the right way.

## PLANNED AND UNPLANNED CHANGE

Many of the changes that affect industries and organizations are both unplanned and planned. The effects on organizations of rapid new technology diffusion, changing workforce demographics and diversity, government regulation or deregulation, and shifting national boundaries and ideologies are **unplanned**. However, changes in organizational strategies, structure, technologies, products, and services aimed at effectively responding to shifts in the environment can be **planned**. We have been concerned with planned changes throughout this book and with the models, approaches, and concepts that can affect organizational behavior by design instead of by chance.

## PREPARING FOR PLANNED CHANGE

Assume that you are a manager in a medium-sized manufacturing firm that increased sales 12 percent annually over the last 10 years until last year when the sales figures showed a significant slump. Corporate staff has met with you and other selected managers and informed all of you that 10 percent of the workforce must be cut, systems streamlined, costs reduced, and revenues increased. In addition, the company is losing market share and new markets to competitors who are organizing, communicating, and selling on the Web. Unless this company streamlines, refocuses, and uses Internet technologies to expand geographically, it is in serious trouble. You are now part of a task force to examine the organization's current systems and readiness and resistance for change and then to report back with a plan and ideas on changing the company to meet these new requirements. Where do you begin?

Jack Welch, change champion at GE, was handed a similar mandate several years ago. He began by defining two business priorities for GE:

> We have two basic premises. The first is that we will run only businesses that are number one and number two in their global markets—or, in the case of services that have a substantial position—and are of scale and potential appropriate to a $50 billion enterprise.
> The second premise is that in addition to the strength, resources, and reach of a big company, which we have already built, we are committed to developing the sensitivity, the leanness, the simplicity, and the agility of a small company. We want the best of both.[5]

Welch then set out to accomplish this vision by changing GE's strategy (selling and closing $10 billion of product lines and businesses), restructuring and flattening the company, and transforming its culture and systems. By 1991, revenue, earnings, and productivity had grown by 3 to 4 percent. Shareholders received a 38 percent return that same year, with an 8 percent dividend increase. By 1999, Welch had made the number 1 ranking for two consecutive years on America's Most Admired Companies published in *Fortune.* He has managed to transform GE with every new turn of technology, market competitiveness, innovation, and responsible management.[6]

It is not only the GEs of the world that must change; small- and medium-sized companies must also implement planned changes in their companies to survive and be competitive. As you read this chapter, think of the approaches that would best fit the situation of a firm for which you work or have worked or are familiar with; or think of GE's example. As a task force member, your job is to suggest where to begin planning a major change effort with your company. Use an approach and concepts that will help your planning effort.

This chapter presents several models for diagnosing and studying behavior and change that affect organizations and individuals externally and internally. These frameworks have been used throughout the text and are referenced here regarding large-scale change. Some of the models complement and extend those presented in Chapter 1. These frameworks (1) provide a holistic approach for studying organizations as interactive systems, internally and with the environment; (2) are dynamic—that is they include the process of change and innovation; and (3) view individuals and groups as intentional actors whose values and activities effect change. We also return to the questions that we have confronted throughout the text: Change for what, whom, and toward what end? Diagnosis for what, whom, and toward what end? Characteristics of exemplary organizations and high-performance members are offered as success factors (i.e., milestones of excellence) for addressing this question: What are organizations striving for and what should they strive for?

### Success Factors for Planned Change

*Effectiveness* is doing the right thing; *efficiency* is doing things right. High-performance organizations and members are both effective and efficient. As stated in Chapter 1, high-performance organizations empower their teams and employees in their learning and performing. No one success factor or standard, company, team, or individual can illustrate to us the most successful or effective style for change. There are many, and some change as global competition, technologies, environments, and industry standards change. The following discussion of organizational success factors—taken from peer reviews of leading companies and research in this area—illustrates standards of excellence that companies can use as a benchmark to measure their change efforts.

*Fortune* magazine annually asks companies to rank firms in their industry on eight attributes: (1) quality of management, (2) quality of product or service, (3) innovativeness, (4) value as a long-term investment, (5) financial soundness, (6) ability to attract, develop, and keep talented people, (7) community and environmental responsibilities, and (8) use of corporate assets.[7] As mentioned, these attributes serve as benchmarks for companies striving to meet and exceed standards that their peers and competitors select as indicators of excellence. The list of most admired companies changes annually. Several companies have appeared on the list many times, changing only in rank—GE, Microsoft, Dell Computer, Intel, Merck, Southwest Airlines, Wal-Mart, and Motorola, to name a few.

In addition to these attributes, the following success factors, taken from a number of leading academic and business publications, also are characteristics of organizational effectiveness:

- Externally focused; market-driven

- Customer-centered

- Strategically networked with business alliances

- Mobilized toward a shared vision

- Focused on creating value in products and services

- Committed to positive continuous learning and continual change

- Determined to fulfill ethical responsibilities to all stakeholders (customers, employees, suppliers, society)

- Committed to measuring progress against world-class standards of excellence

Two companies that continue to excel according to these factors are GE and Ford.

### GE: A Profile

General Electric has many products (aircraft engines, electric motors, lighting, locomotives, factory automation, medical diagnostic imaging) that consistently rank among the top production of the United States and the world in terms of quality and competitiveness. The GE Value Statement lists the following business characteristics:

- Lean: Reduce tasks and the people required to do them to develop world-cost leadership.

- Agile or de-layered: Create fast decision making in a rapidly changing world through improved communication and increased individual response.

- Creative: Develop new ideas. Be innovative. Increase customer satisfaction and operating margins through higher value products and services.

- Ownership: Have self-confidence to trust others. Delegate. Involve higher levels in issues critical to the business and corporation; more individual responsibility, capability to act quickly and independently. Increase job satisfaction and improve understanding of risks and rewards.

- Reward: Recognition and compensation commensurate with risk and performance to attract and motivate types of individuals to accomplish GE's objectives. A number 1 business should provide number 1 people with number 1 opportunity.[8]

The GE Value Statement also describes individual characteristics:

- Reality: Describe the environment as it is—not as we hope it to be; this is critical to developing a vision, winning strategy, and gaining universal acceptance for implementation.

- Leadership: Maintain sustained passion for commitment to a proactive, shared vision and its implementation; rally teams toward achieving a common objective.

- Candor and openness: Have complete and frequent information sharing with individuals and organizations; let employees know where they, their efforts, and their business stand.

- Simplicity: Strive for brevity, charity, the "elegant, simple solution"; less is better.

- Integrity: Never bend or wink at the truth; live within the spirit and letter of the law in every global business arena. Every constituency—shareholders, customers, community, employees—depends, expects, and deserves our unequivocal commitment to integrity.

- Individual dignity: Respect and leverage the talent and contribution of every individual in good and bad times; teamwork depends on trust, mutual understanding, the shared belief that the individual will be treated fairly in any environment.[9]

GE actively practices these values through its Work-Out program in the entire organization. This six-step program is tailored for each business unit; outside consultants facilitate it. The process is as follows:

Step 1: Tie business imperatives to ineffective work practices.

Step 2: Enlist involvement in the Work-Out process.

Step 3: Overview wasteful work practices.

Step 4: Audit by functional groups.

Step 5: Audit by cross-functional groups.

Step 6: Contract, make recommendations, and wrap-up.

In effect, this is GE's change management program.[10]

### Ford: A Profile

Ford's Taurus and Sable designs and quality set the industry standard for automobile design in the 1990s. Its organizational and team performance and quality standards helped usher the U.S. automobile industry back into world-class competition. Ford's

President, Jacques Nasser, is now taking the company into the twenty-first century.[11] Ford uses what it calls an Employee Involvement (EI) process to implement its mission, values, and guiding principles statements. These dimensions lead and guide other organizational change transformations. Ford's mission, values, and guiding principles are the basis for change.[12]

*Mission:* The Ford Motor Company is a worldwide leader in automotive and automotive-related products and services as well as in newer industries such as aerospace, communications, and financial services. Our mission is to improve our products and services continually to meet our customers' needs, allowing us to prosper as a business and to provide a reasonable return for our stockholders, the owners of our business.

*Values:* How we accomplish our mission is as important as the mission itself. Fundamental to success for the Company are these basic values: People—Our people are the source of our strength. They provide our corporate intelligence and determine our reputation and vitality. Involvement and teamwork are our core human values. Products—Our products are the end result of our efforts, and they should be the best in serving customers worldwide. As our products are viewed, so are we viewed. Profits—Profits are the ultimate measure of how efficiently we provide customers with the best products for their needs. Profits are required to survive and grow.

*Guiding Principles:* Quality comes first—To achieve customer satisfaction, the quality of our products and services must be our number one priority. Customers are the focus of everything we do—Our work must be done with our customers in mind, providing better products and services than our competition. Continuous improvement is essential to our success—We must strive for excellence in everything we do: our products, in their safety and value—and in our services, our human relations, our competitiveness, and our profitability. Employee involvement is our way of life—We are a team. We must treat each other with trust and respect. Dealers and suppliers are our partners—The company must maintain mutually beneficial relationships with dealers, suppliers, and our other business associates. Integrity is never compromised—The conduct of our Company worldwide must be pursued in a manner that is socially responsible and commands respect for its integrity and for its positive contributions to society. Our doors are open to men and women alike without discrimination and without regard to ethnic origin or personal beliefs. Nasser, Ford's president, has a game plan to quickly move the company into the global Internet arena as a leader.

GE and Ford provide examples of the implementation of large scale, planned change. In the following section, we review models and methods for planning organizational changes.

## VISION, MISSION, VALUES, CORE COMPETENCIES (CUSTOMER, CUSTOMER, CUSTOMER)

Answering the key questions in Figure 14–1, "What business are we in? What is our product or service? Who is our customer? What are our core competencies?" is the

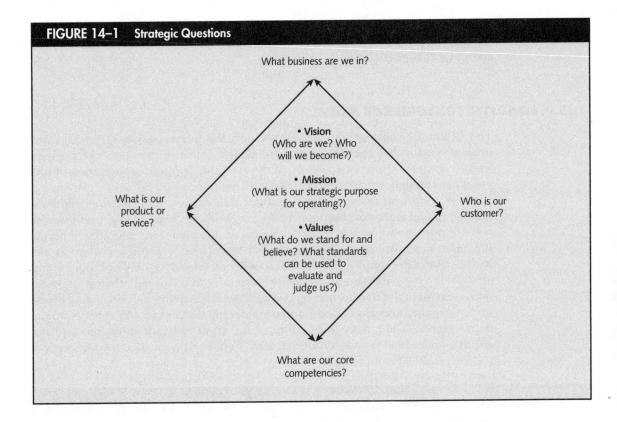

**FIGURE 14–1    Strategic Questions**

What business are we in?

- **Vision**
(Who are we? Who
will we become?)

- **Mission**
(What is our strategic purpose
for operating?)

What is our
product or
service?

Who is our
customer?

- **Values**
(What do we stand for and
believe? What standards
can be used to
evaluate and
judge us?)

What are our core
competencies?

first step leaders can and often do take to begin a change effort. More recently, company leaders have begun to ask "What is our value proposition?" (which we discussed in Chapter 10). McDonald's, for example, does not only sell hamburgers, but also a fast, fairly priced, predictable experience that customers expect and want. (You can always expect the same Big Mac quality anywhere you buy McDonald's products.) UPS defined its business as "moving parcels by trucks" until Federal Express showed a decade later that air transport was more competitive.[13] Since then, UPS has upgraded its business to offer customers the experience they want: fast and reliable delivery of information. UPS now competes with Federal Express by acknowledging that its business is accomplished by air as well as by ground; however, Federal Express maintains a competitive advantage in its real-time, online information systems with self-supporting and self-owned air/ground transportation systems.

Ford's leadership orchestrated the identification of its vision, mission, and values statements, using diverse talent throughout the company. The leader's role then, is continually important in setting the course of change. Jeff Bezos of Amazon.com started by selling books. He has now expanded his vision to selling music, toys, and a host of other products—offering one-stop shopping. Bezos knows that what Amazon.com really sells is user-friendly customer convenience, choice, and product selection.

After the purpose and direction of the company is set, (re)defining and integrating the people and systems to deliver the services and products are the next steps in a change process.

## THE DIAGNOSTIC CONTINGENCY MODEL

The diagnostic contingency model[14] presents the interrelationships of organizations as systems that operate together to exploit opportunities in markets. Figure 14-2 (repeated from Chapter 1) illustrates the **input-transformation-output** processes through which organizations, working on- and off-line with customers as partners, transform resources into products and services. The basic logic underlying this model is that at the input phase, organization leaders interpret environmental opportunities and obtain resources to plan and mobilize internal capabilities to produce defined outputs. If leaders listen to their customers and high-performance employees as well as to other stakeholders, they can begin to successfully interpret markets and mobilize resources to adapt and change organizational systems in the transformation phase. When the systems are managed to fit and stretch together to exploit market opportunities, the outputs should satisfy customer requirements. While many transactions of the input-transformation-output phases are being eliminated and consolidated by Web-based networks, the concepts of

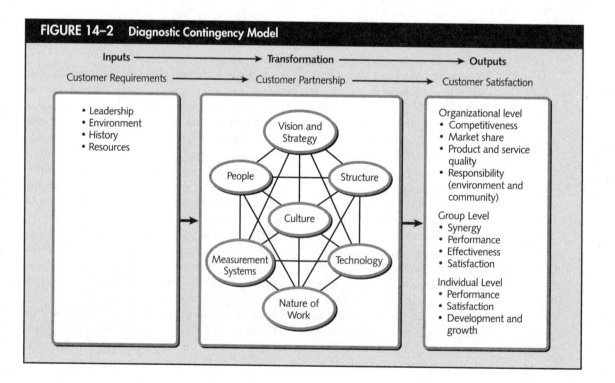

**FIGURE 14-2    Diagnostic Contingency Model**

what constitutes the value proposition and actual content of what customers want in terms of price, service, and delivery capability still holds. For planning purposes, this model is relevant for configuring and streamlining organizations to facilitate and support new technologies.

Figure 14-2 illustrates how interrelated and relevant an organization's systems are during the transformation phase where resources are moved from input to output. An organization's **leaders, managers, and other champions** in partnership with customers must translate their vision into a **strategy**—that is, they must set the course. Strategy serves other transformation purposes as well: it can position the organization more advantageously in its environment; it can identify requirements and relationships with other stakeholders such as customers, regulators, competitors, suppliers; and it can define other system needs and requirements such as professional skills, structure, technologies, nature of work, types of measurement systems, and cultural direction. Of course, a corporate strategy is ultimately broken down into different business and product or service strategies and specific plans. It infuses the way business will be done from top to bottom.

A company's **culture** includes the glue and the compass that define, direct, and hold the systems and people. Culture is the sum of the values, norms, principles, and rules that the leadership, heroes, and pivotal groups within the company form and pass on in myths, stories, and legends. Culture is at the center of Figure 14-2 because of its importance in motivating and influencing other organizational dimensions (how work gets done, how technology is used, how people group together, how ethical practices are modeled). McDonald's culture, for example, reflects consistency, speed, and efficiency. Ford now emphasizes speed, globalization, quality, continuous improvement, and employee involvement. GE's culture reflects agility, speed, ownership of work processes, and leanness.

The people, expertise, level of professionalism, and skills in an organization directly reflect its strategy, vision, mission, values, and core competencies. The selection, training, and retention of talented, skilled people is a key ingredient in an organization's effectiveness. As stated in Chapter 1, flexible knowledge workers will be in more demand as industries move into the Information Age. The fit (congruence) of people and skills with other organizational dimensions is essential for a successful transformation.

The **structure** of an organization, its division and differentiation of labor, is determined by its vision and strategy. Current global strategies and technology are making structures less centralized. This in turn affects the culture and the type of people who will make the best fit in the desired end state. Chapter 11 described variations in structure in more detail.

**Technology** is the means by which work is accomplished. It is the way raw materials are transformed into products and services. Technology, as we discussed in Chapter 9, has traditionally been described as (1) craft (customized and skilled tasks), (2) routine (clear, limited amounts of quantitative information used in analyzing somewhat simple tasks), (3) nonroutine (large amounts of rich information in completing complex tasks), or (4) engineering technology (e.g., large amounts of mostly quantitative information with high and complex task variety).[15]

Technology, then, affects the way work is performed. IBM transformed itself from a proprietary mainframe and laptop to an E-business—selling, networking, and consulting e-solutions in an open systems, online environment.

**Information technology**, in particular, is increasingly becoming a dominant force in the way work (and even organizations) is organized and communicated. Don Tapscott and Art Caston argue this point in their book *Paradigm Shift: The New Promise of Information Technology*.[16] Information technology, these authors argue, is changing organizations in the following ways: (1) extending the enterprise by recasting external relationships and networking more people faster than ever before; (2) integrating the organization by networking suppliers with vendors, thereby making communication across space, time, and people also faster and easier; and (3) initiating the high-performance teams required for working on cross-functional tasks and business processes.

## INPUT-THROUGHPUT-OUTPUT: AUTOMATING THE LINKAGES

The Internet and Web-based technologies are transforming many of the **input-transformation-output** processes by linking and networking customer, supplier, and vendor transactions online. The role of many intermediaries is removed. Intranets and extranets (secure internal and external networks that use digital technology to enable instant information sharing) provide this capability.[17]

Understanding the **nature of work** is important in the transformation phase of the diagnostic contingency model for determining whether the right people, expertise, and skills fit with other organizational dimensions. Work, like technology, can be defined along several continua: routine to nonroutine, mass production to customized, specialized to standardized, bricks and mortar to Web-centric systems management and selling.

As stated in Chapter 1, the knowledge worker will be more in demand as nonroutine, creative work is required by teams of specialists and generalists using information technology to work concurrently on multiple projects. A cluster of skills is important here: technical, relationship-building, teamwork, innovative and critical-thinking skills and the ability to adapt and respond to change. Of course, particular skills depend on the situation and various contingencies.

**Measurement systems**, or metrics, collect, evaluate, and disseminate information, both the activities of people and evaluating progress toward planned milestones and objectives. Measurement systems include, for example, financial ratios; the number of "hits" and items sold as recorded on a Web site each day; human resource mechanisms; the processes of selecting, training, and developing people; and reward systems that identify and determine benefits, bonuses, promotions, pay, and nonmonetary aspects (such as career development, job assignments, job placement, and counseling). The form, management, and substance of measurement systems are determined by the vision and strategy and the particular structure. Self-designing work teams may not have the same measurement systems that headquarter managers have.

To summarize, the theory underlying the transformational phase of the diagnostic contingency model is that the organizational systems and their respective individuals and groups should fit, stretch, and operate congruently according to the vision, mission, and strategy of the company to produce planned outputs.

The **output phase** of the model is organized into three levels: organizational, group, and individual. At the organizational level, the products or services should competitively position the company in its industry as indicated by market share, return on investment, and other financial indicators. The quality and innovativeness of the products and services are indicators of how effectively the input and transformational phases function. An organization's effectiveness is also demonstrated by its legal and ethical responsibilities to the environment, community, and other stakeholders.

At the group/team level, effectiveness is measured by the performance and process of products and services produced. In a related way, team effectiveness is demonstrated by the synergy evidenced: Did the teams produce value that exceeded the effort and resources expended? Was there satisfaction with the product? Did growth, learning, and development occur as a result of the project? We discussed characteristics of high-performance work teams in a previous chapter. Many of the indicators that identify group effectiveness also apply at the individual level: performance, learning, satisfaction, development, and growth. Outputs at this level relate to the individual's fit and satisfaction with work processes such as skill variety, task identity and significance, and autonomy. Individual output also includes feedback about the process and the quality of the results. Individual performance and background characteristics have been discussed throughout the text.

After identifying and refocusing the organizational dimensions for change, implementation planning follows.

## MOBILIZING PLANNED CHANGE: A FIVE-PHASE APPROACH

The five-phase model (introduced in Chapter 1) is summarized here because it addresses an overview of a mobilization process for implementing a planned or unplanned change effort.[18] If an organization's leaders have refocused the vision and direction of the company, as outlined here, it may be necessary to develop an implementation change plan, as outlined in Figure 14-3. First, **motivating change** involves creating readiness and overcoming resistance; resistance factors are discussed later in this chapter. Second, **creating a vision** for the change with valued outcomes, conditions, and midpoint goals of the change is required. Using the results from Figure 14-1, the change implementers can identify what the change will produce, thus reducing uncertainty and fears in individuals. Third, it is important to **develop political support** for the change. Here it is important to identify the key stakeholders who are affected and who can help influence the changes. Fourth, **managing the change** transition requires a plan, commitment from the top, and agreement on how the organizational structure will be mobilized. Fifth, providing

## FIGURE 14–3　The Five-Phase Approach

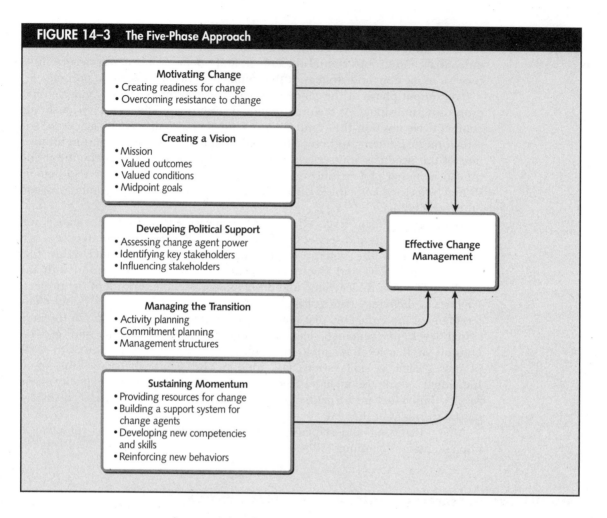

resources for **sustaining the change** involves building support and enabling change agents to reinforce and reward new behaviors.

It is also important to understand and anticipate organization members' readiness, reactions, and actions toward changes. The following discussion summarizes these human dimensions, which accompany each of the five stages in Figure 14–3: **Stage 1, ignoring**: There is usually unawareness or no intention to change. There may be denial, resistance, or people may be demoralized about their ability to change. In effect, the organization is immobilized to change. **Stage 2, attending**: The organization moves to an awareness state but does not make a commitment or is not ready to begin change. The decision to change or not to change must be made. **Stage 3, planning**: The decision is to move to change and to act soon. Action plans begin, as does resource mobilization to change. At this stage, it is important to ensure that all persons affected adversely by the change will be responsibly informed and responded to during the next stage. **Stage 4, executing**: Major investments of resources are mobilized to implement change in this stage. The organization visibly recognizes and implements change action plans, but the risk is high for a possible relapse. Emotionally and cognitively, people may still be unstable. The aim here is to **empower** the people implementing the change and those who will be taking on new roles after the change. It is important to ensure that accurate information is given to all employees affected by the change. Implementing legal and morally responsible actions to protect those who will be dismissed and to ensure fairness is also important at this stage. **Stage 5, embedding**: In this stage, the change is consolidated; work is done to prevent relapse. Continual modification and adjustment to institutionalize the change occurs within and among people and groups. It is a period of stabilizing the change in attitudes, beliefs, values, policy directives, and work.

## CHANGE AGENTS AND ORGANIZATIONAL DEVELOPMENT INTERVENTIONS

Who helps plan and implement the changes? Change agents may be executives, managers, employees, or internal or external consultants who are skilled in organizational development techniques and interventions for assisting change activities. During large-scale organizational changes, change agents can diagnose, plan, implement, monitor, and support systems and human factors before, during, and after a change. At the systems level, change agents can assist in diagnosing the systems' readiness: structures, technologies, space arrangements, and job redesign. Regarding human factors, change agents can design and implement surveys; run sensitivity, management, and skills training; perform career counseling; assist with role negotiation and team building; and write human resources policies and procedures.[19] Understanding the resistance factors to change is necessary in any change management activity.

### Resistance Factors to Organizational Change

Planning and implementing change effectively in organizations should consider the people involved or affected as well as the systems. Often this is not the case. A beginning step for understanding the human factors of change is to identify resistance to change. Organizational resistance to change stems from the factors identified in the next section:[20]

**Three Fears: Failure, the Loss of the Familiar, and the Unknown**

People generally resist change for both rational (self-interest) and psychological reasons. Those who resist change due to self-interest may also experience the psychological factors of fear of the unknown, of the loss of the familiar, and of failure. When all three fears are experienced together, significant stress may develop in individuals, which we discuss later.

- **Personality conflicts**: Change affects how people feel about themselves and others. Personality conflicts within and between individuals are not unusual as a resisting factor to change.

- **Disruption of relationships**: Change that disrupts interpersonal work relationships can also breed resentment and resistance to change. The bonds developed between people at work are important motivators and part of a person's belonging to a place. Changes in these relationships may create anxiety and resistance.

- **Disruption of cultural traditions and group norms**: Underlying—sometimes even unconscious—assumptions, traditions, and unwritten rules of behavior are part of the organizational culture that holds people together and empowers teams. Change that disrupts such bonds can lead to strong resistance and stress. Depending on the culture of affected employees, this type of disruption may cause a more serious reaction.

### Stages of Individual Reactions to Change

Resistance to change can be viewed as a series of stages. Kubler-Ross first outlined what appears to be an almost universal sequence of responses experienced by the survivors of traumatic personal loss.[21] These stages have been used to understand individual reactions to planned change because there are loss and pain in change, even though the ultimate end state is an improvement. These stages are as follows: (1) **denial**: a psychologically buffering reaction that avoids confronting the reality of loss; (2) **anger**: the response immediately following denial (person asks "why did this happen to me"); "How could someone have done this to me?" (3) **depression**: after the anger lessens, the reality of the loss takes hold, causing waves of anguish and depression; (4) **bargaining**: the psychological struggle to regain or restore the lost state or object; and (5) **acceptance**: coming to terms with the loss and moving forward. Knowing this progression can assist managers in developing useful interventions at each phase and in having patience and being mindful that human behavior sometimes occurs nonlinearly.

Moore and Gergen identify four stages of transition which we repeat here:

**Stage 1: Shock**. People experience impending change as a threat. They shut down thinking and as many systems as possible (just as in physiological shock). People need warm blankets and rest, that is, recovery time, emotional support, information, and an opportunity to share the experience with others. Productivity is low. People cannot think clearly and do not remember. **What to do:** Help people in shock look for common ground, build support networks, and give them information again and again. Managers should give visible support. Do not involve these people in planning. Provide safety (i.e., clear expectations, reward systems, support systems, and available resources).

**Stage 2: Defensive retreat**. In this stage, people are holding on and attempting to maintain old ways. They have a great deal of anger and refuse to let go of the past. People and organizations can get stuck here or go back to Stage 1 as each element of change is introduced. **What to do:** Help people

## THE CHANGING WORKPLACE

### Understanding and Managing Ten Challenges to Change

**Step 1**: Select an organization with which you are familiar or interview someone from an organization to help you with this exercise. The organization may be going through a planned change, may have been through such a change, or may be preparing to undergo a change. First, describe the change. Then, identify the people who led the change ("the pilot team"). Be objective and answer, or have the person you may interview answer, each of the 10 items regarding the change.

**Step 2**: For each of the following 10 items, which are challenges to organizational change, answer these two questions:

a.  How *effectively* did the "pilot group"—the team leading the change—address, handle, and deal with this "challenge?" Answers may include excellent, not very well, poorly, and not at all. Explain the answer; offer an example.

b.  What should have (could be) done by the pilot or lead team to effectively address, handle, and deal with this challenge? Be specific and offer examples. (Note: The "Pilot Group" is the group planning and leading the organizational changes.)

### Challenges of Initiating Change: 10 Items

1.  **Control**: Individuals involved in a pilot change group have enough control over their schedules to give the change effort the time required.

2.  **Support**: The pilot group needs support, coaching, and resources to learn to do the work effectively.

3.  **Advocacy**: People are needed who can advocate for change and connect new skills developed to the real work of the business.

4.  **Talk the talk; walk the walk**: People who are supporting and directing the change may not do what they say they will do.

### Challenges of Sustaining Momentum

5.  **Fear and anxiety**: Members of the pilot group will be challenged by personal fear and anxiety and question the change.

6.  **Measurement problems**: Measuring the new change effort and results will be difficult early on when new metrics do not meet expectations of the old.

7.  **Arrogance**: The pilot change group may become arrogant and behave in cult-like ways, labeling people in the company "nonbelievers" and "believers."

### Challenges of Systemwide Redesign and Rethinking

8.  **Autonomy**: The pilot change group will need more autonomy; those in power will want to keep control.

9.  **New Habits**: Each group undergoing change will feel it has to keep starting from scratch—reinventing the wheel—instead of building on previous wins and achievements.

10. **Purpose and Direction**: Daily, routine activities will blur the major question of the change: Can the organization redefine and achieve success?

---

**Step 3**: Summarize your findings under each of these three headings: Challenges of Initiating Change, Challenges of Sustaining Momentum, and Challenges of Systemwide Redesign and Rethinking.

**Step 4**: What lessons were observed and learned? Identify any items from the chapter or your own experience and research that are (or would have been) relevant to assisting and improving this change effort.

SOURCE: Adapted from Peter Senge, *The Dance of Change: The Challenges to Sustaining Momentum in Learning Organizations* (Doubleday/Currency, 1999).

---

identify what they are holding on to and how to maintain it in the new situation or how to let it go. Identify areas of stability. Give information continually and consistently. Ask people to identify what is risky and provide safety in those areas.

**Stage 3: Acknowledgment**. People at this stage experience a sense of grief and sadness over loss. They are letting go, beginning to see the value of what is coming, and looking for ways to make it work by considering the pros and cons. Their ability to take risks begins here, and it takes the form of exploring new ways to look at things and to do things. This stage can lead to high energy if managed well. **What to do**: Involve people in exploring options and planning through the use of a careful decision-making process as a structure and/or support. Overtly encourage and support risk taking by pointing out ways that the organization will support it. Emphasize that everyone is learning.

**Stage 4: Adaptation and Change**. What has been coming has arrived. People are ready to establish new routines and to help others. Risk taking comes into full bloom at this stage relative to changing methods, products, or whatever is called for. **What to do**: Implement plans. Encourage and support risk taking using the supports and structures developed in Stage 3. Establish feedback loops so that information travels in all directions, new learning occurs, and mid-course corrections can be made when necessary.[22]

Individuals can also react behaviorally to change in four ways, through disengagement, disidentification, disenchantment, and disorientation.[23] **Disengagement** is a psychological removal from the effects of change. Symptoms of disengagement include absence of mental attention, drive, commitment, ownership of work, and motivation. Employees may actually be absent from work. Fear is a major cause of this behavior. Managers and co-workers can assist employees who show disengagement reactions by confronting them and identifying their behavior for them. If the employees are unaware of or need assurance, engage them assertively; this may start a dialogue, create awareness, and lead to acceptable performance.

**Disidentification**, another possible reaction to change, occurs when a person feels victimized and threatened by change. When a person's identity is bound to work, a job, or a skill and those are changed, the person feels threatened and vulnerable. A job, skill, or responsibility area may have been taken away from someone who had a sense of mastery and accomplishment in that area. Symptoms may include dwelling on and continued remembrances of the past. Verbal statements that reflect the loss and separation of identity may be reiterated. Managers and co-workers can assist the person by exploring feelings with him and transferring positive identifications from the past situation to the changed one.

**Disenchantment** is reaction to change in which the employee expresses anger over the loss of the past. This anger may be expressed in sabotage, backstabbing, political coalition building, and other reactive behaviors such as starting rumors and spreading gossip. Managers and co-workers can assist an employee showing behavioral patterns of disenchantment by first neutralizing the negative feelings and behavior—allowing the employee to "blow off steam" and then acknowledging her anger without revenge or disapproval, which enables the person to begin to identify the core cause of the disenchantment.

Finally, **disorientation** is a reaction that shows confusion and a sense of feeling lost. People who are accustomed to structure, rules, and organized ways of doing things can, with sweeping changes, become disoriented. Disoriented employees may seem like they are "running in circles," overperforming routine tasks, analyzing too much, and needlessly inquiring about what they are supposed to be doing. Managers and co-workers can help by showing such people the overall plan, direction, and nature of the changes. More detailed and individual planning can also help to orient attitudes toward the new systems and to create constructive behaviors.

## PLANNED CHANGE METHODS

Change management is rarely, if ever, a linear or straightforward set of activities. Organizational and individual change is best seen as a process. If it is a planned process, appropriate models, interventions, and skills are needed to improve the probability of enduring success. Acknowledging and managing individual reactions to change accelerates the success of the change efforts at all levels of the organization. Change agents use the following methods to guide the human and systems dynamics of planned change.

### Force Field Analysis

Kurt Lewin's force field analysis is a model for diagnosing and developing strategies for managing the dynamics of change.[24] Force field analysis can be used at any stage of a change process. It is an excellent method for engaging employees and managers in identifying issues, problems, and opportunities related to a desired end state to be achieved, a plan to be implemented, an initiative to be tested. Lewin's model is based on laws of physics that hold that an object at rest will remain so unless the forces exerted on the object (to move it) are greater than the forces working against it (to keep it at rest). Similarly, a behavior that is positioned between two forces, one opposing change and one pushing to change, will not change if the opposing forces are equal and thus cancel each other. Behavioral change will occur, according to this model, if (1) the forces for change are strengthened, (2) the forces against change are weakened, or (3) a combination of options 1 and 2 is applied.

Figure 14–4 illustrates Lewin's force field analysis using an organizational initiative as an example. The following steps can be used to identify the forces for and against change regarding a particular situation, problem, or opportunity:

1. Describe the opportunity, problem, or issue.

2. Identify the desired end state.

3. List the potential benefits derived from having achieved the end state.

4. Identify the driving forces, strategies, and tactics for change toward the end state.

5. Identify the resisting forces against change toward the end state.

6. Identify tactics that can be used to weaken the forces against change, blocking the desired end state.

7. List tactics to use to strengthen the forces for change to reach the desired end state.

8. Develop an action plan.

For example, suppose you wish to open and operate a franchise so that you can leave an organization where you believe you are about to be terminated. You might define this opportunity as the chance *to develop a feasibility plan for starting*

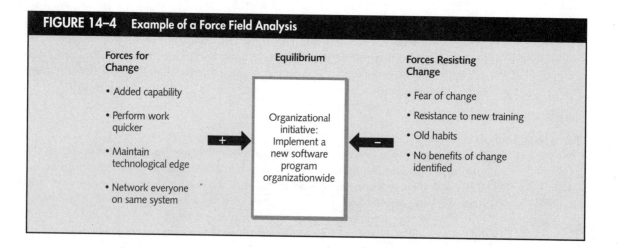

**FIGURE 14–4   Example of a Force Field Analysis**

| Forces for Change | Equilibrium | Forces Resisting Change |
|---|---|---|
| • Added capability | | • Fear of change |
| • Perform work quicker | Organizational initiative: Implement a new software program organizationwide | • Resistance to new training |
| • Maintain technological edge | | • Old habits |
| • Network everyone on same system | | • No benefits of change identified |

*and managing a franchise with McCord's Chicken.* Your end state might be *to operate a fully functioning, profitable franchise store through McCord's Chicken by the end of August 2002 and to earn $150,000 and develop my role and responsibilities as franchise manager and store operator.* The benefits derived from having achieved this end state might include *I will be my own boss; I will be able to hire and manage two or three other people; I will operate a store not more than 20 minutes from my residence; my break-even point of $50,000 is carefully planned and can be arranged; and I can earn at least as much as I'm making at my present job.*

The forces driving for change toward this end state might include a high probability of losing the current job by the end of the year, excitement, energy, and state of mind to go into business, the lack of McCord franchise outlets in a radius of 80 miles from the planned site, and a 90 percent chance of obtaining funding to proceed.

Forces resisting the change might include having never run a franchise business before, a weak economy and possibility that consumer demand might falter; and the need for feasibility and marketing studies, which would require money, time, and energy. Tactics that might be used to weaken the forces against resistance factors to change could include taking McCord's free seminars on the basics of operating a franchise, two studies showing that chicken franchises in the region have done well despite economic downturns, and the opportunity to use student interns at a nearby college to help sample the market. Tactics to strengthen the driving forces for change could be the ability to start the franchise six months before losing the current job to protect assets, the availability of a low-cost loan to bolster finances and confidence, $15,000 saved toward this goal, personal research on three McCord's Chicken stores in a nearby region, and family members who successfully operate similar franchise operations, to offer advice and counseling. The last step involves developing a feasibility action plan with a budget.

### Unfreezing, Moving/Changing, Refreezing in the Force Field
Lewin's force field analysis also argues that there are three stages of change.

**Unfreezing.** The focus here is creating a felt need for change by increasing motivation to change. Individuals are encouraged to abandon old behaviors and attitudes and become open to accept new ones. Managers can participate in this stage by reducing barriers to change, creating incentives to change, and introducing rewards for new behaviors. Individuals begin to unfreeze old behaviors and attitudes when they can see and experience their uselessness.

**Moving/Changing.** During this stage, employees start to experience changes in their attitudes and behaviors. New information, behavioral models, and skills are introduced to employees. New organizational vision, mission, strategy, structure, and technology facilitate new directions for change. Mentors, role models, and training assist employees in the transition from old to new attitudes and behaviors.

**Refreezing.** During this stage, the focus is on reinforcing and institutionalizing new behaviors and attitudes. Enabling employees to practice and integrate new behaviors with appropriate rewards helps to stabilize changes during this phase. Managers must ensure that the culture, structure, and reward system support the new behaviors.

This model can assist managers in developing orientation and training programs before, during, and after planned changes to address individual needs in a changed work environment.

## FACILITATING INDIVIDUAL CHANGE: SIX STRATEGIES

Kotter and Schlesinger have identified six strategies for facilitating change and overcoming resistance.[25] Table 14–1 presents these strategies and identifies when each should be used, and the advantages and drawbacks of each. These strategies can be used when an organization is deciding how best to implement planned change programs of any scale. **Education and communication** and **participation and involvement** are not always appropriate change strategies in every situation. When information is lacking and/or inaccurate, these strategies are commonly used even though they require significant time, effort, and resources. Sometimes **manipulation and co-optation** are recommended when other approaches will not work. **Explicit and implicit coercion** is recommended only when change agents have substantial power, time is short, and resources are scarce. These strategies are risky in that negative consequences and problems can surface later in the form of dissatisfied people and unacceptable productivity. **Facilitation and support** are recommended when a high degree of resistance exists. **Negotiation and agreement** are used with a win/lose situation in which one party has the power to react. This strategy to managing change can be expensive and sends a message to others that negotiation is an acceptable tactic.

In practice, a combination of these strategies can be used more flexibly than the model suggests. Change agents must always be sensitive to the specific context, the audience and the customers as well as the end states and goals of the organization's desired changes when selecting a specific change approach. No universally accepted situations or answers dictate the use of these strategies for implementing change.

### Espoused Theories and Theories in Use

The process of assisting people to move effectively through planned organizational change can be accelerated if a change agent knows what individuals are actually thinking and feeling. Two experts on individual change, Argyris and Schon, argued that "interpersonal competence" and behavior are influenced by "theories in action" (i.e., cognitive maps and assumptions about what constitutes effective action).[26] These cognitive maps have two dimensions: **espoused theories** (what people say) are public explanations of what people say they use in choosing their behaviors and **theories in use** (the theory behind people's actions) are what people most often do. Theories in use are mental models consisting of rules and

## TABLE 14–1    CHANGE APPROACHES

| Approach | Commonly Used in Situations | Advantages | Disadvantages |
|---|---|---|---|
| Education and communication | When there is a lack of information or inaccurate information and analysis | Once persuaded, people will often help with the implementation of change | Can be very time consuming if lots of people are involved |
| Participation and involvement | When the initiators do not have all the information they need to design the change and when others have considerable power to resist | People who participate will be committed to implementing change | Can be very time consuming if participators design an inappropriate change |
| Facilitation and support | When people are resisting because of adjustment problems | No other approach works as well with adjustment problems | Can be time consuming and still fail |
| Negotiation and agreement | When someone or some group will clearly lose out in a change and when that group has considerable power to resist | Sometimes it is a relatively easy way to avoid major resistance | Can be too expensive in many cases if it alerts others to negotiate for compliance |
| Manipulation and co-optation | When other tactics will not work or are too expensive | It can be a relatively quick and inexpensive solution to resistance problems | Can lead to future problems if people feel manipulated |
| Explicit and implicit coercion | When speed is essential and the change initiators possess considerable able power | It is speedy and can overcome any kind of resistance | Can be risky if it leaves people mad at the initiators |

**Source:**  Reprinted by permission of *Harvard Business Review*.  An exhibit from "Choosing Strategies for Change," by J. P. Koster and L. A. Schlesinger (March/April 1979).  Copyright © 1979 by the President and Fellows of Harvard College; all rights reserved.

programs that govern how individuals act in different settings. Argyris and Schon found discrepancies between what managers said they would do and what they actually did. Managers would say they were rational, open, authentic, and empathetic, but they would act competitively, controlling, and with their own self-interests in mind.

This method is helpful in diagnosing and managing individual behavior in planned change situations since espoused theories can be identified and separated from theories in use, especially those of leaders and managers. Then the discrepancies can be addressed. Behavior and organizational system changes can then be planned and implemented more effectively. Acceptance to change is facilitated when individuals can openly express their feelings and have dialogue with managers.

Bolman and Deal, drawing on Argyris and Schon, state that managers have a self-protective, "mastery-mastery" theory-in-use model about effective interpersonal behavior that allows them to "get what they want while protecting themselves from the hazards of organizational life."[27] This self-protective model identifies six postures that managers tend, unfortunately, to use with interpersonal problems. A manager may use the following model:

1. Assume that the problem is caused by the other person(s).

2. Develop a private, unilateral diagnosis and solution.

3. Get the other person, the cause of the problem, to change by using one or more of three strategies:

    a. Facts, logic, and rational persuasion (i.e., argue your solution and point of view).

    b. Indirect influence (manipulate the person by asking leading questions).

    c. Direct critique (confront the other person with what he is doing wrong and tell him how to change).

4. Confirm that the other person caused the problem if he is defensive or resists.

5. Handle resistance by intensifying pressure, protecting the other person, and/or rejecting him.

6. Feel no personal responsibility if the person fails at his efforts; it is his fault.

These are recipes for failure. Resistance to change is the most likely result.

Bolman and Deal propose that strategies from Argyris and Schon can be used to break through the resistance model just described to achieve interpersonal effectiveness. These strategies consist of the following actions: emphasize common goals and mutual influence in relationships, communicate openly and publicly, test assumptions and beliefs, and combine advocacy (statements that communicate what individuals think, know, want, and feel) with inquiry (behavior that seeks to learn what others think, know, want, and feel). Being integrative is the highest combination between advocacy with inquiry. Showing passiveness is the lowest level of integration between advocacy and inquiry. Being accommodative shows a high level of inquiry and a low level of advocacy. Being assertive shows a high level of inquiry and a low level of advocacy.

## MANAGING CHANGE ETHICALLY

Organizational changes and transformation involve the redistribution of power, information, resources, status, authority, and influence. Therefore, individuals' rights, dignity, and privileges can be at risk. Owners, executives, managers, and change agents responsible for the planning and implementation may consider the following ethics-related issue while planning a change program:

**Do the change plan, policies, implementation process and planned outcomes consider the following:**

- **Rights** of individuals affected by the change (e.g., the right to know, the right to privacy, the right not to be terminated without just cause, the right to due process).

- **Justice** of individuals affected by the change (e.g., how fairly the benefits and burdens of the process and outcomes have been distributed, how clear and fair the procedures for distributing the costs and benefits of the change were explained, and how those who were treated unfairly will be compensated).

- **Fairness** of plans, implementation, and methods used in the change (e.g., were the needs, welfare, and dignity of those affected by the change respected? Were manipulation, force, deceit, or coercion used that may have harmed those involved emotionally, physically, or in any other material way?).

These ethical principles can be applied to any process, OD intervention or method, procedure, policy, informational session, training, or briefing before, during, and after the change activity or program is executed.[28]

## CONCLUDING COMMENTS

The models and approaches in this chapter are presented as a reference for preparing for planned organizational change. Several approaches were discussed since organizational development consultants rely on many of these diagnostic tools, depending on the situation. There is no one best organizational change model. Change agents must consider a number of levels and dimensions when diagnosing, planning, and implementing organizational change. Applying an appropriate model to the situation at hand requires judgment and choice. Understanding the nature of human resistance to change and methods for aligning organizational

## THE CHANGING WORKPLACE

### The Ethics of Planning and Implementing Change

**Step 1**: Describe a change that occurred or is occurring in an organization in which you are or were involved, that you researched on the Web or in a business publication, or that you became familiar with through a friend or family member.

**Step 2**: Write a brief *ethical analysis* of the results or ongoing activities of the *effects of the change* on individuals or groups involved using these ethical principles as criteria. You may consider the effects of such activities in the change as these following:

- Methods and procedures used

- Goals and objectives of the change

- Misrepresentation or misuses of data

- Conflicts of interest of people

- Manipulation/accurate use of data, facts

- Intended and unintended motivations

- Material and emotional harm/help done to individuals, groups

- Treatment of people

- Unclear/clear or confusing straightforward communication

- Creation of a hostile or helping environment

Note that the change could be an exemplary activity noteworthy of high ethical standards.

Ethical Principles (consult the chapter for specifics of each principle):

- Rights

- Justice

- Duty

**Step 3**: Using your written analysis, answer the questions with another member of your class:

a.  What were your major findings?

b.  What did you learn from this exercise?

c.  Suggest specific activities and methods that the planners and implementers of the change could have used to avoid or change the outcomes you discovered or identify the exemplary and noteworthy aspects of the effects of the change.

interests and goals to those of individuals may also require several methods, as this text illustrates. Planned change requires organizing. This chapter and the text as a whole can serve as a resource toward this endeavor.

## SCENARIO AND EXERCISE: A SCENARIO

**Step 1**: Read the following scenario. Identify the problems and opportunities you see in this situation.

Rite Company is a 20-year-old manufacturing firm that has 1,000 employees located in five sites across the United States. The firm is losing revenue and profitability for the third consecutive year. The firm's second CEO has just retired; his replacement is a younger person who holds an MBA degree. The top level management team consists of several people who plan to retire in eight years. Those on the team who have been hired in the last three years are restless and afraid they may lose their jobs if the company doesn't "turn the corner" soon. The age of about half the present workforce is over 45. The products the company manufactures are in demand, but Rite Company has problems processing and shipping orders on time, moving inventory, communicating with suppliers, and marketing itself to new and potential users of its operations. Here's a sample of what key employees and top team members have said about the situation.

*Bill (new employee):* "I'm frustrated because our equipment is old. Much of it needs replacement. I could be more productive if I didn't have to do so much by hand. My supervisor is slower in making decisions than the equipment. I may not stay here for another year."

*Louise (employee for two years):* "I'm one of ten women in this plant with 200 men. The bureaucracy is so heavy that I feel I'm working for five bosses. I'm not listened to, I think, because I am a woman, and even if I were listened to, nothing would be changed. We don't even have our inventory online. There are three computers on this site, and I'm not sure what they're used for."

*Ralph (member executive team, 15 years with the company):* "We know we have to change, but change takes time. Even though I'll probably retire in six years, I want to stay with the company as long as I can help. We have a lot to offer but we're not organized well. I'm on a committee now that's working with some of these problems."

*Jim (new CEO):* "We have four major competitors in our manufacturing niche. Three of these firms are almost fully automated and have online ordering and Intranet communication systems in which suppliers, dealers, and customers talk regularly with those companies' key managers. We're working in a 1950s environment here. Our board of directors wants change. I have some ideas but turning this place around isn't going to be easy. A lot of employees feel—and many are—entitled; they've been here half if not all their working lives. Still, for those who want to keep their jobs, we're going to have to get competitive and fast."

**Step 2**: Write what you see as the key problems from this scenario.

**Step 3**: Jim, the new CEO, has brought you into the company from the local college/university as an intern/change agent/consultant. Using chapter information and methods, outline a change program with OD interventions to help Jim get started.

**Step 4**: Share your suggestions with a small group of classmates. Combine your suggestions into one format and share with the entire class.

## REVIEW QUESTIONS

1. Identify some significant external forces that cause or pressure organizations to change. Which force has an organization in which you work or have worked experienced? What did the organization do or not do to respond or react to that change? Why?

2. Characterize some specific changes that the Internet is bringing that will affect changes on the way you study and/or do business. How would you evaluate these changes on your performance? Your working habits? Your work product satisfaction? Explain.

3. List five success factors that organizations can use as end states to guide a major change. Suggest other success factors that can be used to evaluate how effectively or ineffectively an organization performs after a change.

4. Locate a website that describes the firm's vision, mission, and values. Evaluate the company's statements with the vision, mission, and values you believe are important for a company.

5. Locate a website of a consulting company that does "change management." Describe one of the techniques of change on this site. How does the technique compare and differ from methods in this chapter (or book)? Explain.

6. Identify some steps you would use to plan a major change for an organization in which you are a member, student, or employee. Explain why you believe or do not believe the change process you outline would work in the organization you identified.

7. Identify three or more of the resistance factors to change you have experienced in an organization you have been part of as a student or a professional. Why did you experience these factors?

8. Sketch a brief force field analysis to a problem, issue, or opportunity you have but are not sure what the outcome will be. Follow the steps in the chapter. After you finish the exercise, answer this question: What did you learn about the problem, issue, or opportunity? What did you learn about your thinking regarding the topic?

9. What are your general feelings and attitudes toward change that affects you? What do you like about change? Why? What do you dislike? Why?

10. Would you rather (a) plan and implement an organizational change or (b) be the receiver of the change? Explain. How does your answer to this question differ from what you stated in Question 9? Is there a relationship between your answers to these questions? Explain.

## CHAPTER 1

1. P. Coy and N. Gross, "21 Ideas for the 21st Century," *Business Week*, 30 August 1999, 81–162.
2. B. Gates, *Business @ the Speed of Thought: Using a Digital Nervous System* (New York: Warner Books, 1999).
3. M. Hammer and J. Champy, *Reengineering the Corporation: A Manifesto for Business Revolution* (New York: Harper Business, A Division of Harper Collins Publishing, 1993).
4. E. Schwartz, *Digital Darwinism* (New York: Broadway Books, 1999).
5. P. Drucker, "The Coming of the New Organization," *Harvard Business Review*, January–February 1988, 45. Also see R. Reich, "The Company of the Future," *Fast Company*, November 1998, 127–150.
6. Drucker, "The Coming of the New Organization," 50.
7. P. Arredondo, *Successful Diversity Management Initiatives*. (Thousand Oaks, Calif.: Sage, 1996); D. Jamieson and J. O'Mara, *Managing Workforce 2000: Gaining the Diversity Advantage* (San Francisco: Jossey-Bass, 1991); C.M. Dominguez, "The Challenge of Workforce 2000," *The Bureaucrat, The Journal for Public Managers*, Winter 1991–1992, 15–18.
8. R.R. Kanter, "The New Managerial Week," *Harvard Business Review*, November–December 1989, 85–92.
9. L. Bolman and T. Deal, *Reframing Organizations* (San Francisco: Jossey-Bass, 1991).
10. Ibid., 1–12.
11. Ibid., 15–16.
12. P. Senge, *The Fifth Discipline: The Art and Practice of the Learning Organization* (New York: Doubleday/Currency 1990). Also, for an update on Senge's views, see A. Webber, "Learning for a Change," *Fast Company*, May 1999, 178–191.
13. R. Quinn, S. Faerman, M. Thompson, and M. McGrath, *Becoming a Master Manager* (New York: John Wiley, 1990), chap. 1.
14. F. W. Taylor, *The Principles of Scientific Management* (New York: Harper and Brothers, 1991); also H. Fayol, *General and Industrial Management*, trans. C. Storrs (London: Pitman, 1949).
15. M. Weber, *The Theory of Social and Economic Organization*, ed. and trans. A.M. Henderson and T. Parsons (New York: Oxford University Press, 1947); also M. Weber, *Essays on Sociology*, ed. and trans. H.H. Gerth and C.W. Mills (New York: Oxford University Press, 1947).
16. C.E. Snow, "A Discussion of the Relation of Illumination Intensity to Productive Efficiency" in *Management and the Worker*, ed. E. J. Roethlisberger and W. J. Dickson (Cambridge: Harvard University Press, 1939).
17. K. Lewin, "Forces Behind Food Habits and Methods of Change," *Bulletin of the National Research Council*, 108, 1943, 35–65; also L. Loch and J.R.P. French, Jr., "Overcoming Resistance to Change," *Human Relations* 1, 1948, 512–533.

18. J.G.March and H.A. Simon, *Organizations* (New York: John Wiley, 1958); see also H. Simon, *Administrative Behavior*, 2nd ed. (New York: John Wiley, 1958).

19. D. McGregor, *The Human Side of Enterprise* (New York: McGraw-Hill, 1960); also E.H. Schein, *The Hawthorne Group Studies Revisited: A Defense of Theory Y* (Cambridge, Mass.: MIT Sloan School of Management Working Paper), December 1974, 756–774.

20. R.F. Bales, "Task Roles and Social Roles in Problem-Solving Groups," in *Readings in Social Psychology*, 3rd ed., ed. E. Maccoby, T.M. Newcomb, and E.L. Hartley, (New York: Holt, Rinehart, and Winston, 1958).

21. E.K. Trist and K.W. Bamforth, "Some Social and Psychological Consequences of the Long Wall Method of Goal Getting," *Human Relations*, 4, 1951, 3–38; also A.K. Rice, *The Enterprise and Its Environment* (London: Tavistock, 1963); and F.E. Emery and I.L. Trist, "Socio-Technical Systems" in *Management Science: Models and Techniques*, vol. 2 (London: Pergamon, 1960).

22. D. Katz and R.L. Kahn, *The Social Psychology of Organizations*, 2nd ed. (New York: John Wiley, 1978); also D.A. Nadler and M.L. Tushman, "A Diagnostic Model for Organizational Behavior" in *Perspectives on Behavior in Organizations*, ed. J.R. Hackman, L.W. Porter, and E.E. Lawler III (New York: McGraw-Hill, 1977).

23. H. Mintzberg, *Structure in Fives: Designing Effective Organizations* (Englewood Cliffs, NJ: Prentice Hall, 1983).

24. T. Burns and G.M. Stalker, *The Management of Innovation* (London: Tavistock, 1961).

25. J. Woodward, *Industrial Organizations: Theory and Practice* (London: Oxford University Press, 1965); also P. Lawrence and J. Lorsch, *Organization and Environment* (Boston: Harvard University Graduate School of Business, Division of Research, 1967).

26. C. Reeves and D. Bednar, "Defining Quality: Alternatives and Implications," *The Academy of Management Review*, July 1994, 419–445.

27. G. Bounds, L. Yorks, M. Adams, and G. Ranmey, *Beyond Total Quality Management: Toward the Emerging Paradigm* (New York: McGraw Hill, 1984), 11.

28. W. Deming, *Quality, Productivity and Competitive Advantage* (Cambridge: MIT Center for Advanced Engineering Study, 1982).

29. R.B. Reich, "Who Is Us?" *Harvard Business Review*, January–February 1990, 58.

30. Ibid., 55. The statistics are also based on this article (55–64).

31. J. Schermerhorn, *Managing Organizational Behavior* (New York: John Wiley, 1991), 71–72.

32. R.T. Moran and P.R. Harris, *Managing Cultural Synergy* (Houston, Tex.: Gulf Publishing, 1981), chap. 15, p. 3; also quoted in N. Adler, *International Dimensions of Organizational Behavior*, 2nd ed. (Boston, Mass.: PWS-Kent, 1991), 105.

33. D. Hellriegel, J. Slocum, Jr., and R. Woodman, *Organizational Behavior*, 8th ed. (Cincinnati, Ohio: International Thomson Publishing, 1998), 8.

34. W.B. Johnston, "Global Work Force 2000: The New World Labor Market," *Harvard Business Review*, March–April 1991, 115–127.

35. R.R. Thomas, "From Affirmative Action to Affirming Diversity," *Harvard Business Review*, March–April 1991, 109.

36. R. R. Thomas, "The Concept of Managing Diversity," *The Bureaucrat, The Journal for Public Managers*, Winter 1991–1992, 19–22.

37. T. Cox, Jr., *Cultural Diversity in Organizations, Theory, Research & Practice* (San Francisco: Berrett-Koehler, 1993), 3–40.

38. R.R. Thomas, "The Concept of Managing Diversity," *The Bureaucrat, The Journal for Public Managers*, Winter 1991–1992, 19.

39. T. Cox, Jr., *Cultural Diversity in Organizations,* 226; see also note 32.
40. J.W. Weiss, *Business Ethics, A Stakeholder and Issues Management Approach,* 2nd ed. (Philadelphia: The Dryden Press, 1998), 6. This section is based on perspectives and material from this book.
41. Ibid., 7, 8.
42. Ibid. Also, *The Wall Street Journal,* Tuesday, 30 November 1999: A, 1
43. L. Ackerman, "Development, Transition or Transformation: The Question of Change in Organizations," *OD Practitioner,* December 1986, 1–8.
44. This discussion is based on Chapter 8 in T. Cummings and C. Worley, *Organization Development and Change,* 5th ed. (Minneapolis/St. Paul: West, 1993).

## CHAPTER 2

1. R. Charan and G. Colvin, "Why CEOs Fail," *Fortune,* 21 June 1999, 69–78.
2. J. Royce, "Personality Integration: A Synthesis of the Parts and Wholes of Individual and Individual Theory," *Journal of Personality,* December 1983, 783–796.
3. A. Fisherly, "Making Change Stick," *Fortune,* 17 April 1995, 121.
4. G. Colvin, "How to Be a Great e-CEO," *Fortune,* 24 May 1999, 107.
5. L. Tobias, *Psychological Consulting to Management: A Clinician's Perspective* (New York: Brunner/Mazel, 1990), 148–156.
6. P. Sellers, "These Women Rule," *Fortune,* 25 October 1999, 101, 108.
7. K. Lewin, "Formalization and Progress in Psychology," in *Field Theory in Social Science,* ed. D. Cartwright (New York: Harper, 1951).
8. N.S. Endler and D. Magnusson, "Toward an Interactional Psychology of Personality," *Psychological Bulletin,* 83, 1976, 956–974.
9. J.R. Terborg, "Interactional Psychology and Research on Human Behavior in Organizations," *Academy of Management Review,* 6, 1981, 561–576; also quoted in D. Nelson and J. Quick, *Organizational Behavior* (Minneapolis/St. Paul: West, 1994), chap. 3.
10. See A. Cohen, H. Gadon, S. Fink, and R. Willits, with N. Josefowitz, *Effective Behavior in Organizations,* 4th ed. (Homewood, Ill.: Irwin, 1988), 199–212.
11. Ibid.
12. P. Jacob, J. Flink, and H. Schuchman, "Values and Their Function in Decision Making," *American Behavioral Scientist,* Vol. 5, 1962 (Supplement 9) 6–38; M. Rokeach, *The Nature of Human Values* (New York: Free Press, 1973).
13. M. Rokeach, *Beliefs, Attitudes, and Values* (San Francisco: Jossey-Bass, 1968).
14. D. Jamieson and J. O'Mara, *Managing Workforce 2000: Gaining the Diversity Advantage,* (San Francisco: Jossey-Bass, 1999), 28–29.
15. J. Cherlin, "I'm O.K., You're Selfish," *The New York Times Magazine* 1999, 44–50.
16. P. Kruger and K. Mieszkowski, "Stop the Fighting!" *Fast Company,* September, 1998, 93–111.
17. A. DeVito, J. Carlson, and J. Kraus, "Values in Relation to Career Orientation, Gender, and Each Other," *Counseling and Values,* July 1984, 202–206.
18. M. Rokeach and J. Regan, "The Roles of Values in the Counseling Situation," *Personnel and Guidance Journal,* May 1980; also R. Kreitner and A. Kinicki, *Organizational Behavior,* 2nd ed. (Homewood, Ill.: Irwin, 1992), 106.
19. D. McGregor, *The Human Side of Enterprise* (New York: McGraw-Hill, 1975).

20. M. Fishbein and I. Ajzen, *Beliefs, Attitude, and Behavior: An Introduction to Theory and Research* (Reading, Mass.: Addison-Wesley, 1975).

21. J. Gibson, J. Ivancevich, and J. Donnelly, Jr., *Organizations, Behavior, Structure, Processes*, 8th ed. (Burr Ridge, Ill.: Irwin, 1994), chap. 4.

22. Based on a presentation at Bentley College in Waltham, Massachusetts, 1994. Also see H. Levinson, *Executive* (Cambridge, Mass.: Harvard University Press, 1981).

23. L. Festinger, *A Theory of Cognitive Dissonance* (Evanston, Ill.: Row Peterson, 1975).

24. D. Weiss, R. Davis, G. England, and L. Lofquist, *Manual for the Minnesota Satisfaction Questionnaire* (Minneapolis: Industrial Relations Center, University of Minnesota, 1967).

25. S.B. Gustafson and M.D. Mumford, "Personal Style and Person-Environment Fit: A Pattern Approach," *Journal of Vocational Behavior*, April 1995, 163–188.

26. R.R. McCrae, "Why I Advocate the Five-Factor Model, Joint Factor Analyses of the NEO-PI with Other Instruments," in *Personality Psychology: Recent Trends and Emerging Directions*, ed. D.M. Buss and N. Cantor, (New York: Springer-Verlag, 1989), 237–245.

27. R. Tett, D. Jackson, and M. Rothstein, "Personality Measures as Predictors of Job Performance: A Meta-dialytic Review," *Personnel Psychology*, 44, 1991, 703–741; also J. Cortina, M. Schmitt, G. Kaufman, and R. Smith, "The Big Five Personality Factors in the IPI and MMPI: Predictors of Policy Performances," *Personnel Psychology*, 45, 1992, 119–140; and J. Greenberg and R. Baron, *Behavior in Organizations*, 5th ed. (Englewood Cliffs, N.J.: Prentice Hall, 1995), chap. 3.

28. S. Freud, "Psychopathy of Everyday Life," in *The Complete Works of Sigmund Freud*, standard edition, ed. J. Stachey (London: Hogarth Press, 1960).

29. C. Rogers, *On Personal Power: Inner Strength and Its Revolutionary Impact* (New York: Delacorte, 1977).

30. D.D. Clark and R. Hoyle, "A Theoretical Solution to the Problem of Personality-Situational Interaction," *Personality and Individual Differences*, 9, 1988, 133–138; also D. Byrne and L. J. Schulte, "Personality Dimensions and Predictors of Sexual Behavior," in *Annual Review of Sexual Research*, Vol. 1, ed. J. Bancroft (Philadelphia: Society for the Scientific Study of Sex, 1990).

31. J. George and A. Brief, "Feeling Good-Doing Good—A Conceptual Analysis of the Mood at Work-Organizational Spontaneity Relationships," *Psychological Bulletin*, 112, 1992, 310–329.

32. J. George, "Personality, Affect, and Behavior in Groups," *Journal of Applied Psychology*, 75, 1990, 107–116.

33. C.G. Jung, *Psychological Types* (New York: Harcourt & Brace, 1923).

34. S. Hirsch and J. Kummerow, *Life Types* (New York: Warner Books, 1989).

35. Cortina, et. al. 6, "The Big Five Personality Factors in the IPI and MMPI" 119–140. M.J. Schmit and A.M. Ryan, "The Big Five in Personnel Selection: Factor Structure in Applicant and Nonapplicant Populations," *Journal of Applied Psychology*, December 1993, 966–974. R. Kreitner and A. Kinicki, *Organizational Behavior*, 4th ed., 1998, see chap. 3.

36. Ibid.

37. M.P. Cronin, "This Is a Test," *Inc.*, August 1993, 64–68.

38. R. Benfari and J. Know, *Understanding Your Management Style* (Lexington, Mass.: Lexington Books, 1991).

39. C. Walck, "Training for Participative Management: Implications for Psychological Type," *Journal of Psychological Type*, 21, 1991, 3–12.

40. J.B. Rotter, "Internal versus External Control of Reinforcement: A Case History of a Variable," *American Psychologist*, April 1990, 489–493.

41. P. Nystrom, "Managers' Salaries and Their Beliefs About Reinforcement Control," *The Journal of Social Psychology*, August 1983, 291–292; also P. E. Spector, "Behavior in Organizations as a Function of Employees' Locus of Control," *Psychological Bulletin*, May 1982, 482–497; and D.R. Norris and R.E. Niebuhr, "Attributional Influences on Job-Performance Satisfaction Relationship," *Academy of Management Journal*, June 1984, 424–431.

42. A. Goldstein and M. Sercher, *Changing Supervisor Behavior* (New York: Pergamon Press, 1974); also S. Mayer and J. Russell, "Behavior Modeling Training in Organizations: Concerns and Conclusions," *Journal of Management*, Spring 1987, 21–40.

43. A. Farnham, "How to Nurture Creative Sparks," *Fortune*, 10 January 1994, 94–100.

44. A.S. Phillips and A.G. Bedeian, "Leader-Follower Exchange Quality: The Role of Personal and Interpersonal Attributes," *Academy of Management Journal*, August 1994, 990–1001; and Spector, "Behavior in Organizations as a Function of Employees' Locus of Control", 482–497.

45. M. Freidman and R. Roseman, *Type A Behavior and Your Heart* (New York: Alfred A. Knopf, 1974); also W. Kiechell III, "Attack of the Obsessive Managers," *Fortune*, 16 February 1987, 127–128.

46. J. Schaubroek, D.C. Ganster, and B.E. Kemmerer, "Job Complexity, 'Type A' Behavior, and Cardiovascular Disorder: A Prospective Study," *Academy of Management Journal*, 37, 1994, 426–439.

47. P. Pelham and W. Swann, Jr., "From Self-Conceptions to Self-Worth: On the Sources and Structure of Global Self-Esteem," *Journal of Personality and Social Psychology*, 57, 1989, 672–680; also A. Baumgardner, C. Kaufman, and P. Levy, "Regulating Affect Interpersonally: When Low Esteem Leads to Greater Enhancement," *Journal of Personality and Social Psychology*, 56, 1989, 906–921.

48. B. Sclenker, M. Weingold, and J. Hallem, "Self-Serving Attributions in Social Context: Effects of Self-Esteem and Social Pressure," *Journal of Personality and Social Psychology*, 57, 1990, 855–863.

49. A. Bandura, "Regulation of Cognitive Processes Through Perceived Self-Efficacy," *Development Psychology*, September 1989, 729–735.

50. K. Thomas and B. Velthouse, "Cognitive Elements of Empowerment: An 'Interpretative' Model of Intrinsic Task Motivation," *Academy of Management Review*, 15, 1990, 381–394.

51. J. Pierce, D. Gardner, L. Cummings, and R. Duhman, "Organization-Based Self-Esteem: Construct Definition, Measurement, and Validation," *Academy of Management Journal*, September 1989, 625.

52. Ibid., 622–648.

53. J. Matejka and R. Dunsing, "Great Expectations," *Management World*, January 1987, 16–17.

54. T. Cox, Jr., *Cultural Diversity in Organizations, Theory, Research, and Practice* (San Francisco: Berrett-Koehler, 1993), 65.

55. S. Budner, "Intolerance of Ambiguity as a Personal Variable," *Journal of Personality*, 30, 1962, 29–50.

56. M. Ijzendoorn, "Moral Judgment, Authoritarianism, and Ethnocentrism," *Journal of Social Psychology*, 1989, 37–45.

57. Cox, 65–66 (see note 54).

58. P. Senge, *The Fifth Discipline* (New York: Doubleday/Currency, 1990), 139.
59. Ibid., chap. 9.
60. Ibid., 148.
61. Ibid., 149.
62. Ibid., 143.
63. S. Covey, *The 7 Habits of Highly Effective People* (New York: Simon & Schuster, 1989), 47.
64. Ibid., 188.
65. Ibid., 207.
66. Ibid., 264.
67. Ibid., 284.
68. Ibid., 288.
69. J. Collins and F. Schmidt, "Personality, Integrity, and White Collar Crime: A Construct Validity Study," *Personnel Psychology*, 46, 1993, 295–311; also J. Richardson, *Annual Editions: Business Ethics 93/94* (Guilford, Conn.: Dushkin, 1993); and Greenberg and Baron, *Behavior in Organizations*, 94.

## CHAPTER 3

1. R. Hof, "A New Era of Bright Hopes and Terrible Fears: The Internet Age," *Business Week*, 4 October 1999, 84, 86.
2. B. O'Reilly, "360 Feedback Can Change Your Life," *Fortune*, 17 October 1994, 93–100.
3. B.K. Boyd, G.G. Dess, and A.M.A. Rasheed, "Divergence Between Archival and Perceptual Measures of the Environment: Causes and Consequences," *Academy of Management Review*, April 1993, 204–226.
4. S. Fiske and S. Taylor, *Social Cognition* (Reading, Mass.: Addison-Wesley, 1984).
5. This four-step process model, the social information processing model, is derived from S. Fiske and S. Taylor, *Social Conditioning* (Reading, Mass.: Addison-Wesley, 1984); see also D. Schneider, "Social Cognition," *Annual Review of Psychology*, 4(2), 1991; 527–561.
6. B. Bass, *Organizational Decision Making* (Homewood, Ill.: Richard D. Irwin, 1983).
7. K.J. Williams and G.M. Alliger, "Role Stressors, Mood Spillover, and Perceptions of Work-Family Conflict in Employed Parents," *Academy of Management Journal*, August 1994, 837–868.
8. S. Fiske and S. Neuberg, "A Continuum of Impression Formation, from Category-Based to Individuating Processes: Influences of Information and Motivation on Attention and Interpretation," in *Advances in Experimental Social Psychology*, ed. M. Zanna, Vol. 23 1–74 (New York: Academic Press, 1990).
9. M. Levine and J. Shefner, *Fundamental of Sensation and Perceptions* (Reading, Mass.: Addison-Wesley, 1981); also G.T. Chao and S. Kozlowski, "Employee Perceptions on the Implementation of Robotic Manufacturing Technology," *Journal of Applied Psychology*, 71 (1) 1986, 70–76; and S.F. Cronshaw and R.G. Lord, "Effects of Categorization, Attribution, and Encoding Processes in Leadership Perceptions," *Journal of Applied Psychology*, 72 (1) 1987; 97–106. See also J. R. Schermerhorn, Jr., J. G. Hunt, and R. N. Osborn, *Managing Organizational Behavior*, 5th ed. (New York: John Wiley, 1994), 154.

10. R. Wyer and T. Srull, "The Processing of Social Stimulus Information: A Conceptual Integration," in *Person Memory: The Cognitive Basis of Social Perception*, ed. R. Hastie, T. Ostrom, E. Ebbesen, R. Wyer, Jr., D. Hamilton, and D. Carlston, (Hillsdale, N.J.: Erlbaum, 1980).

11. J.C. Wofford, "An Examination of the Cognitive Processes Used to Handle Employee Job Problems," *Academy of Management Journal*, 1994, 180–192.

12. T. Cox Jr. and R. Beale, *Developing Competency to Manage Diversity* (San Francisco: Berrett-Koehler 1997); 96–97.

13. See J. Sherman, "Development and Mental Representation of Stereotypes," *Journal of Personality and Social Psychology*, June 1996, 1126–1141.

14. Cox and Beale, *Developing Competency to Manage Diversity*, 96–97.

15. Oleson, "Maintaining Stereotypes in the Face of Disconfirmation: Constructing Grounds for Subtyping Deviants," *Journal of Personality and Social Psychology*, April 1995, 565–579; and R. Kreitner and A. Kinicki, *Organizational Behavior*, 4th ed., (Boston: Irwin McGraw-Hill, 1998), chap. 6.

16. E. Robinson and J. Hickman, "The Diversity Elite," *Fortune*, 19 July 1999, 62–70.

17. B. Avolio, D. Waldman, and M. McDaniel, "Age and Work Performance in Nonmanagerial Jobs: The Effects of Experience and Occupational Type," *Academy of Management Journal*, June 1990, 407–422. E.G. Burkins, "Work Week: A Special News Report About Life on the Job—and Trends Taking Shape There," *The Wall Street Journal*, 5 May 1996, A1; A.M. and S. Rhodes, "Age-Related Differences in Work Attitudes and Behavior: A Review and Conceptual Analysis," *Psychological Bulletin*, March 1983, 38–367.

18. P. Kruger and K. Mieszkowski, "Stop the Fight!" *Fast Company*, September 1998, 104.

19. Ibid.

20. B. Allen, "Gender Stereotypes Are Not Accurate: A Replication of Martin (2986) Using Diagnostic vs. Self-Report and Behavioral Criteria," *Sex Roles*, May 1995, 583–600.

21. V. Schein, R. Mueller, T. Lituchy, and J. Liu, "Think Manager—Think Male: A Global Phenomenon?" *Journal of Organizational Behavior*, January 1996, 33–41.

22. J. Weiss, *Business Ethics: A Stakeholder and Issues Management Approach*, 2nd ed. (Fort Worth, Tex.: The Dryden Press, 1998), 193.

23. D. Dearborn and H. Simon, "Selective Perception: A Note on the Departmental Identification of Executives," *Sociometry*, June 1958, 140–144; and M. Waller, G. Huber, and W. Glick, "Selective Perception," *Academy of Management Journal*, August 1995, 953–974; and J. Bunderson, "Work History and Selective Perception: Fine-Tuning What We Know," in *Academy of Management Best Papers Proceedings*, ed. D. Moore (Vancouver, BC: Academy of Management Conference, 2995, 459–563.

24. H. Kelley, *Attribution in Social Interaction* (New York: General Learning Press, 1971); also "The Processes of Causal Attribution," *American Psychologist*, February 1973, 107–128.

25. B. Schneider, "The People Make the Place," *Personnel Psychology*, 40, 1987, 437–453.

26. J. Olson and M. Ross, "Attribution: Past, Present, and Future," in *Attribution: Basis Issues and Applications*, ed. J. Harvey and G. Wells, (New York: Academic Press, 1988), 282–311.

27. C. Torres and M. Bruxelles, "Capitalizing on Global Diversity," *HR Magazine*, December 1992, 30.

28. T. Cox, Jr., *Cultural Diversity in Organizations, Theory, Research, & Practice* (San Francisco: Berrett-Koehler, 1993), 64.
29. Ibid.
30. Ibid., 92.
31. S. Rhinesmith, "Global Mindsets for Global Managers," *Training & Development*, October 1992, 63.
32. Ibid., 64.
33. N. Chikudate, "Cross-Cultural Analysis of Cognitive Systems in Organizations: A Comparison Between Japanese and American Organizations," *Management International Review*, 31 (3), 1991, 213–219.
34. N. Abramson, H. Lane, H. Nagai, and H. Takagi, "A Comparison of Canadian and Japanese Cognitive Styles: Implications for Management Interaction," *Journal of International Business Studies*, Third Quarter 1993, 575–587.
35. Ibid.
36. Cox, *Cultural Diversity*, 130.
37. S. Jenner, "The British Roots of Business Ideology," *Journal of General Management*, 10(1), 44–56; and R. Edfelt, "A Look at American Managerial Styles," *Business*, 36(1), 51–54.
38. T. Adorno, E. Frenkel-Brunswik, D. Levinson, and R. Sanford, *The Authoritarian Personality* (New York: Harper Collins, 1950); also M. Ijzendoorn, "Moral Judgment, Authoritarianism, and Ethnocentrism," *Journal of Social Psychology*, 129, (1) 37–45.
39. See Cox, *Cultural Diversity*, 133; and D. Taylor and V. Jaggi, "Ethnocentrism and Causal Attribution in a South Indian Context," *Journal of Cross-Cultural Psychology*, 5 (19), 162–177.
40. B. Schlenker, *Impression Management: The Self-Concept, Social Identity and Interpersonal Relations* (Monterey, Calif.: Brooks/Cole, 1980); also eds. R. Giacolone and P. Rosenfeld, *Impression Management in Organizations* (Hillsdale, N.J.: Erlbaum, 1990); J. Tedeschi and V. Melburg, "Impression Management and Influence in the Organizations," in *Research in the Sociology of Organizations*, eds. S. Bacharach and E. Lawler, (Greenwich, Conn.: JAI Press, 1984), 31–58.
41. S. Wayne and K. Kacman, "The Effects of Impression Management on the Performance Appraisal Process," *Organizational Behavior and Human Decision Processes*, 18, 1991, 70–88; D. Gilmore and C. Ferris, "The Effects of Applicant Management Tactics on Interviewer Judgments," *Journal of Management*, December 1989, 557–564.
42. J.C. Wofford, "An Examination of the Cognitive Processes Used to Handle Employee Job Problems," *Academy of Management Journal*, February 1994, 190.
43. Ibid.
44. R. McIntyre and M. Capen, "A Cognitive Style Perspective on Ethical Questions," *Journal of Business Ethics*, 12, 1993, 629–634. (note limitations of this study that are pointed out on page 633, for example, that the sample consists of business students; however, the typical ethical questions in the study tend to be most commonly encountered by salespersons); related studies on this topic include J. Fleming, "A Suggested Approach to Linking Decision Styles with Business Ethics," *Journal of Business Ethics*, 4, 1985, 137–144; and A. Dubinsky and T. Ingram, "Correlates of Salespeople's Ethical Conflict: An Exploratory Investigation," *Journal of Business Ethics*, 3, 1984, 343–353.

45. C.G. Jung, *Psychological Types*, trans. H.G. Baynes, rev. R.F.C. Hull (Princeton, N.J.: Princeton University Press, 1971).

46. McIntyre and Capen, "A Cognitive Style Perspective," 629–634.

## CHAPTER 4

1. *Fast Company* survey, "How Much Is Enough?" July–August, 1999, 108–119.

2. A. Deutschman, "The Managing Wisdom of High-Tech Superstars," *Fortune*, 17 October 1994, 197–206.

3. S. Shellenbarger, "What Job Candidates Really Want to Know: Will I Have a Life," *The Wall Street Journal*, 17 November 1999, p. B1.

4. A. Maslow, *Motivation and Personality* (New York: Harper & Row, 1954); also, "A Theory of Human Motivation," *Psychological Review*, July 1943, 370–396.

5. A. Maslow, "Critique of Self-Actualization Theory," *Journal of Humanistic Education and Development*, March 1991, 103–108.

6. L. Bolman and T. Deal, *Reframing Organizations, Artistry, Choice, and Leadership* (San Francisco: Jossey-Bass, 1991), 131.

7. D. McGregor, *The Human Side of Enterprise* (New York: McGraw-Hill, 1960).

8. Ibid.

9. Ibid., 61.

10. Ibid.

11. Bolman and Deal, *Reframing Organizations* 127.

12. C. Alderfer, *Existence, Relatedness, and Growth: Human Needs in Organizational Settings* (New York: Free Press, 1972); and "An Empirical Test of a Need Theory of Human Needs," *Organizational Behavior and Human Performance*, April 1969, 142–175.

13. J. Gordon, R. Mondy, A. Sharplin, and S. Premeaux, *Management and Organizational Behavior* (Boston: Allyn and Bacon, 1990).

14. J. Wamous and A. Zwany, "A Cross-Sectional Test of Need Hierarchy Theory," *Organizational Behavior and Human Performance*, February 1977, 78–97.

15. F. Herzberg, B. Mausner, and B. Synderman, *The Motivation of Work* (New York: John Wiley, 1959); C. Alderfer, "One More Time: How Do You Motivate Employees?" *Harvard Business Review*, January–February 1968.

16. A. Korman, *Industrial and Organizational Psychology* (Englewood Cliffs, N.J.: Prentice Hall, 1971), 148–150; and E.E. Lawler III, *Motivation in Work Organizations* (Monterey, Calif.: Brooks/Cole, 1973), 72.

17. D. McClelland, *The Achieving Society* (Princeton, N.J.: Van Nostrand, 1961); and D. McClelland and D. Winter, *Motivating Economic Achievement* (New York: Free Press, 1971).

18. J. Hall and J. Hawker, *Power Management Inventory* (The Woodlands, Tex.: Telemetrics International, 1988); also D. Nelson and J. Quick, *Organizational Behavior* (Minneapolis/St. Paul: West Publishing, 1994).

19. P. Miron and D. McClelland, "The Impact of Achievement Motivation Training in Small Businesses," *California Management Review*, Summer 1979, 13–28.

20. J. Miller and J. Kilpatrick, *Issues for Managers: An International Perspective* (Homewood, Ill.: Irwin, 1987); J. Schermerhorn, Jr., J. Hunt, and R. Osborn, *Managing Organizational Behavior*, 5th ed. (New York: John Wiley, 1994).

21. D. McClelland, *The Achieving Society* (Princeton, N.J.: Van Nostrand, 1961); and D. McClelland and D. Winter, *Motivating Economic Achievement* (New York: Free Press, 1971).

22. D. McClelland and R. Boyatzis, "Leadership Motive Pattern and Long-Term Success in Management," *Journal of Applied Psychology*, 67, 1982, 737–743.

23. P. Machungiva and N. Schmitt, "Work Motivation in a Developing Country," *Journal of Applied Psychology*, February 1983, 31–42; J. Gibson, J. Ivancevich, and J. Donnelly, Jr., *Organizations*, 8th ed. (Burr Ridge, Ill.: Irwin, 1994).

24. J. Stacey Adams, "Toward an Understanding of Equity," *Journal of Abnormal and Social Psychology*, November 1963, 422–436.

25. M. Carrell and J. Dittrich, "Equity Theory: The Recent Literature, Methodological Considerations, and New Directions," *Academy of Management Review* 3, 1978, 202–210.

26. J. Greenberg and G. Leventhal, "Equity and the Use of Overreward to Motivate Performance," *Journal of Personality and Social Psychology* 34, 1976, 179–190.

27. R. Huseman, J. Hatfield, and E. Miles, "A New Perspective on Equity Theory: The Equity Sensitivity Construct," *Academy of Management Review*, 12, 1987, 222–234.

28. J. Greenberg, "Equity and Workplace Status: A Field Experiment," *Journal of Applied Psychology*, November 1988, 606–613.

29. R. Cosier and D. Dalton, "Equity Theory and Time: A Reformulation," *Academy of Management Review*, April 1983, 311–319.

30. R. Folger and M. Knovsky, "Efforts of Procedural and Distributive Justice on Reactions to Pay Raise Decisions," *Academy of Management Journal*, March 1989, 115–130.

31. V. Vroom, *Work and Motivation* (New York: John Wiley, 1964).

32. R. Mowday, "Equity Theory Predictions of Behavior in Organizations," in *Motivation and Work Behavior*, 4th ed., ed. R. Steers and L. Porter (New York: McGraw-Hill, 1987), 89–110.

33. L. Porter and E.E. Lawler III, *Managerial Attitudes and Performance* (Homewood, Ill.: Irwin, 1968).

34. J. Wanous, T. Keon, and J. Latack, "Expectancy Theory and Occupational and Organizational Choices: A Review and Test," *Organizational Behavior and Human Performance*, August 1983, 66–86; also E. Pulakos and N. Schmitt, "A Longitudinal Study of a Valence Model Approach for the Prediction of Job Satisfaction of New Employees," *Journal of Applied Psychology*, May 1983, 307–312.

35. S. Kerr, "On the Folly of Rewarding A, While Hoping for B," *Academy of Management Journal*, December 1975, 769–783.

36. L. Miller, *Behavior Management* (New York: John Wiley, 1978); also F. Luthans, *Organizational Behavior* (New York: McGraw-Hill, 1985); and Gibson, Ivancevich, and Donnelly, *Organizations*.

37. K. O'Hara, C. Johnson, and T. Beecher, "Organizational Behavior Management in the Private Sector: A Review of Empirical Research and Recommendations for Further Investigation," *Academy of Management Review*, October 1985, 848–864.

38. E. Locke, "The Myths of Behavior Modification in Organizations," *Academy of Management Review*, October 1977, 543–553.

39. A. Locke and G. Latham, *A Theory of Goal Setting and Task Performance* (Englewood Cliffs, N.J.: Prentice Hall, 1990).

40. Ibid.

41. G. Doran, *Management Review* (New York: American Management Association, 1981), also see J. Weiss, *5-Phase Project Management: A Professional Implementation Guide* (Reading, Mass.: Addison-Wesley, 1992).

42. E. Locke, K. Shaw, L. Saari, and G. Latham, "Goal Setting and Task Performance: 1969–1980," *Psychological Bulletin*, July 1981, 129.

43. E. Locke, G. Latham, and M. Erez, "The Determinants of Goal Commitment," *Academy of Management Review*, 13, 1988, 23–39.

44. E. Locke and G. Latham, *A Theory of Goal Setting and Task Performance* (Englewood Cliffs, N.J.: Prentice Hall, 1990).

45. E. Locke, E. Frederick, C. Lee, and P. Bobko, "Effect of Self-Efficacy, Goals, and Task Strategies on Task Performance," *Journal of Applied Psychology*, 69, 1984, 241–251.

46. E.E. Lawler III, "Reward Systems" in *Improving Life at Work*, ed. J.R. Hackman and J.L. Suttle (Santa Monica, Calif.: Goodyear, 1977).

47. This discussion is based in part on N. Adler, *International Dimensions of Organizational Behavior*, 2nd ed. (Boston: PWS-Kent Publishing, 1991).

48. G. Hofstede, "Motivation, Leadership and Organization: Do American Theories Apply Abroad?" *Organizational Dynamics*, Summer 1980, 42–63.

49. E. Nevis, "Using an American Perspective in Understanding Another Culture: Toward a Hierarchy of Needs for the People's Republic of China," *The Journal of Applied Behavioral Science*, 19 (3), 1983, 249–264.

50. Ibid.

51. Ibid.

52. G. Hines, "Cross-Cultural Differences in Two-Factor Theory," *Journal of Applied Psychology*, 58 (5), 1973, 375–377.

53. R. Crabbs, "Work Motivation in the Culturally Complex Panama Canal Company," *Academy of Management Proceedings*, 1973, 119–126.

54. D.A. Nadler and E.E. Lawler III, "Quality of Work Life: Perspectives and Directions," *Organizational Dynamics*, II, 1973, 157.

55. J. Miller and J. Kilpatrick, *Issues for Managers: An International Perspective* (Homewood, Ill.: Irwin, 1987).

56. A. Deutschman and D.S. Cooper, "What 25-Year-Olds Want," *Fortune*, 27 August 1990, 42. Also see "Stop the Fight, Battle of the Generations 20 Somethings vs 40 Somethings," *Fast Company*, September 1998, 93–113.

57. D. Jamieson, and J. O'Mara, *Managing Workforce 2000: Gaining the Diversity Advantage* and 2nd ed. (San Francisco: Jossey-Bass, 1991, 1999), 17.

58. Ibid., 17.

59. Ibid., 22.

60. T. Cox, Jr., *Cultural Diversity in Organizations, Theory, Research, & Practice* (San Francisco: Berrett-Koehler, 1993), 83.

61. Ibid., 85, as based on R. Rosenthal, *On the Social Psychology of the Self-Fulfilling Prophecy: Further Evidence for Pygmalion Effects and Their Mediating Mechanisms* (New York: MSS Modular Publications), 53.

62. J. Weiss, *Business Ethics: A Stakeholder, Issues Management Approach*, 2nd ed. (The Dryden Press, 1998).

63. R. Katzell and D. Thompson, "Work Motivation: Theory and Practice," *The American Psychologist*, February 1990, 144.

64. Ibid.
65. Ibid.
66. Ibid.


# CHAPTER 5

1. C. Dahle,"Xtreme Teams," *Fast Company*, November, 1999, 320–326.
2. J.R. Katzenbach and D.K. Smith, "The Discipline of Teams," *Harvard Business Review*, March-April 1993, 112. Also see their book, *The Wisdom of Teams: Creating the High Performance Organization* (Boston, Mass.: Harvard Business School Press, 1992).
3. M. Shaw, "Group Dynamics," *The Psychology of Small Group Behavior*, 3rd ed. (New York: McGraw Hill, 1981), 11.
4. Katzenbach and Smith (1993), "The Discipline of Teams," 113.
5. J. Gordon, "Work Teams, How Far Have They Come?" *Training*, October 1992, 59–65.
6. B. Dumaine, "The Trouble with Teams," *Fortune*, 5 September 1994, 86–92.
7. J. Weiss and H. Thamhain, "Strategies for Effectively Managing Geographically Dispersed Projects," Paper presented at the IAMOT conference, Miami, Florida, February 2000.
8. Ibid.
9. Ibid.
10. Ibid.
11. P. Harris and R. Moran, *Managing Cultural Differences*, 2nd ed. (Houston: Gulf Publishing, 1987), 168, 169. Used with permission.
12. J. Moosbruker, "Developing a Productive Team: Making Groups at Work Work," in *Team Building: Blueprints for Productivity and Satisfaction*, ed. W. Reddy and K. Jamison (Alexandria, Va.: NTL Institute for Applied Behavioral Science, 1988); also, J. Gordon, *A Diagnostic Approach to Organizational Behavior*, 4th ed. (Boston: Allyn and Bacon, 1993), 184.
13. S. Buchholz and T. Roth, *Creating the High Performance Team*, (New York: John Wiley, 1987), xi, 17.
14. R. Kreitner and A. Kinicki, *Organizational Behavior*, 2nd ed. (Homewood, Ill.: Irwin, 1992), 415; R.S. Wellins, W.C. Byham, and J.M. Wilson, *Empowered Teams* (San Francisco: Jossey-Bass, 1991), 4.
15. D. Whetten and K. Cameron, *Developing Management Skills*, 4th ed. (Reading, Mass.: Addison-Wesley), 35–173.
16. S. Caminiti, "What Team Leaders Need to Know," *Fortune*, 20 February 1995, 93.
17. Ibid., 94–98.
18. Ibid.
19. L. Holpp, "Making Choices, Self-Directed Teams or Total Quality Management?" *Training*, May 1992, 72.
20. R. Brough, "Total Quality Management in State Government: The Eight Rules for Producing Results," *The Journal of State Government*, 1992, 4–8.
21. C. Miller, "U.S. Firms Lag in Meeting Global Quality Standards," *Marketing News*, 15 February 1993, 1, 16; and J. Schermerhorn, Jr., J. Hunt, and R. Osborn, *Managing Organizational Behavior*, 5th ed. (New York: John Wiley, 1994) chap. 2.

22. P. Harris and R. Moran, *Managing Cultural Differences*, 2nd ed. (Houston: Gulf Publishing, 1987), 168–169. Copyright 1991 by Gulf Publishing Company, Houston, TX.

23. K. Benne and P. Sheats, "Functional Roles of Group Members," *Journal of Social Issues*, 4, (1948), 473–506.

24. N. Adler, *International Dimensions of Organizational Behavior*, 2nd ed. (Boston: PWS-Kent, 1991).

25. Ibid., 135.

26. Ibid.

27. Harris and Moran, *Managing Cultural Differences*, 311, see note 11.

28. N. Phillips and B. Ridge, *Managing International Teams* (Homewood, Ill.: Irwin, 1994).

29. K. Price, "Decision Responsibility, Task Responsibility, Identifiability, and Social Loafing," *Organizational Behavior and Human Decision Processes*, 40, 1987, 330–345.

30. P. Schindler and C. Thomas, "The Structure of Interpersonal Trust in the Workplace, "*Psychological Reports*, October 1993, 563–573.

31. J. Butler and R. Cantrell, "A Behavioral Decision Theory Approach to Modeling Dyadic Trust in Superiors and Subordinates," *Psychological Reports*, August 1984, 19–28.

32. L. Nash, "Ethics Without the Sermon," *Harvard Business Review*, November-December 1981, 88; also J. Weiss, *Business Ethics, A Managerial, Stakeholder Approach* (Belmont, Calif.: Wadsworth, 1994), chap. 3.

33. I. Janis, "Groupthink," *Psychology Today*, November 1971, 43–46.

34. I. Janis, *Victims of Groupthink*, 2nd ed. (Boston: Houghton Mifflin, 1982).

35. Ibid.

36. These techniques are discussed in G.P. Huber, *Managerial Decision Making* (Glenview, Ill.: Scott Foresman, 1980).

37. A.L. Delbecq, A.L. Van de Ven, and D.H. Gustafson, *Group Techniques for Program Planning: A Guide to Nominal Groups and Delphi Techniques* (Glenview, Ill.: Scott Foresman, 1975); and W.M. Fox, "Anonymity and Other Keys to Successful Problem-Solving Meetings," *National Productivity Review*, Spring 1989, 145–156.

38. H.A. Linstone and M. Turoff, eds., *The Delphi Methods: Techniques and Applications* (Reading, Mass.: Addison Wesley, 1975).

39. J.W. Weiss and R.W. Wysocki, *5-Phase Project Management: A Practical Planning and Implementation Guide* (Reading, Mass.: Addison-Wesley, 1992).

40. H. Kerzner, *Project Management: A Systems Approach to Planning, Scheduling, and Controlling* (New York: Van Nostrand Reinhold, 1979).

## CHAPTER 6

1. D. Coleman, ed., *GroupWare: Collaborative Strategies for LANs and Intranets* (Upper Saddle River, N.J.: Prentice Hall, 1997).

2. J. Kelly, "Executive Behavior, Classical and Existential," *Business Horizons*, January 1993; and A. Deutschman, "The CEO's Secret of Managing Time," *Fortune*, 1 June 1992, 135. Also see R. Charan and G. Colvin, "Why CEOs Fail," *Fortune*, 21 June 1999, 68–80.

3. P. Newman, "Polaroid Develops Communications System—But Not Instantly," in *Readings in Organizational Behavior*, ed. R. Sims, D. White, and D. Bednar (Boston: Allyn and Bacon, 1994, 169–177).

4. Ibid., 176.

5. H. Lasswell, *Power and Personality* (New York: W.W. Norton, 1948) 37–51. Also see J. Gibson, J. Ivancevich, and J. Donnelly, Jr., *Organizations* (Burr Ridge, Ill.: Irwin, 1994).

6. A. Cohen, S. Fink, H. Gadon, R. Willitts, and N. Josefowitz, *Effective Behavior in Organizations*, 5th ed. (Homewood, Ill.: Irwin, 1992), 279.

7. See J. Weiss and H. Thamhain, "Strategies for Effectively Managing Geographically Dispersed Teams and Groups." Paper delivered at the IAMOT Conference, Miami, Florida, February 1999.

8. R. Bolton, *People Skills* (New York: Simon & Schuster, 1979).

9. J. Waters, "Managerial Assertiveness," *Business Horizons*, September-October 1982, 24–29.

10. Bolton, *People Skills*, 17.

11. D. Tannen, *You Just Don't Understand: Women and Men in Conversation* (New York: William Morrow, 1990); also L. Glass, *He Says, She Says: Closing the Communication Between the Sexes* (New York: G.P. Putnam's Sons, 1992).

12. J. Hall and M. Williams, *The Personal Relations Survey* (Woodlands, Tex.: Telometrics International). Johari's Window was developed by Drs. Joseph Luft and Harry Ingham.

13. L. Sussman, "Managers on the Defensive," *Business Horizons*, 34, 1991, 81–87.

14. A.S. Phillips and A.G. Bedeian, "Leader-Follower Exchange Quality: The Role of Personal and Interpersonal Attributes," *The Academy of Management Journal*, August 1994, 990–1001.

15. Based on A. Athos and J. Gabarro, *Interpersonal Behavior, Communication and Understanding Relationships* (Englewood Cliffs, N.J.: Prentice Hall, 1978), 87.

16. T.A. Stewart, "Managing in a Wired Company," *Fortune*, 11 July 1994, 56.

17. Ibid., 46.

18. Ibid., 44.

19. Ibid.

20. O. Baskin and A. Aronoff, *Interpersonal Communications in Organizations* (Santa Monica, Calif.: Goodyear, 1989).

21. J. Moreno, "Contributions of Sociometry to Research Methodology in Sociology," *Sociological Review*, 12, 1947, 287–292.

22. Stewart, "Managing in a Wired Company."

23. R. Smith, "FedEx's Key to Success," *Management Review*, July 1993, 23–25.

24. N. Adler, *International Dimensions of Organizational Behavior*, 2nd ed. (Boston: PWS-Kent, 1991).

25. P. Harris and R. Moran, *Managing Cultural Differences* (Houston: Gulf Publishing, 1987),

26. Copyright 1991 by Gulf Publishing Company, Houston, TX.

27. E. Hall, *Beyond Culture* (Garden City, N.Y.: Anchor Press/Doubleday, 1976).

28. Ibid.

29. J. Weiss and S. Bloom, "Managing in China: Expatriate Experiences and Training Recommendations," *Business Horizons*, May–June 1990, 26.

31. L. Trevino and K. Nelson, *Managing Business Ethics* (New York: John Wiley, 1995).

## CHAPTER 7

1. D. Tapscott, *Digital Economy, Promise and Peril in the Age of Networked Intelligence* (New York: McGraw-Hill, 1995), 249–251.
2. Ibid.
3. D. Yoffe and M. Cusumano, "Building a Company on Internet Time: Lessons from Netscape," *California Management Review*, Spring 1999, 8.
4. Ibid., 11–27.
5. T. Stewart, "Leaders of the Future: Have You Got What It Takes?" *Fortune*, 11 October 1999, 318–322
6. J. Kotter, *Leading Change* (Boston: Harvard Business School Press, 1996).
7. F. Fiedler, "Research on Leadership Selection and Training: One View of the Future," *Administrative Science Quarterly*, June 1996, 241–250.
8. J.P. Kotter, *A Force for Change: How Leadership Differs from Management* (New York: Free Press, 1990).
9. R.E. Kelley, "In Praise of Followers," *Harvard Business Review*, November–December 1988, 143.
10. Ibid., 147.
11. S.C. Lundin and L. Lancaster, "Beyond Leadership: The Importance of Followership," *The Futurist*, May-June 1990, 18–22.
12. D.S. Alcorn, "Dynamic Followership: Empowerment at Work," *Management Quarterly*, Spring 1992, 10.
13. Lundin and Lancaster, "Beyond Leadership: The Importance of Followership," 20.
14. Ibid.
15. J. Huey, op. cit. 48, "The New Post-Heroic Leadership," *Fortune*, 21 February 1994; 42–50.
16. Kelley, "In Praise of Followers," 145.
17. W. Bennis and B. Nanus, *Leaders: The Strategies for Taking Charge* (New York: Harper & Row, 1985), 26–81.
18. P.J. Schoemaker, "How to Link Strategic Vision to Core Capabilities," *Sloan Management Review*, Fall 1992, 67.
19. Ibid., 78. For an update on Apple Computer's strategies and leadership, see D. Kirkpatrick, "The Second Coming of Apple," *Fortune*, 9 November 1998, 87–92.
20. J.M. Kouzes and B. Posner, *The Leadership Challenge: How to Get Extraordinary Things Done in Organizations* (San Francisco: Jossey-Bass, 1991), 113.
21. G. Colvin, "How to be a Great e-CEO," *Fortune*, 17 April 1995, 121.
22. Ibid., 131–160.
23. C.A. O'Reilly and K.H. Roberts, "Information Filtration in Organizations: Three Experiments," *Organizational Behavior and Human Performance*, 11, 1974, 253–265.
24. Bennis and Nanus, *Leaders: The Strategies for Taking Charge*, 55–78,
25. A. Cohen, S. Fink, H. Gadow, R. Willits, with N. Josefowitz, *Effective Behavior in Organizations*, 5th ed. (Homewood, Ill.: Irwin, 1992), 314–319.
26. C. C. Manz, "Developing Self Leaders Through SuperLeadership," *Supervisory Management*, September 1991, 3.
27. Ibid.
28. C.C. Manz and H.P. Sims, Jr., "Superleadership: Beyond the Myth of Heroic Leadership," *Organizational Dynamics*, Spring 1991: 23, 30; see also their book *Superleadership: Leading Others to Lead Themselves* (New York: Prentice Hall, 1989); see also note 32.

29. B. O'Reilly, "360 Feedback Can Change Your Life," *Fortune*, 17 October 1994; 93–100.

30. N.M. Tichy and M.A. Devanna, *The Transformational Leader* (New York: John Wiley, 1990); also N.M. Tichy, *Managing Strategic Change* (New York: John Wiley, 1983); and B.J. Avolio and B.M. Bass, "Transformational Leadership, Charisma, and Beyond," in *Emerging Leadership Vistas*, ed. J.G. Hunt, B.R. Baliga, H.P. Dachler, and C.A. Schriesheim, (Lexington, Mass.: Lexington Books, 1988).

31. Tichy and Devanna, *The Transformational Leader*, 33.

32. This discussion is based on the following sources: B.M. Bass, "Leadership, Good, Better, Best," *Organizational Dynamics* March 1987, 26–40; J.J. Hater and B.M. Bass, "Superiors' Evaluations and Subordinates' Perceptions of Transformational and Transactional Leadership," *Journal of Applied Psychology* March 1987, 695–701; I.C. MacMillan, "New Business Development: A Challenge to Transformational Leadership and the Falling Dominoes Effect," *Group and Organizational Studies*, March 1987, 73–87.

33. J.A. Conger and R.N. Kanungo, *The Charismatic Leader: Behind the Mystiques of Exceptional Leadership* (San Francisco: Jossey-Bass, 1991), 14.

34. J.M. Kouzes and B.Z. Posner, op. cit., 14.

35. Tichy and Devanna, 271–280.

36. S. Sherman, "Leaders Learn to Heed to Voice Within," 93, *Fortune*, 22 Auagust 1994, 92–100.

37. For a theoretical overview of administrative and leadership "logics of action," see J.W. Weiss, "The Historical and Political Perspective on Organizations of Lucien Karpik," in *Complex Organizations, Critical Perspectives,* ed. M. Zey-Ferrell and M. Aiken, (Glenview, Ill.: Scott, Foresman, 1981); and *Organization and Environment: Theory, Issues, and Reality*, ed. L. Karpik, (Beverly Hills, Calif.: Sage, 1978). For a study of the observed leadership "logics of action," see J.W. Weiss, *The Management of Change, Administrative Logics and Actions* (New York: Praeger, 1986).

38. J.A. Conger, "The Dark Side of Leadership," *Organizational Dynamics*, 19, 2, 1990; 4–55.

39. J.M. Howell and B.J. Avolio, "The Ethics of Charismatic Leadership: Submission or Liberation?" *Academy of Management Executive*, 6, 2, 1992, 43–54.

40. B. Bass, *Bass and Stoddill's Handbook of Leadership*, 3rd ed. (New York: The Free Press, 1990).

41. J.M. Kouzes and B. Posner, *The Leadership Challenge*, (San Francisco: Jossey-Bass, 1995), and *Credibility*, (San Francisco: Jossey-Bass, 1993).

42. A.K. Korman, "Consideration, Initiating Structure, and Organizational Criteria: A Review," *Personnel Psychology*, 19, 1966, 349–361.

43. R. Charan and G. Colvin, "Why CEOs Fail," *Fortune*, 21, June 1999, 70.

44. F.E. Fiedler, *A Theory of Leadership Effectiveness* (New York: McGraw-Hill, 1967).

45. F.J. House, "A Path-Goal Theory of Leadership Effectiveness," *Administrative Science Quarterly*, September 1971; 321–338.

46. A. Sagie and M. Koslowsky, "Organizational Attitudes and Behaviors as a Function of Participation in Strategic and Tactical Change Decisions: An Application of Path-Goal Theory," *Journal of Organizational Behavior*, Volume 15, January 1994, 37–47.

47. V.H. Vroom and P.W. Yetton, *Leadership and Decision Making* (Pittsburgh: University of Pittsburgh Press, 1973); also V.H. Vroom and A.G. Jago, *The New Leadership: Managing Participation in Organizations* (Englewood Cliffs, N.J.: Prentice Hall, 1988).

48. J.B. Miner, "The Validity and Usefulness of Theories in an Emerging Science," *Academy of Management Review* 1984, 196–306.

49. J. Gordon, *A Diagnostic Approach to Organizational Behavior*, 6th ed. (Boston: Allyn and Bacon, 1999).

50. G.A. Yukl and J. Clemence, "A Test of Path-Goal Theory of Leadership Using Questionnaire and Diary Measures of Behavior," *Proceedings of the Twenty-First Annual Meeting of the Eastern Academy of Management*, 1984, 174–177; also J. Fulk and E.R. Wendler, "Dimensionality of Leader-Subordinate Interactions: A Path-Goal Investigation," *Organizational Behavior and Human Performance*, 30, 1983; 241–263.

51. P. Harris and R. Moran, *Managing Cultural Differences*, 2nd ed. (Houston: Gulf Publishing, 1987), 392. Copyright 1991 by Gulf Publishing Company, Houston, TX.

52. G. Hofstede, *Cultures and Organizations: Software of the Mind* (London: McGraw-Hill, 1991); also "Motivation, Leadership, and Organization: Do American Theories Apply Abroad?" *Organizational Dynamics*, Summer 1980, 42–63.

53. T. Cox, Jr., *Cultural Diversity in Organizations* (San Francisco: Berrett-Koehler Publishers, 1993), 230. This section is based on Chapters 2 and 14 of this book. Also see T. Cox, Jr. and R. Beale, *Developing Competency to Manage Diversity* (San Francisco: Berrett-Koehler, 1997).

54. Ibid., 231.

55. Ibid., 230.

56. Ibid., 239.

57. P. Sellers, "These Women Rule," *Fortune*, 1999, 94–134.

58. Ibid., 98.

59. Ibid., 120.

60. J. Rosener, "Ways Women Lead," *Harvard Business Review*, November–December 1990, 119–125.

61. This discussion is based on L. Paine, "Managing for Organizational Integrity," *Harvard Business Review*, March–April 1994, 106–117.

62. Sherman, "Leaders Learn to Heed the Voice Within," August 1994, 92–100.

63. L. Spears, *Reflections on Leadership: How Robert K. Greenleaf's Theory of Servant-Leadership Influenced Today's Top Management Thinkers*, (New York: John Wiley, 1995).

## CHAPTER 8

1. B. Morris and P. Sellers, "What Really Happened at Coke," *Fortune*, 10 January 2000, 114–116.

2. Ibid.

3. Ibid.

4. L. Cushmir, "Personalized Versus Socialized Power Needs Among Working Women and Men," *Human Relations*, February 1986, 149.

5. J.R. French and H.H. Raven, "The Bases of Social Power," in *Studies in Social Power*, ed. D. Cortwright, (Ann Arbor, Mich.: Institute for Social Research, 1959); also see P. Podsakoff and C. Schriesheim, "C.A. Field Studies of French and Raven's Bases of Power: Critique, Re-analysis, and Suggestions for Future Research," *Psychological Bulletin*, 97, 1985, 387–411.

6. D. Tannen. "The Power of Talk: Who Get Heard and Why," *Harvard Business School*, September–October 1995.

7. R. Daft, *Organization Theory and Design,* 4th ed. (St. Paul, Minn.: West Publishing, 1987), 388; R. Middlemist and M. Hitt, *Organizational Behavior: Managerial Strategies for Performance* (St. Paul, Minn.: West Publishing, 1988).

8. See J. Pfeffer, *Power in Organizations* (Marshfield, Mass.: Pitman, 1981), 31.

9. K. Labich, "Why Companies Fail," *Fortune,* 14 November 1994, 64–68.

10. H. Leavitt, "Pathfinding Problem Solving, and Implementing: The Management Mix," in *Psychological Dimensions of Organizational Behavior,* 2nd ed., ed. B. Stran (Englewood Cliffs, N.J.: Prentice Hall, 1995), 497.

11. D. Kirkpatrick, "IBM Moves to Fix Its Microsoft Problem," *Fortune,* 10 July 1995, 105.

12. These are *Fortune* magazine's characteristics of "America's Most Admired Companies," cited previously in this book.

13. This section is based on Daft, *Organization Theory and Design,* chap. 12.

14. R. Kanter, "Power Failure in Management Circuits," *Harvard Business Review* July–August 197, 65–75.

15. Daft, *Organization Theory and Design,* 416–420, see also J. Salancik and J. Pfeffer, "Who gets Power—And How They Hold Onto It: A Strategic-Contingency Model of Power," *Organizational Dynamics,* Winter 1977; 3–21.

16. D. Hickson, C. Hinings, C. Lee, R. Schneck, and J. Pennings, "A Strategic Contingencies Theory of Intraorganizational Power," *Administrative Science Quarterly* 16, 1971, 216–229.

17. Ibid.

18. J. Pfeffer, *Power in Organizations,* 101–108.

19. See D. Beeman and T. Sharkey, "The Use And Abuse of Corporate Politics," *Business Horizons,* March–April 1987, 26–30.

20. D. Madison, R. Allen, L. Poerter, P. Renwick, and B. Mayes, "Organizational Politics: An Exploration of Managers' Perceptions," *Human Relations,* February 1980; 79–100; see also R. Kreitner and A. Kinicki, *Organizational Behavior,* 3rd ed. (Burr Ridge, Ill. Irwin, 1995).

21. M. Clarke and D. Butcher, "The Art of the Possible," *Director,* December 1998, 27, 28.

22. D. Buchanan and R. Badham, "Politics and Organizational Change: The Lived Experience," *Human Relations,* May 1999, 609–629.

23. D. Beeman and T. Sharkey, "The Use and Abuse of Corporate Politics," *Business Horizons,* March-April 1987, 30. Quoted with permission.

24. T. Stewart, 57.

25. C. Cockbum, *In the Way of Women: Mens' Resistance to Sex Equality In Organizations* (Ithaca: N.Y.: ILR Press, 1991), 142.

26. J. Weiss, *Business Ethics: A Stakeholder and Issues Management Approach,* 2nd ed. (Fort Worth: The Dryden Press, 1998), 200–203.

27. J. Kotter, "Power, Success and Organizational Effectiveness," *Organizational Dynamics,* Winter 1978, 29.

28. R. Quinn, S. Faerman, M. Thompson, and M. McGrath, *Becoming a Master Manager: A Competency Framework* (New York: John Wiley, 1990), 274.

29. J. Kotter, *Power in Management* (New York: AMACOM, 1979), 16.

30. This section is based on the Kumar/Thibodeaux model and approach. See K. Kumar and M. Thibodeaux, "Organizational Politics and Planned Organizational Change," *Group and Organizational Studies,* 15, 4 (Sage Publications, Inc., 1990), 357–365.

31. Ibid., 364.

32. D. Kipnis, S. Schmidt, and I. Wilkinson, "Intraorganizational Influence Tactics: Explorations in Getting One's Way," *Journal of Applied Psychology*, August 1980; 440–452; also see G. Yukl and C. Falbe, "Influence Tactics and Objectives in Upward, Downward, and Lateral Influence Attempts," *Journal of Applied Psychology*, April 1990, 132–140; and R. Kreitner and A. Kinicki, chap. 10.

33. T. Bonoma and G. Zaltman, *Psychology for Management* (Boston: Kant Publishing Co., 1981) also quoted in Quinn, Faerman, Thompson, and McGrath, *Becoming A Master Manager: A Competency Framework* (New York: John Wiley, 1990).

34. See R. Daft, *Organization Theory and Design*, 411–413.

35. Pfeffer, *Power in Organizations*, see note 8.

36. R. Kanter, *Power Failure in Management Circuits*, 65–75, Pfeffer, *Power in Organizations*.

37. R. Frey, "Empowerment or Else," *Harvard Business Review*, September–October 1993, 80–94.

38. Kreitner and Kinicki, op. cit., 275.

39. W. Burke, "Leadership as Empowering Others" in *Executive Power*, ed. S. Srivastya et al. (San Francisco: Jossey-Bass, 1986), 73.

40. N. Adler, *International Dimensions of Organizational Behavior*, 2nd ed. (Boston: PWS Kent, 1991), 50–51. See also G. Hofstede, "Motivation, Leadership, and Organizations: Do American Theories Apply Abroad?" *Organizational Dynamics*, Summer 1980, 42–63.

41. A. Laurent, "The Cultural Diversity of Western Conceptions of Management," *International Studies of Management and Organization*, Spring–Summer 1983, 75–96; see also N. Adler, *International Dimensions*, 42–43.

42. N. Adler, *International Dimensions*, 43.

## CHAPTER 9

1. B. Kabanoff, "Potential Influence Structures as Sources of Interpersonal Conflict in Groups and Organizations," *Organizational Behavior and Human Decision Processes,* 36, 1985; 115; R.E. Walton, *Interpersonal Peacemaking: Confrontations and Third Party Consultation* (Reading, Mass.: Addison-Wesley, 1969); see also J.R. Gordon, *A Diagnostic Approach to Organizational Behavior*, 4th ed. (Boston, Mass.: Allyn & Bacon, 1993), 448; and J.R. Schermerhorn, Jr., J.G. Hunt, and R.N. Osborn, *Managing Organizational Behavior*, 4th ed. (New York: John Wiley, 1991), 409.

2. J. Gibson, J. Ivancevich, and J. Donnelly, Jr., *Organizations: Behavior, Structure, Processes*, 8th ed. (Burr Ridge, Ill.: Irwin, 1994), 352.

3. J. Rosenfeld, "She Stands on Common Ground," *Fast Company*, January– February 2000, 72–82.

4. D. Katz and R. Kahn, *The Social Psychology of Organizations*, 2nd ed. (New York: John Wiley, 1978); see also, R. Kahn et al., *Organizational Stress; Studies in Role Conflict and Ambiguity* (New York: John Wiley, 1964).

5. J. Greenhaus and N. Beutell, "Sources of Conflict Between Work and Family Roles," *Academy of Management Review*, 10, 1985, 76–88.

6. See C. Fisher and R. Gitelson, "A Meta-analysis of the Correlates of Role Conflict and Ambiguity," *Journal of Applied Psychology*, 68, 1983, 320–333.

7. R. Likert and J. Likert, *New Ways of Managing Conflict* (New York: McGraw-Hill, 1970).

8. R. Baron, "Reducing Organizational Conflict: An Incompatible Response Approach," *Journal of Applied Psychology*, May 1994, 272–279.

9. K. Thomas, "Conflict and Conflict Management," in *Handbook of Industrial and Organizational Psychology*, ed. M. Dunnette (New York: John Wiley, 1976), 900.

10. R. Quinn, S. Faerman, M. Thompson, and M. McGrath, *Becoming A Master Manager: A Competing Framework* (New York: John Wiley, 1990).

11. Ibid.

12. R. Cosier and C. Schwank, "Agreement and Thinking Alike: Ingredients for Poor Decisions," *Academy of Management Executive*, February 1990, 71; see also D. Schweiger, W. Sanberg, and P. Rechner, "Experimental Effects of Dialectical Inquiry, Devil's Advocacy, and Consensus Approaches to Strategic Decision Making," *Academy of Management Journal*, December 1989, 745–772.

13. W. Kiechel III, "How to Escape the Echo Chamber," *Fortune*, 18 June 1990, 130; also R. Kreitner and A. Kinicki, *Organizational Behavior*, 3rd ed. (Burr Ridge, Ill.: Irwin, 1995), 286.

14. D. Kipnis and S. Schmidt, "An Influence Perspective in Bargaining Within Organizations," in *Bargaining Inside Organizations*, ed. M. Bazerman and R. Lewicki (Beverly Hills, Calif.: Sage). See also D. Whetten and K.S. Cameron, *Developing Management Skills*, 4th ed. (Reading, Mass.: Addison Wesley Longman, 1998) chap. 7.

15. R. Adler, "Satisfying Personal Needs: Managing Conflicts, Making Requests, and Saying No," in *Confidence in Communications: A Guide to Assertive and Social Skills*, (New York: Holt, Rinehart and Winston); T. Gordon, *Parent Effectiveness Training*, (New York: Wyden, 1970); S. Kim and R. Smith, "Revenge and Conflict Escalation, *Negotiation Journal* 9, 1993, 37–44; and Whetten and Cameron, *Developing Management Skills*, 1984, 340–341.

16. Whetten and Cameron, *Developing Management Skills*, 340–341.

17. K. Kressel and D. Pruitt, *Mediation Research: The Process and Effectiveness of Third Party Intervention* (San Francisco: Jossey-Bass, 1989); R. Karambayya and J. Brett, "Managers Handling Disputes: Third Party Roles and Perceptions of Fairness," *Academy of Management Journal*, 32, 1989, 687–704; T. Morris and Sashkin, *Ten Ways to Fails as a Mediator*, and Whetten and Cameron, *Developing Management Skills*.

18. "Mr. Learning Organization," Fortune, 17 October, 1994, 150.

19. P. Senge, *The Fifth Discipline* (New York: Doubleday Currency, 1990).

20. R. Bramson, *Coping With Difficult People* (New York: Dell, 1981).

21. R. Moran and W. Stripp, *Successful International Business Negotiations* (Houston: Gulf Publishing, 1991), 72.

22. Ibid., 71–72.

23. M. Neale and M. Bazerman, "Negotiating Rationally: The Power and Impact of the Negotiator's Frame," *Academy of Management Executive*, August 1992, 42–52.

24. M. Bazerman and M. Neale, *Negotiating Rationally* (New York: The Free Press, 1992); see also, R. Kreitner and A. Kinicki, *Organizational Behavior*, 4th ed. (Boston: McGraw-Hill, 1998), chap. 11.

25. R. Fisher and D. Ertel, *Getting Ready to Negotiate: The Getting to YES Workbook* (New York: The Free Press, 1992).

26. W. Ury, *Getting to Yes* (New York: Penguin Books, 1993); also Quinn, et al. *Becoming a Master Manager*, 425–429.

27. Adapted from D.A. Whetten and K.S. Cameron, *Developing Management Skills* (New York: Scott, Foresman, 1984), 425–426; also Quinn et al., *Becoming a Master Manager*, 290–292.

28. J. Wall, Jr., and M. Blum, "Negotiations," *Journal of Management*, June 1991, 278–282.

29. C. Wathson and L. Hoffman, "Managers as Negotiators: A Test of Power versus Gender as Predictors of Feelings, Behavior, and Outcomes," *Leadership Quarterly*, Spring 1996, 63–85.

30. N. Adler, *International Dimensions of Organizational Behavior*, 2nd ed, (Boston: PWS-Kent, 1991), 179–217.

31. L. Copeland and L. Griggs, *Going International: How to Make Friends and Deal Effectively in the Global Marketplace* (New York: Random House, 1985); also Moran and Stripp, *Successful International Business Negotiations*, 84–85.

32. Reardon and Spekman, 78.

33. J. Kohls and P. Buller, "Resolving Cross-Cultural Ethical Conflict: Exploring Alternative Strategies," *Journal of Business Ethics*, 13, 1994, 33.

34. See J. Weiss, *Business Ethics: A Managerial Stakeholder Approach* (Belmont, Calif.: Wadsworth, 1994), chap. 2.

## CHAPTER 10

1. J. Byrne, "The Search for the Young and Gifted," *Business Week*, The Internet Age issue, 4 October, 1999, 108–116.

2. Ibid.

3. Ibid.

4. Ibid. 114, quoted from Andersen Consulting Economist Intellgience Unit.

5. J. Greenberg, ed., "Motivation Through Job Design," in *Organizational Behavior: The State of the Science* (New Jersey: Lawrence Erlbaum Associates, 1994), 23.

6. K.H. Hammonds, K. Kelly, and K. Thurston, "The New World of Work," *Business Week*, 17 October 1994, 76.

7. J. Case, "The Rapidly Vanishing American Job," *The Boston Globe*, 12 October, 1994, 46. Quoted with permission.

8. D. Mills, *Rebirth of the Corporation* (New York: John Wiley, 1991), 139–140.

9. M. Mundel and D. Danner, *Motion and Time Study: Improving Productivity*, 7th ed. (Englewood Cliffs, N.J.: Prentice Hall, 1994), 218–219; J. Wagner III and J. Hollenbeck, *Management of Organizational Behavior*, 2nd ed. (Englewood Cliffs, N.J.: Prentice Hall, 1994), 527–528.

10. E.E. Lawler III, *High Involvement Management* (London: Jossey-Bass, 1986), 86.

11. F. Herzberg, "One More Time: How Do You Motivate Employees?" *Harvard Business Review*, September–October 1987, 109–120.

12. This section is based in part on J. Hackman and G. Oldham, *Work Design* (Reading, Mass.: Addison Wesley, 1980).

13. J. Thomas and R. Griffin, "The Social Information Processing Model of Task Design: A Review of the Literature," *Academy of Management Review*, 8, 1983, 672–682; also G. Salancik and J. Pfeffer, "A Social Information Processing Approach to Job Attitudes and Task Design," *Administrative Science Quarterly*, 23, 1978, 224–253.

14. E. Trist and K. Bamforth, "Some Social and Psychological Consequences of the Long-Wall Method of Goal Getting," *Human Relations*, 4, 1951, 3–38; A. Rice, *Productivity and Social Organization: The Ahmedabad Experiments* (London: Tavistock, 1958).

15. Based on J. McMalman and D. Buchanan, "High Performance Work Systems: The Need for Transition Management," *International Journal of Product Management*, 10(2), 1992, 10–25.

16. D. Dewar, *The Quality Circle Handbook* (Red Bluff, Calif.: Quality Circle Institute, 1980), 17–104.

17. *SAM Advanced Management Journal*, 54(1), 1989, 4–12; also E.E. Lawler III and S. Mohrman, "Quality Circles After the Fad," *Harvard Business Review*, January–February 1985, 71–75.

18. K. Bradley and S. Hill, "Quality Circles and Managerial Interests," *Industrial Relations*, Winter 1987, 68–82; R. Griffin, "Consequences of Quality Circles in an Industrial Setting: A Longitudinal Assessment," *Academy of Management Journal*, 31, 1988, 338–358.

19. I. Bluestone, "How Quality-of-Worklife *Projects Work for the United Auto Workers*," *Monthly Labor Review*, July 1980, S. Fuller, "How Quality-of-Worklife Projects Work for General Motors," *Monthly Labor Review*, July 1990, 39–41.

20. M. Conlin and P. Coy, "The Wild New Workforce," *Business Week*, 6 December 1999, 39–44.

21. M. Hequet, "Virtually Working," p. 30.

22. B. Shaamir and I. Salomon, "Work-at-home and the Quality of Working Life," *Academy of Management Review*, 10, 1985, 455–464; H. Lewis, "Exploring the Dark Side of Telecommuting," *Computerworld*, 12 May 1997, 37.

23. Conlin and Coy, "The Wild New Workforce," 40.

24. D. Jamieson, and J. O'Mara, *Managing Workforce 2000: Gaining the Diversity Advantage* (San Francisco: Jossey-Bass, 1991), 35.

25. Ibid., 37.

26. This section is based on E.E. Lawler III, "From Job-Based to Competency-Based Organizations," *Journal of Organizational Behavior*, 1994, 3–15.

27. Ibid., 6.

28. J. Hackman, G. Oldham, R. Janson, and K. Purdy, "A New Strategy for Job Enrichment," in *Psychological Dimensions of Organizational Behavior*, 2nd ed., ed. B. Straw (Englewood Cliffs, N.J.: Prentice Hall, 1985), 59–76.

29. B. Cunningham and T. Eberle, "A Guide to Job Enrichment and Redesign" in *Readings in Organizational Behavior*, ed. R. Sims, D. White, and D. Bednair, (Boston: Allyn and Bacon, 1992), 266–268.

## CHAPTER 11

1. B. Gates, *Business @ The Speed of Thought* ( New York: Warner Books, 1999), 408, 409.

2. G. Day, "Aligning Organizational Structure to the Market," *Business Strategy Review*, Autumn 1999, 33–46.

3. G. Hamel and C. Prahalad, *Competing for the Future* (Boston: Harvard Business School, 1994). J. Child, "Organizational Structure, Environment, and Performance: The Role of Strategic Choice," *Sociology*, 1972, 1–22; also G. Jones, *Organizational Theory*, 2nd ed. (Reading, Mass.: Addison-Wesley, 1996), chap. 6.

4. B. Lawrence and J. Lorsch, *Organization and Environment* (Boston: Graduate School of Business Administration, Harvard University, 1967).

5. P. Lawrence and J. Lorsch, "Differentiations and Integration in Complex Organizations," *Administrative Science Quarterly*, June 1967, 1–47.

6. T. Burns and G. Stalker, *The Management of Innovation*, (London: Tavistock, 1961); A. Courtright, G. Fairhurst, and L. Rogers, "Interaction Patterns in Organic and Mechanistic Systems," *Academy of Management Journal*, 1989, 773–802.

7. D. Pugh, D. Hickson, C. Hinnings, and C. Turner, "Dimensions of Organizational Structure," *Administrative Science Quarterly*, 1968, 65–91; also R. Daft, *Organization Theory and Design*, 4th ed. (St. Paul, Minn.: West Publishing, 1992); D. Nelson and J. Campbell, *Organizational Behavior* (St. Paul, Minn.: West Publishing, 1994).

8. Daft, *Organizational Theory and Design*, 203.

9. See T. Chi and P. Nystron, "An Economic Analysis of the Matrix Structure, Using Multinational Corporations as an Illustration," *Managerial & Decision Economics*, May 1998, 141–156.

10. C. Bartlett and S. Ghoshal, *Managing Across Borders: The Transnational Solution*, (Boston: Harvard Business School Press, 1991); K. Ohmae, "Managing in a Borderless World," *Harvard Business Review*, May–June 1989, 152–161; S. Yound and W. Nie, *Managing Global Operations* (Westport, Conn.: Greenwood, 1996); W. Joyce, *Megachange: Reforming the Corporation* (Homewood, Ill.: Irwin, 1997); R. Ashkenas, D. Ulrich, T. Jick, and S. Kerr, *The Boundaryless Organization* (San Francisco: Jossey-Bass, 1995).

11. C. Snow, R. Miles, and H. Coleman, Jr., "Managing 21st Century Network Organizations," *Organizational Dynamics*, Winter 1992, 8.

12. Ibid., 13.

13. Q. Mills, *Rebirth of the Corporation* (New York: John Wiley, 1991).

14. J.W. Weiss, "Strategies for Effectively Managing Geographically Dispersed Projects," paper presented at Miami, Florida, February, 2000.

15. Mills, *Rebirth of the Corporation*, 302.

16. This section is based on K. Keidel, "Rethinking Organizational Design," *Academy of Management Executive*, (4), 1994, 12–27; see also P. Senge, *Fifth Discipline: The Art & Practice of the Learning Organization* (Doubleday/Currency, 1990), and *The Dance of Change: Challenges to Sustaining Momentum in Learning Organizations* (Doubleday/Currency, 1999); M. Hammer and J. Champy, *Reengineering the Corporation: A Manifesto for Business Revolution* (New York: Harper Business, 1993), 84, 85; and M. Hammer, *Beyond Reengineering* (New York: Harper Business, 1996).

17. K. Cameron quoted in R. Melcher, "How Goliath's Can Act Like David's," *Business Week/Enterprise*, 1993, 193.

18. Keidel, "Rethinking Organizational Design," 18.

19. Ibid., 20.

20. Gates, *Business @ the Speed of Thought*, 15–21.

21. Ibid., 21.

22. Ibid., 15.

23. Keidel, "Rethinking Organizational Design," 22–25.

24. Gates, *Business @ the Speed of Thought*, 21.

## CHAPTER 12

1. A. Delbecq and J. Weiss, "The Business Culture of Silicon Valley," *Journal of Management Inquiry*, March 2000, 2.

2. E. Schein, *Organizational Culture and Leadership* (San Francisco: Jossey-Bass, 1985), 6–9; G. Hofstede, "Cultural Constraints in Management Theories," *Academy of*

*Management Executive*, February 1993, also, L. Smirich, "Concepts of Culture and Organizational Analysis," *Administrative Science Quarterly*, 28, 1983, 339–358.

3. G. Steinmetz, "German Firm Grows, Silicon Valley Style," *The Wall Street Journal*, 11 April, 1995, A16. For similar profiles of this region's companies, see R. Rosenberg, "Tethered, But Thriving: Key Components of State's Industry Continue to Flourish After Becoming Annexed to Silicon Valley," *The Boston Globe*, August 1998, 15, 17.

4. H.M. Trice and J.M. Beyer, "Studying Organizational Cultures Through Rites and Ceremonials," *Academy of Management Review*, 9, 1984, 653–659.

5. R. Johnson, "A Strategy for Service—Disney Style," *The Journal of Business Strategy*, September–October, 1991, 38.

6. A. Buono and J. Bowditch, "Merger and Countercultural Tensions: Employee Resistance to Organizational Culture Change Efforts," *Eastern Academy of Management Proceedings*, The George Washington University, 1987, 105–108; and *The Human Side of Mergers and Acquisitions* (San Francisco: Jossey-Bass 1989).

7. E. Cundiff and M. Hilger, *Marketing in the International Environment*, 2nd ed. (Englewood Cliffs, N.J.: Prentice Hall, 1988); see also N. Adler, *International Dimensions of Organizational Behavior*, 2nd ed. (Boston: PWS-Kent, 1991); P. Harris and R. Moran, *Managing Cultural Differences*, 4th ed. (Houston, Tex.: Gulf Publishing 1996).

8. M. Czinkota and I. Ronkainen, *International Marketing* (Chicago: The Dryden Press, 1988); C. Gibson and G. Marcoulides, "The Invariance of Leadership Styles Across Four Countries," *Journal of Managerial Issues*, Summer 1995, 176–193; D. Welsh, F. Luthans, and S. Sommer, "Managing Russian Factory Workers: The Impact of US-Based Behavioral and Participative Techniques," *Academy of Management Journal*, February 1993, 58–79; R. Kreitner and A. Kinicki, *Organizational Behavior*, 4th ed. (Boston: McGraw-Hill, 1998).

9. R.S. Wellins, W.C. Byham, and J.M. Wilson, *Empowered Teams* (San Francisco: Jossey-Bass, 1991), 229.

10. A. Saxenian, *Regional Advantage: Culture and Competition in Silicon Valley and Route 128* (Cambridge, Mass.: Harvard University Press, 1994); also see Delbecq and Weiss, "The Business Culture of Silicon Valley."

11. G. Gordon, "Industry Determinants of Organizational Culture," *Academy of Management Review*, 16, (2) 1991, 396–415.

12. Ibid., 404.

13. Ibid., 403.

14. Ibid.

15. Steinmetz, "German Firm Grows."

16. D. Denison, *Corporate Culture and Organizational Effectiveness* (New York: John Wiley, 1990), chap. 1.

17. E. Schein, "How Culture Forms, Develops, and Changes," in *Gaining Control of the Corporate Culture*, ed. R. Kilmann, M. Saxton, R. Serpa, and Associates, (San Francisco: Jossey-Bass, 1986), 42.

18. These characteristics are based on, but not limited to those described by T. Deal and A. Kennedy, *Corporate Cultures: The Rites and Rituals of Corporate Life* (Reading, Mass.: Addison-Wesley, 1982), 3–19.

19. T.J. Peters and R.H. Waterman, Jr., *In Search of Excellence* (Cambridge, Mass.: Harper & Row, 1982), 103.

20. L. Trevino, "A Cultural Perspective on Changing and Developing Organizational Ethics," in *Research in Organizational Change and Development*, vol. 4, ed. W. Pasmore and R. Woodman (Greenich, Conn.: JAI Press, 1990), 195.

21. M. Pastin, "Lessons from High Profit, High Ethics Companies: An Agenda for Managerial Action," in *The Hard Problems of Management: Gaining the Ethics Edge,* ed. M. Pastin, (San Francisco: Jossey-Bass, 1986), 218–228.

22. G. James, "Whistle Blowing: Its Moral Justification," in *Business Ethics: Readings and Cases in Corporate Morality,* 2nd ed., ed. M. Hoffman and J. Moore (New York: McGraw-Hill, 1990), 332. For a practical discussion on whistle blowing, see J. Weiss, *Business Ethics: A Managerial, Stakeholder Approach* (Belmont, Calif.: Wadsworth, 1994), 207–211.

23. R. DeGeorge, *Business Ethics,* 3rd ed. (New York: McMillan Publishing, 1990), 208–214.

24. T. Cox, Jr., *Cultural Diversity in Organizations: Theory, Research, & Practice* (San Francisco: Berrett-Koehler, 1993), 229; T. Cox, Jr., and R. Beale, *Developing Competency to Manage Diversity* (San Francisco, Berrett-Koehler, 1997).

25. Ibid., 243–261.

26. P. Frost, L. Moore, M. Louis, C. Lundberg, and J. Martin, eds., *Organizational Culture* (Beverly Hills, Calif.: Sage, 1985).

27. T. Cummings and C. Worley, *Organizational Development and Change,* 5th ed. (Minneapolis/St. Paul: West, 1993).

28. V. Sathe, *Culture and Related Corporate Realities* (Homewood, Ill.: Richard D. Irwin, 1985), 403.

29. Adapted from E. Schein, *Organizational Culture and Leadership* (San Francisco: Jossey-Bass, 1985), 52.

30. Ibid., 66.

31. Cummings and Worley, *Organizational Development and Change,* 535–536, see note 29.

32. Based on D. Kirkpatrick, "INTEL Goes for Broke," *Fortune,* 16 May, 1994, 62–68.

33. C. O'Reilly, "Corporations, Culture, and Commitment: Motivation and Social Control in Organizations," *California Management Review,* Summer 1989, 9–25.

34. This discussion is based on Cummings and Worley, *Organizational Development and Change,* chap. 8.

35. A. Wilkins and K. Patterson, "You Can't Get There From Here: What Will Make Culture-Change Projects Fail," in *Gaining Control of the Corporate Culture,* ed. R. Kilman, M. Saxton, R. Serpa, and Associates (San Francisco: Jossey-Bass, 1985), 264.

36. J. Weiss and A. Filley, "Retrenchment Consulting in the Public Sector: Issues and Recommendations," *Consultation,* Spring 1986, 55–64.

37. R. Beckhard and R. Harris, *Organizational Transitions: Managing Complex Change,* 2nd ed. (Reading, Mass.: Addison-Wesley, 1987); also see J. Weiss, *5-Phase Project Management* (Reading, Mass.: Addison-Wesley, 1992) for a guide for planning and implementing organizational change projects.

## CHAPTER 13

1. M. Arthur, K. Inkson, and J. Pringle, *The New Careers* (London: Sage, 1999), 1–18.

2. R. Koonce, "Becoming Your Own Career Coach," *Training and Development,* January 1995, 18.

3. S. Ornstein and L. Isabella, "Making Sense of Careers: A Review, 1989–1992," *Journal of Management* 19, 1993, 243–267.

4. L. Richman, "Getting Past Economic Insecurity," *Fortune,* 17 April 1995, 166.

5. W. Kiechel III, "A Manager's Career in the New Economy," *Fortune*, 4 April 1994; 68. Also refer to the nature of career changes and surveys in E. Peck, "It's Your Choice," *Fast Company*, January–February 2000, 200–212.

6. M. London and S.A. Stumpf, "Individual and Organizational Career Development in Changing Times" in *Career Development in Organizations*, ed. D.T. Hall and Associates (San Francisco: Jossey-Bass, 1986), 21–36.

7. K. Labich, "Kissing Off Corporate America," *Fortune*, 20 February 1995; 44–52.

8. Ibid., 44. See also *Fortune*, 2 August 1999.

9. S. Hirsch and J. Kummerew, *Life Types* (New York: Warner Books, 1989).

10. London and Stumpf, "Individual and Organizational Career Development in Changing Times," 70.

11. Ibid., 68–69.

12. B. O'Reilly, "The New Deal: What Companies and Employees Owe One Another," *Fortune*, 13 June 1994, 44–52.

13. J. Feldman, "A Contingency Theory of Socialization," *Administrative Science Quarterly*, 21, 1976, 433–452.

14. J. Feldman, "A Socialization Process That Helps New Recruits Succeed," *Personnel*, 57, 1980, 11–23.

15. J. Wanous and A. Coella, "Organizational Entry Research: Current Status and Future Directions" in *Research in Personnel and Human Resources Management*, vol. 7, ed. G. Ferris and K. Rowland, (Greenwich, Conn.: JAI Press, 1989), 59–120.

16. E. Morrison, "Newcomer Information Seeking: Exploring Types, Modes, Sources, and Outcomes," *Academy of Management Journal*, 36, 1993, 557–589.

17. D.J. Levinson, *The Seasons of a Man's Life* (New York: Alfred A. Knopf, 1978). See also D.T. Hall, *Careers in Organizations* (Santa Monica, Calif.: Goodyear, 1975).

18. D. Hall, "Breaking Career Routines: Mid Career Choice and Identity Development," in *Career Development in Organizations*, ed. D. Hall and Associates, (San Francisco: Jossey-Bass, 1986).

19. D. Hall, "Protean Careers of the 21st Century," *The Academy of Management Executive*, November 1996, 9.

20. Ibid.,10.

21. L.K. Savery, "Comparing Plateaued and Nonplateaued Employees," *Journal of Managerial Psychology*, 1989, 12–15; see also S.K. Stour, J.W. Slocum, Jr., and W.L. Cron, "Dynamics of the Career Plateauing Process," *Journal of Vocational Behavior*, February 1988, 74–91; and D.C. Feldman and B.A. Weitz, "Career Plateaus Reconsidered," *Journal of Management*, March 1988, 69–80.

22. J. VanMaanen, People Processing: Strategies of Organizational Socialization," *Organizational Dynamics*, Summer 1978, 21.

23. J. Greenhaus, *Career Management* (Fort Worth, Tex.: The Dryden Press, 1987).

24. E. Schein, "Individuals and Careers," in *Handbook of Organizational Behavior*, ed. J. Lorsch (Englewood, Cliffs, N.J.: Prentice Hall, 1987), 155.

25. Ibid., 157. Also see E. Schein, "Career Anchors Revisited: Implications for Career Development in the 21st Century," *The Academic of Management Executive*, November 1996, 80–88.

26. Op. cit.

27. G. Dalton, P. Thompson, R. Price, "The Four Stages of Professional Careers—A New Look at Performance by Professionals," *Organizational Dynamics*, Summer 1977; L. Baird and K. Kram, "Career Dynamics: Managing the Superior/ Subordinate Relationship," *Organizational Dynamics II*, 1983, 46–64; D. Seper, "A

Life-Span, Life-Space Approach to Career Development," *Journal of Vocational Behavior,* 16 1980, 282–298.

28. L. Richman, "How to Get Ahead in America," *Fortune,* 16 May 1994, 48.

29. L.K. Savery, "Comparing Plateaued and Nonplateaued Employees."

30. J. Russel, "Career Development Interventions in Organizations," *Journal of Vocational Behavior,* 38, 1991, 237–287.

31. G. Colvin, "The 50 Best Companies for Asians, Blacks, and Hispanics," *Fortune,* 19 July 1999, 52–59.

32. D. Turban and T. Doherty, "Role of the Protege Personality in Receipt of Mentoring and Career Success," *Academy of Management Journal,* 37, (3) 1994, 688–672.

33. K. Kram, *Mentoring at Work* (Glenview, Ill.: Scott, Foresman, 1985); also T. Cox, Jr., *Cultural Diversity in Organizations, Theory, Research, and Practice* (San Francisco: Berrett-Koehler, 1993).

34. T. Cox, Jr., *Cultural Diversity in Organizations* (San Francisco: Berrett-Koehler, 1993), 205, based on L. Phillips-Jones, "Establishing a Formalized Mentoring Program," *Training & Development Journal,* 37, 1983; 38–42, and R. Klauss, "Formalized Mentor Relationships for Management and Executive Development Programs in the Federal Government," *Public Administration Review* 41, 1991, 489–496; see also T. Cox, Jr,. and R. Beale, *Developing Competency to Manage Diversity* (San Francisco: Berrett-Koehler, 1997).

35. D. Feldman "Careers in Organizations: Recent Trends and Future Directions," *Yearly Review of Management,* June 1989, 135–156; see also, C. Jones and R. DeFillippi, "Back to the Future in Film: Combining Industry and Self-knowledge to Meet the Career Challenges of the 21st Century," *The Academy of Management Executive,* November 1996, 89–103.

36. D. Estrine, "Planning a Career in a World Without Managers," *Fortune,* 20 March 1995; 72–80.

37. J. Kotter, *The General Managers* (Cambridge, Mass.: Harvard Business School Press, 1995).

38. D. Estrine, "Planning a Career," 77.

## CHAPTER 14

1. G. Hamel and J. Sampler, "The e-Corp," *Fortune,* 7 December 1998, 81.

2. Ibid., 82–92.

3. Ibid.

4. W. Johnston, "Global Work Force 2000: The New World Labor Market," *Harvard Business Review,* March–April 1991,115–127; J. Reingold and D. Brady, "Braindrain," *Business Week,* 20 September 1999, 113–126.

5. C. Bartlett, "General Electric: Jack Welch's Second Wave (A)," *Harvard Business School Case # 9-391-248,* p. 1.

6. Ibid.

7. E. Brown, "America's Most Admired Companies," *Fortune,* 2 March 1999, 68.

8. C. Bartlett, op. cit.

9. Ibid., 213.

10. Adapted from R. T. Pascale, *Managing on the Edge: How the Smartest Companies Use Conflict to Stay Ahead* (New York: Simon & Schuster, 1990), 212.

11. K. Kerwin with K. Naughton, "Remaking Ford," *Business Week*, 11 October 1999, 138.
12. C. Bartlett, op. cit.
13. Adapted from Pascale, *Managing on the Edge*.
14. D. Nadler and M. Tushman, "A Diagnostic Model for Organizational Behavior," in *Perspectives on Behavior in Organizations*, eds. J. Hackman, E. Lawlett III, and L. Porter (New York: McGraw-Hill, 1977), 85–100; M. Weisbord, "Organizational Diagnosis: Six Places to Look for Trouble With or Without a Theory," *Group and Organizational Studies*, 1, 1976; 430–437.
15. R. Daft and N. Macintosh, "A New Approach to Design and Use of Management Information," *California Management Review*, 21, 1978; 82–92; see also M.G. Morgan, *Images of Organization* (Newbury Park, Calif.: Sage Publications, 1986); see also H. Tsoukas, "The Missing Link: A Transformational View of Metaphors in Organizational Science," *Academy of Management* 16 (3), 1991: 566–585.
16. D. Tapscott and A. Caston, *Paradigm Shift: The New Promise of Information Technology* (New York: McGraw-Hill, 1992).
17. J. Papows, *enterprise.com*, (Reading, Mass.: Perseus Books, 1998).
18. T. Cummings and C. Worley, *Organization Development and Change*, 5th ed. (St. Paul, Minn.: West Publishing, 1993), 91.
19. D. Nadler, "Concepts for the Management of Organizational Change," in *Perspectives on Organizational Behavior*, ed. J. Hackman, E. Lawler III, and L. Porter (New York: McGraw-Hill, 1983); J. Bartunck and M. Moch, "First-Order, Second-Order, and Third-Order Change and Organizational Development Interventions," *Journal of Applied Behavioral Science*, 23(4), 1978, 483–500.
20. J. Klein, "Why Supervisors Resist Employee Involvement," *Harvard Business Review* 62, 1984, 87–95; J. Brehm, *A Theory of Psychological Reactance* (New York: Academic Press, 1966); B. Armentrout, "Have Your Plans for Change Had a Change of Plan?" *HRFOCUS*, 19 January 1996; A. Judson, *Changing Behavior in Organizations: Minimizing Resistance to Change* (Cambridge, Mass.: Blackwell, 1991).
21. E. Kubler-Ross, *On Death and Dying* (New York: Macmillan, 1969).
22. H. Woodward and S. Buchholz, *Aftershock: Helping People Through Corporate Change* (New York: John Wiley, 1987).
23. O. Nelson and J. Quick, *Organizational Behavior: Foundation, Realities, and Challenges* (Cincinnati: South-Western College Publishing, 2000).
24. K. Lewin, "Frontiers in Group Dynamics," *Human Relations* 1, 1947; 5–41.
25. J. Kotter and L. Schlesinger, "Choosing Strategies for Change," *Harvard Business Review*, March–April 1979.
26. C. Argyris and D. Schon, *Theory in Practice: Increasing Professional Effectiveness* (San Francisco: Jossey-Bass, 1974).
27. L. Bolman and T. Deal, *Reframing Organizations, Artistry, Choice, and Leadership* (San Francisco: Jossey-Bass, 1991).
28. J.W. Weiss, *Business Ethics: A Stakeholder and Issues Management Approach*, 2nd ed. (Fort Worth: The Dryden Press, 1998), chap. 3 and 6.